INTERNATIONAL RELATIONS

for **UPSC & State PSC Civil Services Mains Examinations**

IAS SATHI

S.CHAND
PUBLISHING

S Chand And Company Limited
(ISO 9001 Certified Company)

S Chand And Company Limited
(ISO 9001 Certified Company)
Head Office: D-92, Sector–2, Noida 201301, U.P. (India), Ph. 91-120-4682700
S. CHAND
PUBLISHING
Registered Office: A-27, 2nd Floor, Mohan Co-operative Industrial Estate, New Delhi – 110 044
Phone: 011-49731800
www.schandpublishing.com; e-mail: info@schandpublishing.com

Marketing Offices:

Chennai	:	Ph: 23632120, chennai@schandpublishing.com
Guwahati	:	Ph: 2738811, 2735640 guwahati@schandpublishing.com
Hyderabad	:	Ph: 40186018, hyderabad@schandpublishing.com
Jalandhar	:	Ph: 4645630, jalandhar@schandpublishing.com
Kolkata	:	Ph: 23357458, 23353914, kolkata@schandpublishing.com
Lucknow	:	Ph: 4003633, lucknow@schandpublishing.com
Mumbai	:	Ph: 25000297, mumbai@schandpublishing.com
Patna	:	Ph: 2260011, patna@schandpublishing.com

First Edition 2024
Second Edition 2025

ISBN: 978-93-6468-944-1 **Product Code:** H1IRE47GENL20ENAB25O

PRINTED IN INDIA
By Vikas Publishing House Private Limited, Plot 20/4, Site-IV, Industrial Area Sahibabad, Ghaziabad – 201 010 and
Published by S Chand And Company Limited, A-27, 2nd Floor, Mohan Co-operative Industrial Estate, New Delhi – 110 044

CONTENTS

1 INTERNATIONAL ORDER & FOREIGN POLICY – ORIGIN & DEVELOPMENT

INTERNATIONAL RELATIONS – NATURE AND RELATED CONCEPTS

International Relations is the study of interactions between political entities, focusing on the connections between economics, law, power, and politics in the global arena. It examines how states and non-state actors interact, driven by national interests, and seeks to understand why states cooperate, compete, and the impacts of their actions on both domestic and international levels. In today's interconnected world, this field is vital for addressing challenges like climate change, globalization, terrorism, and WMD proliferation. By analyzing historical patterns, trends, and theoretical frameworks, International Relations offers crucial insights into global issues and institutions shaping international affairs.

A. NATION AND STATE

A nation is usually defined as **a group of people with a common language, history, culture, and (usually) geographic territory**. However, there is no common set of characteristics which is visible in all nations. In essence, a nation is an 'imagined' community held together by collective aspirations and belief systems of members. According to **Benedict Anderson** nations may be defined as **"imagined communities" that are "limited and sovereign."**[1]

According to academician **Guibernau**, a nation is a 'human group conscious of forming a community, sharing a common culture, attached to a clearly demarcated territory, having a common past and a common project for the future and claiming the right to rule itself'. Thus, **a nation is limited to a cultural identity without 'statehood'.**[2]

Example - **Palestinians**, who live in and near the nation of Israel, fit in this category. Though Palestinians share a national identity, elect their own government, and share cultural beliefs, they do not have an internationally recognized nation of their own.

General assumptions regarding a 'Nation'
- Shared beliefs
- Continuing historical identity
- Shared living (territory)
- Shared political vision/existence

The State can be characterized as a particular type of human organization that sets itself apart from other social groups due to its primary objective of maintaining order and security. It achieves this goal through various means, including the creation and enforcement of laws. Essentially, the State is a collective agreement among individuals on the methods by which conflicts are resolved, encapsulated in the form of legal frameworks. A State is thus, a political organisation of society, or more precisely the institutions of government.

In the **1933 Montevideo convention on the rights and duties of state** (the *locus classicus* of statehood) a state is considered a legal person in international law if it satisfies four criteria: it has (1) a permanent

[1] Johnson, G.J. (2018), "Oxford Dictionary of Critical Theory (2nd Edn.)", Reference Reviews, Vol. 32 No. 7/8, pp. 23-24
[2] Faas, D. (2009). [Review of *The Identity of Nations*, by M. Guibernau]. *Insight Turkey*, *11*(2), 144–147. http://www.jstor.org/stable/26331181

population, (2) a defined territory, (3) a government and (4) the capacity to enter into relations with other states.

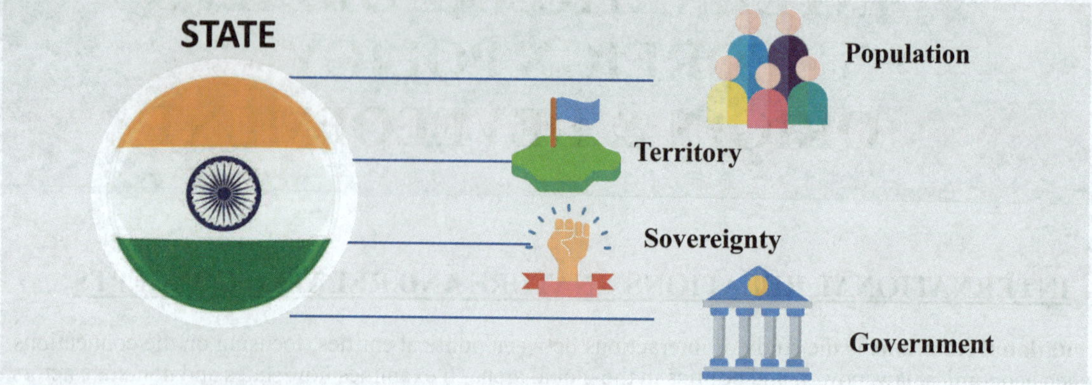

SOVEREIGNTY

When states refer to themselves as 'sovereign,' they assert their sole authority to govern their individual territories according to their own methods. Additionally, States also exercise sovereignty in their interactions with other states, engaging in actions such as declaring war, achieving peace, negotiating treaties, and various other diplomatic endeavors.

For the English utilitarians of the 19th century, the state was an artificial means of producing a unity of interest and a device for maintaining stability. The ideas of the state in the 20th and early 21st centuries ranged from **anarchism**, which believed the state was not important and even harmful because it used some form of coercion, to the **welfare state**, which believed the government was in charge of ensuring the survival of its citizens by providing food to those who were in need.

Nation-State: It is a form of **political organization under which a relatively homogeneous people inhabit a sovereign state**. It is thus an independent political state formed from a group of people who share a common national identity (historically, culturally, or ethnically); (more generally), any independent political state.

B. INTERNATIONALISM

According to Merriam Webster '*internationalism*' is a '**policy of cooperation among nations; an attitude or belief favouring such a policy**'. Although definitions may vary, it definitely denotes an opposition to isolationism and nationalism. It aims to establish an idea that cooperation among countries would be beneficial of all.

A project of internationalism, more significantly, 'liberal internationalism', has been unfolding over the last two centuries which focuses on building a world order that is open, loosely rules-based and progress oriented. Certain dramatic moments in history changed the thinking of the world leaders – the World Wars, the fall of the Berlin Wall, the collapse of Soviet communism, the end to Cold War. Old ideological divides seemed to collapse, while a new global era beckoned.

In the aftermath of World War II, the allies along with its partners worked to create a system organized around open trade, cooperative security, democratic solidarity, and multilateralism, backed by regional and global institutions. By the end, revolutionary ideas of socialism and fascism etc. seemed to be fading and a global consensus seemed to have arrived on the virtues centered around **liberal democracy** and **market capitalism.**

C. FOREIGN POLICY

The Cambridge Dictionary defines foreign policy as, '**the official ways in which a government has decided to deal with other countries, in relation to trade, defence, etc.**'[3]

As per Britannica, foreign policies are '**general objectives that guide the activities and relationships of one state in its interactions with other states**'.[4]

It is thus, a set of pre-established strategies designed and implemented systematically to manage a country's relationships with other nations. They are structured guidelines that regulate international political dealings. Simply put, **foreign policy is a country's national interest pursued abroad.**

D. DIPLOMACY

Diplomacy may be described as the means for implementing foreign policy of a state. Diplomacy encompasses the expertise, profession, and art of effectively handling a country's relationships with other nations, aiming to accomplish the goals outlined in its foreign policy. Stephen McGlinchey has defined it as **'a process between actors (diplomats, usually representing a state) who exist within a system (international relations) and engage in private and public dialogue (diplomacy) to pursue their objectives in a peaceful manner'**.[5] Broadly, Diplomacy can be political, economic or cultural, and ideally should work in tandem. As a rule, the diplomacy is pursued through established diplomatic channels and mechanisms. At times it can be pursued through back-door channels or through informal Track 1.5 /Track 2 mechanisms.

Paradiplomacy is a term used to describe the growing role of subnational actors, such as states, provinces, regions, cities, and other non-state actors, in international relations. It refers to the ability of these actors to conduct foreign policy and engage in international activities, often in areas that fall outside the traditional scope of national diplomacy. Examples of such diplomacy include - Sister city relationships, regional trade among states/provinces in different nations etc.

ORIGIN - WESTPHALIAN SYSTEM

Foreign policy, as now understood, is an outcome of the Westphalian system of modern state, territorial integrity and sovereignty, originating from the **Peace of Westphalia signed in 1648 in Europe**. According to this system, legitimate states were intended to align with nations, which are groups of people united by language and culture. These nation-states then became the principal institutional actors within a system of inter-state relations. International relations became a public concern as well as an important field of study and research only consequent upon the two devastating World Wars.

Peace of Westphalia, signed in 1648, ended the *Thirty Years War* (1618-1648) and the *Eighty Years Wars* (1568-1648) and created the blueprint for modern international relations. The concepts of state sovereignty, mediation and diplomacy between nations all find their origins in the text of this treaty written more than three hundred and fifty years ago. This peace was the first attempt at modern international diplomacy and formally secured the beginnings of religious toleration from a political angle. Subsequently, international politics revolved around the interactions between states exclusively, disregarding other political entities. All states were considered formally equal, with equal rights and responsibilities. Collectively, these states engaged with one another within a system lacking a centralized authority or hegemon.

The important issues dealt by the Treaty which had far-reaching consequences included-

1. **Wider formal religious freedom** - Prior to the Peace of Westphalia, states evaluated foreign nations and policies through the lens of moral judgment, considering their own perspective as good and anything

[3] Cambridge Business English Dictionary © Cambridge University Press, https://dictionary.cambridge.org/dictionary/english/foreign-policy

[4] Britannica, T. Editors of Encyclopaedia (2023, May 17). *foreign policy. Encyclopedia Britannica.* https://www.britannica.com/topic/foreign-policy

[5] McGlinchey, S. (2022). Foundations of International Relations. London: Bloomsbury Publishing, https://www.e-ir.info/2017/01/08/diplomacy/#:~:text=For%20those%20looking%20for%20a,objectives%20in%20a%20peaceful%20manner.

contrary as evil. The treaty mandated that any state signing it should disregard objections based on religious superiority from both Catholic and Protestant leaders. With the ratification of the Peace of Westphalia by representatives of each state, the influence of the Christian community of states was superseded by the principle of state consent.

2. **The nature of war and diplomatic profession** – In the past, war was considered an acceptable means of resolving conflicts. However, according to the Peace treaty, it was prohibited to completely destroy any state, and instead, compensation was to be provided to states relinquishing strategically advantageous territories.
3. **The idea of sovereignty** – The treaty established 'territorial superiority in all matters ecclesiastical as well as political' of princes in the Empire. While the German provinces were previously under the rule of the Holy Roman Emperor, the princes could now ratify peace treaties and could levy taxes. They could also declare war and most significantly, war could not be declared by the empire without their consent.

The Peace Treaty has been repeatedly viewed by scholars as the basis for much of modern international law and professional diplomacy. The Westphalian tradition continues to be visible in several modern international communities including the United Nations, European Union etc., and is a landmark instance of how a single conflict can impact the interactions of multiple independent nations for centuries.

CHANGING GLOBAL DYNAMICS

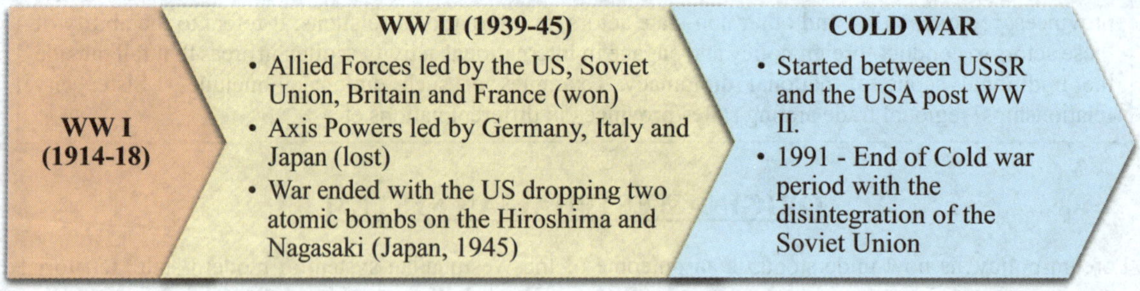

Although the Allied forces stood on the winning side and the United States of America shot up in global hierarchy, the critics of the US's decision to drop the nuclear bombs argue that it was unnecessary to drop them as US knew that Japan was about to surrender. Critics suggest that US action was intended to show their might to Soviet Union, whereas the US supporters contend that this action was necessary to prevent further loss of lives.

COLD WAR

The Cold War refers to the period in international history spanning approximately from 1947 to 1990. During this time, the world was largely divided into two ideological factions aligned with either the **United States** or the **Soviet Union**, known as the 'superpowers'. The term "Cold War" was coined due to the **absence of direct military confrontation** between these powers, although numerous proxy wars supported by the superpowers, such as those in Korea, Vietnam, and Angola, occurred during this period. The Cold War serves as a prominent example of a bipolar system.

The period immediately after the Second World War saw the emergence of two superpowers – the USA and USSR. Both nations wanted to expand spheres and divide the world between two alliance systems. The smaller states used the superpowers to secure their national interests while gaining the promise of protection, economic aid and weapons against their local rivals. The division was first witnessed in Europe, where most countries of western Europe sided with the US (Western alliance) and those of eastern Europe joined the Soviet camp (Eastern alliance).

ALLIANCE SYSTEM

WESTERN	EASTERN	ASIAN
North Atlantic Treaty Organisation (NATO) ♦ Led by the USA ♦ Origin: April 1949 ♦ Association of twelve states which declared that armed attack on any one of them in Europe or North America would be regarded as an attack on all of them.	**Warsaw Pact** ♦ Led by Soviet Union ♦ Created in 1955 ♦ It's principal function was to counter NATO's forces in Europe.	In East and Southeast Asia, as well as in West Asia (Middle East), the United States established an alliance system known as the **Southeast Asian Treaty Organization (SEATO)** and **the Central Treaty Organization (CENTO).** In response, the Soviet Union and China developed strong relationships with regional nations such as North Vietnam, North Korea, and Iraq.

The Cold war had two aspects –

1) **Military Restraint**: The two superpowers and the countries aligned with them were anticipated to act as rational and accountable entities. They were expected to comprehend the dangers associated with engaging in conflicts that could potentially involve the two superpowers and were encouraged to exercise restraint and prevent another large-scale war.
2) **Ideological rift**: The Cold War was accompanied by a genuine ideological conflict, revolving around the most suitable and effective methods of organizing political, economic, and social structures worldwide. The Western alliance, led by the United States, advocated for the ideology of liberal democracy and capitalism, whereas the Eastern alliance, led by the Soviet Union, embraced the ideology of socialism and communism.

COLD WAR DEVELOPMENTS

Time period	Particulars
1947	American President Harry **Truman's Doctrine** about the containment of communism
1947 – 52	**Marshall Plan**: US aid for the reconstruction of the Western Europe
1948-49	Berlin blockade by the Soviet Union and the airlift of supplies to the citizens of West Berlin by the US and its allies
1950 – 53	Korean War
1954	Defeat of the French by the Vietnamese at Dien Bien Phu; Signing of the Geneva Accords, **Division of Vietnam** along the 17th Parallel Formation of SEATO
1954 – 75	American intervention in Vietnam
1955	Signing of the **Baghdad Pact**, later CENTO
1956	Soviet intervention in Hungary
1961	US-sponsored Bay of Pigs invasion of Cuba Construction of the Berlin Wall
1962	Cuban Missile Crisis
1965	American intervention in the Dominican Republic
1968	Soviet intervention in Czechoslovakia
1972	US President Richard Nixon's visit to China

1978-89	Vietnamese intervention in Cambodia
1979 – 89	Soviet intervention in Afghanistan
1985	Gorbachev becomes the President of the USSR; begins the reform process
1989	**Fall of the Berlin Wall**; mass protests against governments in eastern Europe
1990	Unification of Germany
1991	Disintegration of the Soviet Union - End of the Cold War era

DISINTEGRATION OF THE SOVIET UNION

The bipolar world ceased to exist after 1991 when the Soviet System began to deteriorate due to its own internal issues, which primarily included:

- Absence of democratic practices and limitations on freedom of speech.
- The Communist Party of the Soviet Union, representing a one-party system, exercised strict control over all institutions without being accountable to the people.
- Despite the formal existence of fifteen republics within the USSR, Russia held substantial dominance in reality.
- The Soviet Union significantly lagged behind the Western countries in terms of technology, infrastructure (such as transportation and power), and, most importantly, in fulfilling the political and economic aspirations of its citizens.

In order to normalize relations with the West, **Mikhail Gorbachev** introduced structural reforms in USSR.

Main elements of Mikhail Gorbachev's Policy

- ***Glasnost***: 'Openess', mainly of information; loosening of state censorship
- ***Perestroika***: 'Restructuring', specifically of the Communist economy and political system

However, his decision to connect with the West and democratize the Soviet Union backfired and received heavy criticism, both by the people and the East European governments. The disintegration of the USSR became inevitable due to the following reasons –

(a) The **internal weaknesses** of political and economic institutions fell short of meeting the aspirations of the population.

(b) A significant portion of the Soviet economy was allocated towards **maintaining a nuclear and military arsenal**, as well as supporting the development of satellite states.

(c) Ordinary citizens became increasingly **aware of the economic progress in the Western world**, leading to growing dissatisfaction with the Union System.

(d) The **stagnant administrative and political structure** gave rise to various issues. Common people felt disconnected due to slow and suffocating bureaucracy, widespread corruption, and the inability to rectify mistakes.

(e) The **emergence of nationalism** and the **desire for sovereignty** among different republics, including Russia, the Baltic Republics (Estonia, Latvia, and Lithuania), Ukraine, Georgia, and others, ultimately became the primary and immediate cause for the disintegration of the USSR.

Eventually, a coup took place in 1991, and ***Boris Yeltsin*** emerged as the hero. Soon power began to shift from the Soviet Centre to the Republics and in December 1991, under the leadership of Yeltsin, Russia, Ukraine and Belarus, three major republics of the USSR, declared that the Soviet Union was disbanded. The Communist Party of the Soviet Union was banned. Capitalism and democracy were adopted as the bases for the post-Soviet republics. **Russia** was now accepted as the successor state of the Soviet Union.

Although Gorbachev set in motion a lot of reforms to correct the system, he failed miserably. This was because he started reforms which few predicted and lost support fast and the positive steps became impossible to control. Thus, Gorbachev's desire to remove the USSR from economic and social stagnation not only led to the collapse of the USSR but also ended the Cold war.

Consequences of the disintegration of USSR	The ideological dispute ended backed by the power and prestige of the US, the **capitalist economy** was now the dominant economic system internationally.
	Politically, the notion of **liberal democracy** emerged on top.
	It led to the **emergence of new countries**. The Baltic and east European states, wanted to join the European Union and become part of the NATO and the Central Asian countries wanted to take advantage of their geographical location and continue their close ties with Russia while also establishing ties with the West, China and others.

USA HEGEMONY

The sudden collapse of the Soviet Union left one superpower in ruins, however, the other remained with all its power intact, even enhanced. The onset of US hegemony is often associated with the disappearance of Soviet power from the international stage in 1991. However, certain elements of US hegemony trace back to the conclusion of the Second World War in 1945. Moreover, the United States did not immediately exhibit hegemonic behavior starting in 1991.

The word **hegemony**, derived from classical Greek, implies the **leadership or predominance of one state.** The concept of hegemony is employed not only to describe the dominance of a specific state but also to illustrate the methods by which that state's power is upheld. These mechanisms can encompass imperial holdings, military capabilities, economic strength, effective control over multilateral institutions, and more.

The word **hegemony**, derived from classical Greek, implies the **leadership or predominance of one state.** The concept of hegemony is employed not only to describe the dominance of a specific state but also to illustrate the methods by which that state's power is upheld. These mechanisms can encompass imperial holdings, military capabilities, economic strength, effective control over multilateral institutions, and more.

The term hegemony has many facets including the following-

As a 'Hard Power'

- It relates to the **relations, patterns and balances of military capability between states.**
- The US has the most advanced military capabilities on the planet and a major portion of funding is diverted towards military research and development. Thus, it represents a qualitative gap that is difficult to cover

As a 'Soft Power'

- It involves the **capacity to 'manufacture consent'.**
- A dominant power deploys ideological resources to shape the behaviour of competing and lesser powers.
- America is the most seductive, and in this sense the most powerful, culture on earth and has the ability to persuade rather than coerce

As a 'Structural Power'

- The hegemon must possess both the **ability and the desire to establish certain norms for order** and must sustain the global structure.
- This role is played well by the US in providing global public goods. Other examples include sea-lanes of communication (SLOCs), the internet, the share on global economy etc.

While the end of cold war signaled the arrival of a 'unipolar world', the present century has been functioning with the objective of creating a **Multi-Polar World Order** where every sovereign nation, disregarding its resources and global standing, is respected and where the voices of all the nations are heard equally, without bias or discrimination.

The Island of Sri Lanka, also referred to as the **'Pearl of the Indian Ocean'**, was known as Serendib, and Taprobane at different points of time in history. When the country gained independence on 4th February 1948, it chose to retain the Dominion Status within the British Commonwealth and was thus referred to as the **'Dominion of Ceylon'**. The status was eventually withdrawn in May 1972 and the country was renamed as the **'Republic of Sri Lanka'**.

POLITICS AND COMMUNITY

According to the Sri Lankan Constitution, the **Democratic Socialist Republic of Sri Lanka** is an independent, sovereign nation with a **'Unitary State'**. The Parliament consists of members that are elected by universal franchise on proportional representation basis. The President is also elected by the people and exercises executive power including defense.

Communal and Ethnic Disturbances

Even after its independence in 1948, Sri Lanka has been constantly embroiled in communal conflict. The nation's progress has been dented due to the political instability and economic woes that also create uncertainty for the nation's population and the foreign audience. An infamous event that engulfed the country between 1983 and 2009 was the **Civil War** in Sri Lanka. The conflict has its roots in the disenfranchisement of the Tamils of Indian origin. The descendants of the Tamil labourers brought from India by the British plantation owners had considerably altered the Sri Lankan demographics. The Tamil population received a blow in 1949 when through the **Ceylon Citizenship Act,1948** the Tamils of Indian origin were deliberately discriminated and stripped off their Sri Lankan citizenship and became stateless. While the Tamils formed 33 per cent of the population at independence, they were now reduced to less than 20 per cent, which allowed the Sinhalese to procure a majority in Parliament and hold political power.

On one hand, the Tamils grew increasingly alienated with the policies, while on the other hand, the Sinhalese community now wished to regain the supremacy within the country since the colonial leaders had historically sided with the Tamils. **The ethnic tensions culminated into decades long civil war.**

Main reasons behind the Civil War

- Both communities fought to clain the title of being the **'original settlers'** in Ceylon
- **Religion** was a point of rift and reinforced the ethnic consciousness of the two groups i.e. Buddhist-Sinhalese and Hindu-Tamils.
- The victory of the Sri Lanka Freedom Party (SLFP) in 1956 was based on **Sinhalese favouritism** and recognised Tamil as the language of national 'minority'

The war was mainly a clash between the Sinhalese-dominated Sri Lankan government and the **Liberation Tigers of Tamil Eelam (LTTE)** insurgent group. The LTTE had hoped to establish a separate state for the minority ethnic Tamils after decades of discrimination at the hands of the Sinhalese majority.

Liberation Tigers of Tamil Eelam (LTTE)

The LTTE, an insurgent group, was formed under the leadership of **Velupillai Prabhakaran** around **1976**, and it began to campaign for a Tamil homeland in northern and eastern Sri Lanka, where most of the island's Tamils resided. They began an armed struggle demanding a ***Tamil Eelam*** or a separate country for their supporters.

The war claimed over 100,000 lives and lasted for over 25 years. Even after an end to the war in 2009, the country remains bitterly divided on communal lines with reconciliation efforts faltering.

TERRORISM AND RELIGIOUS DISCORD

Sri Lanka's population is diverse, encompassing various ethnicities and religions. The Constitution prioritizes Buddhism, placing a duty on the State to promote it while also protecting the rights of other communities. However, ongoing ethnic and religious tensions persist, with government actions increasingly discriminating against minority communities.

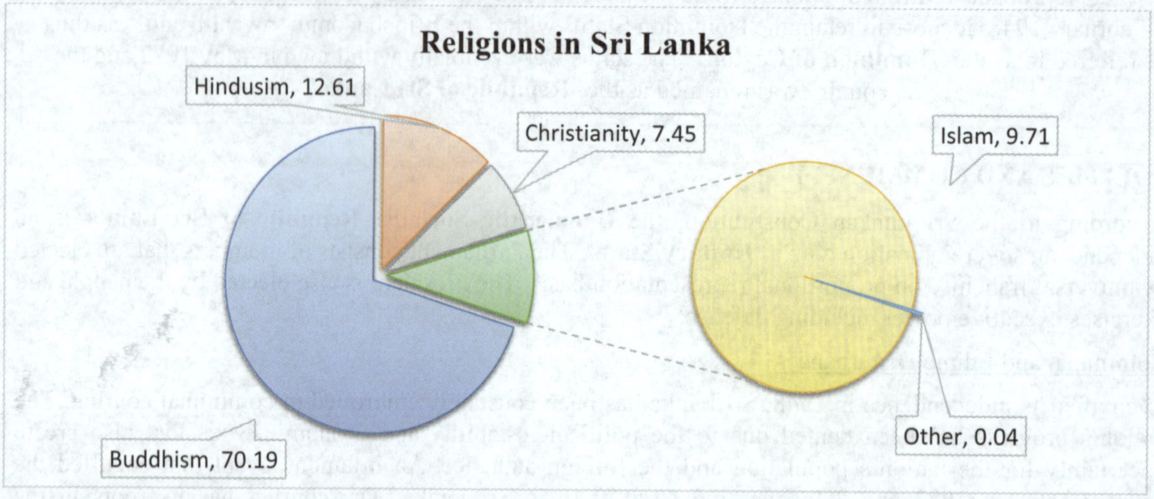

- Sri Lanka's minority communities, particularly Muslims, have faced increasing discrimination and persecution in recent years. Reports from organizations like CSW and USCIRF have documented severe violations of religious freedoms, including the destruction of religious sites and restrictions on religious practices.
- The 2019 Easter Sunday attacks, claimed by the Islamic State, targeted churches and hotels, resulting in significant loss of life and damage to the tourism sector. Additionally, Sri Lankan authorities faced criticism for failing to act on intelligence warnings about the planned attacks.
- The attacks and subsequent discrimination have further strained Sri Lanka's social fabric, exacerbating divisions between different religious communities. The international community has called on Sri Lanka to address religious intolerance and implement reforms to protect minority rights.

ECONOMY & TRADE

- Sri Lanka's economic challenges have deepened since the "Hambantota episode," (discussed later) where the country, burdened by unsustainable loans, was forced to lease its strategic Hambantota Port to China for 99 years. This gave China a strong foothold in the Indian Ocean.
- The economy has been further strained by unforeseen expenditures due to the COVID-19 pandemic, the 2019 Easter Sunday terror attack, and other economic miscalculations. These events severely impacted the $4.5 billion tourism industry, causing Sri Lanka to rely heavily on external support. While China has provided assistance, it often came with strings attached.
- The economic crisis that began in 2022 marked the worst downturn since Sri Lanka's independence. The GDP growth rate plummeted to -3.56% in 2020, and the economy continues to struggle with a balance of payments crisis, successive IMF loans, a collapsing tourism sector, and disastrous agricultural reforms leading to a severe shortage of foreign exchange and mounting sovereign debt. The population has endured crippling inflation, fuel, power, and medical supply shortages, leading to widespread protests and the resignation of the Prime Minister in May 2022.
- In April 2022, facing an unsustainable foreign debt of nearly $25 billion due by 2026, Sri Lankan authorities announced a suspension of $7 billion in debt repayments for the year. Although Sri Lanka had previously sought bailouts from the International Monetary Fund (IMF), these loans often came with restrictive conditions. Despite initial reluctance, the escalating economic crisis and intensifying anti-government protests forced the country to seek IMF assistance again. In early 2022, the IMF demanded that Sri Lanka restructure its massive foreign debt as a precondition for a rescue deal. It wasn't until September 2022 that the IMF approved a preliminary agreement for a $2.9 billion bailout.

As of 2024, Sri Lanka faces the crucial task of correcting its internal economic structures to achieve long-term stability. The country must navigate the delicate balance between IMF conditions and deepening debt to China and other nations. Strategic short-term negotiations are essential to ensure sustainable growth, while addressing the underlying economic issues that have exacerbated the crisis. International pressure, particularly from major powers like the United States and European countries, continues to push Sri Lanka toward meaningful economic reforms and restructuring.

INDIA-SRI LANKA TIES

Among all the other countries with which India shares only maritime borders, Sri Lanka has the closest geographical proximity to India. The *Palk Strait*, spanning a distance of 18 miles, serves as a shallow water body that separates *Jaffna* in northern Sri Lanka from the southernmost tip of India's Tamil Nadu state. Since India's independence in 1947 and Sri Lanka's independence in 1948, both countries have maintained a close relationship. In recent times, this relationship has been characterized by frequent interactions at various levels, leading to enhanced trade, investment, and cooperation in areas such as development, education, culture, and defense. India and Sri Lanka also share a common understanding on significant global matters.

Even though the relationship seems asymmetric in terms of the population, geographical size, military and economic standing and culture etc., however, the relationship between India and Sri Lanka is considered a relationship among equals, since they both are sovereign nations of the 21st century. Both have overcome their colonial baggage and have created a nation well suited to their population. The present times offer plenty of difficulties and but also provides the nations ample opportunity to nourish their relations while leveraging age-old wisdom.

YEAR	KEY EVENTS – INDIA AND SRI LANKA
1947-1950	• The Prime Ministers - Jawahar Lal Nehru (India) and D.S. Senanayake (Sri Lanka) of both nations visited each other. • Sri Lanka also contributed to the relief of victims of Assam during the earthquake in 1950. India gave 15,000 tonnes of rice to Sri Lanka.
1952	Trade Agreement signed
1953	**Nehru-Kotewala Agreement: Efforts to find solution to the ethnic problem**
1956	Ethnic conflict between Sinhalese Buddhist Sri Lankan Tamils begins
1964	**Shastri-Sirimavo Agreement: Issue of State-less people taken up and partially resolved**
1974	Sirimavo Bandaranaike's second visit to India; talks were concluded with Indira Gandhi and an Agreement for the citizenship (division between India and SL) of citizens was agreed upon.
June, 1974	Mrs. Bandaranaike and Mrs. Gandhi concluded a comprehensive agreement on the demarcation of maritime boundary with India accepting Sri Lanka's ownership of the Kacchativu Island.
1976	**Liberation Tigers of Tamil Eelam (LTTE) formed**
1987	**Rajiv-Jayawardene Agreement; Indian Peace Keeping Forces (IPKF) sent**
1991	Rajiv Gandhi assassinated using a suicide bomber (human bomb explosion)

COOPERATION AND CONFLICT

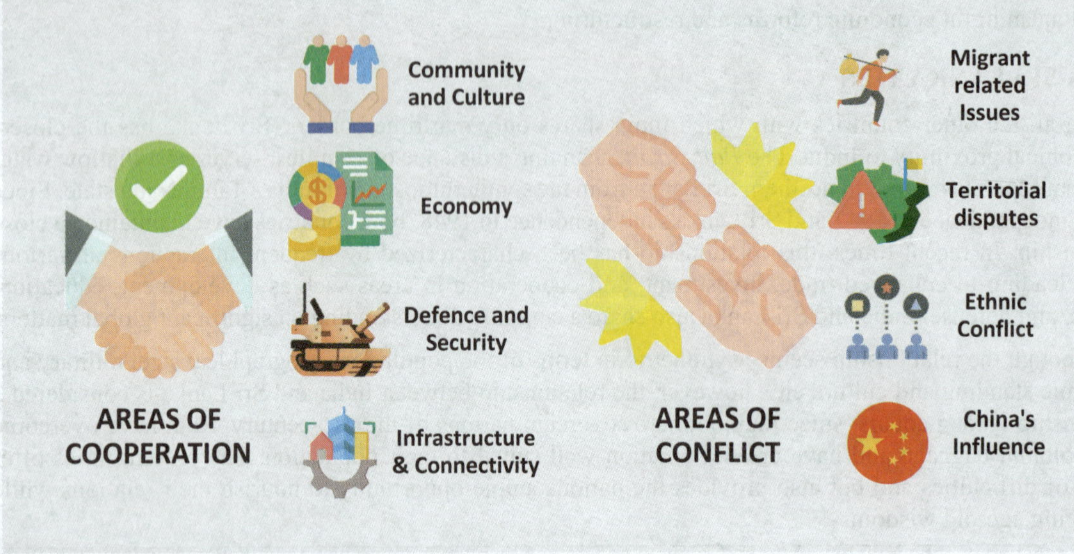

(1) Community & Culture

Historical Linkages - The relationship between India and Sri Lanka is over 2,500 years old and both sides have built upon their historical linkages based on intellectual, cultural, religious and linguistic interaction. The history of bilateral and cultural relations between India and Sri Lanka dates back to the time of Ashoka who had sent his son ***Mahinda*** and daughter ***Sangamitra*** to Ceylon (Sri Lanka) for the propagation of Buddhism. Chola kings ***Rajaraja I*** and ***Rajendra I*** conquered the northern part of Ceylon.

Religion – Sri Lanka is one of the oldest and most important centers of Buddhism outside of India. Buddhism was introduced to Sri Lanka from India in the 3rd century BCE, and many of Sri Lanka's most important Buddhist sites, such as the Temple of the Tooth Relic in Kandy, have strong Indian connections. Sri Lanka's Hindu population has historically had close ties with southern India, particularly Tamil Nadu. The Hindu temples in Sri Lanka, such as the **Koneswaram Temple** in Trincomalee, have significant Indian influence.

The recently renovated **Thiruketheeswaram temple** in Mannar, located in Sri Lanka's Northern Province, has become a symbol of the close connections between Tamil Nadu and Sri Lanka. The restoration of the temple was carried out with the involvement of the Government College of Architecture and Sculpture in Mamallapuram. This temple holds significant importance as one of the five major abodes of Lord Shiva in Sri Lanka and has a historical association with the revered **Saivite saint Thirugnanasambandar**. During the prolonged civil war that concluded in May 2009, the temple suffered damages. Another notable religious site, **Kataragama** in the southern region of Sri Lanka, was traditionally considered one of the six abodes of Lord Muruga by the people of Tamil Nadu. It continues to attract devotees and houses shrines dedicated to **Muruga, Shiva,** and **Deivanai Amman**. Historians also highlight the presence of ongoing trade links between the two regions, as evidenced by the discovery of Sinhala Prakrit inscriptions on pottery in Tamil Nadu.

Diaspora - The cultural relations between the two neighbours have continued to flourish, consisting of its own unique highs and lows. The **People of Indian Origin (PIOs)** comprise Sindhis, Borahs, Gujaratis, Memons, Parsis, Malayalis and Telugu speaking persons who have settled down in Sri Lanka (most of them after partition) and are engaged in business. According to Government census figures (2011), the population of Indian Origin Tamils is about 1.6 million.[11]

Government Initiatives – The Cultural Cooperation Agreement, established in 1977, serves as the foundation for regular Cultural Exchange Programs between the governments of India and Sri Lanka. India plays a significant role in the redevelopment efforts in the Northern and Eastern regions of Sri Lanka. Additionally,

---

[11] India-Sri Lanka Bilateral Relations. Consulate General of India. https://www.cgihambantota.gov.in/page/india-srilanka-relations/

the India-Sri Lanka Foundation, created in December 1998 as an intergovernmental initiative, focuses on strengthening scientific, technical, educational, and cultural cooperation through exchanges among civil society organizations and fostering connections between the younger generations of both countries.[12]

In 2011, India and Sri Lanka jointly celebrated the **2600th anniversary of Lord Buddha's enlightenment** (***Sambuddhathva Jayanthi***) through collaborative events. Education holds significant importance in their cooperation, with India providing approximately 290 scholarship opportunities annually to Sri Lankan students. Additionally, a historic pilgrimage to Bodh Gaya for Sri Lankan Armed Forces personnel and their families was organized from 24-26 June 2018, marking a significant milestone.

In 2015, Prime Minister Modi made a visit to Sri Lanka where he toured **Anuradhapura, Talaimannar,** and **Jaffna**. He returned to Sri Lanka in May 2017 as the Chief Guest for the International Day of Vesak celebrations. During this visit, he inaugurated the Dickoya hospital, delivered a speech at Norwood's ground, and sought blessings at the **Sri Dalada Maligawa temple** in Kandy. In 2019, the Prime Minister made a brief visit to Sri Lanka to show solidarity with the people following the **Easter Sunday attacks**.

India is extensively associated in the redevelopment process in the North and East of Sri Lanka. Government of India formally launched the **e-Tourist Visa (eTV) scheme** for Sri Lankan tourists on 14 April 2015 to increase the people to people contact. During a visit in March 2022, External Affairs Minister S. Jaishankar signed a Memorandum of Understanding (MoU) in the presence of the Sri Lankan PM to give **a $15 million for the maintenance of important Buddhist sites in Sri Lanka**. He additionally inaugurated (virtually) the-state-of-the-art theatre in Jaffna Cultural Centre constructed with India's grant assistance for the benefit of the people of Northern Province.

(2) Migrants and Ethnic conflicts

Post its independence in 1948, Sri Lanka maintained cordial relations with India, however over time the issue of immigrants and other ethnic conflicts between the Tamil and Sinhalese community in Sri Lanka ended up somewhat souring the relations. The policy pursued by the government towards the disenfranchisement of the Tamils severely ruptured the ties.

The **Nehru-Kotelawala Pact of 1954** was signed between the Prime Ministers of the two nations, Jawaharlal Nehru and John Kotelawala. The Pact ensured that the Sri Lankan Government registered the names of people of Indian origin who desired to stay permanently in Sri Lanka, while the others could be sent back. More importantly, it helped to maintain a check on illegal migration.

However, despite the efforts by the two nations, a large number of persons of Indian origin could not get citizenship of Sri Lanka and they became 'stateless persons'. This created tensions in India-Sri Lanka relations which was aggravated by the **1956 language disturbances**. The conflict began in 1956 when the Sinhalese Buddhist nationalism triumphed and, consequently, a sense of alienation among the Sri Lankan Tamil minority grew strong due to electoral interest-driven chauvinistic policies of the SLFP led government of S.W.R.D. Bandaranaike

Main Issues –

- **Original settlers**: Both the Sinhalese and the Tamils claim to be the original settlers in Ceylon. Which of these two groups came first is a dispute between the two. The Tamils are of Dravidian origin and are predominantly Hindus.
- **Religious disharmony**: Religion played (and still plays) a very important role in reinforcing the ethnic consciousness of the two groups i.e., Buddhist-Sinhalese and Hindu-Tamils.
- **Official Language**: The victory of Sri Lanka Freedom Party (SLFP) led by Bhandaranaike in the 1956 was based on its "Sinhala only" platform. Bandaranaike converted the Sri Lankan polity to a Sinhalese Buddhist state.

Eventually, the **Bandaranaike-Chelvanayakem Pact of 1957** recognised Tamil as the language of national minority and the language of administration in the northern and eastern provinces. But this pact could not be enforced on account of violent agitations by militant Sinhala Buddhists.

[12] India-Sri Lanka Bilateral Relations. Consulate General of India. https://www.cgihambantota.gov.in/page/india-srilanka-relations/

The **Shastri-Shrimavo agreement of 1964** sough to redress the problem of over nine lakh stateless persons (Indian Tamils) in Sri Lanka. About 3 lakhs of these people were to be granted Sri Lankan citizenship, and about 5 lakh 25 thousand persons were to be given citizenship of India. These people were allowed 15 years' time during which period they were to shift to India in installments. Prime Minister Sirimavo Bandaranaike visited India in January 1974 and her talks with Prime Minister Indira Gandhi resulted in a fresh agreement, whereby half of these persons were to be given citizenship of Sri Lanka and the rest would become Indian nationals.

While the nations were sorting out immigrant related issues, ethnic conflicts had erupted in Sri Lanka which threatened to destabilize the entire country. India was previously wary of a separate Tamil state, the ethnic riots in 1983 and the subsequent **civil war between the Sri Lankan army and the LTTE** (discussed previously) led to an emotional upsurge in Tamil Nadu in favour of Tamils of Sri Lanka.

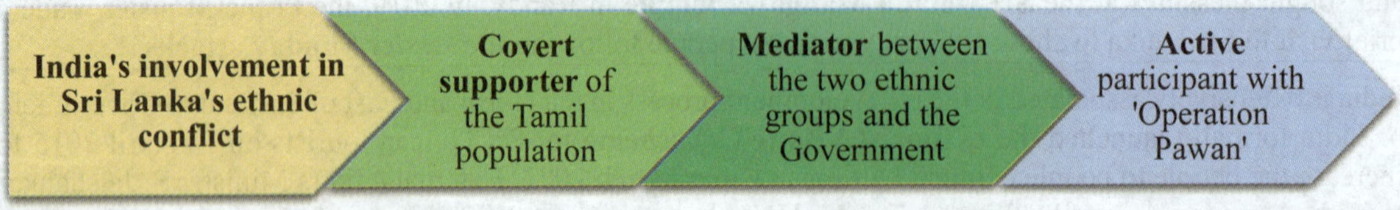

<u>India's decision to support the peace process in Sri Lanka was two-fold</u> –

(1) Peace in Sri Lanka was critical since there was a threat of a **potential spillover of ethnic violence** in India upon the creation of a separate Tamil nation and could fuel separatist tendencies in South India and North-Eastern states.

(2) The involvement was meant to **check the American domination** in Sri Lanka which could intrude in India's sphere of dominance.

On the invitation of Sri Lankan Government, **Rajiv Gandhi** paid a two-day visit to Colombo in 1987. President Jayawardene and Rajiv Gandhi signed an agreement which came to be referred as **Rajiv Jayawardene Agreement, 1987** or the **Indo-Sri Lankan Accord**.

IMPORTANT PROVISIONS

- The **constitution of an autonomous unit** comprising the northern and eastern provinces (Tamil concentration).
- The **elections to provincial councils** were to be completed by 31 December 1987, in the presence of Indian observers.
- **Emergency was to be lifted from northern and eastern provinces.**
- Tamil, Sinhalese and English would be the official languages of Sir Lanka.
- To provide for **Indian Peace Keeping Force (IPKF)** to be posted in Sri Lanka to restore normalcy in the strife-torn areas.

Under '***Operation Pawan***' the **IPKF** was to take control of Jaffna from the LTTE in late 1987 to enforce the disarmament of the LTTE as a part of the **Indo-Sri Lankan Accord**. While the operation had to be peaceful, the Indian forces ended up engaging in a series of battles with the LTTE. Eventually, IPKF failed to attain its objectives and began withdrawing in 1989 and exited completely by 1990.

During the lead-up to the Lok Sabha election in 1991, former **Prime Minister Rajiv Gandhi was assassinated in a suspected suicide bomb attack.** It is believed that his murder was part of a conspiracy involving individuals linked to the Sri Lankan ethnic conflict. Following the assassination, India took on the role of an impartial observer of the conflict.

In the last two decades, India has supported the right of the Government of Sri Lanka to act against terrorist forces, while at the same time, it has conveyed its deep concern at the plight of the Tamil civilian population, emphasizing that their welfare must be addressed. India has consistently taken a position in favour of a negotiated political settlement, which is acceptable to all communities, while being consistent with democracy and having a wider respect for human rights.

(3) Economy and Development

Sri Lanka has been a priority destination for investment from India. Trade and investment have grown and there is cooperation in the fields of development, education, culture and defence. The two nations had signed a Free Trade Agreement (FTA) in 1998, and the **India-Sri Lanka Free Trade Agreement (ISFTA)** came into force in **2000**. Over the years, the nations have partnered in several areas including infrastructure, connectivity, transportation, housing, health, livelihood and rehabilitation, education, and industrial development. The bilateral trade between the two nations has grown exponentially from US$ 658 million in 2000 to US$ 3.3 billion in 2020.

Important exports from India (US$ 3.3 B)	Refined Petroleum, Raw sugar, passenger and Cargo ships, technical textiles, packaged medicaments, chemicals etc.
Important imports from Sri Lanka (US$ 740 M)	Animal food, refined petroleum, nuts and spices, natural rubber etc.

With an aim to widen the ambit of ISFTA, a **Joint Study Group (JSG)** was set up in April 2003 and based on the report's recommendations, **Comprehensive Economic Partnership Agreement (CEPA)** negotiations had begun in 2005. During the 15th SAARC Summit in 2008, both nations were to pen down an agreement, however due to certain reservations expressed by the Government of Sri Lanka, the agreement hasn't been signed so far. The island nation feared that the Indian firms may have end up overpowering the domestic economic space which would've resulted in job losses for the native population.

After a change of Government in Sri Lanka in 2015, talks were resumed under a new framework called the **'Economic and Technological Cooperation Agreement (ETCA)**. The ETCA aims to address the challenges faced during the CEPA negotiations and seeks to boost cooperation in technical areas, scientific expertise and research, boost standards of goods and services and improve opportunities for manpower training. Although the agreement is yet to be finalized, it could serve as a crucial reform towards enhanced partnership with Sri Lanka.

As of 2022, India has the 2nd largest Foreign Direct Investment (FDI) in Sri Lanka and during the period 2005 to 2019, FDI from India amounted to about US$ 1.7 billion. Major areas of investment include petroleum retail, information technology, financial services, real estate, telecommunication, hospitality and tourism, banking and food processing (tea and fruit juices) and infrastructure development (railway, power, water supply).

Indian Companies operating in Sri Lanka

- Dabur
- Asian Paints
- Jet Airways
- Taj Hotels
- Indian Oil
- Airtel
- Ashok Leyland
- Tata Communications
- Ceat
- Apollo etc.

Some Indian Banks functioning in Sri Lanka

- State Bank of India
- ICICI Bank
- Axis Bank
- Indian Bank
- Indian Overseas Bank

Sri Lankan investment in India

- Brandix (about US$ 1 billion to set up a garment city in Vishakapatnam) MAS holdings
- John Keels
- Hayleys
- Aitken Spence (Hotels)
- other investments in the freight servicing and logistics sector

Credit support

The Reserve Bank of India (RBI) had signed a **currency swap agreement** with the Central Bank of Sri Lanka under the **SAARC Currency Swap Framework 2019-22**. The agreement was to be valid till November 2022. However, the year 2021-22 saw Sri Lanka grappling with a severe economic crisis and in such a scenario, India stepped up support and in August 2022, the RBI extended the duration of the US$ 400 million currency swap for the Central Bank of Sri Lanka.

A **US$ 100 million LoC** for undertaking **solar projects in Sri Lanka** has been signed between the Government of Sri Lanka and EXIM Bank in June 2021. The projects will include rooftop solar units for Government buildings, rooftop solar units for low-income families and a floating solar power plant.

India additionally provided a **$55 million Line of Credit to Sri Lanka** in June 2022 for the import of fertilisers, with an objective of helping Sri Lanka tide over its food scarcity. India, being the most consistent lender for Sri Lanka, has reiterated its support to the nation with a renewed emphasis on trade. India also secured an agreement which allows the Indian Oil Corporation access to the British-built Trincomalee oil tank farm. Additionally, India also aims to develop a 100MW power plant near Trincomalee.

India emerged as the top lender to Sri Lanka during the first four months of 2022 and extended credit worth $376.9 million, much more than the $67.9 million from China.

(4) Territorial and Fishermen Issues

Katchatheevu Island is an uninhabited offshore island in the Palk Strait. While it was historically owned by a **King of Ramnad** (present-day Ramanathapuram, Tamil Nadu), during the British rule, it was administered jointly by India and Sri Lanka. Dispute arose when India protested against the presence of Sri Lankan police during the St. Anthony's festival for worship at the local Church on the Island. The Prime Ministers of both nations met and decided on a status quo while ensuring that neither would send its officials during the festival. However, it took another five years to conclude a final agreement with regard to Katchatheevu Island.

In 1974 India, under the leadership of **Indira Gandhi**, ceded the Katchatheevu island to Sri Lanka, through a joint agreement. However, owing to rising demands by the fishermen in India, as of September 2022, the Centre has been making efforts to retrieve the Katchatheevu Island from Sri Lanka.

Two years later through an accord, India further gave up its fishing rights in the region. This development, however, didn't go down well with the local population in India which had been dependent on the waters for their survival and livelihood since decades. Given the proximity of the territorial waters of both countries, especially in the **Palk Straits** and the **Gulf of Mannar**, incidents of straying of fishermen became common. Both countries eventually agreed on certain practical arrangements to deal with the issue of bona fide fishermen of either side crossing the International Maritime Boundary Line.

Overtime, the arrests of Indian fishermen in the territorial waters of Sri Lanka became frequent which created tensions for both governments. Indian government introduced the '**deep-fishing policy**' to stop poaching by the Indian fishermen in Sri Lankan waters. But the policy could not stop poaching by Indian fishermen in Sri Lankan waters, who blame climate change, rising costs and a fall in the fish count on the Indian side, as the reasons for their acts of protest. Other issues include the damaging economic and environmental effects of **bottom trawling**.

On the Sri Lankan side, demands are being made to deny the release of captured Indian boats and refuse the Presidential pardon to captive Indian fishermen. Several demands have also been made by Sri Lankan fishermen to take stringent actions against Indian fishermen entering Sri Lankan waters. It is being alleged by anti-India constituencies in Sri Lanka that India is aiming to economically invade their country. Between the maritime political blame-game, the fishermen continue to grapple with increasing economic woes.

According to unofficial figures, nearly 400 Indian Tamilian fishers have been killed by the Sri Lankan Navy for allegedly crossing over into the Sri Lankan Maritime boundary. During the visit of Sri Lankan President Gotabaya Rajapaksa to India in November 2019, it was announced that Sri Lanka would release all the fishing boats under their custody.

(5) Defence and Security

India has always maintained that Sri Lanka forms an integral element in India's larger maritime strategy in the Indian Ocean. Sri Lanka's location in the Indian Ocean Region (IOR) has been of strategic and geopolitical importance, however its significance has catapulted further in the last two decades. Both nations were much concerned to preserve the IOR as **'Zone of Peace'** in the context of the escalation of great power rivalry in the Indian Ocean from the late sixties onwards. Now with the focus shifting towards the Indo-Pacific, a nation that wields substantial influence over Sri Lanka has much to gain in terms of global politics and naval diplomacy.

In recent years, the two sides have steadily increased their military-to-military relationship and the deepening maritime engagement is in consonance with the Indian vision of **'Security and Growth for All in the Region (SAGAR)**.

India and Sri Lanka conduct **joint Military exercise**, ***Mitra Shakti*** and the 8th Edition of the same was conducted in October 2021 in Ampara, Sri Lanka. The exercise focuses on counter insurgency and counter terrorism operations in semi urban terrain and is the largest bilateral exercise being undertaken by the Sri Lankan Army. The two nations also conduct a **Bilateral Maritime Exercise, SLINEX (Sri Lanka–India Naval Exercise)**. The **10th edition or SLINEX-23** was conducted in Colombo, Sri Lanka in April 2023. The 9th Edition of SLINEX was conducted in March 2022 at Vishakhapatnam. The exercise aims to enhance inter-operability, improve mutual understanding and exchange best practices and procedures for multi-faceted maritime operations between both navies.

Over the last two decade, India, Sri Lanka and Maldives have been forging close relations in order to secure the Indian Ocean Region. A **Trilateral Maritime Security Cooperation Agreement** was signed by India, Sri Lanka and the Maldives in 2011 to improve surveillance, anti-piracy operations and reducing maritime pollution in Indian Ocean Region. The second meeting was held in 2013 (Sri Lanka) and the third in 2014 (India), which also saw Mauritius and Seychelles in attendance as guest countries. The latest and **4th NSA Level Meeting** on Trilateral Maritime Security Cooperation was hosted by Sri Lanka in November 2020.

Signaling a boost to the bilateral ties, India and Sri Lanka had signed a **civilian Nuclear Energy Deal** in 2015 which aimed at cooperation to explore nuclear energy for peaceful purposes. Under the deal, India would assist Sri Lanka in building its nuclear energy infrastructure, including training of personnel. In April 2019, India and Sri Lanka had concluded agreement on countering Drug and Human trafficking.

In July 2021, the top defence officials of the three nations held a two-day virtual **trilateral table-top exercise, TTX-2021** to discuss the best practices and procedures for countering common trans-national maritime crime like curbing narcotics and assistance in maritime search and rescue. On a visit to Sri Lanka in March 2022, Indian External Affairs Minister S. Jaishankar signed an MoU to establish a **Maritime Rescue Coordination Centre (MRCC)** with a grant of $6 million from India.

Maritime Rescue Coordination Centres (MRCCs) form a global network established by the International Maritime Organisation (IMO) under the United Nations. Their purpose is to monitor sea lanes and ensure prompt responses to emergencies, including incidents such as distressed vessels, rescue operations, evacuation of individuals, and containment of environmental disasters like oil spills. Each country is assigned its own Search and Rescue Region, and the Navy or Coast Guard in each country takes responsibility for coordinating the MRCC. In India, the Coast Guard serves as the coordinating agency.

India would be providing **Dornier maritime surveillance aircrafts** to Sri Lanka and a 4,000 MT naval floating dock to Sri Lanka Navy. The MRCC is to be set up inside the Sri Lankan Navy Headquarters, including seven sub-units around the country. One such unit would be positioned in the southern city of Hambantota, which has gained prominence due to the Chinese presence there. Sri Lanka additionally agreed to post a naval liaison officer at the **Indian Navy's Information Fusion Centre-Indian Ocean Region (IFC-IOR)** in Gurugram.

The **Information Fusion Centre-Indian Ocean Region (IFC-IOR)** has been established by the Indian Navy in the year 2018. The Centre tracks merchant shipping and monitors threats such as maritime terrorism and piracy in regional waters and other critical developments in the region under a collaborative framework with like-minded countries. The Sri Lankan liaison officer would join counterparts from 10 of India's partner nations, including Australia, France, Japan, the Maldives, Singapore, the UK and the US.

Another MoU was signed during the 2022 visit to implement the **Sri Lanka Unique Digital Identity (SL-UDI)** programme on a grant of Rs 30 crore. Apart from the defence exercises, **Sri Lanka has been one of the biggest beneficiaries of military training programmes offered by India.**

India and Sri Lanka are common members of several multilateral and regional groupings/organisations including **SAARC, BIMSTEC, IORA, NAM, ADB, Commonwealth of Nations, United Nations** etc.

(6) Chinese presence

Disputes between Sri Lanka and India over the Tamil issue, the issue of fishermen, refugees, the island of Kachchativu, and the maritime border have strained relations between Sri Lanka and India. This caused Sri Lanka to look elsewhere for support. The Rajapaksa administration had reduced Sri Lanka's ties with India and expanded its ties with China and Pakistan, who have helped Sri Lanka's economic development and defense from insurgency.

Over the past few decades, China has been consistently engaging with Sri Lanka and forging economic and political agreements to gain the favour and enhance its influence in the region. Sri Lanka forms an integral part of the '**String of Pearls**' hypothesis and recognizing the strategic importance of Sri Lanka and the Indian Ocean, China has built ports, especially ***Hambantota***, and has undertaken various other projects in Sri Lanka. India has been vocal about its discomfort regarding the Chinese presence in Sri Lankan islands closer to Rameswaram on the Tamil Nadu coastline.

The curious case of 'Hambantota'

- In 2007, Sri Lanka signed an agreement with China to construct the Hambantota Port. The project, financed by China Merchants Port Holdings, was aimed at transforming Sri Lanka into a key maritime hub by attracting global shipping traffic.
- However, the terms of the agreement soon sparked controversy. Critics argued that the deal was disproportionately favorable to China, raising concerns that Sri Lanka was at risk of falling into a debt trap—a scenario where excessive debt to China could lead to the loss of strategic assets.
- By 2017, Sri Lanka's inability to repay the loans led to a 99-year lease of the port to China. This lease handed China significant control over the port and its facilities, a move that has since been widely viewed as a manifestation of China's broader "debt-trap diplomacy."
- The Hambantota Port now stands as a powerful symbol of how a major power can exert influence over a smaller nation's economy through strategic financial investments.

Strategic and Economic Implications of Hambantota Port for Sri Lanka and India

1. **Sovereignty and Economic implications** - The Hambantota Port, a strategically located deep-water port in Sri Lanka, has become a focal point of geopolitical and economic interest in the Indian Ocean region. China's significant investment in the port, culminating in a 99-year lease agreement, has raised concerns about Sri Lanka's economic sovereignty and its potential vulnerability to debt-trap diplomacy.
   - While the port offers economic opportunities, such as increased trade and job creation, it also poses risks. Sri Lanka's heavy reliance on Chinese investment could make it susceptible to Beijing's influence and policies. The port's strategic location could also give China a military advantage in the region, potentially undermining India's security interests.
2. **Altering the Balance of Power**: China's control of Hambantota has the potential to alter the balance of power in the Indian Ocean region. The port's location along crucial maritime routes enhances China's

ability to monitor and influence shipping traffic, potentially challenging India's dominance in the region. This development has raised concerns about China's growing strategic presence and its intentions in the Indian Ocean.

3. **India's Response**: India has been closely monitoring the developments at Hambantota and has taken steps to counter China's growing influence in the region. These include:
   - Strengthening Ties with Sri Lanka: India has provided significant financial assistance and development aid to Sri Lanka, seeking to strengthen bilateral ties and counter Chinese influence.
   - Regional Cooperation: India has been actively promoting regional cooperation through initiatives such as the Indian Ocean Rim Association (IORA) and the Colombo Security Conclave (CSC) to counterbalance China's presence in the region.
   - Military Modernization: India has been modernizing its military and enhancing its maritime capabilities to ensure its security and protect its interests in the Indian Ocean.

By August 2024, India-Sri Lanka relations have continued to face challenges, particularly regarding China's influence in Sri Lanka's strategic infrastructure. While the Sri Lankan government has reassured India by limiting China's role in the Hambantota Port's operations, security concerns remain. In 2023, tensions resurfaced when **Chinese naval vessels, including submarines, were allowed to dock in Sri Lanka**, raising concerns in India about growing Chinese military presence in the Indian Ocean region.

In 2021, Sri Lanka signed a **10-billion-yuan currency swap deal** with China, but it remained inactive due to Sri Lanka's ongoing economic crisis and insufficient foreign reserves. To counter China's influence and enhance its strategic position, India has advanced its plans for developing **Trincomalee Port**, a vital asset on Sri Lanka's northeastern coast. This port offers India a strategic maritime advantage, being close to Chennai and providing better regional oversight.

Source: worldatlas.com

Criticality of the Trincomalee Deal

- The location of the port holds **strategic significance** and has been of interest to several countries, including India, Japan and the US
- It would help to **counter-balance China's stronghold** in the area
- Indian companies would benefit from the enhanced maritime **trade route access**
- It will help **decongest the shipping operations** and would boost the supply chain

INCREASING RELEVANCE OF SRI LANKA

(1) **Strategic Location in the Indian Ocean:** Sri Lanka's strategic location in the Indian Ocean Region (IOR) has made it increasingly significant due to China's expanding naval presence and strategic activities in the Indo-Pacific. This has positioned Sri Lanka as a key player in regional geopolitics.

(2) **Balancing Relations with Major Powers:** While Sri Lanka has leveraged its geographical advantages to balance its relationships with major powers, particularly China and India, it often seeks to maximize its influence in foreign and security policies. Despite the asymmetrical power dynamics with India, Sri Lanka attempts to mitigate India's influence by engaging with other global players.

(3) **Impact on India's Security:** Sri Lanka's importance to India's coastal security and interests in the IOR cannot be overstated. The growing ties between China and Sri Lanka directly impact India's defense and security, raising concerns about the potential for future geopolitical shifts that could affect regional stability.

(4) **India's Strategic Response:** In response to these developments, India has maintained a policy of strategic independence while bolstering maritime and naval cooperation with the United States, Japan, and France. This approach aims to safeguard India's interests in the Indo-Pacific and counterbalance China's growing influence in Sri Lanka and the wider region.

(5) **Diplomatic Efforts and Challenges:** Efforts to stabilize relations between India and Sri Lanka have been ongoing. In September 2022, the Sri Lankan High Commissioner to India referenced former President Mahinda Rajapaksa's remarks, highlighting the cultural and historical ties between the two nations, where **China is seen as a close friend, but *India is regarded as a "brother and sister*."** However, these diplomatic gestures underscore the complexity of the relationship, as Sri Lanka continues to navigate its ties with both China and India.

The international community, including the United States and other key players, is closely monitoring the evolving dynamics between Sri Lanka, China, and India. The increasing relevance of Sri Lanka in global geopolitics will likely have long-term implications for regional security and stability, making it a focal point for future diplomatic and strategic engagements.

FUTURE OPPORTUNITIES AND APPROACHES

(1) **Strengthening Bilateral Relations**: Since its independence, Sri Lanka has navigated through significant challenges and milestones. India has consistently provided support during these periods, and it remains crucial for both nations to strengthen their bilateral relations to ensure mutual economic prosperity in the future. Building trust through confidence-building measures should be a priority, with India being particularly sensitive to Sri Lanka's concerns as a smaller nation to alleviate any fears or suspicions.

(2) **Addressing Illegal Fishing and Maritime Issues**: One pressing issue that needs attention is the illegal poaching by Tamil Nadu fishing trawlers in the Palk Strait and Sri Lankan territorial waters. Resolving this problem is essential for reducing tensions and fostering better relations. Alongside this, while military ties between the two countries are commendable, there should be a greater focus on expanding economic activities and enhancing people-to-people connections through cultural and religious exchanges.

(3) **Combatting Transnational Crimes**: India and Sri Lanka must collaborate to combat transnational crimes such as money laundering, arms smuggling, drug trafficking, and human trafficking. Joint task forces and collaborative efforts can ensure seamless follow-up actions across borders. Periodic reviews and assessments of evolving situations would further enhance mutual understanding and cooperation.

(4) **Tackling Religious Extremism and Enhancing Fisheries**: Addressing religious extremism and terrorism through coordinated policies is vital for both nations. Additionally, diversifying the capacities of Indian fishermen and improving the skills of their Sri Lankan counterparts in inland aquaculture and fish processing could help ease tensions in the fishing sector, promoting a more harmonious relationship.

(5) **Leveraging India's Role in Sri Lanka's Development**: In recent years, there has been a perception that China has outpaced India in Sri Lanka. However, the economic and political crises in Sri Lanka have provided an unexpected opportunity to strengthen India-Sri Lanka relations. While China has been a significant lender to Sri Lanka, India is emerging as a major provider of aid, offering support that is seen as more generous and rooted in goodwill.

Thus, instead of competing with external forces to win Sri Lanka's favor, India should chart a unique path that leverages its historical connections and shared values with Sri Lanka. By focusing on development and prosperity in the island nation, India can create a lasting partnership that benefits both countries, fostering long-term stability and growth in the region.

BHUTAN

ABOUT THE COUNTRY

The Kingdom of Bhutan is a landlocked South Asian nation situated between India and People's Republic of China. Except for a narrow strip of subtropical plains in the far south known as the Duars, the entirety of the country is mountainous. The Duars Plain, located south of the Himalayan range, forms Bhutan's border with the Indian states of West Bengal and Assam. Bhutan also shares borders with the Indian states of Arunachal Pradesh to the east and Sikkim to the southwest.

'Bhutan' may be derived from the Sanskrit word **'Bhu-Uttan'** which means 'High Land'. However, some Bhutanese call their country **'Druk Yul'**, meaning Land of the Thunder Dragon and its inhabitants **'Drukpa'** or Dragon People. The Dzongkha (and Tibetan) name for the country is 'Druk Yul'. Similarly, their head of state is called the **'Druk Gyalpo'** or "Dragon King." The Druk appears on the Bhutanese flag and is the national symbol.

POLITICS & ADMINISTRATION

- Since Bhutan transitioned to a **democratic constitutional monarchy** from an absolute monarchy in 2008, the country has embarked on a development strategy founded on the principle of **Gross National Happiness**.
- The King, the Druk Gyalpo, is the head of state, while the executive power rests with the Council of Ministers, headed by the Prime Minister. The legislative power is vested in a bicameral parliament consisting of the National Assembly (lower house) and the National Council (upper house).
- A unique aspect of Bhutan's governance is the role of Buddhism. The **Dratshang Lhentshog**, the monastic body, holds significant influence in shaping the country's policies and values.
- In terms of international relations, Bhutan has maintained a policy of **neutrality** and **non-alignment**, and has established diplomatic relations with over 50 countries around the world.
- In 2015, Bhutan was the first country in the world to adopt the **Sustainable Development Goals** (SDGs) as its national development agenda, and has made significant strides in areas such as poverty reduction, healthcare, education, and environmental conservation.

ECONOMY & TRADE

- Despite its small size, Bhutan has a unique standing in the international platform due to its unique culture, commitment to environmental conservation, and its development philosophy of **Gross National Happiness (GNH).**

Gross National Happiness

GNH or **Gross Domestic Happiness** as is often referred, is a concept by which the Bhutan measures its economic and moral development. It is a measure of collective happiness in a nation which relies on four main factors/pillars -

Good Governance	Sustainable socio-economic development	Cultural preservation	Environmental conservation

- **Bhutan's GDP** has grown steadily over the past decade, with an average annual growth rate of around **7 percent**. Bhutan's economic development has been guided by the principle of **GNH**.

- According to the World Bank, Bhutan is a **lower-middle income country** and rapid economic growth in Bhutan has contributed to substantial poverty reduction over the last two decades.
- In December 2020, the UN General Assembly officially recognized Bhutan's progress, confirming its **transition from Least Developed Country (LDC) status**. Improvements in human development indicators, such as health, education, and income levels, have played a crucial role in Bhutan's graduation.
- **Key economic sectors** –
  1) Hydropower: Bhutan possesses abundant hydropower resources, and the sector is a major contributor to the economy, with most of the electricity exported to India.
  2) Agriculture: Despite modernization efforts, agriculture remains a primary source of livelihood for a significant portion of the population.
  3) Tourism: Bhutan's pristine natural beauty and unique cultural heritage have attracted a growing number of tourists, contributing to economic growth.
  4) Industry: The industrial sector is relatively small but is gradually expanding, with a focus on hydropower, cement, and wood products.
- **Bhutan's main exports** include **hydropower**, **agricultural products,** and **processed minerals**. Agricultural products such as cardamom, apples, and oranges are also significant exports, with some of it going to Bangladesh, Nepal, and other countries in the region.
- Bhutan's exports of **processed minerals** such as calcium carbide and ferrosilicon go to countries such as Bangladesh, Japan, and South Korea.
- The valleys in Bhutan, rich in water resources, provide favorable conditions for harnessing renewable energy through the development of hydropower. This has contributed to the country's economic growth by ensuring widespread availability of affordable electricity.

DID YOU KNOW?

The Government of Bhutan approved the country's **accession to the World Trade Organization (WTO)** in April 2023. Bhutan's decision to join the WTO signifies the country's commitment to greater economic integration and participation in the global trading system. Bhutan stands to benefit from increased market access, trade liberalization, and potential foreign investments. This decision comes as Bhutan is also graduating from the **Least Developed Country (LDC) status** [Bhutan has met certain economic development criteria set by the United Nations], underscoring its economic progress.

CULTURE & PEOPLE

According to the latest estimates, Bhutan's population is around 771,608 people, as of 2021. Bhutan is a **predominantly Buddhist country**, and Buddhism plays an important role in the country's culture and society. The official language of Bhutan is **Dzongkha**, but several other languages, including Nepali and English, are also spoken. The population of Bhutan is ethnically diverse, with three main ethnic groups: **Ngalongs, Sharchops,** and **Lhotshampas**. Bhutan's society is deeply rooted in traditional values, and there is a strong emphasis on community and family ties. Social interactions in Bhutan are often governed by traditional etiquette, including the use of formal greetings, respectful language, and dress codes.

INDIA and Bhutan Ties

The longstanding and distinctive bilateral relations between India and Bhutan are built on a foundation of trust and mutual understanding that has evolved over time. Irrespective of political affiliations, both countries have maintained a strong and enduring relationship. The economic ties between India and Bhutan, which are mutually advantageous, have played a significant role in shaping the bilateral relations. The relations between India and Bhutan have evolved in mainly three phases –

Phase I (1960-1980)	Phase II (1980-2000)	Phase III (2000-Present)
• Indian support provided for physical infrastructure creation in Bhutan	• Indian assistance provided for development of democratic values and decentralisation for transition to democracy	• Diversification of developmental assistance - IT, education, skill development and hydroelectricity

YEAR	KEY EVENTS
747 AD	Buddhist monk Padmasambhava went from India to Bhutan and led the Nyingmapa sect of Buddhism.
1910	As per the Treaty of Punakha, between China–Tibet and Bhutan, Bhutan was not officially annexed (part of British Empire) but the legal status of Bhutan itself remained undefined.
1947	Post-independence, Pandit Nehru went on a horseback to Bhutan to build relations and advised King J D Wangchuk to build relations with India.
1949	**India and Bhutan concluded a 'Treaty of Friendship and Cooperation'.**
1968	Diplomatic relations between India and Bhutan are established with the establishment of a special office of India in Thimphu
1971	Bhutan exhibits an independent attitude in foreign affairs by joining the United Nations.
2003-2004	The Royal Bhutan Army conducts operations against anti-India insurgents of the United Liberation Front of Assam (ULFA) that were operating bases in Bhutan.
2007	Domestic and Bilateral relations revised with Dr. Manmohan Singh conducting a visit to Bhutan in 2008, supporting its move towards democracy.
2014	Prime Minister Narendra Modi chooses Bhutan as his first foreign destination. He inaugurates the Supreme Court Complex on his visit and promises assistance in the digital sector.
2015-16	India's budgetary support to Bhutan which stood at US $600 million in 2012-13, rises steadily to US$985 million by 2016 under India's 'Economic stimulus package' for Bhutan.
2020	• February – BBIN nations deliberate Memorandum of Understanding (MoU) to implement the Motor Vehicle Agreement to regulate vehicular traffic. • A MoU is signed between the two nations for peaceful use of outer space.
2021	• June – India and Bhutan jointly launch the "**Tax Inspectors Without Borders (TIWB)**" – a joint initiative of UNDP and OECD. • July - Bhutan becomes the first neighbouring country to adopt India's **BHIM-UPI payment system**. • November – Both nations in talks to add seven additional entry and exit points to increase trade connectivity.
March 2024	• PM Modi was conferred the **Order of Druk Gyalpo Award** (Highest Civilian Award) in Bhutan, as recognition of PM Modi's contribution to strengthening India-Bhutan friendship.

India-Bhutan Treaty of Friendship, 1949

- India recognises the sovereignty, independence and territorial integrity of Bhutan.
- India and Bhutan have agreed to extend '*national treatment*' to each other i.e. Indian citizens have same right for employment in Bhutan as Bhutani nationals do in India.
- There would be an open-border system – right of movement into each other's territory without a visa.
- Bhutan agreed to let India "guide" its foreign policy and decided that the two nations would consult closely on foreign and defense affairs.
- The treaty establishes free trade and extradition protocols.
- The treaty discussed cultural cooperation, sports development, cooperation in science and technology and healthcare.

Economy and Infrastructure

- India has been the largest trade and development partner of Bhutan and since the launch of the First Five Year Plan (FYP) of Bhutan in 1961, India has been extending generous financial assistance to Bhutan's FYPs.
- India is Bhutan's largest trading partner, accounting for the majority of the country's exports and imports. The two countries have a free trade agreement that allows for duty-free trade in a wide range of goods. India is also the largest market for Bhutan's hydropower exports, which is a major source of revenue for the country.
- Indian banks, such as the SBI and Bank of Baroda, have presence in Bhutan. Indian firms are undertaking work related to hydroelectric power, minerals exploration and construction in Bhutan.
- Indian imports from Bhutan include minerals, hydropower, wood and chemicals. Bhutan's main imports include fuel, vehicles, and machinery, which mostly come from India. India has also provided financial and technical assistance for the development of Bhutan's road network and other infrastructure.
- India has provided significant amounts of aid and grants to Bhutan for various development projects. This includes funding for education, healthcare, and rural development projects. India is a major source of tourism for Bhutan, with Indian tourists accounting for a significant proportion of the country's total tourist arrivals.

NOTE

National Payments Corporation of India (NPCI) has signed agreements with the **United Arab Emirates** and **Bhutan** to enable **cross-border payments using the UPI system.**

Hydropower and Energy

Bhutan has close economic and geopolitical ties with India, which serves as its primary commercial partner, provider of international aid, and funder and buyer of excess hydropower.

Hydropower is Bhutan's largest export, with most of it going to India. India has made significant investments in Bhutan's economy, particularly in the areas of hydropower and infrastructure. **Indo-Bhutan hydropower cooperation began in 1961** with the signing of the **Jaldhaka agreement**. The Jaldhaka project is situated on the Indian side of Indo-Bhutan border in West Bengal. A major part of power produced at Jaldhaka hydropower plant was exported to southern Bhutan.

India's assistance in the growth of Bhutan's hydropower sector holds a central position in the economic cooperation between the two countries and serves as a significant pillar of their bilateral relations. The revenue generated from the sale of hydropower constitutes a substantial portion of Bhutan's GDP, making it a crucial export commodity and contributing around 63% of the country's total exports. The **Druk Green Power Corporation**, responsible for managing all electricity generation facilities in Bhutan, is the largest taxpayer in the country.

A significant milestone occurred in 1987 when the **Chukha Hydropower Project (CHP)** was completed, marking Bhutan's first major power project. The project was fully funded by the Government of India, with 60 percent provided as a grant and 40 percent as a loan at a 5 percent interest rate, repayable over 15 years following its commissioning. The successful implementation of the Chukha project laid the foundation for future collaborations in the field of hydropower. Another noteworthy venture, the 1,020 MW **Tala Hydroelectric Project**, which stands as one of the largest joint initiatives between India and Bhutan, was also financed by the Government of India, with a similar funding structure of 60 percent grant and 40 percent loan.

The two countries signed the **Agreement on Cooperation in the Field of Hydroelectric Power (HEP) in July 2006**, which outlines the framework for cooperation in the field of Hydropower. In **May 2008**, both nations signed the **Protocol to the 2006 Agreement** concerning Cooperation in the Field of Hydroelectric Power and agreed to increase the scale of power projects from 5,000 MW to 10,000 MW by the year 2020.[13]

- Of these, two projects totalling 2220 MW (1200 MW Punatsangchu-I, 1020 MW Punatsangchu-II) are under construction.
- Out of the remaining 7 HEPs, 4 totalling 2120 MW (600 MW Kholongchhu, 180 MW Bunakha, 570 MW Wangchu and 770 MW Chamkarchu) were to constructed under a Joint Venture (JV) model.
- Under the May 2008 Protocol, the two governments also established the **Empowered Joint Group** to expedite the development of hydropower projects in Bhutan.

During PM Modi's visit to Bhutan in 2014, he laid the foundation stone of the **600 MW Kholongchu hydro-electric project** which would be a **joint venture**. In 2019, the **720 MW Mangdechhu hydroelectric project** was jointly inaugurated.

Th ongoing projects include the **1200 MW Punatsangchu I** (expected to be completed by 2024-2025) and the **1020 MW Punatsangchu II** (it was expected to be commissioned by 2022 but is delayed). The Punatsangchhu-I project, situated along the **Punatsangchhu river**, is a significant run-of-the-river hydroelectric scheme. It is located between 8.5 km and 18.5 km downstream of the **Wangduephodrang bridge** and is considered the largest hydro power project ever undertaken in Bhutan. Furthermore, it holds the distinction of being the initial 10,000 MW project jointly undertaken by the Royal Government of Bhutan and the Government of India.

Diplomacy and Security

- Bhutan's strategic importance to India lies in its geographical location as it is situated between India and China in the Himalayas. This positioning acts as a buffer between the two neighboring giants.
- Unlike other South Asian countries, Bhutan has consistently prioritized India's security concerns and refrained from participating in initiatives such as China's Belt and Road Initiative (BRI) and other forms of assistance like grants and loans.
- The Indian military plays a vital role in safeguarding Bhutan from external and internal threats, and the Eastern Command of the Indian Army and Air Force have integrated Bhutan's defense into their responsibilities. **The Indian Military Training Team (IMTRAT)** also provides training to Bhutanese security personnel.
- Since 1961, the Border Roads Organisation has been running **Project Dantak**, which focuses on constructing roads, telecom infrastructure, educational institutions, and other important infrastructure projects in Bhutan.

NOTE

In March 2024, PM Modi was conferred the **Order of Druk Gyalpo Award** (Highest Civilian Award) in Bhutan.

[13] Bhutan-India Hydropower Relations. Royal Bhutanese Embassy (New Delhi, India) https://www.mfa.gov.bt/rbedelhi/bhutan-india-relations/bhutan-india-hydropower-relations/#:~:text=Manmohan%20Singh%20to%20Bhutan%2C%20the,MW%20by%20the%20year%202020.

India and Bhutan are common members of several multilateral and regional groupings/organisations including **SAARC, BBIN (Bangladesh, Bhutan, India, and Nepal), WTO and United Nations**.

CONTENTIOUS ISSUES

- Wedged between China and India, Bhutan is located at a very strategically significant location due to which **India sees Bhutan as a "buffer state"** against Chinese aggression and military adventures. Securing Bhutan's present borders especially its western border is clearly important for India.
- Bhutan's proximity to the **Siliguri Corridor**, or "**chicken's neck**," which is a narrow strip of land that connects India to the rest of the North-East Region (NER), has only heightened fears of a Chinese invasion and potential isolation of the NER from the rest of the mainland.
- **Chumbi valley** is a tri-junction between Bhutan, India and China. Chumbi valley holds significance for China as it connects Tibet and Sikkim and China wants to expand its manoeuvres here.
  - o The Bhutan–China border problem began in 1950 when China published a map and claimed the West Bhutan area.
  - o China's claims over Bhutanese territory are indirect, stemming from its claims over Tibet.
  - o Over the past several years, China has employed both coercive and persuasive methods to woo Bhutan into solving the territorial disputes but to no avail.

As for India, **any claim over the Chumbi Valley** is dangerous as it is barely 500 km from the **Siliguri corridor** and could result in the severance of the only territorial linkage between the NER and the rest of the country.

- It is important to understand that China's policy and territorial disputes with Bhutan are largely defined by its external and internal calculations that are not necessarily linked only to Bhutan. Internally, Bhutan's 'neutral' or 'friendly' stance could help in legitimizing China's control in Tibet since Bhutan shares cultural and ethnic similarities with the region. Externally, the unresolved border issues and a Bhutan's strong posture pose a credible challenge to China's global standing and aspirations.
- While Bhutan has so far resisted the temptations of China, Bhutan's private sector is keen to benefit from Chinese investment and has been making requests to initiate agreements. With its assiduous construction of trade and transport links in and across the Himalayas, China has begun to erode India's geographic advantage in Bhutan.

In the case of Bhutan, there is a need to revisit the existing bilateral treaties, to harmonise their tenor with the aspirations of the present populace, while safeguarding the security imperatives of India.

MALDIVES

ABOUT THE COUNTRY

The Maldives is a small island nation located in the Indian Ocean, southwest of India and Sri Lanka. It is made up of 26 atolls, with a total of over 1,000 coral islands. The Maldives is known for its beautiful beaches, clear blue waters, and rich marine life, making it a popular tourist destination.

POLITICS & ADMINISTRATION

- Politically, the Maldives is a **presidential representative democratic republic**. The President of the Maldives is both the head of state and head of government, and is elected by popular vote for a five-year term. The Maldives has a **multi-party system**, with several political parties competing for seats in the legislature and the presidency. The most prominent political parties in the Maldives include the Maldivian Democratic Party (MDP), the Progressive Party of Maldives (PPM), and the Adhaalath Party.
- **Islam is the state religion**, and nearly 100% of the population are Sunni Muslims. The legal system in the Maldives is based on Sharia law, which governs aspects of both public and private life. This includes family law, criminal law, and social behavior, reflecting the deep intertwining of religion and state.

- The Maldives also has a decentralized system of government, with each atoll and island having its own administrative body known as the Atoll Council and Island Council, respectively. These councils are responsible for providing basic services and infrastructure to their respective communities.
- In recent years, the Maldives has faced political turmoil, with allegations of corruption, human rights abuses, and authoritarianism. However, the country has also taken steps towards democratization, including the adoption of a new constitution in 2008 and the establishment of a Human Rights Commission.

ECONOMY & TRADE

- The Maldives has a small but rapidly growing economy, heavily dependent on tourism, fishing, and related services. The construction sector is growing, driven by the development of new resorts, housing, and infrastructure projects.
- As of 2023, Maldives GDP (Current US$) was 6.6 billion, with an annual growth of 4.0%.
- Tourism is the backbone of the Maldivian economy, contributing around 70-80% of its GDP and generating the majority of its foreign exchange earnings. The Maldives is renowned for its luxury resorts, pristine beaches, and vibrant marine life, attracting tourists from around the world.
- Fishing is the second-largest industry and has traditionally been the livelihood of many Maldivians. The country is known for its tuna exports, particularly to Europe and Japan.

KEY CHALLENGES FACED BY MALDIVES AS A 'SIDS'

The Maldives, an archipelago nation in the Indian Ocean, is a prime example of a **Small Island Developing State (SIDS).** Characterized by its low-lying geography, limited landmass, and heavy reliance on the ocean, the Maldives epitomizes the vulnerabilities faced by such nations.

CLIMATE CHANGE VULNERABILITY

As one of the world's lowest-lying countries, the Maldives is highly susceptible to sea-level rise, posing an existential threat to its very existence.

ECONOMIC DEPENDENCE

The nation's economy is heavily reliant on tourism, making it vulnerable to economic shocks and external factors

RESOURCE CONSTRAINTS

Limited land area and natural resources restrict development options.

GEOGRAPHICAL ISOLATION

The Maldives' remote location poses challenges in terms of transportation, communication, and access to global markets.

- **Challenges to the economy** - The Maldivian economy is highly vulnerable to external factors such as global economic downturns, natural disasters, and the impacts of climate change. Rising sea levels and environmental degradation pose significant risks to the Maldives, given its low-lying geography. The government has recognized the need to diversify the economy beyond tourism and fisheries. The Maldives has seen a rise in public debt, partly due to large-scale infrastructure projects funded by external borrowing. Managing this debt is crucial for long-term economic stability.
- **Future Prospects** - The government is promoting the concept of the "blue economy," which emphasizes the sustainable use of ocean resources for economic growth, improved livelihoods, and jobs while preserving the health of the ocean ecosystem. There are also efforts to reduce dependence on imported fuel by developing renewable energy sources, such as solar and wind power, are gaining momentum

CULTURE & PEOPLE

- Islam is the state religion and Islamic practices and values are integral to Maldivian life, influencing daily routines, laws, and customs. The practice of Islam is mandatory, and religious observances, such as daily prayers and Ramadan fasting, are strictly followed.
- The official language of the Maldives is Dhivehi, an Indo-Aryan language with its own script, Thaana. It has been influenced by Arabic, Hindi, and English, reflecting the country's historical trade links and interactions.
- Traditionally, Maldivian society has been patriarchal, with men playing dominant roles in public life and women primarily responsible for household duties. However, women in the Maldives enjoy relatively high levels of education and participation in the workforce, particularly in sectors like education, healthcare, and civil service.
- The rise of tourism has introduced global influences into Maldivian society, particularly in urban areas like Malé. While embracing modernization, Maldivians continue to uphold their traditions and cultural identity.
- While being deeply rooted in Islamic traditions, the society is community-oriented with a rich heritage of music, dance, and crafts.

INDIA AND MALDIVES TIES

India and Maldives have deep-rooted connections based on ethnic, linguistic, cultural, religious, and commercial ties, dating back to ancient times. The two countries maintain a close, friendly, and diverse relationship. India was among the first nations to acknowledge Maldives' independence in 1965 and establish diplomatic ties with the country. In line with India's "Neighbourhood First Policy," India is committed to fully supporting the socio-economic development of the Maldives. Similarly, the Maldivian government has expressed its commitment to an "India First policy," emphasizing close collaboration with the Indian government on all matters. Bilateral cooperation between India and Maldives is guided by a set of principles based on the framework of South-South cooperation and building solidarity and partnership between developing nations in the post-colonial phase. Maldives occupies a special place in the **SAGAR** (Security and Growth for All in the Region) vision of Government of India.

Apart from being a neighbouring nation that India supports, Maldives is critical for India on mainly two factors –

Geostrategic relevance	Maritime Economy
• The Maldives holds a strategic position in the Arabian Sea, with its northernmost waters located just 100 km away from the Indian island of **Minicoy**. It is approximately 380 km away from **Kavaratti** and a mere 425 km from the closest point on the Indian mainland, the coast of Thiruvananthapuram. • China's strategic interests and logistical limitations in the Indian Ocean have provided an impetus to it to increase its presence in the Indian Ocean.	• The two vital passages situated at the southern and northern ends of the island chain serve as the only safe routes for ships to navigate. These **sea lanes of communication (SLOCs)** play a crucial role in facilitating maritime trade between the **Gulf of Aden** and **Gulf of Hormuz** in West Asia, as well as the Strait of Malacca in Southeast Asia. • The Indian Ocean is recognized as a **vital route for global trade and energy transportation**, and the Maldives holds a significant position as a strategic point of access. It serves as a crucial transit point for energy supplies originating from Gulf countries.

YEAR	KEY HISTORICAL EVENTS
1558-1573	Occupation by the Portuguese, which eventually ends after expulsion by the locals.
17th century	Islands become a protectorate of the Dutch rulers of Ceylon (Sri Lanka). In 1796, the British take control of Ceylon with the islands coming under them.
1887	The islands become an 'internally self-governing' British protectorate.
1932	First democratic Constitution is proclaimed, and the sultanate becomes an elected position.
1953	It becomes a republic within the Commonwealth and the sultanate is abolished, but restored within months.
1965	Full independence as a sultanate outside Commonwealth.
1968	Sultan deposed after referendum and the Republic is reinstated with Ibrahim Nasir as president.
1976	India and Maldives sign a maritime boundary treaty.
1981	India and Maldives sign a comprehensive trade agreement.
1985	Both nations become **founding members of SAARC** (among other founding members)
1988	A coup attempt involving Sri Lankan mercenaries is foiled with the help of Indian commandos – **Operation Cactus**
1999	Parliamentary elections take place with over 120 independent candidates contesting 40 seats.
2003-2004	• Male witnesses unprecedented anti-government riots • The President promises Constitutional changes including the permission to allow formation of political parties. • State of Emergency imposed after a pro-democracy demonstration turns violent. • The nation suffers sever damage in December of 2004 when a tsunami generated by a powerful undersea earthquake off the Indonesian coast hits the islands.
2006	Indian Navy gifts a Trinkat Class Fast Attack Craft to Maldives National Defence Force's Coast Guard.
2008	• President Gayoom ratifies **new constitution** that paves the way for first multi-party presidential elections. • October – Opposition leader Mohamed Nasheed defeats President Gayoom.
2014	India provides assistance to Male when it witnessed a drinking water crisis. Humanitarian relief efforts are also undertaken.
2011-15	Maldives' first democratically elected president from 2008 to 2012 Mohammed Nasheed, was arrested on 22 February 2015 on terror charges. India and US expressed concern over Nasheed's arrest and manhandling.
2020	India extends help to Maldives to tackle the COVID crisis, in the form of financial, material and logistical support. Under '**Operation Sanjeevani**' the Indian Air Force provided essential medicines and hospital consumables to the islands.
2021	The two nations sign a $500 million infrastructure project for a bridge and causeway link to connect Male with the islands of Villingli, Gulhifalhu and Thilafushi.

COOPERATION AND CONNECTIONS

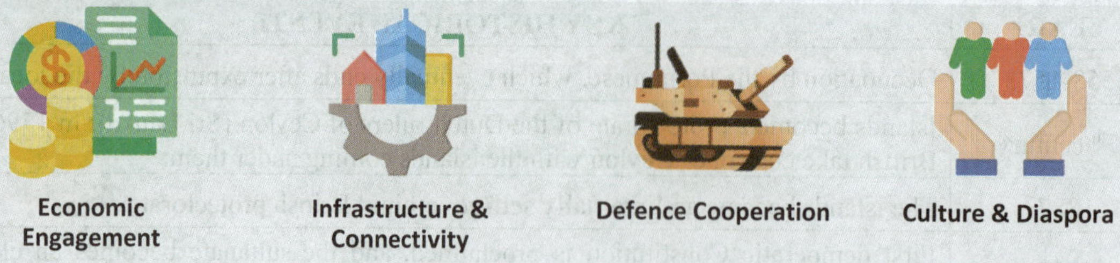

Economic Ties

India is Maldives 2nd largest trading partner (Dec 2022). In 2021, the bilateral trade between India and Maldives exceeded the milestone of $300 million, reaching an impressive amount of USD 323.9 million. This marked a significant growth of over 31% compared to the previous year. The **trade agreement** signed between India and Maldives in 1981 enables the export of essential commodities between the two countries.

Indian imports from Maldives	• Petroleum Gas, Scrap iron and Petroleum Coke. • During the last 26 years the exports of Maldives to India have increased at an annualized rate of 22.9%, from $230k in 1995 to $48.8M in 2021.
Indian exports to Maldives	• Engineering and industrial products like drugs and pharmaceuticals, radar apparatus, rock boulders, aggregates, cement and agriculture produce like rice, spices, fruits, vegetables and poultry produce etc. • During the last 26 years the exports of India to Maldives have increased at an annualized rate of 10.4%, from $31.6M in 1995 to $416M in 2021.

Since February 1974, the **State Bank of India** has been actively contributing to the economic progress of the Maldives. It has played a crucial role by providing loan assistance to support various initiatives such as the development of island resorts, export of marine products, and establishment of business enterprises.

Several agreements were signed between India and Maldives during the official visit by President Solih in **August 2022**, including-

(i)MoU for cooperation in cyber-security
(ii)MoU for cooperation in Disaster Management
(iii)MoU on Collaboration in potential fishing zone forecast capacity building and data sharing and marine scientific research
(iv)MoU on Capacity Building & Training of Members of Local Councils & Women Development Committee of Maldives
(v)Agreement for Credit Financing of Police Infrastructure in Maldives

Infrastructure and Connectivity

In a virtual meeting held between India's External Affairs Minister and Foreign Minister Shahid in **August 2020**, several projects were announced in favour of Maldives–

(1) The launch of cargo vessel service between India and the Maldives
(2) The setting up of the air travel bubble
(3) India's support for the **Greater Male Connectivity Project (GMCP)**.
(4) Renewal of essential commodities trade agreement
(5) Financial assistance of USD 250 million for budget support.

In August 2021, Afcons, an Indian company, secured a contract for the **Greater Male Connectivity Project (GMCP)**, which is the largest infrastructure undertaking in the Maldives. The project, funded by a separate $400 million Line of Credit (LoC) and a $100 million grant from India, aims to establish connectivity between **Male** and **Villingili**, **Gulhifalhu**, and **Thilafushi** islands through the construction of bridges, causeways, and roads. Additionally, in March 2022, the National College for Policing and Law Enforcement (NCPLE) was inaugurated by India's External Affairs Minister. The NCPLE, supported by a $30 million grant from the Government of India, represents the largest grant project executed by India in the Maldives.[14]

President Solih's official visit to India in **August 2022**, witnessed several announcements being made, which included –

- Extension of USD 100 mn Line of Credit to finance infrastructure projects in Maldives
- Facilitation of duty free tuna exports to India from Maldives
- Gifting of replacement ship for the earlier provided ship-CGS Huravee -to Maldives National Defence Force
- Supply of the second Landing Craft Assault (LCA)
- Gifting of 24 utility vehicles to Maldives National Defence Force.

Previously, in 2019, a **credit line agreement** was signed between Ministry of Finance, Government of Maldives and EXIM Bank of India [under **Exim Bank Line of Credit (LoC) of US$ 800 million**]. As a follow up, in 2022, a **US$ 100 million supplementary LoC** was announced. The following projects are being implemented under the LoCs[15] –

- The projects related to the Water and Sanitation on 34 islands and the Addu Roads projects are well underway.
- **Addu Land Reclamation Project** was awarded in March 2022 by GoM to a Dutch company "Van Oord' to carry out a total reclamation of 194.3 hectares of land.
- A proposed **Cancer hospital** as a model centre and State of Art Cancer Facility in Maldives, connecting their 150+ health centers on various islands. The project will be executed under the supervision of TATA Memorial Centre (TMC).
- The **Gulhifalhu Port Project** has been included with the objective to relocate the congested Malé Commercial Harbour and warehousing from Malé to Gulhifalhu Island. It has been envisaged as a modern, technology driven, globally competitive port inclusive of warehousing and logistic zones that could serve the requirement of Maldives for next 35 years.
- The EXIM Bank of India will support the redevelopment of airports in **Hanimaadhoo** and **Gan**. The Hanimaadhoo International Airport Development project under an Indian credit line will add a brand-new terminal to cater to 1.3 million passengers a year.

Defence and Security

Since 1988, defence and security has been a major area of cooperation between India and Maldives. In 2016, India-Maldives signed the **Comprehensive Action Plan for Defence.** India is the primary provider of training opportunities for the Maldivian National Defence Force (MNDF), fulfilling approximately 70% of their defense training needs. In the past decade alone, India has trained over 1400 MNDF trainees, and in 2021-22, it offered 300 training vacancies, including specialized training in organizations such as the Special Protection Group (SPG), National Security Guard (NSG), and Maritime Interdiction Operations (MIO).

The defense cooperation between the two countries has been consistent and encompasses various aspects such as joint exercises, maritime domain awareness, hardware gifting, and infrastructure development. Notable projects in the defense sector include the Composite Training Centre (CTC) for the MNDF, the Coastal Radar System (CRS), and the construction of a new Ministry of Defence Headquarters.

---

[14] Maldivian govt to sign contract for India-funded Greater Male Connectivity Project today, https://www.aninews.in/news/world/asia/maldivian-govt-to-sign-contract-for-india-funded-greater-male-connectivity-project-today20210826095207/

[15] Ministry of External Affairs. Annual Report 2022. https://mea.gov.in/Uploads/PublicationDocs/36286_MEA_Annual_Report_2022_English_web.pdf

During President Solih visit to India in August 2022, important announcements were made, including –

- Supply of a replacement ship for the earlier provided ship-CGS Huravee -to Maldivian National Defence Force (MNDF)
- Supply of the second Landing Craft Assault (LCA) to MNDF
- Gifting of 24 utility vehicles to MNDF was announced. [The 24 utility vehicles were handed over during Finance Secretary's visit to Maldives in 2022.]

Annual Defence Cooperation Dialogue at level of Defence Secretary was initiated in July 2016 and the 2nd edition was held in Nov 2017. The 3rd edition was conducted in February 2022 in Male after a delay due to the COVID-19 pandemic. Maldives is part of the **Colombo Security Conclave** (Initiated by India) which envisages peaceful cooperation in Indian Ocean along with Sri Lanka and Mauritius.

India and Maldives are both committed to ensuring the security of the **Indian Ocean**, with a focus on countering piracy, drug trafficking, and other transnational crimes. India and Maldives are both active participants in multilateral forums that deal with Indian Ocean security and governance, including the **Indian Ocean Rim Association (IORA)** and the **Indian Ocean Naval Symposium (IONS).** Both countries have been working together to promote greater cooperation and coordination among Indian Ocean states.

JOINT EXERCISES	
Ekuverin	It is an annual **Joint military exercise** that has been in place since 2009. *Ekuverin* means 'friends'. The **11th edition** was conducted at Kandhdhoo Island (Maldives) in December 2021.
Dosti	It is a biennial **trilateral coast guard exercise** involving **India, the Maldives** and **Sri Lanka**. The exercise was initiated in 1991 between India and Maldives, with Sri Lanka joining in 2012. The **15th edition** was held in November 2021 in Maldives.
Ekatha	It is a **Joint exercise between Maldivian National Defence Force (MNDF)** and **the Indian Navy**. The **5th Edition** was held in Sept-October 2022 in Maldives.
Exercise Shield (TTX-2021)	It is a **Tri Nation Table Top Anti-Narcotics & Maritime Search and Rescue exercise** between **MNDF, Sri Lanka Navy** and **Indian Navy**. It was conducted in a virtual mode for the first time in July 2021 with the Indian Navy as the lead agency.

People and Culture

The people-to-people linkages between India and Maldives are deep and historic. The Maldives has a sizable Indian community, consisting of both expatriate workers and descendants of earlier migrations. According to some estimates, there are around 20,000 Indians living in the Maldives. Cultural ties between the two countries are also strong, with shared traditions in music, dance, and cuisine. Indian films and television shows are popular in the Maldives, and many Maldivians travel to India for medical treatment, education, and tourism.

In recent years, there has been a significant increase in the number of tourists visiting the Maldives from India, reflecting the growing popularity of the Maldives as a holiday destination for Indian travelers. Foreign Secretary Harsh Vardhan Shringla visited the Maldives in Nov 2020 and announced India's support to Foreign Minister Shahid for the latter's candidacy for the post of UNGA President in 2022.

CLASHES AND CONFLICTS

1) Politics and People

- Maldives has witnessed political instability in the last 15 years, including the ouster of former President Mohamed Nasheed in 2012, and the state of emergency declared by President Abdulla Yameen in 2018. China's growing economic and strategic influence in the Maldives has raised concerns for India, particularly in light of the Hambantota Port project.
- The Maldives has witnessed the emergence of the **'India Out' campaign**, spearheaded by critics of the government. However, India has consistently advocated for democratic reforms and stability in the Maldives, while also seeking to balance its own interests and counter China's influence.
- The Maldives has experienced further political instability in 2024, with ongoing debates and discussions surrounding democratic reforms and governance. While the "India Out" campaign has remained active, with some critics continuing to express concerns about India's influence in the Maldives.
- The Maldivian government has taken steps to address these concerns and promote democratic reforms. There have been discussions and efforts to amend the Maldivian constitution to strengthen democratic institutions and address concerns about governance.
- In the recently conducted parliamentary elections (April 2024), Maldives President Mohamed Muizzu's party earned a landslide victory. This shift in power has been accompanied by a growing pro-China sentiment within the Maldivian government. The new government has taken a more assertive stance against India, with some officials calling for the removal of Indian military personnel from the Maldives.

2) Maritime Issues

- One of the major issues between India and Maldives has been **fishing rights**. The Maldivian government has often accused Indian fishermen of fishing in Maldivian waters, leading to disputes and tensions.
- India and Maldives have a **maritime boundary dispute in the Arabian Sea**, which has been a longstanding issue. The two countries are working to resolve this issue through dialogue and negotiations.
- In 2019, India and Maldives signed a **treaty on the delimitation of their maritime boundaries**, which resolved some of these issues, but there remain some areas of contention. There have been instances of smuggling and other illegal activities in the Indian Ocean, which have led to tensions between India and Maldives. Both countries have been working to enhance cooperation and coordination to counter these activities.

> **NOTE**
>
> The maritime boundary between India and Maldives was delimited through a **bilateral agreement** that was signed on 28 December 1976 and entered into force on 8 June 1978. The line extends for 545 nautical miles and delimits the Parties' exclusive economic zones.

3) Chinese Influence

- China has been a major investor in the Maldives, funding infrastructure projects such as the China-Maldives Friendship Bridge and the development of airports. The 2017 free trade agreement between China and the Maldives has further deepened economic ties.
- These investments have increased China's strategic presence in the Maldives, positioning it as a key player in the Indian Ocean region.
- Chinese companies have also invested in local media outlets, raising concerns about their influence on public opinion and the media landscape.

- The present government (2024 elections) has been viewed as 'Pro-China' and has expressed interest in exploring opportunities under China's Belt and Road Initiative, suggesting a potential shift in foreign policy orientation.
- Concerns have been raised about the Maldives' growing reliance on China, potentially compromising its economic sovereignty and leading to debt-trap diplomacy. China's support for the previous Maldivian government, despite allegations of human rights abuses, has raised concerns about its role in promoting democratic values.

RISING SIGNIFICANCE OF MALDIVES

(a) **Geopolitics & Security** –
- The Maldives is strategically located in the Indian Ocean, serving as a gateway to the Arabian Sea and beyond. Its proximity to key shipping lanes and chokepoints makes it a vital node for global maritime trade.
- The Maldives' strategic location has heightened its importance for regional and global security. Its stability and security are of direct interest to India, which seeks to maintain a balance of power in the Indian Ocean region.

(b) **Economy& Resources** –
- The Maldives is a renowned tourist destination, attracting visitors from around the world. Tourism is a major contributor to its economy, providing employment and foreign exchange.
- The Maldives possesses rich marine resources, including fisheries and coral reefs, which are vital to its economy and ecosystem.
- The Maldives can serve as a gateway for trade between India and other countries in the region, promoting economic growth and development.

(c) **Environment & Climate Change** –
- The Maldives is highly vulnerable to the impacts of climate change, including sea-level rise and coastal erosion. Its efforts to address these challenges are crucial for its long-term sustainability.
- The Maldives is home to diverse marine ecosystems, including coral reefs and sea turtles. Protecting these ecosystems is essential for the country's economic and environmental well-being.

(d) **Global Influence** – The Maldives, as a small island nation, has a unique perspective and can contribute to global discussions on issues such as climate change, sustainable development, and ocean governance. The Maldives can play a role in promoting regional cooperation and stability in the Indian Ocean region.

FUTURE PROSPECTS

1) **Strengthening Bilateral Ties:**
- India and the Maldives have demonstrated a strong commitment to strengthening their bilateral relationship, despite facing challenges.
- The Maldives is a key component of India's Neighborhood First and Security and Growth for All in the Region (SAGAR) policies.

2) **Addressing Challenges:**
- India must remain engaged with the Maldives, regardless of domestic political changes, to maintain a stable and cooperative relationship.
- India must carefully navigate the growing influence of China in the Maldives, while maintaining its own strategic interests.

3) **Strategic Engagement:**

- **Long-Term Strategy:** India needs a long-term strategy to engage with the Maldives, going beyond short-term measures and addressing the underlying challenges.
- **Regional Cooperation:** India should actively participate in regional forums like SAARC and IORA to address shared concerns and strengthen its relationship with the Maldives.
- **Trilateral Cooperation:** Exploring trilateral mechanisms involving India, Maldives, and Sri Lanka can enhance regional cooperation and address common challenges.

The future of India-Maldives relations is promising, but it requires a sustained commitment to cooperation, understanding, and addressing the challenges that lie ahead. By adopting a strategic approach and prioritizing bilateral engagement, India can strengthen its relationship with the Maldives and contribute to the stability and prosperity of the region.

3 MULTIPOLARITY AND SHIFTING BALANCE OF POWER

INTRODUCTION

In international relations, the concept of balance of power has been an important theme throughout history. It is often seen as a key factor in shaping the behavior of countries and maintaining stability in the international system, as well as in preventing the domination of any single power or group of powers.

Owing to the shift in balance of power over the past two decades, the global community has witnessed a shift away from a unipolar world dominated by the United States towards a more multipolar global system, with several major powers vying for influence and shaping the international order.

SHIFT IN BALANCE OF POWER

A change in the distribution of power and influence among countries or regions.

Factors involved -

- changes in the economic or military capabilities of countries
- shifts in alliances or geopolitical strategies,
- changes in the distribution of resources or demographic factors.

MULTIPOLAR WORLD

A global system in which power is distributed among multiple major powers, rather than being concentrated in the hands of a single dominant power or group of powers or dominated by a single hegemonic power.

Factors involved -

- The rise of new powers
- changes in the balance of power
- The emergence of new global challenges that require collective action by multiple powers.

MULTIPOLARITY

Multipolarity is a system of international relations where multiple states possess approximately equal power, such that no single state is able to dominate the others. This can lead to a more complex and balanced distribution of power, as well as increased competition and cooperation among the major powers. Multipolarity has the potential to offer several benefits to the international community.

Historically, the world has often oscillated between multipolar, bipolar, and unipolar systems. The Concert of Europe, a period following the Napoleonic Wars, is often cited as a classic example of multipolarity. However, the post-World War II era was dominated by a bipolar system, with the United States and the Soviet Union as the two superpowers. In recent decades, there has been a growing consensus that the world is transitioning towards a new multipolar order. The rise of China, India, and other emerging powers has challenged the unipolar dominance of the United States.

A multipolar system can promote economic growth and development by encouraging competition and innovation among major powers. This can lead to greater investment in infrastructure, research, and development, which can ultimately benefit the global economy. Such multiple actors have a stake in global governance, which can encourage greater cooperation and collective action on issues such as climate change, global health, and nuclear nonproliferation.

POTENTIAL BENEFITS OF MULTIPOLARITY

Increased stability and security: Multiple powers can balance each other, reducing the likelihood of conflict.

Greater diversity of perspectives: Various viewpoints contribute to more comprehensive problem-solving.

Enhanced economic growth and development: Competition and cooperation among powers can boost global economy.

Improved global governance: Multiple actors can share responsibility for addressing global challenges.

Greater respect for human rights and democratic values: Competition for legitimacy can promote these ideals.

Additional Benefits

(1) Reduced Risk of Global Conflict: A multipolar world deters aggression by ensuring no single power dominates, encouraging diplomacy and reducing the likelihood of major conflicts.

(2) Increased Innovation and Creativity: Competition among multiple powers spurs innovation and problem-solving, leading to technological and scientific advancements.

(3) More Equitable Distribution of Resources: Multiple influential states promote fairer allocation of global resources, preventing monopolization and benefiting smaller and developing nations.

(4) Strengthened Multilateralism: Multipolarity fosters cooperation in international organizations, enhancing global governance and inclusive decision-making.

(5) Greater Opportunities for Cooperation: Multipolarity enables diverse coalitions to address global issues like climate change and pandemics more effectively.

(6) Check on Hegemonic Tendencies: The presence of multiple powers prevents any single nation from dominating global affairs, promoting a balanced international order.

(7) Localization of Issues: Regional powers can address local issues more effectively, offering tailored solutions based on specific regional contexts.

(8) Resilience: Multipolarity enhances global resilience to shocks, providing multiple avenues for support and recovery.

(9) Diffusion of Power: Power is more evenly distributed, promoting a democratic international order and encouraging regional organizations' growth.

This can lead to stronger and more effective global institutions and norms. In a multipolar system, multiple powers have the ability to promote and uphold human rights and democratic values on the global stage. This can help to counterbalance the influence of authoritarian regimes and promote greater respect for human rights and democratic principles around the world.

Overall, a multipolar international system has the potential to promote greater stability, security, and prosperity for the international community, as well as foster greater cooperation and collective action on global challenges. However, it is important to note that a multipolar system also has the potential to lead to increased competition and conflict among major powers, which could have negative consequences for global peace and stability. Additionally, while the present decade has seen the developed nations taking a substantial lead, the role of the developing and underdeveloped nations cannot be neglected.

In a multipolar world, the shifting balance of power among major nations becomes a crucial aspect of international relations. As global influence shifts from a unipolar to a multipolar framework, the interactions between key players like the United States, China, and Russia are instrumental in shaping the contemporary geopolitical landscape. The following segments explore India's relations with these three influential powers, each of which plays a significant role in the evolving balance of power and multipolar order, with their unique interests, strategies, and policies towards India significantly impacting regional and global stability.

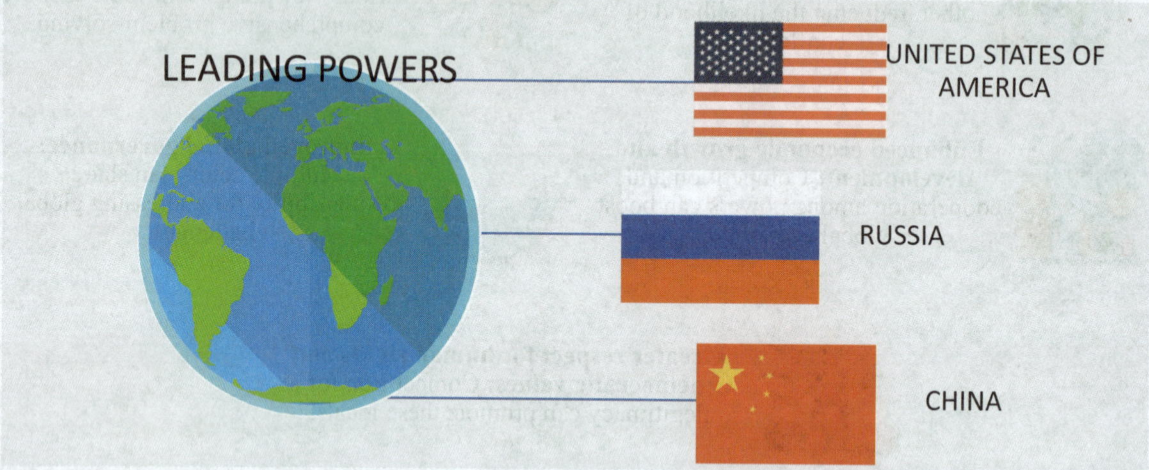

UNITED STATES OF AMERICA

The United States of America, covering a majority of the North American continent, is a **Federal Republic of 50 states**. The USA boasts of a diverse population which is mainly due to a sustained global immigration over the last few decades. The United States is often referred to as a global leader due to its significant economic, military, cultural and other related influence around the world.

Important Statistics*	
Capital	Washington, D.C.
Population	334.9 M (2023)
GDP Growth (annual)	2.5% (2023)
FDI, net inflows (percentage of GDP)	1.5% (2022)
Human Development Index Rank	20 (2023)

*World Bank data

POLITICS AND ADMINISTRATION

The political scene in the United States is complex and dynamic, with a two-party system dominated by the **Democratic** and **Republican** parties. In recent years, the country has faced increasing political polarization and division, with deep ideological differences and partisan divides on a range of issues.

(i) The Democratic Party is generally seen as more liberal and progressive, advocating for policies such as healthcare reform, climate change action, and social justice initiatives.

(ii) The Republican Party is generally seen as more conservative, advocating for policies such as tax cuts, limited government regulation, and a strong national defense.

In recent years, there has been increasing dissatisfaction with the political establishment among voters, leading to the rise of populist movements and candidates on both the left and the right. The **2016 presidential election** saw the unexpected victory **of Donald Trump**, a businessman and reality TV star with no prior political experience, who ran on a platform of "Make America Great Again." The **2020 US presidential election** was highly contested, with incumbent **Donald Trump** running for re-election against former **Vice President Joe Biden**. While Joe Biden became the 46th President of the USA in January 2021, the election was riddled with controversy over mail-in ballots, and legal challenges to the election results.

On January 6, 2021, a mob of supporters of former President Donald Trump stormed the US Capitol building, disrupting the certification of the 2020 presidential election results. The riot resulted in multiple deaths, injuries, and significant damage to the Capitol building. The incident was widely condemned by political leaders and law enforcement officials.

THE YEAR 2024

The U.S. Presidential election is set for November 5, 2024, with the winner serving a four-year term starting January 2025. In July, President Joe Biden announced he would not seek re-election, endorsing Vice President Kamala Harris as the Democratic nominee. Harris's candidacy is historic, echoing her 2020 achievement as the first woman, Black woman, and person of South Asian descent to serve as Vice President. Donald Trump, the 45th U.S. president, secured the Republican nomination for the 2024 election at the party convention in Milwaukee, Wisconsin.

DIPLOMATIC INFLUENCE

The USA wields significant diplomatic influence on the world stage due to its status as a superpower. The political, economic, and military power together help the country to stand out from the rest and take lead in mostly all global developments. The US is a **permanent member of the United Nations Security Council**, and it is often seen as a key player in global diplomacy.

The US has played a key role in leading various **global initiatives** such as the United Nations, NATO, and the World Trade Organization, among others. The US has played a key role in **brokering diplomatic negotiations**, such as the Iran nuclear deal, and has participated in various **peacekeeping efforts** around the world. The US is one of the largest donors of foreign aid in the world, providing **humanitarian and development assistance** to many countries.

In the realm of International Relations, the United States holds a prominent position as a leading global actor. As a key proponent of liberal democracy and free-market capitalism, the U.S. has been instrumental in shaping the post-World War II international order. Its extensive network of alliances, notably through NATO and various bilateral agreements, underpins its influence across different regions.

In recent years, the United States has experienced a notable shift in its global political stance and ideology. A trend toward more inward-looking policies, reflected in "**America First**" rhetoric, has contrasted with its traditional multilateralism. There has been a recalibration of alliances and a more assertive stance on economic and security issues, particularly in relation to China.

ECONOMIC STATUS

- The United States remains the largest economy in the world, with a GDP of approximately **$27 trillion** as of 2023. This accounts for nearly **25% of the global GDP**. The U.S. economy is characterized by a highly diversified structure, with significant contributions from technology, finance, healthcare, manufacturing, and consumer services sectors.
  - **Gross Domestic Product:**
- Nominal GDP (2023): Approximately $27.36 trillion
- Global Ranking: World's largest economy (Rank: 1) globally.
- GDP per capita (current US$ 2023): Approximately $81,700

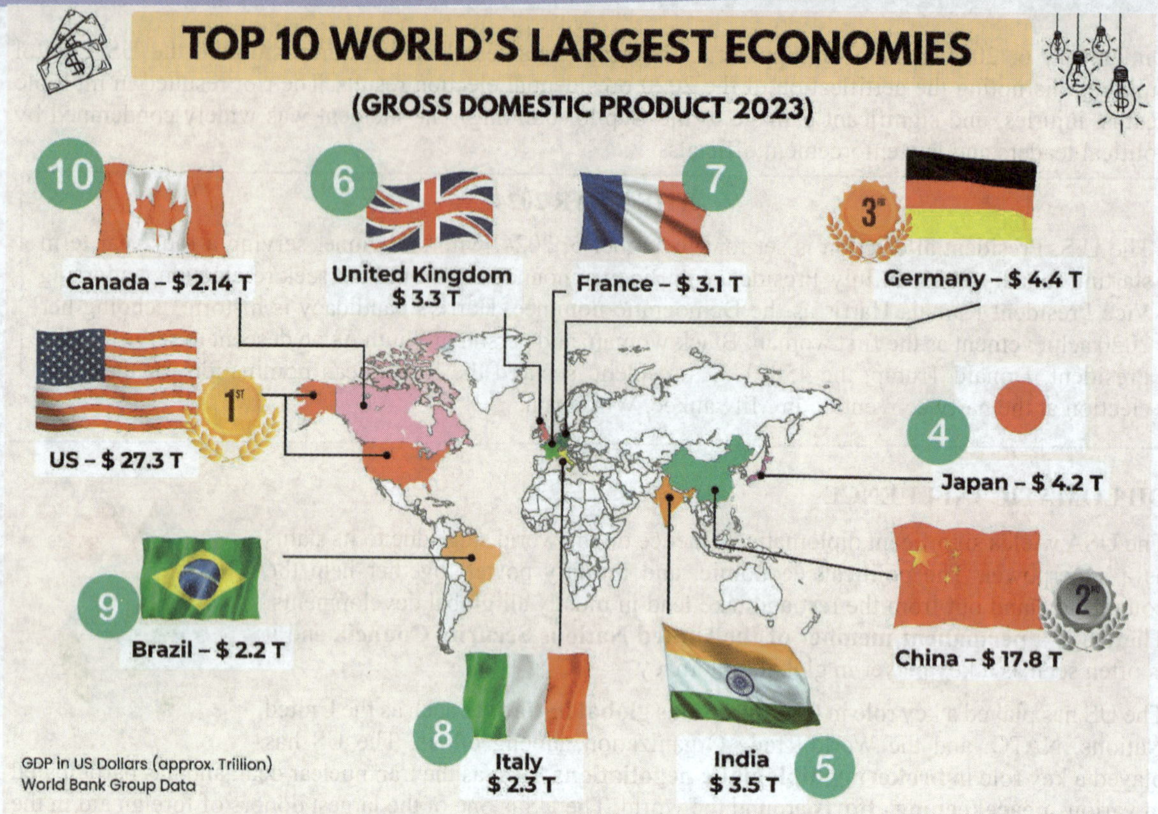

- The U.S. is the **second-largest exporter** and the **largest importer globally**, with a trade deficit of over **$900 billion**.
- The **U.S. dollar** remains the world's primary reserve currency, comprising over 60% of global foreign exchange reserves. U.S. stock markets, particularly the NYSE and NASDAQ, represent over 50% of global equity market capitalization.
- It is home to some of the **largest corporations** in the world offering their services in the fields of technology, retail, finance and healthcare, which play a critical role on the global stage. The major corporations include Apple, Amazon, Alphabet, Microsoft and Walmart.
- The US economy was affected by the COVID-19 pandemic but has shown signs of recovery. A worrisome issue is of the federal debt, which as per latest records, has surpassed **$33 trillion**, raising concerns about long-term fiscal sustainability.

The government has implemented several economic stimulus packages to support businesses and individuals, and unemployment rates have been slowly declining. The Biden administration has proposed a **$2 trillion infrastructure plan** to invest in transportation, broadband, and other critical infrastructure projects across the country. The plan is intended to create jobs, support economic growth, and address long-standing infrastructure needs.

North American Free Trade Agreement (NAFTA)

NAFTA was an agreement signed by the **United States, Canada,** and **Mexico** in **1994**, creating a trilateral trade bloc in North America. The main purpose of NAFTA was to promote free trade between the three countries by eliminating tariffs and other trade barriers, and to create new economic opportunities and jobs. While it was a success, it was also ridden with controversies, with some critics arguing that it led to job losses in the US and Canada as companies moved manufacturing operations to Mexico to take advantage of lower labor costs.

In 2020, NAFTA was replaced by the **United States-Mexico-Canada Agreement (USMCA)**, which includes some revisions to the original agreement such as new provisions for digital trade and higher labor standards.

US-China Trade Wars

- The **US-China trade war** was a significant economic conflict that escalated during the Trump administration. It involved a series of tariffs and trade restrictions imposed by both countries, primarily targeting goods from China. The US imposed tariffs on a wide range of Chinese imports, including consumer goods, machinery, and agricultural products. China retaliated with its own tariffs on US goods.
- As of 2023, trade between the US and China has seen a marked decline. For example, China's exports to the US dropped by 24% year-on-year by mid-2023, reflecting the cooling economic ties. US imports from China also fell, with a shift in supply chains toward other countries like Vietnam and Mexico.
- A major focus of the trade war has been the US's restrictions on Chinese technology companies, most notably Huawei. The US has imposed export controls on advanced semiconductor technology and pressured allies to limit China's access to these critical technologies. In response, China has been accelerating its efforts to achieve self-reliance in key technology sectors.
- Despite the tensions, both countries have engaged in diplomatic efforts to manage the conflict. High-level visits, including those by US Treasury Secretary Janet Yellen and Secretary of State Antony Blinken in 2023, aimed to stabilize relations and reopen communication channels that had been severed during periods of heightened tension.
- As of 2024, the relationship between the US and China remains fragile, with neither side willing to make significant concessions. The upcoming US presidential election in 2024 is expected to add further strain, as candidates from both parties are likely to take tough stances on China. The situation remains precarious, with the potential for further deterioration if new flashpoints arise, such as issues related to Taiwan or the South China Sea.

MILITARY STRENGTH

- The United States maintains the most powerful and technologically advanced military in the world. The U.S. Department of Defense operates with an annual budget exceeding **$800 billion (2023)**, which is more than the combined military spending of the next ten countries.
- In terms of the active personnel, the US has approximately 1.4 million active-duty personnel, with an additional 800,000 in reserve forces. The U.S. maintains around 750 military bases in over 80 countries, ensuring a global reach.
- It also boasts of an enviable nuclear arsenal, with around 3,750 active nuclear warheads, with a total stockpile of about 5,500.
- The U.S. Navy operates 11 aircraft carriers, more than any other nation, providing unmatched global naval capabilities.
- The U.S. leads in the development and deployment of advanced military technologies, including stealth aircraft, unmanned systems, cyber warfare capabilities, and missile defense systems.
- The U.S. Space Force, established in 2019, focuses on maintaining and advancing U.S. dominance in space, particularly in satellite communications, GPS, and missile warning systems.

- The U.S. military has been involved in various **conflicts** and **peacekeeping missions** globally and plays a significant role in maintaining international security and stability. However, some critics argue that the U.S. military's involvement in global affairs can also lead to negative consequences such as **excessive military spending** and **interventionism**.

The United States is a founding member of **NATO** (The North Atlantic Treaty Organization is a military alliance of North American and European countries formed in 1949) and remains the most powerful and influential member of the alliance.

RIMPAC	• It is one of the largest multilateral Naval Exercises, led by the USA (held biennially) • **RIMPAC 2022** was conducted between June and August around the Hawaiian Islands and southern California.

Sea Dragon	• It is a biennial, multi-national naval exercise focused on Anti-Submarine Warfare (ASW) training, tactics, and procedures. It is hosted by the US. • Exercise Sea Dragon 2023 was conducted in March

SCIENCE & TECHNOLOGICAL INNOVATION

The United States continues to be a global leader in scientific research, technology, and innovation, driven by its robust academic institutions, leading technology companies, and significant R&D investments.

- **Investment in R&D:** The U.S. spends over $600 billion annually on research and development, accounting for about 3.2% of its GDP. This high level of investment fuels scientific breakthroughs and technological advancements.
- **Tech Giants:** US is home to many of the world's most successful tech companies based in the US including - Apple Inc., Google (Alphabet Inc.), Microsoft Corporation, Amazon.com Inc., Facebook Inc., Intel Corporation and Tesla Inc, among others, which are collectively worth over $7 trillion. These giants drive innovation and influence global technology trends.
  1) The U.S. hosts the largest number of startups and unicorns (private companies valued over $1 billion), particularly concentrated in Silicon Valley.
- **Nobel prize Legacy:** U.S.-based researchers have won more than 380 Nobel Prizes, more than any other country, highlighting the nation's contribution to scientific advancement.
- **Pioneers in cutting-edge fields:** The United States is at the forefront of **artificial intelligence (AI)** research and development, with many of the leading companies in the field based in the country. Big Data and Blockchain have also taken off well in the country. USA has been working on the development of **electric** and **self-driving vehicles** and has been a major innovator in the transportation industry.
- **Biotech leaders:** The U.S. is a global leader in biotechnology, particularly in areas like gene editing (CRISPR), biopharmaceuticals, and medical diagnostics.
- **Space Exploration:** NASA, along with private companies like SpaceX and Blue Origin, spearheads space exploration efforts, with recent achievements including the **Mars Perseverance rover** and the **Artemis** missions aimed at returning humans to the Moon.
- **Energy efficiency & Renewable Energy:** The U.S. has implemented energy efficiency standards for various appliances and buildings, leading to significant energy savings. Smart grid technologies are being developed and deployed to improve energy efficiency
  - The U.S. has been a major player in the development and adoption of **electric vehicles**, with several domestic and foreign car manufacturers producing electric vehicles for the US market.
  - The United States has seen a surge in solar energy adoption, with numerous solar farms and residential solar installations being built across the country.
  - Wind energy is another major renewable energy source in the U.S., with wind farms located in various regions. There are ongoing efforts to modernize and expand hydropower facilities.
  - Research and development in biofuels, derived from plant materials, is ongoing in the U.S. with the aim of reducing dependence on fossil fuels.

STARLINK PROJECT

It is a satellite-based internet service being developed by **SpaceX**, the private space exploration company founded by Elon Musk. It aims to provide high-speed, low-latency internet access to users all over the world, including remote and rural areas that are currently underserved by traditional internet service providers.

- **Climate change and sustainability**: US-based researchers are at the forefront of climate change research, studying the impacts of climate change and developing solutions to mitigate its effects.
  - o The U.S. has been a leader in the development of various environmental technologies, including water treatment, pollution control, and waste management systems.

CULTURE AND DIASPORA

The diaspora in the USA is a **diverse** and significant population that includes immigrants from many different countries, as well as their descendants. According to the **Migration Policy Institute**, there were over **44 million immigrants** living in the United States in 2019, comprising around 13.5% of the total population. Many of these **immigrants** come from countries such as Mexico, China, India, the Philippines, and Vietnam, but there are also significant diaspora communities from countries across the globe, including Europe, Africa, and the Middle East. **American culture** continues to have a global reach through music, movies, and TV shows, making it a significant soft power asset for the US.

The U.S. is home to 15 of the top 20 universities globally, including institutions like MIT, Harvard, and Stanford, which are pivotal in driving global research. It helps in attracting the younger generations here.

The **death of George Floyd** in police custody in May 2020, however was a major setback for the country's international image. It sparked widespread protests across the US and brought attention to issues of police brutality and racial injustice. The protests led to renewed calls for police reform and efforts to address systemic racism in the US.

With regard to the **environment**, the Biden administration has made addressing climate change a top priority, with plans to invest in clean energy and reduce greenhouse gas emissions. The US has rejoined the Paris climate agreement and is working to promote international cooperation on climate issues.

MISCELLANEOUS CONCEPTS ASSOCIATED WITH USA

CONCEPT	PARTICULARS
1. Neoconservatism	It is a political ideology that emerged in the United States during the 1970s. It combines elements of traditional conservatism with a belief in the active use of American military power to promote democratic values and liberal international order worldwide. Key characteristics of neoconservatism include: (i) **Unilateralism:** A preference for acting alone rather than through international institutions. (ii) **Military interventionism:** A willingness to use military force to achieve foreign policy goals. (iii)**Democracy promotion:** A strong belief in the universal appeal of democracy and the need to spread it globally. (iv)**Anti-communism:** Historically rooted in opposition to communism.
2. Pax Americana	It refers to a period of relative peace and stability in the Western Hemisphere, particularly in the United States, underpinned by American political, economic, and military dominance. This era has been characterized by – (i) Military dominance (ii) Economic influence (iii) Political leadership (iv) Global Stability.
3. Identity Politics	In the US, it refers to political advocacy based on the interests and experiences of specific social groups, often marginalized or discriminated against. These groups can be defined by race, ethnicity, gender, sexual orientation, religion, disability, or other shared characteristics. Ex - Feminist movement (equal pay, reproductive rights etc.), LGBTQ+ rights movement (equality and acceptance of the LGBTQ+ community). Several critics argue that this - 1. Divides society along identity lines. 2. Overemphasizes group differences rather than commonalities.

	3. Can lead to essentialism, reducing individuals to their group identity.
4. National Security Agency (NSA)	It is is the intelligence agency of the US Department of Defense responsible for global monitoring, collection, and processing of information and data for foreign intelligence and counterintelligence purposes.
5. Central Intelligence Agency (CIA)	**The CIA is the primary foreign intelligence agency of the United States.** Created in 1947, its primary function is to gather, process, and analyze national security information from around the world. It performs several roles -including intelligence gathering, covert action, counter intelligence and counter terrorism.
6. Domestic Terrorism & Gun violence	Both these themes significant and contentious issues, often at the forefront of public and political discourse. (1) Domestic terrorism refers to violent acts committed by individuals or groups within the country, motivated by ideological, political, or religious beliefs. This includes far-right extremists, white supremacists, and other radicalized groups. (2) Gun violence, encompassing homicides, mass shootings, and accidental shootings, is exacerbated by the widespread availability of firearms and a deeply entrenched gun culture. The Second Amendment, which protects the right to bear arms, complicates efforts to enact stricter gun control laws. The federal government and state authorities continue to grapple with balancing the right to bear arms with the need to ensure public safety.
7. Cultural Soft Power	The United States employs cultural soft power through various means, leveraging its cultural influence to shape global perceptions and promote American values. Key avenues include – Entertainment industry, education, media & technology, cultural diplomacy and through NGOs and foundations.
8. Climate Action	The United States' stance on climate action has evolved over time, but as of the current administration, it emphasizes a strong commitment to addressing climate change both domestically and globally. The U.S. government acknowledges climate change as a critical issue and prioritizes policies aimed at reducing greenhouse gas emissions, transitioning to clean energy, and promoting sustainable practices.
9. Energy Independence	US aims at achieving energy independence by diversifying its energy sources, increasing domestic production, and enhancing energy efficiency. • **Renewable Energy Expansion**: The U.S. is investing in wind, solar, hydroelectric, and geothermal energy to reduce dependence on imported fossil fuels. • **Energy Technology Innovation**: The U.S. is advancing energy storage technologies and exploring advanced nuclear and hydrogen as clean energy solutions. • **Energy Efficiency**: Efforts focus on reducing energy consumption in industries, transport, and buildings through improved standards and incentives. • **Domestic Production**: The U.S. continues extracting oil and natural gas, using fracking to ensure energy security while transitioning to cleaner energy. • **Infrastructure Upgrades**: Modernizing the grid and energy infrastructure to accommodate new energy sources and enhance resilience. • **Policy and Regulation**: Federal and state policies, including incentives and regulations, support the growth of domestic energy, both renewable and fossil-based.

	• **Reducing Imports**: The U.S. aims to decrease reliance on foreign energy by boosting domestic production and diversifying supply chains.

ALASKA

- Alaska, the largest state in the U.S., is located in the far northwest of North America, bordered by Canada to the east and Russia across the Bering Strait to the west. Known for its vast wilderness, including mountains, forests, and abundant wildlife, Alaska is rich in natural resources, particularly oil, gas, and minerals, making it a key player in U.S. energy production.
- Its strategic location is significant for national security, especially during the Cold War, as it hosts military bases and is a critical point for monitoring Arctic and Pacific regions.
- its proximity to the Arctic highlights its importance in global discussions on climate change and Arctic sovereignty.
- **Aleutian Islands** are a chain of islands that extend from the southwest of Alaska across the North Pacific Ocean toward Russia. They form part of the boundary between the Bering Sea to the north and the Pacific Ocean to the south. They are part of Alaska and are known for their rugged terrain, harsh weather, and active volcanoes. The Aleutians are important for their rich marine life and as a key site for U.S. military installations.

INDIA-USA RELATIONS

The relations between India and the United States have had their share of ups and downs and the journey from President Truman to Biden has been anything but smooth. The Indo-Soviet friendship and the US-Pak alliance were the two historic irritants which stirred the relations of the two democracies. Every US President has come to office with their share of opinions about India which was very well reflected in their foreign dealings with India.

The common foundation of shared democratic values has been a key factor in fostering cooperation between India and the United States. Over time, this cooperation has expanded and deepened, resulting in a strategic partnership of global significance. The bilateral relationship now encompasses various sectors such as trade, investment, defense, security, education, science and technology, cyber security, nuclear energy, space technology, clean energy, environment, agriculture, and health. The interaction between people from both countries adds further energy and strength to this bilateral relationship.

YEAR	KEY HISTORICAL EVENTS
1949	• India makes a formal proclamation of neutrality in Cold War i.e., the Non-Alignment Movement (NAM) • Prime Minister Pandit Jawaharlal Nehru meets with U.S. president Harry S. Truman on a multi-week tour of the United States. • The NAM issue creates constraints within Indo-US relations
Feb, 1959	Inspired by M.K. Gandhi, U.S. civil rights leader **Martin Luther King Jr.** arrives in India for a month-long tour and reaffirms commitment to non-violent resistance.

Dec, 1959	**President Dwight Eisenhower** becomes the first serving U.S. president to visit India.
1962	• One of the initial Indian Institutes of Technology was established with the assistance of nine American universities and the U.S. Agency for International Development (USAID). • During the Kanpur Indo-American Program, American faculty members played a key role in developing academic programs and research laboratories at the newly established university over a period of ten years.
Oct 1962	During the **Indo-China war**, Prime Minister Nehru sends a letter to President John F. Kennedy seeking assistance from the United States. The United States supports India in the conflict, acknowledging the McMahon line as the border and providing air support and weaponry. Strategic and military relations between Washington and Delhi continue to be strong until the 1965 India-Pakistan War.
1963	**Norman Borlaug** traveled to India to start testing high-yield wheat varieties; push towards the 'Green Revolution'.
1971	• India and Pakistan engage in their third conflict while Pakistan undergoes a civil war resulting in the formation of Bangladesh. • Despite evidence of the Pakistani Army's atrocities in East Pakistan, the United States supports Islamabad due to its role in President Nixon's efforts to improve relations with China. • India, departing from its non-alignment stance, enters into a twenty-year Treaty of Friendship and Cooperation with the Soviet Union.
1974	India becomes the first nation outside the UNSC permanent members to detonate a **nuclear device (Pokhran-I).** This began a period of estrangement between USA and India.
1978	• January: **U.S. President Jimmy Carter** visits India on a three-day official trip to meet with Indian President Neelam Sanjiva Reddy and Prime Minister Morarji Desai • June: PM Desai reciprocates with an official six-day visit to Washington
Mar, 1978	The United States passes the **Non-Proliferation Act**, which mandates that countries not party to the Non-Proliferation Treaty, including India, must permit inspections of all nuclear facilities by the International Atomic Energy Agency. India declines to comply, leading to the cessation of all nuclear assistance from Washington to Delhi.
1982	During her visit to the United States, Indira Gandhi engages in diplomatic efforts and meets with President Ronald Reagan. The leaders successfully improve bilateral relations and reach an agreement to enhance cooperation and address a dispute concerning nuclear power.
Dec, 1984	• **Bhopal Gas Leak incident** occurs at an American-owned Union Carbide Pesticide Plant in Bhopal, India which kills thousands. • India unsuccessfully seeks extradition of the company's chief executive from the United States for criminal prosecution as the death and disability toll climbs to the tens of thousands in the ensuing years. • This incident strained Indo-US relations.
1990	Deputy National Security Advisor Robert Gates travels to India and Pakistan to defuse tensions over the rapidly escalating insurgency in Kashmir (fears of potential nuclear warfare)
1991	India launches **Economic Reforms** and expands ties with US.

1998	• India tests **nuclear devices (Pokhran-II)**, surprising U.S. intelligence organizations. The tests draw international condemnation and damages relations with U.S. • President Bill Clinton imposes **economic sanctions**, required under U.S. law.
1999	India-Pakistan clash in Kashmir area. Eventually President Clinton summons PM Nawaz Sharif, after which he withdraws his forces from their positions beyond the Line of Control.
2000	• **President Bill Clinton** makes the first U.S. presidential trip to India since 1978. • The Indo-U.S. Science and Technology Forum is established
2001	**President George Bush lifts all remaining U.S. sanctions imposed after 1998 nuclear test.**
2005	• **Energy Security Dialogue** begins • The signing of the **New Framework for the U.S.-India Defense Relationship** focuses on areas such as maritime security, humanitarian assistance and disaster relief, and counterterrorism.
2005	Landmark **Civil Nuclear Deal** is drafted → India agrees to separate its civil and military nuclear facilities and place all its civil resources under International Atomic Energy Agency (IAEA) safeguards. [Deal completed in July 2007]
2008	• The Nuclear Suppliers Group (NSG) grants India an exemption to its rules, enabling India to participate in nuclear trade. • In November, Chandrayaan-1 successfully lands on the moon, making it the first Indian spacecraft to do so. It carries two scientific instruments developed by NASA scientists, which later make the discovery of water molecules on the moon's surface.
November 26, 2008	LeT Terrorists attack Taj Palace Hotel in Mumbai. The U.S. cooperated by sending FBI investigators and forensic experts
2010	• U.S. Treasury Secretary Launches **Economic and Financial Partnership** • The first U.S.-India Strategic Dialogue is convened. • **President Obama backs India bid for UNSC**
2012	Secretary of Defense Leon Panetta boosts military ties, after Obama administration announced "pivot" to Asia
2014	President Obama invites PM Modi to U.S. reversing an earlier visa ban. In Sept, 2014 PM Modi visits U.S. and events include a sold-out speech in New York's Madison Square Garden and meetings with U.S. business executives.
2015	President Obama's second India visit elevates ties
2016	The U.S. elevates India to a "major defence partner"
June, 2017	President Donald Trump welcomes PM Modi to White House. A Joint statement is released emphasizing defence partnership, cooperation on counterterrorism and boosting economic ties
Sept, 2018	'2+2' dialogue conducted in New Delhi. **COMCASA (Communications Compatibility and Security Agreement)** gives India access to advanced communication technology from U.S. defence equipment and allows real time information sharing.
2019	President Trump ends India's Special Trade Status.
2020	Officials Sign Deal to Boost Intelligence Sharing - **The Basic Exchange and Cooperation Agreement (BECA)**

2021	• 46th President Joe Biden appointed at least 55 Indian-Americans to key leadership positions in his administration, including Vice-President Kamala Harris. • The USA joins the International Solar Alliance
April 2021	US Navy conducts '**Freedom of Navigation**' operation in Indian waters without India's prior consent.
Sept, 2021	The White House hosts the first-ever in-person **QUAD summit**.
2022	• The United States hosted the **fourth 2+2 Dialogue** and the two nations agreed to cooperate on issues of counterterrorism, space, health etc. • US Commission on International Religious Freedom (USCIRF) report on religious freedom recommends that India be designated a 'Country of Particular Concern'. • Prime Minister Narendra Modi and US President Joe Biden met at the Quad Leaders Summit in Tokyo, Japan. • PM Modi made his first state visit to the US, addressing the US Congress and strengthening bilateral ties.
2023	• PM Modi and President Biden met at the G20 Leaders Summit in Bali, Indonesia. • Both nations launched the Critical and Emerging Technology (iCET) Initiative to collaborate on emerging technologies • India and the US announced plans for a joint mission to the International Space Station.
2024	• The Quad Leaders Summit in Tokyo in May 2023 strengthened the India-US partnership. • Both countries have collaborated on global initiatives, such as the Indo-Pacific Economic Framework (IPEF) and the Summit for Democracy.

Cold War and the Aftermath

The Indian leaders had been in constant touch with the events of the USA and diplomatic contacts between India and the US had been initiated in around 1941. However, due to several hurdles, the relations couldn't soar as high as their potentials allowed.

The main factors included –

- The US was too occupied countering the advances of the Soviet Union through the **'containment of Communism'** policy during the Cold War phase to forge any effective bilateral relations with India
- PM Nehru opted for **'non-alignment'** and refused to join the competitive military alliances during the Cold War phase which was regarded by the USA as India's refusal to collaborate - **sign of unfriendliness.**
- The US through Cold war brought rivalry to India's doorsteps by forming two **military organisation SEATO and CENTO with Pakistan** who joined these alliances as a key member. The US military aided Pakistan for checking the spread of communism, but it was used against India contrary to initial assurances.

(a) The **October 1962 war between India and China** introduced a new element in the Indo-US relations. A strong alliance between India-US was advocated by a few to counter the Chinese threat. Once the Chinese invasion scaled up, the Indian officials appealed to the US for military supplies. The then US President John F. Kennedy provided India with small arms and equipment and the US agreed to payment for these arms in rupees.

(b) The relations and goodwill suffered a setback when the US showed reluctance is openly blaming Pakistan for starting the 1965 war against India. While the **US continued to back Pakistan**, the **Vietnam War** further exacerbated the sourness in the Indo-US bilateral relations in the 1960s.

(c) The 1970s were no different and during the Bangladesh War (1971), the US froze its economic assistance to India (bilateral assistance started in 1978 after a long gap) and a part of the US Seventh Fleet was ordered into the Bay of Bengal. The nuclear-powered aircraft carrier USS Enterprise sailed towards the Bay of Bengal in a show of solidarity with Pakistan army.

(d) It was after India hosted President Carter's visit in 1977 that in the spirit of reconciliation, the relations were rekindled. This harmony couldn't survive for very long as the **Soviet invasion of Afghanistan in 1979** had thrown India and United States on opposite sides.

(e) The relations had received several setbacks but continued parallelly. The United States, along with countries like Canada, provided assistance to India in establishing nuclear power stations in 1963. However, this cooperation faced challenges in the 1970s due to India's peaceful nuclear explosion at Pokhran in 1974 and its refusal to sign the **Nuclear Non-Proliferation Treaty**. The US had hoped that India would sign the **Comprehensive Test Ban Treaty (CTBT)** in 1996, but India did not. In May 1998, when India conducted five nuclear tests at **Pokhran** and declared itself a nuclear weapons state, the US imposed military and economic sanctions.

21st Century India-US Ties

In 2000, President Bill Clinton made the first U.S. presidential trip to India since 1978, helping to thaw the coldness in the relations. One of the key turning points in India-USA relations was the signing of the **US-India Civil Nuclear Agreement in 2008**, which ended India's isolation in the global nuclear order and paved the way for closer strategic ties between the two countries. Since then, the two countries have worked to enhance their strategic partnership and have engaged in high-level talks and visits.

Indo-US Civil Nuclear Agreement

The **123 Agreement** signed between the United States of America and the Republic of India is known as the **USA–India Civil Nuclear Agreement** or India-USA nuclear deal. This historic deal effectively rewrote the rules of global nuclear regime by underlining India's credentials as a responsible nuclear state that had to be placed under the umbrella of the global nuclear order. (Discussed in detail in a separate chapter)

COOPERATIONS AND CAMARADERIE

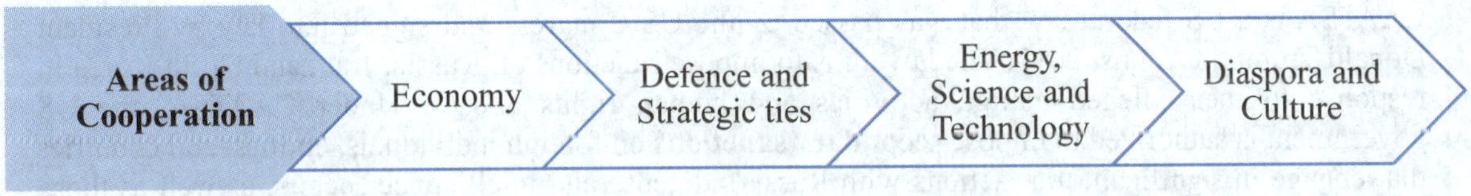

Economic Linkages

- The United States is India's **largest trading partner** and most important export market. Several American companies continue to view India as a critical market and expansion of economic operations have continued successfully. In 2021, overall **U.S.-India bilateral trade in goods and services reached a record $157 billion.**
- In November 2022, Commerce and Industry Minister, Piyush Goyal stated that "in the coming 7-8 years, the bilateral trade could be **USD 500-600 billion by 2030**, when our exports in goods and services will be USD 2 trillion each." As of April 2023, the **US is India's largest export destination**. It accounted for New Delhi's merchandise despatches worth $76 billion in FY22, or **18% of its total exports**.
- The USA and India have signed several trade agreements, including the **US-India Trade Policy Forum**, **the Bilateral Investment Treaty**, and the **Generalized System of Preferences**. However, negotiations on a comprehensive trade deal have been ongoing since 2018, and both sides are working to resolve outstanding issues.
- Indian firms and companies are also equally optimistic about the markets of the USA and have increased their presence. According to official records, by the end of 2020, Indian investment in the United States totaled **$12.7 billion**, supporting over 70,000 American jobs.

- The USA is one of the largest investors in India, with a **cumulative FDI of over $46 billion** in various sectors such as energy, infrastructure, and manufacturing. **US replaced Mauritius** as the **second largest source of foreign direct investment** into India during 2020-21.
- US is one of the top 5 investment destinations for Indian FDI. Indian companies have also invested heavily in the USA, with investments totaling over **$20 billion** in sectors such as IT, pharma, and energy.
- The **digital ties** between the nations have also received a boost. In 2019, the USA removed India from its list of developing countries, which had exempted Indian exports from certain trade rules. India has also taken steps to ease foreign investment rules in its digital sector, which has led to increased investment from US tech companies such as Amazon, Google, and Facebook.

Indo-Pacific Economic Framework for Prosperity (IPEF)

The IPEF was launched jointly by the US and other partner countries of the Indo-Pacific region on **May 23, 2022,** in Tokyo. It is a regional economic cooperation initiative of 14 IPEF partners that represent **40 per cent of the global GDP** and **28 per cent of global goods and services trade**. It is being regarded as a response to the China's Belt and Road Initiative, which has been criticized for its lack of transparency and debt sustainability.

Members - The US, Australia, Brunei Darussalam, Fiji, India, Indonesia, Japan, Korea, Malaysia, New Zealand, the Philippines, Singapore, Thailand, and Vietnam.

Four Pillars - (1) Trade (2) Supply Chains (3) Clean Energy, Decarbonization, and Infrastructure and (4) Tax and Anti-Corruption.

While 13 member countries have joined all four subjects under IPEF, **India has opted out of the trade pillar** as of now (Dec 2022). It has joined the other three subjects.

The United States granted a significant exemption to India by passing a legislative amendment in the US House of Representatives. This exemption allowed India to bypass economic sanctions under the **Countering America's Adversaries Through Sanctions Act (CAATSA)** for its purchase of the S-400 missile defense system from Russia in 2018. The purpose of this purchase was to enhance India's deterrence capabilities against potential aggressors, such as China.

Countering America's Adversaries Through Sanctions Act (CAATSA)

CAATSA is a US federal law that was passed by the US Congress and signed into law by President Donald Trump in August 2017. The law aims to impose sanctions on Russia, Iran, and North Korea in response to their alleged malign activities and human rights abuses. Under CAATSA, the US government is authorized to impose **secondary sanctions** on foreign individuals, entities, and countries that engage in significant transactions with Russia's defense and intelligence sectors, as well as those who engage in significant transactions with Iran's ballistic missile program and support for terrorism. The law also mandates sanctions on North Korea for its nuclear and missile programs.

Overall, CAATSA is seen as part of the US government's broader effort to counter perceived threats from Russia, Iran, and North Korea and to promote US national security interests. The law has been criticized for its potential impact on US allies and for its potential to disrupt global trade and investment.

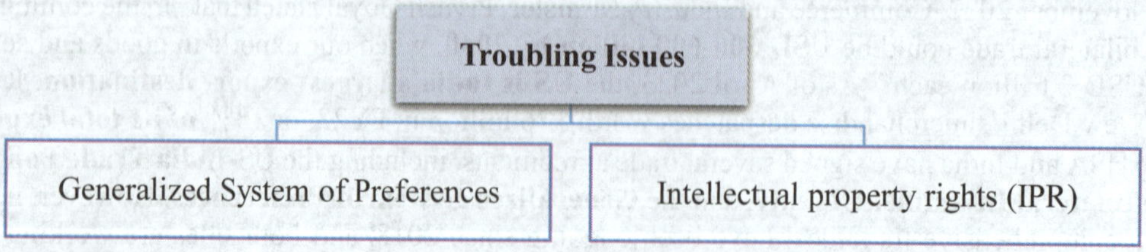

I. India has sought restoration of the **Generalized System of Preferences** (GSP) access to the US market that was revoked by Washington in 2019.
   - The **GSP** is a program that allows duty-free entry of certain products from developing countries into the US market.

- Reasons for revocation of GSP –
  (a) A primary reason cited for the revocation was **India's failure to provide equitable and reasonable access to its markets.** The US claimed that India had implemented a range of trade barriers that made it difficult for American companies to do business in India, like high tariffs, price controls, and restrictions on imports of certain goods.
  (b) Another reason cited by the US was India's **failure to provide adequate protection for US intellectual property rights (IPR).**
  (c) The US raised concerns about **India's e-commerce policies**, including restrictions on foreign investment in the e-commerce sector and data localization requirements.
- Impact of the revocation of GSP status - It resulted in the **imposition of duties on certain Indian exports to the US**, which has made those products less competitive in the US market.
- This has affected sectors such as textiles, engineering goods, and chemical products. For example, Indian exporters of certain aluminum products, such as sheet and plate, are now subject to a 10% tariff when exporting to the US.
- The two sides have reportedly been in talks to resolve the issue, but **as of April 2023, there has been no official announcement regarding the restoration of India's GSP status.**

II. Intellectual property rights (IPR) have been a constant source of conflicts between the two nations that have otherwise had good economic relations

- Patent Disputes: India's pharmaceutical industry has faced allegations of intellectual property infringement, particularly related to generic drug production.
- Data Localization: The US has pushed for India to adopt stricter data localization laws, while India has argued for data sovereignty.
- Copyright Protection: The protection of copyrighted materials, including software and media content, has been a subject of negotiation between the two countries.

(a) India had been placed on the US Trade Representative's **"Special 301" watchlist**, which identifies countries that the US believes are not doing enough to protect intellectual property.
(b) The US has criticized India's patent laws, which it says do not provide adequate protection to US companies' intellectual property, especially with regard to **compulsory licensing**.
(c) The US has accused India of not doing enough to protect copyrighted materials, particularly in the areas of music, movies, and software.

Defence & Strategic partnership

- India and the USA have been increasing their defense cooperation over the past two decades, which covers a wide range of areas, including counterterrorism, maritime security, defense trade, and technology collaboration. India plays a vital role in achieving USA's shared vision for a free and open Indo-Pacific. The USA and India have developed a strong **defense trade partnership**, with the USA becoming India's second-largest arms supplier after Russia.
- In collaboration with various government agencies, the **Political-Military Affairs (PM) Bureau** of the United States plays a crucial role in promoting the defense trade relationship and broader security partnership between the United States and India.
- The defense relationship has become a significant cornerstone of the strategic partnership between the two countries, marked by the signing of the **'New Framework for India-U.S. Defense Relations**' in 2005. This has led to increased cooperation in defense trade, personnel exchanges, joint exercises, collaboration, and maritime security, including counter-piracy efforts. Furthermore, there have been exchanges and collaborations between the three services of both nations.
- A significant development in India-USA relations was the designation of India as a "**Major Defense Partner**" by the USA in 2016, which has facilitated greater cooperation in defense and security matters. As a result of this designation, India was subsequently granted **tier 1 status in the Strategic Trade Authorization in 2018.** This status enables India to access a broad range of military and dual-use technologies regulated by the Department of Commerce without the need for individual licenses.

India has made a number of recent defense purchases from the USA as part of its efforts to modernize its military and strengthen its strategic partnership with the USA. Some of the key defense deals between the two countries include India's purchase of **C-130J Super Hercules transport aircraft, P-8I maritime surveillance aircraft**, **C17 Globemasters**, **Boeing AH-64 Apache** and **Boeing CH-47 Chinook helicopters** from the USA.

- In 2018, India received the first batch of **M777 ultra-light howitzers** from the USA, as part of a $700 million deal for 145 guns. In 2020, India approved the purchase of 30 **Sea Guardian drones** from the USA, which will be used for maritime surveillance and reconnaissance.
- There have been consistent interactions at various levels between India and the USA to discuss bilateral, regional, and global matters. The Foreign Office Consultations, involving the Foreign Secretary of India and the U.S. Undersecretary for Political Affairs, play a crucial role in this dialogue framework.
- Regarding counter-terrorism, there has been notable advancement in cooperation through intelligence sharing, information exchange, operational collaboration, and the provision of counter-terrorism technology and equipment. To further enhance coordination in this area, the **India-US Counter-Terrorism Collaboration Initiative** was established in 2010. Overtime, India and US have completed the "foundational pacts" for deep military cooperation between the two countries–

General Security of Military Information Agreement (GSOMIA)

- **Signed in 2002**.
- It provides for specific measures to ensure security standards for safeguarding critical information shared by the U.S. with India.

Logistics Exchange Memorandum of Agreement (LEMOA)

- **Signed in 2016.**
- It allows the militaries of both nations to **access supplies and services (logistical support)** from each other's bases, land facilities, air bases and ports; the resources can be reimbursed later.

Communications Compatibility and Security Agreement (COMCASA)

- **Signed in 2018** after the first 2+2 Dialogue.
- It enables the military commanders (aircraft/ships) of both nations to **communicate through secure networks** through the provisioning of US encrypted communications equipment and systems.
- It is effective during both war and peace time.

Basic Exchange and Cooperation Agreement (BECA)

- **Signed in 2020.**
- It enables India to get **real-time access to American geospatial intelligence** (information on maps, satellite images, topographical and aeronautical data etc.), which helps to improve accuracy of automated systems and aids in navigation and targeting.
- The geospatial intelligence would also help to respond to natural disasters.

Apart from the other critical diplomatic linkages, US is also India's oldest **2+2 talks partner**. The first dialogue in 2018 served as a key towards unlocking the forward-looking vision of the Indo-US strategic partnership and helped in promoting synergy in diplomatic efforts.

The **2+2 Dialogue** is a format of **meeting of the foreign and defence ministers of India** and **its allies on security and strategic issues**. It is meant to build a stronger and more integrated strategic relationship during the ever-changing geo-political environment. India has 2+2 dialogues with four key strategic partners:

- **USA** – First dialogue: September 2018 (New Delhi).
- **Japan** – First dialogue: November 2019 (New Delhi).
- **Australia** - First dialogue: September 2021 (New Delhi).
- **Russia** - First dialogue: December 2021 (New Delhi).

During the **fourth 2+2 dialogue** between India and the USA, held in April 2022 in Washington, D.C., both countries engaged in discussions regarding India's co-hosting of the **Indo-Pacific Armies Chiefs Conference (IPACC)** and **Indo-Pacific Armies Management Seminar (IPAMS)** in 2023. The ministerial dialogue also focused on the importance of revitalizing the **Defence Technology and Trade Initiative (DTTI)** through collaborative projects involving advanced, emerging, and critical military technologies. As part of the DTTI, India and the USA signed a project agreement for the development of an **Air-launched Unmanned Aerial Vehicle (ALUAV)**.

The **Industrial Security Agreement** (ISA) was signed in **2019** to facilitate the exchange of classified information between the defence industries of both countries. During the ISA Summit in 2021, both sides agreed in-principle to establish the **Indo-US Industrial Security Joint Working Group.** According to officials, the group will meet periodically to align the policies and procedures expeditiously that will allow the defence industries to collaborate on cutting edge defence technologies.

Since the establishment of BIMSTEC, the US has provided more than $145 million in Foreign Military Financing for maritime capacity building in Bangladesh, Sri Lanka, and Maldives to enhance the capacity of civilian and military actors with maritime equities to prevent, detect, and respond promptly to illicit activities within their own areas of responsibility and throughout the Bay of Bengal.

Starting from 2015, the United States has granted India authorization for more than **$3 billion worth of defense articles** through the **Direct Commercial Sales (DCS)** process. The DCS process allows for the export of defense equipment, services, and associated manufacturing technologies that are regulated under the 21 categories of the U.S. Munitions List (USML).

India participates in the **International Military Education and Training (IMET) program** and received at least $1 million of IMET funding annually since 2003. IMET provides professional military education and training to military students and is key to establishing lasting relationships with future leaders.

MILITARY EXERCISES	
Yudh Abhyas	The **Joint Training exercise (Army)** is conducted annually between India and USA with the aim of exchanging best practices, Tactics, Techniques and Procedures between the Armies of the two nations. The **18th edition** started in November 2022 at Auli, Uttarakhand.
Vajra Prahar	It is **Special Forces joint training exercise** that began alternately in 2010 in India and the US. It aims to share best practices and experiences in areas such as joint mission planning and operational tactics as also to improve interoperability between the Special Forces of both Nations. The **13th edition** culminated at Bakloh in Himachal Pradesh in August 2022.

Tiger Triumph	It is an **Indo-US Tri-Services Amphibious HADR (Humanitarian Assistance and Disaster Relief) Exercise**. In was conducted for the first time in November 2019. It sought to improve interoperability between India and the US and create a multinational command and control model for humanitarian assistance in the Indian Ocean Region (IOR). It would help in coordinating disaster relief in the region. The 2nd Edition of the Indo-US
India participates in the U.S.-led **Rim of the Pacific (RIMPAC)** exercise and trilateral **Malabar exercise** with the United States and Japan.	

In order to preserve its ideological and moral authority, the United States must first deal with economic and political weaknesses at home. The idiosyncrasy of lamenting on China's policies and political setup wouldn't assist in long term resolution of its problems and would in reality, generate greater curiosity around China and its policies. Instead, the focus must be directed towards strengthening economic competitiveness, forging internal political cohesion, and working with European and Asian partners to build lasting international relationships.

(1) India and the United States have been interacting regularly in several multilateral organizations, including the **United Nations, G-20, Association of Southeast Asian Nations (ASEAN) Regional Forum, International Monetary Fund, World Bank, World Trade Organization** and more recently, **Quadrilateral Security Dialogue (QUAD)** [Discussed in detail in the upcoming chapters].

(2) India is also one of twelve countries partnering with the United States on the **Indo-Pacific Economic Framework for Prosperity (IPEF)** to make our economies more connected, resilient, clean, and fair. India is a member of the **Indian Ocean Rim Association (IORA)**, at which the United States is a dialogue partner.

(3) The United States has supported India's bid for a place at the **UN Security Council** as a permanent member.

Energy, Science and Technology

India and the USA have been collaborating on a range of energy-related initiatives and have been reflecting on their shared commitment to clean energy and sustainable development. In 2016, the two countries launched the **US-India Clean Energy Finance (USICEF) initiative**, which aims to mobilize private sector investment in clean energy projects in India.

Both nations have launched joint initiatives in the field of clean energy, including the **US-India Energy Dialogue** and **the Partnership to Advance Clean Energy (PACE)**, which aims to accelerate the deployment of clean energy technologies in India. A Ministerial dialogue of **US-India Strategic Clean Energy Partnership (USISCEP)** was held in USA in October 2022. A revamped USISCEP was launched in accordance with **U.S.-India Climate and Clean Energy Agenda 2030.** USA has also provided technical assistance and capacity building support to India's **National Solar Mission**, which aims to increase the share of solar power in India's energy mix.

In 2021, the United States became a member of the **International Solar Alliance**, which is headquartered in India. Additionally, in 2022, Samantha Power, the Administrator of the United States Agency for International Development (USAID), assumed the role of Co-chair of the Governing Council of the Coalition for Disaster Resilient Infrastructure (CDRI), where India holds a permanent co-chair position.

The **India-US Science and Technology Cooperation Agreement** was signed in 2005 which was renewed for a period of ten years in 2019. The USA and India have also been collaborating on nuclear energy, with the USA providing support for India's civilian nuclear program. The two countries signed a **civil nuclear cooperation agreement in 2008**, which paved the way for increased cooperation on nuclear energy and technology transfer. The two countries have collaborated on space research for a long time. But in recent years, this collaboration has expanded to include a range of joint projects and initiatives in areas such as earth observation, satellite navigation, and space exploration.

The two countries have launched a number of joint satellite missions, including the **NASA-ISRO Synthetic Aperture Radar (NISAR) mission** (estimated launch – 2024), which aims to measure changes in the earth's surface and improve our understanding of natural disasters such as earthquakes and floods. India-US have been collaborating on satellite navigation, with **India's NavIC** (Navigation with Indian Constellation) **system** and the **USA's GPS** (Global Positioning System) system interoperable.

In 2023, India and the US launched the **Critical and Emerging Technology (iCET) initiative** to collaborate on emerging technologies like artificial intelligence, quantum computing, and semiconductors.

Both countries developed a roadmap to accelerate defense technological cooperation and joint production.

India recently raised concern over not being part of the US-led Minerals Security Partnership (MSP). The MSP is an international partnership for stable and diverse mineral supply chain. It ensures that critical minerals are produced, processed, and recycled to support the ability of countries to realize full economic development benefit of their geological endowments. It involves **11-members** i.e., Korea, US, Canada, Japan, Germany, UK, EU Commission, Finland, France, Australia, and Norway

Diaspora and Culture

India and the USA have a long history of cultural and people-to-people linkages, which have been strengthened by the growing economic and strategic partnership between the two countries. The **Indian Americans constitute the third largest Asian ethnic group in the US** with a population of 3.18 million. Indian-Americans have made significant contributions to various fields, including business, technology, academia, and the arts, and have played an important role in strengthening the bilateral relationship between the two countries. The nearly 200,000 **Indian students in the United States contribute $7.7 billion annually** to the U.S. economy.

The **Fulbright Program** has been an important mechanism for academic and cultural exchange between the two countries. It is a flagship international educational exchange program sponsored by the U.S. government. Additionally, the **US-India Education Foundation (USIEF)** has been facilitating educational exchange between the two countries since 1950.

Immigration Debates

- The India-US relationship has been characterized by a complex interplay of economic ties, cultural exchange, and immigration concerns. The Indian diaspora in the United States is one of the largest and most influential, with millions of people contributing to various sectors of the American economy. However, immigration has also been a source of tension between the two countries.
- A critical hurdle has been the **high rate of visa denials** and delays for Indian nationals seeking to visit or work in the USA. The United States has faced criticism for its visa policies, particularly for skilled workers and students from India.
- The **H-1B visa program**, which allows US companies to hire foreign workers in specialty occupations, has been a subject of debate, with India seeking reforms to address concerns about visa quotas and processing delays.
- The issue of **illegal immigration** has also been a source of tension between India and the USA, with the USA taking a hard line on illegal immigration and deporting a number of Indian nationals in recent years.
- The issue of **brain drain**, with Indian talent migrating to the United States, has also been a topic of discussion. While the diaspora contributes significantly to the US economy, there are concerns about the loss of talent from India.

US – A DWINDLING POWER

The Second World War, coupled with the rearrangement of the world order around the late 1980s provided a much-needed impetus for the rise of the United States as a global superpower. The United States has been oscillating between two issues over the last decade – the '***America First***' foreign policy (as opined by President Trump) and the policies surrounding its '**global leader**' status.

America Divided: Impact on Foreign Policy

The United States has historically been a global leader, championing liberal international order and engaging in various multilateral initiatives. However, in recent years, domestic political polarization has significantly impacted this role. The nation has grappled with a deepening partisan divide on foreign policy issues, creating a complex landscape for policymakers.	On one hand, a segment of the American public, often aligned with **conservative factions**, has expressed growing isolationist sentiments. This group advocates for reducing foreign commitments, military spending, and international involvement. They argue that the U.S. should prioritize domestic issues over global concerns.
	Conversely, another segment, typically associated with **liberal and centrist views**, emphasizes the importance of American leadership on the world stage. They believe the U.S. has a moral and strategic imperative to maintain its global influence to counter emerging threats, promote human rights, and protect allies.

The global standing of the USA has faced challenges in the past few years due to a number of factors -

Isolationist Policy

- One of the main factors has been the perception that the USA has become increasingly isolationist in its approach to foreign policy, with a focus on prioritizing American interests over international cooperation and engagement.
- This has led to concerns among allies and partners about the reliability of US leadership, and the potential for the USA to disengage from key global challenges.

Decline in Democratic values

- There has been an erosion of trust in US institutions and democratic values, both domestically and internationally.
- The contentious US presidential election in 2016, and the subsequent impeachment proceedings and protests, have raised concerns about the strength of US democratic institutions and the rule of law.

International relations

- The recent mishandling of international relationships, including its approach to trade and economic issues, and its shifting stance on key security alliances such as NATO.
- These developments have led to concerns about the USA's reliability as a partner and a global leader, and have contributed to a sense of uncertainty and instability in the international system.

Handling of Global issues

- The USA has faced criticism for its handling of issues such as immigration, racial justice, and climate change and its withdrawal from the Paris climate agreement, which have been viewed by some as evidence of a declining commitment to global leadership.

On the international agenda, the provisioning of global public goods is accorded a high pedestal since it determines the effective functioning of the world order. While in domestic politics, individual governments help to sustain public goods like policing services, clean environment among other things, however, on a global level this task must be delegated to a few selected nations who can successfully shoulder the burden. Since the smaller nations have little incentive to pay for such global public goods along with the fact that their contributions would make little dents, such global goods, namely financial systems, economic stability, freedom of navigation in seas and oceans are hence provided by a coalition of the largest powers.

Post the World War II, the United States became the flag bearer for the provisioning of such global public goods. Over the recent years, this status seems to be diluting with the United States falling into a

Kindleberger trap, showing a greater focus on its national issues, and gradually creating a vacuum which is being effectively filled by China.

> The term "**Kindleberger Trap**" was coined by **Joseph Nye**, a Harvard professor, based on the ideas of Charles Kindleberger, an economic historian. While both the Thucydides Trap and the Kindleberger Trap emphasize the risks associated with power shifts, the Kindleberger Trap differs by attributing the failure of the international system to a lack of adequate provision of global public goods, rather than focusing solely on the threats posed by a rising power.

Overall, the USA's global standing has faced significant challenges in the past few years, but the country continues to be an important global power with significant economic, military, and cultural influence. The USA's ability to address these challenges and strengthen its global leadership will depend on a range of factors, including its ability to rebuild trust and confidence among allies and partners, and its willingness to engage constructively with the international community on key global issues.

USA-CHINA AND THE THUCYDIDES TRAP

The tensions between USA and China date back to the formation of the Peoples Republic of China in 1949. The relations have suffered innumerable wounds and the two nations have locked horns on several occasions ranging from the Korean crisis to the Tibetan uprising and from the Taiwan issues to the Hong Kong protests. The relationship in the last decades has been volatile with both nations investing heavily in military capabilities. The relations took a nosedive in 2018 when President Trump imposed punitive tariffs on China, casting a shadow of economic doom throughout the globe. The two nations imposed retaliatory tariffs on each other's exports over the next few years, mainly on account of 'unfair trade practices'.

The scholars now point towards an intensifying rivalry between the two powers which circles around **mutual perceptions of threat and an expectation of potential future military conflicts**. While the Trump administration saw chaos reign in on the relationship between US and China, the Biden administration has chosen a less confrontational and more predictable route. The defining question for this generation however would be whether the two superpowers can escape the ***Thucydides trap*** and a war from which neither would get away unscathed.

> The **Thucydides Trap** theory suggests that when a rising power emerges, it is likely to challenge the dominant position of an existing hegemon. The fear and concerns of the established power regarding the rising power's ascent can create competitive dynamics that may escalate tensions and potentially lead to conflict.

The **South China Sea** is increasingly become a bone of contention for both the nations and the US has taken a number of steps to increase its presence in the region in recent years, in response to China's increasing assertiveness in the region –

- **Freedom of navigation operations**: The USA has conducted a series of freedom of navigation operations (FONOPs) in the South China Sea, which involve sailing US Navy ships through waters claimed by China. These operations are designed to challenge China's excessive maritime claims and demonstrate the USA's commitment to freedom of navigation in the region.
- **Military presence**: The USA has increased its military presence in the region, with the deployment of additional ships, aircraft, and personnel. The USA has also conducted joint patrols with its allies and partners, and established new military installations, such as the Marine Corps base in Darwin, Australia. The USA has increased the frequency and scale of military exercises with its allies and partners in the region, including India, Japan, and Australia. These exercises are intended to improve interoperability among regional militaries and enhance their ability to operate together in the event of a conflict.
- **Diplomatic engagement**: The USA has engaged in diplomatic efforts to build a coalition of countries to push back against China's assertiveness in the region. This has included strengthening partnerships with countries such as India, Japan, and Australia, and promoting a rules-based order in the region.
- **Technology cooperation**: The USA has sought to cooperate with its allies and partners in the region on advanced military technologies, such as unmanned aerial vehicles and missile defense systems.

While USA' approach is said to reflect its commitment to maintaining freedom of navigation and promoting a rules-based order in the region, however, it has also raised concerns about the risk of escalating tensions and potential conflict with China.

The United States has maintained a policy known as the "**One China" policy** since the 1970s, recognizing Taiwan as part of China. However, it also maintains unofficial ties with Taiwan, employing a strategy of deliberate ambiguity. Taiwan is located within the "first island chain," which consists of several US-friendly territories crucial to US foreign policy. This chain serves as a maritime boundary between the East China Sea, Philippine Sea, South China Sea, and Sulu Sea. It includes strategic chokepoints for China, such as the Bashi Channel and the Miyako Strait. The concept of the first island chain was formulated by the US in 1951 as part of its **Island Chain Strategy**, aimed at containing the former USSR and China by establishing naval bases in the western Pacific region to restrict their sea access.

Source: Oxford Analytica

The United States has previously recognized the Indo-Pacific as vital to their security and prosperity. The Second World War reminded the US that their country could only be secure if Asia was, too. And hence in the post-war era, the nation solidified its ties with the region, through ironclad treaty alliances with Australia, Japan, the Republic of Korea (ROK), the Philippines, and Thailand, laying the foundation of security that allowed regional democracies to flourish. Amidst the growing concerns in the region, the White House recently released an **Indo-Pacific Strategy document** to solidify its commitment towards the island nations. The accelerated efforts of China to engage with the Pacific islands made the US scramble which immediately took measures to reconnect with the island nations.

The USA has taken a range of steps in recent years to tackle the emerging role of China and address what it sees as China's increasing challenge to the global order. These steps include:

- **Diplomatic Pressures** - The USA has engaged in diplomatic efforts to build a coalition of countries to push back against China's assertiveness in areas such as the South China Sea and Hong Kong. The USA has also taken a more critical stance on China's human rights record, particularly with regard to the treatment of Uighur Muslims in Xinjiang.
- **Economic pressure**: The USA has imposed tariffs and other trade restrictions on Chinese goods, and taken steps to restrict Chinese investment in sensitive sectors such as technology and infrastructure. The USA has also sought to promote alternative supply chains to reduce dependence on China.
- **Military pressure**: The USA has increased its military presence in the Indo-Pacific region, and conducted freedom of navigation operations in the South China Sea to challenge China's territorial

claims. The USA has also stepped up military cooperation with countries in the region to bolster their defense capabilities.

- **Technology competition**: The USA has sought to limit China's access to advanced technologies such as 5G, and imposed export controls on certain technologies with military applications, while developing emerging technologies like artificial intelligence and quantum computing.

Thus, USA's approach to China reflects a growing recognition of the strategic and economic challenges posed by China's rise, and a determination to protect and promote US interests in the face of this challenge. However, this approach has also raised concerns about the risk of escalating tensions and a potential new Cold War between the two countries.

The ongoing trade disputes between China and the US has resulted in uncertainty about trade policy on a global scale. The higher tariffs led to the reprising of risk assets, slower growth and tighter financing conditions. The USA, once the epitome of free trade, has widened the scope of its **protectionist shield** to reduce its trade deficit. The resultant changes could lead to the fragmentation of global trading framework and **weakening of the rules-based system**. According to reports, the economic slowdown and the trade war combined, resulted in a loss of USD 550 billion in import tariffs, majorly aimed at Beijing. The World Bank has predicted a significant slowdown in the global economy backed by a poor economic growth in US and China.

Impact on India

The overall impact of the USA-China conflict for India can be summarized under the following heads –

Economic implications	▪ According to experts, the USA-China rivalry has the potential **to reshape global trade and investment patterns.** ▪ The trade war provided a 'natural experiment' to the nations next in line to become **manufacturing powerhouses.** ▪ The economic instability has resulted in **trade diversification** in favour of other exporting nations, including but not restricted to, Vietnam, Indonesia, Mexico, South Korea, Japan, Bangladesh and India. ▪ According to a UNCTAD study, several nations are set to benefit from the trade tensions - Vietnam, with 5% export gains, Australia (4.6%), Brazil (3.8%), India (3.5%), and Philippines (3.2%). India has always been considered as the replacement of China as the 'world's factory'. ▪ On the flip side, **India could face increased competition from both the USA and China** in areas such as technology and innovation, and could be negatively impacted by disruptions to global trade flows.
Security implications	▪ The strategic competition between the USA and China is playing out in the **Indo-Pacific region**, where **India is a major player**. ▪ India is likely to be increasingly drawn into the strategic rivalry, which could have security implications for the country. ▪ For instance, India may need to balance its relationships with the USA and China, and may face pressure to take sides in the rivalry.
Diplomatic implications	▪ The rivalry could create tensions between the diplomatic relations of India with these nations. India has historically maintained a **policy of non-alignment**, but the increasing pressure from both the USA and China to take sides could make this more difficult. India will need to navigate its relationships with both countries carefully in order to avoid being drawn into the rivalry and maintain its sovereignty.
Regional implications	▪ Both USA and China are looking to leverage the economic and diplomatic relations with the regional powers in the Indo-Pacific in order to garner greater support. ▪ With several nations taking sides in the rivalry, it could likely create tensions between the relations of India with such countries in the future. For example, India may need

	to navigate its relationship with China's close ally, Pakistan, in the context of the rivalry.

Thus, the two major democracies – India and the US, have a great deal of work ahead of them backed by their convergent economic, geopolitical and strategic interests. However, the personal predilections of Prime Ministers and Presidents may threaten the ties and could potentially rupture the bond. While the ties continue to improve, the pace of development of relations will depend on the knowledge of facts and influence of people around the respective national leaders. Since the nations face unprecedented and multifaceted domestic and global changes, they must look towards carefully balancing the interests of each other. They must continue to work towards finding solutions that support their shared economic and strategic interests, while also addressing the concerns of their citizens.

RUSSIA

ABOUT THE COUNTRY

Russia is a vast country that spans two continents - Europe and Asia - and is the largest country in the world (area) with a total area of 17,098,242 Km² (6,601,665 mi²) and a land area of 16,376,870 Km² (6,323,142 mi²), equivalent to 11% of the total world's landmass. Its capital city is Moscow, and it has a population of over 144 million (2022). The **1993 constitution** declares Russia a **democratic, federative, law-based state with a republican form of government**. Historically, Russia has played a significant role in global politics and has a complex and diverse cultural heritage. It was founded in the 9th century and went through various stages of development, including the Tsarist period, the Soviet era, and its transition to a democratic country in the 1990s.

Important Statistics*

Capital	Moscow	
Population	143 M	(2023)
GDP Growth (annual)	3.6%	(2023)
FDI, net inflows (percentage of GDP)	(-) 1.8%	(2022)
Human Development Index Rank	56	(2023)

*World Bank data

In International Relations, Russia is a pivotal actor with a complex and influential role. As a major power with significant military capabilities, a vast natural resource base, and a permanent seat on the United Nations Security Council, Russia exerts substantial influence on global affairs. Its foreign policy is often characterized by a realist approach, prioritizing state sovereignty, regional dominance, and strategic interests.

Aftermath of the Cold War

The end of the Cold War profoundly affected Russia, leading to significant political and economic changes. After the Soviet Union's collapse in 1991, Russia transitioned from communism to democracy and from a command economy to a market-oriented one. The 1990s were marked by economic turmoil, including hyperinflation, high unemployment, and declining GDP, along with political instability and corruption. Despite these challenges, Russia undertook reforms in privatization and market liberalization.

In the 2000s, Russia saw economic recovery, driven by rising oil prices and improved political stability. Reforms aimed to enhance the investment climate and reduce reliance on natural resources. However, concerns about democratic regression persist, with issues like election rigging, media censorship, and human rights abuses. The annexation of Crimea in 2014 and involvement in Syria and Ukraine have also drawn criticism. Overall, Russia's post-Cold War era has been marked by both progress and controversy

POLITICS AND ADMINISTRATION

- Russia is a **federal semi-presidential republic**. The **President** is the head of state, and the **Prime Minister** is the head of government. ***Vladimir Putin*** has been the dominant figure in Russian politics since 2000, either as President or Prime Minister. His governance is characterized by centralized power, conservative policies, and nationalism.

VLADIMIR PUTIN

- Born in 1952, Putin is a prominent Russian politician and former intelligence officer. He has served as the President of Russia since May 7, 2012, and previously held the position from 2000 to 2008. Between his presidential terms, Putin was the Prime Minister of Russia from 1999 to 2000 and from 2008 to 2012.
- He served for 15 years as a foreign intelligence officer in the KGB, the foreign intelligence and domestic security agency of the Soviet Union.
- Putin's tenure has been marked by efforts to centralize power, assert Russian influence on the global stage, and manage economic reforms.

- The **Federal Assembly** consists of two chambers—*State Duma* (lower house) and *Federation Council* (upper house). The **United Russia** party, closely aligned with Putin, holds a majority.
- Russia has **85 federal subjects** (including republics, territories, and cities), each with varying degrees of autonomy.
- Russia's political system has been criticized for its suppression of opposition, curbs on freedom of speech, and control over media. Several Opposition leaders including **Alexei Navalny** have faced imprisonment and persecution.

DIPLOMATIC INFLUENCE

- Russia is a **permanent member of the UN Security Council** and has significant influence in global geopolitics. It uses its veto power to shape international decisions, particularly on issues like Syria, Ukraine, and Iran.
- Russia leads the **Eurasian Economic Union (EAEU)** and is influential in the **Commonwealth of Independent States (CIS)**, extending its influence over former Soviet states.
- Russia is a prominent member of **BRICS** (Brazil, Russia, India, China, South Africa) and the **Shanghai Cooperation Organization (SCO)**, promoting multipolarity and challenging Western hegemony.
- Russia's annexation of Crimea in 2014 and its 2022 full-scale invasion of Ukraine have significantly altered its diplomatic relations. The war has led to sanctions from the West, isolation from G7 nations, and deteriorated relations with NATO and the EU.

ECONOMY & TRADE

- Russia's economy is heavily reliant on its natural resources, particularly energy. It is one of the world's largest producers and exporters of oil, natural gas, and coal. These resources contribute significantly to the country's GDP and foreign exchange reserves.
- It holds the **world's largest natural gas reserves** and is the second-largest exporter of crude oil.
- **Gross Domestic Product:**
  - → Nominal GDP (2023): Approximately $2 trillion
  - → Global Ranking: Eleventh (11th) largest global economy
  - → GDP per capita (current US$ 2023): Approximately $13,800

- While the economy has diversified in recent years, with a growing focus on sectors such as manufacturing and services, the energy sector remains a dominant force. Russia's vast territory and abundant natural resources offer significant potential for economic growth and development.
- Since 2014, Russia has faced **economic sanctions** from Western nations, particularly after the Crimea annexation and the 2022 Ukraine war. These sanctions have limited Russia's access to international financial markets, technology imports, and foreign investment. In response to sanctions, Russia has pursued a strategy of import substitution, especially in sectors like agriculture, manufacturing, and defence.
- Major trading partners include China, India, Turkey, and members of the Eurasian Economic Union (EAEU). Trade with the EU has significantly declined due to sanctions.
- Russia's economy has struggled with inflation, and the **ruble** has faced volatility due to international sanctions, oil price fluctuations, and capital outflows.

MILITARY STRENGTH

- Russia has the **second-largest military** in the world by several measures, with a budget of approximately **$85 billion USD** in 2023.
- The **Russian Armed Forces** have around **1 million active personnel** and over **2 million in reserves**.
- Conventional Forces:
  - ✓ Army: Equipped with a significant number of tanks (about 12,000), artillery, and armoured vehicles.
  - ✓ Navy: Comprises surface vessels and one of the largest submarine fleets in the world. Russia is focusing on expanding its naval presence in the Arctic and Mediterranean.
  - ✓ Air Force: Operates a fleet of advanced fighter jets, bombers, and transport aircraft. The Su-57 is Russia's most advanced stealth fighter.
- Russia possesses the world's largest stockpile of nuclear warheads (around **5,889**), and it maintains a **nuclear triad** (air, land, and sea-based nuclear capabilities).
- Russia is a key player in the **Collective Security Treaty Organization (CSTO)**, a military alliance with post-Soviet states like Belarus, Kazakhstan, and Armenia.

SCIENCE AND TECHNOLOGY

- Russia, through **Roscosmos**, is a major player in space exploration. It has a rich legacy as a pioneer of space technology, with notable achievements like launching the first satellite (*Sputnik*) and sending the first human into space (*Yuri Gagarin*).
- Russia is a global leader in **nuclear technology** for both civilian and military purposes. It provides nuclear reactors and fuel to countries worldwide through its state-run company, Rosatom.
- Russia is known for its advanced capabilities in **cyber warfare** and **cyber espionage**, often targeting governments and organizations globally. It has a sophisticated network of hackers and intelligence services that conduct cyber-attacks.
- Russia has invested in **AI** and **robotics** for both civilian and military applications, though it still lags behind global leaders like the U.S. and China.
- Russia prioritizes the development of **cutting-edge defence technologies**, including hypersonic missiles, anti-satellite systems, and advanced missile defence systems like the S-400 and S-500.

RESOURCE WEALTH AND RUSSIA'S FAR EAST

The Far Eastern region, which constitutes a significant portion of Russia's landmass, holds great economic and strategic importance. As a result, various Asian nations are actively seeking to capitalize on the region's advantages. The **Far Eastern Federal District (FEFD)** is situated in the easternmost part of Russia and shares borders with the Pacific and Arctic oceans, as well as five countries: China, Japan, Mongolia, the United States, and North Korea.

This expansive region encompasses approximately one-third of Russia's territory and boasts abundant natural resources, including fish, oil, natural gas, timber, diamonds, coal, and various minerals. The Russian government has pursued a strategic development approach for the region, aiming to establish connections between Russia and the trading routes of Asia. China stands as the primary investor in the region, accounting for 90% of total investments, followed by South Korea and Japan.

Significance of Russia's far eastern region

- It is an area rich in **natural resources** ranging from: Fisheries, Oil, Natural gas, Wood, diamonds, other minerals. India could engage in joint exploration for the production of said resources.
- It is **strategically located** between Asia and North America. India could benefit from the development of the Northern Sea Route, which could significantly reduce transportation time and costs between Asia and Europe.
- Russia's Far East is home to a significant number of military installations. India could explore opportunities for military cooperation with Russia, including joint military exercises and technology transfer.
- The **sparsely populated region** provides significant potential for Asian nations such as India to utilize their human resources and create economic opportunities for their populations while also exploring the region's resources.
- Additionally, the region can serve as a **gateway for facilitating Russia's movement towards Asia and Asia's movement towards Russia**, including the Arctic maritime routes.

In order to harness the economic and strategic advantages of Russia's Far East, India is actively seeking to engage with the region through the following approaches:

- In 2019, India extended a $1 billion line of credit to support infrastructure development in the region.
- Business representatives from Gujarat and the Republic of Sakha have initiated agreements in the diamond and pharmaceutical industries.

Moving forward, India aims to enhance its involvement in Russia's Far East by directing more investments and human resources into the region. Utilizing para diplomacy can be a means to strengthen economic connectivity with the region. Overall, there exists substantial potential for cooperation between India and Russia's Far East across various sectors, with both countries able to benefit from each other's strengths and resources.

Eastern Economic Forum (EEF)

The EEF was created in **2015** as a platform to attract foreign investments to Russia's Far East (RFE) region. It serves as a showcase for the economic potential, favorable business environment, and investment prospects in the region. The forum focuses on establishing connections between the Far East and the Asia Pacific region. In September 2022, Prime Minister Modi participated in the **7th Eastern Economic Forum**, which was hosted by Russia in Vladivostok, through virtual means.

RUSSIA-UKRAINE CONFLICT

Ukraine is the **largest country entirely within Europe**, both in terms of land area and population. It is bordered by Belarus to the north, Russia to the northeast and east, Poland, Slovakia, Hungary, and Romania to the west, and Moldova and the Black Sea to the south. It has diverse geography, including vast plains, plateaus, and the Carpathian Mountains in the west. With over 44 million people, it is the second-most populous country in Europe after Russia. Its size and population contribute to its economic potential, market size, and influence in regional affairs.

Ukraine was part of various empires and kingdoms throughout its existence, including the Kyivan Rus, the Polish-Lithuanian Commonwealth, the Russian Empire, and the Soviet Union. Ukraine declared independence from the Soviet Union in 1991. Presently, Ukraine is a semi-presidential republic with a multi-party system. The President is the head of state and the Prime Minister is the head of government.

Ukraine officially gained its independence on August 24, 1991. This independence came as a result of the dissolution of the Soviet Union. Prior to that, Ukraine had been part of the Soviet Union since 1922. Following a referendum held in December 1991, the people of Ukraine overwhelmingly voted for independence, leading to the establishment of the independent state of Ukraine.

Ukraine is located at the crossroads of Europe and Asia, making it a **crucial transit country for energy resources and trade routes**. Its **proximity to Russia and the European Union** gives it strategic importance and makes it a focal point of regional dynamics. Ukraine was a significant player in **nuclear disarmament efforts**. After gaining independence, Ukraine voluntarily gave up the world's third-largest nuclear arsenal, which it inherited from the Soviet Union. Ukraine's aspirations for closer integration with the European Union have been a focal point of its foreign policy.

Conflicts and Clashes

The origins of the Russia-Ukraine conflict can be traced back to a combination of historical, political, and territorial factors. One key event that sparked the conflict was the Euromaidan protests in late 2013 and early 2014 in Ukraine. The protests initially began as a response to then-**President Viktor Yanukovych's decision to abandon plans for closer integration with the European Union and instead seek closer ties with Russia**. The protests grew in size and intensity, with demonstrators demanding political and economic reforms, an end to corruption, and closer alignment with Western institutions. The Ukrainian government responded with force, leading to violent clashes and a rising death toll. Eventually, President Yanukovych fled the country, and a **transitional government was formed**.

In this context, Russia became increasingly concerned about Ukraine's political shift towards the West and saw it as a threat to its influence in the region. In response to the changing political landscape in Ukraine, **Russia annexed Crimea**, a region with a significant Russian-speaking population, in March 2014. Following the annexation, **pro-Russian separatist movements emerged in eastern Ukraine**, leading to a violent conflict between Ukrainian government forces and separatist groups supported by Russia. The conflict has been characterized by ongoing clashes, ceasefire violations, and humanitarian crises, resulting in a significant loss of life and displacement of people.

ANNEXATION OF CRIMEA

The forcible incorporation of Crimea into the Russian Federation in 2014 marked a significant escalation of tensions between Russia and Ukraine. This event followed political unrest in Ukraine, including the ousting of pro-Russian President Viktor Yanukovych.

In February 2014, Russian troops entered Crimea, seizing control of key infrastructure and government buildings. A controversial and widely criticized referendum was held in March, in which a majority allegedly voted to join Russia. Despite international condemnation and claims of illegitimacy due to lack of transparency and the presence of Russian military forces, Russia officially annexed Crimea, incorporating it as a federal subject. The annexation has been widely condemned by the international community, including the United Nations, which considers Crimea to be part of Ukraine. The event led to significant geopolitical tensions, particularly between Russia and Western countries, and resulted in sanctions against Russia. The situation continues to be a major point of contention in international relations.

The Russian Invasion

The Russian invasion into Ukraine is the largest conventional military attack seen since World War II. **The invasion which began in February 2022, has continued unabated for over 2 and a half years (September 2024).**

CRITICAL DEVELOPMENTS	
2022	(a) **February 24:** • Russian President Vladimir Putin officially recognizes the independence of the self-declared *Donetsk People's Republic* (DPR) and *Luhansk People's Republic* (LPR) in eastern Ukraine. • Russia launches a full-scale invasion of Ukraine. (b) **Zaporizhzhia Nuclear Power Plant**, Europe's largest nuclear plant, is seized by Russian forces, raising fears of nuclear disaster. (c) Russia announces the annexation of four Ukrainian regions: Donetsk, Luhansk, Zaporizhzhia, and Kherson. (d) **Miscellaneous**– (a) The United Nations General Assembly passed a resolution that held Russia responsible for all damage caused to Ukraine by the invasion and demanded reparations. (b) The European Parliament declared Russia a "state sponsor of terrorism" for the way it had systematically attacked civilians and committed war crimes.
2023	1) Ukrainian forces advance in southern regions, targeting **Russian logistics hubs** in **Crimea** and the **Sea of Azov** coast. Ukraine's forces push towards **Melitopol** in an attempt to cut off the Russian land corridor to Crimea. 2) Both sides increasingly rely on **drone warfare.** Russia intensifies its attacks on Ukrainian infrastructure, targeting energy facilities and civilian areas - leading to a humanitarian crisis. 3) Ukraine launches a major counteroffensive in the eastern Donbas region, making significant gains. 4) In October, the **US** and **EU** announce additional military aid packages to Ukraine, including more advanced air defence systems.
2024	• While Ukraine has regained some territories, much of the eastern regions, including **Donetsk** and **Luhansk**, remain under Russian control. • Both sides face **economic strain** and **exhaustion** but remain resolute. Diplomatic efforts to mediate a peace agreement have stalled due to irreconcilable demands. • On 3rd September, at least 58 people were killed in a Russian missile Strike (Poltava) and over 300 were injured. anu • According to records from the Office of the High Commissioner for Human Rights (OHCHR), Russia's invasion of Ukraine (from February 2022 to July 2024) has resulted in over 11,500 civilian deaths and more than 24,000 injuries.

The resultant transgression of sovereignty and territorial integrity of Ukraine has been frowned upon by a heavy majority. The "unprovoked and unjustified attack" by Russia has invited sanctions from the countries including USA and the European Union. These are expected to have an impact on the global economy, including through disruption of supply chains. Apart from the crucial humanitarian crisis, the global economy will feel the effects of faster inflation and slower growth.

Impacts of Ukraine Conflict	Higher prices for commodities including food and energy will push up inflation, further eroding the value of incomes and weighing on demand.
	Neighboring economies in particular will grapple with disrupted trade, supply chains, and remittances including a surge in refugee flows.
	Reduced business confidence and higher investor uncertainty will weigh on asset prices, tightening financial conditions and potentially spurring capital outflows from emerging markets.

The **Ukraine-Russia region** is recognized as a significant global **"breadbasket"** and holds a crucial position as a major food producer. It plays a vital role not just as an exporter of essential commodities like wheat but also as a major supplier of fertilizers worldwide. **Approximately 30% of global wheat exports and 65% of sunflower exports originate from the Ukraine-Russia region**. These markets are tightly interconnected, and any minor disruption in the supply chain can have an impact on prices due to their interdependence.

The ripple effect from the **increased inflation** is likely with a resultant tightening of global financial conditions. The Middle East and African nations could be severely impacted due to their dependence on import of about 80 percent of wheat from Ukraine and Russia, with the tourism sector also facing a major setback. Socio-economic issues could exacerbate globally which had worsened due to the pandemic.

NATO-Ukraine Relations

NATO's (North Atlantic Treaty Organization - intergovernmental military alliance) involvement in the Ukraine-Russia conflict primarily revolves around its support for Ukraine and its commitment to the principles of territorial integrity, sovereignty, and the right of nations to choose their own path. While **Ukraine is not a NATO member**, the alliance has provided political and practical support to Ukraine, including diplomatic pressure, economic assistance, and military aid.

Dialogue and cooperation between Ukraine and NATO began after Ukraine gained independence and became a member of the North Atlantic Cooperation Council in 1991 and the Partnership for Peace program in 1994. The signing of the 1997 Charter on a Distinctive Partnership further enhanced the relationship and established the NATO-Ukraine Commission (NUC) to facilitate ongoing cooperation.

YEAR	CRITICAL DEVELOPMENTS – NATO Specific
2014	Since Russia's illegal annexation of Crimea & aggression in Eastern Ukraine, **NATO has reinforced its support for Ukraine.** NATO also increased presence in Black Sea.
2017	The Ukrainian Parliament adopted legislation **reinstating membership in NATO as a strategic foreign and security policy objective.**
2020	President Zelensky approved Ukraine's new National Security Strategy - providing for development of the **distinctive partnership with NATO** with the aim of membership in NATO.
2022	NATO unequivocally condemned Russia's illegal attempt to annex four regions of Ukraine – **Donetsk, Luhansk, Kherson** and **Zaporizhzhia.**
2023-2024	• **NATO Vilnius Summit (2023):** It was a significant development, where allies agreed to remove Ukraine's Membership Action Plan (MAP) requirement, signaling a clear path to NATO membership. • **Enhanced Support Package:** NATO members pledged long-term support to Ukraine, including military assistance, training, and financial aid. This package aims to bolster Ukraine's defense capabilities and prepare it for eventual NATO membership. • **NATO-Ukraine Council:** The creation of the NATO-Ukraine Council elevated Ukraine's status within the alliance, providing a platform for regular consultations and decision-making. • **Continued Military Aid:** NATO member states continue to provide substantial military aid to Ukraine, including advanced weaponry, ammunition, and training. This support has been crucial in Ukraine's defense against Russian aggression.

NATO condemns Russia's actions in Ukraine, imposing sanctions and boosting its military presence in Eastern Europe. It supports Ukraine through joint exercises, defense capacity-building, and reforms, while continuing to monitor and promote regional stability amid ongoing conflict.

Recent Developments

Since the invasion began in February 2022, the sight of missiles in the Ukrainian air has become a common sight. During an **'Emergency Special Session on Ukraine'** held in April 2022, the United Nations General Assembly passed a resolution urging the suspension of Russia from the Human Rights Council. According to the 2006 resolution that established the UN Human Rights Council, a country can be suspended from membership if it engages in severe and consistent human rights violations. The resolution obtained the required two-thirds majority of votes, excluding abstentions, with 93 nations supporting the resolution and 24 nations opposing it, out of the 193-member Assembly.

Among the nations that voted against the resolution included Russia, China, Cuba, North Korea, Iran, Syria, Vietnam etc. The Chinese ambassador claimed that the resolution would be like 'adding fuel to fire' and could set a new 'dangerous precedent'. While EU lauded the Assembly's decision and stated that it 'sent a strong signal of accountability, which would prevent and discourage more violations of human rights', the United States described the resolution as 'an important and historic moment.'

On **17 March 2023**, Pre-Trial Chamber II of the International Criminal Court (ICC) issued a warrant of arrest for **Mr. Vladimir Vladimirovich Putin** in the context of the **situation in Ukraine**. The charges read – "the President of the Russian Federation, is allegedly responsible for the **war crime of unlawful deportation of population (children)** and that of **unlawful transfer of population (children) from occupied areas of Ukraine to the Russian Federation**". [16]

India's take on the Ukraine Conflict

- During the UN's Emergency Session in 2022, **India was among the 58 nations that chose to abstain from voting**, with the others including Brazil, South Africa, Egypt, Saudi Arabia, Indonesia etc. The Russia-Ukraine conflict will have far-reaching effects including trade and diplomatic relations. The conflict placed the Indian community in Ukraine in direct danger, however the '*Operation Ganga*' helped to divert the crisis.
  - India's neutral stance on the Russia-Ukraine conflict could lead to several challenges. Diplomatically, it risks straining ties with key partners like the **U.S.** and **EU**, who support Ukraine.
  - Economically, its trade relations with both Russia and Ukraine could be impacted.
  - India's perceived indifference to global security concerns may harm its own security interests and alienate allies. This could result in diplomatic isolation on certain international issues.
- As of 2024, **India's stance on the Russia-Ukraine conflict** remains one of **strategic neutrality** and **balanced diplomacy**. India has refrained from explicitly condemning Russia, maintaining a neutral position in international forums like the **UN**, where it has abstained from key votes criticizing Russia.
- India has emphasized the importance of '*dialogue* and *diplomacy'* to resolve the conflict, calling for a peaceful settlement that respects international law and sovereignty. While it has expressed concern over the humanitarian impact, India continues to uphold its strong economic and defence ties with Russia, particularly in energy imports and military equipment. However, India has also engaged with Western powers, maintaining relations with the US, EU, and Ukraine, reflecting its broader diplomatic approach of balancing relationships with both Russia and the West.
- India advocates for **multilateral engagement** to address the crisis and has avoided taking sides directly, positioning itself as a potential **mediator** for peace, while prioritizing its own national interests and global strategic autonomy.

[16] Situation in Ukraine: ICC judges issue arrest warrants against Vladimir Vladimirovich Putin and Maria Alekseyevna Lvova-Belova. (2023, March 17). International Criminal Court. https://www.icc-cpi.int/news/situation-ukraine-icc-judges-issue-arrest-warrants-against-vladimir-vladimirovich-putin-and

PM MODI IN UKRAINE (2024)

In late August, Indian Prime Minister Narendra Modi made a historic visit to Kyiv, becoming the first Indian leader to visit Ukraine since its independence in 1991. His trip was seen as part of international efforts to achieve a peaceful resolution to the Russia-Ukraine war. It was also viewed as a demonstration of India's diplomatic balancing act, as the country seeks to mitigate negative perceptions of its strong economic and defense ties with Moscow while asserting itself as an emerging geopolitical power.

Prior to his visit to Ukraine, PM Modi had met with Russian President Vladimir Putin in July, demonstrating India's continued engagement with Russia on various issues.

MISCELLANEOUS CONCEPTS ASSOCIATED WITH RUSSIA

CONCEPTS	PARTICULARS
KGB	The KGB (Komitet Gosudarstvennoy Bezopasnosti - 1954 to 1991) served as both the foreign intelligence and domestic security agency of the Soviet Union. In addition to these roles, during the Soviet era, the KGB was responsible for safeguarding the nation's political leadership, overseeing border troops, and conducting general surveillance of the population. The KGB gradually expanded its foreign intelligence operations to become the world's largest foreign intelligence service (at the time). As the Cold War intensified, the KGB came to be viewed as a counterpart of the U.S. Central Intelligence Agency (CIA).
Kremlin	*Kremlin* meaning citadel, is a group of buildings in the center of Moscow that serves as the official seat of the government of Russia.
Tsar	It is the title associated with rulers of Russia. A "Tsar" (also spelled ***Czar*** or ***Tzar***) refers to a monarch or emperor who ruled over Russia from the late 16th century until the Russian Revolution of 1917. The term is derived from the Latin word 'Caesar', reflecting the title's association with imperial authority. The Tsar was the supreme ruler of the Russian Empire, holding both political and religious authority.
Détente	The term **détente** refers to the easing of tensions between rival countries, particularly during the **Cold War** between the Soviet Union and the United States. In the context of Russia, **détente** is most notably associated with the **1970s** when both the U.S. and the Soviet Union sought to reduce the risk of nuclear war and improve diplomatic relations. Key milestones during this period included **arms control agreements** like the **Strategic Arms Limitation Talks (SALT I)** and the **Helsinki Accords**, which sought to establish norms of behavior between the superpowers.
Gazprom, Rosneft & Oil	Russia is one of the world's largest producers and exporters of oil and natural gas. These industries are vital to Russia's economy, providing much of the government's revenue and influencing its foreign policy. **Gazprom** and **Rosneft** are two of Russia's largest state-owned energy companies, playing critical roles in the global energy market and Russian economy.
Arctic Passage or the Northern Sea Route (NSR)	The **Arctic Passage**, or the **NSR**, is a shipping lane along the northern coast of Russia, within the **Arctic Ocean**. As climate change leads to the melting of Arctic ice, this route is becoming increasingly accessible for commercial shipping. The **NSR** significantly shortens the travel distance between Europe and Asia compared to traditional routes, such as the **Suez Canal**. This has led to growing interest from global shipping companies and states, including China, which sees the NSR as part of its **Polar Silk Road**.

INDIA AND RUSSIA – 'THE ALL-WEATHER FRIENDS'

The phrase 'All-Weather Friend' is the most widely accepted view of India and Russia relations. Since India's independence, the two nations have shared a unique relationship which is the envy of many. The partnership between the two countries developed after the 1971 Indo-Soviet Treaty of Peace, Friendship, and Cooperation, following escalating tensions with Pakistan and US support for the latter (provided military aid) and President Richard Nixon's closeness with Pakistani President Yahya Khan during the 1971 Indo-Pakistani War.

YEAR	HOSTORICAL TIMELINE
1955	The Indian PM and Soviet leader made visits to USSR and India respectively; a Soviet-Indian agreement on the construction of the Bhilai Steel Plant was signed.
1957	• New agreement was signed for construction of several new enterprises of heavy machine-building, mining, energy production, including oil and gas drilling. • The Soviet Union applied its first veto on a resolution on Kashmir in the Security Council sponsored by UK, USA, Australia & Cuba
Beginning of 1960s	• Soviet-Indian trade expanded and grew by 30 times compared with 1953 • Soviet-Indian relations were affected by changes in the Chinese foreign policy
Nov, 1962	Soviet Union started arm selling to India, partly to help her in her military build-up against China, partly to counter American and British military aid to India.
1971	• It became the peak of Soviet-Indian cooperation marked by signing 'the Soviet-Indian Treaty of Peace, Friendship and Cooperation'. • It proved to be a strong support for India in the war with Pakistan which received support from China and USA. • At the UN Security Council, the USSR thrice vetoed resolutions on the situation on the Indian Peninsula.
1980s	• Despite India's diversification efforts, it was almost 80% dependent on Soviet arms supply. • Moscow offered New Delhi generous terms of loans and signed agreements, granting long-term credit, repayment by export of Indian merchandise rather than by hard currency and even allowed licensed production of arms and did some technology transfer.
1985	During an official visit to USSR, the then PM Rajiv Gandhi entered into an agreement on guidelines for trade, economic, scientific and technical cooperation in the establishment of a number of specific projects in India for further expansion of mutually beneficial contacts.
1988	Gorbachev visited India and focused on the importance of good relations between Soviet Union, India and China for solving the problems of Asia-Pacific region.
1991	• End of Cold War → Dissolution of USSR → Commonwealth of Independent States. • Russia was recognized as "state-continuator of the erstwhile Soviet Union".
Post 1991	India's ties with Russia have been uncertain on many grounds.
2000	**Declaration on "Strategic Partnership"**
2010	**Special and Privileged Strategic Partnership**

2017	During 17th Annual Summit, a joint statement 'Partnership for global peace and stability' and a 'Road map of events' was adopted to celebrate the 70th anniversary of establishment of diplomatic relations between India and Russia. In October, India and Russia sign a major agreement for the purchase of the **S-400 Triumf air defense system**, which is a significant component of India's defense modernization efforts.
2018	• India and Russia hold their first **2+2 dialogue**, involving foreign and defense ministers, to strengthen strategic partnerships. • India participates in the **Vostok-2018** joint military exercises held in Russia, focusing on improving military interoperability.
2019-2022	• **Russia-India-China Trilateral** (Jan 2019): The trilateral dialogue with China is renewed, focusing on enhancing strategic cooperation among the three countries. • Russian President Vladimir Putin visits India for the **India-Russia Summit** (Sept 2019), where both nations reaffirm their strategic partnership and discuss various issues including trade, defense, and energy. • India and Russia collaborate in combating the COVID-19 pandemic, with Russia sending medical aid to India. • The **21st India-Russia Annual Summit** (Dec 2021) takes place, with discussions on various strategic and economic issues, including defense cooperation and energy partnerships. • India maintains a neutral stance on Russia's invasion of Ukraine (Feb 2022), emphasizing dialogue and diplomatic resolution. • The **22nd India-Russia Annual Summit** (Dec 2022) emphasizes the continued strategic and economic partnership amid global geopolitical shifts.
2023	• India and Russia enhance energy cooperation, with India increasing imports of Russian oil and gas despite Western sanctions on Russia. • Amidst the ongoing Ukraine conflict, India and Russia continue to engage diplomatically, with discussions on various global issues and regional stability.
July 2024	PM Modi met with Russian President Vladimir Putin, demonstrating India's continued engagement with Russia on various issues.

INDO-RUSSIA COOPERATION AND COLLABORATION

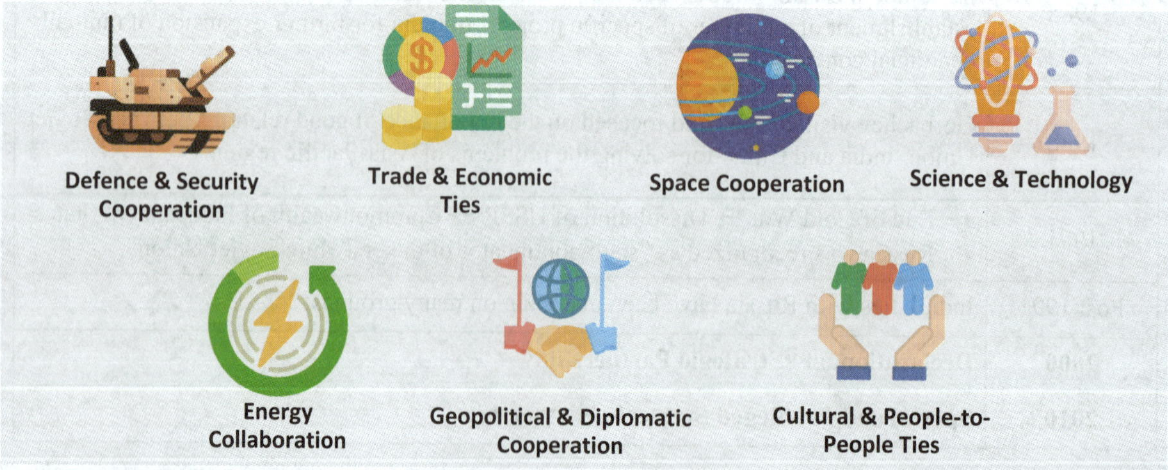

A. Defence and Security

Historical Significance: The foundation of India-Russia defence ties was laid during the Cold War when India relied heavily on Soviet military equipment. This trend continued post-Soviet Union, with Russia being a dominant supplier of advanced weapons and military technology to India.

(a) Arms Trade:

- Russia remains India's largest supplier of defence equipment, accounting for over 60-70% of India's military imports. Significant purchases include Su-30 MKI aircraft, MiG-21 Bison, MiG-29 fighters, T-90S tanks, and the advanced **S-400 Triumf** air defence system. The defence trade between the two nations has exceeded $15 billion since 2018.
- In response to Russia's exclusion from the SWIFT system, India and Russia have agreed on the **Rupee-Rouble payment arrangement** to continue their arms trade despite global sanctions.

> **NOTE**
> India's first and only overseas military base — the **Gissar Military Aerodrome (GMA)** in **Tajikistan**, was secured with Russian aid in the late 1990s and developed in the early 2000s.

(b) Joint Ventures:

- A hallmark of India-Russia defence cooperation is joint development projects, such as the **BrahMos cruise missile**, which is the world's fastest cruise missile with a range of 400 km.
- Other collaborations include the **production of AK-203 assault rifles** in India under the 'Make in India' initiative, licensed production of **Mango Armor-piercing rounds** for T-90 tanks, and ongoing construction of **stealth frigates** under Project 1135.6.
- Agreements have also been made for the production of **Ka-226T helicopters** in India and for spare parts of Russian-origin military equipment.

(c) Technology Transfer and Indigenous Development:

- India's focus on self-reliance in defence production has been bolstered by Russia's willingness to transfer critical defence technologies. This includes support in developing India's indigenous defence industry through the co-production of equipment.
- Russia has played a crucial role in the development of India's indigenous **nuclear submarines**, particularly in the construction of their onboard nuclear power plants.

(d) Strategic Assets:

- Russia has provided India with key strategic military platforms, including leasing **nuclear-powered attack submarines** to the Indian Navy—an arrangement unique to India. Russia also supplied India's **INS *Vikramaditya***, currently the Indian Navy's only operational aircraft carrier.

(e) Inter-Governmental Mechanisms:

- The **India-Russia Inter-Governmental Commission on Military Technical Cooperation (IRIGC-MTC)**, co-chaired by the Defence Ministers of both countries, is the primary forum for advancing military ties. It oversees joint projects, new contracts, and initiatives to enhance military cooperation.

(f) Shifts in Defence Procurement:

- While Russia continues to be India's primary arms supplier, India has been reducing its reliance on Russian imports, focusing instead on domestic defence manufacturing. Some large-scale deals have been deferred in favor of promoting the 'Make in India' initiative.
- Despite the reduction in the volume of imports, Russia remains an indispensable partner, especially in providing critical defence technology and military services that are difficult to replace.

JOINT EXERCISES	
Indra	It is a bilateral, bi-annual military exercise. The 12th Edition of joint military Exercise was held at Volgograd, Russia from 01 to 13 August 2021.
Indra Navy	It is a biennial bilateral maritime exercise. In July, 2021, the 12th edition of the military exercise INDRA NAVY was held in the Baltic Sea. The 11th edition had taken place in September 2020; due to COVID-19 restrictions, it was conducted in a 'non-contact, at sea only' format.
Avia Indra	It is a Joint India-Russia Air Force exercise.

B. Trade & Commerce

- According to India's Ministry of Commerce and Industry, bilateral trade with Russia reached **USD 65 billion** by the end of 2023, a 1.8-fold increase from 2022.
- India's exports to Russia totalled **USD 4.06 billion**, with pharmaceutical products contributing **USD 245.7 million**, the largest share. At the same time, imports from Russia stood **at USD 67.07 billion**, as reported by the United Nations COMTRADE database.
- India's trade deficit with Russia rose to **USD 57.18 billion** in FY24, a 33% annual increase driven by higher crude oil imports. Imports from Russia reached **USD 61.44 billion** in FY24, up 33%, while exports increased by 35% to USD 4.26 billion.
- **Crude oil imports** alone saw a significant 49.82% rise, reaching **USD 46.49 billion** in FY24, compared to USD 31.03 billion the previous year.

NOTE

In July 2024, during talks between Prime Minister Narendra Modi and President Vladimir Putin, both nations announced plans to elevate bilateral trade to **USD 100 billion by 2030.** They also aim to establish a settlement system using national currencies and introduce digital financial instruments. This surge in trade has been especially prominent since 2022, with Indian companies purchasing discounted Russian crude despite Western criticism.

- Previously, India and Russia had set a bilateral trade target of USD 30 billion by 2025, focusing on sectors like energy, infrastructure, and agriculture. While oil and gas have long been key areas of cooperation, both nations are now exploring economic diversification beyond these traditional sectors.
- Russia, historically India's top supplier of military hardware, became its leading **crude oil supplier** in March 2023, overtaking Iraq.
  (i) Key imports from Russia include mineral fuels, oils, pearls, precious stones, nuclear reactors, electrical machinery, and fertilizers.
  (ii) In contrast, India's top exports to Russia are pharmaceutical products, electrical machinery, and nuclear reactors.
- India and Russia are working on enhancing connectivity to facilitate trade through initiatives like the **International North-South Transport Corridor (INSTC)**, which aims to reduce transportation costs and time for goods moving between India, Russia, and Central Asia.
- As of April 2023, India and Russia were in advanced negotiations for a new **Bilateral Investment Treaty (BIT)** to boost investor confidence. This new agreement will address investor protections, including Double Tax protection and reduced taxes through Withholding Tax provisions, with a focus on investment rather than trade. The existing BIT, established in 1994, is considered outdated.
- In addition, India and Russia are exploring the possibility of a **Free Trade Agreement (FTA)** with the Russian-led Eurasian Economic Union to further strengthen commercial ties.

C. Space Cooperation

India and Russia share a long-standing and significant partnership in the field of space exploration, which has evolved over several decades. Their collaboration has ranged from launching India's early satellites to the latest advancements in space technology and human spaceflight programs. Below are the key aspects of this collaboration:

1) **Historical Collaborations**:
   - The space cooperation between India and Russia dates back to the 1970s when the Soviet Union played a pivotal role in launching India's first satellites, including **Aryabhata-I**, **Bhaskara-I**, and **Bhaskara-II**.
   - A significant milestone in this partnership was when Indian astronaut **Rakesh Sharma** became the first Indian to travel to space as part of a Soviet space mission in 1984. This event symbolized the deep-rooted cooperation between the two nations in space exploration.

2) **Technology Transfers and Launch Systems**:
   - Russia has been instrumental in providing critical space technology to India, particularly **cryogenic engine technology** for India's **Geosynchronous Satellite Launch Vehicles (GSLV)**, enabling India to enhance its satellite launch capabilities.
   - Over the years, the **Indian Space Research Organisation (ISRO)** and Russian space agencies have worked together on multiple satellite launches and technical exchanges, cementing their cooperation in satellite technology.
   - During the 19th Bilateral Summit, a Memorandum of Understanding (MoU) was signed between ISRO and ROSCOSMOS to strengthen collaboration in the **Human Spaceflight Programme**. This agreement paved the way for joint activities, including astronaut training and potential future space missions.

3) **Joint Space Missions**:
   - Under a 2004 **Inter-Governmental Agreement**, India and Russia collaborated on the **Chandrayaan-1** and **Chandrayaan-2** missions. Russia was involved in developing a lander for these missions, aimed at expanding lunar exploration.
   - In recent years, the focus has shifted toward joint human spaceflight endeavors. Russia has been actively supporting India's **Gaganyaan** mission—India's first manned space mission. **Glavcosmos**, a subsidiary of **ROSCOSMOS**, provides commercial services for India's human spaceflight initiatives, and Indian Air Force pilots have undergone cosmonaut training at Russia's **Institute of Aerospace Medicine**.

4) **Satellite Navigation Systems**:
   - India and Russia have collaborated on satellite-based navigation systems, particularly through joint work on the **NavIC-GLONASS ground stations** and **Global Navigation Satellite Systems (GNSS)** augmentation. This partnership helps enhance satellite navigation capabilities in both nations.
   - India has also become a supplier of **GLONASS chipsets**, which reflects the growing technological synergy between the two countries in the space domain.

While India's dependence on Russian space technology has diminished over time due to advancements in indigenous capabilities, the two countries continue to maintain strong ties in space exploration. Russia's role in providing critical space technologies and commercial services for India's space ambitions remains indispensable.

D. Science & Technology

India and Russia have maintained a long-standing partnership in science and technology, underpinned by shared strategic interests and mutual benefits. Over the years, this collaboration has grown across sectors like nuclear energy, defense technology, and information technology. In recent years, particularly in 2023 and 2024, both countries have worked on enhancing these ties with a focus on high-tech, digital, and innovation-driven areas.

1) **Nuclear Energy Cooperation**
   - The **Kudankulam Nuclear Power Plant (KKNPP),** built with Russian collaboration, remains the most prominent symbol of Indo-Russian nuclear energy cooperation. Units 1 and 2 are already operational, while construction on Units 3 and 4 is underway, with plans for additional reactors.
   - In 2023, India and Russia reinforced their partnership in the nuclear sector by announcing further advancements in nuclear energy production and the continuation of reactor construction at Kudankulam.
   - In addition to power generation, India and Russia are collaborating on nuclear research. There have been discussions in 2023–2024 to further expand R&D into areas like nuclear fuel cycle technology, nuclear waste management, and fast reactors.
2) **Defense Technology and Research**
   - A major success in this partnership is the development of the **BrahMos supersonic cruise missile**, a joint venture between India's DRDO and Russia's NPO Mashinostroyeniya.
   - In 2023, both nations agreed to boost BrahMos production and explore new export markets. They are also co-developing next-generation military technologies, including hypersonic weapons and advanced aircraft.
   - By 2024, their defense R&D efforts expanded to focus on cutting-edge battlefield technologies.
3) **Advanced IT and Cybersecurity**
   - India and Russia have strengthened cooperation in digital technologies, particularly in AI, big data, and blockchain.
   - In 2023, new initiatives were launched to enhance AI research and IT infrastructure, while 2024 saw joint efforts in cybersecurity to protect critical infrastructure.
   - Additionally, technological exchanges between Russia's Skolkovo Innovation Center and Indian tech hubs are fostering collaboration in areas like robotics, fintech, and AI, driving mutual innovation.
4) **Pharmaceuticals and Biotechnology**
   - The partnership in pharmaceuticals gained momentum during the COVID-19 pandemic, with India producing Russia's Sputnik V vaccine. This collaboration continued through 2023–2024, focusing on vaccine development and biotechnology innovations.
   - Joint research in agriculture and health has also expanded. By 2024, India had become a major exporter of pharmaceuticals to Russia, with exports reaching USD 245.7 million in 2023.
5) **Innovation in Agriculture and Space Technologies:** India and Russia extended their partnership into agri-tech, launching joint programs in 2023 to develop innovative solutions like precision farming. They also use space technology for agriculture monitoring and disaster management, improving food security and climate resilience by 2024.
6) **Bilateral Investment in Technology:** India and Russia are updating their Bilateral Investment Treaty (BIT) to enhance investor protection and support science and technology investments. Negotiations in 2023 focused on R&D and technology transfer.

E. Energy and Environment Collaboration

Energy security is a vital component of the India-Russia partnership, especially in the context of India's growing energy demands.

- **Oil and Gas**: India and Russia have expanded their cooperation in the field of hydrocarbons. Indian companies, such as ONGC Videsh, have invested in Russian oil fields like the Sakhalin and Vankor projects. India is also exploring opportunities in the Arctic region, where Russia is one of the leading players.
- **Liquefied Natural Gas (LNG)**: Russia's Gazprom has been supplying LNG to India, diversifying India's sources of natural gas imports.
- **Nuclear Energy**: Nuclear collaboration between the two countries is a key component of their strategic relationship. The **Kudankulam Nuclear Power Plant** in Tamil Nadu, built with Russian assistance, is

the flagship project of this collaboration. Plans to expand nuclear energy production through more reactors at Kudankulam and other potential sites reflect the significance of this partnership.

- **Arctic Cooperation**: India has shown interest in the Russian Arctic, particularly in areas of energy exploration, shipping, and scientific research, as the Arctic opens up due to climate change.
- **Green Energy**: Both countries are exploring opportunities in renewable energy, including cooperation on solar and wind energy projects, which aligns with India's climate goals.

F. Geopolitical & Diplomatic Cooperation

- India and Russia share a long-standing partnership grounded in mutual respect and shared geopolitical interests. Both nations are staunch advocates of a multipolar world order, emphasizing the importance of a balanced international system governed by the principles of international law and the UN Charter.
- The **1971 Treaty of Peace, Friendship, and Cooperation** still serves as a cornerstone of their strategic alliance, shaping South Asia's geopolitical landscape.
- Their vision aligns in promoting a **rules-based global order** where emerging economies and developing nations play a larger role in decision-making.
- India's advocacy for **multipolarism** reflects its pursuit of a more equitable global system, balancing its relationships with major powers like Russia, China, and the United States. Similarly, Russia has built strategic partnerships with various global players, including India, to uphold a balanced power dynamic in international relations.
- While challenges exist, such as India's growing alignment with Western powers through initiatives like the **Quad**, and Russia's closer ties with China and Pakistan, both countries have managed to maintain a strong diplomatic rapport. Despite concerns over these developments, their ties remain resilient, exemplifying their status as "***all-weather friends***."
- India and Russia also collaborate extensively on regional and global security issues. **Counterterrorism** efforts are a shared priority, particularly within multilateral platforms like the Russia-India-China (RIC) trilateral and bilateral agreements.
- Both nations are committed to stability in Afghanistan and Central Asia, a region where their cooperation became increasingly vital following the U.S. withdrawal.
- In multilateral forums, such as the UN, BRICS, Shanghai Cooperation Organisation (SCO), and G20, their collaboration remains strong. Russia continues to support India's bid for a permanent seat on the UN Security Council, reflecting their shared vision of a more representative global governance system.
- Overall, India and Russia's geopolitical cooperation is defined by shared values, trust, and the ability to navigate complex global dynamics, ensuring their partnership remains robust despite changing international realities.

G. Cultural and People-to-People Ties

- The historical, cultural, and educational exchanges between India and Russia also play a key role in fostering deeper ties.
- Many Indian students pursue higher education in Russia, especially in the field of medicine. Russian universities are a popular destination for Indian students.
- The two countries regularly organise cultural festivals and film festivals that showcase each other's heritage. The **Days of Russian Culture in India** and vice versa promote mutual understanding.
- Russia is a growing destination for Indian tourists, and similarly, Indian tourists are drawn to Russian historical and cultural sites.

RUSSIA-CHINA RELATIONS

The two nations have had their share of ups and downs, but the relationship gained impetus with the signing of the China-Russia **Friendship Treaty** in July 2001.

The Russian annexation of Crimea in 2014 had previously invited western sanctions and had forced Russia to seek deeper economic ties with China. A repetition of the phase of China-Russia closeness is underway in 2021-22 due to the ongoing Ukraine-Russia war. While the western nations including NATO have taken a strong counter-position against the Russian efforts to invade Ukraine, this period is seeing an increased backing by China in favour of Russia. The imposition of harsher sanctions on Russia coupled with a volatile Ruble and unstable markets, has propelled Russia in China's direction for support.

Such intimacy between the nations could have serious implications for the Indian national security, with India currently being heavily dependent on Russian resources especially in the defence sector. China's rising power and relevance in the global arena has the potential to undermine Russia's commitments towards India.

The following are certain outcomes of the Russia-Sino closeness -

The Russia-China partnership could create **strategic challenges** for India, particularly in the areas of security and defense. The two countries have recently conducted joint military exercises and have been working to strengthen their defense cooperation. This could create a more challenging security environment for India.

→

The two countries have been working to increase their trade and economic ties, which could potentially affect India's **economic interests** in the region. India may face increased competition in areas such as energy and natural resources.

→

Russia and China have been working to coordinate their positions on a range of global issues, including the situation in Afghanistan and the ongoing conflict in Syria. India may find itself in a more **difficult position diplomatically**, particularly if it is forced to choose between aligning with Russia or China on certain issues.

Overall, the growing closeness between Russia and China is a complex issue for India, and the outcome will depend on how India navigates the changing regional dynamics and builds its own relationships with both countries.

CHINA

ABOUT THE COUNTRY

China is a country located in East Asia and is the third-largest country in the world in terms of land area, covering an area of approximately 9.6 million square kilometers. China has a long history and rich culture, with a written history dating back more than 5,000 years. The country has been ruled by various dynasties and emperors throughout its history, and it was established as a communist state in 1949, with Beijing as its capital.

Important Statistics*

Capital	Beijing	
Population	1.41 B	(2023)
GDP Growth (annual)	5.2%	(2023)
FDI, net inflows (percentage of GDP)	1.0%	(2022)
Human Development Index Rank	73	(2020)

*World Bank data

In International Relations, China stands as a formidable global power, significantly influencing the contemporary international system. As the world's second most populous nation and second-largest economy, China's rise has reshaped geopolitical dynamics.

Guided by a strategic blend of **realism** and **assertive diplomacy**, China prioritizes national sovereignty and territorial integrity particularly concerning Taiwan, Hong Kong, the South China Sea, and Xinjiang. Over the past decade, China has been working to enhance global connectivity and extend its influence through infrastructure investments. The nation's approach to international relations is characterized by a commitment to multipolarity and a cautious engagement with the West.

POLITICS AND ADMINISTRATION

- The administration of China is deeply rooted in its unique system of governance, which is shaped by the **Communist Party of China (CPC)**, state institutions, and a rigid hierarchical structure.
- Unlike multiparty systems, the CPC exercises a monopoly on power, and political pluralism is absent. No other political party can contest elections independently. CPC has maintained uninterrupted power since 1949.
- The governance model of China is deeply influenced by **Marxism-Leninism**, **Mao Zedong Thought**, **Deng Xiaoping Theory**, and **Xi Jinping Thought on Socialism with Chinese Characteristics for a New Era**.
- The **President** of China is the head of state, formally representing the country in diplomatic affairs and other ceremonial roles.

XI JINPING

- As of 2024, the President of China is Xi Jinping. Born on June 15, 1953, Xi is a prominent Chinese politician and the paramount leader of the People's Republic of China. He assumed office as President on March 14, 2013, and has been a key figure in Chinese politics, also serving as the General Secretary of the Communist Party of China (CPC) and the Chairman of the Central Military Commission, making him the top leader of the country.
- Xi Jinping's leadership has been marked by a strong emphasis on consolidating power, anti-corruption campaigns, and a robust foreign policy aimed at increasing China's global influence.

- **The National People's Congress (NPC)** is China's legislative body and, in theory, the highest state authority. It consists of nearly 3,000 delegates elected from provincial governments and various social groups.
- China operates a highly centralized administrative structure, but with significant delegation of authority to regional and local governments for practical governance. China is divided into 34 provincial-level administrative units, including 23 provinces, 5 autonomous regions, 4 direct-controlled municipalities (Beijing, Tianjin, Shanghai, and Chongqing), and 2 special administrative regions (Hong Kong and Macau).
- Autonomous regions like **Tibet** and **Xinjiang** have been granted a degree of administrative autonomy, particularly in cultural and language policies. However, the central government maintains strict control over political matters, and tensions related to ethnic minorities, especially in Tibet and Xinjiang, have led to heavy government surveillance and suppression of dissent.
- The government employs sophisticated surveillance technologies, including the **Social Credit System**, which monitors citizens' behavior.
- The CPC tightly controls the media, internet, and academic spaces. Freedom of expression is limited, and the state actively censors dissent, using tools like the **Great Firewall** to block foreign websites and monitor online activity.
- The country has made significant progress in recent decades in areas such as poverty reduction, education, and healthcare. However, it still faces challenges such as income inequality, environmental degradation, and human rights issues.

Military and the Role of the People's Liberation Army (PLA)

The **People's Liberation Army (PLA)** is a key player in China's political and administrative structure, owing allegiance directly to the CPC rather than the state. The integration of civilian and military objectives in state governance has been a characteristic feature of China's political structure. The military has significant involvement in public administration, domestic infrastructure, and strategic decision-making. Under Xi Jinping, the PLA has undergone significant modernization, focusing on enhancing its technological and combat capabilities. The military plays an essential role in enforcing domestic stability and projecting China's power abroad.

ECONOMY & TRADE

(1) China is the **second-largest economy globally**, after the United States. Its economic rise has been one of the most remarkable stories of the past few decades, transforming from a largely agrarian society to a global industrial powerhouse.

(2) **Gross Domestic Product:**
- Nominal GDP (2023): Approximately $17.8 trillion
- Global Ranking: Second largest economy globally
- GDP per capita (current US$ 2023): Approximately $12,700

(3) China is often referred to as the "**world's factory**" due to its dominant position in global manufacturing. It accounts for approximately 30% of global manufacturing output. The country produces a vast array of goods, from consumer electronics and textiles to machinery and vehicles.

(4) It is a leading producer and exporter of a wide range of goods, including electronics, textiles, and machinery. It is also home to many of the world's largest tech companies, including Huawei, Alibaba, and Tencent.

(5) China has a vast and growing domestic market, with over **1.4 billion consumers**. The rise of the middle class has fueled domestic consumption, making it an increasingly important driver of economic growth.

(6) Through initiatives like the BRI and investments in Africa, Latin America, and Southeast Asia, China is becoming a **leading global investor and creditor**. The country is also a major player in international organizations like the World Trade Organization (WTO), International Monetary Fund (IMF), and the Asian Infrastructure Investment Bank (AIIB).

(7) China is the **world's largest exporter and a leading importer**, with total trade exceeding $6 trillion in 2023. It is a key trading partner for countries across Asia, Europe, Africa, and the Americas. The Belt and Road Initiative (BRI) has further expanded China's trade links by investing in infrastructure projects across more than 60 countries.

INFRASTRUCTURE DEVELOPMENT & BELT AND ROAD INITIATIVE

The **Belt and Road Initiative (BRI)**, also known as **One Belt One Road (OBOR)**, is a comprehensive economic development and trade project proposed by Chinese President Xi Jinping. It aims to enhance connectivity and foster cooperation among numerous countries spanning Asia, Africa, and Europe. Initially, the concept comprised **the Silk Road Economic Belt (SREB)** and **the Maritime Silk Road (MSR).** These two initiatives were eventually combined into the broader framework known as One Belt One Road (OBOR) Initiative, later renamed as the Belt and Road Initiative (BRI).

BRI has continued to expand since its inception in 2013, with new projects and investments announced regularly. According to World Bank estimates in 2021, close to **US$500 billion was invested in belt and toad initiative projects spread over 50 developing nations between 2013 and 2018**. As of 2024, recent estimates suggest that BRI-related investments have surpassed the US$1 trillion mark.

Significance of BRI

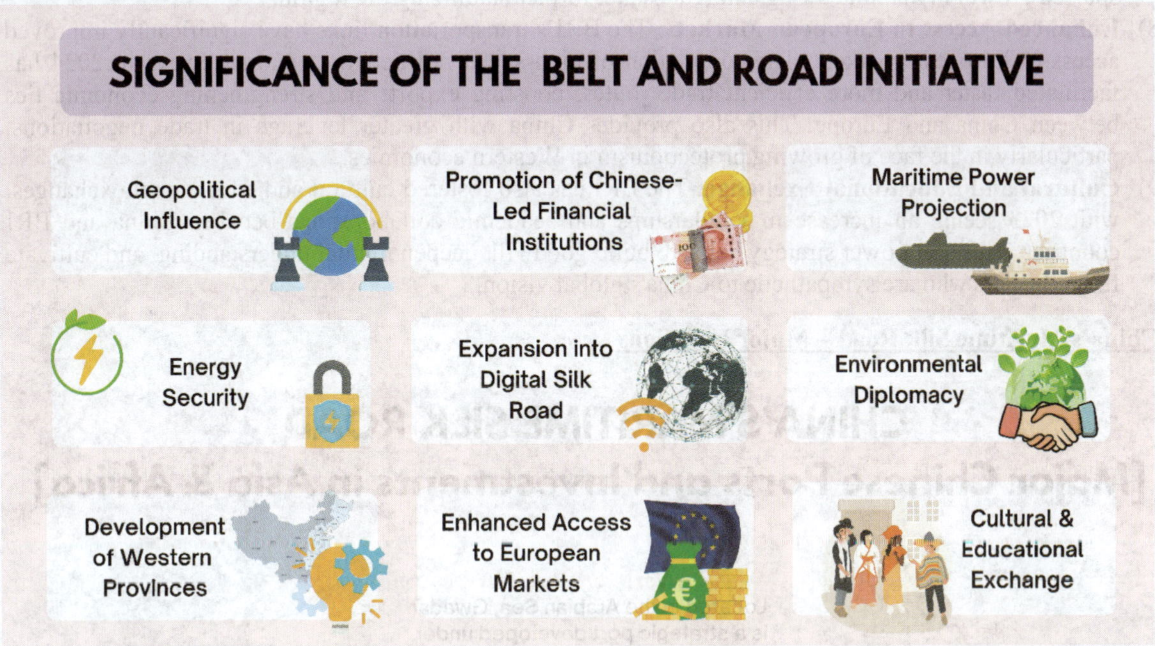

1) **Geopolitical Influence**: The BRI continues to expand China's geopolitical influence, particularly in Africa, Central Asia, and Southeast Asia. By financing and constructing critical infrastructure, China has secured long-term strategic partnerships, access to natural resources, and political influence. This expansion has been met with both cooperation and resistance from other global powers, especially as the U.S. and EU launch alternative initiatives to counterbalance China's influence.
2) **Promotion of Chinese-Led Financial Institutions**: The BRI helps to bolster Chinese financial institutions like the Asian Infrastructure Investment Bank (AIIB), with recent expansions in 2023. AIIB's growing membership and capital base underline China's increasing influence in global financial governance, providing alternatives to Western-led financial institutions and enhancing China's soft power.
3) **Maritime Power Projection**: The BRI has solidified China's status as a maritime power, particularly with the completion of key ports and naval bases in the Indian Ocean Region by 2024. This has allowed China to secure critical sea lanes, ensure uninterrupted trade, and enhance its strategic military presence, particularly in response to growing U.S. naval activities in the Indo-Pacific.
4) **Energy Security**: New energy corridors established under the BRI in 2023 have enhanced China's energy security by providing alternative routes from the Middle East, Africa, and Central Asia. These routes bypass chokepoints like the Strait of Hormuz and the Malacca Strait, reducing China's vulnerability to geopolitical tensions and securing its energy needs for the future.
5) **Expansion into Digital Silk Road**: Since 2023, the BRI has increasingly focused on the "Digital Silk Road," investing in telecommunications, data centers, and e-commerce infrastructure across participating countries. This expansion into digital infrastructure not only promotes technological connectivity but also reinforces China's role in shaping global digital standards and governance.
6) **Environmental Diplomacy**: In 2024, China has positioned the BRI as a vehicle for promoting green infrastructure and sustainable development. The initiative now emphasizes renewable energy projects, green financing, and eco-friendly transportation, aligning with global climate goals. This shift enhances China's leadership in global environmental diplomacy, countering criticism of the BRI's environmental impact.
7) **Development of Western Provinces**: The BRI remains central to the development of China's western provinces, especially Xinjiang, which continues to be a focus in 2024. The region's designation as the "Core Zone of the Silk Road Economic Belt" has attracted increased investment, helping to address

ethnic tensions through economic integration. The Chinese government's incentives in 2023 have spurred growth in manufacturing and real estate, further stabilizing the region.

8) **Enhanced Access to European Markets**: The BRI's transportation links have significantly improved access to European markets. The completion of high-speed rail networks and roadways in 2024 has facilitated faster and more efficient trade routes, boosting exports and strengthening economic ties between China and Europe. This also provides China with greater leverage in trade negotiations, particularly in the face of growing protectionism in Western economies.
9) **Cultural and Educational Exchange**: The BRI has also fostered cultural and educational exchanges, with 2023 seeing an increase in scholarships and academic collaborations between China and BRI countries. This soft power strategy helps to build goodwill, deepen mutual understanding, and cultivate future leaders who are sympathetic to China's global vision.

<u>China's Maritime Silk Road – Major Locations</u>

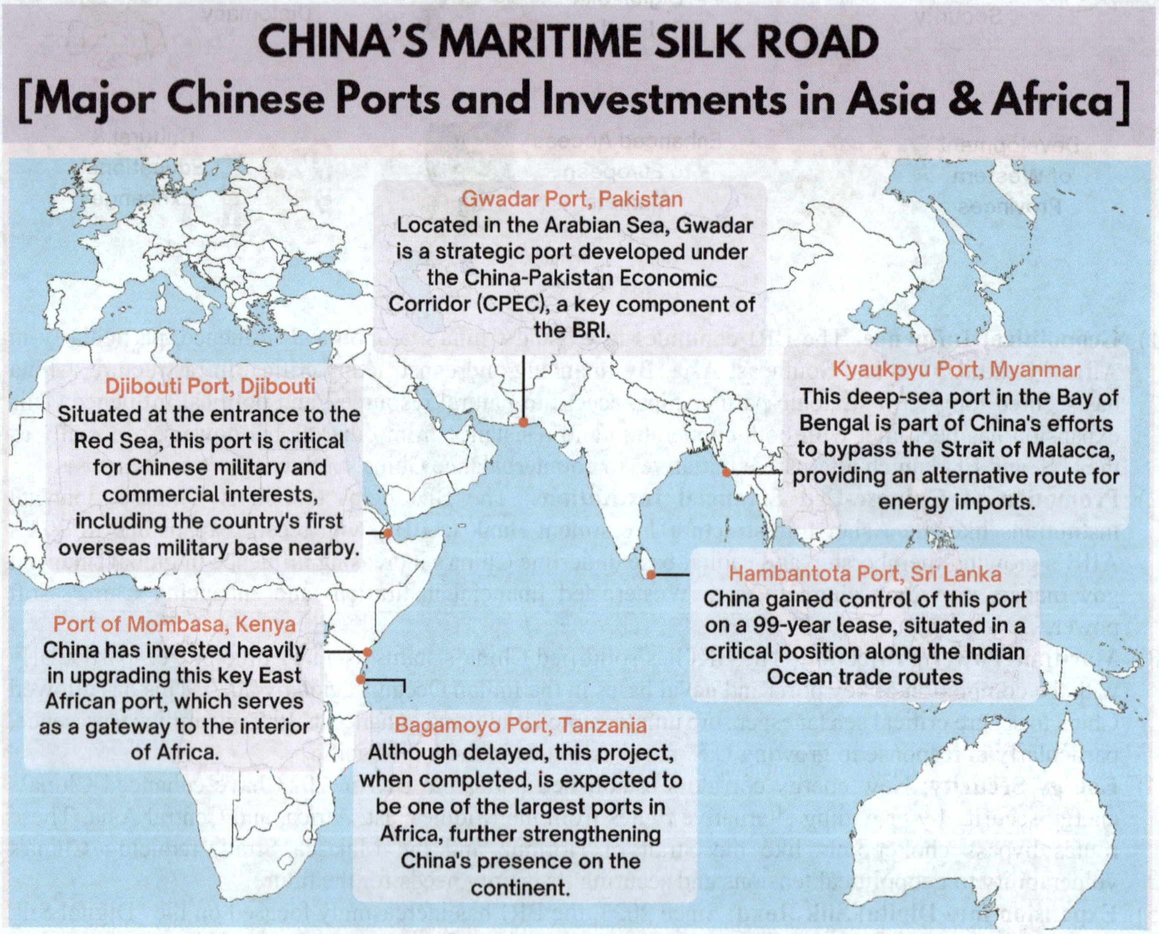

Other Locations of Chinese Ports and Investments	
EUROPE	1) **Port of Rotterdam, Netherlands**: The Port of Rotterdam is Europe's largest port and a critical hub for global trade. Chinese companies, including COSCO, have made significant investments in the port's infrastructure, particularly in the development of new terminals and logistics centers. 2) **Port of Hamburg, Germany**: The Port of Hamburg is one of Europe's busiest ports and a vital gateway for trade between China and Germany. In recent years, Chinese companies have acquired stakes in key terminals, and COSCO's involvement has increased.

	3) **Port of Valencia, Spain**: The Port of Valencia is the largest port on the Mediterranean coast in Spain and a major entry point for Chinese goods into Southern Europe. Chinese companies have invested in terminal operations, making it a crucial part of the Maritime Silk Road, which connects China to Europe via the Mediterranean. 4) **Port of Piraeus, Greece**: Managed by China Ocean Shipping Company (COSCO), this port is a key entry point for Chinese goods into Europe and serves as a strategic hub for Chinese trade. 5) **Zeebrugge Port, Belgium**: Acquired by COSCO, this port serves as an important logistics hub for Chinese goods entering Northern Europe.
MIDDLE EAST	1) **Port of Haifa, Israel**: China is involved in the construction of a new terminal at this strategic Mediterranean port, enhancing its access to European and Middle Eastern markets. 2) **Khalifa Port, UAE**: Managed by COSCO, this port near Abu Dhabi enhances China's presence in the Gulf region, facilitating trade and logistics.
LATIN AMERICA & OCEANIA	1) **Panama Ports, Panama**: China has invested in various port projects in Panama, taking advantage of the country's strategic location at the crossroads of global shipping routes. 2) **Puerto La Plata, Argentina**: China has been involved in the modernization and expansion of this port, enhancing its influence in Latin American trade routes. 3) **Port of Darwin, Australia**: Leased to a Chinese company for 99 years, this port has raised concerns due to its strategic location in Northern Australia.

While China has been expanding its influence world-over, the BRI has had a crippling effect on several nations. The rising Chinese debt has made the nations cautious of its future engagements. According to estimates from insurance groups, ten African and Latin American countries that have benefitted from strong Chinese engagement since 2010 – Argentina, Brazil, Ecuador, Angola, Egypt, Ethiopia, Ghana, Kenya, South Africa and Zambia – will face an external financing gap of US$47 billion by 2025 as a result of any gradual disengagement from financing by China.

The unsustainable lending in the past now threatens to destabilize Beijing's economy. China seems to be rationalizing future flows and recalibrating its strategy especially post-Covid.

SILK ROADSTER

It is a new initiative launched by China to foster cooperation and exchanges with Southeast and South Asian countries. As outlined in the concept paper, the platform aims to facilitate:

- **Technical skills training**
- **People-to-people exchanges**
- **Enterprise cooperation**
- **Cultural events**

MILITARY STRENGTH

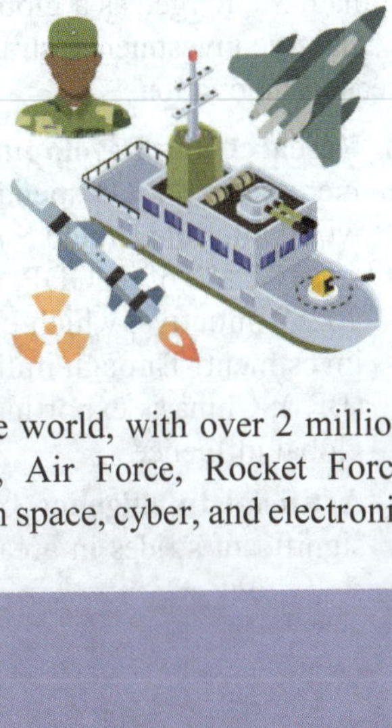

- China has emerged as one of the foremost military powers globally, second only to the United States in terms of overall military capabilities. Its rapid military modernization has significantly altered the security landscape in the Asia-Pacific region and is increasingly shaping the broader global military balance.
- As a recognized **nuclear power**, China's strategic capabilities further enhance its standing, solidifying its role as a dominant force in both conventional and nuclear military strength.
- The **People's Liberation Army (PLA)** is the largest military force in the world, with over 2 million active-duty personnel. The PLA comprises the Ground Force, Navy, Air Force, Rocket Force (responsible for strategic missiles), and Strategic Support Force (focused on space, cyber, and electronic warfare).

- China's military modernization has been a top priority for the government, with a goal to transform the PLA into a world-class military by 2049 (centenary of the founding of the People's Republic of China).
  - China's **Rocket Force** has developed a range of advanced ballistic and cruise missiles, including the DF-21D "carrier killer" missile and the DF-41 intercontinental ballistic missile (ICBM), which can reach the U.S. mainland.
  - The **PLA Navy** (PLAN) has seen rapid expansion, becoming the world's largest navy by the number of ships. This includes aircraft carriers like the Liaoning and the domestically built Shandong, along with advanced submarines, destroyers, and amphibious assault ships.
  - The **PLA Air Force** (PLAAF) is the largest in Asia and the third-largest in the world. It has acquired advanced fighter jets such as the J-20 stealth fighter and is developing long-range bombers and drones to enhance its strategic reach.
  - China's **Strategic Support Force** focuses on cyber, electronic, and space warfare capabilities. China has developed anti-satellite weapons, demonstrated by its 2007 test that destroyed a defunct satellite, and is advancing its space-based military assets.
- China maintains a growing and increasingly sophisticated **nuclear arsenal**, estimated to include around 350 nuclear warheads as of 2024. The country adheres to a "**no first use**" policy but has been expanding its nuclear triad capabilities, ensuring it can deliver nuclear weapons via land, sea, and air. The development of new ICBMs, submarine-launched ballistic missiles (SLBMs), and strategic bombers underlines China's focus on enhancing its nuclear deterrent.

Regional and Global Military Influence

China has increasingly engaged in military diplomacy, participating in joint exercises and arms sales with various countries, particularly in Africa, Southeast Asia, and Central Asia. The Shanghai Cooperation Organization (SCO), which includes China, Russia, and several Central Asian countries, has become a platform for military cooperation, counterterrorism, and regional security.

- **South China Sea**: China has aggressively expanded its presence in the South China Sea, building artificial islands, deploying military assets, and establishing naval bases. This has allowed China to assert its territorial claims and control key maritime routes, challenging the U.S. and its allies' presence in the region.
- **Indian Ocean Region**: The expansion of the PLA Navy into the Indian Ocean, Africa, and the Mediterranean reflects China's broader strategic ambitions. The establishment of a military base in Djibouti and increased naval patrols in the Indian Ocean showcase China's intent to protect its interests along critical global trade routes.
- **Taiwan and East Asia**: The PLA's focus on Taiwan remains a central aspect of China's military strategy. China has conducted large-scale military exercises near Taiwan, signaling its resolve to reunify the island with the mainland, by force if necessary. This has heightened tensions with the U.S., which has a commitment to Taiwan's defense.

SCIENCE AND TECHNOLOGY

China has emerged as a global powerhouse in science and technology, driven by massive investments, strategic policies, and a clear ambition to lead in key areas of innovation.

1) **Research and Development (R&D) Investments**: China has significantly increased its R&D spending, becoming the second-largest spender in the world after the United States. By 2023, China's R&D expenditure reached nearly 2.5% of its GDP, a substantial increase from previous years. The government's "Made in China 2025" initiative, which emphasizes innovation in high-tech industries, has been a major driver of this investment. Through initiatives like the ***Digital Silk Road***, a component of the Belt and Road Initiative (BRI), China is exporting its technology and standards to developing countries, further expanding its global influence.
2) **Artificial Intelligence (AI)**: China is at the forefront of AI research and development and has made significant strides in areas like facial recognition, natural language processing, and machine learning.

Chinese tech giants like Baidu, Alibaba, Tencent, and Huawei are leading global AI research, backed by strong government support.

3) **Quantum Computing and Communications**: China is a global leader in quantum technology, particularly in quantum communication and computing. The country launched the world's first quantum satellite, ***Micius***, in 2016, and has since made significant advancements in quantum encryption and quantum key distribution. As per reports in 2024, China was reportedly close to achieving practical quantum supremacy, positioning itself ahead of other major powers in this critical field.
4) **5G Technology**: China has taken a dominant position in the global 5G race. Huawei, one of the world's leading 5G technology providers, has been at the forefront of developing and deploying 5G networks worldwide. By 2023, China had already rolled out extensive 5G networks domestically, with tens of millions of users accessing these high-speed services.
5) **Space Exploration**: China's space program has made remarkable achievements, establishing the country as a leading space-faring nation. The successful landing of the Chang'e 4 mission on the far side of the moon in 2019 was a significant milestone. In 2021, China further demonstrated its capabilities with the successful landing of the Tianwen-1 rover on Mars. By 2023, China had completed its own space station, Tiangong, marking its place as one of the few countries with an active space station in orbit. China's other programs include plans for lunar bases, Mars exploration, and further deep-space missions.
6) **Biotechnology and Pharmaceuticals**: China has also made substantial progress in biotechnology and pharmaceuticals. The country was one of the first to develop and deploy COVID-19 vaccines, with Sinovac and Sinopharm vaccines being distributed globally. Chinese biotech firms are increasingly engaged in cutting-edge research, including gene editing, stem cell research, and synthetic biology. In 2023, China continued to expand its capabilities in drug discovery, precision medicine, and biotechnology.
7) **Renewable Energy and Green Technology:** China is a global leader in renewable energy technologies, particularly in solar and wind power. The country is the largest producer of solar panels and has the world's largest installed capacity of solar and wind energy. In 2023, China continued to push forward its green energy initiatives as part of its commitment to achieving carbon neutrality by 2060. The country is also advancing in electric vehicles (EVs) and battery technology.

DIPLOMACY AND FOREIGN RELATIONS

China is a permanent member of the United Nations Security Council and plays a significant role in global affairs. It has diplomatic relations with nearly all countries in the world and is a member of several international organizations, including the World Trade Organization, the International Monetary Fund, and the World Health Organization.

China's diplomacy and foreign relations in the 21st century have been marked by assertiveness and strategic engagement. Under President Xi Jinping, China has embraced a more confident global stance, shifting from the "peaceful rise" narrative to what is called "major-country diplomacy." Key aspects include:

1. **Belt and Road Initiative (BRI)**: Launched in 2013, this large-scale infrastructure project aims to connect Asia, Africa, and Europe through trade routes, ports, and energy corridors. It is a cornerstone of China's strategy to expand its influence, increase economic ties, and secure raw material supplies.
2. **United Nations and Multilateralism**: China has significantly increased its participation in multilateral forums such as the UN, World Trade Organization (WTO), and BRICS (Brazil, Russia, India, China, South Africa). Beijing has positioned itself as a defender of globalization and free trade while challenging Western dominance in global governance.
3. **Territorial and Maritime Assertiveness**: In regions like the South China Sea, China's assertive territorial claims and island-building activities have drawn international scrutiny and regional tensions. This aspect of China's foreign policy has caused friction with neighboring countries and the United States.
4. **Engagement with Developing Nations**: China has been heavily involved in Africa, Latin America, and Southeast Asia, often through economic assistance, infrastructure development, and resource extraction.

The BRI plays a significant role in this outreach, but China has also built military and diplomatic ties with several states in these regions.

5. **Diplomatic Soft Power**: China has increased its use of soft power through cultural diplomacy, media outlets, and Confucius Institutes globally. These efforts aim to improve China's image and promote its values and development model.
6. **Geopolitical Tensions with the West**: The trade war with the U.S., tensions over Taiwan, Hong Kong, and Xinjiang, as well as human rights issues, have increasingly soured China's relations with Western nations. China's strategic alignment with Russia has also reinforced its position against Western geopolitical frameworks.
7. **Post-Pandemic Diplomacy**: China's handling of the COVID-19 pandemic and its subsequent "vaccine diplomacy" saw it providing medical aid and vaccines to several developing nations, positioning itself as a leader in global health efforts.

IMPORTANT TERMINOLOGY CONCERNING CHINA	
Wolf Warrior Diplomacy	It refers to China's more assertive and confrontational diplomatic stance, named after a popular Chinese action film series. Chinese diplomats under this approach aggressively defend China's policies and criticize Western nations, particularly on issues like human rights, Taiwan, and trade. It reflects a shift from traditional, cautious diplomacy to a more nationalistic and combative tone.
Debt-trap Diplomacy	A criticism associated with China's Belt and Road Initiative (BRI), where China is accused of offering massive infrastructure loans to developing nations, which may struggle to repay, leading to dependency on Beijing. Sri Lanka's Hambantota Port is often cited as an example, where the country leased the port to China after defaulting on debt.
Panda Diplomacy	Refers to China's use of giant pandas as diplomatic gifts or loans to other countries. This practice, which dates back to the Tang dynasty, is used to foster goodwill and strengthen bilateral relationships. For instance, pandas are often sent to countries with which China seeks closer ties.
Sharp Power	This phrase describes how China uses coercive measures—ranging from economic influence to digital surveillance—to assert its influence in foreign nations, often manipulating information and controlling narratives about China abroad.
China's Red Line	This idiom is often used to describe non-negotiable issues for China, such as its sovereignty over Taiwan, Hong Kong, or the South China Sea. Crossing a "red line" is considered a direct challenge to China's core interests.

ONE CHINA POLICY

The One China Policy refers to the diplomatic stance that recognizes the People's Republic of China (PRC) as the sole legal government of China, and considers Taiwan to be a part of China. The policy was first articulated by the Chinese government in the 1950s, following the Chinese Civil War, which ended in victory for the Communist Party and the establishment of the PRC.

Under the One China Policy, **countries that maintain diplomatic relations with the PRC must also acknowledge the PRC's sovereignty over Taiwan**. This means that they cannot have formal diplomatic relations with the government on Taiwan, which is known as the Republic of China (ROC).

China commemorated the 25th **anniversary of Hong Kong's return** and reaffirmed its authority over the region through the **One Country, Two Systems (OCTS)** framework. This arrangement allows Hong Kong and Macau to maintain distinct economic and political systems while remaining part of China. As Special Administrative Regions, both regions have their own currencies, economic structures, and legal systems, although defense and foreign affairs are under the control of China. Notably, Hong Kong enjoys certain democratic rights, including freedom of assembly and speech, that are not typically available in mainland China.

TAIWAN ISSUE

Taiwan, officially known as the **Republic of China (ROC)**, is an island separated from China by the Taiwan Strait. **Taiwan and China split in 1949** after the Communists won a civil war on the mainland. Both sides state they are one country but disagree over which government is entitled to national leadership. **Taiwan has been governed independently of mainland China**, officially the People's Republic of China (PRC), since **1949**. However, Beijing has always maintained that Taiwan is an integral part of the territory and has **vowed to eventually 'unite' Taiwan with the mainland China**, even by using coercive methods if necessary.

TAIWAN

Capital	Taipei City
Area	35,980 square kilometers
Population	23 million (Jan 2023)
Form of government	Semi-Presidential Republic
GDP	$ 829 Billion (2022); Per Capita - $ 35, 513 (2022)
Languages	Mandarin Chinese (official), Minnan, Hakka dialects, Indigenous languages
Religions	Buddhism 35%, Taoism 33%, Christianity 4%, folk 10%, none or unspecified 18% (2005)

Taiwan has its own **democratically elected government with a President**. The current President's party, **Democratic Progressive Party (DPP)**, favors independence and has repeatedly rebuked Beijing's efforts to undermine the democracy in the nation.

Beijing asserts that Taiwan is obligated to adhere to a diplomatic understanding referred to as the **1992 Consensus**, which was reached between the **Chinese Communist Party (CCP)** and the **Kuomintang (KMT) party**, which governed Taiwan at the time. However, the People's Republic of China (PRC) and the Republic of China (ROC) have differing interpretations of the consensus as it was not intended to address the legal status of Taiwan. The **Democratic Progressive Party** (DPP), the primary rival of the KMT, has never endorsed the principles outlined in the 1992 Consensus. However, this hasn't dissuaded the PRC's efforts and Beijing has been constantly mounting political and military pressures on Taipei.

China has increased the scale and frequency of patrols of PLA bombers, fighter jets, and surveillance aircraft over and around Taiwan.

→ China has increasingly sailed its warships and aircraft carriers through the Taiwan Strait in shows of force.

→ Taiwan has reported of thousands of cyberattacks on a daily basis from China which have been targeting government agencies, their data and personal information.

→ In 2016, China suspended a cross-strait communication mechanism with the main Taiwan liaison office.

→ It restricted tourism to Taiwan, and the number of mainland tourists visiting Taiwan fell from a high of over 4 million in 2015 to 2.7 million in 2019.

→ China has pressured global corporations, including airlines and hotel chains, to list Taiwan as a Chinese province.

→ In August 2022, there was a major escalation in Taiwan after the island detected 21 Chinese military aircraft and 6 Chinese naval ships in and around the Taiwan Strait.

→ In 2023, the United States maintained its support for Taiwan, providing military aid and conducting arms sales. This further aggravated the relationship between China and the US.

→ In 2024, China is expected to maintain its aggressive military posture towards Taiwan, seeking to deter Taiwan from any moves towards independence. China may increase economic pressure too.

In a 2019 speech, the **President Xi Jinping of People's Republic of China (PRC)** reiterated China's long-standing proposal for Taiwan: that it be incorporated into the mainland under the formula of "**one country, two systems**." This formula has also been used for Hong Kong, which was guaranteed the ability to **preserve its political and economic systems and granted a "high degree of autonomy**." However, the leaders of Taiwan and the general public have vehemently opposed this status and demanded greater independence.

DID YOU KNOW?

Despite ongoing tensions in the cross-strait relations, **Taiwan has emerged as the leading global contract manufacturer of semiconductor chips**. Its semiconductor industry is thriving, catering to a wide range of electronic devices such as smartphones, computers, vehicles, and even AI-based weapon systems.

Taiwan and World

The approach of the **United States** is governed by the One-China Policy. It acknowledges the Chinese position that "**there is one China and Taiwan is part of China**" and that the PRC is the "sole legal government of China". The main agenda of the United States' is to maintain peace and stability in the **Taiwan Strait**, and it has encouraged both Beijing and Taipei to maintain the status quo. The top US analysts have been hinting at an all out conflict between China and Taiwan, which could result in the involvement of US since it hasn't outrightly ruled out defending Taiwan if China attacks. Russia's invasion of Ukraine in early 2022 has exacerbated the situation and reignited the debate, with analysts arguing that Moscow's moves could embolden Beijing to similarly invade Taiwan.

China has rejected Taiwan's participation as a member of the UN agencies among other international organisations. Taiwan holds member status in over forty organisations (mostly regional) including Asian

Development Bank, Asia-Pacific Economic Cooperation forum, as well as in the World Trade Organization. However, only **thirteen states maintain official diplomatic ties with Taiwan**.

Taiwan and India

- Currently, **India and Taiwan do not have formal diplomatic ties** and India adheres to the **One-China policy**. However, the trade and people to people ties are getting stronger and the relations have witnessed transformative changes since 2020. With the initiation of the **'Look East policy'** by India in 1991, Taiwan and India started to approach each other and loosen visa restrictions.
- In 1995 the two countries established **representative offices** in each other's capitals, namely Taipei Economic and Cultural Center in India (TECC) for ROC (Taiwan) in New Delhi and India-Taipei Association (ITA) for India in Taipei. India and Taiwan signed "**Double Taxation Avoidance Agreement**" and "**Customs Mutual Assistance Agreement**" in July 2011.
- In 2022 bilateral Deputy Ministerial Meetings on Economic Consultation as well as Science and Technology Cooperation was held with remarkable progress. **Taiwan's reputation as the world leader in semiconductor and electronics complements India's leadership in ITES (Information Technology-Enabled Services).**

While China has been using its bullying tactics against Taiwan, for instance the **build-up around Taiwan Strait (latter half of 2022)**, India has maintained a studied silence and reacted by **opposing any unilateral action to change the Status Quo and to maintain peace and stability in the region.**

ECONOMY AND TRADE

- Bilateral trade has grown nearly six-fold from USD 1.19 billion in 2001 to almost **USD 7.7 billion in 2021**.
- India ranks as **Taiwan's 14th largest export destination** and **18th largest source of imports**.
- As of the end of 2021, around 106 Taiwanese companies have set up business operations in India, with the total investment amount of USD 1.5 billion.
- Main fields of interest include information and communication technology, medical devices, automobile components, machinery, steel, electronics, construction, engineering, financial services, etc.

SCIENCE AND TECHNOLOGY

- The **MOU on Scientific and Technological Cooperation** was signed between Taipei Economic and Cultural Center in India (TECC) and India-Taipei Association (ITA) in 2007.
- As of 2023, a total of 115 projects and joint proposals have been carried out while 25 seminars have been held bilaterally.
- Cooperation revolves around the fields of agricultural and food science; sustainable energy and storage devices; health care including functional genomics, drug development and biomedical devices; earth, atmosphere and ocean sciences & digital including cloud computing.

CULTURE & COOPERATION

- Out of the 1,30,000 **foreign students** studying in Taiwan, **2,800 students hail from India**.
- In 2019, Foundation for International Cooperation in Higher Education of Taiwan signed an MOU with Association of Indian Universities, by which **academic degrees and certificates recognized by one will be recognized by the other**.
- In 2018, the Youth Ambassadors delegation visited India and a **Taiwan Film Festival** was held by TECC in New Delhi.
- In 2022, the Dance Troupe of the College of Indigenous Studies from National Dong Hwa University was invited to attend an international folk culture event **Udbhav Utsav** in Madhya Pradesh.

India and Taiwan continue to forge healthy relations going ahead. While India has maintained its 'One-China' policy, Chinese wolf warrior diplomacy has resulted in the need for India to reconsider the ties with Taiwan. China's takeover of the island nation or a cross-strait conflict would have serious implications for India and merits a serious discussion on the country's military, diplomatic and economic response, which has been missing from the Indian policy discourse. Going ahead, Taiwan-India ties have the potential to be a pivotal relationship in the Indo-Pacific region, but only if both nations lose their hesitation and become proactive in engaging with one another.

HONG KONG

Hong Kong is a former British colony that became a **special administrative region of China in 1997**, when Britain's 99-year lease of the New Territories, north of Hong Kong island, expired.

In 1842, China had ceded the Hong Kong island to Britain after the First Opium War. In 1898, China leased the New Territories (along with 235 islands) to Britain for 99 years. Hong Kong was occupied by Japan during the Second World War (1941-45).

Hong Kong operates under the framework of "**one country, two systems,**" in which China has committed to granting the region a significant level of autonomy and maintaining its economic and social structures for a period of 50 years following the handover.

HONG KONG

Administrative Centre	Tamar
Area	2,755 sq km
Languages	Chinese and English
Population	7.2 million (2022)
Leader	Chief executive: John Lee Ka-chiu (Sept 2024)

- **Beijing has retained the power to veto changes to the political system** and the pro-democracy actors/organisations in Hong Kong have been vehemently arguing against the constant interference of People's Republic of China in the functioning of Hong Kong and the allow paced of political reform.
- During 2014, there was a significant demonstration in Hong Kong as **pro-democracy protesters occupied the city center** for several weeks. The protest was in response to the Chinese government's

decision to impose restrictions on voters' options in the upcoming 2017 Hong Kong leadership election. At its peak, the Occupy Central protests drew participation from over 100,000 individuals.

- It was in **2017 when Chinese President Xi Jinping visited Hong Kong** on an official work, but used the opportunity to **warn against any attempt to undermine China's influence over the special administrative region**.
- The year **2019 witnessed anti-government and pro-democracy protests** spread like wildfire in Hong Kong. These also involved violent clashes with the police and the protests were targeted against a proposal to allow extradition to mainland China.
- In 2021, Beijing implemented **changes to Hong Kong's electoral system** in order to exert greater control over the region. These changes included reducing the number of directly elected seats in the Legislative Council and introducing a requirement for all candidates to undergo vetting and approval by a committee appointed by Beijing.

India and Hong Kong

Historical ties between India and Hong Kong go back to the **Treaty of Nanking**, which ended the First Opium War and made Hong Kong a British territory, in the 1840s. From the early 19th century (1840 forward) commerce connections, linkages now cover industries such investment banking, services, marine, shipping, logistics, culture, education, and trade. Starting from January 2017, the Hong Kong government implemented a mandatory Pre-Arrival Registration for Indian nationals planning to visit Hong Kong without a visa for a duration of 14 days. Hong Kong remains an important partner for India, ranking 7th in terms of import sources.

ECONOMY AND TRADE

- **India-Hong Kong bilateral trade was US$ 30.08 billion in FY 2021-22**, with a year-on-year increase of 18.73%.
- In FY 2023-24, Hong Kong was India's **12th largest export market**, with Indian exports totaling approximately $9.89 billion. The value of exports of goods from India to Hong Kong increased by 8.09% over a year earlier to **$10.98 billion**.
- Hong Kong remains an important partner for India, ranking **7th in terms of import sources**. India imported goods worth **$19.1 billion** from Hong Kong, which is a continuation of the strong upward trend observed in recent years.
- Hong Kong holds the **14th position in terms of foreign direct investment (FDI)** equity inflows into India, with a cumulative FDI amount of **US $4.7 billion** recorded from April 2000 to Sept 2023.

CULTURE AND COMMUNITY

- The **Indian community** in Hong Kong is believed to consist of around **42,569 individuals**, including Indian nationals and People of Indian origin. Out of this population, approximately 32,796 individuals hold Indian passports.
- **Sindhis, Gujaratis** and **Punjabis** (Sikh) form the largest component of the community.
- The MoU on "Establishment of the ICCR visiting professorship of Indian Studies" (2015) was renewed in 2019.
- The **International Day of Yoga** is celebrated in Hong Kong every year since its inception.
- Film festivals, exhibitions, competitions, and art workshops to help promote Indian art and culture are held on a regular basis.

Major Indian export items

- Pearls, precious & semi-precious stones, Iron & Steel, Electrical Machinery, Meat & edible meat, Machinery, Mineral fuels
- Fish & crustaceans, Raw hides & skins, Optical & medical instruments and Pharmaceutical products.

Major import items from Hong Kong

- Electrical machinery, Pearls, precious and semi-precious stones, Machinery, Optical & medical instruments,
- Plastic & articles thereof, Organic Chemicals, Iron & steel and Pulp of wood.

MACAU

It is a **special administrative region of China** (1999) located near Hong Kong and occupies a small peninsula and two islands off **China's southern coast**. Colonized by the **Portuguese** in the 16th century, Macau was the first European settlement in the Far East. With an area spanning **33 sq km**, the mainstay of Macau's economy is tourism and gambling industry. Macau continues to capitalize on its long history as a 'gambling centre'.

The total trade between India and Macau was worth **US$ 17.75 million** in FY 2022-23, wherein India's exports to Macau were valued at US$ 04.35 million and Macau's exports to India were valued at US$ 13.4million..

Human Rights Violations

The ***Uyghurs*** (or Uighurs) are a **Turkic ethnic group (predominantly Muslims) and the largest minority group in Xinjiang, almost 12 million in population**. The community members consider themselves as culturally and ethnically close to Central Asian nations. Over the past decades, China has been accused of targeting the Uyghur community, their religious figures and practices and even destroying mosques and tombs. There have been reports that the authorities in Xinjiang have detained thousands of Uyghurs, Kazakhs and other Turkic Muslims in internment camps or 're-education camps'. It was previously reported that China sentenced thousands of Muslims to prison terms declaring them as 'terrorists'. Many nations, including the US, UK and Canada have gone to the extent of accusing China of committing 'genocide' and 'crimes against humanity'. Additionally, the past years have witnessed a big inflow of Han Chinese (majority in China) into the Xinjiang region which was allegedly meant to dilute the minority population in the region.

Xinjiang, officially the ***Xinjiang Uyghur Autonomous Region (XUAR)*** is a vast area consisting of mountains, forests and deserts in the far northwestern China, bordering Russia, Central Asian nations and Pakistan. The significance of the region lies in its wealth of natural resources which includes oil, rare earth minerals and gas and more importantly because of its strategic relevance for acting as a buffer for China against its neighbours.

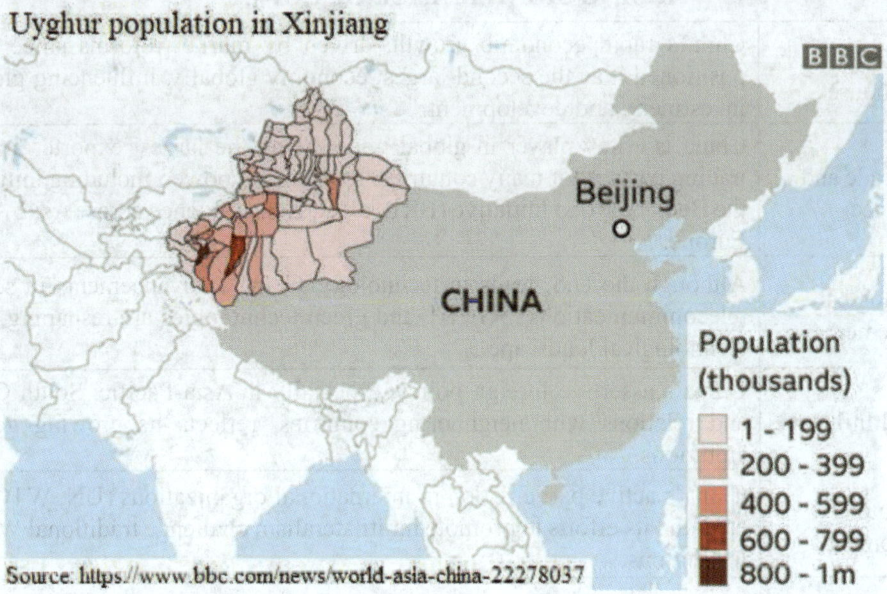

In August 2022, the United Nations (UN) released a long-awaited report focusing on the human rights violations in the Xinjiang region which was welcomed by human rights advocates world over. The report documents the human rights abuses in the region which have been targeted against Uyghurs and other Muslim ethnic minorities. The Chinese administration was however quick to rebut the claims and accused the Western powers of concocting lies to contain China and diminish its credibility. The authorities suggested that the crackdown was aimed at quashing separatism, terrorism and religious extremism.

RISE OF CHINA

- The rise of China has significantly shifted the global balance of power, traditionally dominated by the West. Since 1945, China has drawn on its rich cultural heritage to advance its global standing. While both China and India have gained prominence, their bilateral relations have been strained by ideological differences and conflicting views on global politics.
- According to the IMF, China's economic reforms since 1978—promoting private businesses, liberalizing trade, and investing in industrial and educational growth—transformed it into an economic powerhouse. Although the U.S. remains the technological leader, China has secured a dominant role in global finance and trade.
- Recent efforts to ease tensions along the Line of Actual Control (LAC) reflect ongoing diplomatic work between India and China, particularly highlighted during the 2020 Russia-India-China (RIC) meeting. India's External Affairs Minister emphasized adherence to international law and multilateralism.
- As China continues its rise, the Thucydides Trap theory suggests a potential conflict with the U.S., as a rising power challenges an established one. China's growing influence, particularly in foreign aid, development, and rare earth minerals, has positioned it as a key player, especially as the U.S. retreats from its global commitments.

The **Kindleberger Trap** was coined by Harvard professor Joseph Nye but derived from the late economic historian Charles Kindleberger. While both the *Thucydides Trap* and the *Kindleberger Trap* highlight the danger involved in the shifting balance of power, however unlike the former, which focuses on the threats from a strong aspirant power, the Kindleberger Trap attributes the failure of the international system to the under-provisioning of global public goods.

RISING SIGNIFICANCE OF CHINA	
Economic Powerhouse	China's rapid economic growth, driven by market reforms since 1978, has positioned it as the second-largest economy globally, influencing global trade, investment, and development.
Global Trade and Finance	China is a key player in global trade, being the largest exporter and a major trading partner for many countries. Its financial power, including initiatives like the Belt and Road Initiative (BRI), extends its influence across Asia, Africa, and Europe.
Technological Advancements	Although the U.S. leads in technology, China's advancements in sectors like telecommunications (5G), AI, and green technologies are reshaping the global technological landscape.
Geopolitical Influence	China's assertive foreign policy, especially in Asia-Pacific, South China Sea, and relations with neighboring countries, reflects its growing geopolitical ambitions.
Multilateral Engagement	China's active participation in international organizations (UN, WTO, BRICS, etc.) and its efforts to promote multilateralism challenge traditional Western-led institutions.
Global Governance and Leadership	China's leadership in climate change negotiations, global health (during COVID-19), and its role in development aid and infrastructure projects in developing nations enhance its global standing.
Military Modernization	China's increasing military capabilities and strategic initiatives, such as expanding its naval reach, have implications for regional and global security dynamics.
Soft Power Expansion	Through cultural diplomacy, investments in education, and media influence, China is enhancing its soft power across the world.

Issues in the rise of China

It must be noted that China's path towards becoming a world leader isn't likely to be a smooth sail and to achieve the ambitious global targets, the nation must tackle its domestic issues first; an important one being the establishment of a reliable and transparent governance system. President Xi has cited the Tacitus Trap as a way to emphasize the importance of preserving government credibility to safeguard the legitimacy and power status of the Party. To prevent potential threats, the Chinese state must strive for increased transparency, enhance its legitimacy, and reshape the relationship between the state and society.

> The Chinese have introduced the concept of the **Tacitus Trap**, which draws inspiration from the works of the Roman historian Tacitus. This term refers to a scenario where the actions and statements of the government are met with skepticism or distrust, regardless of their content or intentions. In such a situation, the government's credibility is compromised, and its actions are perceived negatively by the public.

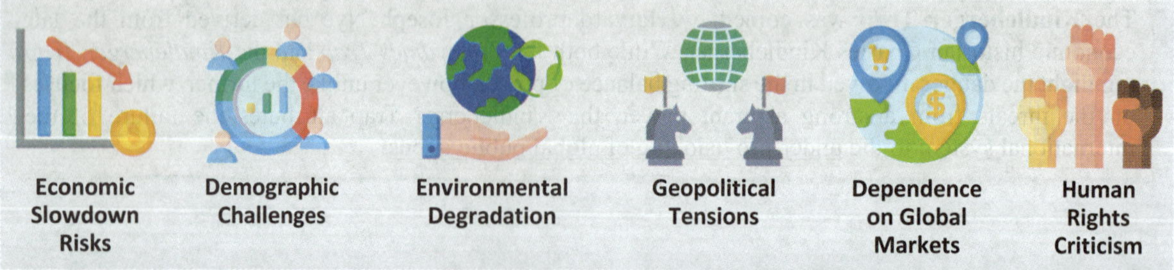

- Despite years of rapid growth, China faces a slowing economy due to declining productivity, rising debt, and an aging population. This could hinder its ability to sustain global economic influence.
- China's shrinking workforce and aging population, a consequence of the one-child policy, are placing enormous pressure on its social security systems and long-term economic prospects.
- Rapid industrialization has led to severe environmental issues, including pollution, deforestation, and water scarcity. China's ability to balance growth with sustainable development is crucial for its global leadership aspirations.
- China's territorial disputes, particularly in the South China Sea, strained relations with India, and a growing rivalry with the U.S. increase the likelihood of regional conflicts, potentially limiting its global rise.
- China's heavy reliance on global supply chains and international markets makes it vulnerable to trade disputes, economic sanctions, and shifts in global trade dynamics.
- China's approach to governance, especially concerning human rights in regions like Xinjiang and Hong Kong, has led to widespread international criticism, undermining its soft power and global credibility.

INDIA-CHINA RELATIONS

India and China are two of the oldest extant civilizations, which were perceived as the seats of legendary wealth, especially by the Europeans. The nations witnessed respective periods of stagnation, poverty and weakness. The mid-twentieth century was the nadir for both the nations. Jawaharlal Nehru envisaged a post-colonial world in which both India and China played a major role in global affairs. In one of his earliest recorded works, *Glimpses of World History*, J.L. Nehru had referred to China as a great country and friend of India.

While India was looking forward to the dawn of independence, China was being plunged into a civil war. The latter witnessed a military struggle from 1945 to 1949 between the Nationalists (Kuomintang) under ***Chiang Kai-shek*** and the Communists under ***Mao Zedong***, for retaining the absolute control of China. While the Nationalists had initial success, the Communists had a series of decisive victories and turned the balance in their favour by 1949, followed by the disintegration of the Nationalist government, which retreated to **Taiwan**.

TIMELINE OF INDIA-CHINA RELATIONS	
1949	China and India established diplomatic relations, making India the second non-communist country, following Burma, to do so.
1951	China compelled the Tibetan Governor of Chamdo to relinquish complete suzerainty over Tibet.
1954	China and India enter into an agreement known as the Five Principles of Peaceful Coexistence or Panchsheel.
1959	The Dalai Lama, along with approximately 80,000 followers, escapes from Tibet and establishes a "government-in-exile" in India.
1962	India and China engage in a short-lived border conflict, resulting in New Delhi's defeat.
1975	China criticizes the integration of Sikkim into India.
1976	India and China resume full diplomatic relations following a 15-year break.
1986	Beijing expresses disapproval of India's decision to elevate Arunachal Pradesh, a region bordering China, to a fully recognized state.
1988	Prime Minister Rajiv Gandhi visits China, and both countries agree to establish a joint working group to address boundary disputes.

1991	Chinese Premier Li Peng concludes his historic visit to India, marking the first visit by a Chinese premier in 31 years.
1993	Indian Prime Minister P.V. Narasimha Rao reciprocates the gesture and visits China, where they sign an agreement on maintaining peace and tranquility along the Line of Actual Control (LAC).
1995	Subsequently, both India and China reach an agreement to withdraw their troops in the eastern sector.
1996	Chinese President Jiang Zemin visits India, leading to an agreement between the two nations to reduce military presence along the disputed border and commit to non-aggression.
1998	Tensions arise when India conducts nuclear tests, resulting in verbal exchanges with Beijing after Defense Minister George Fernandes identifies China as a significant security threat.
2003	During a significant visit by Indian Prime Minister Atal Behari Vajpayee, China and India come to a de facto agreement on the status of Tibet and Sikkim.
2004	The issue of Sikkim loses its relevance as the Chinese foreign ministry's annual yearbook no longer recognizes it as an "independent nation."
2005	India and China established a 'Strategic and Cooperative Partnership for Peace and Prosperity'.
2006	During a visit by Indian Defence Minister Pranab Mukherjee, China and India commit to enhancing military exchanges.
July 2006	The Nathu La pass, which connects the northeastern Indian state of Sikkim with Tibet in China, is reopened for trade.
2010	China started issuing stapled visas to people from J&K
2013	President Xi Jinping promoted Belt and Road initiative
2016	India declined Chinese invite to attend BRI summit
2017	Doklam standoff
2017	India and Pakistan admitted to Shanghai Cooperation Organization
2018	Wuhan Summit (1st informal summit)
2019	Mamallapuram Summit (2nd informal summit)
2020	(1) 70 years of India-China friendship (2) Sikkim and Pangong Tso (Galwan Valley) standoffs (3) In response, India implemented several economic measures against China, including banning over 200 Chinese apps, restricting Chinese investments, and increasing scrutiny of Chinese companies operating in India.
2021-22	• After several rounds of military and diplomatic talks, both India and China agreed to a phased disengagement of troops from some of the friction points in Ladakh, including the north and south banks of Pangong Tso. • In 2022, India and China continued to engage in military and diplomatic talks, holding multiple rounds of Corps Commander-level meetings to resolve the standoffs at the LAC. • Despite tensions, bilateral trade between India and China reached a record high in 2022, surpassing $125 billion.

2023	• Both India and China continued to strengthen their border infrastructure. • Diplomatic engagements continued, with both sides participating in multilateral forums like the BRICS Summit and the Shanghai Cooperation Organisation (SCO).
2024	In 2024, India continued to diversify its military and diplomatic alliances, particularly with countries like the United States, Japan, and Australia through the Quad. China responded by strengthening its ties with Pakistan and increasing its presence in South Asia through initiatives like the Belt and Road Initiative (BRI).

Historical Burdens

Free India began its relationship with China on a very friendly note. After it became to Nehruji that the Communist victory was inevitable, he emphasized on serving national interests by establishing early contact with them. After the Chinese revolution, Mao Zedong proclaimed the formal establishment of the People's Republic of China and things began changing post October 1949. Ambassador Panikkar had been in China since September 1949 for discussing diplomatic negotiations regarding issues affecting India but had to return post the change in regime which no longer recognized previous diplomatic envoys. On his return the Ambassador pressed the Indian side for an early recognition of the Chinese regime. The main reasons why India contemplated early recognition of Communist regime in China included the following–

- Safeguarding India's northern frontier and helping to define its relationship to the status of Tibet.
- The Indian thinking was getting reshaped with the growing Communist movement in the country.
- Enhancement of India's global stature and a way to demonstrate that it didn't follow the dictates of others.
- It could help towards achieving Nehruji's vision of India and China working in friendship for 'Asian resurgence'.

While the foreign policy decision to recognize the new government was being debated, a group of stalwarts including India's Deputy Prime Minister Vallabhbhai Patel and Governor General of India C. Rajagopalachari urged Prime Minister Nehru to rethink the decision. However, eventually such ideas were overshadowed by tremendous support in favour of recognizing the new regime.

> India had had cordial relations with Kuomintang (Nationalists, China) and its leader Chiang Kai-shek before independence, who in turn had voiced his support for the cause of self-determination for India after the war. However, after the Civil War, the Communist Party had made it mandatory for any country wishing to have diplomatic relations with the new regime, to withdraw all recognition from the Chiang Kai-shek regime. They wanted the nations to provide full recognition to the new government i.e., People's Republic of China or nothing.

The hasty recognition became a bone of contention for some time and a substantial issue of discussion owing to the following reasons –

- There was an absence of wider political consultations within the Indian leadership and Jawaharlal Nehru's opinions had probably shrouded critical opinions.
- India repeatedly made attempts to reassure China that it wouldn't align with the west against them, due to which India lost a crucial tactical advantage that might have helped to extract assurances from the new regime.
- India was coerced into severing ties with the Nationalist government (settled in Taiwan) without even being able to bring the issue to the discussion table.
- While the Chinese side laid out a list of preconditions, India didn't place any substantive demands to be fulfilled by the former in exchange for recognition, thereby letting go of an advantageous position.
- The Indian side had been extremely erroneous in presuming that recognition of the new regime in China would automatically result in the establishment of diplomatic relations with China. Their hopes were shattered when Zhou Enlai revealed their government's expectations regarding negotiations for formal establishment of diplomatic relations to be conducted in Beijing.

India and China eventually took different routes to effectively enter the global sphere and gain complementary strengths. The joint enunciation of ***Panchsheel***, the Five Principles of Peaceful Coexistence, by the Indian Prime Minister Nehru and the Chinese Premier Zhou Enlai in 1954 was a step in the direction of stronger relationship between the two countries. At the time when independent India was making attempts to stabilize domestic affairs, China's **'Great Leap Forward'** (1958-60s) under Mao Zedong gave them a much-needed push from a predominantly agrarian society to a modern one. However, India's harvest failures and famine in 1965-66 and massive breakdown of the Great Leap Policy, brought the nations to their proverbial knees in terms of foreign policies.

Panchsheel Principles

- Mutual respect for sovereignty and territorial integrity
- Mutual non-aggression
- Non-interference in each other's internal affairs
- Equality and mutual benefit
- Peaceful coexistence

Some critical events that changed the trajectory of Indo-Sino relations –

1. Boundary disputes: India and China witnessed several boundary disputes over next decade, immediately succeeding the independence. The areas in dispute were Aksai Chin and parts of Arunachal Pradesh. Between 1957 and 1959, the Chinese occupied the Aksai-chin area and built a strategic road there. The border disputes erupted further in 1960 and the talks between **PM Nehru** and **Mao Tsetung** to resolve the differences, proved futile.

Until 1947, three lines defined the boundaries of Ladakh. These were the **Johnson Line** (1865), the **Johnson-Ardagh Line** (1897) and the **Macartney-MacDonald Line** (1899The Johnson Line was established approximately ten years after the initiation of the Great Trigonometric Survey of India in 1855. The survey focused on mapping the northeastern region of Ladakh and the route from Leh to the Karakoram Pass. **WH Johnson** was assigned the task and was supported by ***Maharaja Gulab Singh*** of Jammu and Kashmir, who wanted the northeastern boundaries of his kingdom, extending beyond the Karakoram Pass, to be accurately represented.

2. China annexed Tibet in 1950: China annexed Tibet, which was opposed by the Tibet population. After being curtailed by the Panchsheel principle of 'non-interference', India conceded China's claim over Tibet to avoid animosity between the nations.
3. Asylum to Dalai Lama in 1959: After an armed uprising, Dalai Lama sought refuge in India which was granted on 3rd April 1959 after Dalai Lama met PM Nehru in Mussoorie. This was considered as an outright interference in internal affairs of China (against the *Panchsheel* principles) and greatly ruptured the Indo-Sino ties.
4. India-China War, 1962: In 1962, the two sides fought a four-week war over a border dispute that left thousands dead on the Indian side. Beijing retained Aksai Chin. A futile attempt to work out a peaceful settlement between the two countries was made by Sri Lanka under **Colombo Proposal**. Eventually, China declared a unilateral ceasefire and the troops withdrew to their original position. The war came to an end with a truce and the formation of the *de facto* boundary, known as the **Line of Actual Control (LAC)**.

Consequences of the 1962 War

- India's **image received a setback**, both on the national and international front. While the nation was humiliated, it also infused a sense of nationalism and a desire to undo the damage.
- The Defence Minister V. Krishna Menon and PM Nehru were heavily criticized for their **lack of military preparedness** and the former even had to leave the cabinet.
- The political setup within India received a jolt. The rift between China and USSR created **issues within the Communist Party of India (CPI)**. The party split in 1964 – (i) the pro-USSR faction remained within the CPI and also strengthened ties with the Congress (ii) the other faction, which was pro-China, remained distant from Congress and formed the Communist Party of India- Marxist (CPI-M).
- The Indian government shifted its focus to the **north-eastern** region and began the process of reorganization.
- India-China relations remained stagnant for over a decade. Eventually, **full diplomatic relations were restored in 1976**.

Atal Behari Vajpayee was the first top level leader (the then External Affairs Minister) to visit China in 1979.

According to the Indian perspective, political and military occurrences during that period led to a deep-seated distrust of China, which continues to significantly influence public perceptions. This historical legacy is further fueled by more recent controversies.

Great Leap Forward
(1958 to the early 1960s)

The campaign was undertaken by the Chinese communists to organize its population, especially in large-scale rural communes, to meet China's industrial and agricultural problems. It was aimed at making China a major industrial power overnight by rapidly raising agricultural and industrial production. During this period, farmers were encouraged to make steel instead of growing crops, peasants were forced onto unproductive communes and grain was exported at the time people were starving.	In the end industrialization was pushed too fast, resulting in the overproduction of inferior goods and the deterioration of the entire industrial sector. Normal market mechanisms broke down and the goods that were produced were unusable. Agriculture was neglected and the Chinese people were exhausted. These above stated factors along with bad weather caused three successive crop failures in 1959, 1960 and 1961

China's global influence grew significantly after the 2000s, driven by economic growth and changing international dynamics. This rise led to increased assertiveness in its foreign policy, impacting neighboring countries and regional structures. Tensions with nations like Japan, Philippines, and Vietnam escalated due to China's actions in the South China Sea, including island building and territorial disputes. Despite these challenges, China has maintained a complex relationship with the United States, balancing cooperation in some areas while competing in others.

Continuing Distress

"If the logic of a multipolar world leads to a 'unipolar Asia' led by China, India might find itself in the fire rather than the frying pan."

\- C. Raja Mohan

The relations between India and China have continued to remain complicated. Considering how the nations could have a flourishing trade, being two of the largest economies, however such convergence cannot be insulated from their basic socio-economic makeup and past divergences. While competitive sources can be used to expand trade or build infrastructure, however such measures couldn't be utilized due to defects on the Indian side –

1. The Indian controls are less effective and cheap imports undercut the growth of its domestic capabilities.
2. India hasn't shown the skills of China in absorbing the technologies and creating its own.

While both the nations have made attempts in the recent times to bridge gaps and sustain bilateral relations on the basis of an international political setup, uneasiness continues to prevail over their relationship. Even as the two Asian giants sign loftily worded documents on one hand to sustain a healthy environment, the distrust between the nations rises unabated as they continue their ascent in the global inter-state hierarchy. Cheng Ruisheng, who served as China's ambassador to India in the mid-1990s, summed up the relationship as follows: "Inadequacy of mutual trust remains despite the rapid development of relations."

India-China Issues

- Border Disputes
- Water related disagreements
- Chinese expansionist policy
- Infrastructure Development & BRI

Border Disputes

The border between India and China is not clearly demarcated everywhere and the root cause of all major issues is the ill-defined **3,488 km long disputed boundary** with **no mutually agreed real control line (LAC)** according to India, however the Chinese consider it to be only **2,000 km**. China occupied the **Aksai Chin** (38,000 sq. km) which was part of India's erstwhile Princely State of Jammu and Kashmir. It continues to assert claims regarding Arunachal Pradesh and has kept the Line of Actual Control (LAC) disputed and un-delineated. The face-offs have increased over the recent years, with the latest being in **Galwan**. While the boundary remains ill-defined, the rivers, lakes and snowcaps along the frontier mean the line can shift, bringing soldiers face to face at many points, sparking a confrontation.

Western Sector — **Johnson line extending to Kunlun mountains; Aksai Chin and Ladakh**

- The issue pertains to the **Johnson Line**, a proposal made by the British in the 1860s, which defined the border extending to the Kunlun Mountains and included Aksai Chin within the territory of the princely state of Jammu and Kashmir at that time.
- India uses the Johnson Line and claims Aksai Chin as its own.
- China doesn't recognize Johnson Line and instead accepts McDonald Line which puts Aksai Chin under its control

Middle Sector — **Uttarakhand and Himachal Pradesh**

- The dispute is comparatively minor. Here LAC is the least controversial except for the precise alignment to be followed in the Barahoti plains.
- India and China have exchanged maps on which they broadly agree.

Eastern Sector — **McMohan Line; Arunachal Pradesh and Sikkim**

- The boundary dispute in this region concerns the **McMahon Line**, which was established in 1914 during a meeting in Shimla involving representatives from China, India, and Tibet.
- India maintains that based on this line, the Tawang Tract is a part of its territory, as per the 1951 position. On the other hand, China claims that the Tawang Tract belongs to its territory.

Some notable skirmishes	
Nathu La clashes (1967)	Nathu La became a significant point of contention, being India's highest mountain pass located in the northeastern state of Sikkim. Situated between Bhutan, Chinese-administered Tibet, and Nepal, the area witnessed a series of confrontations that involved artillery fire. New Delhi reported the loss of approximately 80 Indian soldiers and estimated up to 400 casualties on the Chinese side.
Tulung La skirmish (1975)	This skirmish marked the last instance where official reports confirmed shots being fired across the disputed border. In Arunachal Pradesh, four Indian soldiers were ambushed and killed along the dividing line. New Delhi accused Beijing of trespassing into Indian territory, an allegation that China denied and dismissed.
Doklam Standoff (2017)	A prolonged standoff took place between India and China in the high-altitude region of Doklam in Bhutan. The Indian army deployed troops to prevent China from constructing a road in the area. The Doklam plateau holds strategic importance as it grants China access to the "chicken's neck," a narrow strip of land connecting India's northeastern states with the rest of the country. Both China and Bhutan claim sovereignty over the region, with Bhutan being an ally of India. The dispute was eventually resolved through diplomatic negotiations.
Ladakh confrontation (2020)	A violent clash occurred on June 15, resulting in the death of 20 Indian soldiers and the injury of 76 others in hand-to-hand combat. This incident followed several weeks of simmering tensions, which began with minor scuffles between Indian and Chinese soldiers in high-altitude fistfights along the Sikkim state border in early May. According to Indian officials, Chinese troops subsequently crossed the demarcation line and encroached further west into the Ladakh region. In response, India deployed additional troops to face off against the Chinese forces.
Tawang Sector, Arunachal Pradesh (December 2022)	The latest conflict occurred in December 2022 when troops clashed for the first time in more than a year. The area of conflict was near the Tawang sector of Arunachal Pradesh state, the eastern tip of India. Some soldiers suffered minor injuries.

In 2018, news regarding the construction of a road by China in the strategic **Shaksgam Valley** caught wind. The valley is a 5,400 sq km in the northernmost portion of Siachen and being narrow, the Indian Army had previously suggested that any construction in the said area was difficult.

The year 2020 marked a significant setback in India-China relations, with violent clashes along the Line of Actual Control (LAC) in the Galwan Valley. These clashes, following earlier skirmishes in Pangong Tso and Naku La, eroded trust and cooperation between the two nuclear powers. While partial troop disengagement has taken place, complete de-escalation remains elusive. The root causes of the clashes are complex, with factors such as military buildup, territorial disputes, and differing perceptions of the status quo playing a role.

Beyond the immediate security concerns, the India-China relationship is also shaped by broader geopolitical dynamics. As China's economic influence grows, India faces the challenge of competing for regional and global leadership. Strengthening connectivity, infrastructure, and economic development are crucial for India to enhance its standing and effectively counter China's rising power.

Development has been made post the Galwan clashes, however friction points continue to exist. The episode in Ladakh prompted a 'Change of orientation' with the military now looking northwards. The Pakistan-China 'collusivity' must also not be dismissed which is fast becoming more virulent than ever before. As

India looks to tackle the two-front threat, it has also proceeded with '**Theaterisation**' on the sidelines; however, efforts must continue to cater for self-sustaining Northern and Western fronts.

Major Border Dispute settlement mechanism – India & China

1. 1993 – Agreement on the Maintenance of Peace and Tranquility along the LAC
2. 1996 – Agreement on Confidence building measures in the Military Field along the LAC
3. 2005 – Protocol on Modalities for the Implementation of Confidence-Building Measures in the Military Field along the LAC
4. 2012 – Agreement on the establishment of a working mechanism for the consultation and Coordination – India-China Border Affairs.
5. 2013 – Border Defence Cooperation Agreement

DOKLAM ISSUE

The Doklam issue is a territorial dispute between India and China over a remote plateau in the Himalayas known as Doklam or Donglang in Chinese. The plateau is located at the **tri-junction of India, Bhutan, and China**, and it has been claimed by both China and Bhutan. In 2017, Chinese troops began construction of a road in the Doklam area, which Bhutan and India claimed was a violation of Bhutan's sovereignty. Indian troops intervened and stopped the construction, leading to a military standoff between India and China that lasted for 73 days. Both sides deployed troops and equipment to the region, raising tensions between the two countries. The standoff ended on August 28, 2017, after both India and China agreed to withdraw their troops from the disputed area. The agreement also included a commitment by both sides to maintain peace and stability in the region.

Why is India supporting Bhutan's side on Doklam Issue?

- Bhutan has a very strategic position considering India's geography. It acts as a buffer against Chinese aggression.
- India enjoys a strong and friendly relationship with Bhutan, which stands in contrast to its relationship with China. In order to strengthen this bond, India and Bhutan signed a "Friendship Treaty" in 2007. This treaty includes commitments from India to safeguard Bhutan's interests and promotes close coordination between the two countries' militaries.
- India has expressed concerns about the potential completion of the road, as it could provide China with increased access to India's strategically sensitive "**chicken's neck**" region, which connects the seven northeastern states to the rest of the Indian mainland.

Water Related Disagreements

The trans-boundary water issues between India and China, particularly concerning the Brahmaputra River, have been a source of ongoing tension. The river, known as the Yarlung Tsangpo in China, is a crucial water resource that flows through Tibet, India, and eventually empties into the Bay of Bengal. China's hydropower projects on the Brahmaputra and other shared rivers have raised concerns in India regarding potential downstream impacts.

The Brahmaputra River and China's Hydropower Projects

- Geographical Significance: The Brahmaputra River originates in Tibet and is known as the Yarlung Tsangpo in China.The river flows through India before merging with the Ganges and eventually emptying into the Bay of Bengal.
- China's Hydropower Developments: China has constructed several hydropower dams on the Brahmaputra, including the ***Zangmu*** project, which became fully operational in 2015.

1. Under its 12th Five Year Plan (2011-2015), China planned to develop additional projects: ***Jiacha***, ***Dagu***, and ***Jiexu***. The Jiacha project became operational in August 2020, and the Dagu project has achieved partial operationalization.
2. Since 2023, China has continued its aggressive hydropower development on Brahmaputra. The most alarming development is the planned construction of a massive "**super dam**" in the Medog region (where Yarlung Tsangpo/Brahmaputra Grand Canyon, the world's deepest and longest canyon, is located) near the Indian border. The **Medog Project** is a proposed Chinese dam in Tibet that would be the world's largest hydroelectric dam. This project, expected to generate 60 gigawatts of electricity, has raised concerns in India and Bangladesh about potential water diversion and ecological impacts downstream.

- **Concerns from India and Indian government's response**:
  (a) India is concerned that these projects may reduce downstream water flows, potentially affecting water availability and agriculture.
  (b) Despite several rounds of talks, no formal agreement has been reached between India and China on the Brahmaputra issue.
  (c) The **Medog Project** is seen as a potential tool for China to exert geopolitical pressure, particularly given the strategic location of the Brahmaputra as it flows into India through Arunachal Pradesh, a region that China claims as part of its territory. This raises fears of water being used as a leverage point in broader territorial disputes.
  (d) Despite repeated requests from India for more transparency, China has not publicly released detailed plans or hydrological data concerning its projects. This opacity exacerbates mistrust and fuels speculation in India about the potential for a "water war" between the two countries.
  (e) The Indian government closely monitors developments in China's hydropower projects on the Brahmaputra. As a lower riparian state, India has repeatedly communicated its concerns to China, emphasizing that the interests of downstream states must be safeguarded.
  (f) India and China have held multiple rounds of talks aimed at reaching an understanding on the issue, but a concrete agreement remains elusive.

Other Trans-Border Rivers

- The Indus River: The Indus River, which flows through India and Pakistan, also originates in the Himalayas. China has been building dams on tributaries of the Indus in Tibet, causing concerns in both India and Pakistan regarding downstream water flow impacts.
- Sutlej, Beas, and Ravi Rivers: India has expressed concerns over China's activities on other shared rivers, including the Sutlej, Beas, and Ravi. China's construction of dams and water diversion activities on these rivers poses additional challenges for water sharing between the two nations.

Chinese Expansionist Policy

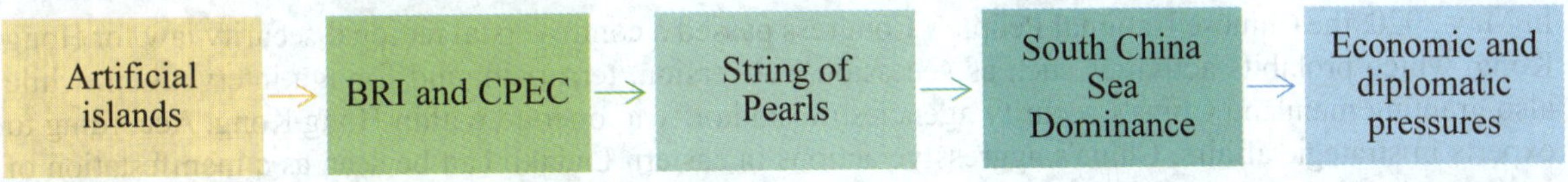

(1) An issue that has caught international attention is the fact that China has built a series of **artificial islands** in the South China Sea, which has allowed it to establish a more permanent presence in the region. These islands have been equipped with runways, ports, and military facilities, which has raised concerns among other countries in the region over China's intentions. China has constructed runways and fortified artificial islands in the **Spratly islands** of the South China Sea. The presence of garrisons, airfields, and missile sites connected by advanced road and rail networks signifies China's strong position on the Tibetan plateau.

(2) Notably, China has also developed the **China-Pakistan Economic Corridor (CPEC)**, which provides a pathway from Xinjiang to the Pakistani port of **Gwadar** via Gilgit-Baltistan, establishing access to the Arabian Sea. Furthermore, China has built a new harbor in **Hambantota** and upgraded the Colombo port in Sri Lanka.

The CPEC is a collection of infrastructure projects that are under construction throughout Pakistan since 2013, as a part of the Belt and Road Initiative.

- **Aim**: upgrade Pakistan's required infrastructure and strengthen its economy by the construction of modern transportation networks, numerous energy projects, and special economic zones.
- **India's Concerns**: The CPEC passes through Pakistan-Occupied Kashmir (Gilgit-Baltistan). As both India and Pakistan claim all of Kashmir, the area is considered a disputed territory by India. According to India, it undermines India's strategic interests and territorial integrity.

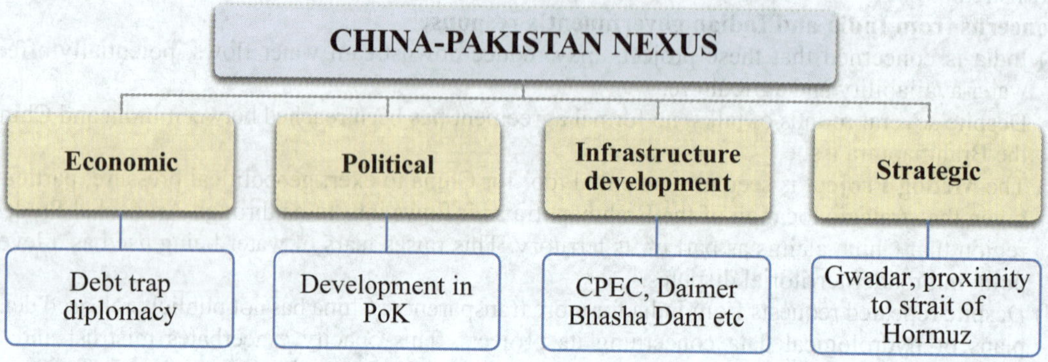

(3) The **Chinese string of pearls strategy** around Indian Ocean has encircled India strategically and endangering its strategic interest in the region. It refers to the network of Chinese military and commercial facilities and relationships along its sea lines of communication extending from the Chinese mainland to Port Sudan in the Horn of Africa.

(4) China has also increased its military presence in the **South China Sea**, deploying naval vessels and aircraft to the region. This has included the construction of military bases on some of the artificial islands, as well as the deployment of fighter jets, warships, and missile systems. China has also been increasing its maritime law enforcement activities in the South China Sea, including through the deployment of coast guard vessels and the establishment of administrative structures to manage the region's waters. This has led to confrontations with other countries in the region, including the Philippines and Vietnam.

(5) China has been using its **economic** and **diplomatic leverage** to pressure other countries in the region to recognize its territorial claims in the South China Sea. This has included offering economic incentives to countries that support its position, as well as using its veto power at the United Nations to block resolutions critical of its actions.

In May 2020, the Chinese National People's Congress passed a controversial national security law for Hong Kong, which prohibits activities such as secession, subversion, terrorism, and foreign intervention, while also granting mainland China's security agencies the authority to operate within Hong Kong. According to experts in strategic affairs, China's aggressive actions in eastern Ladakh can be seen as a manifestation of its expansionist agenda, which was met with a resolute and effective response from the Indian army.

(China's disputes with the other nations have been covered alongside the respective nation)

Xi Jinping has reiterated his ambitions for China to become a major player on the global stage by 2035. The rise of China seems inevitable, but now it is possible that India would have to deal with a much more assertive and belligerent China. The proactive leadership coupled with the '**resurgent nationalism**' in China due to the sustained economic growth has now created a **Leviathan** which might have to be restrained in future. The leapfrogging witnessed in military technologies apart from the economic front, has challenged the might of all major nations, including USA.

Owing to the unwavering rise of China, India has chosen to step up engagement with the QUAD, a Japan, Australia and US grouping to effectively contain China in the Indo-Pacific region.

Areas of Cooperation

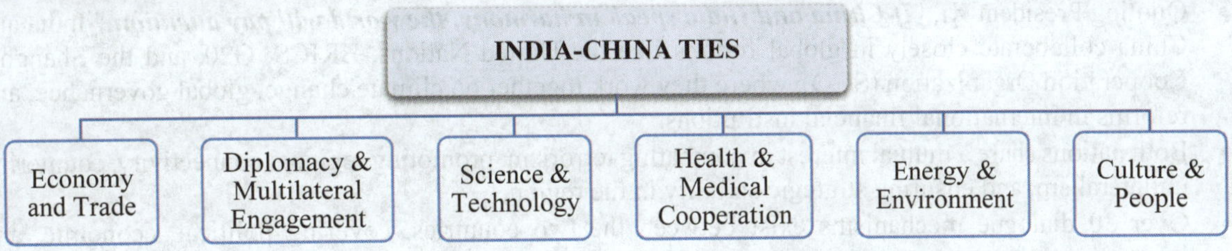

Economy and Trade

- Trade and economic engagement are pivotal to India-China relations, despite imbalances. China is India's largest trading partner, and bilateral trade reached $135.98 billion in 2022.
- In 2022, India's trade deficit with China surpassed $100 billion for the first time. China's exports to India reached $118.5 billion, while India's exports to China fell to $17.48 billion. Major imports include active pharmaceutical ingredients (APIs), chemicals, machinery, and medical supplies.
- By the end of 2021, Chinese investments in India stood at $5.4 billion, while Indian investments in China amounted to $943.96 million. Despite the economic imbalance, both nations recognize the importance of trade and economic cooperation for mutual growth.
- The **Joint Group on Economic Relations, Science, and Technology (JEG),** established in 1988, continues to serve as a platform for discussing trade cooperation. The **Strategic Economic Dialogue (SED)**, created in 2010, focuses on macroeconomic cooperation in areas like infrastructure, energy, and high technology.
- Another initiative is the NITI Aayog-DRC Dialogue, created during Prime Minister Modi's 2015 visit, which promotes discussions on global economic cooperation.

DID YOU KNOW?

After almost 44 years, in 2006 India and China reopened ***Nathu La*** (mountain pass situated in eastern Himalayas), ending the decades long disconnect between Tibet & Sikkim.

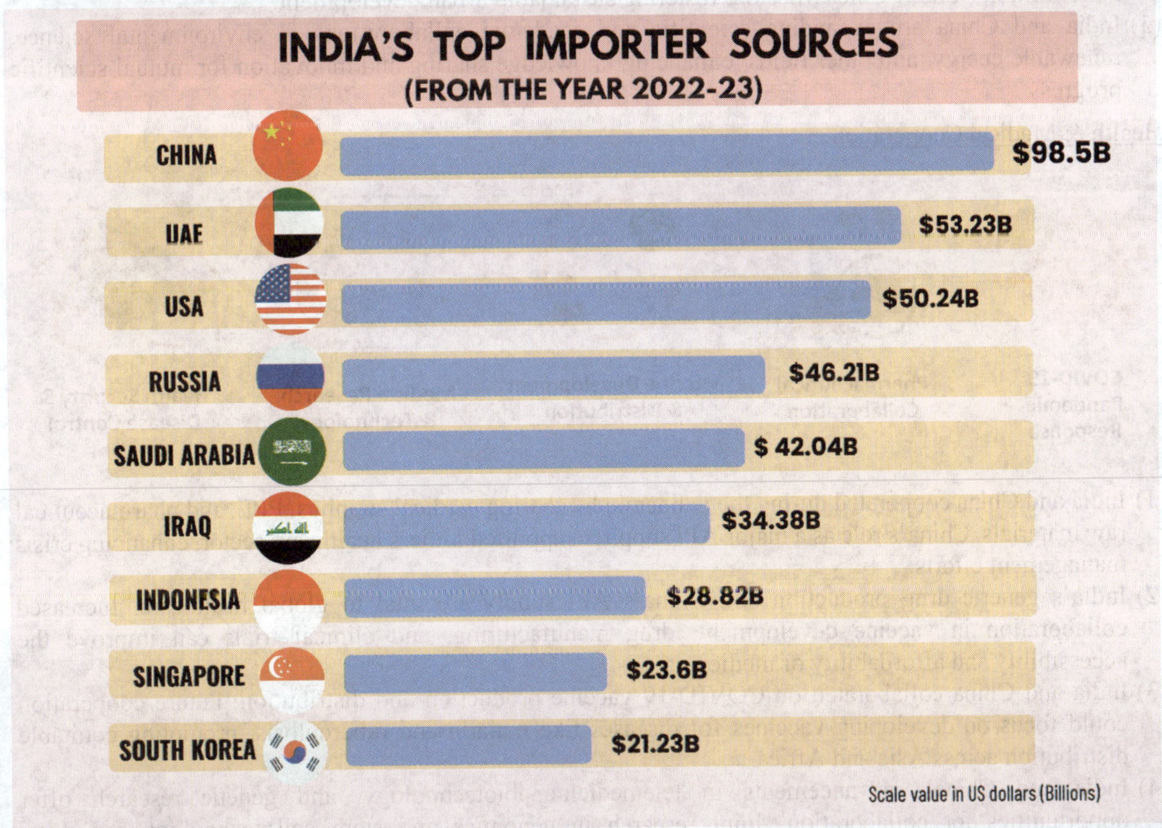

Diplomacy and Multilateral Engagement

- Quoting President Xi, "***If China and India speak in harmony, the world will pay attention***." India and China collaborate closely in global forums like the United Nations, BRICS, G20, and the Shanghai Cooperation Organization (SCO), where they work together on climate change, global governance, and reforms in international financial institutions.
- Both nations share a mutual interest in combating terrorism, promoting regional connectivity, countering unilateralism, and ensuring strategic stability in the region.
- Over 30 dialogue mechanisms exist between the two countries, covering political, economic, and international matters.

Science & Technology

(1) India and China are collaborating in high-tech sectors like AI, big data, 5G, and biotechnology. Joint R&D in these fields aims to advance innovation and address shared challenges.
(2) India and China are exploring collaboration in space programs, focusing on satellite technology and expertise sharing. Joint efforts could enhance regional environmental monitoring and disaster management.
(3) With rapid digitization, India and China are discussing joint cybersecurity frameworks to protect infrastructure and bridge the digital divide amidst growing cyber threats.
(4) India and China are advancing smart city projects. China's expertise in urban tech and infrastructure can benefit India's Smart Cities Mission, fostering sustainable urban development.
(5) India and China are expanding scientific and academic collaborations in environmental science, renewable energy, and other fields, enhancing knowledge sharing and innovation for mutual scientific progress.

Health & Medical Cooperation

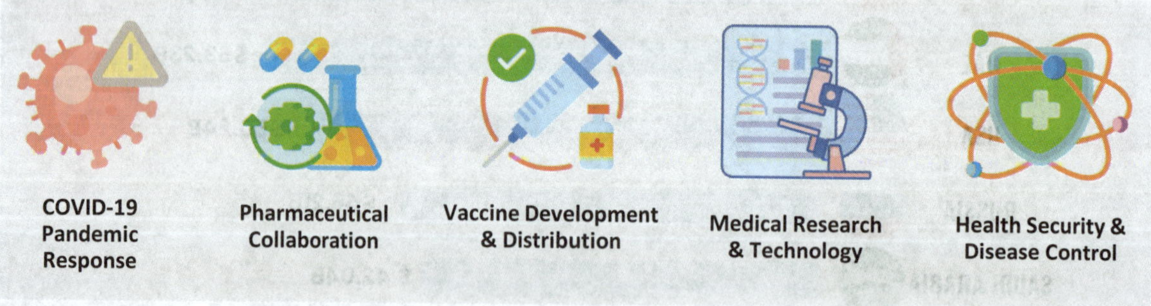

(1) India and China cooperated during the pandemic by sharing medical supplies, PPE, and pharmaceutical raw materials. China's role as a major API supplier supported India's healthcare sector, enhancing crisis management efforts.
(2) India's generic drug production and China's API supply are vital to global healthcare. Increased collaboration in vaccine development, drug manufacturing, and clinical trials can improve the accessibility and affordability of medicines.
(3) India and China collaborated on COVID-19 vaccine production and distribution. Future cooperation could focus on developing vaccines for diseases like malaria and tuberculosis, promoting equitable distribution across Asia and Africa.
(4) India and China's advancements in telemedicine, biotechnology, and genetic research offer opportunities for collaboration. Joint research in genomics and stem cell technology can drive

breakthroughs in personalized medicine and healthcare innovation. India's Ayurveda and China's Traditional Chinese Medicine have potential for collaboration in herbal medicine and integrative treatments. Exploring synergies between these systems can lead to innovative preventive healthcare solutions.

(5) India and China can collaborate on combating infectious diseases like tuberculosis, malaria, and HIV/AIDS. Joint efforts in disease surveillance, research, and expertise sharing can strengthen regional health security and preparedness.

Energy & Environment

(i) **Energy Cooperation**: Both countries share an interest in sustainable energy development and have engaged in talks to enhance collaboration in renewable energy projects, addressing mutual concerns about energy security.

(ii) **Climate Change**: As the world's two largest developing nations, India and China are key players in climate change negotiations. They have the potential to lead global efforts toward reducing emissions and promoting green technologies.

(iii) **Health and Medical Cooperation**: The COVID-19 pandemic underscored the need for closer collaboration in health security. Both countries have shared expertise and medical supplies during crises, creating opportunities for future cooperation in healthcare.

Culture

- India and China have shared cultural ties dating back thousands of years. The influence of ancient Indian monk-scholars and Chinese pilgrims like *Fa Xian* and *Xuan Zang* enriched both cultures through the exchange of ideas and Buddhism.
- Cultural exchanges continue today, with yoga becoming increasingly popular in China. The establishment of the high-level mechanism on Cultural and People-to-People Exchanges in 2018 further strengthened cooperation in areas such as media, sports, tourism, and city-level exchanges.
- Historical trade routes like the *Silk Road* fostered cultural connections, allowing the exchange of goods, such as Indian textiles and Chinese ceramics, contributing to the long-standing cultural bond.

ROAD TO THE FUTURE

Going ahead, India and China should engage in continuous diplomatic dialogues to resolve the issues between the two countries. Both sides should engage in constructive talks to address their differences and find solutions to their problems. India and China should work towards better border management and improving the mechanisms for resolving border disputes. There is an urgent need for a single nodal agency to coordinate the functioning of the multiple bodies involved in safeguarding India's borders. Operational control over the Line of Control (LoC) and the actual line of control must belong to the military. The operational capacity of paramilitary forces must be strengthened as a priority.

Confidence-building measures can help in reducing tensions and increasing trust between India and China. These measures can include the exchange of visits between the leaders of both countries, cultural exchanges, and joint military exercises. India and China should work towards increasing trade relations and removing trade barriers. Improved economic ties can be an important factor in improving the overall relationship between the two countries.

Both India and China have rich cultural traditions, and people-to-people contacts can help in building bridges between the two countries. This can include educational exchanges, tourism, and cultural exchanges.

India and China now agree on the importance of supporting and strengthening the rules-based multilateral trading system at a time when globally agreed trading practices and standards are being challenged selectively. An honest attempt to build a new paradigm of trust between India and China should be based on shared historical and cultural awareness, as well as on the collective wisdom of ordinary citizens on both sides. It is important for both countries to work towards building mutual trust, understanding, and respect for each other's interests and concerns.

4 THE CONTINENT OF EUROPE

Europe is composed of the westward-projecting peninsulas of Eurasia (the great landmass that it shares with Asia) and occupying nearly one-fifteenth of the world's total land area. The European continent is known for its high quality of life and prosperous developed countries. It offers abundant opportunities for learning and personal growth, with strong economic credentials and well-established political institutions. Given this context, it is crucial for India to establish strong and meaningful connections with European countries.

EUROPEAN UNION

Source: https://european-union.europa.eu/easy-read_en

The Second World War dismantled the world structures thoroughly and shook the age-old foundations of various regimes. Europe was no exception and the leaders grappled with the idea of 'Europe' for future. The United States provided significant financial assistance through the **'Marshall Plan'** and played a key role in establishing NATO, a collective security organization. The Marshall Plan involved the creation of the **Organisation for European Economic Cooperation (OEEC)** in 1948, which aimed to provide aid to Western European states. Additionally, the **Council of Europe** was established in 1949 to enhance political cooperation among European countries. Initially, only six countries participated in economic cooperation in 1951, but more countries gradually joined over time. This process of economic integration among European capitalist nations led to the formation of the **European Economic Community in 1957**. The political aspect of this integration was further emphasized with the establishment of the European Parliament.

TIMELINE OF EUROPEAN INTEGRATION

- **1951 April -** Six west European countries, France, West Germany, Italy, Belgium, the Netherlands and Luxembourg sign the Treaty of Paris establishing the European Coal and Steel Community (ECSC).
- **1957 March 25** - These six countries sign the Treaties of Rome establishing the **European Economic Community (EEC)** and the **European Atomic Energy Community (Euratom).**
- **1973 January** - Denmark, Ireland and the United Kingdom join the European Community (EC).
- **1979 June**: First direct elections to the European Parliament.
- **1981 January**: Greece joins the EC.
- **1985 June:** The Schengen Agreement abolishes border controls among the EC members.
- **1986 January**: Spain and Portugal join the EC.
- **1990 October**: Unification of Germany.
- **1992 February**: **The Treaty of Maastricht** was signed establishing the European Union (EU).
- **1993 January**: **The single market was created.**
- **1995 January**: Austria, Finland and Sweden join the EU.
- **2002 January**: Euro, the new currency, was introduced in the 12 EU members.
- **2004 May**: Ten new members, Cyprus, the Czech Republic, Estonia, Hungary, Latvia, Lithuania, Malta, Poland, Slovakia and Slovenia join the EU.
- **2007 January**: Bulgaria and Romania join the EU. Slovenia adopts the Euro.
- **2009 December**: The Lisbon Treaty came into force.
- **2012**: **The EU is awarded the Nobel Peace Prize.**
- **2013**: Croatia becomes the 28th member of the EU.
- **2016**: Referendum in Britain, 51.9 per cent voters decide that Britain exit (Brexit) from the EU.

The European Union currently (as in September 2022) comprises of **27 EU countries**. The **United Kingdom withdrew from the European Union on 31 January 2020.**

The **European flag** symbolises both the European Union and, more broadly, the identity and unity of Europe. The circle of 12 gold stars on a blue background stands for the ideals of unity, solidarity and harmony among the peoples of Europe.

The **EURO** (€) is the official currency of 19 out of 27 EU countries. These countries are collectively known as the **EUROZONE**.

CORE EU INSTITUTIONS

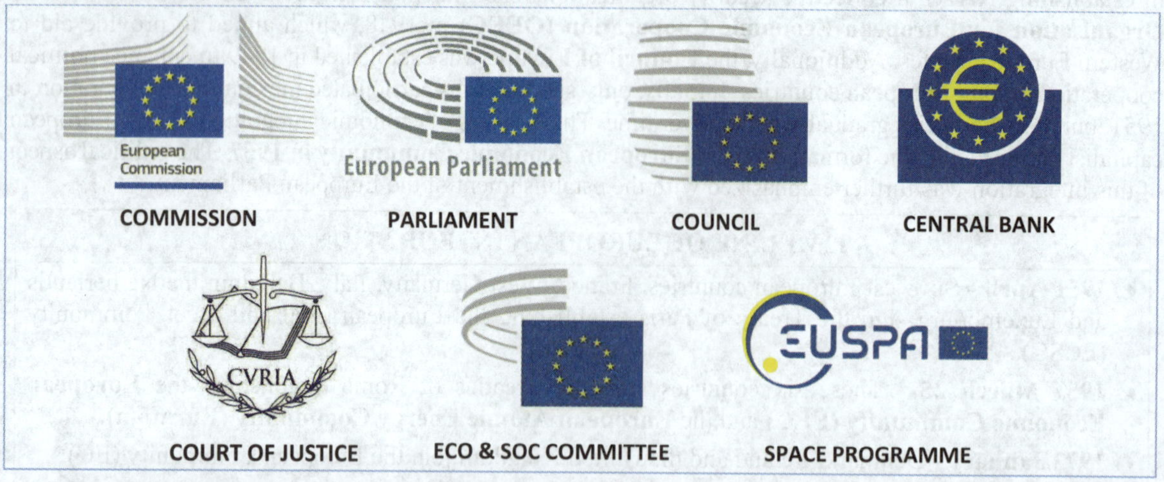

1. **<u>European Commission</u>:** The European Commission is the EU's politically independent executive branch. It is solely responsible for drafting proposals for new European legislation and implementing the decisions made by the European Parliament and the Council of the EU.
   - <u>Establishment</u> – 1958
   - <u>Location</u> – Brussels (Belgium)
   - <u>Role</u> – Promotes the general interest of the EU by proposing and enforcing legislation as well as by implementing policies and the EU budget
   - <u>Members</u> – A team or 'College' of Commissioners, 1 from each EU country.
2. **<u>European Parliament</u>:** It is the EU's law-making body. It is directly elected by EU voters every 5 years. The last European elections took place in June 2024. Important features include –
   - <u>Establishment</u> – 1952 as Common Assembly of the European Coal and Steel Community, 1962 as European Parliament → first direct elections in 1979.
   - <u>Location</u> – Strasbourg (France), Brussels (Belgium), Luxembourg
   - <u>Role</u> – Directly-elected EU body with legislative, supervisory, and budgetary responsibilities
   - <u>Members</u> – 720 MEPs (Members of the European Parliament).
3. **<u>The Council of the European Union</u>** – In the Council of the EU, also informally known as the Council, government ministers from each EU member country convene to discuss, amend, and adopt laws, as well as to coordinate policies. These ministers have the authority to commit their respective governments to the decisions made during the meetings. Together with the European Parliament, the Council is the main decision-making body of the EU.
   - <u>Establishment</u> – 1958 (as Council of the European Economic Community).
   - <u>Location</u> –Brussels (Belgium)
   - <u>Role</u> – Voice of EU member governments, adopting EU laws and coordinating EU policies
   - <u>Members</u> – Government ministers from each EU country, according to the policy area to be discussed.

> **NOTE** – Do not confuse it with the ***European Council***- quarterly summits, where EU leaders meet to set the broad direction of EU policy making.

4. **<u>European Council</u>** – The European Council unites EU leaders to establish the political agenda of the European Union. It represents the highest level of political collaboration among EU member states. It:
   - <u>Establishment</u> – 1974 (informal forum), 1992 (formal status), 2009 (official EU institution).
   - <u>Location</u> –Brussels (Belgium)
   - <u>Role</u> – Defines the general political direction and priorities of the EU
   - <u>Members</u> – Heads of state or government of EU countries, European Council President, European Commission President.

Important works -

(a) Determines the EU's overall direction and political priorities, but **does not legislate**.
(b) Addresses complex or sensitive issues that cannot be resolved at lower levels of intergovernmental cooperation.
(c) Defines the EU's common foreign and security policy, considering the Union's strategic interests and defense implications

5. **European Central Bank (ECB)** – The ECB (established in 1998) oversees the management of the euro and formulates and executes the EU's economic and monetary policy. Its primary objective is to maintain price stability, which in turn supports economic growth and the creation of jobs.
   - Location – Frankfurt (Germany)
   - Role – To manage the euro, keep prices stable and conduct EU economic & monetary policy
   - Members – ECB President and Vice-President and governors of national central banks from all EU countries.

6. **Court of Justice of the European Union (CJEU)** – The CJEU (established in 1952) interprets EU law to ensure uniform application across all member states and resolves legal disputes between national governments and EU institutions. Additionally, under certain conditions, individuals, companies, or organizations can bring cases against an EU institution if they believe their rights have been violated.
   - Location – Luxembourg
   - Role – Ensuring EU law is interpreted and applied the same in every EU country; ensuring countries and EU institutions abide by EU law.
   - Members – Court of Justice: judge from each EU country, plus 11 advocates general; General Court: 2 judges from each EU country.

7. **European Economic & Social Committee** – It is an EU advisory body (established in 1957) made up of representatives from workers' and employers' organizations, as well as other interest groups. It provides opinions on EU matters to the European Commission, the Council of the EU, and the European Parliament, thereby serving as a link between the EU's decision-making institutions and its citizens.
   - Location – Brussels (Belgium)
   - Role – Advisory body representing employers' and workers' organisations and other interest groups
   - Members – 329 from all EU countries

8. **European Union Agency for the Space Programme (EUSPA)** – EUSPA (setup in 2004) supports the EU's objective of maximizing the return on its investment in space by focusing on: security, user benefits, economic growth and competitiveness.
   - Partners – European Commission, European Space Agency (ESA)
   - Location – Prague (Czech Republic)
   - Role – EUSPA manages public interests related to the European Global Navigation Satellite System (GNSS) programmes EGNOS (European Geostationary Navigation Overlay System) and Galileo, the Earth observation (EO) programme Copernicus, and the European Union Governmental Satellite Communications (GOVSATCOM) programme.

European Space Agency (ESA)

It is an intergovernmental organization dedicated to the exploration of space, coordinating European space missions, research, and technological development for peaceful purposes and global collaboration.

CERN (European Organization for Nuclear Research)

CERN is a leading global laboratory for particle physics research, known for operating the Large Hadron Collider. It focuses on fundamental studies of subatomic particles and the forces that govern them.

IMPORTANT FEATURES OF THE EU

(1) **Maastricht Treaty** - Signed in 1992, the Maastricht Treaty marked a pivotal moment in European integration, formally establishing the European Union (EU). Apart from laying the groundwork for the Euro as a common currency, it introduced three important pillars:

I. **European Community**: Focused on economic cooperation, including the single market.

II. **Common Foreign and Security Policy (CFSP)**: Established a framework for cooperation on foreign and security matters.

III. **Justice and Home Affairs (JHA)**: Addressed issues related to immigration, asylum, and police cooperation.

(2) **Lisbon treaty** - The Lisbon Treaty, which entered into force in 2009, amended the Maastricht Treaty to streamline the EU's decision-making processes and enhance its global role. In short, it modernized the EU and equipped it to address the challenges of the 21st century. The key changes included:

(a) **Enhanced role of the European Parliament:** Increased the Parliament's legislative powers.

(b) **Simplified decision-making:** Introduced new voting procedures to make the EU more efficient.

(c) **Strengthened external action:** Gave the EU a stronger voice on the global stage, including in foreign policy and security.

(d) **Charter of Fundamental Rights:** Made the Charter of Fundamental Rights legally binding.

(3) **The Schengen Area** – The Schengen Area is a remarkable achievement of the EU, providing a border-free zone that allows for the free movement of over 425 million EU citizens, as well as non-EU nationals legally residing or visiting the EU for tourism, study, or business. Established in 1985, the Schengen Area has expanded to include almost all EU Member States and some associated non-EU countries.

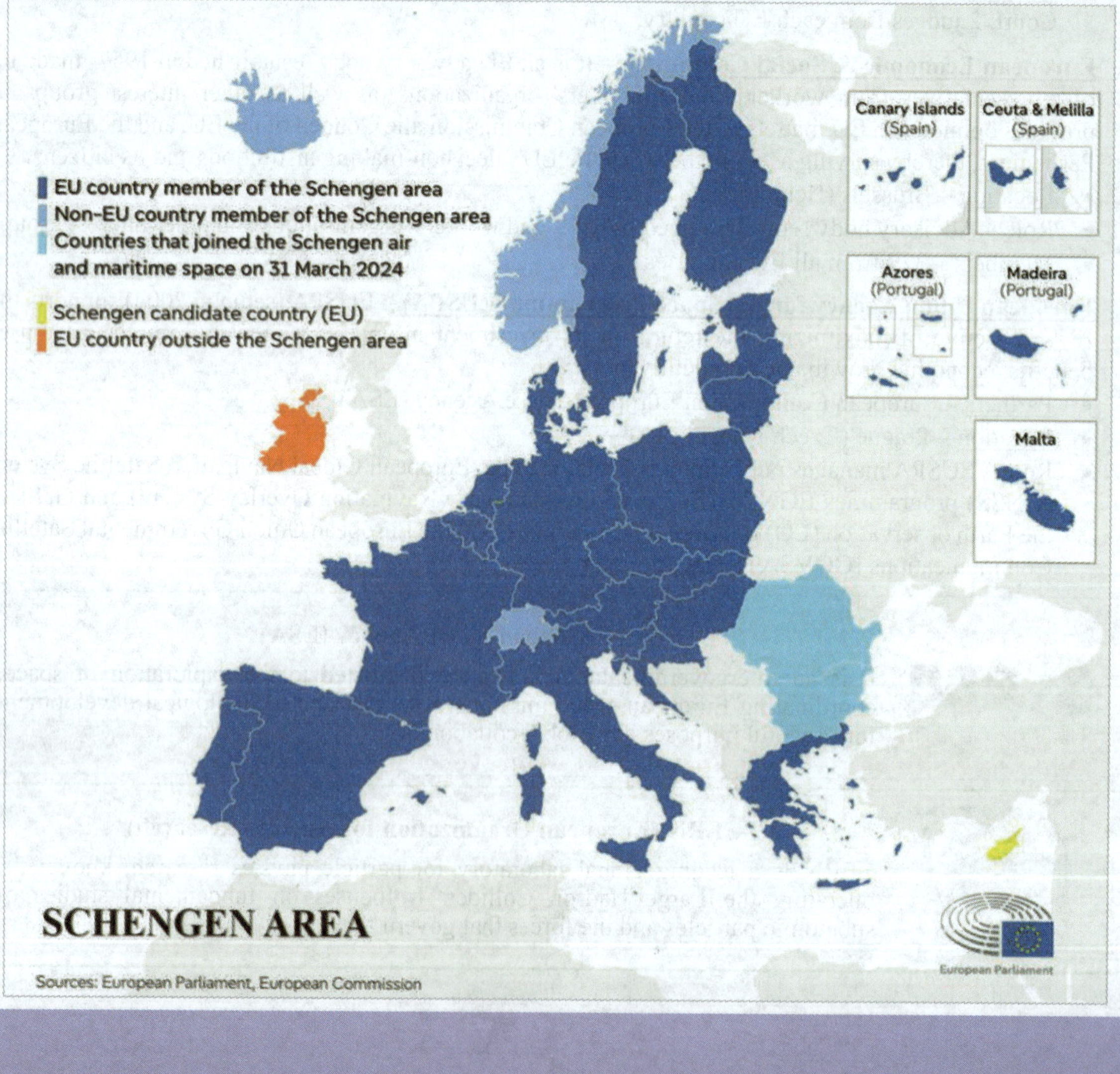

As of 31 March 2024, **Bulgaria** and **Romania** joined the Schengen Area, which already included most EU countries except for Cyprus and Ireland. Although internal air and sea border checks have been removed for these new members, a unanimous decision on lifting internal land border checks is pending. Additionally, non-EU countries such as **Iceland, Norway, Switzerland,** and **Liechtenstein** are also part of the Schengen Area, allowing for seamless movement across these regions.

(4) **<u>Economy & Trade</u>** – EU has developed a comprehensive set of economic and trade policies designed to promote growth, stability, and competitiveness within the EU and globally.

(i) **Single market** – It enables the free movement of goods, services, capital, and people across member states. It aims to eliminate barriers to trade and investment, creating a more efficient and competitive market environment.

(ii) **Economic and Monetary Union (EMU)** - It is a cornerstone of the EU aimed at achieving economic convergence and monetary integration among its member states. It represents a significant step towards European integration, fostering economic stability, trade, and investment within the Eurozone. Key components -

- ✓ **Single Currency:** The adoption of the Euro as a common currency for most EU member states.
- ✓ **Coordination of Economic Policies:** Member states coordinate their economic policies to ensure stability and growth.
- ✓ **Independent Central Bank:** The European Central Bank (ECB) is responsible for monetary policy in the Eurozone.
- ✓ **Fiscal Discipline:** Member states adhere to fiscal rules to maintain budgetary stability.

(iii) **European Economic Area (EEA)** - The European Economic Area (EEA) is a treaty between the European Union (EU) and three members of the European Free Trade Association (EFTA): **Iceland, Liechtenstein,** and **Norway.** It essentially extends the EU's single market to these three EFTA countries.

- Although the EEA offers significant benefits, it's not a full membership in the EU.
- EFTA countries do not participate in EU policies outside the single market, such as common agricultural policy or common foreign and security policy.

<u>Key features of the EEA</u>:

(a) **Free movement of goods, people, services, and capital**: This is the cornerstone of the EEA, allowing for unrestricted trade and movement within the area.
(b) **Common rules**: EEA countries adopt most of the EU's laws related to the single market, ensuring a level playing field for businesses and individuals.
(c) **Cooperation**: The EEA involves close cooperation between the EU and the EFTA members on various economic and political issues.

<u>Benefits of EEA</u>:

1. **Access to the EU market:** EEA countries gain unrestricted access to the EU's vast market of over 450 million consumers.
2. **Economic growth:** Free trade and movement of people and capital stimulate economic growth and job creation.
3. **Political influence:** EEA countries participate in shaping the rules of the single market.

EUROPEAN FREE TRADE ASSOCIATION (EFTA)

EFTA is an intergovernmental organization established to promote free trade and economic integration among its member states. Currently, the EFTA consists of four European countries: **Iceland, Norway, Switzerland & Liechtenstein.**

<u>NOTE</u>: While Iceland, Liechtenstein, and Norway are not members of the European Union (EU), they are part of the European Economic Area (EEA) which grants them access to the EU's single market. **Switzerland,** on the other hand, maintains a closer relationship with the EU through bilateral agreements.

(5) **<u>Regulation of Foreign Policy & Diplomatic relations</u>**- The EU has developed comprehensive foreign policy aimed at promoting peace, security, and stability both within Europe and globally. The policies

are guided by the principles of democracy, rule of law, and respect for human rights. The EU's approach to foreign policy is characterized by a commitment to multilateralism, diplomatic engagement, and cooperation with international partners.

(i) The **CFSP** or **Common Foreign and Security Policy** is the EU's framework for coordinating foreign policy actions among its member states. It aims to preserve peace, prevent conflicts, and strengthen international security. The CFSP covers a wide range of activities, including diplomatic relations, economic sanctions, humanitarian aid, and crisis management.

(ii) The **High Representative**, who also serves as Vice-President of the European Commission, is responsible for representing the EU in international affairs and coordinating the CFSP.

(iii)The EU **Global Strategy**, adopted in 2016, outlines the EU's strategic priorities in foreign policy, including promoting a rules-based international order, advancing human rights, fostering regional stability, and enhancing resilience against security threats.

(iv)The EU's **Neighbourhood Policy** focuses on fostering stability, security, and prosperity in neighbouring regions, including Eastern Europe, the Mediterranean, and the Middle East. The EU also pursues **enlargement policies**, supporting potential candidate countries in meeting the criteria for EU membership.

(6) **Defence Policies** – The EU's defense strategy, primarily organized under the CSDP, focuses on enhancing the EU's ability to act as a cohesive and capable security actor. The strategy aims to strengthen the EU's capacity to address internal and external security challenges, promote peace, and ensure the security of its member states.

(i) **Common Security and Defence Policy (CSDP)** – It is the EU's course of action in the fields of defense and crisis management. It's a key component of the EU's Common Foreign and Security Policy (CFSP). While the CSDP is not a common defense policy, it has evolved into a framework for coordinating and conducting military operations. Important elements include –

✓ The EU can deploy civilian and military missions to prevent conflicts, contribute to peacemaking, peacekeeping, and peacebuilding efforts.

✓ Member states provide forces for EU-led operations.

✓ The EU and NATO have a strategic partnership, with many member states being part of both organizations.

(ii) **Permanent Structured Cooperation (PESCO)**: It is a framework for deeper defense cooperation among EU member states willing to pursue enhanced integration. It includes joint projects to develop military capabilities, improve operational readiness, and foster interoperability among member states' armed forces. PESCO projects cover a range of areas, including cyber defense, military mobility, and joint training.

(iii)**The European Defence Fund (EDF)** aims to enhance the EU's defense capabilities by funding research and development projects and encouraging cooperation among member states in defense technologies.

(iv)**The Strategic Compass**, adopted in 2022, provides a shared vision and actionable goals for the EU's security and defense policy. It addresses threats such as cyberattacks, hybrid warfare, and terrorism, and outlines measures to enhance the EU's strategic autonomy and capacity to act independently when necessary.

(v) The EU's defense strategy includes **cooperation with international organizations** like NATO, the United Nations, and regional partners. This cooperation enhances the EU's ability to respond to global security challenges and supports capacity-building efforts in partner countries.

(7) **Digital Security** - The EU has been aiming at advancing a legislation to strengthen the security requirements for all software products and digital hardware.

(i) The **Cyber Resilience Act (CRA)** was formally adopted by the European Parliament in March 2024. This critical legislation aims to enhance the cybersecurity of digital products placed on the EU market.

- The CRA introduces mandatory cybersecurity requirements for manufacturers and importers of products with digital elements, ranging from smartphones and household appliances to industrial equipment and software.
- The goal is to improve the overall resilience of the EU's digital ecosystem.

- The legislation is aimed at curbing cybercrime which according to Cybersecurity Ventures costed the global economy €5.5 trillion in 2021. According to rough estimates, by 2025, cybercrime damages are expected to surpass €10 trillion.

(ii) The **EU general data protection regulation (GDPR)** governs how the personal data of individuals in the EU may be processed and transferred. It is the strongest privacy and security law in the world. The GDPR defines:

✓ individuals' fundamental rights in the digital age
✓ the obligations of those processing data
✓ methods for ensuring compliance
✓ sanctions for those in breach of the rules

The GDPR also covers the transfer of personal data to non-EU countries and international organisations. The European Commission is in charge of assessing the level of protection given by a territory or processing sector in a non-EU country.

Economy

- The European Union operates as a single market made up of 27 countries. The total value of all goods and services produced (GDP) in the EU in 2021 was € 14.5 trillion.
- As per the World Bank data, EU's GDP per capita (current US$) was estimated to be $18.35 trillion in 2023; while the GDP growth (annual %) was pegged at 0.5%.
- The EU accounts for around 14% of the world's trade in goods. The EU, China and the United States accounted for around 45 % of global imports as well as exports of goods.
- The EU had a trade surplus of €119.8 billion in January 2023, down from €128.3 billion in the previous month.
- EU received over €300 billion in FDI in 2021.
- It is the world's second most important source of space and communications technology.

Politics & International Affairs

- EU is an important bloc in international economic organisations, like WTO.
- Among the current members, **France** holds a permanent seat on the UN Security Council. The EU includes several non-permanent members of the UNSC.
- The EU is one of the largest donors of foreign aid in the world, providing billions of euros in development assistance to countries around the globe.
- EU has played a key role in negotiating international agreements such as the Paris Climate Accord and the Iran Nuclear Deal.

Important Multilateral Engagements

- **Transatlantic Trade and Investment Partnership (TTIP)**: While not finalized, this proposed trade agreement with the US aimed to create the world's largest free trade area.
- **Comprehensive Economic and Trade Agreement (CETA)**: A landmark trade deal between the EU and Canada, representing one of the most progressive trade agreements globally.
- **EU-Japan Economic Partnership Agreement (EPA)**: A significant trade deal enhancing economic ties between the EU and Japan.
- **Global Climate Action**: The EU has been a leading force in international efforts to combat climate change, including the Paris Agreement.

CRITICAL DEVELOPMENTS AND TERMINOLOGY

European Green Deal	It is a comprehensive set of policy initiatives by the European Commission with the overarching goal of making the European Union climate-neutral by 2050. It aims to transform the EU's economy into a sustainable one, ensuring no net emissions of greenhouse gases. It encompasses a wide range of policies, including those related to energy, transportation, agriculture, industry, and building renovation. Key objectives include: • **Climate neutrality:** Achieving zero net greenhouse gas emissions by 2050. • **Green transition:** Transforming the EU economy into a sustainable and resource-efficient one. • **Social fairness:** Ensuring a just transition that leaves no one behind. • **Innovation:** Driving research and innovation for green technologies.
Sovereign Debt Crisis or Eurozone Crisis	It was a financial crisis that emerged in the late 2000s, affecting several Eurozone countries. The crisis began in the wake of the global financial crisis of 2007-2008, which weakened economies and strained public finances. It was characterized by the difficulty or inability of several EU member states to repay or refinance their government debt without the assistance of third parties. As a result, the **European Financial Stability Facility (EFSF) and European Stability Mechanism (ESM)** were established by EU to provide temporary stability support to Eurozone countries in financial distress.
Defence Strategies	The EU has developed comprehensive foreign policy aimed at promoting peace, security, and stability both within Europe and globally. The policies are guided by the principles of democracy, rule of law, and respect for human rights. The EU's approach to foreign policy is characterized by a commitment to multilateralism, diplomatic engagement, and cooperation with international partners.
Nord Stream Pipelines	They are natural gas pipelines that run from Russia to Germany via the Baltic Sea. They were at the centre of geopolitical tensions in the second half of 2022 as Russia was accused of intentionally causing damage to the pipelines in a suspected retaliation against Western sanctions following its invasion of Ukraine.
Euroscepticism	It refers to opposition to, or skepticism about, European integration. It encompasses a range of views, from those who advocate for reform of the EU to those who call for its complete dissolution. The key drivers of this ideology include – (a) Sovereignty concerns: Some believe that EU membership erodes national sovereignty and decision-making power. (b) Economic impact: Critics argue that EU membership has a negative impact on national economies, particularly in terms of regulations and competition. (c) Immigration and security: Concerns over immigration and security have fueled Eurosceptic sentiment in some countries. (d) Democratic deficit: Critics argue that the EU's decision-making process is undemocratic and lacks transparency.

CHALLENGES AND OBSTACLES

1) **Demographic changes** – The EU is experiencing an aging population and declining birth rates, leading to concerns about labour shortages, economic growth, and the sustainability of social welfare systems.
2) **Euroscepticism** – The EU has faced growing Euroscepticism in some member states, fueled by economic disparities, immigration concerns, and perceived loss of national sovereignty. This has led to challenges in decision-making and maintaining unity.
3) **Migration and Refugee Crisis** – The migrant and/or refugee crisis in Europe began intensifying in 2015, with a significant influx of refugees and migrants, primarily from Syria, Afghanistan, and Iraq,

seeking asylum in EU countries. The influx of migrants and refugees has strained EU member states, leading to disagreements over burden-sharing and asylum policies. This has exposed divisions within the EU and posed challenges to the Schengen Area. The critical challenges include –

- **Unequal distribution** of refugees among EU member states, leading to tensions and accusations of free-riding.
- The **cost of accommodating and integrating refugees** has raised concerns about the economic burden on host countries.
- Fears of potential **security threats** among refugees have fueled anti-immigration sentiment.
- The crisis has **tested the solidarity** of the EU, highlighting differences in national interests and approaches to migration.

CONFLICTS & CRISIS

Conflict and instability in regions such as the Middle East and North Africa have forced millions of people to flee their homes and seek refuge in neighboring countries and in Europe. The Syrian civil war, in particular, has been a major driver of refugee flows into Europe since 2015. As per UNHCR, in 2021, more than 114,000 people risked their lives trying to reach Europe by sea; over 3,200 of them are dead or missing. While EU has been doing its bit to secure a place for such refugees, more recently, EU has been attempting to secure its borders in a step to curtail the large number of people trying to illegally enter the European borders.

4) **Cyberwarfare** – The increasing frequency and sophistication of cyberattacks pose significant threats to the EU's critical infrastructure, economy, and security.
5) **Energy Security** – The EU's reliance on energy imports, particularly from Russia, has highlighted its vulnerability to supply disruptions and geopolitical pressures. The transition to renewable energy sources is a complex process.
6) **NATO alliance** – Balancing the EU's Common Security and Defense Policy (CSDP) with NATO membership is a complex issue. Ensuring effective cooperation between the two while maintaining European strategic autonomy is a challenge.
7) **Terrorism and Radicalization** – The threat of terrorism continues to be a significant challenge for the EU, requiring coordinated efforts to prevent radicalization, counter extremism, and enhance security measures.

CHINA AND EU LINKAGES

- The rail networks between China and Europe form a crucial element in China's **'Pivot to Europe'** strategy, while the links serve as important trade routes for European economies. The rail routes are spread over China, Kazakhastan, Russia, Belarus and beyond. It connects important Chinese centres including Yiwu (Zhejiang province), Xi'an (Shaanxi), Zhengzhou (Henan), Chengdu (Sichuan) and Wuhan (Hubei) to European cities including Moscow, Hamburg, Minsk, Milan, Warsaw, Munich and Madrid.

In 2021, China was the third largest partner for EU exports of goods (10.2 %) and the largest partner for EU imports of goods (22.4 %). Over the last decade, the rail links between China and Europe have been forged as part of President Xi's **'Silk Road Project'**, (now Belt and Road Initiative).

- The Russia-Ukraine conflict ruptured the trade routes between China and Europe and as a consequence over a million containers which were usually transported using the railway link connecting Western Europe and Eastern China via Russia, now have to settle on costlier routes by sea, threatening to exacerbate the global supply chain madness.
- With the main Kazakhastan-Russia rail route to Europe now cut off, rail freight had to be shifted south in favour of the multi-modal route using the Caspian Sea, which includes either **China-Kazakhastan-Europe** or **China-Uzbekistan-Turkmenistan** to Europe.
- Both use Caspian Sea Ports to access Azerbaijan's **Baku port**, additional rail connectivity across Georgia and Turkey, to Black Sea Ports with the southern EU. Additionally, with the Russian ports being inaccessible, the other ports are witnessing unprecedented congestions.

In June 2022, the Kyrgyz President made an announcement regarding the commencement of the **China-Kyrgyzstan-Uzbekistan (CKU)** railway project in 2023. It would link China, Kyrgyzstan and Uzbekistan to Central and Eastern Europe via Iran and Turkey.

INDIA AND THE EUROPEAN UNION

The relationship between India and the European Union (EU) has strengthened significantly in recent years, characterized by increased cooperation in various areas, including trade, investment, technology, and security. Both sides share a commitment to a rules-based international order, multilateralism, and sustainable development.

Areas of Cooperation

- **Trade and Investment**: The EU is one of India's largest trading partners, and bilateral trade has continued to grow steadily. The EU is also a major source of foreign investment in India.
- **Technology**: India and the EU are collaborating on a wide range of technological areas, including artificial intelligence, quantum computing, and semiconductors.
- **Climate Change**: Both sides are committed to addressing climate change and have collaborated on initiatives to promote clean energy and sustainable development.
- **Defense and Security**: India and the EU have strengthened their cooperation in the areas of defense and security, including counter-terrorism and maritime security.
- **Connectivity**: India and the EU are working together to enhance connectivity, including through infrastructure projects and digital partnerships.

Challenges & Opportunities

- **Trade Barriers**: Despite the growing economic relationship, there are still some trade barriers that need to be addressed, such as tariffs and non-tariff measures.
- **Geopolitical Issues**: The EU and India have different perspectives on some geopolitical issues, which can sometimes create tensions in the relationship.
- **Potential for Deeper Cooperation**: There is significant potential for further deepening the India-EU partnership, particularly in areas such as technology, climate change, and sustainable development.

- The **European Union (EU) is India's largest trading partner**, with bilateral trade in goods reaching €124 billion in 2023, representing 12.2% of India's total trade—surpassing both the USA (10.8%) and China (10.5%).
- The EU is also the second-largest destination for Indian exports, accounting for 17.5% of the total, just behind the USA at 17.6%, while China ranks fourth at 3.7%.
- On the EU side, India is its **9th largest trading partner**, contributing **2.2%** to the EU's total trade in goods in **2023**, which is significantly lower compared to the USA (**16.7%**), China (**14.6%**), and the UK (**10.1%**). Over the past decade, trade in goods between India and the EU has seen nearly a **90% increase**.
- Trade in services between the two regions has also expanded, reaching **€50.8 billion** in **2023**, up from €30.4 billion in 2020.
- The EU's foreign investment stock in India grew to **€108.3 billion** in **2022**, up from €82.3 billion in 2019, although it remains lower than the EU's investment stocks in **China (€247.5 billion)** or **Brazil (€293.4 billion)**.
- Additionally, around 6,000 European companies operate in India, directly employing 1.7 million people and indirectly supporting 5 million jobs **across** diverse sectors.

THE UNITED KINGDOM

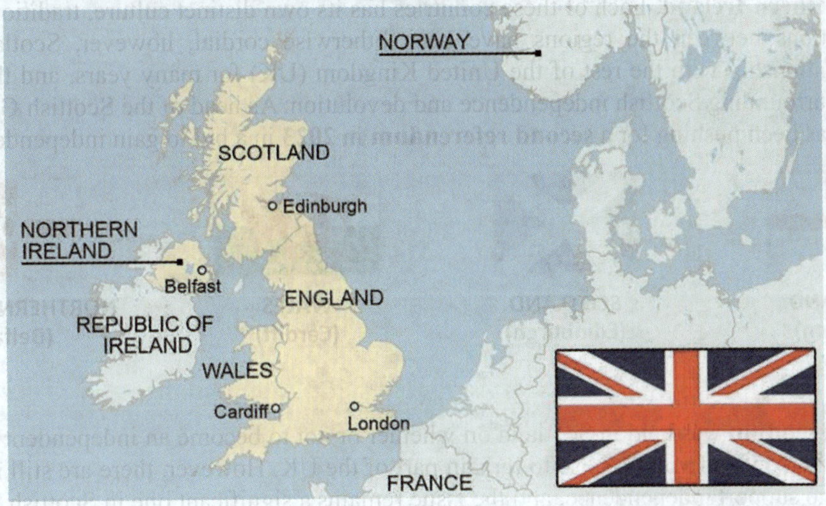

The United Kingdom (UK) is a **constitutional monarchy** with a **parliamentary system of government.** The present UK monarch is **King Charles III**, but the Prime Minister serves as the head of government. As of August 2024, the Prime Minister is **Keir Starmer** of the Labour Party (became PM in July 2024). The UK has a multi-party system, with the two largest parties being the ***Conservative Party*** and the ***Labour Party***. Other important parties include the Scottish National Party (SNP), the Liberal Democrats, and the Democratic Unionist Party (DUP). The UK has a long history of democracy and political stability, although there have been some notable periods of political turmoil, such as during the Brexit process.

Capital: **London**	Head of State: **King Charles III**	Prime Minister: **Keir Starmer**	GDP (current US$): **3.34 trillion** (2023)

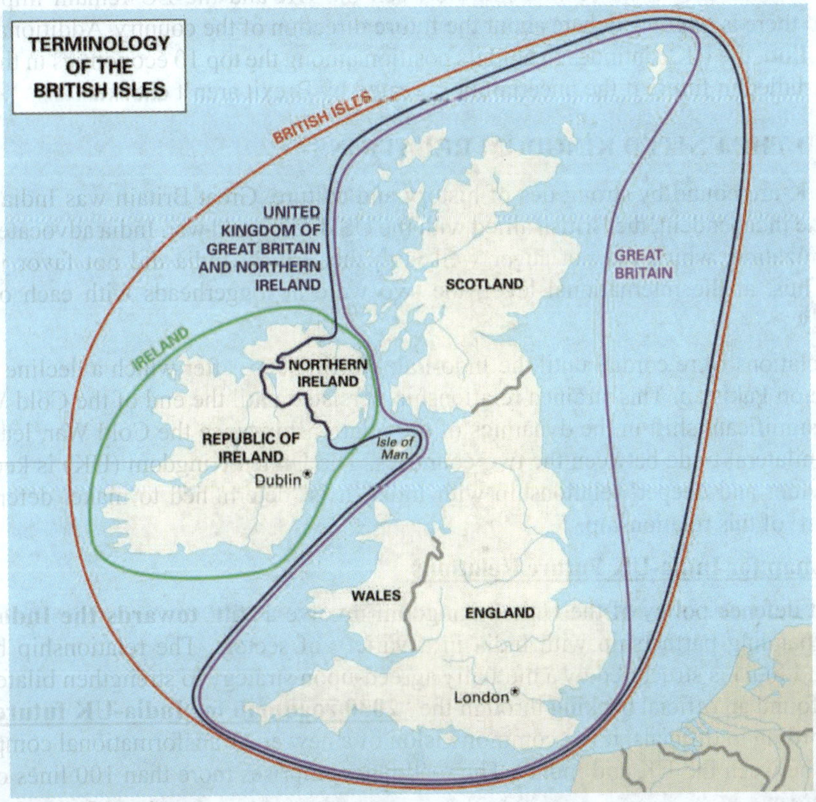

Source: Britannica

The United Kingdom (UK) is a political union composed of four constituent countries: **England, Scotland, Wales, and Northern Ireland**. Each of these countries has its own distinct culture, traditions, and history. While the relations between the regions have been otherwise cordial, however, Scotland has had a complicated relationship with the rest of the United Kingdom (UK) for many years, and there have been various issues surrounding Scottish independence and devolution. As head of the Scottish Government, the First Minister has been pushing for a **second referendum** in **2023** in a bid to gain independence.

ENGLAND (London)

SCOTLAND (Edinburgh)

WALES (Cardiff)

NORTHERN IRELAND (Belfast)

In 2014, a **referendum** was held in Scotland on whether or not to become an independent country, and the result was that 55% of voters chose to remain part of the UK. However, there are still many people in Scotland who support independence, and the issue remains a significant one in Scottish politics.

Important Statistics - UK		
Population	68 M	(2023)
GDP Growth (annual)	0.1%	(2023)
FDI, net inflows (percentage of GDP)	1.5%	(2022)
Human Development Index Rank	15	(2023)

*World Bank data

The UK is a major player in international affairs, with a strong economy, military, and diplomatic presence in the world. UK's **nuclear arsenal** gives it a positive strategic posture in the global interactions. The **post-Brexit** process and the future relationship between the UK and the EU remain important issues in UK politics, and there is ongoing debate about the future direction of the country. Additionally, with a real GDP of **$2.76 trillion**, the UK continues to hold its position among the top 10 economies in the world. The growth could be curtailed in future if the uncertainties created by Brexit aren't checked.

INDIA AND THE UNITED KINGDOM RELATIONS

India and UK are bound by strong ties of history and culture. Great Britain was India's colonial ruler. As India became independent, the British allied with the US during cold war. India advocated for non-alignment and decolonization, which did not auger well with the British. India did not favor joining any military alliances. Thus, at the international level, the two were at loggerheads with each other politically and ideologically.

India-UK relations were cordial until the Indo-Pak War in 1965, after which a decline occurred due to the UK's stance on Pakistan. This strained relationship persisted until the end of the Cold War. However, there has been a significant shift in the dynamics of the relationship since the Cold War, leading to a consistent increase in bilateral trade between the two countries. The United Kingdom (UK) is keen on establishing a 'stronger, wider and deeper' relationship with India. It is 'determined to make' defence cooperation 'an essential part' of this relationship.

2030 Roadmap for India-UK Future Relations

Foreign and defence policy of the United Kingdom involve a **'tilt' towards the Indo-Pacific area**. This involves expanding partnership with India in a variety of sectors. The relationship between the United Kingdom and India is structured by a mutually agreed-upon strategy to strengthen bilateral relationships by 2030. This found an official backing through the "**2030 roadmap for India-UK future relations**" (4 May 2021). According to officials, it is a common vision of a new and transformational comprehensive strategic partnership between the UK and India". The roadmap comprises more than 100 lines of activity. It covers five major areas –

- **Connecting our countries and people** – The nations would upgrade institutional mechanisms" to help them achieve goals in all areas of cooperation and strengthen avenues for people-to-people connections in education, research and innovation, capacity building, employment and culture.
- **Trade and prosperity** – India and the UK would create shared prosperity and deliver leadership in global economic governance. An enhanced trade partnership would unlock the potential for the relationship from our dynamic private sectors.
- **Climate** – As per the roadmap, both nations were committed to safeguarding the planet and building a more environmentally sustainable future and achieving the goals of the Paris Agreement. This included mobilising investment and climate finance.
- **Health** – Both nations would use their combined research and innovation strength to address the biggest global health challenges, save lives and improve health and well-being.
- **Defence & Security** - The UK and India would work together in a strategic partnership to tackle cyber, space, crime and terrorist threats and develop a free, open and secure Indo-Pacific region.

<u>**Areas of Cooperation**</u>

<u>Trade & Commerce</u>

- The India-UK economic relations received a vibrant upward direction after the establishment of **Joint Economic and Trade Committee (JETCO)** in 2005 to tackle trade barriers and promote business links. India and the UK have been working to increase their bilateral trade and investment ties.
- In 2020, the UK became India's second-largest trading partner outside the EU. The two countries have also signed several agreements to enhance economic cooperation and facilitate investment.
- As per official UK government data (2022), India-UK bilateral trade stood at around GBP 29.6 billion a year. **India accounts for 1.7 percent of total UK exports** and India was the 12th largest export market for the UK in the four quarters to the end of Q3 2022.
- As per officials figures, about 70 percent of India-UK trade is dominated by the services sector. In 2020, UK foreign direct investment (FDI) in India amounted to £14.9 billion.
- In 2021, the UK and India signed several investment agreements, including a £240 million investment by the UK's CDC Group in India's National Investment and Infrastructure Fund (NIIF), and a £240 million investment by India's Serum Institute in the UK's vaccine industry.
- Both India and the UK have stated that they want to establish a **comprehensive strategic partnership**. The move towards achieving this will be guided by a mutually agreed **'2030 roadmap for India-UK future relations'**, which was published on 4 May 2021.
- In a step towards achieving this agenda, India and the United Kingdom have been initiating talks towards a **bilateral Free Trade Agreement (FTA)** since a few years, but the negotiations began formally in January 2022. The seventh round of India-UK FTA discussions took place in London from February 6-10, 2023.
- The latest development came in on April 13 (2023), when UK's ex PM Rishi Sunak spoke with PM Narendra Modi and agreed to accelerate the process of resolving any "outstanding issues" in the FTA negotiations.

<u>Education & Research</u>

- India and the UK have a history of commitment to further educational ties as India is one of the biggest contributors to the British Higher Education system. As of 2019-2020, there are over 53,000 Indians enlisted in the UK educational institutions.
- In a recent development, the two countries have signed a **Memorandum of Understanding (MoU) on Education**, which includes a focus on maritime education. This agreement aims to facilitate the

recognition of academic qualifications and duration of study in higher educational institutions between India and the other country. However, it is important to note that professional degrees like engineering and medicine are not covered under this MoU. Additionally, the MoU also encompasses maritime education, ensuring the mutual recognition of certificates, competency, and endorsements of seafarers issued by both sides.

- In 2019, the UK and India launched the **India-UK Global Health Security Partnership**, which aims to strengthen collaboration on global health security. The partnership focuses on enhancing capacity in areas such as disease surveillance, outbreak response, and laboratory networks. The UK and India have also collaborated on several joint research initiatives aimed at addressing global health challenges. For example, the **UK Medical Research Council and India's Department of Biotechnology** have jointly funded research on infectious diseases such as tuberculosis and dengue fever. In August 2020, the UK government had launched a 3-million pound innovation challenge fund in India to support scientists in academia and industry to tackle the most acute global challenges such as COVID-19 and the threat to the environment.
- Furthermore, in January 2023, India and the UK reached an agreement on a reciprocal **UK-India Young Professionals Scheme**. This scheme aims to provide annual visas to 3,000 graduates aged between 18 and 30, allowing them to live and work in either country for a period of up to two years.

Energy & Resources

- The UK and India have collaborated on several renewable energy initiatives, such as the **UK-India Energy for Growth Partnership**. This partnership aims to promote the development of renewable energy and low-carbon solutions in India, with a focus on solar and wind energy. Additionally, the **UK-India Joint Working Group on Energy Efficiency** focuses on sharing best practices and promoting energy efficiency in areas such as buildings, industry, and transport. In 2021, the UK and India announced several initiatives to enhance cooperation in the energy sector, including a partnership on clean energy and climate change, and an agreement to collaborate on hydrogen and fuel cell technology.
- The UK and India have also collaborated on natural resources issues, such as the **UK-India Joint Working Group on Mining.** This group aims to promote sustainable mining practices and address environmental and social challenges in the mining sector. Additionally, the **UK-India Water Quality and Security Programme** focuses on promoting sustainable water management practices and addressing water quality and security challenges in India.

Defence & Security

- The UK and India share a natural partnership in the field of defense, with a focus on research, development, and training. The Indo-Pacific region has gained increasing importance for the UK, as it is central to global economic growth and holds significant geostrategic value. Recognizing the significance of the Indo-Pacific, the UK has made substantial investments in defense equipment capabilities to enhance its role in the region.
- Under the **Defence and International Security Partnership (DISP)**, the UK and India have established six bilateral working groups as subgroups to the **Defence Consultative Group**. These working groups facilitate collaboration and development in areas such as the Army, Navy, Air Force, Science & Technology, Equipment, and Joint Environment. The nations have been discussing the expansion of cooperation under the **DISP** which was agreed in 2015.
- The UK and India have also collaborated on defence trade and technology transfer, with the UK serving as a key supplier of defence equipment to India. The two countries have also worked together on joint research and development projects in areas such as aerospace and defence. The nations have also collaborated on maritime security, with the two countries conducting joint naval exercises and sharing expertise on issues such as piracy and maritime domain awareness.

JOINT EXERCISES	
Indradhanush	It is a joint air force exercise that began in 2006. The 5th edition took place in February 2020.

Ajeya Warrior	It is a joint military exercise. The emphasis is on counter-terrorist operations in Urban and Semi-Urban areas. The latest 6th edition took place in October 2021 at Chaubatia, Uttarakhand.
Konkan	It is a joint military exercise and the latest edition took place in 2021 on the English Channel.

Culture & Society

India and UK signed a MoU on Cultural Cooperation in July 2010. The Nehru Centre (TNC), established in 1992 in London, is the cultural outreach of the High Commission of India in UK India is the second largest source of students studying in UK and the number of Indian students in UK is approximately 38,000. **The UK-India Education and Research Initiative (UKIERI)** was initiated in 2006, aiming to enhance collaboration in higher education, research, schools, and professional and technical skills between the two countries. The Indian community in the UK constitutes one of the largest ethnic minority groups, with approximately 1.5 million individuals of Indian origin recorded in the 2011 census. This population accounts for nearly 1.8% of the total British population.

BREXIT and its Impact on India

Brexit refers to the United Kingdom's (UK) decision to leave the European Union (EU), which was voted on in a referendum held on June 23, 2016. The referendum resulted in 52% of voters in favour of leaving the EU and 48% in favour of remaining. The Brexit process officially began on March 29, 2017, when the UK formally triggered Article 50 of the Lisbon Treaty, which outlines the process for leaving the EU. Negotiations between the UK and the EU began, and after several rounds of talks, an agreement on the terms of the UK's departure was reached on November 14, 2018. The **United Kingdom withdrew from the European Union on 31 January 2020.**

The UK's departure from the EU has led to changes in trade, immigration, and other policies, and has raised questions about the future of the UK's relationship with the EU and other countries around the world. The major impact of consequences of BREXIT include –

- The U.K. is no longer part of the customs union and single market with the EU.
- Free movement between the U.K. and EU has ended. European nationals living in U.K. need documents to suggest that they have been allowed residence by government.
- The U.K. must negotiate new trade agreements with countries outside of the EU, which had more than 40 trade agre ements with 70 countries already in place.
- The U.K. must pay a "divorce bill" of 25 billion pounds by 2057. This is to fulfill any remaining financial commitments made while a member of the EU.

The UK is an important trading partner for India, and Brexit has the potential to impact **bilateral trade**. However, the UK and India have been working to strengthen trade ties, with negotiations for a free trade agreement (FTA) underway. India is a significant investor in the UK, and Brexit has raised concerns about the impact on **Indian companies** with operations in the UK. However, some experts suggest that Brexit could also present new opportunities for Indian companies, such as in the areas of technology and innovation. Brexit has led to changes in **immigration policies** in the UK, which could impact Indian students and professionals who want to study or work in the country. However, the UK government has stated that it remains committed to attracting the "brightest and best" from around the world, including from India. Occasions

Illegal Migration and the UK

- One prominent aspect of illegal migration in the UK is the **crossing of the English Channel** by small boats or other means by migrants attempting to reach the UK from France or other European countries. These crossings have increased significantly in recent years, leading to concerns about border security and the well-being of migrants. Illegal migration may very often involve human trafficking and smuggling networks that exploit vulnerable individuals.
- The **issue of illegal migration intersects with the UK's asylum system**. Some individuals who enter illegally may subsequently claim asylum, seeking protection based on fear of persecution or other grounds. The processing of asylum claims and determining the status of individuals can be a complex and time-consuming process.
- Illegal migration has been a **subject of public and political debate** in the UK, with differing opinions on how to address the issue. Discussions often focus on border control, immigration policy, the human rights of migrants, and the strain on public services and resources.
- One of the **top priorities of Prime Minister Rishi Sunak's government is cracking down on illegal migration** (the 'stop the boats' plan). He has on several occasions announced his commitment to tackle abuse of laws and border demarcations. Addressing the issue of economic burden, the PM had revealed that the 'British taxpayers were spending around £6 million a day on housing illegal migrants.'

FRANCE

OFFICIAL FLAG

France is a **semi-presidential republic** with a President as the head of state and a Prime Minister as the head of government. As of July 2024, the President of France is **Emmanuel Macron**. France has a **multi-party system** with a number of parties represented in the National Assembly, the lower house of the French Parliament. France has a long history of **secularism** and separation of church and state. This principle is enshrined in the French Constitution and is a defining feature of French society. France has a rich cultural heritage and is known for its art, literature, and cuisine. Paris, the capital city, is home to many world-renowned museums, such as the Louvre and the Musée d'Orsay.

Capital: **Paris**	President: **Emmanuel Macron**	Prime Minister: **Gabriel Attal**	GDP (current US$): **3.03 trillion** (2023)

Important Statistics		
Population	68 M	(2023)
GDP Growth (annual)	0.7%	(2023)
FDI, net inflows (percentage of GDP)	3.8%	(2022)
Human Development Index Rank	28	(2023)
*World Bank data		

France is considered to be one of the world's great powers and has significant influence in international affairs. It is a **permanent member of the United Nations Security Council**, which gives it the ability to veto resolutions, and is also a member of the G7, G20, and other international organizations. It has one of the largest armies in Europe and has been involved in numerous military operations around the world, including in Africa and the Middle East. France also maintains a **nuclear arsenal**, which is an important element of its strategic posture. As per the World Bank records of 2021, France's GDP estimate represents **$2.96 trillion**. At present over 70% of the nation's GDP stems from the service sector. France is also the global leader in the arenas of automotive, railway and aerospace.

The **French Declaration on the Rights of Man and Citizen** was a document adopted by the National Assembly of France on August 26, 1789, during the French Revolution. It is considered to be one of the most important documents in the history of human rights and played a significant role in shaping the modern concept of citizenship and individual liberty. The Declaration was inspired by the Enlightenment ideas of natural law, individual rights, and popular sovereignty.

Time period	Important developments
1939-45	During the Second World War, Germany occupies a large territory of France. The rising friction among groups gives impetus to French Resistance.
1944	Allied forces land at France leading to its liberation.
1946-58	Fourth Republic – Marks the beginning of economic reconstruction and the process of independence for many of France's colonies.
1951	Six west European countries including France, sign the Treaty of Paris establishing the European Coal and Steel Community (ECSC).
1957	Formation of the European Economic Community (EEC)
1968	National strike against the government policies and lack of social reform
1992	France signs Maastricht Treaty on European union.
1995-1996	A group of Six nuclear tests (underground explosions) conducted in the Pacific – France attracts international condemnation.
2002	Euro coins and notes replace franc in entirety
2010	France concludes military and nuclear accord with UK – cooperation in testing nuclear warheads.
2015	The Charlie Hebdo Shooting – series of terrorist attacks takes place
2016	Islamic State takes responsibility of lorry attack in crowd which killed 84 people.
2017	Emmanuel Macron wins the presidential election
Nov-Dec 2018	The 'Yellow-Vest' protests erupt in an attempt to curb fossil fuel use through price hikes which turn violent – Partial government climb-down erupt.

The **"yellow vest" movement**, also known as the "Gilets Jaunes" movement, began in France in November 2018 and quickly spread to other European countries. The movement was initially sparked by a proposed fuel tax hike in France, but quickly evolved into a broader protest against government policies and economic inequality. Protesters demanded a range of reforms, including a decrease in fuel taxes, an increase in the minimum wage, and greater government transparency and accountability. The movement gained significant attention and support across Europe, with protests and demonstrations taking place in countries such as Belgium, the Netherlands, Spain, and Germany.

India France Relations

India and France share a robust and multi-faceted relationship, with cooperation extending across various domains, including defense, space, nuclear energy, trade, and culture. The strategic partnership, established in 1998, has matured over the years, with both nations working closely on regional and global issues.

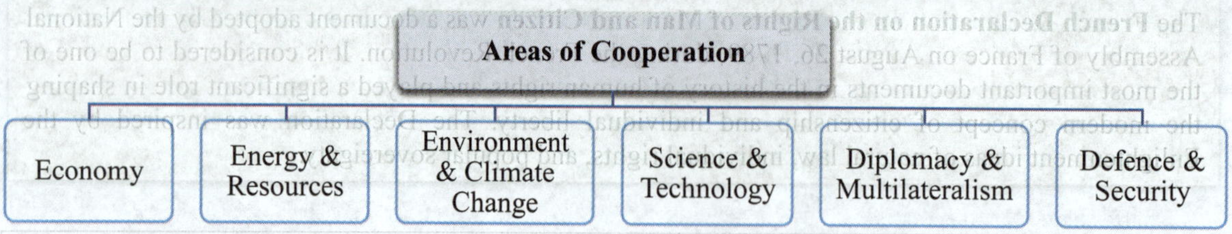

(a) **Economy** – The year 2023 marked the 25th anniversary of Indo-French strategic partnership. France is one of India's key trading partners in the European Union, with trade encompassing a wide range of goods and services. French companies have a significant presence in India, particularly in sectors like automobiles, aerospace, and luxury goods. Meanwhile, Indian companies are increasingly investing in France, particularly in the IT, pharmaceuticals, and energy sectors. India has a trade surplus with France and bilateral trade stood at nearly $8 billion in 2022. As part of their cooperation in the Indo-Pacific, India and France agreed to work towards the establishment of an Indo-Pacific Trilateral Development Cooperation Fund in 2022, which would aim to support India-based innovators and start-ups.

(b) **Energy & Resources** – Energy cooperation is a cornerstone of the India-France relationship, especially in the field of civil nuclear energy. France has been a key partner in India's nuclear energy development, with agreements in place for the construction of nuclear reactors in India. Additionally, both countries collaborate in renewable energy, particularly solar energy, with the International Solar Alliance being a significant joint initiative.

(c) **Environment & Climate Change** – India and France are committed to addressing global environmental challenges. Both nations played key roles in the Paris Agreement and continue to work together on climate change mitigation. France supports India's efforts in renewable energy and sustainability, with joint projects focusing on clean energy, urban sustainability, and biodiversity conservation. The partnership also emphasizes sustainable development goals and climate finance. The International Solar Alliance is a joint initiative of India and France and was launched during COP21 to promote solar energy. India had joined the French-led initiative called High Ambition Coalition for Nature and People which aims at protecting at least 30% of the world's Lands and Oceans by 2030.

(d) **Science & Technology** – Cooperation in science and technology is a dynamic aspect of India-France relations. Both countries collaborate on cutting-edge research in fields like space exploration, biotechnology, and information technology. The Indian Space Research Organisation (ISRO) and the French space agency CNES have a long history of collaboration, including satellite launches and joint missions. In 2021, India and France signed an agreement for cooperation towards India's first human space mission – **Gaganyaan**. Additionally, academic exchanges and joint research programs in various scientific fields are regularly conducted. The two countries collaborate on the development and operation of nuclear power plants, as well as on nuclear research and development. India is also a member of the International Thermonuclear Experimental Reactor (ITER) which is a multi-national consortium established to construct an experimental fusion reactor located in Cadarache (France).

(e) **Diplomacy & Multilateralism** – India and France share a commitment to multilateralism and work closely in international forums like the United Nations, G20, and UNESCO. Both countries advocate for reforms in global governance institutions, particularly the UN Security Council. Their cooperation extends to issues like counter-terrorism, cyber security, and global health, where they have taken joint initiatives to strengthen international norms and cooperation.

(f) **Defence & Security** – The defence relationship includes extensive collaboration in defense procurement, joint military exercises, and intelligence sharing. France is a major supplier of defense equipment to India, with key deals including the Rafale fighter jets. Additionally, both countries cooperate in maritime security, counter-terrorism, and cybersecurity, reflecting their shared commitment to regional and global security.

On **September 19, 2022**, on the margins of the United Nations General Assembly in New York, the Foreign Ministers of **France, India, and the UAE met for the first time in a trilateral format**. The major objective of the meet was to explore potential cooperation in the **Indo-Pacific region** including in Maritime Security, Humanitarian Assistance and Disaster Relief (HADR), Blue Economy, Regional Connectivity, Cooperation in Multilateral Fora, Energy and Food Security, Startups etc.

Training Exercises	
Garuda	It is a bilateral air exercise between the Air Forces of India and France. Garuda-VII was held in Jodhpur (Rajasthan) in Oct-Nov 2022.
Varuna	It is an annual naval exercise between India and France. The 21st edition of Varuna was conducted in January 2023 on the Western Seaboard, Goa.
Shakti	It is a bilateral joint military exercise between the Armies of India and France. The 6th edition – EX Shakti 2021, was conducted at the Military School of Draguignan, France in November 2021.

GERMANY

OFFICIAL FLAG

Germany is a **federal parliamentary republic** with a **President** as the head of state and a **Chancellor** as the head of government. As of August 2024, the Chancellor of Germany is **Olaf Scholz**, who assumed office in December 2021. As of March 2023, with a real GDP of **$3.84 trillion**, Germany occupies the fourth place among the top five economies on the globe. After a brief plummeting in 2009, Germany's economy bounced forward with 4.0% expansion a decade back. It is known for its strong manufacturing sector, particularly in the automotive and machinery industries. Germany has a strong welfare state with a comprehensive social security system that provides healthcare, education, and other benefits to citizens. It also has a strong tradition of workers' rights and labor protection.

Capital: **Berlin**	President: **Frank-Walter Steinmeier**	Chancellor: **Olaf Scholz**	GDP (current US$): **4.46 trillion** (2023)

Important Statistics

Population	84 M	(2023)
GDP Growth (annual)	-0.3%	(2023)
FDI, net inflows (percentage of GDP)	1.5%	(2022)
Human Development Index Rank	07	(2023)

*World Bank data

Germany was divided into two during the Cold War, with East Germany under Soviet control and West Germany aligned with the United States. The **fall of the Berlin Wall in 1989** and **reunification in 1990** marked a major turning point in German history.

India and Germany Relations

Areas of Cooperation → Trade & Industry → Energy & Resources → Education & Research → Sci & Tech → Healthcare

In 2021, **Germany held the position of both the largest importer of goods from India and the largest exporter of goods to India**. In May 2022, the Indian Prime Minister and the German Chancellor co-chaired the 6th plenary session of the **Inter-Governmental Consultations (IGC).** During this session, the two nations agreed to strengthen the **India-Germany Strategic Partnership** across various areas, including shared values and regional interests, green and sustainable development, trade, investment, and digital transformation, political and academic exchange, scientific cooperation, workforce and people mobility, and global health. During the events, the Foreign Secretary of India also initialed the **Comprehensive Migration & Mobility Partnership Agreement** with State Secretary of Ministry of Interior of Germany.

Germany had also signed a **$10.5 Billion Green Deal** (Green and Sustainable Development Partnership (SDGs)) to Boost Clean Energy Use. The deliverables under the partnership include –

- Develop an Indo-German **Green Hydrogen Roadmap**.
- Establish an Indo-German **Renewable Energy Partnership** with focus on innovative solar energy and other renewables.
- Establish a lighthouse cooperation on "**Agroecology and Sustainable Management of Natural Resources**".
- Deepen cooperation in **restoring forest landscapes** under the Bonn Challenge.
- Furthering Collaboration on **Green Energy Corridors**, e.g. Leh-Haryana transmission line and project of carbon neutral Ladakh.

Other critical Indo-German initiatives include –

- The **NITI Aayog-BMZ Dialogue** focuses on enhancing the localization of Sustainable Development Goals (SDGs) at the city level.
- The **Indo-German Energy Programme (IGEN)** assists in the implementation of the Energy Conservation Act of 2001.
- The **Indo-German Partnership on Green Urban Mobility** promotes the integration of sustainable modes of transportation, including metros and light metros.
- In June 2022, **India** and the **G7** agreed to collaborate on the establishment of a **Just Energy Transition Partnership (JETP)** with the aim of advancing a fair transition towards cleaner energy sources.

ITALY

Italy is a parliamentary republic with a bicameral legislature and a ceremonial head of state. Italy faces challenges such as corruption, economic stagnation, and regional disparities. Italy has a mixed economy, with both public and private sectors playing significant roles. The Italian economy is driven by sectors such as manufacturing, tourism, and agriculture. Italy is a major exporter of goods and services, with significant trade relationships with the European Union and other countries.

OFFICIAL FLAG

Capital: **Rome**	President: **Sergio Mattarella**	Prime Minister: **Georgia Meloni**	GDP (current US$): **2.25 trillion** (2023)

Important Statistics	
Population	58.8 M (2023)
GDP Growth (annual)	0.9% (2023)
FDI, net inflows (percentage of GDP)	3.0% (2022)
Human Development Index Rank	30 (2023)
*World Bank data	

Italy is a founding member of the North Atlantic Treaty Organization (NATO), contributing to collective defense and security. Italy has a well-equipped military and participates in international peacekeeping missions. Italy faces increasing cybersecurity threats and is investing in measures to protect its digital infrastructure. Italy is a founding member of the European Union and plays an active role in EU decision-making. Italy has a strong interest in the Mediterranean region and is involved in regional cooperation initiatives. Italy maintains strong diplomatic relations with countries around the world, including the United States, Russia, and China.

India & Italy Relations

1. **Growing Ties**: India and Italy have seen a significant boost in their relationship, marked by enhanced diplomatic, economic, and cultural engagements. The relationship has deepened, especially in recent years, as both nations seek to strengthen cooperation across various strategic sectors, such as trade, innovation, technology, energy, and defense. High-level visits and summits, such as the India-Italy Strategic Partnership, have led to agreements on shared goals, further enhancing the scope of bilateral cooperation.
2. **Economic Ties**:
   - India and Italy are major economic partners, with bilateral trade between India and Italy reaching a value of **US$14.25 billion** in 2022-23, reflecting a strong and growing economic relationship, driven by sectors like manufacturing, automobiles, pharmaceuticals, and textiles.
   - Italy ranks as **India's 5th largest trading partner in the European Union (EU),** with Italian companies increasingly investing in Indian industries like renewable energy, infrastructure, and agriculture.
   - Italy is the **18th largest foreign investor** in India, with a cumulative FDI inflow of **US$3.40 billion** from April 2000 to September 2023.
   - Both countries are committed to expanding their trade volume and improving market access, especially as Italy is a key supporter of India's participation in global value chains.
3. **Defense Cooperation**: The defense relationship between India and Italy has evolved significantly, with both countries engaging in joint defense collaborations. In recent years, there has been an increased focus on defense manufacturing and technology transfers, with discussions around the joint development of military equipment like fighter jets, naval systems, and advanced surveillance technologies. Italy's defense sector, which includes aerospace companies like *Leonardo*, has sought deeper ties with India as part of its broader ***Make in India*** initiative aimed at boosting indigenous production and reducing dependence on imports.
4. **Cultural Exchange**: Both nations share a deep cultural heritage, fostering an enduring relationship through people-to-people exchanges. India and Italy promote cultural diplomacy through events, festivals, and academic collaborations that highlight their shared historical legacies in art, architecture, music, and cuisine. The Indian diaspora in Italy, numbering over 200,000, also plays a significant role in strengthening this cultural connection, contributing to Italy's economy and fostering mutual understanding.

THE NORDIC REGION

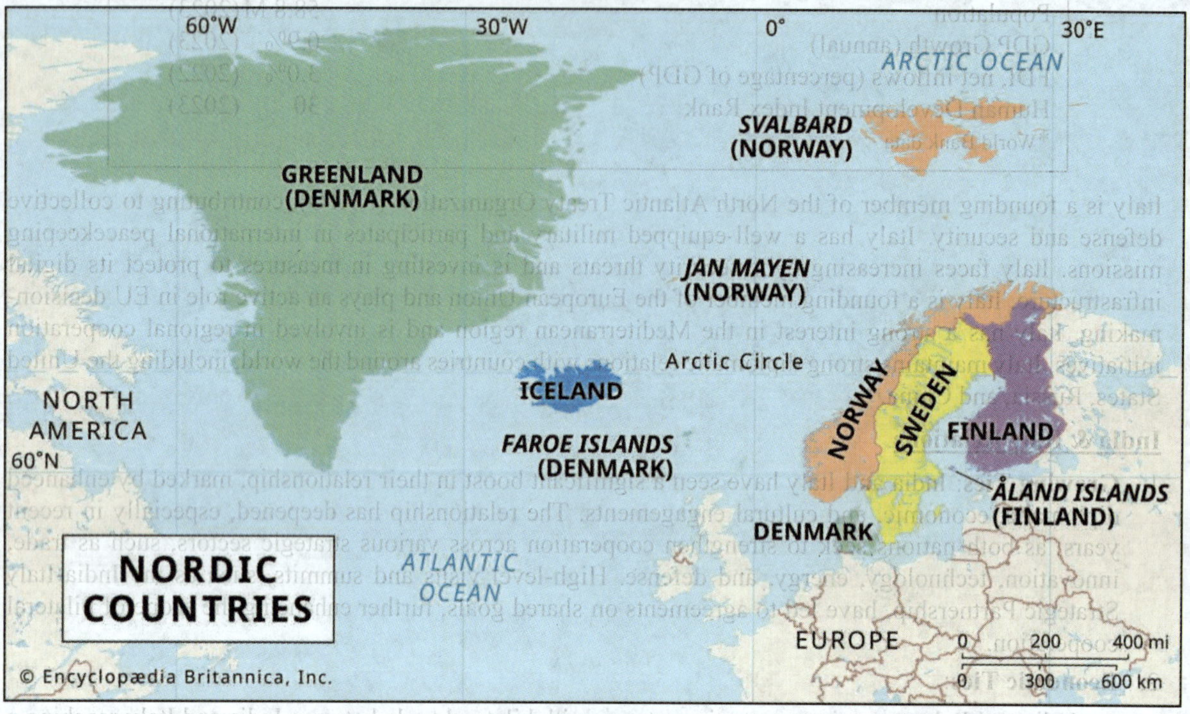

- The Nordic Region consists of **Denmark, Norway, Sweden, Finland, and Iceland**, as well as the **Faroe Islands (Denmark), Greenland (Denmark), and Åland (Finland).** These countries are known for their high quality of life, strong social welfare systems, and deep commitment to democracy, human rights, and sustainable development.
- The Nordic nations are known for their strong welfare states, often referred to as the "**Nordic model**." This model combines a free market economy with a comprehensive welfare system, providing universal healthcare, free education, and a strong social safety net. The region ranks highly in global indices of prosperity, equality, and quality of life.
- The Nordic countries are known for their strong cooperation in international affairs, often working together in global forums. They are members of various international organizations, including the United Nations (UN), the European Union (EU) (except Norway and Iceland), and the Schengen Area. Additionally, they participate in the Nordic Council and the Nordic Council of Ministers, which foster inter-parliamentary and intergovernmental cooperation.
- The nations are leaders in environmental sustainability and green technology. They prioritize renewable energy, environmental protection, and sustainable urban planning. The region is also known for its high levels of innovation, particularly in sectors such as technology, design, and green industries.

The Nordic countries collectively represent a model of social democracy, welfare states, and environmental sustainability, making them influential in global discussions.

COUNTRY	CAPITAL	POPULATION (2023)	HUMAN DEVELOPMENT INDEX (2023-24) RANKING	GDP GROWTH % (Annual), 2023
India	New Delhi	1.39 billion	134	8.9
Denmark	Copenhagen	5.9 million	5	1.9
Sweden	Stockholm	10.5 million	5	(-)0.2
Norway	Oslo	5.5 million	2	0.5
Finland	Helsinki	5.5 million	12	(-)1.0
Iceland	Reykjavik	393,600	3	4.1

*World Bank data

GEOPOLITICAL SIGNIFICANCE

- **Bridge between East and West:** Situated at the crossroads of Europe and the Arctic, the Nordic countries have historically acted as a bridge between East and West. Finland, in particular, has played a crucial role in maintaining balanced relations with both Russia and the West.
- **Arctic Sovereignty:** With significant portions of their territories within the Arctic Circle, the Nordic nations are key players in Arctic governance and resource management. Their cooperation in this region is vital for ensuring stability and sustainable development.
- **European Integration:** All Nordic countries, except Iceland, are members of the European Union, contributing to the region's economic and political integration.
- **Military Neutrality:** While Finland and Sweden recently joined NATO, traditional Nordic neutrality has shaped their foreign policies for decades. This neutrality has allowed them to act as mediators and facilitators in international conflicts.
- **Global Actors:** Despite their relatively small size, the Nordic nations have established themselves as global actors, with influence in areas such as climate change, human rights, and development aid.

SCANDINAVIA or NORDIC?

FEATURE	SCANDINAVIAN COUNTRIES	NORDIC COUNTRIES
Countries included	Consists of Denmark, Norway, and Sweden.	Encompass the Scandinavian nations (Denmark, Norway & Sweden) along with Finland, and Iceland.
Geographical basis	Based on geographical location - the Scandinavian Peninsula.	A broader term based on cultural, historical, and linguistic similarities.
Language	North Germanic languages	Primarily Nordic languages (Finnish is Finnic)
Landmass	Primarily peninsular	Includes both peninsular and island nations.

DENMARK

Denmark, the most southerly of the Nordic countries, is a small, densely populated country, made up of a large archipelago skirted by lovely beaches. Known for its ***hygge*** (pronounced 'hue-gah') lifestyle, Denmark boasts a strong emphasis on work-life balance, social equality, and environmental sustainability. Copenhagen, its capital, is a modern metropolis renowned for its architecture, culture, and harbour.

Although Denmark may be a small European nation, it stans out on the international stage as a 'global powerhouse'. Known for its progressive policies and strong commitment to international cooperation, Denmark is a vocal advocate for human rights, climate action, and global development. As a founding member of the European Union and NATO, Denmark plays a crucial role in European security and integration. Its strong economy and emphasis on innovation have positioned it as a global leader in various sectors, from renewable energy to life sciences.

NORWAY

For many, Norway is synonymous with oil and mountains. Its dramatic, beautiful scenery stretches from the beaches and cliffs in the south through the mountainous areas in the middle to the midnight sun at the North Cape. Norway is a kingdom with a strong maritime tradition and a significant focus on sustainable development. Its fjords, glaciers, and northern lights are world-renowned, attracting tourists from around the globe.

Norway, rich in natural resources, particularly oil and gas, has solidified its position as a significant global actor. The country has leveraged its wealth to foster a robust welfare state and actively engage in international development and humanitarian aid. While maintaining a neutral stance on many global conflicts, Norway has been a vocal advocate for peace and disarmament. Its membership in NATO and the Nordic Council has shaped its foreign policy, emphasizing cooperation and stability in the region and beyond.

SWEDEN

The largest country in the Nordic Region is also the one with the biggest population. For many, Sweden is synonymous with the production of high-quality cars, iron, and steel. However, Sweden is also a pioneer in sustainable living and renewable energy. Its expansive forests, pristine lakes, and vibrant cities offer a high quality of life for its citizens.

Sweden has a long-standing tradition of neutrality and humanitarianism. Its foreign policy is characterized by a strong commitment to multilateralism and international law. As a member of the European Union, Sweden actively participates in European integration while maintaining a distinct Nordic identity. The country is a leading donor of development aid and has been at the forefront of global efforts to address climate change. Sweden's reputation for innovation and social progress has solidified its position as a respected global actor.

> **NOTE**
>
> **Sweden** is the Nordic nation that most recently joined NATO. It officially became a member in March 2024.

FINLAND

Lakes and forests characterize the expansive Finnish landscape. Finland is also renowned for mobile phones, design, and Moomins. A strong sense of national identity and a deep connection to nature define Finnish culture. Known for its excellent education system and high-tech industries, Finland is a leading Nordic country in innovation and technology.

Finland's geographical location has shaped its foreign policy, positioning it as a bridge between Eastern and Western Europe. Historically neutral, Finland has maintained strong relations with both Russia and the West. The country has actively participated in European and Nordic cooperation while also fostering ties with its Eastern neighbours. Known for its expertise in technology and education, Finland has emerged as a global leader in innovation and sustainable development.

ICELAND

Iceland, the volcanic island in the north Atlantic, is famous for its hot springs and dramatic scenery. This sparsely populated country offers a unique blend of natural wonders, including glaciers, volcanoes, and geysers. Iceland has a strong emphasis on renewable energy, particularly geothermal and hydropower. Its vibrant cultural scene and literary heritage have gained international recognition.

Despite its small size, Iceland has made a significant impact on the global stage. The country has been at the forefront of environmental protection, with a strong commitment to renewable energy and sustainable development. Iceland's active participation in international forums, such as the United Nations and the Nordic Council, has allowed it to contribute to global governance. While maintaining a neutral stance on defense, Iceland is a strong supporter of NATO and transatlantic cooperation.

The **NORDIC COUNCIL** is the official body for formal inter-parliamentary cooperation among the Nordic countries. Established in 1952, it brings together representatives from all the regions of the Nordic (including the islands). The Council works to promote cooperation in various areas, including:	**Economy:** Trade, investment, and sustainable development.
	Environment: Climate change, biodiversity, & natural resources
	Culture: Language, literature, and the arts.
	Social affairs: Education, health, and social welfare.
	Justice and home affairs: Police cooperation and judicial matters

INDIA AND THE NORDIC NATIONS

India-Denmark

- India-Denmark relations have witnessed a steady growth in recent years. The two countries share a strong commitment to multilateralism and global governance. Their relationship has been strengthened through various high-level visits and dialogues.
- In recent years, the two countries have focused on expanding cooperation in sectors like renewable energy, urban development, and digitalization.
- The economic relationship between India and Denmark is robust, with trade focusing on pharmaceuticals, machinery, textiles, and food products. Both nations are keen on expanding trade, particularly in the green energy sector. Denmark is a leader in wind energy, and India has benefited from Danish expertise and investment in this area.
- A significant milestone was the signing of the **Migration and Mobility Partnership Agreement** in February 2024. This agreement aims to facilitate student and professional exchanges between the two countries.
- Denmark, a global leader in renewable energy, continues to be a key partner for India in this sector. Key areas of collaboration include green technologies, water management, and smart cities. The **'Green Strategic Partnership'** established in 2020 underlines their commitment to addressing global challenges like climate change. The two countries also cooperate in areas of maritime security and sustainable development. India had also agreed to join the **International Centre for Anti-Microbial Resistance (ICARS)** as mission partner.
- Cultural exchanges, particularly in the fields of tourism, education and arts, have contributed to strengthening bilateral ties. Indian culture, particularly cuisine and festivals, is appreciated in Denmark.

India-Norway

- India and Norway share a long-standing relationship built on mutual respect and cooperation. The two countries have frequent diplomatic engagements and share common views on multilateralism.

- As India becomes an increasingly interested observer in the Arctic region, cooperation with Norway, a key Arctic nation, has gained importance. Both countries have shown interest in collaborating on sustainable fisheries and aquaculture.
- While specific large-scale trade deals might not have been concluded, there has been a steady growth in bilateral trade and investment.
- Trade between India and Norway includes petroleum products, seafood, and IT services. Norway's sovereign wealth fund has invested significantly in India, indicating strong economic ties.
- Renewable energy, particularly offshore wind, is a key area of interest. Norway is a significant investor in India's energy sector, particularly in offshore oil and gas exploration.
- The two countries collaborate on issues of climate change, ocean governance, and sustainable development. Cooperation extends to maritime affairs, where both countries are exploring sustainable use of ocean resources. They also collaborate on health, particularly in combating non-communicable diseases and promoting public health.
- Cultural exchanges, including academic exchanges and research collaborations, have further strengthened the bilateral relationship. Norway has a small but growing Indian community, contributing to cultural diversity.

India-Sweden

- India and Sweden share a strong historic relationship, with the first diplomatic ties being established in 1949. India and Sweden enjoy strong relations based on shared democratic values and a commitment to multilateralism. They have a long-standing and dynamic relationship, highlighted by cooperation in technology, innovation, and sustainability. High-level visits and strategic dialogues have deepened this partnership.
- Trade relations are robust, with major Swedish companies operating in India, and vice versa. Key sectors include automotive, telecommunications, and pharmaceuticals. Sweden is a major investor in India, with a focus on clean technology, telecommunications, and automotive sectors.
- Significant cooperation exists in areas like innovation, research and development, and start-ups. Given Sweden's reputation as a global innovation hub, collaboration in areas like IT, telecommunications, and cleantech has been a priority.
- The **'Sweden-India Innovation Partnership'** aims to boost collaboration in these fields. Environmental sustainability and health are other critical areas of mutual interest.
- India and Sweden have cultivated a robust defense partnership over the years. A foundational **Memorandum of Understanding (MoU) on Defense Cooperation** was inked in 2009, fostering regular dialogue through the Joint Working Group. The relationship deepened significantly with the **General Security Agreement** of 2019, enabling seamless sharing of classified information.
- The **India-Sweden Virtual Summit** of March 2021 marked a pivotal moment, underscoring defense and security as pillars of the bilateral relationship. Prime Minister Modi extended an open invitation to Swedish defense companies to leverage India's burgeoning defense manufacturing ecosystem, particularly through the **Make in India** initiative and dedicated **defense production corridors** in Tamil Nadu and Uttar Pradesh. Defense Minister Rajnath Singh further emphasized this call to action, urging Swedish defense majors to establish manufacturing footprints within India.
- Cultural exchanges, including the presence of a large Indian diaspora in Sweden, have contributed to strengthening the bilateral relationship. Cultural exchange programs, film festivals, yoga, cuisine and academic partnerships have further strengthened the ties between India and Sweden.

India-Finland

- India and Finland share a growing partnership based on mutual interests in technology, innovation, and sustainable development. Regular business delegations and trade fairs have been organized to foster economic cooperation between the two countries.
- Given Finland's geographical location, there has been increasing interest in Arctic cooperation between the two countries.

- Trade between India and Finland has grown steadily, with key exports including electronics, machinery, and pharmaceuticals. Finland's expertise in information technology, and clean energy is highly valued in India.
- Both nations collaborate extensively in education, particularly in research and higher education. They also work together on clean technologies and environmental sustainability.
- Finland is a significant investor in India's IT and telecommunications sector. The two countries collaborate in areas of education, healthcare, and clean energy.
- Cultural exchanges, including academic and artistic collaborations, have contributed to strengthening the bilateral relationship. Finnish literature, music, and design have found an audience in India, while Indian festivals and traditions are celebrated by the Indian community in Finland.

India-Iceland

- India and Iceland share a growing interest in cooperation in areas of renewable energy, fisheries, and climate change. While the bilateral relationship is relatively young, there is potential for growth in trade, investment, and tourism.
- Trade relations are modest but growing, with a focus on fisheries, pharmaceuticals, and IT services. Iceland is interested in exploring renewable energy cooperation, particularly geothermal energy, where it has considerable expertise.
- A significant development took place in March 2024 when India signed a **Trade and Economic Partnership Agreement (TEPA)** with the **EFTA** (discussed under the European Union section), which includes Iceland. This agreement is expected to boost trade and investment between the two countries.
- India and Iceland collaborate in areas such as geothermal energy, Arctic research, and oceanic studies. Both countries share a strong interest in promoting sustainable and green technologies.
- Cultural exchanges are limited but growing, with efforts to promote tourism and cultural awareness. Academic and scientific collaborations, can contribute to strengthening the bilateral ties.

In May 2022, the Indian Prime Minister attended the **second India-Nordic Summit** in Copenhagen, Denmark, following the inaugural summit in Stockholm in 2018. The leaders discussed the importance of global cooperation to tackle critical issues such as climate change, the COVID-19 pandemic, biodiversity loss, and food and energy security. The Nordic nations reiterated their support for India's bid to become a permanent member of a reformed and expanded United Nations Security Council. The Indian Prime Minister emphasized India's Arctic Policy as a means to enhance collaboration with the Nordic countries in the Arctic. He also encouraged Nordic companies to invest in India's blue economy, particularly in the **Sagarmala Project**.

Overall, India's relations with the Nordic nations have gained significant momentum in recent years, driven by shared interests in areas such as trade, investment, technology, and sustainable development. These countries have emerged as important partners for India's economic and social development.

THE BALTICS

Source: Britannica

ESTONIA (Tallin)

LATVIA (Riga)

LITHUANIA (Vilius)

- The Baltic states comprise Estonia, Latvia, and Lithuania. Located in Northeastern Europe on the coast of the Baltic Sea, they share a common history marked by periods of foreign domination, culminating in Soviet occupation.
- All three Baltic states endured prolonged periods of Soviet occupation, fostering a strong sense of national identity and resilience. The Baltic Way demonstrations in 1989 marked a turning point, leading to independence for all three countries.
- Following independence, the Baltic states underwent swift economic transitions, embracing market economies and European integration. All three countries are members of the EU and NATO, aligning themselves closely with Western institutions.

GEOPOLITICAL SIGNIFICANCE

- **Bridge between East and West:** The Baltic states serve as a bridge between the European Union and Russia, making them important geopolitical players.
- **NATO's Eastern Flank:** As NATO's easternmost members, they play a crucial role in European security.
- **Vulnerability to Russian Influence:** Due to their geographical location and historical ties, the Baltic states remain vigilant about potential Russian influence.

- **Challenges** - Key challenges for the Baltic States include addressing demographic issues like population decline and aging, ensuring energy independence, and managing relations with Russia. Economic disparities within the region and the need for further technological advancement also present ongoing challenges.
- **Regional Cooperation** - Several regional organizations and initiatives aim to promote cooperation and stability in the Baltic region, including:
  (i) The Council of the Baltic Sea States (CBSS): Focuses on regional cooperation in areas like economic development, environmental protection, and security.

(ii) The Baltic Assembly: An inter-parliamentary organization for promoting cooperation among the Baltic States.

(iii)The Baltic Sea States Subregional Co-operation (BSSSC): Involves local and regional authorities around the Baltic Sea.

INDIA AND THE BALTICS

India has been developing friendly and cooperative relations with the three Baltic nations and the cooperation has majorly been focused around economy and cultural exchanges. The Baltic states are strategically located between Western Europe and Russia. Their proximity to the Baltic Sea and their position as a gateway to the Nordic region and Central Europe make them important in terms of trade routes and transportation corridors. The region also plays a vital role in energy security, particularly in terms of natural gas and oil transit routes.

- **Multilateral Platforms**: India has been actively engaging with the Baltic nations at various international forums such as the United Nations, Non-Aligned Movement (NAM), and the European Union. India has also supported the inclusion of the Baltic nations in various international organizations such as the World Trade Organization (WTO), the United Nations Security Council, and the Organization for Security and Cooperation in Europe (OSCE).
- **Economic Ties:** While the overall trade volume is relatively modest, there's a growing interest in expanding economic cooperation. Areas of potential growth include information technology, pharmaceuticals, and renewable energy. India had signed bilateral agreements with Estonia, Latvia, and Lithuania to promote economic cooperation and investment. In 2021, the trade volume between India and the Baltic nations was around **$540 million**, with a potential for further growth.
- **Digital Cooperation:** The Baltic states, particularly Estonia, are known for their digital advancements. India, with its growing digital economy, sees opportunities for collaboration in areas like e-governance, cybersecurity, and fintech.
- **Defense and Security:** Given the Baltic states' geopolitical location, India has shown interest in strengthening defense cooperation, including counter-terrorism and maritime security.
- **Cultural Exchange:** India has been promoting cultural ties with the Baltic nations through various initiatives such as the **Indian Council for Cultural Relations (ICCR)** scholarships, cultural events, and festivals. In 2021, the Baltic-Indian Cultural Centre was inaugurated in Estonia, which aims to promote cultural exchange and understanding between the two regions.
-

CHALLENGES - Despite the growing cooperation, certain challenges persist. Geographic distance, relatively small economies of the Baltic states, and competing priorities can sometimes hinder the pace of bilateral relations. However, the potential for growth in areas like digital economy, start-ups, and renewable energy presents significant opportunities for both sides.

THE BALKANS

- The Balkan Peninsula is located in **southeastern Europe** and consists of **Albania, Bosnia and Herzegovina, Bulgaria, Croatia, Greece, Kosovo, Montenegro, North Macedonia, Romania, Serbia, Slovenia** and **westernmost part of Turkey**. The term "Balkans" comes from the Turkish word "*balkan*" which means "mountain".
- The Balkan region has historically been a crucible of **geopolitical complexities**, shaped by a confluence of historical, cultural, religious, and economic factors. The region's history is marked by ethnic, religious, and linguistic divisions, often leading to conflict and instability.
- The Balkans has frequently been a battleground for competing great powers, from the Ottoman Empire to the Cold War superpowers. Path to European Integration: Most Balkan countries have joined the EU, but the process has been uneven, with some countries facing challenges in meeting membership criteria.
- **Russia** maintains significant influence in the region, often competing with Western interests.

- On the security front, the region continues to grapple with issues of organized crime, corruption, and ethnic tensions, impacting security and stability. Economic disparities within and between Balkan countries have further fueled social and political tensions.

GEOPOLITICAL SIGNIFICANCE

- **Gateway to Central Europe:** The Balkans is strategically located at the **crossroads of Europe, Asia, and the Mediterranean,** making it a strategically important location.
- **Resources & Trade:** The region possesses valuable natural resources, including minerals and agricultural products, which have attracted external interest. Its position between the Adriatic, Ionian, and Aegean Seas gives it access to major shipping routes and makes it a key transit point for trade and transportation between different regions.
- **EU and NATO Aspirations:** Several Balkan countries have joined the EU and NATO, aligning the region more closely with Western institutions.
- **Crossroads of Civilizations:** The Balkans have been a meeting point of various cultures, religions, and empires throughout history, leading to a complex ethnic and religious mosaic.**Great Power Competition:** The region has often been a battleground for competing great powers, contributing to instability and conflict.
- **Geopolitical Fault Line:** The Balkans remain a sensitive region with potential for instability due to unresolved issues and the influence of external actors.

As of mid-2024, the Balkans continue to grapple with a complex array of security challenges. While significant progress has been made since the turbulent 1990s, the region remains vulnerable to ethnic tensions, organized crime, and the influence of external powers. On the path to EU and NATO integration, while progress has been made, challenges remain for some countries in meeting the membership criteria of these organizations.

INDIA AND THE BALKANS

- India's interactions with the Balkans have been limited historically, but there have been some notable interactions and developments in recent years. India has shown interest in investing in infrastructure projects in the Balkans, aiming to improve connectivity.
- In terms of political and diplomatic relations, India has maintained good relations with the Balkan countries and has been actively engaged in promoting bilateral ties.
- While the overall trade volume is relatively modest, there is significant potential for growth, especially in IT, pharmaceuticals, and agriculture. India has also been a participant in various regional forums and initiatives in the Balkans, such as the **Southeast European Cooperative Initiative (SECI)** and the **Central European Free Trade Agreement (CEFTA).**
- India has been exploring opportunities to expand trade and investment with the Balkan countries and has signed various bilateral agreements to facilitate this process. For example, in 2018, India signed a **double taxation avoidance agreement (DTAA)** with Serbia, which is expected to boost trade and investment flows between the two countries.
- India has been promoting cultural ties with the Balkans through events such as the annual Balkan-India Cultural Festival, which showcases the rich cultural heritage of both regions. Additionally, there have been efforts to increase educational exchanges between India and the Balkan countries, including scholarships and training programs for students and professionals.

NOTABLE DEVELOPMENTS	
Albania	It is emerging as a potential strategic partner for India in the Balkan region. The country's strategic location, coupled with its growing economy and aspirations for European integration, makes it an attractive proposition for India. Albania's growing economy presents potential for Indian businesses to invest in sectors like infrastructure, IT, and pharmaceuticals.
Bulgaria	Both India and Serbia have focused on enhancing economic cooperation, particularly in the areas of agriculture, pharmaceuticals, and IT.
Croatia	India and Croatia have signed agreements on trade and economic cooperation. They also collaborate in cultural and educational fields.
Romania	The relationship between India and Romania has gained momentum in recent years, with a focus on trade, investment, and cultural exchange. Both countries have signed several agreements to boost trade and investment.
Serbia	The historical ties between India and Serbia, dating back to the Non-Aligned Movement era, have been strengthened in recent years. Serbia has been a consistent supporter of India's candidature for a permanent seat in the UN Security Council. India and Serbia have signed agreements in various fields, including agriculture, tourism, and pharmaceuticals. Both countries have expressed interest in expanding economic and cultural ties.

CHALLENGES - The geographical distance between India and the Balkans can pose challenges in terms of transportation and logistics. Moreover, the relatively smaller economies of the Balkan nations compared to India might limit the scope of trade and investment.

5

EAST & SOUTH-EAST ASIA

JAPAN: LAND OF THE RISING SUN

Japan, an island nation in East Asia, is comprised of a chain of islands extending approximately 1,500 miles (2,400 km) in a northeast-southwest direction across the western North Pacific Ocean. The majority of its land area is occupied by four main islands: ***Hokkaido***, ***Honshu***, ***Shikoku***, and ***Kyushu***, spanning a total of 377,974 square kilometers. Despite being the only country to experience the devastation of nuclear bombs, Japan made significant progress in the aftermath of World War II.

Following a **parliamentary democracy**, **Japan is the only Asian member of G-7**. While Japan is famous as the **world's third-largest economy** after the United States and China, it also has a rich history and culture, and is known for its advancements in technology, science, and engineering.

IMPORTANT DETAILS	
Capital	Tokyo
Monarch	Emperor Naruhito
Prime Minister	Fumio Kishida
Population (2023)	124 M
Human Development Index Rank (2023)	24
GDP Growth (annual % - 2023)	1.9

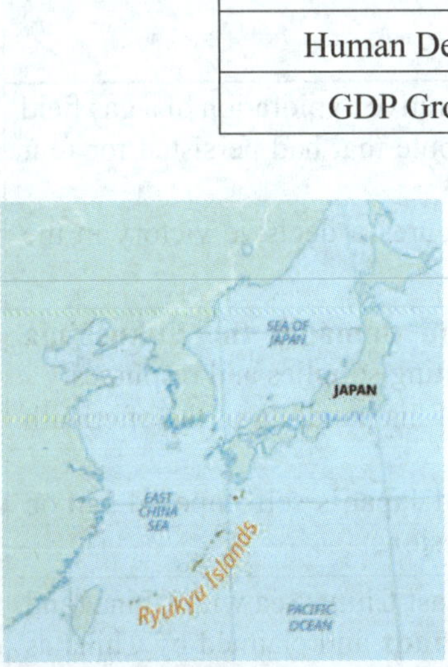

RYUKYU ISLANDS

- **Location**: The Ryukyu Islands are an archipelago that stretches southwest from the southern tip of Japan's main islands to Taiwan, forming a chain in the East China Sea.
- **Significance**: These islands are part of Japan and include Okinawa, the largest and most populous of the islands. The Ryukyu Islands have a unique cultural identity, influenced by both Japanese and Chinese traditions. Historically, the Ryukyu Kingdom was an independent entity before being annexed by Japan in the 19th century. Okinawa, in particular, holds significant strategic military importance due to the presence of U.S. military bases.

HISTORICAL DEVELOPMENTS OF JAPAN - TIMELINE	
1939	Outbreak of **Second World War** in Europe.
1941	Japan launches attack on US Pacific fleet at **Pearl Harbor**, Hawaii.
1942	• Japan occupies nations including Dutch East Indies, Burma, Philippines, Burma and Malaya. • US aircraft carriers defeat the Japanese at the 'Battle of Midway'.
1945	• **US planes drop two atomic bombs on Hiroshima and Nagasaki**. • Emperor Hirohito surrenders and relinquishes divine status. • Japanese forces disbanded and Japan placed under US military government.
1947	• Japan **renounces war and pledges not to maintain forces** for that purpose (Pacifist Constitution). • The new Constitution establishes parliamentary system with universal suffrage. • The Emperor is granted a ceremonial status.
1951	**Japan signs peace treaty with US and other nations.**
1956	**Japan joins the United Nations.**
1994	The anti-LDP coalition collapses and an administration supported by the LDP and Socialists takes control.
1995	The **Great Hanshin earthquake** (Kobe earthquake) of 7.2 Richter magnitude hits central Japan.
2003	• The Government announces decision to install **'purely defensive' US-made missile shield.** • The **Japan Aerospace Exploration Agency (JAXA)** is formed by merging three previously independent organizations.
2006	• **Shinzo Abe becomes the Prime Minister**. • In a first since World War II, the Parliament approves the creation of a full-fledged defence ministry.
2007	• Prime Minister Abe suggests establishing the **Quadrilateral Security Dialogue (Quad)** as an official multilateral discussion involving Japan, Australia, and the United States. • Prime Minister Abe steps down from his position.
2008-09	• Japan and China come to an agreement for the collaborative exploration of a gas field in the East China Sea, resolving a long-standing dispute that had persisted for four years. • The opposition Democratic Party of Japan (DPJ) secures a decisive victory in the general election.
2011	• **An offshore earthquake and subsequent tsunami damages the Fukushima nuclear plant** causing a radiation leak and contaminating supplies and resources. • The PM Naoto Kan steps down following criticism of his handling of the aftermath of the Fukushima nuclear crisis. • December – The government announces relaxation of Japan's self-imposed ban on arms exports, mainly for supporting humanitarian missions.
2012	• Dispute over ownership of a group of islands in the East China Sea with China (and Taiwan) - administered by Japan as the **Senkaku Islands** and claimed by China as the **Diaoyu Islands.**

	• Shinzo Abe elected as Prime Minister and promises a successful economic recovery plan.
2013-14	• Japan approves the relocation of a US military airbase on its southern island of Okinawa. • The cabinet approves a **new national strategy** and increased defence spending. A new security policy paves the way for its military to fight overseas.
2015	**Japan restarts first nuclear reactor at Sendai plant since the Fukushima disaster, under new safety rules.**
2016-19	• After Emperor Akihito indicates his readiness to abdicate, the Parliament passes a bill to allow him to abdicate. • Emperor Akihito abdicates in favour of his son, Crown Prince ***Naruhito***. • November 2019 - The **first India-Japan 2+2 Foreign and Defence Ministerial Meeting** held.
2020	PM Abe steps down citing health concerns and is succeeded by chief cabinet secretary Yoshihide Suga.
2021	Fumio Kishida becomes the Prime Minister.

POLITICS & ADMINISTRATION

- Japan is a **constitutional monarchy** with a **parliamentary government**. The **Emperor** serves as the ceremonial head of state, while the Prime Minister is the head of government and holds executive authority.
- The **National Diet** is the national legislature of Japan. It is composed of a lower house, called the House of Representatives, and an upper house, the House of Councillors.
- Administratively, Japan is divided into 47 prefectures, each with its own local government headed by an elected governor. These prefectures are further subdivided into municipalities.
- Japan's judiciary is independent and includes a Supreme Court and lower courts. The legal system is based on civil law, with influences from European legal traditions.
- The central government exercises significant influence over local governments, although decentralization reforms have granted more autonomy to local entities.
- Japan's administrative structure supports a highly organized and efficient government, known for its stable political environment and robust bureaucracy.

ECONOMY & TRADE

- Based on the real GDP forecast, the Japanese economy ranks third globally (April 2023) at an estimate of **$5.05 trillion**. According to official OECD figures, Japan's real GDP growth is projected at 1.8% in 2023 and 0.9% in 2024.
- In the 1960s, 70s, and 80s, Japan experienced significant economic growth, but its performance during the 1990s was less remarkable. The rapid growth during that period was largely attributed to the remarkable **expansion of industrial production and the establishment of a large domestic market**, supported by a proactive export trade policy. The emphasis on trade was driven by Japan's limited availability of natural resources, particularly fossil fuels and various minerals, necessary to sustain its industrial economy.
- Japan has built a very **diverse industrial and service sector**, and it is one of the world's leading manufacturers of **automobiles, steel,** and **high-technology manufactured goods** (particularly consumer electronics).
- Japan has been actively engaged in negotiating and implementing **free trade agreements (FTAs)** to expand its market access and boost economic growth. Some notable treaties include–

- <u>Comprehensive and Progressive Agreement for Trans-Pacific Partnership (CPTPP)</u> - A successor to the TPP, the CPTPP covers a wider range of issues than traditional trade agreements, including digital trade, labor, and environmental protection. Japan is a key member and has been actively promoting the agreement as a model for high-standard trade liberalization. (Discussed in detail later)
- <u>Regional Comprehensive Economic Partnership (RCEP)</u> - RCEP is a massive free trade agreement involving 15 countries in the Asia-Pacific region. It is the world's largest free trade agreement in terms of GDP, creating new opportunities for Japanese businesses. (Discussed in detail later)
- <u>Japan-EU Economic Partnership Agreement (EPA)</u>: A comprehensive trade agreement covering goods, services, investment, and other areas.
- <u>Japan-US Trade Agreement</u>: This bilateral agreement aims to deepen economic ties and address trade imbalances.

- Over the past decade, Japan has been doing its best to grow its economy. However, the COVID-19 pandemic hit the economy hard, provoking a marked downturn. The Japan's economy has been showing signs of recovery.

However, Japan still faces several economic challenges, including an **aging population**, a **shrinking workforce**, and **high levels of government debt**. To address these issues, the government has been implementing a range of policies aimed at boosting economic growth, such as increasing investment in infrastructure and promoting innovation and entrepreneurship.

SCIENCE AND TECHNOLOGY

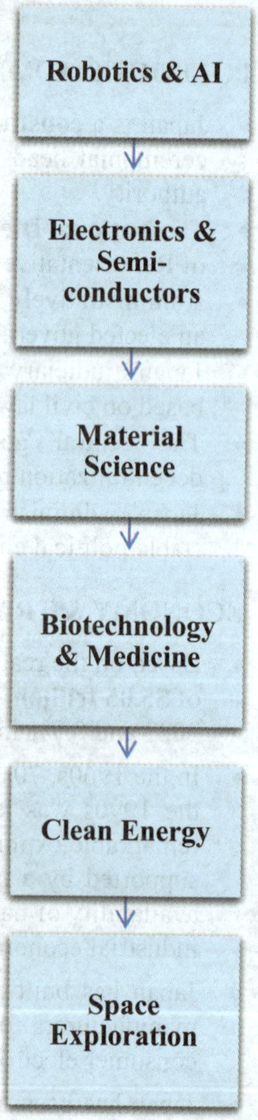

- Japan is known for its advancements in science and technology and has made significant progress in the field. Japan is a leader in **robotics** including developing the first industrial robot in the 1960s. Presently, advancements in artificial intelligence (AI) are being integrated into various sectors, from healthcare to transportation.
- In recent years, Japan has been focusing on developing **humanoid robots** for various applications, including elderly care, disaster response, and entertainment.
- Japan has a strong **electronics industry**, and many well-known brands, including Sony, Panasonic, and Toshiba, are based in Japan. Moreover, Japan has been a pioneer in **semiconductor technology**, and continues to be a major player in the global electronics industry.
- The country has made significant contributions to **materials science**, including the development of high-strength steel and carbon fiber composites. Over the past few years, Japan has been developing new materials for applications like energy storage and conversion.
- Japan has a strong **biotechnology industry** and advancements in biotech and **medical research** have led to breakthroughs in areas like regenerative medicine and drug discovery. The domestic companies have developed several drugs, including Tamiflu, a medication used to treat influenza.
- With a focus on renewable energy sources, Japan is investing heavily in technologies such as solar, wind, and hydrogen power.
- It has made significant contributions to **space technology**, including launching several satellites and spacecraft, such as the **Hayabusa probe**, which successfully landed on an asteroid and returned to Earth with samples.
- Additionally, Japan has developed its own positioning system called the **Quasi-Zenith Satellite System (QZSS)**. QZSS is a satellite-based augmentation system that provides positioning, navigation, and timing services to users in Japan and the surrounding region. It works in conjunction with other global navigation satellite systems (GNSS) such as the Global Positioning System (GPS) to enhance positioning accuracy and reliability.

FOREIGN POLICY & DIPLOMACY

- Japan is considered a major player in global affairs and boasts of a considerably well-off international standing. It is a member of the **United Nations, the G7, the G20,** and **the Asia-Pacific Economic Cooperation (APEC).**
- The **Abe Doctrine** has played a significant role in Japanese diplomatic policy. It refers to the foreign and security policy framework implemented by former Japanese Prime Minister Shinzo Abe during his tenure. It marked a significant departure from Japan's post-World War II pacifist stance.

KEY ELEMENTS OF THE ABE DOCTRINE:	**Proactive pacifism:** A shift from Japan's traditional pacifist stance to a more assertive role in international affairs while maintaining its commitment to peace.
	Strengthening the US-Japan alliance: Reinforcing the bilateral security alliance as the cornerstone of Japanese security.
	Expanding Japan's security role: Increasing Japan's military capabilities and expanding its role in regional security, including through participation in peacekeeping operations.
	Economic diplomacy: Utilizing economic power to enhance Japan's global influence.
	Addressing historical issues: Making efforts to improve relations with neighboring countries, particularly South Korea and China.

- <u>**Free and Open Indo Pacific Concept**</u> – It is a strategic vision championed by Japan to promote peace, stability, and prosperity in the Indo-Pacific region. Japan has been a leading proponent of the FOIP, aiming to counter China's growing influence and promote a rules-based order in the region. An important grouping considering this is the **QUAD** or the **Quadrilateral Security Dialogue** (This part has been discussed in detail in the chapter – 'Global Waters & Maritime Outlook').

The **Quadrilateral Security Dialogue (QUAD)** is a strategic forum comprising four nations: the United States, India, Japan, and Australia. It emerged in the early 2000s as an informal dialogue focused on common interests in the Indo-Pacific region. The group aims to promote a free, open, and inclusive Indo-Pacific, ensuring stability, security, and adherence to international law, particularly in light of China's growing influence in the region. Former Japanese Prime Minister Shinzo Abe was a key architect in the revival and strengthening of the QUAD framework. Abe first proposed the idea of the QUAD during his first term as Prime Minister in 2007. He envisioned a partnership among democratic nations in the Indo-Pacific to promote peace and stability.

- **Territorial Disputes** - Japan is involved in several territorial disputes with neighbouring countries, complicating its diplomatic relations. The two important ones include the following –

SENKAKU ISLANDS (Diaoyu Islands)

- Claimed by Japan**, China, & Taiwan**.
- Located in the East China Sea, the islands are strategically important due to potential oil and gas reserves and control over vital shipping lanes.
- Frequent maritime confrontations between China and Japan over the islands have heightened tensions.

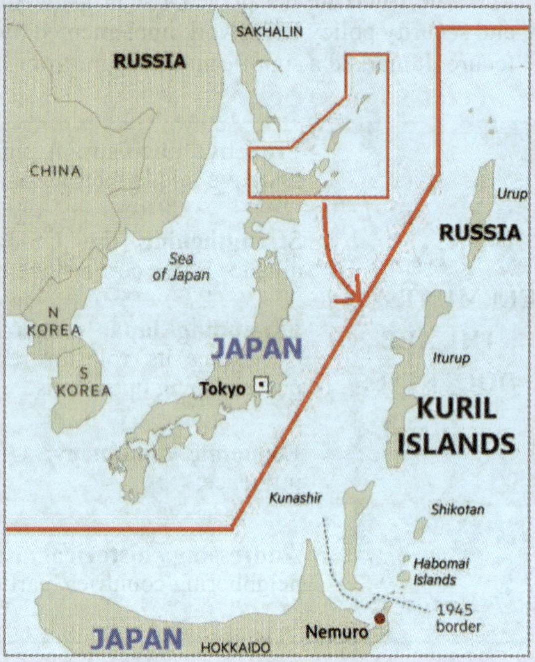

NORTHERN TERRITORIES (Kuril Islands)

- Disputed with **Russia**.
- Japan claims sovereignty over four islands in the southern Kuril chain, occupied by Russia since the end of World War II.
- The issue has prevented the signing of a formal peace treaty between the two countries.

- Japan has maintained a steadfast stance on **North Korea's nuclear and missile programs**, working closely with the US and other partners to address the issue.
- Japan has also been actively involved in international **peacekeeping efforts** and has contributed troops to UN missions.
- Efforts to **improve relations with South Korea** have been a priority for Japan, although challenges persist. The relationship between Japan and South Korea has been marked by historical tensions stemming from Japan's colonial rule over the Korean Peninsula from 1910 to 1945.

SECURITY & DEFENCE

TIMELINE OF MILITARY & DEFENCE DEVLOPMENTS IN JAPAN	
1947	Japan's defense and security policy gets shaped by its **pacifist Constitution**, particularly **Article 9**, which **'renounces war and prohibits maintaining armed forces for warfare'**.
1951	The **Treaty of Mutual Cooperation and Security** was signed between Japan and the United States, whereby the US guaranteed Japan's security in exchange for maintaining American bases on Japanese soil.

1952	National Police Reserve renamed to **National Safety Force** → The maintenance of armed forces was challenged and the Supreme Court ruled that "**Article 9 does not deny the right to self-defense** inherent in our nation as a sovereign power."
1954	The National Safety Force was reconstituted as the **Self-Defense Forces (SDF)**, its current designation. Article 9 has been interpreted to permit Japan to possess weapons considered necessary for self-defense at a minimal level. While **Japan can maintain "defensive" weapons, it is restricted from acquiring "offensive" weapons**, such as intercontinental ballistic missiles (ICBMs) and strategic bombers.
2007	In a major shift, under the direction of then-Prime Minister Shinzo Abe, the Japanese Defense Agency is turned into a ministry and renamed the Japanese **Ministry of Defense**.
2014	The Japanese Cabinet approved a decision to develop comprehensive security legislation aimed at ensuring the country's survival and protecting its citizens. Citing "complex and significant national security challenges," the legislation permits Japan to exercise collective self-defense under specific circumstances.

ARTICLE 9 OF THE JAPANESE CONSTITUTION

"Article 9. Aspiring sincerely to an international peace based on justice and order, the Japanese people forever renounce war as a sovereign right of the nation and the threat or use of force as means of settling international disputes.

In order to accomplish the aim of the preceding paragraph, land, sea, and air forces, as well as other war potential, will never be maintained. The right of belligerency of the state will not be recognized."

- The post-World War II **Treaty of Mutual Cooperation and Security** that was signed between Japan and the United States remains a cornerstone of Japan's defense, providing a nuclear umbrella and ensuring regional stability. This cornerstone of Japanese security has been further solidified through joint military exercises, intelligence sharing, and coordinated diplomatic efforts.
- Recent security challenges, such as North Korea's missile tests and China's maritime assertiveness (especially in the Indo-Pacific region), have led Japan to strengthen its defense capabilities, including increased defense spending and constitutional reinterpretations to allow **collective self-defense**.
- Additionally, Japan emphasizes **non-traditional security issues**, like cybersecurity and disaster response. Balancing its pacifist principles with regional security demands, Japan continues to adapt its defense posture to address evolving threats while engaging in diplomacy to maintain peace and stability in the Asia-Pacific region.
- Former Japanese Prime Minister Shinzo Abe was a strong proponent of the **"Free and Open Indo-Pacific" (FOIP)** vision. The FOIP concept, championed by Japan and strongly supported by other QUAD members, reflects a vision for a stable, inclusive, and rules-based regional order.

The key strategic interests Japan has in FOIP are as follows -

Security & Stability: Promotes peaceful dispute resolution and adherence to international law, ensuring regional security.

Maritime Security: Ensures freedom of navigation and protects critical trade routes vital for Japan's economy.

Economic Prosperity: Enhances trade, investment, and infrastructure development, ensuring stable supply chains and fair economic practices.

Partnerships & Alliances: Strengthens ties with like-minded countries for collective defense and strategic cooperation.

Democratic Values & Human Rights: Promotes democracy, human rights, & the rule of law in the Indo-Pacific.

Countering Regional Coercion: Counters coercive actions & regional dominance, particularly from assertive actors.

Humanitarian Assistance and Disaster Relief (HADR): Supports humanitarian aid and disaster relief, enhancing regional stability and Japan's soft power.

DIASPORA AND CULTURE

- Japan's society is often characterized by a strong sense of **collectivism, social harmony, and respect for traditions and cultural norms.** The society lays emphasis on teamwork, consensus-building, and group decision-making.
- The society overall places high value on social harmony and promotes harmony while avoiding conflict. Japan has a rich cultural heritage, and traditions and cultural norms are highly valued and respected. This is reflected in various aspects of Japanese society, including language, arts, religion, and cuisine.
- Japan has been particularly successful in the area of **cultural export**, leveraging its unique cultural heritage to enhance its global image and economic interests. Cultural export refers to the dissemination of a nation's cultural products and values to other countries. This includes – anime & manga, video games, fashion & design, cuisine and technology.
- A recent issue has been Japan's **declining population growth**. The population growth (annual %) as of 2023 was (-)0.5 (World Bank data).

DEMOGRAPHIC DECLINE

Japan has one of the world's oldest populations! Japan's birth rate has been declining for many years, and this trend is expected to continue. This means that the country's population is expected to continue aging. This could result in issues related to healthcare, pensions, and social welfare, including a shortage of a young-healthy workforce and mounting healthcare costs for the elderly. The Japanese government has implemented various policies to address the aging population issue, including initiatives to encourage families to have more children and to increase immigration.

INDIAN-JAPAN CONNECT

India and Japan share a strong relationship based on cultural, economic, and strategic ties. The diplomatic relations between the two countries were established in **1952**, and since then, the two nations have been cooperating in various areas such as technology, trade, defense, and security. In recent years, the relationship between India and Japan has grown stronger.

Economy and Infrastructure

- The two countries have set a target of increasing this to $50 billion by 2025. Both the countries had adopted the **Comprehensive Economic Partnership Agreement (CEPA)** in August **2011**. There has been a trade imbalance as **India's exports to Japan** stood at just **$6.2 billion in FY22**, while its **imports** hit **$14.4 billion**. The trade deficit has prompted Indian officials to review the FTA in order to restore greater trade balance.

- In 2021-22, the total bilateral trade amounted to over US$ 20 billion where India's imports from Japan amounted to over **US$ 14 billion**, while Indian exports to Japan stood at around **US$ 6 billion**. India was the 18th largest trading partner for Japan, and Japan was the 13th largest trading partner for India in 2021.
- Japan has been a major investor in India's economy, particularly in the infrastructure and manufacturing sectors. Japanese companies have invested in a range of sectors in India, including **automobiles, electronics, and renewable energy.** In 2020, Japan's total FDI in India was **$6.14 billion**, making it the third-largest investor in the country.
- In 2017, Japan pledged to invest **$40 billion** in India's **infrastructure projects over the next five years**, including the development of smart cities, high-speed railways, and industrial corridors. The **Mumbai-Ahmedabad High-Speed Rail Project** is a flagship project of India and Japan's collaboration, which involves building a **high-speed railway line** between the cities of Mumbai and Ahmedabad. The project is expected to be completed by **2027** and is being funded by a soft loan from Japan worth **$12 billion.**
- Japan is one of the major partners in the **Delhi-Mumbai Industrial Corridor** project that aims to create a high-tech industrial zone along a 1,500 km long corridor between Delhi and Mumbai. Japan has committed to investing **over $4.5 billion** in various infrastructure projects along the corridor. Japan has expressed interest in partnering with India to develop the **Chennai-Bengaluru Industrial Corridor** and have signed a Memorandum of Understanding (MoU) to explore opportunities for collaboration.
- Japan has been collaborating with India on the development of **smart cities** and have signed an MoU to work together on various aspects of smart city development, including urban planning, transportation, and energy management. Japan has expressed interest in funding the **North-East Connectivity Project**, which is estimated to cost around **$10 billion.** India and Japan had also signed a memorandum of understanding to set up **'India Japan Act East Forum'**.
- Under India's "Act East Policy" and Japan's vision for a "Free and Open Indo-Pacific," the Act East Forum provides a platform for India and Japan to collaborate in the North-Eastern region. The **sixth joint meeting** of the India-Japan Act East Forum (AEF) was held in March 2022 in New Delhi.
- India has also been the largest recipient of Japanese Official Development Assistance (ODA) Loan for the past decades. Delhi Metro is one of the most successful examples of Japanese cooperation through the utilization of ODA.

> The agreement to establish the **Act East Forum** was signed in **2017**. The objectives include the identification of specific projects for the economic modernization of India's North-East region, such as connectivity, developmental infrastructure, industrial linkages, and people-to-people contacts through tourism, culture, and sports-related activities.

Defence and Security

- During Prime Minister Singh's visit to Japan in October 2008, two leaders issued "the Joint Declaration on Security Cooperation between Japan and India". Other frameworks for security dialogue include the **India-Japan 2+2 Dialogue** (Foreign and Defense Ministerial Meeting), annual **Defense Ministerial Dialogue** and **Coast Guard-to-Coast Guard dialogue**. In September 2022, the second "2+2" meeting was held in Tokyo.
- Japan has been working closely with India in the strategic **Andaman and Nicobar Islands**, which are located near the critical sea lanes of the Indian Ocean. The proximity of these islands to the **Malacca Strait** places them in a strategic position with regards to surveillance of the crucial sea lines of communication. Japan has been providing assistance to India to improve maritime security and infrastructure in the A&N islands, as well as to promote sustainable development and tourism.
- India and Japan conduct regular joint military exercises, including the annual **'Dharma Guardian'** exercise, which focuses on counter-terrorism and urban warfare training. India and Japan have been collaborating on **technology development** and **transfer in defense**, including unmanned ground vehicles, robotics, and artificial intelligence. The defense collaborations between India and Japan are expected to grow stronger in the future, given the shared strategic interests and security concerns in the Indo-Pacific region.

Science and Technology

- India and Japan have been collaborating on various **ICT projects**, including the development of 5G technology, artificial intelligence, and robotics. Both countries have also been cooperating on cybersecurity and data protection.
- India and Japan have been collaborating on the establishment of **science and technology parks**, including the India-Japan Technology Park in Rajasthan. These parks aim to promote technology transfer, research and development, and innovation. Both countries have also been collaborating on **space exploration**, including lunar and Mars missions.
- **Life sciences**, **biotechnology**, and **nanotechnology** are the other fields of collaborative efforts between the two nations. Both countries have also been collaborating on joint research projects in agriculture and food processing.
- Both nations have also joined hands on **energy technology**, including renewable energy and energy efficiency. Both countries have also been cooperating on **nuclear energy**, including the development of nuclear power plants.

International Partnership

India's **special strategic and global partnerships with Japan** is a critical aspect in India's post-Cold War strategy. The overlapping interests and shared concerns on global matters has further strengthened the relationship between India and Japan. The cooperation mainly revolves around their **economic complementarity, their ideology to promote an equitable and sustainable growth for all, denuclearization and issues regarding the rise of China** and its expanding footprint in the region.

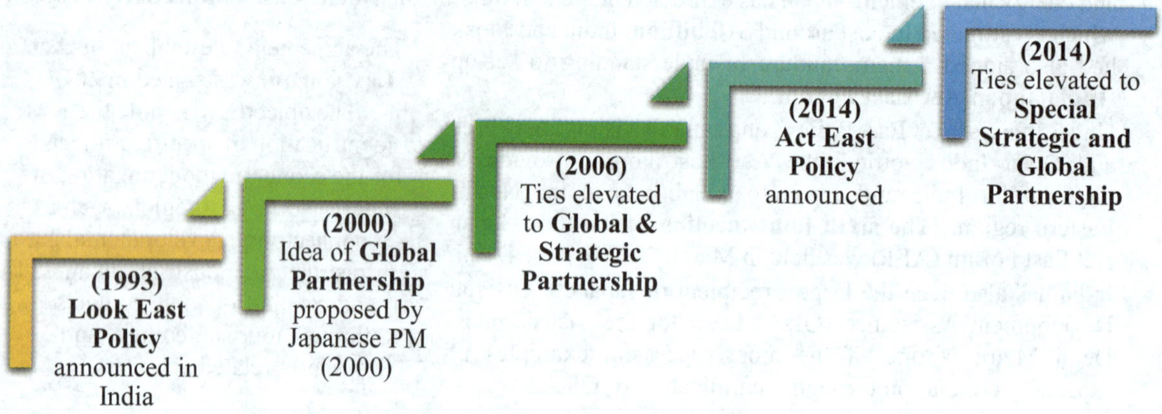

The past decades have witnessed the strengthening of India-Japan partnerships on various levels, including **bilateral (India–Japan), trilateral (India–Japan–United States) and quadrilateral (India–Japan–United States–Australia).** In addition, Japan has expressed support for India's bid for a **permanent seat on the UN Security Council.**

Culture and Population

- The friendship between India and Japan has a long history rooted in **spiritual affinity** and **strong cultural** and **civilization ties** dating back to the visit of Indian monk **Bodhisena** in 752 AD.
- In contemporary times, prominent Indians associated with Japan were Swami Vivekananda, Nobel laureate Rabindranath Tagore, entrepreneur JRD Tata and freedom fighter Netaji Subhash Chandra Bose. As of June 2022, over 40,000 Indian nationals have been residing in Japan.
- The year **2012** commemorated the **60th Anniversary of the establishment of diplomatic relations between Japan and India**. During Prime Minister Modi's visit to Japan in November 2016, both leaders declared 2017 as the Year of Japan-India Friendly Exchanges, aiming to further strengthen people-to-people interactions between the two countries. Additionally, 2017 marked the 60th anniversary since the Cultural Agreement between Japan and India was enacted in 1957.

- Japan has designated 2022 as the "**Japan-Southwest Asia Exchange Year,**" with the objective of elevating Japan's relations with the countries of Southwest Asia to new levels of cooperation and engagement.

COUNTERING CHINA'S ASSERTIVENESS

Japan has a **boundary dispute** with China over **Senkaku Island** in East China Sea. In November 2013, China suddenly announced the creation of an Air Defence Identification Zone (ADIZ) over the Senkaku/Diayou islands in East China Sea. India has been at the receiving end of China's attitude since Independence particularly in **Ladakh** and **Arunachal Pradesh**. Therefore, synergy has developed between the two nations against the rise of China in claiming territories. India and Japan share concerns about **China's assertiveness in the South China Sea** and its growing military presence in the Indo-Pacific region. Both countries have been calling for a rules-based order in the region and have emphasized the importance of freedom of navigation and overflight.

The Quadrilateral Security Dialogue, or **Quad** aims to promote a free, open, and inclusive Indo-Pacific region. It has been seen as a way to enhance security and stability in the region, and India and Japan have been active participants in this forum. India and Japan have also been working together to promote regional connectivity and infrastructure development as an alternative to China's Belt and Road Initiative (BRI). The two countries have been collaborating on several infrastructure projects, including the **Asia-Africa Growth Corridor**, which aims to promote economic cooperation and connectivity between Asia and Africa.

ASIA-AFRICA GROWTH CORRIDOR (AAGC)

It is a joint initiative between **India** and **Japan**, aimed at promoting economic cooperation and connectivity between Asia and Africa. The initiative was first announced during the visit of Japanese Prime Minister Shinzo Abe to India in 2016, and it was formally launched in **2017**. The AAGC has three pillars of cooperation:

(1) Infrastructure and Industrial Development
(2) Quality Growth and Development
(3) People-to-People Partnership

OPPORTUNITIES AHEAD

The future prospects of India-Japan relations look very promising, given the growing strategic partnership between the two countries and the shared values and interests they have in common. India and Japan are likely to deepen their economic cooperation, particularly in the areas of trade, investment, and infrastructure development. Additionally, defence and security cooperation has also been on the rise while collaborations in technology and innovation have been ever-increasing.

Going ahead, India can undertake further economic reforms to create a more business-friendly environment, which can attract more Japanese investment and businesses. India can deepen its defense cooperation with Japan by increasing joint exercises, sharing intelligence, and collaborating on defense equipment procurement.

While such steps are being undertaken to enhance cooperation, it must be understood that the partnership between India and Japan should be based on mutual complementarities with the aim of ensuring security and stability in the region, as well as inclusive development for the people of both countries. Stepping into the future, the India-Japan strategic and global partnership is set to have a decisive impact on the Asian balance of power.

SOUTH KOREA

CULTURAL POWERHOUSE AND TECH GIANT

South Korea, officially known as the **Republic of Korea**, is a country located in East Asia. It shares a land border with North Korea to the north and is surrounded by the Sea of Japan and the Yellow Sea. South Korea has a highly developed and globally integrated economy, with a focus on technology and innovation. The country is a major exporter of electronics, automobiles, and other manufactured goods, and has a large service sector. South Korea is also known for its advanced infrastructure, including high-speed internet and transportation systems.

The **38th PARALLEL** is a line of latitude that roughly divides the Korean Peninsula into North Korea and South Korea. It was established at the end of World War II when the United States and the Soviet Union agreed to divide Korea into occupation zones. A heavily fortified buffer zone separates the two Koreas along the 38th parallel.

POLITY & ECONOMY

South Korea has a democratic government, with a president as the head of state and a National Assembly as the legislative body. The country has a well-trained and modern military, with a focus on defending against potential threats from North Korea. South Korea is an active participant in regional and global diplomacy, with a focus on promoting peace and security on the Korean peninsula and in the Asia-Pacific region. The country is a member of the United Nations, the G20, and the World Trade Organization, among other international organizations.

IMPORTANT DETAILS	
Capital	Seoul
President	Yoon Suk Yeol
Prime Minister	Han Duck-soo
Population (2023)	51.7 million
Human Development Index Rank (2023)	19
GDP Growth (annual % - 2023)	1.4

- South Korea is a well-developed mixed economy and ranks as the fourth largest economy in Asia, with a **per capita income surpassing $33,000**.
- Despite experiencing the impact of the Great Recession, the country has maintained its status as one of the fastest growing developed nations globally. It is projected to be the tenth largest economy in terms of real GDP, valued at $1.63 trillion.
- Over the years, South Korea's GDP has experienced significant growth, surpassing **$1.80 trillion** from a modest $2.3 billion in 1962, and it currently stands as the tenth largest in the world based on 2021 GDP rankings.
- Despite its reliance on imported natural resources such as crude oil and essential minerals, South Korea has successfully achieved economic transformation. In 1996, it became the 29th member country of the Organization for Economic Cooperation and Development (OECD).

- Additionally, **South Korea typically ranks among the world's top eight or nine holders of foreign exchange reserves, reaching approx. $412 billion in June 2024**. [India holds the 4th position in the forex reserves with approx. $471 billion.]

INDUSTRY & TECHNOLOGY

- South Korea is renowned for its advanced industrial base and cutting-edge technology sector, making it one of the world's leading economies. The country has transformed from an agrarian society into a global industrial powerhouse within a few decades.
- South Korea is home to some of the world's largest **electronics companies**, such as Samsung and LG, which are global leaders in smartphones, semiconductors, displays, and home appliances. Hyundai Motor Company and Kia Motors are among the world's top **automobile manufacturers**, known for their innovation and quality.
- South Korea boasts the **largest shipbuilding industry globally** and is recognized as one of the leading producers of **semiconductors** and electronic goods. The country also holds a prominent position in the automotive manufacturing sector, having successfully produced more than 3.5 million vehicles in 2021.
- South Korea is investing heavily in robotics and **artificial intelligence**, aiming to lead in these future industries. The country is a pioneer in developing smart cities and autonomous technologies. In recent years, South Korea has been focusing on **renewable energy sources**, aiming to reduce its dependency on fossil fuels and promote sustainability.
- The South Korean government plays an active role in fostering innovation through policies that support research and development, technology startups, and global partnerships.

DIPLOMACY AND INTERNATIONAL RELATIONS

- South Korea has a proactive and dynamic approach to diplomacy and international relations, with a focus on maintaining peace and stability in Northeast Asia and beyond. South Korea maintains a close alliance with the United States, which is a cornerstone of its foreign policy and national security. The **U.S.-ROK alliance** is crucial for deterring North Korean aggression and ensuring regional security.
- South Korea is an active member of the United Nations, the World Trade Organization, the G20, and other international organizations. It has been a non-permanent member of the UN Security Council and is a strong advocate for multilateralism, global trade, and sustainable development.
- Under its "**New Southern Policy**," South Korea is expanding its diplomatic and economic engagement with Southeast Asia and India, aiming to diversify its partnerships and reduce dependency on traditional allies.
- South Korea has transitioned from a recipient of international aid to a donor, providing **development assistance** to various countries, particularly in Asia and Africa. It is also active in global humanitarian efforts, contributing to disaster relief and peacekeeping missions.
- **Relations with North Korea** remain a central issue in South Korea's foreign policy. South Korea seeks peaceful reunification and has engaged in various diplomatic initiatives, including inter-Korean summits, to reduce tensions and promote dialogue.

CULTURE & DIASPORA

- South Korea has a rich cultural heritage that blends traditional and modern elements, and its global cultural influence has grown significantly in recent years, particularly through the phenomenon known as the "Korean Wave" or "Hallyu".
- South Korea's traditional culture is preserved and celebrated through its art forms, including traditional music, dance, hanbok (traditional clothing), and tea ceremonies. Festivals like Chuseok (Korean Thanksgiving) and Seollal (Lunar New Year) are important cultural celebrations.
- South Korea places a strong emphasis on education, with a highly competitive system that produces skilled professionals, particularly in science and technology. The country's education system and cultural emphasis on hard work have contributed to its rapid development and global competitiveness.
- The country leverages its cultural assets as a form of soft power, using cultural diplomacy to enhance its international image and build cultural connections globally.

INDIA AND SOUTH KOREA TIES

India and South Korea interact in various fields, including trade, defense, science and technology, and culture. The two countries have a strategic partnership and have been strengthening their bilateral ties over the years.

India played a significant role in Korean affairs following Korea's independence in 1945. **K.P.S. Menon** chaired the United Nations Commission, consisting of nine members, which was established in 1947 to conduct elections in Korea. During the **Korean War (1950-1953)**, a resolution sponsored by India was accepted by both sides of the conflict, leading to a ceasefire on July 27, 1953. **Lt. General K.S. Thimayya** of India later chaired the **Neutral Nations Repatriation Commission (NNRC)** and contributed to addressing humanitarian issues resulting from the war. The state visit of **President Dr. APJ Abdul Kalam** to Korea in February 2006 marked a new dynamic phase in India-RoK relations.

Areas of Cooperation → Economy → Defence and Strategic ties → Energy, Science and Technology → People and Culture

Economy & Trade

- India and South Korea have a **bilateral trade agreement**, which was signed in **2009**. The bilateral **Comprehensive Economic Cooperation Agreement (CEPA)**, set in place since 2010, has spurred the trade and investments both ways. It is Korea's first free trade agreement with a member of the BRICS countries.
- The trade and economic relations between India and Republic of Korea (Korea) have gathered momentum in recent years with annual bilateral trade reaching **US$23.7 billion** in **2021** (as per data from Korea International Trade Association), highest ever bilateral trade figure till now.
- Korea is an export-driven economy and is drawn by India's huge market. Korea developed considerable expertise in shipbuilding, steel, nuclear energy, heavy electrical machinery etc. and has been keen to invest in India in these areas. In 2021, Korea's investment to India recorded **US$218 million**. Among Korean companies that have invested in India, **Hyundai Motor Group, Samsung Electronics** and **LG Group** have been the leaders. **Kia Motors**, a sister company in the Hyundai Group, announced an investment of US$ 1.6 billion in two phases to set up two manufacturing units in Ananthapur, Andhra Pradesh.
- India and South Korea have been promoting startups and innovation in their respective countries and have even been collaborating with each other in this regard. Korea's total FDI to India from 1980 up to December 2021 stands at **US$7.27 billion.** India is Korea's 16th biggest source for imports and 7th biggest export market as of 2021.

Major exports to India	Automobile parts, telecommunication equipment, hot rolled iron products, petroleum refined products, base lubricating oils, nuclear reactors, mechanical appliances, electrical machinery & parts and iron & steel products.
Major imports from India	textiles, light oils and preparations (naphtha), pharmaceuticals, cereals and agricultural products.

During Prime Minister Narendra Modi's State visit to Seoul on 18 May 2015, a revised **Double Taxation Avoidance Agreement** was signed. Subsequently, in July 2018, President Moon Jae-in visited India, during which Prime Minister Modi and President Moon set a **target of achieving bilateral trade worth $50 billion by 2030**.

One major area of disconnect between India and South Korea is the **trade imbalance**. South Korea is always among India's top 5 trading partners, but India is South Korea's ninth-largest trading partner. South Korea has consistently maintained a trade surplus with India, which has led to concerns in India about the impact on its domestic industries. India has sought to address this issue by seeking greater access to the South Korean market for its goods and services.

Defense and Security

India and South Korea have been cooperating in defense and security matters. The two countries have held joint military exercises and have signed agreements for defense cooperation, including for the transfer of defense technology. South Korean defense companies have also shown interest in participating in India's defense sector.

RIMPAC	• It is one of the largest multilateral Naval Exercises, led by the USA (held biennially) • The Rim of Pacific Exercise involves 26 counties including India and South Korea. • **RIMPAC 2022** was conducted between June and August around the Hawaiian Islands and southern California.
Sea Dragon	• It is a biennial, multi-national naval exercise focused on Anti-Submarine Warfare (ASW) training, tactics, and procedures. • India and Korea participate in this exercise which is hosted by the US. • Exercise Sea Dragon 2023 was conducted in March
Sahyog - Hyeoblyeog	• Indo-Korean joint anti-piracy, search and rescue exercise. • The 2018 edition was conducted on 5th April 2018 off the Chennai coast, in Tamil Nadu.

Energy and Science & Technology

The two nations have been collaborating in science and technology, with a focus on research and development. Together they have established **joint research centers** and have been exchanging scientific and technological expertise. The **Indo-Korean Science and Technology Center** was established in **2010** to promote collaborative research in areas such as nanotechnology, biotechnology, and materials science.

South Korea is a **global leader in the electronics and IT sector**, while India has a growing IT industry. The two countries have been collaborating in the electronics and IT sector, with South Korean companies such as Samsung and LG investing in India.

The two countries have also been working together to develop **5G technology**. They have also been collaborating in the areas of artificial intelligence and blockchain technology. The two countries have also established a **startup center** in Seoul to facilitate collaboration between Indian and South Korean startups.

They have also been collaborating in **space research and development**. They have established a joint working group on space cooperation, which has resulted in several joint projects, including the development of a geostationary satellite for meteorological observations. Moreover, India and South Korea have signed agreements for defense cooperation, including for the **transfer of defense technology**. South Korean defense companies have shown interest in participating in India's defense sector, and the two countries have been collaborating in the areas of **unmanned aerial vehicles** and **underwater robotics**.

People and Culture

India and South Korea have a rich cultural heritage, and there has been a growing interest in cultural exchanges between the two countries. South Korean TV dramas and music have gained popularity in India, while Indian movies and music have found an audience in South Korea. The two countries have also been collaborating in the areas of art, literature, and education. During PM Modi's visit to South Korea in 2019, he unveiled a bust of Mahatma Gandhi at prestigious Yonsei University to commemorate **150th birth anniversary of Mahatma Gandhi**. He also accepted the **Seoul Peace Prize** conferred upon him by Seoul Peace Prize Foundation.

THE CHINESE ANGLE

South Korea has been focusing on its relationship with China, especially since the two nations have significant economic ties. However, the bilateral relationship has been complex off late and has fluctuated over time. For instance, China and South Korea have different approaches to dealing with North Korea. China has historically been North Korea's closest ally and has sought to maintain a stable relationship with the country, while South Korea has sought to engage with North Korea but has also emphasized the need for denuclearization and regional security.

Another potential security challenge for South Korea and China is territorial disputes in the region. China has territorial disputes with several countries in the region, including Japan, Taiwan, and Vietnam, and has asserted its claims to various islands and maritime areas. These disputes have led to tensions between China and South Korea.

NORTH KOREA

THE AUTHORITARIAN REGIME

OFFICIAL FLAG

North Korea, officially known as the **Democratic People's Republic of Korea (DPRK)**, is a country located on the northern part of the Korean Peninsula in East Asia. It shares borders with China to the north, and South Korea to the south, and is separated from Japan to the east by the Sea of Japan. The country has a population of around 25 million people and its capital and largest city is Pyongyang.

North Korea is a one-party state with the ruling **Workers' Party of Korea**, led by the **Kim family**, in control of the government. North Korea's economy is centrally planned and heavily controlled by the government. It is largely based on heavy industry, with an emphasis on military production. The country is known for its isolationist policies, with limited interactions with the outside world. The government tightly controls access to information and limits internet access to a select few individuals and institutions.

IMPORTANT DETAILS	
Capital	Pyongyang
Supreme Commander	Kim Jong Un
Population	25,88725 million

Isolationist Policies

(a) **Juche Ideology:** The cornerstone of North Korea's isolationist policies is the Juche ideology, which emphasizes self-reliance and independence from foreign influences. Established by Kim Il-sung, the country's founder, Juche advocates for economic and political self-sufficiency and has been a guiding principle for North Korean policy.

(b) **Limited Foreign Relations**: North Korea maintains a very limited network of diplomatic relations. It has formal ties with a few countries, including China, Russia, and a handful of others, but its diplomatic engagement is otherwise minimal.

(c) **Economic Autarky:** North Korea pursues a policy of economic autarky, striving to minimize reliance on international trade and investment. This policy has resulted in a heavily controlled economy with limited foreign direct investment.

(d) **Isolation from Global Economy:** The DPRK's isolation is also reflected in its limited participation in the global economy. Sanctions imposed by the international community, particularly by the United Nations, have further isolated North Korea economically, targeting its nuclear and missile programs and exacerbating the country's economic challenges.

ECONOMY AND TRADE

- North Korea has a centrally planned economy, with most aspects of economic activity controlled by the state. The state-run economy prioritizes military spending and the development of key industries, often at the expense of consumer goods and private enterprise.
- The economy is heavily focused on agriculture and heavy industry. Key sectors include mining (especially coal and minerals), steel production, and military-related industries. Agriculture, particularly rice and maize cultivation, is crucial but often suffers from inefficiencies and food shortages.

- The combination of economic autarky, international sanctions, and limited foreign trade has contributed to significant economic hardship and food insecurity within North Korea. The country faces frequent shortages of basic goods and services.
- North Korea lags behind in technological innovation and development compared to global standards. While there are efforts to develop certain technologies, such as in the military and space sectors, the overall technological infrastructure is underdeveloped.
- Internet access is highly restricted and censored, with most citizens having no access to the global internet. Instead, a domestic intranet is used, which limits exposure to global technological advancements and information.

DEFENCE AND DIPLOMACY

- North Korea maintains one of the largest standing armies in the world relative to its population. The military plays a central role in the country's politics and economy, with substantial resources allocated to defense spending.
- North Korea's nuclear weapons program is a major aspect of its defense strategy. The country has conducted several nuclear tests and developed intercontinental ballistic missiles (ICBMs), which have drawn international condemnation and resulted in severe sanctions.
- North Korea's diplomatic relations are limited, with formal ties maintained with a few countries, including China, Russia, and some smaller states. The country has historically maintained a degree of isolation from the broader international community.

North Korea began its nuclear program in the **1980s** with the assistance of Soviet and Chinese technologies. The program initially focused on **developing nuclear reactors for energy production**. North Korea conducted its **first nuclear test in 2006**. Since then, it has carried out several more tests.

North Korea has developed a range of **ballistic missiles**, including short-range, medium-range, and intercontinental ballistic missiles (ICBMs). The development of ICBMs has raised international concerns about the potential for long-range nuclear strikes.

The international community, led by the United Nations, has **imposed extensive sanctions** on North Korea in response to its nuclear weapons program. These sanctions target various sectors, including trade, finance, and technology, aiming to pressure North Korea into denuclearization.

PEOPLE AND SOCIETY

- North Korea's culture is deeply influenced by its traditional Korean heritage, including Confucian values, Korean Buddhism, and folklore. Traditional Korean music, dance, and art are preserved and promoted by the state.
- The North Korean government exerts extensive control over social life, including education, media, and cultural activities. The regime promotes a highly controlled and homogeneous society, with limited personal freedoms.
- The movement of both North Korean citizens and foreigners within the country is tightly controlled. Ordinary North Koreans require permission from the government to travel, and international travel is highly restricted. Foreign visitors, including diplomats and aid workers, face stringent regulations and monitoring during their stay.
- The closed nature and isolationist policies allow the North Korean regime to maintain a high degree of control over its population and suppress dissent. This control is reinforced by extensive surveillance, a powerful security apparatus, and a cult of personality surrounding its leaders.

INDIA AND NORTH KOREA

- India and North Korea have maintained diplomatic relations since the 1970s, and India has been one of the few countries to maintain a diplomatic mission in Pyongyang, North Korea's capital. Relations between India and DPR Korea have been generally characterised by friendship, cooperation and understanding. However, the relationship between the two countries has been somewhat limited and has fluctuated over time.
- India strongly condemned DPR Korea's nuclear tests and frequent ballistic missile tests and also urged DPR Korea to restrain from further nuclear and ballistic missile tests to ease tensions on the Korean Peninsula. In 2017, India voted in favor of United Nations Security Council (UNSC) resolutions imposing sanctions on North Korea in response to its nuclear and missile tests.
- However, India has also sought to maintain a dialogue with North Korea and has hosted North Korean officials for talks. In 2018, India's Minister of State for External Affairs, General (Retd.) V.K. Singh, visited North Korea and met with senior officials to discuss issues of mutual interest, including regional security and economic cooperation.

MONGOLIA

THE HEART OF ASIA

Mongolia, a landlocked country in East Asia, is known for its vast steppes and nomadic culture. Its strategic location between China and Russia has shaped its foreign policy and economic relations. Mongolia has pursued a policy of neutrality and non-alignment, seeking to balance its relationships with its powerful neighbors.

Mongolia's rich cultural heritage, including its nomadic traditions and Buddhist philosophy, has contributed to its unique identity and attracted tourists from around the world.

IMPORTANT DETAILS	
Capital	Ulaanbaatar
President	Ukhnaagiin Khurelsukh
Prime Minister	Oyun-Erdene Luvsannamsrain
Population (2023)	3.4 million
Human Development Index Rank (2023)	96

POLITY & ADMINISTRATION

- Mongolia is a **parliamentary republic with a multi-party system.** The country adopted its first democratic constitution in 1992, transitioning from a socialist state to a democracy.
- The President of Mongolia is the head of state, elected for a four-year term, while the Prime Minister is the head of government, leading the executive branch. The Mongolian parliament, known as the *State Great Khural*, is a unicameral body with 76 members, also elected for four-year terms.
- Mongolia's administrative divisions include 21 provinces (aimags) and the capital city, Ulaanbaatar, which is an autonomous municipality.

ECONOMY & TRADE

- After decades of communist rule, Mongolia embraced democracy and a market economy, positioning itself as a bridge between East and West. Mongolia's economy is largely driven by its vast mineral resources, making mining the backbone of its economy.
- Key exports include coal, copper, gold, and other minerals, primarily destined for China, Mongolia's largest trading partner. The agricultural sector, particularly livestock farming, is also significant, with Mongolia being known for its production of cashmere, wool, and meat products.
- The economy is susceptible to fluctuations in global commodity prices and has been seeking to diversify, with efforts to develop other sectors like agriculture, manufacturing, and tourism.
- Mongolia's geographic location makes it a landlocked country with economic dependencies on its neighbors, especially China and Russia, but it has been working to expand its trade partnerships beyond the region.
- In recent years, Mongolia has been actively engaged in economic development and modernization. It has attracted foreign investment, particularly in the mining and energy sectors. However, the country continues to face challenges such as poverty, unemployment, and environmental degradation.

DEFENCE & DIPLOMACY

- Mongolia maintains a policy of neutrality, emphasizing peaceful coexistence and non-alignment.
- Its defence strategy focuses on maintaining a small but professional military force, primarily tasked with defending the country's sovereignty and participating in international peacekeeping missions.
- Mongolia's military, known as the Mongolian Armed Forces, participates in joint exercises with international partners, including the United States and various NATO countries, under its **"Third Neighbor" policy**, which seeks to engage with countries beyond its two dominant neighbors, Russia and China.
- The 'Third Neighbour Policy' seeks to diversify Mongolia's diplomatic and economic relations by engaging with countries like the United States, Japan, South Korea, India, and members of the European Union.
- Mongolia is a member of the United Nations, the World Trade Organization, and various regional organizations. It has positioned itself as a proponent of democracy and human rights, hosting international conferences and contributing to global peace and security through its participation in peacekeeping missions.

CULTURE & DIASPORA

- Mongolia has a rich cultural heritage deeply rooted in its nomadic traditions. The majority of Mongolians are ethnic Mongols, with Buddhism being the predominant religion, influenced by Tibetan Buddhism. Shamanism is also practiced, reflecting the country's ancient spiritual beliefs.
- Mongolian culture is characterized by its epic literature, music, and traditional practices such as ***throat singing*** (khöömei) and the Naadam festival, which features traditional sports like wrestling, horse racing, and archery.

Despite modernization, many Mongolians continue to live nomadic or semi-nomadic lifestyles, herding livestock across the vast steppes. The country's culture and identity are strongly tied to the legacy of **Genghis Khan**, who founded the Mongol Empire, one of the largest empires in history.

INDIA AND MONGOLIA

- India and Mongolia established **diplomatic relations** in 1955, and their ties are characterized by mutual respect and shared values, particularly in terms of democratic governance and Buddhism, which is a significant cultural connection. India was the first country outside the Soviet bloc to establish diplomatic relations with Mongolia.

- The relationship was elevated to a "**Strategic Partnership**" in 2015, during Indian Prime Minister Narendra Modi's historic visit to Mongolia, marking the first-ever visit by an Indian Prime Minister to the country. Both nations cooperate closely in multilateral forums such as the United Nations, and India supports Mongolia's participation in regional organizations like the Shanghai Cooperation Organisation (SCO).
- **Economic and trade relations** between India and Mongolia are modest but growing, with both countries looking to enhance cooperation in various sectors. Bilateral trade primarily involves Mongolia exporting minerals, raw materials, and animal products to India, while India exports pharmaceuticals, machinery, and consumer goods to Mongolia. There is significant potential for growth in sectors such as mining, agriculture, renewable energy, and information technology. India has provided economic assistance to Mongolia, including lines of credit for infrastructure projects, and both countries are exploring ways to increase bilateral trade and investment.
- Defence and security cooperation have been expanding, reflecting their strategic partnership. The two countries conduct regular joint military exercises, such as the annual "Nomadic Elephant" exercises, which focus on counter-insurgency and peacekeeping operations. India has also provided training to Mongolian military personnel and supports capacity-building initiatives.
- Both nations share an interest in promoting **regional security and stability**, and Mongolia views India as a key partner in its "***Third Neighbor***" policy, which seeks to build ties with countries other than Russia and China. Defence cooperation also includes dialogue on regional security issues, with an emphasis on maintaining peace and stability in Asia.
- **People-to-people relations** between India and Mongolia are strong, with deep cultural and historical ties, particularly through Buddhism. India is seen as the land of Buddha, and this spiritual connection is a cornerstone of the relationship. Cultural exchanges, including the celebration of Buddhist festivals and academic exchanges, have strengthened mutual understanding. Educational cooperation is also significant, with Indian scholarships and training programs offered to Mongolian students and professionals.

'ASEAN' COUNTRIES

THE GROUP

The Association of Southeast Asian Nations (ASEAN) is a regional intergovernmental organization comprising ten member states in Southeast Asia. ASEAN was established on August 8, 1967, in Bangkok, Thailand, with the signing of the ASEAN Declaration by its founding members, Indonesia, Malaysia, the Philippines, Singapore, and Thailand. Since then, Brunei, Cambodia, Laos, Myanmar, and Vietnam have also joined as members.

The ASEAN region has a combined population of over 650 million people and a total GDP of more than **$3 trillion**, making it one of the fastest-growing and most dynamic regions in the world. ASEAN works towards regional integration, economic cooperation, and political and security collaboration among its member states. ASEAN promotes economic cooperation among its members through initiatives such as the ASEAN Free Trade Area (AFTA), which aims to reduce barriers to trade and investment among member states.

ASEAN also plays an important role in regional security, with initiatives such as the ASEAN Regional Forum (ARF) and the ASEAN Defence Ministers' Meeting (ADMM) promoting cooperation and dialogue among member states and with external partners on issues such as counterterrorism, maritime security, and disaster management. The respect for national sovereignty is critical to the functioning of ASEAN. On the lines of EU, ASEAN agreed to establish an ASEAN Community comprising three pillars, namely,

- the ASEAN Security Community
- the ASEAN Economic Community
- the ASEAN Socio-Cultural Community

Country	Capital	Population (approx. 2023)	GDP (current US$), 2023 (approx. billion)	Human Development Index Rank (2023)
INDIA	**NEW DELHI**	**1.43 billion**	**3.55 trillion**	**134**
Brunei Darussalam	Bandar Seri Begawan	450,000	15	55
Cambodia	Phnom Penh	17 million	31.7	148
Indonesia	Jakarta	275 million	1.37 trillion	112
Laos (Lao PDR)	Vientiane	7.5 million	15.8	139
Malaysia	Kuala Lumpur	33 million	399	63
Myanmar	Naypyidaw	55 million	64	144
Philippines	Manila	115 million	437	113
Singapore	Singapore	5.9 million	501	9
Thailand	Bangkok	70 million	514.9	66
Vietnam	Hanoi	98 million	429	107

NOTE: 'Myanmar' has been discussed in the initial chapters.

THAILAND

Thailand, often referred to as the "***Land of Smiles***," is a Southeast Asian country with a rich cultural heritage. The country has experienced significant economic growth, driven by tourism, manufacturing, and agriculture. Thailand is a founding member of ASEAN and plays a crucial role in regional stability and cooperation. However, challenges such as political instability and income inequality persist.

Rising relevance in International Relations

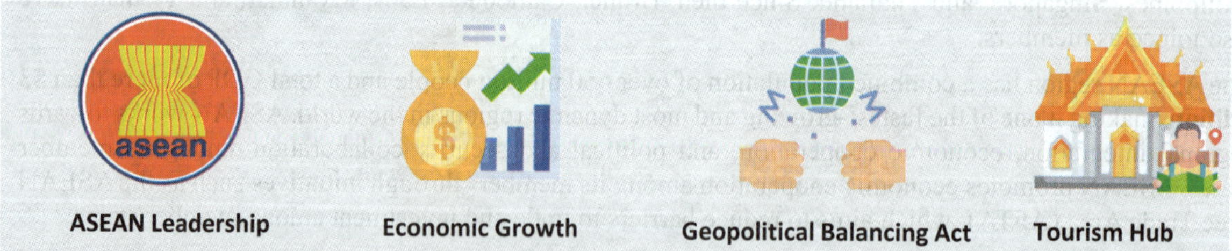

1. **ASEAN Leadership**: Thailand, as a founding member of ASEAN, has played a pivotal role in shaping the bloc's trajectory. Its diplomatic acumen and economic influence have contributed significantly to ASEAN's cohesion and effectiveness. Bangkok's strategic location has made it a natural choice for hosting ASEAN summits and initiatives, solidifying its position as a regional leader.
2. **Economic Growth**: Thailand's sustained economic growth has positioned it as a key player in Southeast Asia. Its robust manufacturing sector, coupled with a growing service industry, has contributed to its economic success. The country has successfully diversified its economy, reducing reliance on agriculture and tourism. As a result, Thailand has become an attractive destination for foreign investment and a regional economic hub.
3. **Geopolitical Balancing Act**: Thailand has skilfully navigated complex geopolitical challenges, maintaining balanced relationships with major powers such as the United States and China. This

diplomatic dexterity has allowed Thailand to protect its national interests while contributing to regional stability.

4. **Tourism Hub**: Thailand has transformed itself into a world-renowned tourist destination, attracting millions of visitors annually. The tourism industry is a major contributor to the nation's GDP, creating employment opportunities and fostering cultural exchange. Beyond economic benefits, Thailand's soft power has been enhanced through its reputation as a welcoming and hospitable country.

A. Politics & Administration

- Thailand operates as a constitutional monarchy. The King, as the head of state, is revered as a symbol of national unity and stability. However, the political power rests with the Prime Minister and the elected government.
- The country has experienced a complex political history, marked by periods of democratic rule interspersed with military coups. The most recent coup took place in 2014, leading to military rule until 2019.
- The 2017 constitution, drafted by the military junta, has been criticized for its provisions that strengthen the military's influence over politics.
- Current issues in Thailand's governance include debates over the role of the monarchy, demands for greater democratic reforms, and concerns about human rights, freedom of expression and excessive influence of the military in politics.

B. Economy & Trade

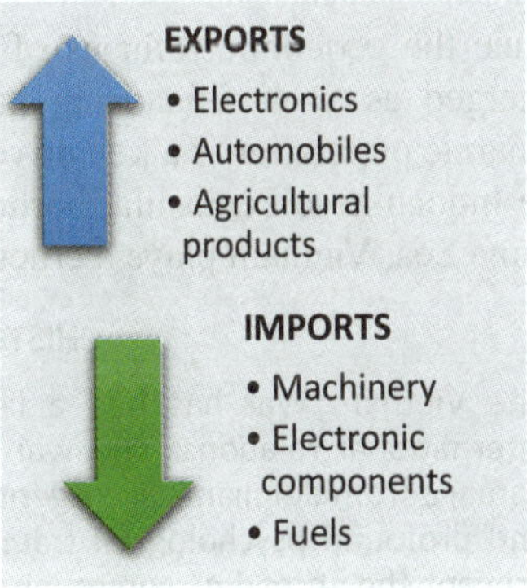

- In the present decade, Thailand's economy is one of the largest in the region and has undergone significant transformation, evolving from an agrarian to an industrial and service-based economy.
- The **Thai Baht** is a relatively stable currency and is considered a reserve currency in the region. Thailand's GDP in 2023 was almost **$515 billion**, ranking it as the second-largest economy in Southeast Asia after Indonesia.
- Key sectors driving growth include tourism, electronics, automotive manufacturing, and agriculture. The country is a major exporter of rice, rubber, and seafood.
- Thailand has been a significant recipient of Foreign Direct Investment (FDI), primarily in the manufacturing and services sectors.
- While enjoying macroeconomic stability, Thailand faces challenges such as income inequality and regional disparities.
- **India-Thailand**: Bilateral trade has experienced significant growth in recent years, encompassing a wide range of products and services. India's exports to Thailand primarily include gems and jewelry, machinery, and transport equipment, while imports from Thailand consist of electronic components, rubber, and agricultural products. Both countries have encouraged investments from each other. Enhanced connectivity through air and sea routes has facilitated trade and people-to-people exchanges.

C. Defence and Security

- Thailand's strategic location at the heart of Southeast Asia necessitates a robust defense capability. The Royal Thai Armed Forces plays a crucial role in maintaining internal security and territorial integrity.
- As a central player in ASEAN, Thailand actively engages in regional cooperation and economic integration efforts.
- Its strategic location at the heart of the Indochinese Peninsula makes it a pivotal player in regional trade and logistics. Challenges such as human trafficking, drug smuggling, and transnational crime remain areas of concern.

D. Culture & Diaspora

- Thailand is renowned for its rich cultural heritage, characterized by its unique blend of Buddhist, Hindu, and indigenous traditions.

- The country's vibrant arts, music, and cuisine have gained global recognition.
- The Thai diaspora, particularly in North America and Europe, contributes significantly to the economy through remittances and cultural exchange.

E. Diplomatic Relations

- Thailand has traditionally pursued a policy of neutrality and balance in its foreign relations.
- Thailand's foreign policy balances relationships with major global powers, including China and the United States, while maintaining strong ties with its ASEAN neighbors.
- Thailand has also been involved in various peacekeeping missions and humanitarian aid efforts, enhancing its international standing.
- **India -Thailand**: Both nations collaborate within regional frameworks like ASEAN and BIMSTEC to promote economic integration and cooperation.

VIETNAM

Vietnam is a Southeast Asian country with a rich history and a dynamic present. Shaped by centuries of foreign influence, particularly from China, Vietnam emerged as an independent nation in the 20th century. The country endured a long and arduous war for independence, followed by a period of communist rule.

Since the economic reforms of the 1980s, Vietnam has undergone a remarkable transformation. It has emerged as a manufacturing hub, attracting significant foreign investment. The country's young and dynamic population is a key driver of economic growth. Geographically, Vietnam is strategically located on the Indochinese Peninsula, bordering China, Laos, and Cambodia. With a long coastline along the South China Sea, Vietnam plays a crucial role in regional maritime affairs and trade.

HISTORICAL BITS – THE VIETNAM WAR (1955-1975)

The Vietnam War has had a lasting impact on present-day Vietnam, shaping its society, economy, and international relations. The war left deep scars, including widespread physical destruction, environmental damage from defoliants like **Agent Orange** (herbicide mixture used by the U.S. military during the Vietnam War), and profound psychological trauma. The conflict stemmed from Cold War tensions and the U.S.'s desire to prevent the spread of communism in Southeast Asia. It ended with the fall of Saigon in 1975, leading to the reunification of Vietnam under communist control. The post-war period saw a challenging reconstruction process marked by poverty and international isolation.

A. Politics & Administration

- Vietnam is a **socialist republic** with a **single-party system** dominated by the **Communist Party of Vietnam** (**CPV** holds a monopoly on political power).
- The country's political system is characterized by centralized control and a strong emphasis on maintaining the party's leadership in all aspects of governance and society.
- The **National Assembly** is the country's unicameral legislature, but its powers are limited compared to the CPV. The **President** is the head of state, while the **Prime Minister** is the head of government.

EXPORTS
- Electronics & Electric equipment
- Textile and Garments
- Footwear
- Agricultural Products

IMPORTS
- Machinery & equipment
- Raw materials for fabrics/textiles
- Steel, Iron & Automobile parts
- Chemicals & Petroleum Products

- The judiciary in Vietnam is also not independent and is influenced by the CPV.
- While the country has experienced significant economic growth and modernization, political pluralism and freedoms remain tightly controlled. The government maintains control over media and civil society, and freedom of expression and assembly are limited.

B. Economy & Trade

- Vietnam has embraced economic reforms since the 1980s (**Doi Moi**), leading to substantial growth and integration into the global economy. The country has transitioned from a centrally planned economy to a "**socialist-oriented market economy**," which has been instrumental in its economic success.
- The country's GDP growth rates have typically been among the highest in Southeast Asia, frequently exceeding 6% annually. Vietnam's GDP in 2023 was approximately **$430 billion**, with a GDP growth (annual %) of 5.0 in 2023.

DOI MOI is the Vietnamese term for "renovation" or "renewal." It refers to the comprehensive economic reforms initiated by the Communist Party of Vietnam in 1986. The country was facing economic stagnation and poverty following the Vietnam War, and the centrally planned economy was proving unsustainable. The key aspects include -	**Market-Oriented Reforms:** The reforms shifted Vietnam towards a market-oriented economy, allowing for greater private enterprise and foreign investment. **Agriculture Transformation:** The agricultural sector was reformed to increase productivity and efficiency, leading to a significant reduction in rural poverty. **Open-Door Policy:** Vietnam began to open its economy to foreign trade and investment, attracting global companies and technology transfer. **Infrastructure Development:** Investments in transportation, telecommunications, and energy infrastructure were prioritized to support economic growth.

- Key sectors include manufacturing & industry, agriculture, and services, with a burgeoning tech industry.
- The **foreign direct investment (FDI)** plays a crucial role in Vietnam's economic development, bringing in capital, technology, and management expertise. The FDI, net inflows (% of GDP) as of 2022, was **4.4%**.
- The country is an active participant in several international trade agreements, including the Comprehensive and Progressive Agreement for Trans-Pacific Partnership (CPTPP), the Regional Comprehensive Economic Partnership (RCEP), and a free trade agreement with the European Union (EVFTA).
- Vietnam demonstrated considerable resilience during the COVID-19 pandemic, maintaining positive economic growth in 2020 when many other countries experienced contractions. This was due to effective pandemic control measures, a diversified economy, and strong government support.

C. Defence and Security

- Vietnam's strategic location along the South China Sea and its extensive coastline make it a critical player in regional maritime security. Vietnam's defence strategy is primarily focused on territorial integrity, national sovereignty, and economic development.
- The military, known as the **Vietnamese People's Army** has undergone modernization efforts, acquiring advanced weaponry and equipment to enhance its capabilities. The CPV maintains strict control over the military, ensuring its loyalty to the party.
- The South China Sea dispute with China remains a primary security concern. Vietnam has invested in coastal defense and maritime capabilities to protect its territorial waters.As a member of ASEAN, Vietnam advocates for regional stability, economic cooperation, and adherence to international law, particularly in maritime disputes.
- The country recognizes the link between economic growth and national security, focusing on infrastructure development and human capital development to strengthen its overall resilience.

D. Culture & Diaspora

- Vietnam's culture is a rich tapestry woven from centuries of history, influenced by Chinese, French, and American cultures.

- The philosophies of Confucianism, Buddhism, and Taoism have deeply influenced Vietnamese values, emphasizing family, community, and respect for elders. The Vietnam war's legacy fostered a strong sense of nationalism and resilience.

E. Diplomatic Relations

- The country's foreign policy seeks to balance relations with major powers, including China and the United States, while enhancing its role in regional and global affairs.
- Vietnam has normalized relations with former adversaries (Vietnam War), including the United States, and has become an active participant in global trade and diplomacy, striving for peace and stability in the region.

India and Vietnam

India and Vietnam established diplomatic relations in 1972 (year before the US withdrawal from Vietnam), and the relationship has grown significantly over the decades, particularly after the launch of India's "Look East Policy" in the 1990s, which later evolved into the "Act East Policy." The relationship was elevated to a "Strategic Partnership" in 2007 and further to a "Comprehensive Strategic Partnership" in 2016, reflecting the deepening ties between the two nations.

Both countries cooperate closely in regional and multilateral forums, such as ASEAN, the East Asia Summit, and the United Nations, and share common interests in promoting peace, stability, and prosperity in the Indo-Pacific region.

- **Economic and trade relations** between India and Vietnam have grown rapidly, with Vietnam becoming one of India's key trading partners in ASEAN. Bilateral trade has been expanding, covering sectors such as textiles, pharmaceuticals, agricultural products, electronics, and machinery.
- India is also a significant **investor** in Vietnam, particularly in sectors like oil and gas exploration, energy, and manufacturing. Both countries have been working to further enhance trade and investment, focusing on areas like information technology, renewable energy, and infrastructure development. The India-ASEAN Free Trade Agreement has further facilitated increased trade.
- **Defence and security cooperation** are pillars of the India-Vietnam relationship. Both countries share strategic interests in the Indo-Pacific region, particularly concerning maritime security and freedom of navigation in the South China Sea.
- Both nations conduct regular **high-level defence dialogues** and have signed several agreements to deepen military cooperation, including in areas like training, capacity building, and joint exercises. India has also extended a Line of Credit to Vietnam for defence procurement, and both countries collaborate on counterterrorism, cyber security, and disaster management.
- **People-to-people ties** between India and Vietnam are marked by deep cultural and historical connections, particularly through shared Buddhist heritage. Educational cooperation is also significant, with scholarships and training programs offered to Vietnamese students and professionals in India. Tourism is another important aspect of the relationship. The Indian community in Vietnam, though small, contributes to the local economy and serves as a bridge between the two nations.

Rising relevance in International Relations

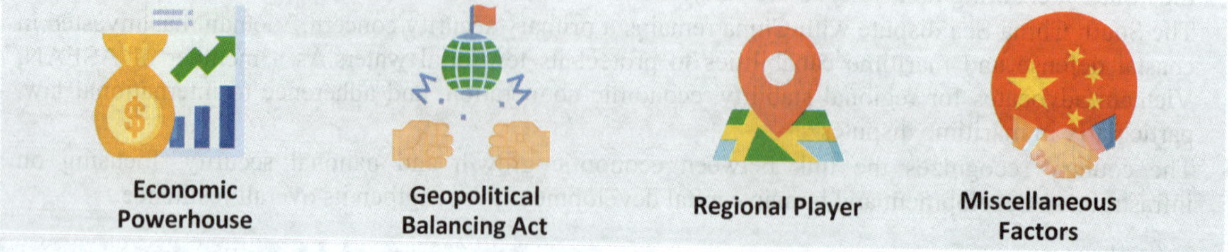

1. **Economic Powerhouse:** Vietnam's economic transformation since the "Doi Moi" reforms of the late 1980s has been remarkable. The country has transitioned from a centrally planned economy to a dynamic market-oriented one, achieving impressive growth rates. As a major player in global supply chains,

particularly in textiles, electronics, and footwear, Vietnam has attracted significant foreign direct investment. Its membership in the CPTPP has further boosted its export competitiveness.

2. **Geopolitical Balancing Act:** Vietnam's geographic location in Southeast Asia places it at the crossroads of major powers. The South China Sea disputes with China have underscored the complexities of its foreign policy. To counterbalance China's influence, Vietnam has been strengthening ties with the United States and other Western countries. The normalization of relations with the US has been a significant step in this direction.
3. **Regional Player:** Vietnam has also played an increasingly active role in regional affairs, particularly within ASEAN. Its membership in the bloc has enabled it to contribute to regional stability and economic integration. As the Indo-Pacific region gains strategic importance, Vietnam is positioning itself as a key player, balancing its relationships with major powers while pursuing its own national interests.
4. **Miscellaneous Factors:**
   - Indonesia's stance on the **Belt & Road Initiative (BRI)** is one of selective engagement. While the promise of infrastructure development and increased connectivity is alluring, the country is cautious about debt traps and potential geopolitical implications. Indonesia has prioritized projects that align with its national development goals and has sought to balance its participation in the BRI with its relationships with other major powers
   - Vietnam is experiencing rapid growth in its **digital economy**, with a young and tech-savvy population. Moreover, the government is investing heavily in **infrastructure** to support economic growth and development.
   - As an archipelagic nation highly vulnerable to the impacts of **climate change**, Vietnam has emerged as a leader in climate action. The country has set ambitious targets for reducing greenhouse gas emissions and has been actively involved in international climate negotiations.
   - The nation's **human rights record** has not been one to boast. Vietnam has faced international criticism regarding the issues of freedom of speech, assembly, and religion. Balancing economic growth with respect for human rights is a complex challenge for the country.
   - Additionally, Vietnam's rapid industrialization has raised **concerns about labor practices**, including working conditions and wages. The country has taken steps to improve labor standards, but challenges persist.

INDONESIA

Indonesia, the **world's largest archipelago nation**, is a sprawling nation of over 17,000 islands (Java, Sumatra, Borneo (shared with Malaysia and Brunei), and Sulawesi) and is a diverse country with a significant Muslim population. As the fourth most populous country globally, Indonesia plays a crucial role in regional and global affairs. Rich in natural resources, including oil, gas, and minerals, the country has experienced economic growth in recent decades. Indonesia has transitioned from decades of authoritarian rule to a robust democracy, with a vibrant political landscape and active civil society.

A. **Politics & Administration**

International observers widely consider **SUHARTO** to have been a military dictator, leading Indonesia under an authoritarian regime from 1967 until his resignation in 1998 amidst widespread unrest.

- Indonesia's diverse cultural and ethnic tapestry is united under a **democratic system** that has steadily evolved since the end of authoritarian rule in the late 20th century.
- Indonesia is a **unitary state** and operates as a **presidential republic** with a multi-party system. The country has made strides in democratic consolidation since the fall of the **Suharto** regime.
- The political structure is defined by the 1945 Constitution, which has undergone several amendments to enhance democratic governance and decentralization. The complex interplay between the central government and regional authorities is a key feature of Indonesian politics.
- The President of Indonesia serves as both the head of state and government, elected directly by the people for a five-year term, with a maximum of two terms.
- Since the fall of the New Order, Indonesia has pursued **decentralization**, granting substantial autonomy to its 34 provinces and numerous regencies (kabupaten) and cities (kota). This decentralization aims to enhance governance, accountability, and responsiveness to local needs, recognizing Indonesia's diverse cultural and ethnic landscape.
- Presently, challenges such as corruption, regional disparities, and terrorism persist.

B. **Economy & Trade**

- Indonesia's economy is **Southeast Asia's largest**, bolstered by abundant natural resources including oil, gas, and minerals, a growing manufacturing sector, and an expanding digital economy.

Indonesia is **rich in natural resources, including oil, natural gas, coal, tin, bauxite, and gold**. The mining and energy sectors have historically been significant contributors to the economy. Indonesia is one of the world's largest exporters of thermal coal and the leading global producer of palm oil. In 2021, the mining sector contributed approximately 7% to Indonesia's GDP.

- The **manufacturing sector** is a vital component of the Indonesian economy, accounting for around 20% of GDP. Key industries include automotive, textiles, electronics, and food processing.
- **Agriculture** remains an essential sector, employing around 30% of the workforce. Major agricultural products include palm oil, rubber, cocoa, coffee, rice, and spices. Indonesia is a leading global exporter of palm oil and rubber.
- The **services sector** has been growing, driven by tourism, retail, and finance. Tourism is a significant foreign exchange earner, with destinations like Bali, Jakarta, and Yogyakarta attracting millions of international visitors annually.

Key export commodities include palm oil, coal, petroleum gas, and rubber

Significant imports consist of machinery, chemicals, fuels, and foodstuffs.

China, the United States, Japan, and India are among Indonesia's largest trading partners.

- The **digital economy** is also rapidly expanding, fueled by a tech-savy new generation. E-commerce, fintech, and digital services are burgeoning, with internet penetration exceeding 70%. The government has launched initiatives to support digital startups and infrastructure, aiming to be the largest digital economy in Southeast Asia by 2025. In 2020, the digital economy contributed approximately $44 billion, projected to reach **$124 billion** by **2025**.
- Indonesia continues to attract substantial **FDI**, particularly in sectors like mining, manufacturing, and real estate. In 2021, FDI inflows reached approximately $30 billion, demonstrating investor confidence in the country's economic prospects.

- Indonesia is actively engaged in **regional and global economic integration** through initiatives like ASEAN, The Asia Pacific Economic Cooperation (APEC), the World Trade Organization (WTO) and the G20.
- **Challenges** such as infrastructure development, corruption, and inequality need to be addressed to fully realize its economic potential.

C. Defence and Security

- Indonesia faces various security challenges, including maritime disputes, terrorism, and natural disasters.
- The Indonesian Armed Forces (TNI) play a crucial role in maintaining internal security and territorial integrity.
- The country is a member of ASEAN and participates in regional security cooperation efforts. Balancing economic development with defense spending is a key challenge for the government.

D. Culture & Diaspora

- Indonesia is a nation of immense cultural diversity, with over 300 ethnic groups and numerous religions.
- The country's rich cultural heritage, including traditional arts, music, and dance, is a source of national pride.
- The Indonesian diaspora, particularly in Malaysia and the Middle East, contributes to the country's economy and maintains strong ties with their homeland.

E. Diplomatic Relations

Indonesia's foreign policy, often described as independent and active, seeks to balance relations with global powers while asserting its influence in regional and international forums. As a member of the G20, Indonesia's voice is increasingly important in global economic discussions, and its strategic maritime location underscores its significance in global trade and security.

India and Indonesia

India and Indonesia established diplomatic relations in 1951, and their ties are underpinned by shared historical and cultural connections. Both countries are large democracies with significant global influence, and they work closely in multilateral forums such as ASEAN, the G20, and the United Nations. The strategic partnership was elevated in 2018 during the visit of Indian Prime Minister Narendra Modi to Indonesia, where both nations agreed to enhance cooperation in various sectors, including maritime security, counterterrorism, and economic development.

- Indonesia is one of India's largest **trading partners** in ASEAN. The trade relationship is diverse, covering sectors such as coal, palm oil, petroleum products, automobiles, textiles, and agricultural commodities. Both countries are working to further enhance trade and investment, with a focus on sectors like infrastructure, manufacturing, and renewable energy.
- The **Comprehensive Economic Cooperation Agreement (CECA)** between India and ASEAN, of which Indonesia is a key member, has facilitated increased trade and investment flows. There is also growing interest in enhancing cooperation in areas like digital economy, tourism, and small and medium enterprises (SMEs).
- Both nations share concerns over **maritime security** in the Indo-Pacific region, particularly in the context of the strategic importance of the Indian Ocean and the South China Sea. The two countries conduct regular joint military exercises, and collaborate on capacity building, training, and intelligence sharing. In 2018, India and Indonesia signed a defence cooperation agreement to further deepen military ties and enhance coordination on regional security challenges, including counterterrorism and disaster response.
- **People-to-people relations** between India and Indonesia are vibrant and rooted in strong cultural and historical ties. Both countries share a rich cultural heritage, with significant Hindu and Buddhist influences evident in Indonesian culture, particularly in regions like Bali and Java.

- Cultural exchanges, educational collaborations, and tourism are key components of the relationship. Indian films, music, and dance forms are popular in Indonesia, while traditional Indonesian arts and culture are appreciated in India. The Indian diaspora in Indonesia, though relatively small, plays an important role in strengthening these ties.

Rising significance in International Relations

1. **Strategic Location:** Indonesia's archipelagic nature, comprising over **17,000 islands**, positions it strategically as a maritime crossroads. With an Exclusive Economic Zone (EEZ) spanning millions of square kilometers, the country commands significant maritime resources and strategic influence in the region. As a leading member of ASEAN, Indonesia plays a pivotal role in regional cooperation and security
2. **Economic Potential:** As **Southeast Asia's largest economy**, Indonesia boasts a substantial domestic market and a growing middle class. Its abundant natural resources, including oil, gas, minerals, and timber, contribute significantly to the economy. However, the country is transitioning towards a more diversified and service-oriented economy. With a large and young population, Indonesia is poised to benefit from a demographic dividend, driving economic growth and development.
3. **Geopolitical Considerations:** Indonesia's geographic location places it at the intersection of major geopolitical interests. The South China Sea disputes, involving territorial claims with China, have underscored Indonesia's strategic challenges. Balancing relations with China, the US, and other regional powers is crucial for its national interests. The country has adopted a non-aligned stance, emphasizing the importance of regional stability and cooperation.
4. **Increased Global Role:** Indonesia's hosting of the G20 summit in 2022 marked a significant milestone in its global ascent. The presidency provided a platform to showcase the country's leadership on global issues, including economic recovery, climate change, and health. As a champion of democracy and pluralism in the Islamic world, Indonesia has emerged as a voice of moderation on the global stage.
5. **Miscellaneous factors:**
   - **Belt and Road Initiative (BRI):** Indonesia is a key participant in China's Belt and Road Initiative (BRI). Indonesia stands to benefit significantly through improved connectivity, increased trade, and investment in infrastructure. However, the country also faces challenges in balancing its participation in the BRI with its broader geopolitical interests.
   - **Free Trade Agreements (FTAs):** Indonesia has been actively pursuing free trade agreements to boost its economy and expand market access. FTAs with countries like China, India, Australia, and the EU have been instrumental in promoting trade, investment, and economic growth.
   - **Climate Change:** As an archipelagic nation, Indonesia is highly vulnerable to the impacts of climate change, including sea-level rise, extreme weather events, and environmental degradation. The country has emerged as a leader in climate action, advocating for global cooperation and implementing domestic policies to mitigate climate change.
   - **Digital Economy:** Indonesia has witnessed rapid growth in its digital economy, driven by increasing internet penetration and smartphone adoption. The country has the potential to become a digital powerhouse, with opportunities in e-commerce, fintech, and digital services.

While Indonesia's rise is evident, challenges such as corruption, inequality, and infrastructure development persist. However, the country's vast potential, coupled with its strategic location and growing global influence, positions it as a key player in the evolving geopolitical landscape.

MALAYSIA

Malaysia is a diverse and dynamic Southeast Asian nation known for its economic growth and multicultural society. The country comprises Peninsular Malaysia and the states of Sabah and Sarawak on the island of Borneo. The country has experienced rapid economic growth since the 1970s, driven by exports and foreign investment. Malaysia is a significant player in the international arena. Its strategic location, economic growth, and active participation in regional and global organizations have solidified its position

A. Politics & Administration

- The country practices a unique form of constitutional monarchy and parliamentary democracy, balancing between traditional monarchy and modern governance.
- The country is a federation of 13 states and three federal territories, each with a degree of administrative autonomy.
- Malaysia's monarchy is distinct in that it is a rotating system among nine Malay states, where the sultans serve as the heads of their respective states.
- Every five years, one of these sultans is elected as the Yang di-Pertuan Agong, or King, by the Conference of Rulers. The King serves as the ceremonial head of state, performing roles such as granting royal assent to bills and appointing the Prime Minister.
- The Malaysian Parliament is bicameral, consisting of the House of Representatives (Dewan Rakyat) and the Senate (Dewan Negara).

The judiciary is independent, with the Federal Court being the highest judicial authority. Malaysia's legal system is based on English common law, Islamic law (sharia) in personal matters, and customary law for indigenous peoples.

B. Economy & Trade

- Malaysia's economy is one of the region's most advanced and diversified, with key sectors including manufacturing, services, and natural resources such as oil and palm oil.
- Malaysia is rich in natural resources, including oil, natural gas, and palm oil. It is **one of the world's largest producers and exporters of palm oil** and has significant reserves of oil and gas.
- The manufacturing sector is a cornerstone of the Malaysian economy, contributing about 23% to GDP. It includes industries such as electronics, automotive, petrochemicals, and machinery.
- Malaysia is also a leading global exporter of semiconductors and electronic equipment.
- The services sector is the largest component of the Malaysian economy, accounting for approximately 54% of GDP. Key areas include finance, tourism, education, and healthcare. Kuala Lumpur, the capital, is a major financial hub in the region.
- Malaysia has an open economy, highly integrated into global trade networks. It is a member of the WTO, ASEAN, RCEP, CPTPP, among others.

C. Defence and Security

- Malaysia's strategic position along the Strait of Malacca—a critical maritime chokepoint—gives it significant geopolitical importance. The country's defense and security policies are shaped by this strategic location and its commitment to regional stability.
- The Malaysian Armed Forces (Angkatan Tentera Malaysia, ATM) consist of the Malaysian Army, Royal Malaysian Navy, and Royal Malaysian Air Force.
- Given the importance of the Strait of Malacca, Malaysia prioritizes maritime security, working closely with neighboring countries like Indonesia and Singapore to ensure safe passage through this vital sea route. The Malaysian Maritime Enforcement Agency (MMEA) plays a crucial role in enforcing maritime law, combating piracy, and ensuring maritime safety.
- The country also invests in modernizing its military capabilities, including acquiring advanced naval and air assets.

- Malaysia is an active participant in regional defense and security forums, including the ASEAN Defense Ministers' Meeting (ADMM) and the Five Power Defence Arrangements (FPDA), which include Australia, New Zealand, Singapore, and the United Kingdom.

D. **Culture & Diaspora**

- Malaysia is a multi-ethnic and multicultural society, with a rich tapestry of traditions, languages, and religions. The population is composed primarily of Malays, Chinese, Indians, and various indigenous groups, each contributing to the country's cultural diversity.
- Bahasa Malaysia is the official language, but English is widely spoken and serves as an important second language. Other languages, including Mandarin, Tamil, and indigenous languages, are also spoken.

E. **Diplomatic Relations**

- Malaysia's foreign policy focuses on maintaining friendly relations with all nations, with a particular emphasis on regional cooperation and Islamic solidarity.
- While Malaysia is committed to multilateralism, it also maintains a neutral and non-aligned foreign policy, seeking peaceful and cooperative relations with all countries. It emphasizes non-interference in the internal affairs of other nations and promotes peaceful resolution of conflicts.
- Malaysia is an active member of ASEAN and plays a significant role in regional diplomacy, advocating for economic cooperation, political stability, and security in Southeast Asia.
- As a predominantly Muslim country, Malaysia is an active member of the Organisation of Islamic Cooperation (OIC), advocating for the rights and interests of Muslim communities worldwide.

India and Malaysia

India and Malaysia established diplomatic relations in 1957, soon after Malaysia gained independence. The relationship is built on historical and cultural ties, with both countries being members of the Commonwealth and sharing a colonial past. High-level visits and regular dialogues, such as the India-Malaysia Strategic Partnership established in 2010, have reinforced bilateral ties. Both nations cooperate closely in regional and multilateral forums like ASEAN, the East Asia Summit (EAS), and the Non-Aligned Movement (NAM), working together on issues of mutual interest, including regional security and economic development.

- **Economic and trade relations** between India and Malaysia are robust, with Malaysia being one of India's largest trading partners in ASEAN. Bilateral trade is diverse, covering sectors such as palm oil, electronics, machinery, petroleum products, and pharmaceuticals.
- The **Comprehensive Economic Cooperation Agreement (CECA)** between the two countries, signed in 2011, has significantly boosted trade and investment. Malaysia is a key destination for Indian investments, particularly in sectors like infrastructure, construction, and information technology.
- The two countries have signed several agreements to enhance **defence collaboration**, including joint military exercises, training programs, and high-level defence dialogues. India and Malaysia conduct joint naval exercises and cooperate on maritime security, particularly in the strategically important *Strait of Malacca*. Both nations are also collaborating on counterterrorism, intelligence sharing, and capacity building to address common security challenges.
- Malaysia is home to a significant **Indian diaspora**, predominantly of Tamil origin, which has contributed to Malaysia's socio-economic development and cultural diversity. The cultural ties are celebrated through the exchange of arts, festivals, and religious practices, with Indian festivals like Diwali and Thaipusam widely celebrated in Malaysia.
- **Educational and academic exchanges** are also growing, with students from both countries pursuing higher education and research opportunities in each other's institutions. **Tourism** is another important aspect, with Malaysia being a popular destination for Indian tourists and vice versa.

SINGAPORE

Singapore is a unique **city-state** located at the southern tip of the Malay Peninsula in Southeast Asia. Its strategic position has been instrumental in its rise as a global financial and commercial hub. As a small island nation with limited natural resources, Singapore has excelled in leveraging its human capital, technology, and strategic location to become a prosperous and influential player on the world stage. The nations rapid transformation from a British colony to a global metropolis is a remarkable example of economic development and nation-building.

<table>
<tr><td rowspan="3">Singapore is termed a "city-state" because it encompasses both a city and an independent sovereign state within a single geographic boundary.</td><td>Geographical Size: Singapore is a small island nation with a land area of approximately 728 square kilometers, making it about the size of a large city rather than a typical country with diverse urban and rural areas.</td></tr>
<tr><td>Single Urban Entity: The entire country is essentially one large metropolitan area. There is no division between urban and rural regions as seen in larger countries.</td></tr>
<tr><td>Unified Government Structure: Unlike other countries, Singapore has a centralized government that governs the entire nation. There are no subdivisions like states or provinces; instead, the government manages the country's administration from a central point, similar to a city government but on a national scale.</td></tr>
</table>

A. Polity & Economy

- Singapore operates as a **parliamentary republic** with a dominant-party system. The **People's Action Party (PAP)** has held power since independence in 1965. The government emphasizes meritocracy, efficiency, and a clean governance model.
- The Prime Minister is the head of government, and the President, who has a more ceremonial role, is the head of state. The political system is characterized by stability and a strong focus on economic development.
- Singapore is often termed as an '**economic miracle**' and is a **global financial center** and a **major trading hub**. Its strategic location, coupled with a business-friendly environment, has attracted significant foreign investment.
- It operates a **free-market economy**, with minimal corruption, open markets, and a well-established legal framework. The government has prioritized education and technological advancement, fostering a skilled workforce.
- Key sectors driving the economy include **finance, trade, manufacturing, and tourism**. Singapore is a vocal advocate for free trade and has been instrumental in shaping regional economic integration. The country has a high per capita income, with its economy driven by exports in electronics, biotechnology, and financial services.

Urban planning in Singapore is characterized by meticulous, long-term strategic planning and efficient land use management, crucial for optimizing the limited space available in this small island nation. There is a strong emphasis on sustainability, economic growth, and quality of life for its residents. Singapore aims to reduce car ownership through policies like the Certificate of Entitlement (COE) system and road pricing. Singapore continuously adapts its urban infrastructure to address future challenges. This includes the development of smart city technologies, digital infrastructure, and resilient designs to tackle issues like climate change and aging infrastructure.

B. Defence and Security

- Singapore's defense policy is predicated on the twin pillars of **deterrence** and **diplomacy**. The nation recognizes the importance of a strong military to protect its territorial integrity and economic interests.

- **Compulsory national service** is mandatory for all male citizens. This is meant to foster a strong sense of civic duty and military preparedness.
- Given its size, geographical location and limited natural resources, the city-state has invested heavily in developing a robust and **advanced military technology**, including unmanned aerial vehicles, missile systems, and cyber defense.
- The country actively participates in regional security initiatives, such as **ASEAN Defence Ministers Meeting (ADMM)** and **Five Power Defence Arrangements (FPDA)**, to enhance cooperation and address shared security challenges.

> **Total Defence Capability** - This comprehensive approach involves not only the Singapore Armed Forces (SAF) but also the civilian population in national defense, encompassing the 6 pillars viz. Military, Civil, Economic, Social, Digital and Psychological Defence.

C. Culture & Diaspora

- Singapore is a multicultural society with a harmonious blend of Chinese, Malay, Indian, and Eurasian cultures.
- This multiculturalism is a cornerstone of Singaporean identity and is celebrated through numerous festivals, cuisines, and cultural practices. The government has also promoted multiculturalism and religious tolerance.
- The country's global influence has led to a significant Singaporean diaspora, particularly in Southeast Asia, North America, and Australia.

LANGUAGES

Singapore has four official languages: ***English***, ***Mandarin***, ***Malay***, and ***Tamil***.

D. Diplomatic Relations

Singapore's foreign policy is characterized by pragmatism, foresight, and a strong emphasis on economic diplomacy. Singapore's emphasis on education, culture, and tourism has enhanced its global image. The country has successfully leveraged its soft power to build goodwill and influence.

India and Singapore

India and Singapore established diplomatic relations in 1965, and over the decades, their partnership has grown into one of the most comprehensive in the region. Singapore is a key partner in India's "Act East Policy," and the two countries maintain close cooperation in regional and global forums, such as ASEAN and the United Nations. The relationship is marked by shared values, including a commitment to multilateralism, free trade, and regional stability.

> **NOTE**
>
> Prime Minister Narendra Modi will embark on official visits to Brunei and Singapore in early September of 2024. He would be visiting after nearly six years. During the visit, there would be an interaction with the CEOs and other business leaders in Singapore.

- **Economic and trade relations** between India and Singapore are a cornerstone of their bilateral ties. Singapore is one of India's largest trading partners in ASEAN and a major source of foreign direct investment (FDI) into India.
- The **Comprehensive Economic Cooperation Agreement (CECA)** signed in 2005 has significantly boosted trade, investment, and economic cooperation. Singaporean companies are heavily invested in sectors such as infrastructure, real estate, and financial services in India, while Indian businesses have a strong presence in Singapore, particularly in information technology, pharmaceuticals, and education.
- The two countries are also collaborating on emerging technologies, such as fintech, cybersecurity, and green energy.
- **Defence and security** cooperation has been expanding with the two nations conducting regular joint military exercises (army, navy and air force) underlining their strategic alignment. The 'India-Singapore Defence Ministers' Dialogue', established in 2015, provides a structured framework for deepening defence ties.

- **Maritime security**, especially in the strategically important Straits of Malacca, is a key area of collaboration, with both nations working closely to ensure the safety and freedom of navigation in these vital sea lanes. **Cybersecurity** and **counterterrorism** are also emerging areas of cooperation.

Significance on the Global Stage

1. **Geostrategic Location**: Singapore's geographical position at the crossroads of major shipping lanes in Southeast Asia has been instrumental in its economic rise. The Strait of Malacca, a crucial chokepoint for global trade, passes nearby, making Singapore a pivotal maritime hub. This strategic location has enabled the city-state to develop a world-class port infrastructure, handling a substantial portion of global container traffic.
2. **Economic Miracle:** Singapore's transformation from a British colonial outpost to a global financial center is a remarkable story. The government's emphasis on free-market policies, a skilled workforce, and a corruption-free environment has attracted significant foreign investment. With a GDP per capita among the highest globally, Singapore has established itself as a leading financial center, home to numerous multinational corporations.
3. **Trade and Investment**: Singapore is a staunch advocate of free trade and has been instrumental in negotiating numerous trade agreements. As a leading global trading nation, it has cultivated strong economic ties with countries worldwide. The country's pro-business policies, coupled with its strategic location, have made it a preferred destination for foreign investments. Singapore's Changi Airport is consistently ranked among the world's best, further enhancing its connectivity and attractiveness as a global business hub.
4. **Diplomatic Dexterity**: The nation has skillfully navigated complex geopolitical relationships, maintaining strong ties with both the United States and China. This diplomatic dexterity has allowed the city-state to play a crucial role in regional and global affairs. Singapore's role in mediating disputes and facilitating dialogue has earned it respect as a trusted intermediary on the world stage.
5. **Smart Nation Initiative**: Singapore's ambitious Smart Nation initiative aims to leverage technology to improve the lives of its citizens and enhance the country's competitiveness. With a focus on areas like urban planning, transportation, healthcare, and public safety, Singapore is at the forefront of technological innovation. This initiative has positioned Singapore as a model for other cities and nations seeking to harness technology for sustainable development.

CAMBODIA

Cambodia, located in the heart of Southeast Asia, is a nation rich in history and culture, best known for the ancient Angkor Wat temple complex. Emerging from decades of conflict and genocide, Cambodia has made significant strides in economic development and political stability under the leadership of Prime Minister Hun Sen. Despite these advances, the country continues to grapple with issues such as poverty, corruption, and human rights concerns.

A. Politics & Administration

Cambodia has a complex political history, marked by periods of instability and civil war. The country is a **constitutional monarchy**, with the King as the head of state and a Prime Minister as the head of government. The People's Party of Cambodia (CPP) has dominated politics since the 1990s.

B. Economy & Trade

- Cambodia's economy has experienced significant growth in recent years, driven by exports, particularly in the garment and footwear sectors.
- Cambodia's economy is largely driven by agriculture, textiles, and tourism, with growing interests in oil and gas exploration.
- However, the country is heavily reliant on tourism and the economy remains vulnerable to external shocks, such as global economic downturns. The government has been focusing on diversifying the economy and reducing reliance on agriculture.

C. Defence and Security

- Cambodia's defense policy is primarily focused on maintaining internal security and territorial integrity. The Cambodian People's Armed Forces (CPAF) is the country's military force.
- While Cambodia has participated in some UN peacekeeping missions, its defense spending remains relatively low compared to its neighbors.
- The country faces challenges such as human trafficking, drug trafficking, and transnational crime.

D. Culture & Diaspora

- Cambodia boasts a rich cultural heritage, most notably exemplified by the Angkor Wat temple complex. The country has made efforts to preserve its cultural heritage while promoting tourism.
- The Khmer Rouge regime caused significant damage to the country's cultural heritage, and efforts to rebuild and restore cultural sites are ongoing.
- Other important cultural and tourism places include - Preah Vihear Temple, Wat Phnom, Banteay Srei and Phnom Penh Royal Palace, among others.

E. Diplomatic Relations

- Cambodia has sought to balance its relationships with major powers, including China, the United States, and ASEAN member states.
- The country has faced criticism for its growing ties with China, particularly concerning human rights issues. Cambodia plays an active role in ASEAN and has participated in various regional cooperation initiatives.
- The nation has been working to improve its governance and human rights record to attract foreign investment and aid.

India and Cambodia

India and Cambodia established diplomatic relations in 1952, and their ties are deeply rooted in shared cultural and historical connections, particularly through **Buddhism** and the **Hindu influence** on *Khmer* civilization. Both countries have since developed a close partnership, reinforced by regular high-level visits and interactions. India's "Act East Policy" and Cambodia's strategic positioning within ASEAN have contributed to strengthening bilateral relations.

- **Economic ties** between India and Cambodia are growing, though the potential for trade is still largely untapped. Bilateral trade has been increasing, with India exporting pharmaceuticals, machinery, textiles, and agricultural products to Cambodia, while Cambodia exports footwear, apparel, and agricultural products to India.
- Both countries have been exploring ways to enhance economic cooperation, particularly in the fields of tourism, agriculture, and **small and medium enterprises (SMEs).** India has also supported Cambodia through various capacity-building initiatives under the **Mekong-Ganga Cooperation framework**.
- **Defence and security cooperation** have gained momentum in recent years. India has been assisting Cambodia in capacity-building, providing training to Cambodian military personnel, and offering technical assistance in de-mining operations. There are talks about deepening the defence ties, with a focus on maritime security, particularly in the context of the strategic importance of the South China Sea and the broader Indo-Pacific region.

- The **people-to-people relations** between India and Cambodia are characterized by strong cultural and religious ties. India's influence on Cambodia's art, architecture, and religion is evident in the country's many temples and cultural practices. Cultural exchanges, including the celebration of Indian festivals and events in Cambodia, and Cambodian cultural performances in India, have strengthened mutual understanding. Tourism and educational ties have also witnesses a steady growth.

PHILIPPINES

The Philippines, an archipelago of over 7,000 islands, is a Southeast Asian nation with a rich cultural heritage. The country has experienced periods of economic growth and challenges, including corruption and natural disasters. Despite these hurdles, the Philippines has a large and young population, which presents significant opportunities for economic development.

A. Politics & Administration

- The Philippines operates as a democratic republic with a presidential system, characterized by a separation of powers among the executive, legislative, and judicial branches.
- The Philippines polity has experienced significant political and economic transformations, especially since the People Power Revolution in 1986. The country's political system is outlined in its 1987 Constitution, which emphasizes democratic principles and the rule of law.
- The President of the Philippines serves as both the head of state and head of government. Elected by popular vote for a single six-year term, the President has significant powers, including the authority to enforce laws, oversee the executive branch, command the military, and appoint key officials

B. Economy & Trade

- The economy is driven by services, particularly business process outsourcing (BPO), remittances from overseas Filipino workers, and a growing manufacturing sector.
- The country is actively pursuing free trade agreements to boost exports and attract foreign investments.
- However, challenges such as poverty, inequality, and infrastructure development persist.

C. Diplomatic Relations

- The country's foreign policy balances relations with major powers, while promoting its national interests and sovereignty.
- The Philippines has traditionally maintained close ties with the United States, but has also sought to diversify its foreign relations.
- As a member of ASEAN, the Philippines actively participates in regional diplomacy, advocating for issues like maritime security and economic integration.
- The South China Sea dispute with China has been a major foreign policy challenge. The Philippines has also faced internal political divisions and external pressures, affecting its diplomatic standing.

D. Defence and Security

- Its strategic location in the Western Pacific, along with its complex maritime disputes in the South China Sea, underscores its critical role in regional security dynamics. The Philippines faces several security challenges, including terrorism, maritime disputes, and natural disasters.
- The Armed Forces of the Philippines (AFP) is responsible for maintaining internal security and territorial defense.
- The country has sought to modernize its military capabilities through acquisitions of new equipment and training. The Philippines is a key member of ASEAN and participates in regional security cooperation.

SABINA SHOAL is a coral atoll located approximately 75 nautical miles from the Philippine coast, closer to the Philippines than to China. Both China and the Philippines claim sovereignty over Sabina Shoal (and other features in South China Sea).

In August 2024, there occured a collision between a Chinese Coast Guard vessel and a Philippine Coast Guard vessel near **Sabina Shoal**, a disputed feature in the ***Spratly Islands***, which further highlighted the ongoing maritime dispute between China and the Philippines, with both countries asserting their rights to the disputed areas.

The incident has raised concerns about the potential for further escalation in the **South China Sea**, as both countries have deployed naval and coast guard vessels to the region. Several nations (including the USA) have expressed concern over the incident and called for both sides to resolve the dispute through peaceful means.

E. Culture & Diaspora

- The Philippines is known for its warm and hospitable people, with a rich cultural heritage influenced by Spanish, American, and indigenous traditions.
- The Filipino diaspora, particularly in the United States and the Middle East, is a significant source of remittances and cultural exchange.
- The country has made efforts to preserve its cultural heritage while embracing globalization.

Bayanihan

Bayanihan is a Filipino word derived from the word bayan meaning town, nation, or community in general.
It is a Filipino concept of communal unity, work, and cooperation, often symbolized by the image of villagers working together to carry a house.

India and Philippines

India and the Philippines established diplomatic relations in 1949, soon after India's independence and both countries share a multifaceted relationship that has evolved significantly over the years.

- **Bilateral trade** has been expanding, with both countries exploring new areas of economic cooperation. Major exports from India include pharmaceuticals, machinery, and electronic goods, while the Philippines exports electronics, food products, and coconut oil to India. Both nations are also focusing on enhancing trade in services, particularly in information technology and business process outsourcing (BPO) sectors. Additionally, there have been discussions on expanding cooperation in renewable energy, infrastructure development, and investment opportunities.
- **Defence and security cooperation** have become increasingly important in India-Philippines relations. Both countries share concerns over maritime security, particularly in the South China Sea, where the Philippines has territorial disputes. India has expressed support for a rules-based order and the peaceful resolution of disputes. The two nations have signed defence agreements, conducted joint military exercises, and engaged in training programs to enhance interoperability between their armed forces. Other areas of recent partnership include counter-terrorism and cybersecurity.
- Regular high-level exchanges, including visits by heads of state and government, have strengthened **diplomatic ties**. India's "Act East Policy" and the Philippines' "Look West Policy" have further enhanced cooperation, especially in regional and global forums like ASEAN, where India is a dialogue partner.

- The **Indian community in the Philippines**, though small, is well-integrated and contributes to the local economy. **Educational ties** have strengthened, with more Filipino students seeking higher education in India, particularly in medical fields.

BRUNEI DARUSSALAM

Brunei Darussalam, a small oil-rich sultanate located on the northern coast of the island of Borneo, is known for its opulent lifestyle and high standard of living. With a population of just over 450,000, the country enjoys one of the highest per capita incomes globally. While heavily reliant on oil and gas, Brunei is gradually diversifying its economy. Despite its small size and population, the nation enjoys a high standard of living funded by its substantial hydrocarbon income.

A. Politics & Administration

- Brunei is an absolute monarchy, with the Sultan of Brunei serving as both the head of state and government. The current Sultan, Hassanal Bolkiah, has ruled since 1967.
- Brunei's political system is characterized by the concentration of power in the hands of the Sultan, who exercises executive authority with the assistance of a council of ministers.
- The nation operates under the Constitution of 1959, which grants significant powers to the Sultan, including the ability to legislate by decree. Brunei has not held general elections since its independence from British protection in 1984, and political parties are largely inactive.
- The legal system is a combination of English common law and Islamic law (Sharia), with the latter gaining prominence in recent years, particularly since the introduction of the Sharia Penal Code in 2014.

B. Economy & Trade

- Brunei's economy is heavily dependent on oil and natural gas, which account for over 90% of its exports and a significant portion of its GDP. The country has one of the highest per capita incomes in Asia, owing to its substantial energy resources.
- To diversify its economy, Brunei has implemented various initiatives, including promoting sectors like halal manufacturing, Islamic finance, and tourism.
- The government provides extensive welfare programs funded by oil revenues, including free education and healthcare. Brunei's main trading partners include Japan, South Korea, China, and Singapore.
- The country is a member of several international economic organizations, including ASEAN and the World Trade Organization (WTO), and is involved in the Comprehensive and Progressive Agreement for Trans-Pacific Partnership (CPTPP).

C. Defence and Security

- Brunei maintains a relatively small but well-trained and equipped military, known as the **Royal Brunei Armed Forces (RBAF).** The RBAF is composed of the army, navy, and air force. The nation's defence policy is focused on maintaining internal stability, securing its maritime borders, and protecting its sovereignty.
- Brunei relies on strong defence ties with regional and international partners, including the United Kingdom, Australia, and Malaysia. It also participates in regional security initiatives under the ASEAN Defence Ministers' Meeting (ADMM) and engages in joint military exercises with other countries.
- The Sultan remains the supreme commander of the armed forces, reflecting the central role of the monarchy in national security.

D. Culture & Diaspora

Brunei's culture is deeply rooted in Malay traditions and Islamic values. The official language is Malay, and Islam is the state religion, influencing many aspects of daily life. The country celebrates several Islamic holidays and maintains a conservative social environment. Brunei's cultural heritage includes traditional music, dance, and crafts, such as silat (martial arts), gulingtangan (a traditional musical ensemble), and weaving. The Bruneian diaspora is relatively small but is present in countries like Malaysia, Singapore, and

Australia. Cultural exchanges with neighboring Southeast Asian nations, particularly within the ASEAN framework, are an important aspect of Brunei's cultural diplomacy.

E. Diplomatic Relations

- Brunei has diplomatic relations with over 170 countries and maintains embassies in key global capitals. Its foreign policy is guided by the principles of mutual respect, sovereignty, and peaceful coexistence.
- Brunei's diplomatic efforts are also focused on enhancing economic ties, particularly with major economies like China, the United States, and Japan. The country has maintained close ties with Western nations, particularly the United Kingdom, due to its historical colonial relationship.
- Brunei's strategic location along key maritime routes enhances its geopolitical significance, while its Islamic heritage and moderate stance on global issues position it as a unique player in international affairs.
- As a member of ASEAN, Brunei plays an active role in promoting regional cooperation and stability. The country also participates in international organizations such as the United Nations, the Commonwealth, and the Organization of Islamic Cooperation (OIC).

India and Brunei

- India and Brunei enjoy cordial diplomatic relations, underpinned by historical and cultural ties. Both countries share a commitment to multilateralism, and their interactions are strengthened through platforms like ASEAN.
- In 2024, diplomatic engagements have focused on enhancing bilateral cooperation, especially in multilateral forums like ASEAN, where India and Brunei work together on regional issues.
- The economic relationship between India and Brunei is modest but growing. In 2024, both countries have emphasized increasing trade, particularly in energy and hydrocarbons, as Brunei is rich in oil and gas. Efforts are also being made to diversify trade, including IT services and pharmaceuticals from India.
- Defence cooperation remains a smaller aspect of the relationship, but in 2024, both countries have explored expanding collaboration in maritime security, given the strategic location of Brunei in Southeast Asia. Exchanges in defense training and counter-terrorism efforts have also been areas of discussion.
- The Indian diaspora in Brunei is about 14,000 and they comprise a substantial number of doctors and teachers in Brunei. Cultural exchanges and celebrations of Indian festivals have strengthened ties. Over the last few years, there have been initiatives to further promote cultural diplomacy, with increased engagement in educational and professional exchanges.

> **NOTE**
>
> Prime Minister Narendra Modi will embark on official visits to Brunei and Singapore in early September of 2024. During his visit to Brunei on September 3-4, he will meet Sultan Haji Hassanal Bolkiah to enhance bilateral cooperation across various sectors. This visit marks the first time an Indian prime minister has travelled to Brunei for a bilateral engagement and commemorates 40 years of diplomatic relations between India and Brunei.

LAOS (LAO PDR)

Laos, officially known as the Lao People's Democratic Republic (PDR), is a landlocked country in Southeast Asia, known for its mountainous terrain and rich cultural heritage. While one of the least developed countries in the region, Laos has made progress in recent years. The country is rich in hydropower resources and has been focusing on developing its infrastructure to attract foreign investment.

A. Politics & Administration

Laos is a single-party socialist republic, with the Lao People's Revolutionary Party (LPRP) holding a monopoly on political power. The country has been under communist rule since 1975, following the abolition of the monarchy. The LPRP controls all branches of government, and political opposition is not permitted. The President, who is also the General Secretary of the LPRP, serves as the head of state, while the Prime Minister acts as the head of government. Laos operates under a constitution that was first promulgated in 1991 and has been amended several times to reflect changes in governance. The legal system is based on socialist legal theory and is influenced by French civil law traditions.

B. Economy & Trade

- Laos is one of the least developed and most sparsely populated countries in Southeast Asia. Its economy is largely driven by agriculture, which employs a significant portion of the population, though it has been gradually transitioning towards more industrial and service-oriented activities.
- Its strategic location, bordered by China, Vietnam, Cambodia, Thailand, and Myanmar, positions Laos as a crucial conduit for regional trade and investment.
- Hydropower is a major economic driver, with Laos earning substantial revenue from exporting electricity to neighboring countries like Thailand and Vietnam. The government has also been promoting foreign investment, particularly in mining, tourism, and infrastructure development.
- Laos is a member of ASEAN and the World Trade Organization (WTO), and it benefits from regional trade agreements. However, the country faces challenges such as a high level of public debt, dependency on external aid, poverty, infrastructure deficits, and a need for greater economic diversification.

C. Defense and Security

Laos maintains a modest military force, known as the Lao People's Armed Forces (LPAF), which is primarily focused on internal security and border protection. The military is closely aligned with the ruling LPRP and plays a significant role in maintaining the party's control. Laos has limited military capabilities and relies on close relationships with neighboring countries like Vietnam and China for defense and security cooperation. The country also participates in regional security initiatives through ASEAN, including the ASEAN Defence Ministers' Meeting (ADMM). The government's security concerns are largely focused on maintaining internal stability and managing transnational issues such as drug trafficking and illegal logging.

D. Culture

Laos has a rich cultural heritage that reflects its history, ethnic diversity, and Buddhist traditions. The majority of Laotians practice Theravada Buddhism, which plays a central role in the nation's cultural and spiritual life. Traditional music, dance, and festivals are integral to Laotian culture, with celebrations like the Lao New Year (Pi Mai) being widely observed. The country's artistic heritage includes weaving, wood carving, and the making of religious artifacts.

E. Diplomatic Relations

Laos pursues a foreign policy of neutrality, non-alignment, and peaceful coexistence, reflecting its desire to maintain sovereignty and avoid entanglement in regional conflicts. The country has close ties with its neighbors, particularly Vietnam, which has been its most significant ally since the communist takeover in 1975. Laos is a member of several international organizations, including the United Nations, ASEAN, and the Mekong River Commission, where it works on regional issues such as water management and development. The country has also been strengthening its relationships with major powers like China and Japan, seeking economic cooperation and investment.

India and Laos

- India and Laos share a strong diplomatic relationship, rooted in historical and cultural ties. Diplomatic engagements are reinforced through regular high-level visits, and both countries collaborate in multilateral forums like ASEAN.
- The economic relationship between India and Laos is relatively modest but has potential for growth. Trade mainly includes India's exports of machinery, pharmaceuticals, and electronics to Laos, while Laos exports timber and coffee to India. India is also involved in developmental projects in Laos, particularly in the areas of irrigation, agriculture, and power.
- Defence cooperation between India and Laos is limited but includes capacity-building initiatives. India has provided training to Lao military personnel and offers assistance in areas like demining and military medical services. Both countries have discussed expanding cooperation in security and defense.

- People-to-people relations are an important aspect of India-Laos ties, with cultural and educational exchanges playing a key role. India offers scholarships to Lao students and organizes cultural events to promote mutual understanding. The presence of a small Indian community in Laos also contributes to the bilateral relationship, particularly in sectors like education and trade.

INDIA-ASEAN RELATIONS

YEAR	PARTICULARS
1992	India becomes a Sectoral Partner of ASEAN
1996	Indian becomes ASEAN Dialogue Partner
2002	India becomes a Summit-Level Partner of ASEAN
2009	ASEAN-India Trade in Goods Agreement (AITIGA) signed (came into force in 2010)
2012	The Dialogue Partnership gets elevated to 'Strategic Partnership' at the 20-year Commemorative Summit
2014	ASEAN-India Agreement for Trade in Services (AITISA) signed (ratified by all parties in 2018)
2018	The Strategic Partnership to be focused on building cooperation in the maritime domain
December 2019	11th Edition of Delhi Dialogue held in Delhi
2022	30 years to ASEAN-India relations; 2022 designated as ASEAN-India Friendship Year
June 2022	12th Edition of Delhi Dialogue held
July-Aug 2024	5th meeting of ASEAN-India Trade in Goods Agreement (AITIGA) Joint Committee held in Jakarta

The economic strength of ASEAN in the present times has captured the interest of various growing economies, including India. While Indian foreign policy did not adequately prioritize ASEAN during the Cold War era, recent years have witnessed efforts from India to rectify this. Over time, India-ASEAN relations have progressed significantly, with India transitioning from being a Sectoral Dialogue Partner in 1992 to a Summit-level Partner in 2002. In 2012, the relationship was further elevated to a "strategic partnership." Since then, both sides have actively worked towards enhancing cooperation in areas such as economics, security, politics, and culture.

ASEAN is an important region for India due to its strategic location, economic potential, and political significance.

Economic Reasons

- The region offers significant opportunities for Indian businesses, and ASEAN's economic integration initiatives, such as the ASEAN Free Trade Area (AFTA), make it easier for Indian businesses to access ASEAN markets.
- The two-way trade between India nd ASEAN reached over $90 billion in 2020.
- ASEAN is an important trade partner of India with about **11% share in India's global trade.**

Strategic Significance

- ASEAN is a key player in the geopolitics of the Asia-Pacific region, and India has strategic interests in the region. India has been strengthening its ties with ASEAN through its Act East Policy

Regional integration

- ASEAN's regional integration initiatives, such as the ASEAN Economic Community (AEC), could provide opportunities for India to integrate further with the ASEAN region.

Cultural linkages

- India has strong cultural and historical ties with Southeast Asia, and ASEAN countries are home to significant Indian diaspora communities.

ASEAN PLUS SIX (ASEAN+6)

It is a concept that refers to a series of meetings between the ten member states of the Association of Southeast Asian Nations (ASEAN) and six other countries: **China, Japan, South Korea, India, Australia,** and **New Zealand**. The meetings are aimed at strengthening economic cooperation and integration between the ASEAN region and these six countries. The ASEAN+6 meetings were first held in 1997, with the inaugural ASEAN+3 meeting in Kuala Lumpur, Malaysia. In 1999, the group expanded to include Australia and New Zealand, and in 2005, India was also included, making it ASEAN+6.

Some sector-specific Dialogue Mechanisms include -

(1) Energy: The **East Asia Summit Energy Ministers Meeting** at the ministerial level serves as a platform for discussions on energy requirements. In November 2012, the **Ministry of New & Renewable Energy (MNRE)** organized the inaugural **ASEAN-India Ministerial Meeting on New & Renewable Energy** in New Delhi. The meeting focused on various aspects including the policy and regulatory framework for promoting renewable energy, facilitating finance for renewable energy projects, and fostering cooperation in research and development, technology transfer, and resource assessment. The meeting resulted in the adoption of the **'New Delhi Declaration on ASEAN-India Cooperation in Renewable Energy'**, highlighting the commitment to collaboration in the renewable energy sector.

(2) Education: The **Fifth East Asia Summit Education Ministers Meeting** (5th EAS EMM) was convened online on 1 October 2021, in conjunction with the 5th ASEAN Plus Three Education Ministers Meeting (5th APT EMM).

(3) Maritime connectivity: The **ASEAN-India Maritime Transport Working Group (AIMTWG)** helps in expanding ties related to the Maritime transport domain.

(4) Agriculture sector: Cooperation in various fields of agriculture, such as ensuring food security, sharing information and technology, undertaking research and development projects, promoting agriculture and

forestry-related industries, and enhancing human resources development, has been a key focus of ASEAN-India relations. Since 2011, an annual **ASEAN-India Ministerial Meeting on Agriculture and Forestry (AIMMAF)** has been convened regularly to facilitate discussions and collaboration in these areas.

(5) Promoting security sector cooperation including combating terrorism, drug trafficking and transnational crimes: The **Senior Official's Meeting on Transnational Crimes SOMTC + India** tackles the transnational crimes and related issues.

(6) Science and Technology and Space Sector: **ASEAN-India Working Group on Science & Technology** (AIWGST- Secretary level) has been helping to enhance cooperation in S&T. **ASEAN Digital Minister's Meeting** (TELMIN before 2021) **+ India (ADGMIN)** meetings is another step in this direction. ISRO is currently involved in a space cooperation initiative that includes the implementation of various projects. These projects entail the establishment of a **Tracking and Data Reception Station** and **Data Processing Facility** in Ho Chi Minh City, the up-gradation of the **Tracking Telemetry and Command (TTC) Centre** in Biak, Indonesia, and the training of ASEAN personnel in space science and technology at the **Centre for Space Science and Technology Education in Asia and the Pacific (CSSTEAP).**

(7) Small and Medium Enterprises: The collaboration in this area has been facilitated through the establishment of a Joint Working Group. India has established a **Project Development Fund** of approximately **$75 million** to support the development of manufacturing hubs in CLMV countries. Additionally, India has initiated the establishment of an **ASEAN-India Innovation Platform** by increasing the ASEAN-India Science and Technology Development fund **from $1 million to $5 million**. This platform aims to facilitate the commercialization of affordable technologies, technology transfer, and collaborative research and development projects.

(8) Tourism: The cooperation is conducted through the annual **ASEAN-India Tourism Ministers (ATM) Meeting**. During the **3rd ATM +** India meeting in 2012, an important milestone was achieved as India became the **first Dialogue Partner to sign a Memorandum of Understanding (MoU) on Strengthening Tourism Cooperation with ASEAN**. As part of this initiative, an ASEAN Promotional Chapter for Tourism (APCT) was established in Mumbai in 2011.

The Government of India has established three funds to enhance and facilitate cooperation between ASEAN and India: the ASEAN-India Cooperation Fund (AIF), the ASEAN-India Green Fund (AIGF), and the ASEAN-India Science and Technology Development Fund (AISTDF).

ASEAN-India Trade in Goods Agreement (AITIGA)

The 5th AITIGA Joint Committee and related meetings for review of AITIGA were held in ASEAN Secretariat, Jakarta, Indonesia from 29th July to 1st August 2024, marking a significant milestone in enhancing economic cooperation between ASEAN and India. The 4th Joint Committee meeting for the review of AITIGA was held in Putrajaya, Malaysia from 7-9 May 2024.

Apart from the above-stated mechanisms, India participates in other Fora alongside ASEAN –

ASEAN Regional Forum (ARF)

It was established in 1994 as a critical platform for security dialogue in the Indo-Pacific. It comprises of 27 members – 10 ASEAN member nations, 10 ASEAN Dialogue Partners (Australia, Canada, China, the European Union (EU), India, Japan, New Zealand, the Republic of Korea (ROK), Russia and the United States), Bangladesh, the Democratic People's Republic of Korea, Mongolia, Pakistan, Sri Lanka, Papua New Guinea, and Timor-Leste.

The Forum consists of five areas of focus, namely Counter-Terrorism and Transnational Crime, Information and Communications Technology (ICT) Security, Disaster Relief, Maritime Security, and Non-Proliferation and Disarmament. The most recent Ministerial Meeting of the ARF took place in **August 2022** in Phnom Penh, Cambodia, where statements were adopted to uphold Southeast Asia as a Nuclear Weapon Free Zone and to promote peace, stability, and prosperity through confidence-building measures and preventive diplomacy.

Economic Connect[17]

Evolution of India-ASEAN Trade (Billion USD)			
Year	**Export**	**Import**	**Net**
1996-97	2.902	2.934	-0.032
2005-06	10.411	10.883	-0.472
2015-16	25.133	39.909	-14.776
Apr 2021-Feb 22	38.295	60.10	-16.69

(a) ASEAN Economic Ministers-India Consultations (AEM + India): The AEM is an important sectoral body, and the meetings are crucial for economic engagement. The Commerce Ministers attend the meetings, with the ASEAN-India Agreement for Trade in Goods (AITIGA) being the main agenda in recent times.

(b) The ASEAN-India Framework Agreement on Comprehensive Economic Cooperation (2003): It provides the mandate for the creation of an ASEAN-India Free Trade Area. Three major agreements were finalized under it –
- ASEAN-India Trade in Goods Agreement (AITIGA, signed 2009)
- ASEAN-India Agreement for Trade in Services (AITISA, signed 2014)
- Agreement on Investment (signed 2014)

(c) ASEAN-India Business Council (AIBC): It was set up in 2003 to promote Comprehensive Economic Cooperation between India and the ASEAN region. It serves as a private sector mechanism to provide Governments on both sides with authoritative feedback on their current policies and also recommend steps to promote the ASEAN-India economic partnership. A Secretariat for AIBC was established in Malaysia in 2015.

Mekong Ganga Cooperation (MGC)

- The initiative was launched in **November 2000** at Vientiane, Lao PDR by the efforts of six countries - India and five ASEAN countries, namely, Cambodia, Lao PDR, Myanmar, Thailand and Vietnam. The **Ganga** and the **Mekong rivers** hold significant historical and cultural importance, and the MGC initiative aims to promote stronger connections among the communities residing along these two major river basins.
- The primary objective is to enhance cooperation in areas such as tourism, culture, education, transportation, and communication among the member nations. According to statements made by External Affairs Minister, S. Jaishankar, 'Mekong region is of great importance to India and India seeks multi-dimensional engagement with the MGC member nations.' More recently, India has been promoting connectivity in the region beyond the physical barriers, and would include digital, economic and people-to-people connectivity.
- **Mekong-Ganga Senior Officials' Meeting** was held in Phnom Penh, Cambodia, on **August 1, 2022**. The participants discussed priority areas ranging from the promotion of economic recovery in the post Covid-19 period to the participation of the MSMEs in global supply chains. Other issues included strengthening community health capacity and guaranteeing equitable and sustainable access to vaccines, accelerating digital transformation and creating information technology infrastructure in order to develop smart tourism.

[17] Overview of India-ASEAN- Relations. (2022, May 09). https://www.mea.gov.in/Portal/ForeignRelation/ASEAN_India_Brief_May_2022.pdf

Asia Cooperation Dialogue (ACD)

The Asia Cooperation Dialogue (ACD) is a **continent-wide forum** and was first of its kind in Asia. It was inaugurated in **June 2002** in Cha-Am, Thailand. The dialogue saw 18 Asian Foreign Ministers in attendance for the first time. Presently, the **35 countries** are a part of ACD-

- Founding Members (18) – Bahrain, Bangladesh, Brunei Darussalam, Cambodia, China, India, Indonesia, Japan, Republic of Korea, Lao PDR, Malaysia, Myanmar, Pakistan, Philippines, Qatar, Singapore, Thailand and Vietnam.
- New Members – Kazakhstan, Bhutan, Russia, Tajikistan, Kuwait, Iran, Saudi Arabia, Uzbekistan, Oman, Mongolia, Sri Lanka, UAE, Kyrgyz Republic, Afghanistan, Turkey, Nepal and Palestine.

The dialogue aims to **establish an Asian Community by including every Asian nation** without duplicating other organisations or creating a bloc against others in order to fill the existing void within Asia. Among 19 areas of cooperation, **energy, information and communications technology, and transport** are included.

The **main objectives** include –

1. Fostering interdependence among Asian nations across various areas of collaboration by recognizing shared strengths and opportunities, aiming to alleviate poverty and enhance the overall standard of living.
2. Enhancing intra-Asian trade and financial markets, thereby bolstering the negotiating power of Asian countries.
3. Establishing an Asian Community that is capable of engaging with the global community on a more equitable basis, thereby transforming the Asian continent.

The ACD enables the constitution of an informal and non-institutionalized forum for Asian Foreign Ministers to regularly exchange views on issues of mutual interest. The ACD has two main dimensions –

(i) Dialogue- It is aimed at **promoting interaction and participation** of ACD Ministers and Government officials.

(ii) Projects- Countries are encourages to **volunteer to become "primary movers" in cooperative areas of interest** and to advance each project to the benefit of Asian nations.

The Kingdom of Bahrain assumed the Chairmanship of the ACD from 2021-22. The 17th ACD Ministerial Meeting took place virtually in January 2021 in Ankara, Turkey.

Indian Ocean Rim Association (IORA)

It is an inter-governmental organisation formed in 1997 to foster regional economic cooperation. With 23 Member States and 10 dialogue partners, the organisation works on a variety of issues, including disaster risk management, maritime security, fisheries management and tourism and cultural exchanges. With over 80% of the world's seaborne trade in oil, and around 100,000 commercial vessels traversing the Indian Ocean per year, the sea lanes have acquired greater significance in the past couple of decades.

India-ASEAN Indo-Pacific Developments

Indo-Pacific is an interconnected geography and India's vision is premised upon the principle of '**ASEAN-Centrality**'. India has been engaging with the South-East Asian nations, along with East Asian and other Indo-Pacific nations to enhance influence and boost its international standing. India actively engages with the region to advance its vision of an open and inclusive Indo-Pacific, in line with initiatives such as the **Act East Policy (AEP)** and **Indo-Pacific Oceans Initiative (IPOI)**, with the aim of ensuring **security and prosperity for all in the region (SAGAR).**

> The **Asian Infrastructure Investment Bank (AIIB)** is a multilateral development bank (MDB) that aims to improve economic and social outcomes in Asia. It was established in 2005 and is headquartered as **Beijing**, China. AIIB has **106 members**, 92 Full Members and 14 Prospective Members, and is open to accepting additional members.

India advocates for a free, open, and inclusive order in the Indo-Pacific that upholds the sovereignty and territorial integrity of all nations, promotes peaceful resolution of disputes through dialogue, and adheres to international rules and laws. India's concept of the Indo-Pacific emphasizes inclusivity and supports the freedom of navigation and overflight for all in the international seas. The **12th Delhi Dialogue**, which was convened in June 2022, with the theme, "Building Bridges in Indo-Pacific" reinforced and highlighted the importance of the Indo-Pacific region and the role to be played by the two major players, India and ASEAN, around this issue.

> **Delhi Dialogue** is India's premier annual **Track 1.5 mechanism** for engagement of the two partners. This international conference brings together think tanks, dignitaries, senior officials, business leaders, academics, and prominent individuals from both India and ASEAN to discuss ways of enhancing the Strategic Partnership. Since its inception in 2009, twelve editions of the Dialogue have been successfully conducted, with the most recent one concluding in June 2022.

While addressing the ASEAN India Commemorative Summit in New Delhi, Prime Minister Modi stated, "India shares the ASEAN vision for rule-based societies and values of peace. We are committed to working with ASEAN nations to enhance collaboration in the maritime domain. It highlights the importance of our strategic partnership placing ASEAN at the centre of India's Act East Policy."[18]

India-Philippines BrahMos Deal

In January 2022, the two nations signed a US$ 375 million BrahMos deal which has been hailed as a milestone in India's relations with the ASEAN and the greater Indo-Pacific region. According to Atul Dinkar Rane, the head of BrahMos Aerospace, this deal represents India's first export agreement for a complete major weapon system and sets the stage for future similar deals. The deal serves the following benefits –

- It stands as evidence of India's sterling reputation as a supporter of international law.
- It acts as a bridge between India's Act East and Defence Export policies by increasing India's profile as a defence trade partner of technology products.
- It equips the Philippines naval forces with a much-needed deterrent capacity against the rising China and helps to modernize the forces in order to maintain a positive balance of power in its favour.
- Overall, it helps in contributing to the stability of the Indo-Pacific, since the deal includes training for operators and an integrated logistics support package.

---

[18] Opening remarks by the PM at the Plenary Session of the INDIA- ASEAN Commemorative Summit. (2018, Jan 25). https://www.pmindia.gov.in/en/news_updates/opening-remarks-by-the-pm-at-the-plenary-session-of-the-india-asean-commemorative-summit/

EAST ASIA SUMMIT (EAS)

The process for the establishment of the Summit was initiated in **2005** with the convening of the **1st East Asia Summit in Kuala Lumpur, Malaysia**. EAS is regarded as the Indo-Pacific's premier forum for strategic dialogue. The EAS was comprised of 16 participating countries originally – 10 ASEAN member nations, Australia, China, India, Japan, New Zealand, and the Republic of Korea. Russia and the United States were admitted in the year 2011, taking the **total number of members to 18**.

The EAS (East Asia Summit) can be characterized as a prominent forum led by leaders, where dialogue and cooperation take place on a wide range of strategic, political, and economic issues that are of shared interest and concern. The primary objective of the EAS is to foster peace, stability, and economic prosperity in East Asia. The **priority areas for cooperation** include - environment and energy, education, finance, global health issues and pandemic diseases, natural disaster management, and ASEAN Connectivity.

In 2021 EAS members represented 53.1 per cent of the world's population and accounted for 59.5 per cent of global GDP worth an estimated US$57.2 trillion. The **12th East Asia Summit (EAS) Foreign Ministers' Meeting** was convened on **5th August 2022** in Phnom Penh (Cambodia). The meeting saw discussions on strategic challenges facing the region including, Russia's invasion of Ukraine, situation in Myanmar, maritime security and the South China Sea, the Korean Peninsula, counter-terrorism, disinformation and climate change.

Note: The Regional Groupings have been discussed in a separate chapter.

6

WEST & CENTRAL ASIA

DEFINING THE REGION

COUNTRY	CAPITAL	POPULATION (2021)	GDP (current US$), 2021 (billion)	Human Development Index Rank (2023)
INDIA	**NEW DELHI**	**1.39 BILLION**	**3.17 trillion**	**134**
Armenia	Yerevan	2,968,128	13.9	76
Azerbaijan	Baku	10,145,212	54.6	89
Bahrain	Manama	1,748,295	38.9	34
Cyprus	Nicosia	1,215,588	27.7	29
Georgia	Tbilisi	3,708,610	18.7	60
Iran	Tehran	85,028,760	231.55	78
Iraq	Baghdad	41,179,351	207.89	128
Israel	Jerusalem (proclaimed Capital)	9,364,000	481.59	25
Jordan	Amman	10,269,022	45.24	99
Kuwait	Kuwait City	4,328,553	105.96	49
Lebanon	Beirut	6,769,151	18.08	109
Oman	Muscat	5,223,376	85.87	59
Qatar	Doha	2,930,524	179.57	40
Saudi Arabia	Riyadh	35,340,680	833.54	40
Syrian Arab Republic	Damascus	18,275,704	21.45	157
Turkiye	Ankara	85,042,736	815.27	45
United Arab Emirates	Abu Dhabi	9,991,083	358.87 (2020)	17
Yemen	Sana'a	30,490,639	21.06	186
*World Bank Data				

West Asia is known for its rich history, ancient civilizations, and cultural heritage, including the Persian, Babylonian, and Ottoman Empires. The region is home to some of the world's most important religious sites, including ***Mecca, Medina, Jerusalem,* and *Bethlehem***. The Middle Eastern region is particularly known for being a major oil producing region, with significant reserves of natural gas and other minerals.

Islam is the dominant religion in West Asia, followed by Christianity, Judaism, and other minority religions. The Caucasus region has a rich history, with ancient civilizations such as the Urartians and the Georgians and is home to a diverse range of ethnic groups, including Armenians, Azerbaijanis, Georgians, Russians, and others, each with their own unique languages, cultures, and traditions.

The Varied Governance Models of West Asia

The political structures in West Asia are as diverse as their populations and often complex. While countries like *Saudi Arabia, the United Arab Emirates,* and *Qatar* are **monarchies**, where power is concentrated in the hands of a hereditary ruler or royal family, *Iran*, *Iraq*, and *Turkey* are **republics**, where power is vested in elected officials and/or a president. Additionally, Iran is a unique example of a **theocracy**, where political power is closely intertwined with religious authority. The Palestinian territories in the **West Bank** and **Gaza Strip** are not recognized as independent states and are under Israeli occupation.

More importantly, the region has been infamous for being unbalanced and tempestuous. West Asia has experienced political instability and conflict over the years, including ongoing conflicts in Syria, Iraq, and Yemen, as well as the Israeli-Palestinian conflict. Additionally, the levant region continues to face significant political, economic, and social challenges, including ongoing conflicts and humanitarian crises in Syria and Palestine. The past two decades have also witnessed an escalation in conflicts in the region.

Some recent conflicts include -

- The **Syrian Civil War** began in 2011 as a result of protests against the Syrian government. It quickly turned into a full-blown conflict that has resulted in hundreds of thousands of deaths, displacement of millions of people, and significant destruction of infrastructure.
- **Iraq** has been grappling with violence and instability since the US-led invasion in 2003. The country has seen ongoing **sectarian violence**, attacks by ISIS, and political instability.
- The **Yemeni Civil War** began in 2015 when Houthi rebels took over the capital, Sana'a. The conflict has resulted in a humanitarian crisis, with millions of people facing food shortages and disease.
- The **Israeli-Palestinian conflict** has been ongoing for decades, with both sides engaging in violence and political maneuvering. 2021 witnessed escalations in violence in Gaza that had led to significant loss of life and displacement of civilians.
- **Turkey** has been engaged in a conflict with the ***Kurdish*** minority in the country for decades. The conflict has escalated in recent years, with the Turkish government launching military operations in Kurdish-majority areas of Syria and Iraq.
- **Iran** and **Saudi Arabia** have been engaged in a regional power struggle for years, with tensions escalating in recent years over issues such as Yemen and the Syrian conflict.
- As of August 2024, tensions between **Iran** and **Israel** have escalated significantly, particularly in the aftermath of the assassination of prominent figures linked to *Hamas* and *Hezbollah*. Iran has vowed retaliation, with its leadership signaling an impending strike against Israel.

WEST ASIA OR MIDDLE EAST?

In common parlance, both these regions are considered the same. However, Indian academicians prefer to use the term West Asia and not the Middle East. The term Middle East originated with the British Foreign Office in the 19th century. The British divided the world from their country's vantage point by coining terms like the Near East (the area closest to the United Kingdom), the Far East (which was east of British India), and the Middle East (which was between British India and the Near East). But with the collapse of the British empire the term lost its relevance.

Western Asia includes Egypt's 'Sinai Peninsula' (the only Asian part of Egypt), the Levant, the Arabian Peninsula, Turkey (excluding the European part of Turkey), Cyprus, the Caucasus, Iraq and Iran. The only difference between it and the Middle East is that the Middle East includes all of Egypt, and includes all of Turkey, including the European part of Turkey, but excludes the Caucasus.

THE ARABIAN PENINSULA & BOLSTERING TIES

The Arabian Peninsula comprises the following countries:

SAUDI ARABIA (Riyadh)

UNITED ARAB EMIRATES (Abu Dhabi)

OMAN (Muscat)

YEMEN (Sana'a)

KUWAIT (Kuwait City)

QATAR (Doha)

BAHRAIN (Manama)

(1) Saudi Arabia

It is the largest country on the peninsula, occupying the majority of the landmass and is a pivotal actor in the Middle Eastern Geopolitics. Politically, Saudi Arabia is a monarchy governed by the Al Saud family, with the King holding substantial power. The Kingdom's significance extends to its role as the custodian of Islam's two holiest cities, Mecca and Medina, giving it religious authority in the Muslim world.

It holds significant clout due to its vast oil reserves, being one of the world's leading oil exporters. The Kingdom plays a central role in the global energy market and wields substantial influence in the Organization of the Petroleum Exporting Countries (OPEC). Saudi Arabia's Vision 2030 plan, spearheaded by Crown Prince Mohammed bin Salman, aims to diversify the economy and reduce dependency on oil, while also introducing social reforms.

In recent years, Saudi Arabia has been engaged in a regional rivalry with Iran, with both nations competing for influence across the Middle East, notably in Yemen, Syria, and Lebanon. Additionally, the country faces international scrutiny over its human rights record, particularly concerning the treatment of dissidents and the ongoing conflict in Yemen.

(2) United Arab Emirates (UAE)

The UAE is a federation of seven emirates, with Abu Dhabi as the capital and Dubai as its global commercial hub. The UAE has emerged as a key player in regional and international politics, leveraging its wealth, strategic location, and modern infrastructure. Known for its ambitious foreign policy, the UAE has actively engaged in various conflicts across the Middle East and North Africa, including Yemen and Libya, while also normalizing relations with Israel through the **Abraham Accords** in 2020.

In September 2020, the **Abraham Accords** were signed between **Israel, UAE, and Bahrain mediated by the United States**. The agreements establish diplomatic relations, trade, and other cooperation between the countries.

The **Abraham Accords** are a series of agreements that established diplomatic relations between Israel and several Arab nations. Signed in the latter half of 2020, these accords include a broad declaration of peace and cooperation, along with specific bilateral agreements between Israel and the United Arab Emirates, Bahrain, and Morocco. The accords are named after the biblical figure Abraham, considered a common patriarch in both Jewish and Arab traditions, symbolizing a step toward reconciliation and brotherhood in the region.

GOLDEN VISA

It is a long-term residency permit in the UAE that allows foreign professionals and talents to live, work, or study in the country while enjoying a range of exclusive benefits. This visa is available to a select group, including investors, entrepreneurs, scientists, exceptional students and graduates, humanitarian leaders, and frontline workers.

The UAE's leadership, particularly under President (His Highness) ***Sheikh Mohammed bin Zayed Al Nahyan***, has positioned the country as a center of innovation and influence, while also navigating complex relationships with regional powers like Saudi Arabia, Iran, and Turkey. The UAE's **successful lunar mission in 2024** is a groundbreaking achievement. By landing the Emirati-made lunar rover on the moon, the country has positioned itself as a leader in space exploration and technology.

DID YOU KNOW?

India is home to the second largest Muslim population in the world.

(3) <u>Oman</u>

Oman is known for its neutrality and independent foreign policy, distinguishing it from its more assertive neighbors. Under the leadership of the late *Sultan Qaboos bin Said*, Oman adopted a foreign policy of non-interference, earning it a reputation as a mediator in regional conflicts. Oman has maintained balanced relations with both Saudi Arabia and Iran, avoiding entanglement in the rivalry that dominates the region.

Oman stands out among Gulf nations for its **neutral foreign policy** and emphasis on **peaceful coexistence**. Unlike its neighbors, Oman has maintained cordial relations with a wide range of international actors. Known for its **rich cultural heritage** and efforts towards **sustainable development**, Oman presents a unique model for the region.

Economically, Oman has sought to diversify away from oil, investing in sectors like tourism, logistics, and manufacturing through its **Vision 2040** plan. However, the country faces significant challenges, including high youth unemployment, economic diversification, and a growing fiscal deficit. **Sultan of Oman, Sultan Haitham bin Tariq**, continues to uphold Oman's tradition of diplomacy and cautious modernization, while navigating the pressures of maintaining stability in a turbulent region.

(4) <u>Yemen</u>

Yemen, located at the southern tip of the Arabian Peninsula, is one of the region's most fragile states, beset by internal conflict, poverty, and humanitarian crises. The country's strategic location at the **Bab el-Mandeb Strait**, a crucial maritime chokepoint linking the **Red Sea** to the **Gulf of Aden**, makes it geopolitically significant.

Yemen has been embroiled in a devastating civil war since 2015, involving various factions, including the **Houthi movement**, the internationally recognized government, and a Saudi-led coalition.

The conflict has turned Yemen into a **battleground for regional powers**, particularly Saudi Arabia and Iran, who support opposing sides. The war has led to one of the world's worst **humanitarian crises**, with widespread famine, disease, and displacement.

Yemen's weak central government and tribal divisions have historically made it difficult to achieve lasting peace, while the presence of terrorist groups such as Al-Qaeda in the Arabian Peninsula (AQAP) adds another layer of complexity. International efforts to broker peace have so far yielded limited success, leaving Yemen's future uncertain and its impact on regional stability profound.

(5) Kuwait

Kuwait, a small but wealthy nation in the northeastern part of the Arabian Peninsula, has played a unique role in regional and international relations. Known for its relatively open political system and vibrant parliamentary life, Kuwait stands out in a region dominated by monarchies. The **Emir of Kuwait** holds significant power, but the country's relatively open political environment allows for more public discourse and participation than in many of its neighbors.

Its strategic location and significant **oil reserves** have made it a key player in global energy markets and regional geopolitics. Known for its high standard of living, Kuwait has been a major contributor to regional economic development.

Kuwait's foreign policy is characterized by a cautious approach, balancing relationships with neighboring countries while maintaining strong ties with the United States. Economically, Kuwait faces challenges related to over-reliance on oil and the need for diversification, but its substantial sovereign wealth fund provides a cushion against economic shocks.

(6) Qatar

Qatar, a small yet wealthy nation on the northeastern coast of the Arabian Peninsula, has punched above its weight in international affairs. Qatar has undergone rapid urbanization and modernization, transforming into a global business hub. The country's ambitious **Vision 2030 plan** aims to diversify its economy and enhance its global standing, with the successful hosting of the 2022 FIFA World Cup showcasing its soft power capabilities.

Unlike Saudi Arabia, which is primarily an oil-rich nation, Qatar possesses the world's largest **natural gas reserves**, making it a global energy powerhouse. Leveraging its vast natural gas reserves, Qatar has become one of the richest countries in the world per capita, with its wealth enabling an assertive foreign policy.

Qatar-based media outlets, such as **Al Jazeera**, have shaped global discourse and projected the nation's soft power. Qatar's influence extends through its support for various political movements across the Middle East, including Islamist groups.

ALJAZEERA

This support (to media) has often put Qatar at odds with its Gulf neighbors, particularly Saudi Arabia and the UAE, culminating in the 2017 blockade where several Arab countries severed ties with Qatar. The resolution of the blockade in 2021 marked a return to diplomatic relations, but underlying tensions remain. Additionally, Qatar also hosts the largest U.S. military base in the Middle East, further solidifying its strategic importance.

(7) Bahrain

Bahrain, a small island nation in the Persian Gulf, is known for its strategic location and complex political landscape. Bahrain's economy has historically relied on oil, but in recent years, the government has pursued diversification, focusing on sectors like banking, finance, and tourism. Bahrain was one of the first Gulf states to discover oil, but its reserves are smaller than those of its neighbors, prompting an earlier shift towards diversification.

Politically, Bahrain has faced significant internal challenges, particularly since the **Arab Spring** in 2011, which saw widespread protests against the ruling Al Khalifa family. The government, with support from Saudi Arabia, quelled the protests, but underlying sectarian tensions between the Sunni ruling elite and the Shiite majority persist. Bahrain's foreign policy is closely aligned with Saudi Arabia, particularly in its stance against Iran, which it accuses of meddling in its internal affairs.

The country's small size and limited resources mean that it often relies on its larger neighbors for security and economic support, but it continues to assert its sovereignty on the international stage. The country is home to the U.S. Navy's Fifth Fleet, underscoring its importance to Western security interests in the region.

AREAS OF ENGAGEMENT

(1) **Saudi Arabia** –

- India is Saudi Arabia's second-largest trading partner, while Saudi Arabia ranks as **India's fifth-largest trading partner.** The trade relationship between the two countries has shown consistent growth over the years. In the fiscal year (FY) 2023-24, bilateral trade amounted to **USD 43.3 billion**.
- Indian exports during this period reached **USD 11.56 billion**, marking a **7.8% increase**. On the other hand, Saudi exports to India totalled **USD 31.8 billion**.
- In FY 2022-23, Saudi Arabia was India's third-largest supplier of **crude oil and petroleum products**, with India importing **39.5 MMT of crude oil**, accounting for **16.7%** of India's total crude oil imports.
- **LPG imports** from Saudi Arabia were **7.85 MMT**, making up **11.2%** of India's total petroleum product imports during the same period.
- India and Saudi Arabia, as maritime neighbours, enjoy strong naval and defence ties. Two editions of the bilateral naval exercise **'Al Mohed Al Hindi'** have been conducted, enhancing operational cooperation. The two nations are also working closely in **defence industries** and capacity building.
- The first-ever **India-Saudi Joint Land Force Exercise, 'EX-SADA TANSEEQ-I'**, took place from January 29 to February 10, 2024, in Rajasthan.
- During the visit of India's Minister of State for Defence, **Shri Ajay Bhatt,** to Saudi Arabia in February 2024, a **USD 225 million agreement** was signed for the export of defence products from India to Saudi Arabia, led by **Munitions India Ltd.**
- The **Indian community** in Saudi Arabia, numbering more than **2.65 million**, serves as a vital link between the two nations.
- The annual **Hajj pilgrimage** is a significant aspect of Indo-Saudi relations. During the visit of the Saudi Crown Prince to New Delhi in February 2019, India's **Hajj *quota*** was increased by **24,975**, allowing **200,000 Indians** to perform Hajj in August 2019. Following pandemic-related restrictions, India's Hajj quota was restored to **175,025 pilgrims** in 2023.
- The **India-Saudi Arabia Strategic Partnership Council (SPC)** was established in October 2019 during the visit of the Prime Minister of India to Saudi Arabia. The SPC consists of two main committees: the Political, Security, Social, and Cultural Committee, and the Committee on Economy and Investments.
- In September 2022, a ministerial meeting of the SPC took place in Saudi Arabia, yielding significant outcomes, including:
    1. Efforts to facilitate the realization of the Crown Prince's 2019 announcement of USD 100 billion investments in India.
    2. Endorsement of 41 areas of cooperation identified by technical teams in the domains of Agriculture & Food Security, Energy, Technology & IT, and Industry & Infrastructure.
    3. Emphasis on collaboration in the digital fintech sector, with the operationalization of UPI (Unified Payments Interface) and Rupay Card in Saudi Arabia.
    4. Renewed commitment to joint projects, such as the West coast refinery, LNG infrastructure investment, and the development of strategic petroleum storage facilities in India.

(2) United Arab Emirates (UAE) –

- The India-UAE trade relationship has expanded remarkably over the decades. In the **1970s**, trade between the two nations was valued at **US$ 180 million** annually. By **2022-23**, this trade had skyrocketed to **US$ 85 billion**, making the UAE India's **third-largest trading partner** after **China and the US**.
- The UAE is also India's **4th largest source of crude oil** and the **2nd largest source for LNG and LPG**.
- The UAE is India's **second-largest export destination**, with exports totaling nearly **US$ 31.61 billion** in **2022-23**.
- **India's exports** to the UAE are diversified, comprising a broad range of products. Major Indian exports to the UAE include: petroleum products, precious metals, stones, gems, and jewellery, minerals, food items (cereals, sugar, fruits, vegetables, tea, meat, seafood), textiles (garments, synthetic fibres, cotton, yarn), engineering and machinery products and chemicals.
- **India's major imports** from the UAE include: Petroleum and petroleum products, precious metals, stones, gems, and jewellery & Minerals, chemicals, wood, and wood products.
- The UAE is a significant investor in India, with total investments estimated to be around **US$ 20-21 billion** as of March 2023. This includes **US$ 15.5 billion** in **Foreign Direct Investment (FDI)** and the remainder as **portfolio investments.**
- In **2022-23**, the UAE ranked as the **4th largest FDI investor** in India. The UAE has also committed to investing **US$ 75 billion** in India's infrastructure sector over time.
- The **Abu Dhabi Investment Authority (ADIA)**, one of the world's largest sovereign wealth funds, has invested **US$ 1 billion** as an anchor investor in India's **National Infrastructure Investment Fund (NIIF)**.
- The **Indian community** in the UAE, estimated at **3.5 million**, is one of the largest Indian diaspora groups in the world. Their annual remittances are among the highest globally, accounting for **18% of the total remittances to India** as of **2020-21**.

(3) Oman –

- The **Sultanate of Oman** is a strategic partner of India and holds an important position within regional and multilateral fora such as the **Gulf Cooperation Council (GCC)**, **Arab League**, and the **Indian Ocean Rim Association (IORA)**.
- India and Oman share strong ties rooted in **geography, history, and culture**, resulting in warm and cordial relations. Oman is a pivotal part of India's **West Asia Policy** and is its oldest regional strategic partner.
- Bilateral trade between the two nations reached **US$ 9.988 billion** in FY 2021-2022 and surged to **US$ 12.388 billion** in FY 2022-2023. Investment flows are robust, with over **6000 India-Oman joint ventures** operating in Oman, valued at over **US$ 7.5 billion**.
- India is the **second-largest market** for Oman's **crude oil exports** (2022), after China. India is the **second-largest market** for Oman's **non-oil exports** (2022), after Saudi Arabia.
- India ranks as the **third-largest source** of Oman's imports after the UAE and Saudi Arabia.
- India's exports to Oman stood at **US$ 4.477 billion**, making Oman India's **31st largest export market**.
- India's imports from Oman were valued at **US$ 7.911 billion**, positioning Oman as India's **24th largest import source**.
- The Indian community plays a significant role in Oman, with approximately **684,771 Indians** residing in the country, including **531,435 work visa holders**. Several Indian families have been living in Oman for more than **150-200 years**.
- As of July 2023, **1,825 Indian-origin individuals** have acquired **Omani citizenship**, further emphasizing the deep-rooted cultural connections.

(4) Yemen –

- India has been a strong supporter of Yemen's independence and was one of the first countries to recognize the **Yemen Arab Republic (YAR)** in 1962 and the **People's Democratic Republic of Yemen (PDRY)** in 1967. These early diplomatic efforts laid the foundation for India-Yemen relations in the post-colonial era. In 1990, YAR and PDRY merged to form the Republic of Yemen, further solidifying the relationship.
- Yemen is also a member of the **Indian Ocean Rim Association (IORA)** and has consistently supported India's bid for permanent membership in an expanded United Nations Security Council (UNSC).
- The bilateral trade between India and Yemen has been robust. In FY 2021-22, total trade stood at **US$ 1.07 billion - Exports from India to Yemen** amounted to **US$ 847 million**, reflecting a **7.77% growth** year-on-year. **Imports from Yemen** reached **US$ 228 million**, showing a remarkable **873.92% growth** year-on-year.
- **Key Indian exports** to Yemen include: Rice, wheat, and sugar; Pharmaceuticals and processed food products and Textiles, petroleum products, and ceramics.
- India imports from Yemen include: Iron and steel, Petroleum and telecom instruments & aluminium, lead and copper.
- India has also shown interest in Yemen's **petroleum and natural gas industry**. Major Indian oil companies like **Indian Oil Corporation, Bharat Petroleum Corporation Limited, Reliance**, and **Mangalore Refineries** have previously imported Yemeni crude oil.
- Defence cooperation between India and Yemen covers a broad spectrum, including:
  - Participation in **joint military exercises** like **MILAN**.
  - Training of Yemeni officers, cadets, and soldiers at Indian Armed Forces training establishments, at both **junior and senior levels**, as well as in **specialized fields**.
  - Collaboration between the **Indian Navy** and the **Yemen Coast Guard** for **anti-piracy patrols** in the Indian Ocean.
- Given the strategic location of both countries and their historical ties, opportunities exist to further deepen defence cooperation, particularly in Anti-piracy operations, Intelligence sharing, Defence industry collaboration and medical assistance.

(5) Kuwait –

- India and Kuwait have traditionally enjoyed a **friendly relationship**, grounded in history and time-tested bonds. India has been a natural trading partner for Kuwait, with the **Indian Rupee** serving as legal tender in Kuwait until 1961. The year 2021-22 marked the **60th anniversary** of diplomatic relations between the two countries.
- Kuwait remains a **reliable supplier** of **crude oil and LPG** to India, fulfilling a critical component of India's energy needs. To facilitate and enhance this cooperation, a **Joint Working Group (JWG) on Hydrocarbons** meets regularly to address and manage issues related to energy supplies.
- Labour and manpower issues are central to India-Kuwait relations. Indians constitute the **largest expatriate community** in Kuwait, encompassing both white-collar and blue-collar workers. The **Joint Working Group (JWG) on Labour, Employment, and Manpower Development** regularly convenes to address and discuss labour-related matters.
- The Indian community in Kuwait, comprising approximately **1 million people**, is the largest expatriate group in the country. This community includes a diverse range of professionals such as: engineers, doctors, and chartered accountants, scientists, software experts, and management consultants, architects, technicians, and nurses & retail traders and businessmen

(6) Qatar –

- India-Qatar cooperation has been expanding across multiple sectors, supported by historically strong ties and consistent engagement at various levels of government. Regular interactions, including at the highest level, have helped sustain this relationship.

- On December 1, 2023, Prime Minister Narendra Modi met with the Amir of Qatar on the sidelines of the **COP28 Summit** in Dubai. The leaders discussed the potential of strengthening the bilateral partnership and the welfare of the Indian community residing in Qatar.
- In 2023-24, bilateral trade between India and Qatar reached **USD 14.08 billion**, making India Qatar's second-largest trading partner.
- During 2022-23, India exported goods worth **USD 1.96 billion** to Qatar, including cereals, copper articles, iron and steel articles, vegetables, fruits, spices, processed food products, electrical machinery, plastic products, textiles, construction materials, chemicals, precious stones, and rubber. India imported goods valued at USD 16.8 billion from Qatar, including LNG, LPG, chemicals, petrochemicals, plastics, and aluminium articles.
- **India** is one of the **top three export destinations** for Qatar, alongside China and Japan, and is also a key source of imports for Qatar, ranking alongside China and the US.
- On **July 10, 2024**, an Indian delegation, comprising officers from the Department of Commerce and other ministries, held a **Joint Working Group (JWG)** meeting with their Qatari counterparts in Doha. Both sides reviewed the progress of discussions on potential Memoranda of Understanding (MoUs) on Food Safety and the exchange of pre-arrival information to facilitate trade and customs control. They agreed to expedite these discussions and to hold the next JWG meeting in New Delhi in 2025.
- **Qatar is India's largest supplier of LNG**, providing 10.74 million metric tons (MMT) of LNG worth USD 8.32 billion in FY 2022-23. This accounts for over 48% of India's total global LNG imports.
- According to the Qatar Chamber of Commerce and Industry, more than **15,000 Indian companies**, both large and small, operate in Qatar, either wholly owned or as joint ventures. Indian companies are actively collaborating in sectors such as infrastructure, communications and IT, energy, and other areas.
- Defence cooperation forms an important part of India-Qatar relations. India offers training opportunities at its defence institutions to various partner countries, including Qatar. India also regularly participates in the Doha International Maritime Defence Exhibition and Conference (DIMDEX) in Qatar.
- As of December 2023, over 835,000 Indian nationals reside in Qatar, forming the largest expatriate community. These individuals are employed in a wide range of professions including medicine, engineering, education, finance, business, media, and as blue-collar workers.

(7) Bahrain –

- India and Bahrain share excellent bilateral relations marked by strong political, economic, cultural, and people-to-people ties. The historic relationship dates back approximately 5,000 years, with trade and exchanges rooted in the Dilmun Civilization in Bahrain and the Indus Valley Civilization in India.
- At the invitation of His Royal Highness Prince Khalifa bin Salman Al Khalifa, Prime Minister Narendra Modi paid a state visit to Bahrain on **August 24-25, 2019**, further strengthening the bilateral relationship.
- In March 2022, Bahrain became the **86th member of the International Solar Alliance (ISA)** by depositing its Instrument of Accession during the 5th Foreign Office Consultations held in New Delhi.
- Bilateral trade between India and Bahrain has witnessed significant growth. In 2021-2022, trade grew by 54% to reach a record **USD 1.65 billion**. In 2022-2023, bilateral trade grew by an additional 20%, reaching **USD 1.98 billion**, with the trade balance favoring Bahrain.
- India ranks among the top five trading partners of Bahrain.
  - **India's Exports to Bahrain** - Major exports include agricultural products such as rice, boneless meat, shrimp, sugar, fresh fruits, and vegetables, along with machinery, engineering goods, medicaments, jewellery, polymers, private cars, ships, boats, and floating structures.

- India's Imports from Bahrain: Key imports consist of urea, methanol, mineral fuels and oils, iron ore, aluminium, copper, and bridge sections.

- The Indian expatriate community is highly regarded in Bahrain by both the authorities and employers due to their trustworthiness, strong work ethic, and "apolitical" nature.

Gulf Cooperation Council

India is fast emerging as a dominant force and aims to diversify its interests in a rapidly evolving geopolitical scene. The Arabian Peninsula is one such areas of focus in the present decade.

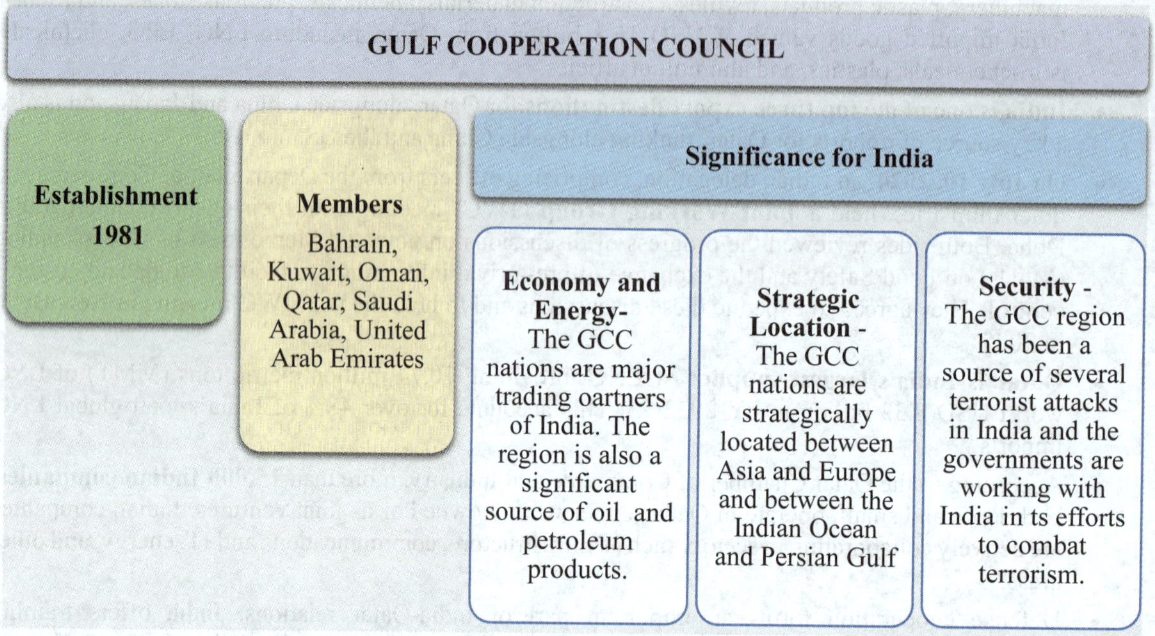

India's trade with the **Gulf Cooperation Council (GCC)** has been experiencing significant growth. The **GCC is presently the largest trading partner bloc for India**, with bilateral trade valued at over USD 154 billion in the fiscal year 2021-22. However, it is important to note that **India and the GCC do not have a Free Trade Agreement (FTA)** in place. In the year 2021-22, the GCC, along with Iraq, contributed to nearly one-fifth of India's total trade. Among the GCC countries, the United Arab Emirates (UAE), Saudi Arabia, and Kuwait have the highest number of non-resident Indians (NRIs), collectively accounting for over half of the NRI population. Additionally, **GCC countries are responsible for more than 50% of the total remittance flow into India.**

The shift towards the Middle Eastern area, especially the Gulf, can be understood due to two critical factors –

1. The economic afnd strategic relevance of the region stands undisputed.
2. Due to such high stakes in the region, India, that aims to become a global leader, cannot be exclusionary in its approach and thus, must engage actively with the region.

AREAS OF DISCONNECT

- Some Arab countries, particularly Pakistan's close allies such as Saudi Arabia and the United Arab Emirates, have expressed concern over the situation in **Kashmir** and the overall situation of **Muslims in India**, and have repeatedly supported Pakistan's stance on the issues. Specifically, they have raised concerns about India's Citizenship Amendment Act (CAA) and the National Register of Citizens (NRC), which they see as discriminatory against Muslims. However, India has rejected any interference in its internal affairs and maintains that the CAA and NRC are necessary measures to address illegal immigration and do not discriminate against any particular religion.

- There have been occasional **trade disputes** between India and some Arab nations over issues such as tariffs, import restrictions, and non-tariff barriers. However, most of these issues have been resolved through negotiations and dialogue.
- There have been some cases of **labor disputes** involving Indian workers in Arab countries, particularly related to issues such as non-payment of wages, poor working conditions, and mistreatment. However, these issues have been addressed through diplomatic channels and by strengthening labor laws and regulations.
- India is heavily dependent on **oil and gas imports** from Arab nations, and since this region has been **unstable** for quite some time, any disruption in the supply chain due to geopolitical or economic factors can affect India's energy security. Thus, India has been working to diversify its energy sources and reduce its dependence on imports.
- The Arab region plays a significant role in India's efforts to **combat terrorism**, as the region is a source of terrorism financing, recruitment, and training. India has been the victim of several major terrorist attacks in recent years, including the 2008 Mumbai attacks, which were carried out by Pakistan-based terrorists with links to militant groups in the Arab region. Terrorist groups operating in the Arab region, such as **ISIS** and **Al Qaeda**, have been known to recruit Indian nationals to carry out attacks in India. The Arab region is a major source of terrorist financing as well. However, India has been working closely with Arab governments to enhance cooperation on these issues.

Middle East Green Initiative (MGI) is a Saudi Arabia led regional dialogue on climate launched in 2021 to bring together leaders from across the MENA region (Middle East/North Africa) and beyond. The critical objectives include –

- Reducing carbon emissions from regional hydrocarbon production by more than 60%.
- Plant 50 billion trees across the Middle East and restore an area equivalent to 200 million hectares of degraded land. (It can help in reducing global carbon levels by 2.5%).

India also participated in the **Second MGI Summit** that was held in November 2022, in Sharm El Sheikh, in tandem with COP27. Saudi Arabia's Crown Prince announced that the kingdom would contribute **$2.5 billion** to a green initiative in the Middle East over the next 10 years, and host its headquarters.

THE CRADLE OF CIVILIZATIONS: EXAMINING EGYPT, IRAQ & IRAN

EGYPT – THE NILE VALLEY POWERHOUSE

Egypt occupies a strategic position in both the Arab world and Africa, serving as a historical leader in the region. More importantly, it controls the Suez Canal, one of the world's most critical maritime chokepoints, which significantly influences global trade and energy flows. Politically, Egypt has long been a key player in Middle Eastern geopolitics, particularly through its role in the Arab-Israeli conflict and as a founding member of the Arab League. Egypt was the first Arab country to sign a peace treaty with Israel in 1979, which has shaped its relations with both Western powers, particularly the United States, and other Arab nations.

The **Sucz Canal**, which **connects the Red Sea to the Mediterranean**, is a crucial shipping route for global trade, allowing ships to bypass the long and expensive journey around the southern tip of Africa.

Domestically, Egypt has faced political instability, especially after the 2011 revolution that ousted President Hosni Mubarak. The current government, led by President Abdel Fattah el-Sisi, has been criticized for its authoritarian practices, but it maintains strong ties with the West due to Egypt's role in regional security, counterterrorism, and as a mediator in the Israeli-Palestinian conflict.

Economically, Egypt is focused on infrastructure projects and attracting foreign investment, yet it faces significant challenges such as high unemployment, poverty, and reliance on external financial support. The country's foreign policy is characterized by balancing relationships with global powers like the U.S., Russia, and China, while maintaining influence within the Arab world and Africa.

Egypt that is often referred to as the '**Gateway to Africa**', is an area of immense opportunity for India, especially in terms of catering to Egypt's economic needs, utilising its strategic location and leveraging its leadership in the region in India's favour. Additionally, Egypt's control of the **Suez Canal** makes it an important player in global trade and a key transit point for oil and gas shipments.

India has been engaging with **Egypt** and recently, both nations have agreed to elevate their engagement to a '**strategic partnership**', through which they aim to "develop a long-term framework for greater cooperation in the fields of politics, security, economics, and science", as stated by PM Modi. The trade between the two countries amounted to **USD 7.26 billion** in 2021-22.

IRAQ - A NATION IN TRANSITION

Iraq is a country with deep historical roots and significant geopolitical importance in the Middle East, largely due to its vast oil reserves and strategic location between Iran and Saudi Arabia. The U.S.-led invasion in 2003, which toppled **Saddam Hussein**, profoundly altered Iraq's political landscape, leading to years of instability, sectarian conflict, and the rise of extremist groups like **ISIS**. The Iraqi government, established post-2003, is a fragile democracy, often marred by corruption, political infighting, and a lack of effective governance.

The **Islamic State of Iraq and Syria (ISIS)** emerged from the chaos that followed the 2003 US invasion of Iraq. It exploited sectarian tensions and a weak central government to establish a self-proclaimed caliphate across parts of Iraq and Syria. ISIS's brutal tactics and extremist ideology posed a significant threat to regional stability and global security. The defeat of ISIS in 2017 marked a turning point, but the group's remnants continue to pose a security challenge for Iraq.

Iraq's foreign policy is heavily influenced by its relations with neighboring Iran, which has substantial political, economic, and military influence in the country, particularly through Shia militias. Iraq also maintains a complex relationship with the United States, balancing the benefits of U.S. military and economic support with the need to appease pro-Iranian factions within its borders. Additionally, Iraq's relations with Turkey are strained due to issues like water rights and the presence of Kurdish groups along the border.

The ongoing challenges of rebuilding infrastructure, addressing sectarian divisions, and integrating diverse ethnic and religious groups continue to dominate Iraq's domestic and international agenda.

In August 2024, Iraq's parliament introduced a controversial bill (proposed by the Iraq Justice Ministry) that would **lower the legal marriage age for girls to 9 and boys to 15**. The move has sparked significant debate within Iraq and internationally, reflecting deep societal divisions over the role of religion, tradition, and modernity in Iraqi law.

IRAN - A COMPLEX PORTRAIT

Iran is a pivotal state in the Middle East, known for its vast energy resources, strategic location, and influence over the Shiite Muslim population across the region. Governed by a theocratic regime since the 1979 Islamic Revolution, Iran's foreign policy is driven by a combination of ideological commitments and pragmatic interests. The country has positioned itself as a counterweight to U.S. and Israeli influence in the region, often supporting non-state actors like ***Hezbollah*** in Lebanon, the ***Houthis*** in Yemen, and various militias in Iraq and Syria.

Iran's **nuclear program** has been a central issue in its international relations, leading to severe sanctions and diplomatic isolation. The 2015 **Joint Comprehensive Plan of Action (JCPOA)** aimed to limit Iran's nuclear activities was a major diplomatic achievement. However, its unraveling following the U.S. withdrawal in 2018 led to increased uranium enrichment and heightened regional and global concerns, particularly with Israel and the Gulf states.

The country's strategic partnership with Russia and China reflects its efforts to circumvent Western sanctions and build alternative alliances. Iran's foreign policy aims to expand its influence while safeguarding its regime against both internal and external threats.

The **Chabahar Port** is situated in **southeastern Iran**, providing direct access to the ocean and serving as the sole Iranian port with such connectivity. It holds significant trade potential for India, Iran, and Afghanistan, facilitating trade opportunities with Central Asian nations. The port consists of two separate sections named **Shahid Kalantari** and **Shahid Beheshti**. The operation of the Shahid Beheshti Port was taken over by the Indian firm India Ports Global Limited.

In 2003, **India and Iran agreed to jointly develop the Chabahar Port**, strategically located outside the Strait of Hormuz near Iran's border with Pakistan. During Prime Minister Modi's visit to Iran in 2016, a contract was signed to enable an investment of up to **$85 million for the port's development**. As per the agreement signed in May of that year, India committed to equipping and operating two berths in Phase-I of the Chabahar Port, with a capital investment of $85.21 million and annual revenue expenditure of $22.95 million under a 10-year lease agreement.

The Significance of Chabahar Port is as follows -

Direct Route to Afghanistan

- It ensures the establishment of a politically sustainable **connectivity between India and Afghanistan**. It helps to reduce India's dependency on Pakistan for connectivity to Afghanistan.

Trade and Commerce

- Trade relations between India and Iran have received a boost with fertilizers, chemicals, cereals, and other commodities being exchanged with less hurdles.
- The port isused to ship crude oil and urea, greatly reducing India's transportation cost. The port significantly **reduces transport costs and freight time** to Central Asia and the Persian Gulf.

Countering China

- It could assist India in countering the **China Pakistan Economic Corridor (CPEC)** as well as Chinese presence in the Arabian Sea which China is trying to ensure by helping Pakistan to develop the **Gwadar port** (It is approx. 70 km away from Chabahar Port).

Humanitarian operations

- From a diplomatic perspective, **Chabahar port** can be used by India as a point from were **humanitarian operations** in Central and South Asia can be coordinated.

Link to the INSTC

- Chabahar port helps boost India's access to Iran, the key gateway to the **International North-South Transport Corridor** that has sea, rail and road routes between **India, Russia, Iran, Europe and Central Asia.**

India's engagement is not limited to South Asia alone, as it recognizes the benefits of expanding its reach to the extended neighborhood, including Iran and Afghanistan. This broader regional involvement not only enhances trade and energy security but also aligns with India's ambitions to attain superpower status. Strong political and economic ties between India and Iran are vital for the successful development of the Chabahar port and the overall economic prosperity of both nations.

IRAN-ISRAEL CONFLICT

As of August 2024, tensions between Iran and Israel have escalated significantly, particularly in the aftermath of the assassination of prominent figures linked to ***Hamas*** and ***Hezbollah***. Iran has vowed retaliation, with its leadership signaling an impending strike against Israel. This comes amid growing concerns over Iran's nuclear ambitions, with U.S. intelligence noting increased discussions among Iranian officials about their ability to produce a nuclear weapon.

In response, Israel has heightened its military readiness, including doubling drone surveillance in its northern regions to pre-empt potential attacks from Hezbollah or Iranian forces. The situation is further complicated by the involvement of Iranian-backed militias along the Jordan-Iraq border, which Jordan fears could be used to launch attacks on Israel.

THE LEVANT REGION

The 'Levant' or Levant region is a historical geographical term referring to the area in the Eastern Mediterranean region of Western Asia. Historically, the Levant has been a crossroads of cultures, religions, and trade routes, making it a region of significant historical and geopolitical importance.

The Levant has historically been a bridge between East and West, serving as a vital hub for trade and cultural exchange. Its strategic location continues to make it a focal point for political and military conflicts. In the last decade, it remains a region of considerable geopolitical importance and instability, with ongoing conflicts, refugee crises, and tensions between different ethnic and religious groups. The complex interplay of historical grievances, territorial disputes, and external influences continues to shape the region's dynamics.

(1) SYRIA

Syria is a focal point in Middle Eastern geopolitics, heavily impacted by the ongoing civil war since 2011. The Assad regime seeks to reclaim full control over Syrian territory and gain international legitimacy, leveraging support from allies like Russia and Iran. Syria's foreign policy is deeply influenced by its need for military and economic aid, and its stance against Israel remains firm, particularly regarding the **Golan Heights**.

The Civil War (since 2011) has drawn in numerous international players, Syria has endured the devastating civil war, leading to widespread destruction and a humanitarian catastrophe. The conflict has drawn in multiple foreign powers including Russia, Iran, Turkey, and the United States, each backing different factions, complicating efforts to restore peace and stability. The country faces immense challenges in rebuilding its infrastructure and addressing the deep divisions within society.

(2) LEBANON

Lebanon's international relations are complicated by internal sectarian divisions and external influences, particularly from Iran and Saudi Arabia. The country is also significantly affected by its relationship with Syria and the presence of Hezbollah, a powerful Shia militia and political group with strong ties to Iran.

Lebanon's foreign policy is often characterized by a delicate balance between maintaining neutrality and navigating the pressures from regional powers. The Lebanese government seeks international aid to manage economic crises and cope with the influx of Syrian refugees, while also dealing with the challenges posed by Hezbollah's activities and Israel's security concerns.

(3) JORDAN

Jordan maintains a stable and strategic role in the Middle East, often acting as a mediator in regional conflicts, particularly between Israel and Palestine. Jordan's foreign policy focuses on maintaining security, economic stability, and regional cooperation. The country balances relations with its Arab neighbors, Israel, and Western allies. Jordan supports a two-state solution to the Israel-Palestine conflict and has played a key role in hosting refugees from regional conflicts.

(4) CYPRUS

Cyprus is strategically located in the Eastern Mediterranean and has complex international relations, particularly due to its division between the Greek Cypriot south and the Turkish-occupied north. Cyprus focuses on resolving the island's division, enhancing regional cooperation, particularly in energy exploration in the Eastern Mediterranean, and strengthening ties with the EU.

It maintains strong ties with Greece, the EU, and increasingly with Israel and Egypt over energy cooperation. Relations with Turkey are tense due to the ongoing dispute over the island's division.

(5) REPUBLIC OF TÜRKIYE (TURKEY)

Southern Turkey, particularly areas like Hatay, has geopolitical significance due to its proximity to Syria and the Eastern Mediterranean. Turkey's foreign policy in this region is shaped by its broader goals of regional influence, countering Kurdish autonomy movements, and managing Syrian refugee flows. It seeks to assert its claims in the Eastern Mediterranean, often leading to tensions with Cyprus, Greece, and the EU. Turkey's policies in southern regions are also influenced by domestic security concerns and the need to stabilize its border with Syria.

NOTE – **Israel** and **Palestine** are covered separately in detail in this chapter later.

REGIONAL MILITIA or NON-STATE GROUPS ACTIVE IN THE REGION	
Hamas	▪ It is a Palestinian Islamist militant organization founded in 1987. It emerged from the Palestinian branch of the Muslim Brotherhood and is known for its dual role as a political party and an armed militant group. ▪ Hamas aims to establish an Islamic state in historical Palestine and is opposed to the state of Israel. Its charter calls for the liberation of Palestinian territories through armed struggle. The group has been involved in numerous conflicts with Israel, conducting rocket attacks and engaging in violent clashes.
Hezbollah	▪ Also known as the Party of God, Hezbollah is a Shiite Islamist militant and political organization based in Lebanon. Founded in the early 1980s during the **Lebanese Civil War**, Hezbollah was initially supported by Iran and Syria, emerging as a resistance group against the Israeli occupation of southern Lebanon. The

	organization operates as both a powerful military force and a political party, holding seats in the Lebanese parliament and influencing the country's political landscape. ▪ Regionally, Hezbollah is a significant player in Middle Eastern geopolitics, acting as a proxy for Iran in its regional power struggle against Israel and Sunni Arab states. The organization is considered a terrorist group by several countries, including the United States, while others view it as a legitimate resistance movement.
Syrian Democratic Forces (SDF)	The SDF is a multi-ethnic coalition of militias formed in 2015 to combat ISIS in northern Syria. It includes Kurdish, Arab, and Assyrian groups, with the Kurdish YPG (People's Protection Units) being the most prominent component. The SDF has played a significant role in the Syrian Civil War, particularly in the fight against ISIS.
Ahrar al-Sham	It is an Islamist rebel group that was active in the Syrian Civil War, founded in 2011. It aims to establish an Islamic state in Syria and is part of the broader opposition to the Assad regime. The group seeks to replace the current Syrian government with an Islamic state governed by Sharia law. It has been involved in numerous battles and sieges throughout Syria. It has received support from various regional powers but has also faced criticism for its hardline views and actions. In recent years, its influence has been somewhat diminished

REPERCUSSIONS OF EMERGING REGIONAL MILITIAS FOR SOVEREIGN GOVERNANCE

These groups often challenge the authority of established governments, leading to **internal conflicts**. For instance, Hezbollah's strong military presence in Lebanon sometimes undermines the Lebanese state's monopoly on the use of force, creating a parallel power structure.

Hezbollah and *Hamas* are often involved in broader regional dynamics, acting as **proxies for larger powers** like Iran. These groups' actions can escalate tensions between regional powers, notably between Iran and its adversaries like Israel and Sunni Arab states.

The militant activities of these groups, including rocket attacks and cross-border incursions, pose **direct security threats** to neighboring countries. Ex - Hamas' rocket attacks from Gaza similarly provoke Israeli military responses, contributing to cyclical violence.

The militant stances of groups like Hamas **complicate efforts to achieve peace agreements** in the region. Hamas' refusal to recognize Israel and its use of violence as a means of resistance undermine potential negotiations and peace efforts, affecting broader Israeli-Palestinian relations.

The activities of these groups often result in significant **civilian casualties and humanitarian crises**. For example, conflicts involving Hezbollah and Hamas have led to destruction in Lebanon and Gaza, respectively, exacerbating the humanitarian situation.

Countries that host or support these groups may face **international sanctions and diplomatic isolation.** For instance, Lebanon faces economic and political repercussions due to Hezbollah's influence, affecting its international relations and access to foreign aid.

ISRAEL-PALESTINE: CONFLICT AND COEXISTENCE

ISRAEL is a highly influential state in the Middle East, despite its small size and population. Established in 1948, Israel's existence and territorial boundaries have been at the heart of the Arab-Israeli conflict, leading to several wars and ongoing tensions with its Arab neighbors. However, Israel's signing of the Abraham Accords in 2020 marked a significant shift, normalizing relations with the UAE, Bahrain, and Morocco, and reflecting a new regional dynamic where shared concerns over Iran overshadow the traditional Arab-Israeli animosity.

Domestically, Israel is a vibrant democracy, but its political scene is deeply divided, especially regarding the **Palestinian issue** (discussed under the heading of 'Palestine'). Israel's continued occupation of Palestinian territories and expansion of settlements remain major points of contention in international diplomacy.

Israel's strategic location, technological innovation, and military capabilities make it a central player in regional and global geopolitics. Israel's foreign policy is characterized by its efforts to ensure security, maintain strategic alliances, and navigate the complex political landscape of the Middle East. Israel's relationship with the United States is one of its most crucial international alliances, providing substantial military aid and diplomatic support, particularly in forums like the United Nations.

Areas of India-Israel Cooperation → Trade & Economy → Research & Development → Agriculture and Technologies → Defence and related R&D

Bilateral trade between the two nations has increased and diversified to include electronic machinery, nuclear products and medical equipment, from US$900 million in 2000 to **US$7.86 billion in 2021**. In the past two years, multiple MoUs have been signed between Israel's Start-Up National Central and Indian entrepreneurship centres.

Both nations have increased the scope of **India-Israel Industrial R&D and Innovation Fund (I4F)** to include sectors like renewable energy and ICT. Israel has an impressive track record of reusing 90 percent of its **wastewater** and India is partnering with Israel to combat its looming water crisis. As of April 2023, there are over 25 Israeli projects in India looking at water distribution and management, wastewater treatment, desalination, and water security.

MOSSAD is Israel's national intelligence agency, established in 1949. It is responsible for intelligence gathering, covert operations, and counterterrorism. Mossad is known for its high level of secrecy and efficiency, and its operations often influence international relations.

India and Israel have been collaborating in the field of **agriculture** since the early 2000s. The collaboration is based on the sharing of expertise and technologies in areas such as irrigation, horticulture, post-harvest management, and seed development. The **Indo-Israeli Agricultural Project (IIAP)** operates 29 Centres of Excellence (CoEs) across 21 states in India. Both countries have signed **a three-year work program (2021-2023)** for development in Agriculture cooperation to benefit local farmers. India and Israel have established several **Centers of Excellence (CoEs)** across India, which serve as demonstration and training centers for farmers. The CoEs provide access to Israeli technologies and best practices in areas such as micro-irrigation, greenhouse cultivation, and precision farming.

The two countries have been collaborating in **defense research and development**, joint military exercises, procurement of defense equipment, and counter-terrorism cooperation. India is one of the largest buyers of Israeli **defense equipment**, with purchases ranging from missiles, drones, electronic warfare systems, and other advanced military technologies. The bilateral defense trade reached $1 billion in 2020. As per SIPRI's 2021 records, Israel accounts for 13% of Indian imports including critical defence technologies and joint developmental projects, that include – Missiles like BARAK-8 and Spike; UAVs like Harop and Heron. In

June 2022, India-Israel Defence Ministers held bilateral talks where **India-Israel Vision on Defence Cooperation** was adopted for enhancing cooperation in the field of Futuristic Defence Technologies.

I2U2 GROUP

Members - **India, Israel, the UAE** and **the US.**

Formation – The foreign Ministers of the four nations formed the bloc in **October 2021** to deepen technological and private sector collaboration in the region and tackle transnational challenges in six focus areas: water, energy, transportation, space, health and food security. It is being referred to as the **West Asia 'Quad'**.

In September 2020, the **Abraham Accords** were signed between Israel, UAE, and Bahrain mediated by the United States. In the wake of the same, the I2U2 was formed to majorly deal with issues concerning maritime security, infrastructure, and transport.

NOTE: Discussed in detail in another chapter.

PALESTINE refers to the geographic region comprising the West Bank and the Gaza Strip, areas that are at the heart of the ongoing Israel-Palestine conflict. Palestine has a long and complex history, deeply intertwined with religious, cultural, and political narratives. It is home to significant religious sites for Muslims, Christians, and Jews.

HISTORICAL BACKGROUND

After the fall of the Ottoman Empire, Palestine was administered by **Britain** under a League of Nations mandate. The **1947 UN Partition Plan** proposed dividing the land into separate Jewish and Arab states, but this led to conflict and the **1948 Arab-Israeli War**, resulting in the creation of Israel and the displacement of many Palestinians. The West Bank came under Jordanian control until the **Six-Day War (1967)**.

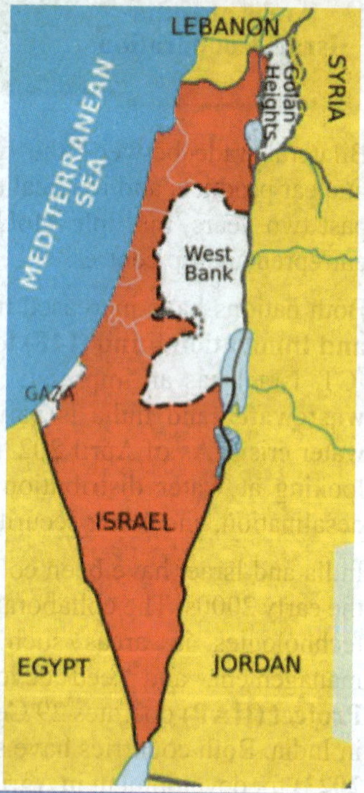

The Palestinian territories have **limited formal international recognition**, but they receive substantial diplomatic support from many countries and international organizations advocating for Palestinian statehood. The Palestinian leadership presently seeks international recognition of statehood, an end to Israeli occupation, and a resolution to the refugee issue. They engage diplomatically with global powers, the UN, and Arab states to garner support for their cause. The divide between the West Bank and Gaza complicates unified foreign policy efforts.

Disputed Regions: West Bank and Gaza Strip

The **West Bank** is a landlocked territory located in the Middle East, bordered by Israel to the west, Jordan to the east, and the Dead Sea to the southeast. It covers an area of approximately 5,655 square kilometers and is home to a Palestinian population, as well as Israeli settlements.

Historically, the West Bank was part of the area known as **Mandatory Palestine** under British administration until 1948. After the **Arab-Israeli War (1948)** and the establishment of the State of Israel, the West Bank came under Jordanian control until the **Six-Day War (1967)**.

Following the **Six-Day War**, Israel occupied the West Bank, and since then, it has been a major point of contention in the Israeli-Palestinian conflict. The territory is recognized by many countries and international organizations as part of the future Palestinian state. The Palestinian Authority, established through the **Oslo Accords** in the 1990s, exercises limited self-rule in certain areas of the West Bank, while Israeli forces maintain overall security control. Moreover, Israeli settlements, considered illegal under international law, have been constructed in the West Bank. These settlements, populated by Israeli civilians, have been a significant source of tension and obstacles to peace negotiations.

OSLO ACCORDS

They were a set of agreements negotiated between **Israel** and the **Palestine Liberation Organization (PLO)** in the early 1990s that aimed to resolve the Israeli-Palestinian conflict through a peace process based on the principle of a two-state solution (two separate sovereign nations). The Accords weren't successful, and the peace process stalled in the years that followed, and many of the key issues, such as the status of Jerusalem, the borders of a future Palestinian state, and the right of return for Palestinian refugees, remain unresolved.

The **Gaza Strip** is a coastal territory located on the eastern coast of the Mediterranean Sea. It is bordered by Israel to the north, east, and west, and Egypt to the south. The Gaza Strip covers an area of about 365 square kilometers and is densely populated, primarily by Palestinians.

Historical Background - The Gaza Strip was also **part of Mandatory Palestine** and came under Egyptian administration after the Arab-Israeli War (1948). After the Six-Day War in 1967, Israel occupied the territory, including East Jerusalem.

In 2005, Israel unilaterally disengaged from the ***Gaza Strip***, dismantling its settlements and withdrawing its military forces. The move aimed to reduce tensions but left the Palestinian Authority responsible for governing the territory. Following the disengagement, the **militant group 'Hamas'** won legislative elections in the Palestinian territories in 2006. Subsequently, a power struggle between Hamas and the Palestinian Authority led to Hamas taking control of the Gaza Strip in 2007. Since then, the Gaza Strip has been under Hamas' **de facto governance**. Israel, along with Egypt, imposes a blockade on the Gaza Strip, restricting the movement of goods and people in and out of the territory.

The **West Bank** and the **Gaza Strip** are integral parts of discussions and negotiations for a peaceful resolution to the Israeli-Palestinian conflict. The status and future of these territories remain key issues in efforts to achieve a lasting and comprehensive solution.

The Israel-Palestine Conflict

The Israel-Palestine conflict is a long-standing dispute over land and national identity. Israel, established in 1948, and the Palestinian territories (West Bank and Gaza Strip) have clashed over borders, security, and sovereignty. Palestinians seek an independent state and criticize Israeli settlements and military actions. Conversely, Israel cites security concerns and historical claims. Peace efforts have stalled, leading to recurrent violence and deep-seated animosity. The conflict involves complex issues, including refugee rights, Jerusalem's status, and mutual recognition.

The Israel-Palestine conflict is driven by several key issues and areas of contention:

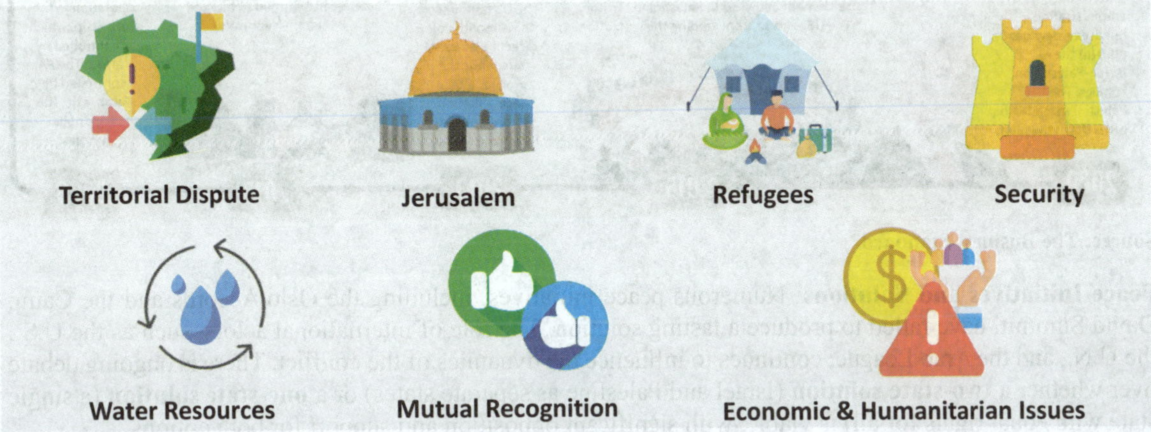

1. The **boundaries of Israel and a potential Palestinian state are highly contested**, particularly regarding the West Bank, Gaza Strip, and East Jerusalem. Israeli settlements in the West Bank are viewed by Palestinians and much of the international community as illegal under international law, while Israel disputes this. The expansion of these settlements is a major point of tension.
2. Both Israel and Palestine claim **Jerusalem as their capital**. The city holds significant religious and historical importance for Jews, Muslims, and Christians. The status of East Jerusalem, which Israel annexed after the 1967 Six-Day War, remains a highly sensitive issue.
3. Millions of **Palestinian refugees and their descendants claim the right to return to their ancestral homes** in what is now **Israel**, from which they or their forebears were displaced during the 1948 Arab-Israeli War. Israel opposes this, citing demographic and security concerns.
4. Ongoing violence, including rocket attacks, suicide bombings, and military incursions, exacerbates tensions. Israel cites **security concerns** as justification for its military operations and control over Palestinian territories. Israel demands security guarantees, including demilitarization of any future Palestinian state, while Palestinians seek an end to Israeli military presence and restrictions in their territories.
5. The **allocation and control of scarce water resources** in the region, particularly in the West Bank, is another area of dispute. Israel controls much of the water supply, leading to accusations of inequity by Palestinians.
6. Palestinians and some Arab states have historically **refused to recognize Israel's right to exist**, although this has gradually shifted with recent peace agreements. Conversely, **Israel has been reluctant to fully recognize a Palestinian state** due to security concerns. While many countries recognize Palestine as a state, Israel and some of its allies do not, arguing that statehood should be the result of direct negotiations.
7. The **Israeli blockade of Gaza**, restrictions on movement, and **economic controls in the West Bank** contribute to widespread poverty and humanitarian issues in Palestinian territories. Both sides accuse each other of human rights violations, including disproportionate use of force, house demolitions, and restrictions on freedom of movement.

Source: The Business Standard

Peace Initiatives and Solutions: Numerous peace initiatives, including the Oslo Accords and the Camp David Summit, have failed to produce a lasting solution. The role of international actors, such as the U.S., the U.N., and the Arab League, continues to influence the dynamics of the conflict. There is ongoing debate over whether a **two-state solution** (Israel and Palestine as separate states) or a **one-state solution** (a single state with equal rights for all) is viable, with significant opposition and support for both options.

India's De-Hyphenated Policy

India's de-hyphenated policy refers to the policy of **treating Palestine as a separate and distinct issue from India's relations with Israel**. Historically, India had maintained a pro-Palestinian stance and had refrained from establishing diplomatic relations with Israel. However, in recent years, India has adopted a more pragmatic approach and has sought to develop relations with both Israel and Palestine independently, without allowing one issue to dictate the other.

India has been a supporter of Palestine's bid for statehood and has consistently voted in favor of pro-Palestinian resolutions at the United Nations. However, over the past decade, India has developed closer ties with Israel, particularly in the areas of defense, technology, and agriculture. In 2022, India and Israel celebrated the 30th anniversary of full diplomatic ties.

Despite its growing ties with Israel, India has maintained its engagement with Palestine and has provided economic and technical assistance to the Palestinian Authority. India's relations with Palestine are based on mutual respect and shared aspirations for peace and stability in the region.

- India established diplomatic relations with Palestine in 1988 and has maintained a diplomatic mission in Ramallah since then.
- India has been providing development assistance to Palestine, including financial and technical assistance, and has supported several development projects in Palestine, particularly in the fields of health, education, and infrastructure.
- Over the past years, the two countries have organized several cultural events, such as film festivals, music concerts, and art exhibitions, to showcase their respective cultures.
- India has been exploring opportunities for business and trade with Palestine, particularly in sectors such as agriculture, pharmaceuticals, and information technology.
- On the diplomatic front, India has been supportive of the Palestinian cause for statehood and has supported Palestine's bid for full membership in the United Nations.

At the **December 2022** session of UNSC, India again asserted that long-term peace in Israel and Palestine can be achieved through negotiation on the **Two-State Solution**. It is a proposed framework for resolving the Israeli-Palestinian conflict by creating two independent and sovereign states - Israel for the Jewish people and Palestine for the Palestinian people. Under this proposal, Israel would retain control over the majority of the land it currently occupies, while Palestine would be established in the **West Bank**, including East Jerusalem, and the Gaza Strip. The two states would share borders and cooperate on issues such as security, water resources, and trade.

The de-hyphenated policy is mostly a delicate balancing act, as it seeks to maintain its traditional support for the Palestinian cause while also developing closer ties with Israel. India has emphasized the need for a peaceful resolution of the Israeli-Palestinian conflict and has called for the establishment of a sovereign, independent, and viable Palestinian state coexisting peacefully with Israel.

INDIA, SOUTH CAUCASUS AND GROWING ENGAGEMENTS

Following the dissolution of the USSR in 1991, 15 independent countries emerged. Among these, Armenia, Azerbaijan, and Georgia form a distinct geographic region referred to as the South Caucasus.

- The Caucasus region is an important transit point for trade between Europe and Asia, with major transport routes such as the **Silk Road** passing through the region. Based on literary records, India's interaction through the Silk Road/Route trade connections was extensive and Armenians, Georgians and Azerbaijanis had all enjoyed the patronage of the Mughal Empire.
- Further ahead in the timeline, India was quick to recognise the independence of the three nations and established diplomatic relations in 1992. However, this didn't lead to any major bilateral relations between the nation due to India's neglection of the area, mainly due to its unstable and tumultuous situation.
- **Georgia** has been committed to its integration with the Euro-Atlantic structures (NATO and EU) and effective bilateral relations with India took off only after 2010. **Azerbaijan**, on the other hand, has been

initiating economic relations with India off late, while **Armenia** continues to rely heavily on Russia as it attempts to follow a policy of multi-engagement with India.

- India has been attempting to engage in a more effective manner without the region, but the efforts are still not at par with those of other global opponents. The Caucasus region is an important energy hub, with significant reserves of oil and natural gas. The **Baku-Tbilisi-Ceyhan pipeline**, which transports oil from Azerbaijan to Turkey, is one of the region's most important energy infrastructure projects. Since the time India has been eyeing to diversify its energy requirements, the Caucasus region has clearly been gaining prominence in the official circles.
- However, the bilateral relations haven't taken off as effectively as India's other diplomatic connections, mainly due to the fact that the Caucasus region has been plagued by conflict and political instability for centuries, including ongoing disputes over territorial claims, ethnic tensions, and regional power struggles.
- The **Nagorno-Karabakh** conflict between **Armenia** and **Azerbaijan** over the disputed Nagorno-Karabakh region has been a significant source of tension in the region for decades. The first armed conflict erupted between 1988 and 1994, while the second conflict erupted into a war in 2020, resulting in thousands of casualties and displacement of civilians. The 2020 conflict was eventually concluded after Russian mediation. Since the region is home to various ethnic groups, the tensions between them have often escalated into civil unrest.

The most recent attempts to conclude peace between Armenia and Azerbaijan through talks/negotiations took place in **Washington** (April 2023), while Russia played host to the leaders of the two nations for a meeting in **Moscow** in May 2023.

The **Lachin Corridor** is of great significance to the region. It connects Armenia and Nagorno-Karabakh region. The corridor is internationally recognised as part of Azerbaijan but populated mainly by ethnic Armenians.

Additionally, the South Caucasus region is of strategic importance to major regional and global powers, including Russia, Turkey, and Iran. These countries have competing interests in the region, and their involvement has often exacerbated tensions and conflicts. Additionally, owing to the resource richness of the region, there is significant economic competition between the countries of the region and their external partners.

CENTRAL ASIAN REGION

DEFINING THE REGION

Central Asian Region (CAR) is a diverse land with many ethnic groups, languages, religions and tribes. The nations which make up Central Asia are five of the former Soviet republics: Kazakhstan, Kyrgyzstan, Turkmenistan, Tajikistan, and Uzbekistan. When the Soviet Union collapsed, all five Central Asian Soviet socialist republics obtained their independence in 1991, becoming sovereign and independent nations. Afghanistan was previously thought to be included in South Asia, but in recent discussions, it has come to be included as a part of Central Asia, though it was never officially part of the Soviet Union.

The fight for hegemony in Central Asia is age old and its location between two powers, Russia and China, further adds to its relevance in the global scenario. CAR is the northern frontier of the Islamic world hitherto unaffected by fundamentalist wave. The Soviet developmental legacy still remains as a bulwark against potential extremist threats emanating from Pakistan and Afghanistan. The phase between 1999 and 2014 was shaped heavily by the resource boom in the region and the revenues from oil and gas successfully floated the nations. When world energy prices fell in 2014 and fluctuations in prices of oil and exchange rates became recurrent, the governments recognised the need for economic diversification and began reorienting their foreign and economic policies.

In 1991, the CAR leaders lacked the necessary faith to diversify in international and global markets, apart from treating them as outlets for cotton, oil and gas or minerals. While Kyrgyzstan joined the World Trade Organisation (WTO) during the 1990s, the other Central Asian nations didn't join until 2012.

Country	Capital	Political System	GDP (current US$), 2023 (billion)	Human Development Index Rank (2023)
INDIA	**NEW DELHI**	**DEMOCRATIC REPUBLIC**	**3.55 trillion**	**134**
Kazakhstan	Nur-Sultan	Presidential Republic	261.4	67
Kyrgyz Republic	Bishkek	Democratic Parliamentary Republic	13.9	117
Turkmenistan	Ashgabat	Presidential Republic	59.8	94
Tajikistan	Dushanbe	Presidential Republic	12	126
Uzbekistan	Tashkent	Presidential Republic	90.8	106
Afghanistan	Kabul	Islamic Republic (Taliban form of government is considered a totalitarian theocracy)	14.5 (2022)	182
*World Bank Data				

CENTRAL ASIAN NATIONS

In recent years, India has shown a growing interest in strengthening its strategic influence in Central Asia; however, it has not fully utilized the potential opportunities available. Over the past twenty-five years, India has cited various obstacles such as limited physical connectivity, hostile relations with Pakistan, and instability in Afghanistan as reasons for its limited engagement with Central Asia. With its full membership in the SCO, India now has the chance to forge closer ties with the region, but it still lacks a clear political and strategic vision.

REPUBLIC OF KAZAKHSTAN is a unitary state with a Presidential system of government. The country's Constitution establishes Kazakhstan as a democratic, secular, legal, and social state that upholds the fundamental values of human life, rights, and freedoms as its highest principles.[19] The country is the largest state in Central Asia and occupies land equal to that of Western Europe but consists of the lowest population density globally (less than 6.93 people per km²).

[19] The Republic of Kazakhstan. Official website. https://www.akorda.kz/en/republic_of_kazakhstan/kazakhstan

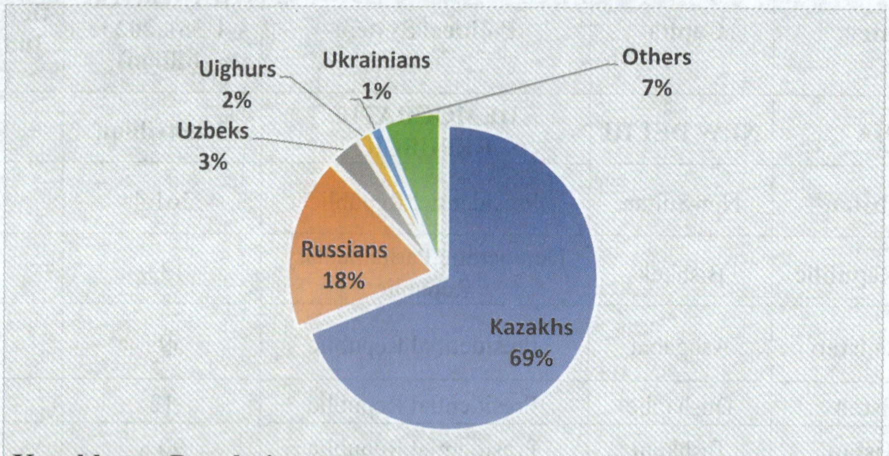

Kazakhstan Population

The nation is proclaimed to have the best-performing economy in the region, backed by successful manufacturing, services and agriculture sectors. The development was fueled by structural reforms, strong domestic demand, foreign direct investment and abundant hydrocarbon resources. The region is significant for creating linkages between the economies of China and South Asia with Russia and Western Europe. The connectivity ranges from road, rail and more importantly through ports. **Aktau, Kuryk** and **Bautino** ports are the important ports of Kazakhstan.

The **Aktau port** lies on Kazakhstan's eastern coastline facing the Caspian Sea. Post 1991, its strategic position at the confluence of numerous international transportation gateways allows it to function as the premier port of the country.

KYRGYZ REPUBLIC (commonly known as Kyrgyzstan) is a landlocked country located at the heart of Central Asia, of which most of the territory is mountainous. While there are more than 90 ethnic groups, the Kyrgyz people comprise 72.6% of the country's population and are traditionally Sunni Muslim. As a **Parliamentary Republic** that holds contested elections, the country has been hailed as the most democratic country in Central Asia. Kyrgyzstan has a unicameral parliament, the **Jogorku Kenesh** ("Supreme Council"). In recent years, the international observers have pointed out the rising instability in the region apart from the concerns about democratic backsliding. The country maintains close political ties with Russia and Russians consists of 5.3% of the total population in the country.

TURKMENISTAN is a **Presidential Republic** and the second largest state in Central Asia (also a landlocked country). It is a democratic, law-based, secular State, located at the centre of the Eurasian continent. **Milli Gengesh** of Turkmenistan (The Parliament) is a representative body having the legislative authority. The country is known for its autocratic government and has a reputation for being an 'island of stability'. The country borders the Caspian Sea, which offers abundant hydrocarbons apart from gas and oil deposits.

Kyrgz Republic Facts

- The village of **Arslanbob** (Kyrgyz Republic) lies in the Chatkal mountain range and is home to the largest walnut forest in the world.
- The **Issyk-Kul Lake** or the 'Pearl of Kyrgyz Republic' is the second largest Salt Lake in the world.
- **Merzbaher's Lake** is a highland lake which disappears every year and reappears again.

According to **Human Rights Watch**, Turkmenistan continues to be a highly **oppressive country where the government tightly controls and limits fundamental rights and freedoms, such as the rights to association, expression, and religion**. Individuals who criticize the government, including activists and independent journalists, are subjected to heightened intimidation, harassment, physical assaults, and imprisonment. The country remains closed off to independent scrutiny or examination.

Lying towards the South-East of Central Asia, the **REPUBLIC OF TAJIKISTAN** is home to the mountains belonging to highest ranges of Central Asia, which comprise 93% of the total area of the country. Tajikistan includes the Gorno-Badakhshan ("Mountain Badakhshan") autonomous region, with its capital at Khorugh (Khorog). Tajikistan encompasses the smallest amount of land among the five Central Asian states. The geography is mostly unsuitable for habitation but the desert and semi-desert lands have been turned into oases, with flourishing cotton plantations, vineyards and gardens. Tajikistan's finance sector is relatively small, predominantly comprising commercial banks that have limited exposure to international markets. The country's currency is susceptible to fluctuations in Russia's economy due to the significant contribution of remittances from Tajik workers in Russia, which make up approximately one-third of Tajikistan's GDP.

The **REPUBLIC OF UZBEKISTAN** is a landlocked country (barring the Aral Sea to its North-West) and the most populous in Central Asia which also boasts of a rich history, culture and diversity. Known to be the 'centre of the Silk Road', the country has been part of several empires. Uzbekistan's subsoil is rich in valuables especially oil, gas, coal and uranium. Uzbekistan has been implementing large-scale reforms in recent years to strengthen its energy industry. Uzbekistan follows a policy of non-alignment with military and political alliances, which means it does not allow foreign military bases or facilities on its territory and its military personnel do not participate in peacekeeping operations. The country's focus in Central Asia is to promote peace and stability in the region and address regional security issues, including contributing to the resolution of the situation in Afghanistan. Uzbekistan actively engages with over 100 international organizations and seeks to enhance cooperation with various multilateral structures.

The **Fergana Valley** (eastern Uzbekistan) is a fertile valley fed by two rivers, **Naryn** and **Kara Darya** and is one of the most densely populated areas of Central Asia. A far cry from the time of ***Babur***, the valley is anow an industrial city and a major producer of cotton (White Gold), fruit, and raw silk.

INDIA'S ENGAGEMENT WITH CENTRAL ASIA

India has a long history of cultural and commercial ties with Central Asia, aided by its geographical proximity. The relations stagnated in the 20th century, due to the Anglo-Russian rivalry and the formation of independent states with differing ideologies post the disintegration of USSR. India had to re-strategize its relations with the newly independent states and sent a semi-official delegation to establish diplomatic relations in 1991-92. India had also provided financial aid of US $ 10-15 million to the region during the economic crisis which was followed by visits to the CAR nations by the Indian Prime Minister Narsimha Rao.

Significance of Central Asian Region for India				
Strategic Location and Diplomacy	Resource and Energy	Connectivity and Infrastructure	Trade and Commerce	Defence and Security

Strategic Location and Diplomacy

Central Asia is located at the crossroads of Europe and Asia, and is situated between Russia, China, the Middle East, and South Asia. Its **strategic location** makes it an important transit point for trade and energy flows, and a key region for regional security and stability.

Due to their geographical location, these countries serve as a connecting point between various regions of Asia and between Europe and Asia. The current geopolitical dynamics in Central Asia resemble a modern version of the historical "great game." Multiple global powers, including Russia, China, the US, Turkey, Iran, Europe, the EU, Japan, Pakistan, India, and Afghanistan, have significant security and economic interests in the region. To leverage their geopolitical advantages and protect their national interests, Central Asian countries have actively engaged with the international community through diverse channels and institutions.

The struggle between the Tsarist Russia and Great Britain over Central Asia in the 19th and 20th century originally known as **"Great Game"**. It was a dispute for political dominance, control and security of the territories and trade routes located between the Russian and British Empires – mainly the Central Asian region.

Resource and Energy

Central Asia is rich in natural resources, particularly oil, gas, and minerals. The region's energy resources are of growing importance to global energy security, and have attracted the attention of major energy consumers such as China, Russia, and the European Union. India also has a growing demand for energy, and the region presents an opportunity for India to diversify its energy sources and reduce its dependence on traditional suppliers. In addition to energy cooperation, India and the Central Asian countries have been working to increase trade in other sectors such as agriculture, pharmaceuticals, and textiles. India has offered to share its expertise in agriculture with the Central Asian countries, and has also signed agreements to import cotton and other agricultural products from the region.

(1) **Kazakhstan's** mineral resource base consists of more than five thousand deposits and the estimated valuation of the deposits is trillions of dollars. The country leads globally in terms of explored reserves of zinc, wolframium and barytes. It holds substantial reserves of silver, lead, chromite, copper, fluorite, and gold. The country has significant oil and gas resources (ninth in the world in terms of explored oil reserves) concentrated in the western regions. Additionally, the country ranks in the top 10 globally for its uranium and coal reserves.

CHINA-CENTRAL ASIA GAS PIPELINE
(Turkmenistan-Uzbekistan-Kazakhstan-China gas pipeline)

As of mid-2024, the **China-Central Asia Gas Pipeline** remains a key pillar in China's energy security strategy. Operational since **December 2009**, this transnational pipeline continues to supply gas to over **500 million residents**, linking **Turkmenistan's gas fields** to China's **West-to-East Gas Pipeline** in **Xinjiang**.

Stretching **1,833 km**, it passes through **Uzbekistan** and **Kazakhstan** and is designed to transmit **60 billion cubic meters** of natural gas annually. In recent updates, China has been exploring the pipeline's **expansion** due to rising domestic demand, focusing on enhancing capacity and ensuring steady gas flows. This is part of China's broader effort to diversify energy sources and reduce dependency on coal. Meanwhile, Central Asian nations, especially **Turkmenistan**, are leveraging the pipeline for greater revenue and regional economic integration.

(2) **Turkmenistan** possesses substantial natural gas reserves, ranking as the **fourth largest in the world and accounting for approximately 10 percent of global reserves**. In addition to its significant gas reserves, the country is also known for its other valuable resources such as petroleum, sulfur, iodine, salt, bentonite clays, limestone, gypsum, and cement. These resources have the potential to serve as essential inputs for industries related to chemicals and construction. It has effectively diversified its economy which consists of oil and gas production, oil refining industries, metal processing and mechanical engineering. Presently, the country boasts of over 60 textile complexes with 80 percent of its manufactured textile products being exported to the countries of European Union, the USA, Canada, Russia, Turkey, China, the Baltic nations etc.

A major investment endeavor aimed at expanding the resource capacity of the industry is the industrial development of Turkmenistan's "Galkynysh" gas field, which is considered the largest in the world. With an estimated volume of nearly 27 trillion cubic meters, it surpasses other fields like "*Yashlar*" and "*Garakyol*". As of 2021, the operating fund of the field includes more than 40 wells, covering an area of over 4 thousand square kilometers.

(3) Kyrgyz Republic relies on its large and medium sized rivers (water resources), making hydropower its most critical energy source, which continues to remain underutilized. The country has about 30 percent of the hydropower resources of the entire Central Asian region and around 90 percent of the total electricity generation is hydro based. The technological hydropower potential is estimated at 142 billion kWh/year and the economic or production potential is 60 billion kWh. Around 70 percent of the hydropower potential remains dormant. The explored coal reserves (over 70 deposits) are estimated at 1.3 billion tonnes (Bt). The Government has been making plans to exploit new well sites for oil and gas, with potential recognized in Ferghana Valley, the Alai Valley, the Naryn Basin, the Issyk-Kul basin and the eastern Chuy Basin.

(4) **Uzbekistan** is rich in minerals ranging from natural gas, lignite and coal, gold, copper, tungsten, bismuth, and oil. The country ranks in the top ten figures globally for its cotton production and gold reserves. It is also among the world leaders for producing and supplying reserves of certain minerals: gold, phosphorites, molybdenum, etc. Uzbekistan is among the top 15 countries with the largest uranium and copper reserves. Besides, their agricultural economy is also an important economic driver. The contemporary level of exploration of minerals is related to opening up of rich deposits of precious, non-ferrous and rare metals, all types of organic fuel — oil, natural and condensed gas, brown and other types of coal, shale oil, uranium, etc. The country's explored reserves are over US$1 billion.

(5) **Tajikistan** has conducted large-scale geological exploration over the years and boasts of deposits of lead and zinc, copper and bismuth, antimony and azoque, precious metal, molybdenum and wolframium, iron, tin, boron raw materials, strontium, fluorite, rock salts, semi-precious and precious stones and other raw materials for the construction industry, anthracite, graphite, oil and gas, ozokerite, underground fresh, thermal and mineral waters, phosphorites, as well as a number of other minerals, in total more than 50 types of mineral resources. Tajikistan has substantial coal with estimated reserves of 4.5 billion tons. Tajikistan's hydropower potential ranks in the top ten globally. The estimated potential of solar energy has been projected at about 25 billion kWh/year. Additionally, horticulture has been important and apricots, pears, apples, plums, quinces, cherries, pomegranates, figs, and nuts are produced.

Kazakhstan and Turkmenistan - are also part of the Caspian coastline, promising to open the door to other Caspian states rich in energy.

Connectivity and Infrastructure

- Central Asia is home to several important transport corridors, including the ancient Silk Road and the more modern Eurasian land bridge. The development of transport infrastructure in the region is seen as key to enhancing regional connectivity and promoting economic growth.
- The **International North-South Transportation Corridor (INSTC)** is a multimodal route that encompasses various modes of transport. It involves shipping from Mumbai to Iran's Chabahar Port, followed by rail transport to Iran's Caspian Sea ports. From there, it **provides connectivity to Russia, Azerbaijan, Turkey, Europe, as well as to Central Asian markets via Kazakhstan and Turkmenistan**. Additionally, there has been a significant increase in rail freight between China and Europe, with the number of containers transported growing from virtually none in 2011 to over 300,000 per year in 2019 and surpassing 550,000 in 2020, despite the challenges posed by the COVID-19 pandemic.
- Because of the lack of access to open sea and ocean (except for the Caspian Sea), a major bulk of Kazakhstan's traffic falls on land transport to take advantage of its geographical position and vast territory. It is implementing a large-scale project called "**New Silk Road**", which aims to revive the country's historical role of being the main connecting link of the continent and turn it into the largest business and transit hub in the region - bridging Europe and Asia.
- Turkmenistan collaborated with India, Pakistan, and Afghanistan to establish a gas pipeline that spans the Turkmenistan-Afghanistan-Pakistan-India (TAPI) route. A ceremony took place in Kabul on September 30, 2020, to promote the advancement of joint infrastructure projects between Turkmenistan and Afghanistan. These projects include the construction of the TAPI gas pipeline, the Turkmenistan-Afghanistan-Pakistan (TAP) electric and fiber-optic communication line, as well as railway construction. The gas pipeline would provide Afghanistan with much needed energy as well as transit income.
- **The Trans-Caspian International Transport Route (TITR)** was established in **2017** with the objective of facilitating the coordination among all stakeholders involved in the transportation of goods and containers along the route from Asia to Europe, and vice versa. It aims to **provide the necessary**

information support for seamless transportation along this route. While it wasn't the preferred route previously, the traffic along TITR grew steadily after 2017, and received a further impetus after the Russia-Ukraine conflict.

The Caspian Sea routes are collectively known as the **Trans-Caspian International Transport Route (TITR)** or the **Middle Corridor** came into existence in 2017 mainly by an agreement among Azerbaijan, Georgia, and Kazakhstan, in coordination with China, Turkey, and Ukraine. The route starts from Southeast Asia and China, runs through Kazakhstan, the Caspian Sea, Azerbaijan, Georgia and further to European countries; more notably the route circumvents Russia.

With Russia under sanctions, the main rail route from China to the European Union has shifted south to the Multi-modal route provided by using the Caspian Sea. Kazakhstan is facing an economic crisis as the war in Ukraine threatens the crude oil exports, which accounts for around 14 percent of GDP and 57 percent of exports. The bulk of these oil exports pass through a pipeline from Kazakhstan's western oil fields through southern Russia to Russia's Black Sea oil terminal at Novorossiysk.

In June 2022, the Kyrgyz President made an announcement regarding the commencement of the **China-Kyrgyzstan-Uzbekistan (CKU)** railway project in 2023. The CKU railway route, with a proposed length of 523 kms, forms the southern portion of the China-Europe freight rail and would link China, Kyrgyzstan and Uzbekistan to Central and Eastern Europe via Iran and Turkey. According to Uzbek officials the railway route will be the shortest route to transport goods from China to Europe and the Middle East, cutting the freight journey by 900 kms and saving seven to eight days in shipping time.

Trade and Commerce

Central Asia possesses a youthful and expanding population, along with an economy that is still in the early stages of development but holds considerable growth prospects. The region's economic potential has played a pivotal role in its growing importance on the global stage. Over the past few decades, the economic performance of Central Asian nations has improved, largely driven by favorable commodity prices. The collective economy of the region surpassed US$ 339 billion, albeit with varying levels of development and purchasing power across the individual countries.

Defence and Security

Central Asia is facing various security challenges, including terrorism, extremism, drug trafficking, and transnational crime. These issues are of global concern, and have led to increased international attention and engagement with the region. Central Asia is a key partner for India in the area of security cooperation. The region is facing various security challenges, including terrorism, extremism, and drug trafficking, and India has been working with the Central Asian countries to address these issues.

AFGHANISTAN - A NATION REBUILDING

Afghanistan is a multiethnic country located in the South-Central Asia. Known officially as the Islamic Republic of Afghanistan, the country is surrounded by land on all sides. Infamous as the **'Graveyard of Empires'**, Afghanistan has been sought by several rulers, with armies undertaking laborious journeys in an attempt to subdue the region but the land eventually laid to rest the fiercest of kingdoms. The continuous instability and war left behind traces of the ideology and culture of previous rulers and the people of Afghanistan failed to unite as a nation overtime. The country continues to thrive as a patchwork of contending ethnic groups and shifting alliances.

AFGHANISTAN

India's engagement with Afghanistan

YEAR	KEY EVENTS
1919	Treaty of Rawalpindi gave Afghanistan the right to be independent of British dominance.
1947	For a brief spell, India shared her contiguous border with Afghanistan.
1948	India-Pakistan War; border contested by both sides
Post 1948	The Durand line, which technically forms the border between India and Afghanistan, was no longer been a point of conflict between India and Afghanistan because it fell in Pakistan occupied Kashmir (PoK) territory.
1949	The Afghan King, Zahir Shah concluded the Treaty of Friendship with India
1979	Soviets invaded Afghanistan → India did not condemn the invasion but began to instead drift away from engaging directly with Afghanistan (as a supporter of NAM)
1989	Withdrawal of the Soviet Union
1996	Rise of Taliban → India joined hands with Russia and Iran in supporting the United Islamic Front for the Salvation of Afghanistan (UIFSA) also called 'Northern Alliance'
Post 2001	Post US Operation 'Enduring Freedom' (Taliban Government toppled) and the Bonn-I conference, India supported the development of Afghanistan and sided with Hamid Karzai.
2011	Strategic Partnership Agreement (SPA) – Assistance to help rebuild Afghanistan's infrastructure and institutions.
2012	School (now human rights activist) Malala Yousafzai gets shot by Taliban gunmen.
2016	India continued to engage with Ashraf Ghani; Afghan-India Friendship Dam jointly inaugurated – Salma Dam
2017	• Moscow Format Talks introduced • Afghanistan invited to participate in the International Solar Alliance Summit meeting being conducted in India
2020	• Doha Peace deal signed – US and Taliban sign deal; US and NATO to pull out gradually from Afghanistan • India signed five agreements for construction of schools and roads worth US$ 2.6 million.
2021	• The US starts backing out from Afghanistan - US forces vacated Bagram Airfield • Taliban return to power in Afghanistan and the Taliban Government (de facto) is established - 'The Islamic Emirate of Afghanistan'.
August 2022	The Taliban celebrates the first Anniversary of the withdrawal of US-led forces from Afghanistan. The Taliban government continues to await recognition from the international community.

While USA's 20-year occupation saw little development in Afghanistan, Beijing's association with the region is witnessing a growth since Afghanistan holds the key to the stability of Central Asian region and both China and Russia have been patiently noting any American incursions in the region. The Shanghai Cooperation Organisation (SCO) is an important participant in the Central Asian region and with Afghanistan as an Observer state, SCO has been developing energy supplies to power reconstruction and manufacturing here.

Area 652,230 sq kms	**Official Language** Dari, Pashto
Religion Islam - 99.7% Sunni: 85-90%, Shia 10-15% Other - 0.3%	**Life expectancy at birth** 65 years (2021)

Taliban Takeover

In **2021**, the Taliban, an **Islamic fundamentalist group**, regained power in Afghanistan following a prolonged insurgency against the government supported by the United States. Since taking control, the Taliban have implemented measures reminiscent of their oppressive rule during the late 1990s. Various human rights organizations, including the United Nations mission in Afghanistan and Amnesty International, have documented multiple instances of human rights violations.

Some crucial issues within Afghanistan under the Taliban rule include –

A. Threat to Human Rights and other freedoms

- Intimidation of journalists and restriction on press freedoms, resulting in the shutting down of several news organizations.
- Continuous monitoring of former government officials, protesters, activists and individuals of religious minorities, with several even disappearing over time.
- Deprivation of livelihood and identity including restrictions on attending secondary school and other occupation/work for women.
- Restrictions are imposed on women, limiting their access to technology and, in some cases, prohibiting them from entering shops and other commercial establishments.
- There has been a significant rise in the number of women who have been arrested for violating discriminatory policies, including rules that mandate women to be accompanied by a male chaperone in public and to fully cover their bodies.
- Increase in the rate of child marriages.

B. Security challenges

- The hurried withdrawal of the US forces from Afghan land was conducted before any major objectives of securing stability were achieved. Additionally, the rush left the Taliban with access to several pieces of advanced machinery, military equipment and weapons, threatening the internal security of the region.
- There is an increasing threat of Afghanistan becoming a safe haven for terrorists, potentially destabilizing both regional and international security structures.
- The sceptics are of the opinion that the anti-west sentiment could result in Taliban facilitating and motivating various rogue terrorist groups to fight any foreign radical thinking which isn't suited to them.
- Even a passive support to the Al Qaeda, LeT, JeM and other groups by Taliban could have disastrous effect on the neighbouring areas, including India.

C. Economic roadblocks

- With the international community pausing support in the form of developmental aid after Taliban's takeover, the country is witnessing a worsening of economic issues with reports suggesting that almost 97 percent of the Afghans could be living in poverty by mid-2022.
- The nation has been isolated from the global banking system and has been denied access to its currency reserves. It is alleged that, guided by the United States, the International Monetary Fund (IMF) has also obstructed Afghanistan from obtaining credit and assets.

- The economic limitations have led to over 90 percent of the population experiencing various levels of food insecurity.
- Due to the liquidity crisis, nearly 5 percent of the workforce (close to 5,00,000) has lost their jobs since the takeover.

Pakistan and Afghanistan share a complex and dynamic relationship in international relations, shaped by their historical, cultural, economic, and geopolitical ties. The two countries have been linked by a long border and have historically shared many ethnic and linguistic similarities. However, their relationship has been complicated by issues such as terrorism, refugee flows, and trade disputes. The Taliban regained control of Afghanistan in 2021, two decades after being removed by U.S. forces. The government and military of Pakistan generally supported a Taliban triumph in Afghanistan. However, supporting the Taliban has carried significant risks. Pakistan has accused Afghanistan of providing safe havens to the ***Tehreek-e-Taliban Pakistan*** (TTP is the largest militant organization fighting against the state in Pakistan) and other militant groups that carry out attacks inside Pakistan. In contrast, Afghanistan has accused Pakistan of supporting the Afghan Taliban and other militant groups that operate in Afghanistan. The takeover by Taliban has far-reaching impacts on India-Pakistan relations as well.

Implications of Taliban Takeover on India

Security Concerns	Regional Stability	China's influence	Refugee Crisis

- Pakistan's supposed support to Taliban could potentially impact **India's security interests**. The Taliban have a history of supporting terrorist groups that target India, such as **Lashkar-e-Taiba (LeT)** and **Jaish-e-Mohammed (JeM)**, both of which are based in Pakistan. These groups have carried out several attacks in India in the past, and any support that the Taliban provides to these groups could further exacerbate the security situation in India.
- The Taliban's takeover of Afghanistan could lead to a destabilization of the region and impact India's strategic interests in the region. Moreover, **India has invested heavily in Afghanistan's development** over the years, and any instability or deterioration of security in the country could impact India's interests in the region. The Taliban's takeover could potentially lead to a rise in extremism and terrorism in the region, which could impact India's interests.
- India also has a **strategic interest** in Afghanistan as a **gateway to Central Asia** and as a potential partner in its efforts to **counter China's growing influence** in the region. China has been increasing its presence and influence in the region, particularly in Afghanistan, and the Taliban's takeover could potentially strengthen China's strategic position in the region. This could impact India's efforts to counter China's growing influence and assert its own strategic interests in the region.
- The Taliban's takeover has led to a large number of Afghan refugees fleeing the country, and India, being a neighboring country, could potentially face an influx of refugees. This could put a strain on India's resources and lead to social tensions.

With regard to **Afghanistan**, USA's withdrawal had left most nations struggling to adapt to the new realities in a short span of time. After sufficient delay which was meant for gaining a global perspective on the issue, **India sent an official delegation to Kabul in June 2022** to initiate dialogue with Taliban. Indian officials met the Taliban administration's acting foreign minister to discuss India-Afghan diplomatic relations, bilateral trade and humanitarian aid. The communications between the two governments conveyed the continuation of a peaceful atmosphere between the two nations, and the Taliban spokespersons welcomed India's prolonged involvement in the development and economic reconstruction of Afghanistan.

India had pulled its officials out of Afghanistan in August 2021 and closed its embassy. As of January 2023, India has '**no formal diplomatic ties**' with the Taliban Government and New Delhi continues to maintain its previous stance against granting official legitimacy to the Taliban Government.

Therefore, going ahead, the need of the hour is to improve regional cooperation to fester the regional tensions surrounding Afghanistan. The neighbouring nations in the region, including India and Russia have been cooperating to avert any destabilizing power vacuum if a terrorist blowback is witnessed in the region.

ROADBLOCKS TO GROWTH OF CAR

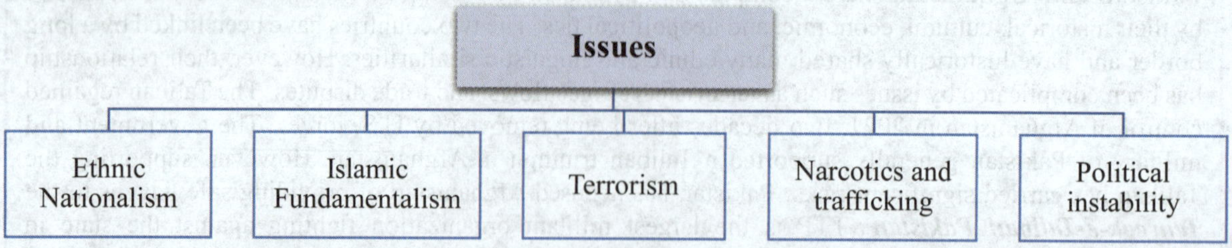

Over time, certain specific problems including terrorism, Islamic fundamentalism and internal instability, have repeatedly created hindrances towards the fulfillment of India's geopolitical interests in the Central Asian Region. Similar issues have been discussed by the other neighboring states as well.

Central Asia is a neighbor of the **"Golden Crescent"** of opium production (Iran-Pak-Afghan) and is also a victim of terrorism and the illegal arms trade. India is also not new to these problems on its Western front. Collaboration and cooperation with Central Asia in this regard benefits the entire region. Religious extremism, fundamentalism and terrorism continue to pose challenges to the societies of Central Asia as well as to regional stability. The **Fergana Valley** remains a Mecca for fundamentalism. The Central Asian republics are seriously threatened by the illegal drug trade from Afghanistan.

To tackle the difficulties, the **Istanbul Protocol** was established in 2011. **It involved the foreign ministers of various nations, such as China, India, Iran, Kazakhstan, Pakistan, and Russia, who pledged to collaborate in addressing terrorism, drug trafficking, insurgencies, and other related challenges**. Furthermore, the representatives at the Summit embraced the 'New Silk Road' strategy, which aimed to position Afghanistan as a pivotal hub for trade in South and Central Asia, fostering its economic dynamism.

While China and Pakistan share their borders with the Central Asian nations, India is dependent on Pakistan and Iran to access the region. Overtime, India has lost its immediate neighbourhood to China, which has developed good political and economic relations with nearly all of India's neighbours, thereby strategically encircling India. Since India views itself as a stabilizer and security provider in the region, it is compelled to improve its relationship with Central Asian countries (*Mandal theory* - your neighbour is your natural enemy and neighbour's neighbour is your friend) in order to serve its vital interest. India is also working to create a stable and peaceful Central Asia for bringing normalcy in Afghanistan. To upgrade its ties with Central Asia, India launched the **'Connect Central Asia Policy'** in 2012 which focused on deepening diplomatic relations through a multipronged strategy which targets political, economic, cultural and security aspects.

During the **India-Central Asia Summit (2022)** the leaders discussed multifaceted issues involving trade and connectivity, development cooperation, defence and security and issues regarding the diaspora. A comprehensive Joint Declaration was adopted by the leaders towards a common vision for a comprehensive India-Central Asia partnership.

On 27 January 2022, PM Modi hosted the first **India-Central Asia Summit** in virtual format which was attended by the Leaders of Kazakhstan, Kyrgyzstan, Tajikistan, Turkmenistan and Uzbekistan. The Summit coincided with the 30th anniversary of establishment of diplomatic relations between India and Central Asian countries.

Chinese ingressions in Central Asia

Prior to the 2000s Central Asia had relatively lower strategic priority for China and the interests were largely restricted to energy needs. The last two decades have witnessed a sustained effort to connect with the region.

The positioning of the region on the globe keeps it in the limelight along with its pool of natural resources and minerals which continues to attract global players.

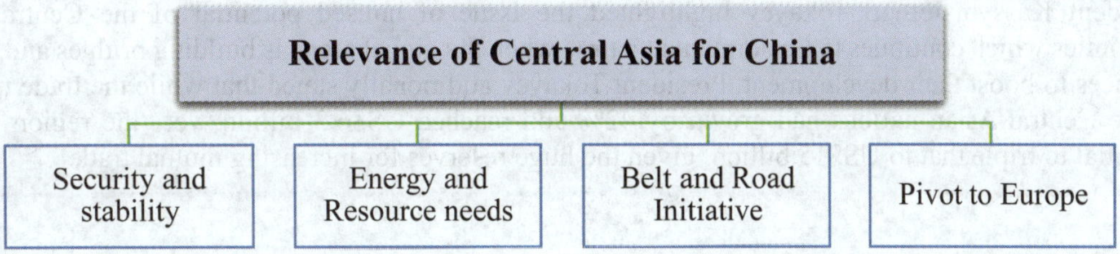

During the Soviet period, China had unsettled borders with Kazakh, Kyrgyz and Tajik Soviet Social Republics which was also the bone of contention between Russia and China. Once the Republics became independent post USSR's disintegration, China worked to settle the border issues with Kazakhstan, Kyrgyzstan and Tajikistan. The eagerness to demarcate territory was rooted in the fact that China wished to ensure peace in the East Turkistan region, christened as **Xinjiang** by China (annexed in 1949 with the assistance of the Soviet Union).

In the race for energy accumulation, China has been the frontrunner is forging a strong relationship with the Central Asian nations. The linkages were further solidified with the foundation of the **Shanghai Five** (China, Kazakhstan, Kyrgyzstan, Russia, and Tajikistan) in 1996 and the expanded version in June 2001, the **Shanghai Cooperation Organisation** (explained in detail in later chapters). The Central Asian commercial and resource interests also hold prominence. The launch of the **Belt and Road Initiative (BRI)** in 2013 by President Xi Jinping during a visit to Astana opened up new dimensions of Chinese economic, security and political interests and also significantly underscored the strategic value of Central Asian region to the West. In its '**pivot to Europe**' BRI is the most potent weapon towards the furtherance of the Chinese policy of expansion. For Central Asian Republics, China has the largest economic footprint in Central Asia and is the biggest source of Foreign Direct Investment as it brings in technological expertise and huge investments. Since the Central Asian nations do not have a direct access to the sea, the Chinese infrastructural projects, railway and road linkages have the potential to address the challenges and ease trading. Apart from external trade, the BRI projects have successfully created jobs and boosted national revenue while also creating stronger bonds between the Central Asian Nations.

In a proposed project for the region, China plans to open a route linking Uzbekistan with Pakistan via Afghanistan by making use of the existing infrastructure built during the late 1800s. As a result, the landlocked nations of Uzbekistan and Afghanistan would get faster and cheaper access to the sea via Pakistan's port.

Recent Developments

The threat of global recession and international conflict has provided an impetus towards accelerated development of regional economic cooperation. The economic disruptions have resulted in the collapse of trade supply chains and have brought to the fore the trend towards regionalization and the Central Asian nations are fast absorbing this reality.

On 25 January 2022, President Xi Jinping hosted the leaders of the five Central Asian nations (Kazakhstan, Kyrgyz Republic, Tajikistan, Turkmenistan, and Uzbekistan) through a Virtual Summit to commemorate the **30th Anniversary of Diplomatic Relations Between China and Central Asian Countries**. The Chinese President made significant announcements to increase the trade target between the nations to US$ 70 billion by 2030 and for a provision of US$ 500 million towards assisting the Central Asian nations over the next three years towards 'socially significant' projects.

Apart from economic troubles, the region has witnessed troubles in border demarcation apart from the security threats, with riots shaking both Uzbekistan and Kazakhstan in 2022. The more recent conflicts between Ukraine and Russia have further enhanced the strategic relevance of Central Asia which serves as the direct supply chain routes between China and European Union.

During the **4th Consultative Meeting of heads of Central Asian states** (July 2022), Kazakhstan's President Kassym-Jomart Tokayev highlighted the issue of unused potential of the Central Asian economies which continues to lie dormant at a time when the global arena is building bridges and forging alliances to boost their development. President Tokayev additionally stated that while the trade turnover of the Central Asian nations had grown by 42% and reached US$6.3 billion, yet "the region had the potential to triple that to US$15 billion, given the huge reserves for increasing mutual trade".

7 THE CONTINENT OF AFRICA

DEFINING THE REGION

Africa is a colossal continent of **54 nations** with a population of around 1.2 billion. However, the continent continues to remain somewhat neglected and poorly understood. The 21st century development around the African continent is testimony to the fact that the world's most powerful nations are once again engaging with the continent and competing for control of its vast natural resources. The sovereign nations gradually realized the strategic and political significance of the African nations and the global waters surrounding the area and hence have accelerated their participation in the region.

Africa has 60% of the world's arable land but it spends more than US$40 billion annually on food imports. This mismatch is due to various reasons including the apathy of the top leadership, the Dutch Disease and the mismanagement of policy executions within the states.

AFRICAN NATIONS: A BRIEF SNAPSHOT

Morocco: A politically stable and progressive nation, Morocco leads in trade & renewable energy but faces ongoing tension over Western Sahara, a major diplomatic issue with Algeria and the Polisario Front.

Algeria: A key oil & gas producer, Algeria shapes North African geopolitics but struggles with economic issues due to declining oil prices and corruption. Political protests and unrest have also emerged.

Egypt: A key Middle Eastern and African power, Egypt struggles economically due to inflation and tourism decline. Protests against the government's economic policies and leadership have intensified amidst political dissatisfaction.

Sudan: Conflict-ridden Sudan faces a severe humanitarian crisis marked by civil war, displacement, and violence, significantly destabilizing the region & hindering development.

Senegal: Senegal's stable democracy and leadership in climate change policy make it a regional model, but the country remains vulnerable to climate impacts like drought and coastal erosion, threatening its sustainability efforts.

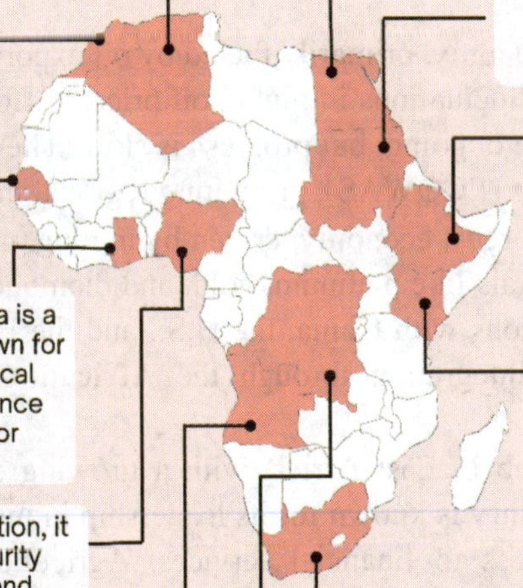

Ethiopia: Emerging as a regional power, Ethiopia's progress is marred by the Tigray conflict, which has caused a severe humanitarian crisis and displaced millions, impacting its stability and development efforts.

Ghana: A stable democracy, Ghana is a regional leader in West Africa, known for its economic development, political stability, and sustainable governance practices, setting an example for neighboring countries.

Kenya: As East Africa's economic hub, Kenya plays a key role in regional peacekeeping and humanitarian efforts, but drought, security threats, and the COVID-19 pandemic have negatively impacted its economy.

Nigeria: Africa's most populous nation, it is a regional power, though security issues like terrorism, banditry, and economic inequality persist. Much of the population still remains in poverty.

South Africa: A regional powerhouse, South Africa influences global diplomacy by advocating for racial equality, social justice, and economic development, positioning itself as a key player in Africa's progress.

Angola: A major oil producer, it holds significant regional influence but faces governance challenges, including corruption and inequality. These issues fuel social unrest and hinder economic and political development.

Democratic Republic of Congo: Despite vast natural resources, the DRC's instability and political crises limit its development. Continuous conflict and leadership changes obstruct its potential for regional influence and sustainable growth.

POLITY AND GOVERNANCE

Africa is home to a variety of political systems, ranging from democracies like South Africa and Botswana to authoritarian regimes like Eritrea and Burundi. Many African countries face significant challenges, including corruption, political instability, and human rights abuses. Regional organizations such as the **African Union (AU)** play a crucial role in promoting peace, security, and development in Africa. The AU has been involved in mediating conflicts, promoting human rights, and fostering economic cooperation among African countries.

- **South Africa** stands as one of Africa's most robust democracies, with a well-established constitution and strong institutions. Despite this, governance is often challenged by corruption, political infighting, and socio-economic inequality.
- **Nigeria**, Africa's most populous nation, is a federal republic that faces persistent governance challenges. Governance in Nigeria is characterized by a delicate balancing act between various ethnic and religious groups, with ongoing debates over federalism and resource allocation.
- **Kenya's** political landscape is dominated by a strong presidential system. Ethnic divisions often influence elections, leading to periodic unrest.
- **Ethiopia** has long been governed by a federal parliamentary republic, but ethnic federalism has often led to tensions among the various regions. The ongoing conflict in the Tigray region, which erupted in 2020, has posed significant challenges to governance under Prime Minister Abiy Ahmed, who came to power on a reformist platform.

ECONOMY & TRADE

Africa is rich in natural resources, including minerals, oil, and gas. Countries like South Africa, Nigeria, and Angola are major producers and exporters of these resources. Many African countries have experienced significant economic growth in recent years, driven by increased trade and investment. For example, Rwanda has achieved impressive economic growth rates, while Ethiopia has emerged as a regional economic powerhouse.

Despite economic growth, Africa continues to face challenges such as poverty, inequality, and infrastructure deficits. Countries like Ghana and Kenya have made progress in addressing these issues, but much remains to be done.

- **Nigeria** boasts Africa's largest economy, primarily fueled by oil exports. However, oil dependency has made the economy vulnerable to fluctuations in global oil prices. Efforts to diversify into agriculture, technology, and manufacturing are ongoing, but progress is slow. The country is part of the Economic Community of West African States (ECOWAS), promoting regional trade and integration.
- **South Africa** is Africa's second-largest economy, driven by mining, manufacturing, and services. The country is a global leader in minerals like platinum, gold, and diamonds. South Africa is a member of BRICS and has strong trade relations with China, the U.S., and the European Union. Its trade policy focuses on expanding regional integration through the **African Continental Free Trade Area (AfCFTA)**.
- **Kenya** is a regional economic hub in East Africa, with a growing economy driven by agriculture, services, and technology. The country is known for its leadership in mobile banking through platforms like M-Pesa, revolutionizing access to financial services. Agriculture, especially tea, coffee, and horticulture, plays a significant role in trade.

African Continental Free Trade Area (ACFTA)

The ACFTA is the **world's largest free trade area** bringing together the **55 countries of the African Union (AU) and eight (8) Regional Economic Communities (RECs).** The overall mandate of the ACFTA is to create a single continental market with a population of about 1.3 billion people and a combined GDP of approximately US$ 3.4 trillion. The ACFTA is one of the flagship projects of **Agenda 2063: The Africa We Want**, the African Union's long-term development strategy for transforming the continent into a global powerhouse. **As of March 2023, 54 African Union states have signed the ACFTA agreement.**

DEFENSE & SECURITY

Africa faces various security challenges, including terrorism, piracy, and armed conflicts. Regional cooperation in defence and security is essential for addressing these challenges. The African Union has established peacekeeping forces to address conflicts in various parts of the continent.

Many African countries are investing in modernizing their militaries to enhance their capabilities. For example, South Africa has a relatively well-equipped military, while Nigeria has been investing in military hardware and training.

- **Nigeria** faces significant security challenges, particularly in the northeast with *Boko Haram's* insurgency and the *Islamic State West Africa Province (ISWAP)*. The government has invested heavily in military operations to combat terrorism, but issues like banditry and separatist movements in other regions complicate security efforts.
- **South Africa's** defense capabilities are the most advanced on the continent, but the country faces fewer external security threats compared to others. Domestically, security challenges stem from high crime rates and unrest related to socio-economic inequality. South Africa plays a leading role in peacekeeping missions within the African Union, notably in conflict zones like the Democratic Republic of Congo (DRC).
- **Ethiopia's** security concerns have intensified due to the conflict in the ***Tigray*** region, which has involved federal forces, regional militias, and foreign actors like Eritrea. The conflict has triggered one of the most severe humanitarian crises in recent African history. Ethiopia's strategic location in the Horn of Africa also places it at the center of broader regional security dynamics, including its involvement in the African Union Mission in Somalia (AMISOM).
- **Somalia's** piracy threat in the Indian Ocean has seen a resurgence in recent years. While the number of attacks has decreased significantly from its peak in the early 2010s, incidents of piracy and hijacking continue to occur. This resurgence is attributed to various factors, including political instability in Somalia, economic hardship, and the ongoing conflict in Yemen. International naval forces have played a crucial role in combating Somali piracy, patrolling the Indian Ocean and disrupting pirate operations.

FOREIGN AFFAIRS & DIPLOMACY

- Africa's influence on the global stage is growing, with countries playing increasingly active roles in international organizations. South Africa, Nigeria, and Egypt are among the most influential African nations on the global stage.
- Africa is strengthening its ties with other developing countries, particularly in Asia and Latin America. Countries like China and India have been investing heavily in Africa, fostering economic and political relationships.
- African countries are seeking to build stronger partnerships with developed nations to promote economic development and address global challenges. For example, the African Union has established partnerships with the European Union and the United States to promote peace, security, and development.

Egypt's foreign policy balances its African identity with its strategic importance in the Middle East. As a founding member of the African Union, Egypt is influential in regional diplomacy, particularly on issues like water rights, exemplified by its involvement in the ***Grand Ethiopian Renaissance Dam (GERD)*** dispute. Egypt's strategic position also makes it a critical player in Mediterranean security and European relations.

ENVIRONMENT & TECHNOLOGY

Africa is particularly vulnerable to the impacts of climate change, including droughts, floods, and desertification. Countries like Kenya and Ethiopia are facing severe water shortages due to climate change.

There is growing interest in renewable energy in Africa, as countries seek to diversify their energy sources and reduce their carbon footprint. Countries like Kenya and South Africa have made significant investments in renewable energy projects. Africa is making strides in technology, with increasing access to mobile phones and the internet. Countries like Rwanda and Ghana are leading the way in digital innovation and e-government.

- **Kenya** leads Africa in renewable energy, particularly in geothermal, wind, and solar power. It is home to the largest wind farm in Africa, the Lake Turkana Wind Power project. Kenya also stands out for its technological innovations, particularly in mobile banking and fintech.
- **Ethiopia** is pursuing green development, focusing on hydropower as a renewable energy source. The Grand Ethiopian Renaissance Dam (GERD) is set to be Africa's largest hydroelectric power plant, though it has sparked tensions with Egypt and Sudan over water rights. Ethiopia's reforestation program, which saw the planting of over 350 million trees in a single day, highlights its environmental efforts.
- **South Africa** is committed to addressing climate change but faces challenges due to its reliance on coal for energy. The country is investing in renewable energy sources, though it remains one of the largest carbon emitters in Africa. In technology, South Africa is a continental leader in research, notably in areas like space science, artificial intelligence, and medical innovations.

THE GREAT GREEN WALL INITIATIVE

It is an African-led initiative and was started in 2007 by the African Union to combat desertification, land degradation, drought. Initially targeting 11 Sahelian nations [Chad, Burkina Faso, Eritrea, Ethiopia, Mali, Niger, Mauritania, Nigeria, Sudan, Senegal, Djibouti], the campaign was built to halt the progress of the Sahara Desert, which has spread by 10 percent since 1920 and engulfed entire villages.

The project aims to restore 100 million hectares of degraded land by 2030. It aims to transform the lives of 100 million Africans by growing 8,000 kilo metre long and fifteen kilo metre wide mosaic of trees, vegetation, grasslands, plants. The initiative aims to sequester 250 million tonnes of carbon and create ten million green jobs.

By 2024, the initiative has restored nearly **20 million hectares**, sequestered millions of tonnes of carbon, and created **over a million green jobs**, contributing to climate resilience and transforming the lives of millions across Africa.

DIASPORA & CULTURE

- Africa has a significant diaspora, with millions of Africans living in other countries. The African diaspora contributes to economic development and cultural exchange between Africa and other regions.
- Africa is home to a rich and diverse cultural heritage, with numerous languages, religions, and traditions. This diversity contributes to the continent's unique identity and cultural vibrancy.
- Africa is a linguistically diverse continent, home to over 2,000 languages spread across a vast number of language families. These languages reflect the continent's rich cultural heritage and history. The major language families include **Afroasiatic** (Arabic, Amharic & Hausa), **Niger-Congo** (Swahili, Yoruba,

Zulu and Xhosa), **Nilo-Saharan** (Dinka, Nuer & Luo) **and Khoisan** (known for their distinctive click sounds). Many countries are multilingual, with indigenous languages coexisting alongside colonial languages like English, French, and Portuguese, as a result of Africa's colonial history.

- The African diaspora plays a vital role in promoting cultural exchange and understanding between Africa and the rest of the world. For example, African music, art, and literature have gained global recognition.

THE NEW SCRAMBLE FOR AFRICA

The term "*Great Game*," historically used to describe the geopolitical confrontations of the 19th century, is now resurfacing in discussions about the growing competition for influence in Africa. Once dominated by European powers, particularly on the East African coast and the Southern Indian Ocean, Africa has seen a dramatic rise in foreign involvement over the past two decades. However, the phrase "Great Game" feels outdated, and instead, the term "*New Scramble for Africa*" is being applied to describe 21st-century developments. Unlike the earlier scrambles, which were primarily exploitative and focused on resource extraction without benefit to Africa, the current wave presents itself as more cooperative, emphasizing partnerships between foreign powers and African nations.

- The **first "scramble"** took place in the 19th century, when European colonists divided and seized African lands, while the **second scramble** occurred during the Cold War, as global powers competed for the allegiance of newly independent African states. Both waves left Africa with limited control over its internal affairs.
- Today, however, Africa is experiencing rapid economic growth, with countries such as Ethiopia, Côte d'Ivoire, Mozambique, Tanzania, Rwanda, and the Democratic Republic of the Congo leading the way. According to the IMF, these nations are among the fastest-growing economies globally, driven by sectors like banking, telecommunications, and infrastructure, which offer significant investment opportunities.
- Moreover, Africa's population is expected to grow from 1.19 billion in 2015 to 4.39 billion by 2100, creating an enormous consumer market. This demographic shift highlights the importance of engaging in Africa's structural economic transformation to fully leverage the continent's growing potential.

Dutch disease: Resource-rich countries generally experience the 'resource curse', or 'paradox of plenty', in which they fail to experience wealth from their resource endowments but rather undergo a cycle of persistent underdevelopment.

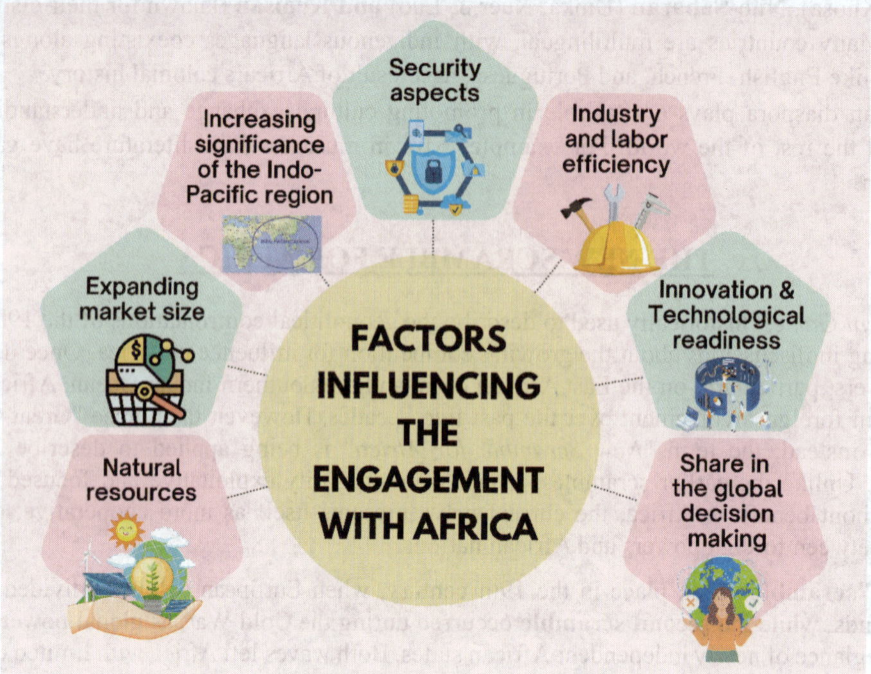

KEY DRIVERS OF THE NEW SCRAMBLE

Natural Resources: Africa remains rich in valuable natural resources such as oil, gas, minerals (like cobalt, lithium, and rare earth elements), and arable land. These resources are critical for global industries, including technology, manufacturing, and energy. Countries like China, the United States, the European Union, and emerging powers like India and Turkey are heavily involved in securing access to these resources through investments and trade deals.

The key factors influencing the rising engagement with Africa include the following -

(1) **Natural and Energy Resources**

- Africa is home to abundant natural resources, including oil, gas, rare minerals, and metals such as cobalt, copper, and lithium, essential for industries worldwide. The continent accounts for about 10% of the world's oil reserves and 8% of natural gas.
- In recent years, major powers like China, the U.S., and Russia have increased their presence to secure access to these resources.
- The rising demand for minerals critical to the global energy transition, such as lithium and cobalt used in electric vehicle batteries, has intensified this engagement.
- Notably, Chinese investments in African mining and energy projects continue to rise, with the Belt and Road Initiative (BRI) further expanding China's footprint in African resource sectors.

(2) **Expanding Market Size**

- Africa's rapidly growing population and emerging middle class offer significant market potential for global businesses.
- The **African Continental Free Trade Area (AfCFTA)**, launched in 2021, aims to create the world's largest free trade zone, unlocking economic potential and promoting intra-African trade.
- This agreement has attracted foreign companies eager to tap into the continent's burgeoning consumer base. Countries such as Nigeria, Kenya, and South Africa are becoming major hubs for retail, technology, and financial services.
- Africa's urbanization and rising consumer demand for digital services, particularly mobile banking and e-commerce, present lucrative opportunities for multinational companies.

(3) Strategic Geopolitical Position

- Africa's location at the crossroads of Europe, Asia, and the Americas enhances its strategic importance.
- Africa's location, controlling key maritime routes like the Suez Canal and the Cape of Good Hope, makes it essential for global trade and energy transport.
- Global powers are vying for influence, with Russia increasing its military presence in countries like Sudan and Libya, while China and the U.S. seek strategic partnerships.
- Countries like Djibouti, home to several foreign military bases, are critical for controlling access to the Red Sea and protecting global shipping lanes.
- Recent developments, such as the U.S. Africa Strategy 2023, aim to counter Chinese and Russian influence while securing strategic military and economic partnerships with African nations.

(4) Increasing Significance of the Indo-Pacific Region

- Africa's eastern coastline, bordering the Indian Ocean, is becoming increasingly important in the broader Indo-Pacific strategy. India, Japan, and Australia are deepening their economic and strategic ties with African nations, as part of their Indo-Pacific outreach.
- India, for instance, has enhanced its maritime collaboration with African countries, seeking to ensure secure sea lines of communication and combat piracy.
- Japan's investments under its Free and Open Indo-Pacific (FOIP) vision also focus on infrastructure projects along the East African coast, enhancing connectivity with the Indo-Pacific region.

(5) Infrastructure Development

- Africa requires extensive infrastructure development in transportation, energy, and digital networks.
- The BRI has spearheaded this drive, with China building railways, ports, and highways across the continent. These investments have increased China's economic and political influence, although concerns about debt dependency persist.
- Other global players like the U.S. and Europe are also entering the competition, offering alternatives to counterbalance Chinese dominance.

(6) Military & Security Aspects

- Africa is increasingly seen as crucial for global security, particularly in counterterrorism, peacekeeping, and anti-piracy efforts.
- Nations such as the U.S., France, and China have military bases or security partnerships across the continent. With the rise of insurgencies in the Sahel region and East Africa, foreign powers are stepping up their military engagement to stabilize these regions.
- Additionally, the African Union and regional organizations like ECOWAS are gaining greater prominence in addressing peace and security issues on the continent.
- Western powers, especially the U.S., have been providing military training and counterterrorism support, particularly against groups such as Boko Haram and Al-Shabaab.

(7) Industry and Labour Efficiency

- Africa offers both a growing labor force and competitive manufacturing prospects. The continent's young and increasingly educated workforce is attracting foreign direct investment in industries like textiles, agriculture, and pharmaceuticals.
- Countries like Ethiopia and Rwanda have been developing their manufacturing sectors, turning into regional production hubs.
- Global supply chain shifts following the COVID-19 pandemic have also drawn attention to Africa as a potential manufacturing base, especially as companies diversify their supply sources away from Asia.

(8) Innovation and Technological Readiness

- Africa has seen significant progress in digital innovation, particularly in mobile technology, fintech, and e-commerce. Countries like Kenya, with its M-Pesa mobile payment platform, are leading technological adoption, attracting interest from global tech giants like Google, Microsoft, and Facebook.
- Foreign investors are increasingly looking at Africa's tech hubs in Lagos, Nairobi, and Cape Town as innovation centers.
- The development of 5G networks, backed by companies from China and other global players, is further boosting Africa's technological landscape, enhancing connectivity and integration into the global economy.

(9) Climate Change & Environmental Issues

- Africa's vulnerability to climate change is driving foreign engagement, with countries competing to lead climate-related investments.
- Projects focusing on renewable energy—such as solar and wind—are increasingly seen as critical to Africa's future.
- Europe and China have particularly focused on green energy projects, while competition for rare minerals like cobalt, essential for renewable technologies, further intensifies global interest.

(10) Share in Global Decision-Making

- Africa's influence on the global stage is steadily increasing. The continent, with 54 nations, is becoming more assertive in multilateral institutions such as the United Nations, the World Trade Organization, and the African Union.
- In recent years, there have been growing calls for African representation in forums like the G20, where South Africa is the only member.
- Additionally, Africa's importance in global climate negotiations, such as the Paris Agreement, is rising as the continent grapples with the impacts of climate change. Efforts to give Africa a greater voice in global governance, particularly regarding trade and climate issues, are expected to intensify in the coming years.

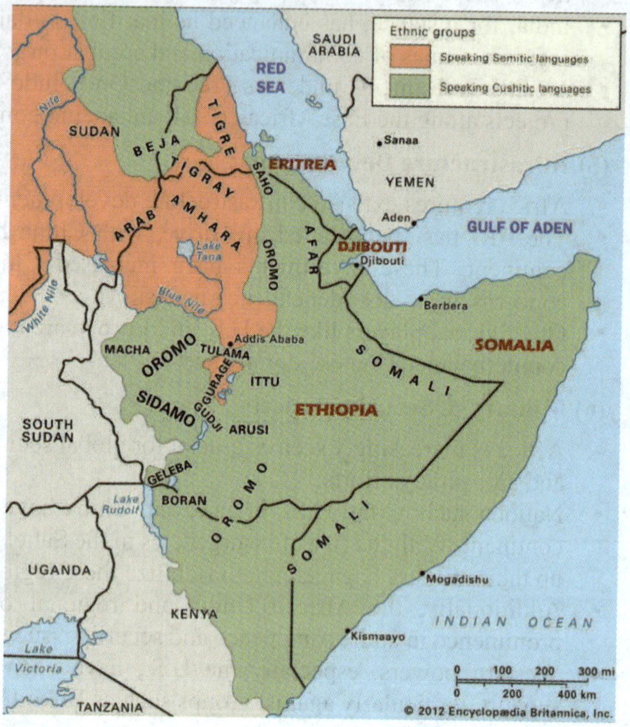

HORN OF AFRICA

It is the peninsula in East Africa, extending into the Arabian Sea (image). It is the easternmost extension of the African continent, comprising countries such as **Somalia, Ethiopia, Eritrea, Djibouti**, and sometimes extending to include **Sudan** and **South Sudan**. It is strategically located near the **Bab-el-Mandeb Strait**, a crucial chokepoint that connects the **Red Sea** to the **Gulf of Aden** and the **Indian Ocean**. This waterway is pivotal for international trade, as it is part of the primary shipping route between Europe, the Middle East, and Asia.

COUNTRIES INVOLVED	
Somalia	▪ Somalia has a diverse population with major ethnic groups including Somalis, Bantu, and other minority communities. The country has a rich cultural heritage but the population experiences high levels of poverty, displacement, and limited access to basic services like healthcare and education. This is mainly due to prolonged conflict and instability. ▪ Somalia remains a focal point for international counterterrorism efforts due to the presence of ***Al-Shabaab***. The country's strategic location by the **Gulf of Aden** has drawn global attention, including military involvement from the **U.S., Turkey**, and **AMISOM**. ▪ Ongoing instability, maritime piracy, and humanitarian crises continue to influence international policy in the region.

Ethiopia	▪ It is a land-locked country on the Horn of Africa and its capital is Addis Ababa. Ethiopia is characterized by its ethnic diversity with over 80 ethnic groups, including the Oromo, Amhara, Tigray, and Somali. It is a federal parliamentary republic with a complex political landscape. ▪ Ethiopia, Africa's second-most populous country, has attracted international focus due to its **Tigray conflict** and key role in the **Nile River dispute**. ▪ The country is a growing hub for Chinese investments under the **Belt and Road Initiative**, while its internal instability raises regional concerns, impacting relations with neighbors like Sudan and Eritrea.
Eritrea	▪ Eritrea is an **authoritarian state** under the leadership of President *Isaias Afwerki*, who has been in power since independence in 1993. The country is known for its strict government control over social and political life. ▪ Eritrea faces challenges including limited freedom of expression, compulsory military service, and a lack of basic freedoms, which have led to significant emigration and a large diaspora. ▪ Eritrea's strategic location by the **Red Sea** has attracted international attention, especially with military involvement in **Yemen** and **Ethiopia's Tigray conflict**. ▪ The country's isolationist policies have led to minimal foreign alliances, except for its military cooperation with Ethiopia and security collaborations with Gulf nations.
Djibouti	▪ Djibouti is a stable country with a relatively authoritarian political system led by President **Ismail Omar Guelleh**, who has been in power since 1999. ▪ Djibouti's population is ethnically diverse, including Somali, Afar, and Arab communities. The country has relatively high literacy rates compared to some neighboring countries. ▪ Djibouti's economy is service-oriented, with significant contributions from port operations and logistics due to its strategic location at the Bab-el-Mandeb Strait. The country has invested heavily in infrastructure, including ports and railways, with support from international partners like China. ▪ Djibouti's critical location at the **Bab-el-Mandeb Strait** makes it a strategic hub for international military bases, including those of the **U.S., China, and France**. ▪ The country plays a key role in global shipping, and its partnerships, particularly with China, through infrastructure projects have enhanced its geopolitical significance in the region.

Bab-el-Mandeb Strait

This narrow strait links the **Red Sea** to the **Gulf of Aden** and is vital for global maritime trade, particularly oil shipments. Control over this strait is highly contested, with several international and regional actors keeping a close watch.

Gulf of Aden

Located to the north of Somalia and south of Yemen, the Gulf of Aden is prone to piracy and has seen increasing international naval presence to secure shipping lanes. This region connects to the **Suez Canal**, making it an essential part of global trade routes.

Red Sea

The Red Sea, bordering **Djibouti, Eritrea, and Sudan**, is a major water body that connects to the Mediterranean via the **Suez Canal**. It has seen growing geopolitical competition, with countries like **Saudi Arabia, Egypt, and China** increasing their influence along the coast.

Ogaden Region

Located in southeastern Ethiopia, bordering Somalia, the Ogaden region is a flashpoint for territorial disputes and insurgencies. It is home to ethnic Somalis and has seen conflicts over self-determination and control of resources like **natural gas (2024)**.

Issues of Concern

(a) Eritrea-Ethiopia Relations: The long-standing border dispute between Ethiopia and Eritrea was partially resolved through the **2018 peace agreement**, which ended a 20-year conflict. However, tensions remain, especially with Eritrea's involvement in the Tigray conflict.

(b) Somalia's Internal Instability: Somalia has faced decades of internal conflict, with **Al-Shabaab**, an extremist group, controlling parts of the country. Somalia's instability has resulted in piracy in the Gulf of Aden, refugee crises, and spillover effects into neighbouring Kenya and Ethiopia. International actors like the **U.S.**, **Turkey**, and **African Union Mission in Somalia (AMISOM)** have been heavily involved in trying to stabilize the country.

(c) Djibouti's Strategic Importance: Djibouti hosts military bases for several global powers, including the **U.S.**, **China**, **France**, and **Japan**, making it a focal point of international interest in the region. Djibouti's location at the mouth of the *Bab-el-Mandeb Strait* gives it strategic control over one of the world's busiest shipping lanes.

(d) Somalia-Kenya Maritime Dispute: A major maritime dispute exists between Somalia and Kenya over oil-rich waters in the **Indian Ocean**. The case was brought before the **International Court of Justice (ICJ)**, which ruled largely in favour of Somalia in 2021, heightening tensions between the two countries.

(e) Humanitarian Crisis: The Horn of Africa faces severe **droughts and famines**, leading to food insecurity for millions. Climate change has exacerbated these conditions, making the region one of the most vulnerable to environmental crises. These challenges contribute to mass displacement and further destabilize the region.

KEY PLAYERS IN THE REGION

China has been the most dominant player in the new scramble, with extensive investments in infrastructure, mining, and energy. China's diplomatic presence is also strong, with African nations increasingly turning to China for loans and development assistance.

While less focused on infrastructure than China, the **United States** is deeply involved in Africa through security partnerships, trade (e.g., the *African Growth and Opportunity Act*), and initiatives like *Power Africa* to boost energy access.

The **European Union** has a historical connection to Africa and remains a significant investor, particularly in infrastructure and development aid. European countries are also deeply involved in security efforts, particularly in the *Sahel* region, to combat terrorism and migration.

Russia has been increasing its influence in Africa, often through arms sales and military cooperation. Russia's role in Africa is more focused on security and geopolitics, often working with African nations to counterbalance Western influence.

India is also expanding its role in Africa, especially in sectors like pharmaceuticals, education, and IT. India is cultivating partnerships based on shared historical and cultural ties, especially with Eastern and Southern African nations.

IMPLICATIONS OF THE NEW SCRAMBLE

Economic Growth vs. Debt Dependency	Sovereignty & Self-Determination	Competition for Influence
• While foreign investments can drive economic growth and development, concerns about debt traps and dependency on foreign powers are growing. • For instance, Chinese loans for infrastructure projects have led to accusations of "debt diplomacy," where African nations risk losing control of strategic assets if they fail to repay.	• The increasing involvement of global powers in Africa's economy and security has raised concerns about the erosion of sovereignty, as foreign interests often dictate national policies and priorities.	• The New Scramble for Africa has transformed the continent into a geopolitical chessboard where global powers compete for strategic advantage. • This has both positive and negative consequences for African nations, as they must navigate external influences while striving to maintain their own interests.

So far, the continent doesn't have an effective unified strategy or institutional capacity to effectively respond to the 'new scramble in Africa'. The African Union has however, introduced the strategic framework '**Agenda 2063**' in 2016. It is Africa's blueprint and master plan to transform it into a future global powerhouse. It is a tangible representation of the pan-African drive for unity, self-determination, freedom, progress, and collective wealth sought under Pan-Africanism and the African Renaissance, and it aspires to achieve its goal of inclusive and sustainable development. While the plan includes Africa's aspirations for the future, it also identifies key flagship programmes that could assist in boosting the economic growth and lead to the rapid transformation of the continent.

MAJOR ISSUES TROUBLING AFRICA

Africa faces a diverse range of challenges across political, economic, social, and environmental dimensions. These issues affect various African nations, each grappling with its own specific set of obstacles. Some of the key issues and the countries impacted include:

(1) **Poverty and Inequality:** Many African countries experience significant poverty and income inequality, with a large portion of the population living in extreme poverty. Countries such as *Nigeria, Chad, Malawi,* and *Zimbabwe* are among those facing severe economic disparities.

(2) **Economic Development and Debt Crisis:** Limited access to capital, inadequate infrastructure, and low levels of industrialization continue to impede economic growth. In addition, many African nations face a critical debt burden:

- Zambia: With a debt-to-GDP ratio of over 100%, Zambia struggles to meet its financial obligations.
- Ghana: Rising debt levels have increased the risk of debt default.
- Ethiopia: Significant debt due to infrastructure projects and ongoing conflict in the Tigray region.
- Kenya: Concerns over debt sustainability persist.
- Mozambique: Grappling with debt issues, exacerbated by hidden debt discovered in 2016.

(3) **Governance and Corruption:** Weak governance structures, corruption, and lack of accountability pose significant barriers to socioeconomic development. Countries such as *South Sudan, Somalia,* and *Nigeria* are examples where corruption remains endemic, impacting public services and economic stability.

(4) **Conflict and Security:** Several African nations face political instability, conflict, and security threats, which hinder development and exacerbate humanitarian crises:

- Sudan: Ongoing conflict has created a severe humanitarian crisis, with widespread displacement and violence.
- Burkina Faso, Mali, and Niger: These nations face regional instability and security challenges.

- Central African Republic and Libya also face prolonged conflicts contributing to regional insecurity.

(5) **Health and Disease Burden:** African countries are severely impacted by a high burden of diseases, including HIV/AIDS, malaria, and tuberculosis. Nations such as *South Africa, Botswana, Eswatini,* and *Lesotho* have particularly high HIV prevalence rates, while *Nigeria* and *Democratic Republic of Congo* are heavily affected by malaria.

(6) **Education and Skills Gap:** Limited access to quality education and skills training contributes to high illiteracy rates and a lack of a skilled workforce, affecting economic growth. Countries like *Somalia, Chad,* and *Mali* are struggling with low literacy levels and inadequate educational infrastructure.

(7) **Climate Change and Environmental Degradation:** Africa is particularly vulnerable to the effects of climate change, such as droughts, desertification, and extreme weather events. Countries like *Kenya, Somalia,* and *Ethiopia* are dealing with frequent droughts, while *Mozambique* and *Madagascar* face devastating cyclones. *Zimbabwe* has also been grappling with prolonged droughts, compounded by economic challenges. *Malawi* has experienced both droughts and floods in recent years, impacting agricultural productivity and exacerbating food insecurity.

(8) **Infrastructure Deficits:** Inadequate infrastructure, including transportation networks, energy systems, and basic utilities, hampers trade and economic growth. Nations such as *Democratic Republic of Congo, Nigeria, Chad,* and *Tanzania* face significant infrastructure gaps, impeding connectivity and development.

(9) **Food Security and Agriculture:** Many African nations struggle with food insecurity, poor agricultural practices, and challenges in achieving self-sufficiency:

- South Sudan and Somalia are experiencing acute food crises due to conflict and climate factors. *Somalia* has faced severe drought conditions for several years, leading to food shortages and widespread hunger.
- Niger, Ethiopia, and Chad also suffer from chronic food insecurity and drought conditions affecting agricultural productivity.

(10) **Migration and Refugee Crises:** Significant migration and refugee movements occur due to conflicts, political instability, and economic hardship:

- South Sudan, Ethiopia, and Central African Republic are grappling with large refugee populations fleeing violence and instability.
- Libya remains a key transit point for migrants attempting to cross into Europe.

(11) **China-Africa Relations:** China's growing economic and political influence in Africa is another significant issue. Chinese investments in infrastructure projects across *Kenya, Nigeria, Ethiopia,* and *Angola* have fuelled economic partnerships, though concerns about debt dependency are rising.

(12) **Technological Advancements:** Despite these challenges, several African countries are witnessing technological progress, with advancements in sectors such as digitalization and renewable energy. Countries like *Rwanda, Kenya,* and *South Africa* are at the forefront of these developments, transforming their economies through technology.

GLOBAL SPOTLIGHT: CONFLICTS & CRIMES

(1) CONFLICTS IN SUDAN

- Sudan has been embroiled in multiple conflicts over the years, the most notable being the Darfur conflict, due to tensions over marginalization, land rights, and political representation. The **Darfur conflict** began in 2003 in the Darfur region of western Sudan, primarily as a rebellion by non-Arab ethnic groups against the Sudanese government. These groups, including the **Fur**, **Masalit**, and **Zaghawa**, accused the government of marginalizing them politically and economically. In response, the Sudanese government, under President Omar al-Bashir, armed and supported Arab militias known as the **Janjaweed**, who carried out brutal attacks on Darfur's villages, committing widespread atrocities including mass killings, rape, and displacement.

- The conflict resulted in a severe humanitarian crisis, with over **300,000 people killed** and **millions displaced**. The International Criminal Court (ICC) indicted President al-Bashir for **genocide**, war crimes, and crimes against humanity. Despite peace agreements and the presence of international peacekeepers, violence and instability have persisted, and Darfur remains volatile, marked by ongoing clashes between rebel factions, militias, and government forces. The conflict has drawn international condemnation and remains one of Africa's most severe humanitarian crises.
- Another significant conflict led to the independence of South Sudan in 2011, following decades of war between the Sudanese government and the Sudan People's Liberation Movement.
- ***Omar al-Bashir***, Sudan's long-time dictator, was ousted in 2019 after mass protests. A transitional government was formed but was overthrown in a 2021 military coup led by *General Abdel Fattah al-Burhan*, resulting in instability. Tensions escalated in 2023 between factions led by *Burhan* and *Gen. Mohamed Hamdan Dagalo* of the Rapid Support Forces (RSF), sparking violent clashes in Khartoum and Darfur. The struggle for control continues, with thousands displaced and civilians severely affected.

NOTE: According to the UN Refugee Agency, over 1,10,000 refugees have crossed from Sudan to neighbouring countries since the start of the conflicts, while about 334,000 people are estimated to have been internally displaced.

THE CIVIL WAR – WORLD'S WORST HUMANITARIAN CRISIS (2023-Present Day)

The ongoing conflict in Sudan, which erupted in April 2023, is a complex and multifaceted crisis with severe humanitarian consequences. The conflict pits the **Sudanese Armed Forces (SAF)** against the **Rapid Support Forces (RSF),** a paramilitary group that was once part of the SAF.

Main Causes

1) **Power Struggle:** The conflict is primarily a power struggle between the Sudanese Armed Forces (SAF) and the Rapid Support Forces (RSF). Both groups are vying for control of the government and the country's resources.
2) **Historical Grievances:** The RSF was formed from former Janjaweed militiamen who were involved in the genocide in Darfur. These groups have long-standing grievances and seek greater political representation.
3) **Economic Inequality:** The economic disparities between different regions of Sudan have contributed to social unrest and fuelled the conflict.
4) **Regional Destabilization:** The conflict in Sudan has destabilized the wider region, with spillover effects in neighbouring countries.
5) **International Interference:** External actors, including regional powers and international organizations, have become involved in the conflict, potentially exacerbating the violence.

The conflict has been marked by intense fighting in *Khartoum* and other major cities, leading to widespread displacement, civilian casualties, and the destruction of infrastructure. The humanitarian situation in Sudan is dire, with millions of people facing food insecurity, lack of access to essential services, and displacement. The conflict has also had a significant impact on the wider region, with refugees fleeing to neighbouring countries such as South Sudan, Ethiopia, and Egypt. The instability in Sudan has created security concerns and disrupted trade flows in the Horn of Africa.

Consequences of the Civil War

Sudan's humanitarian crisis is worsening at an alarming rate. With over 750,000 people facing severe hunger, NGOs are warning of an impending disaster of unprecedented scale in recent decades. For the past 16 months, Sudanese civilians have endured relentless attacks, displacing more than 10 million people and creating the largest displacement crisis globally.

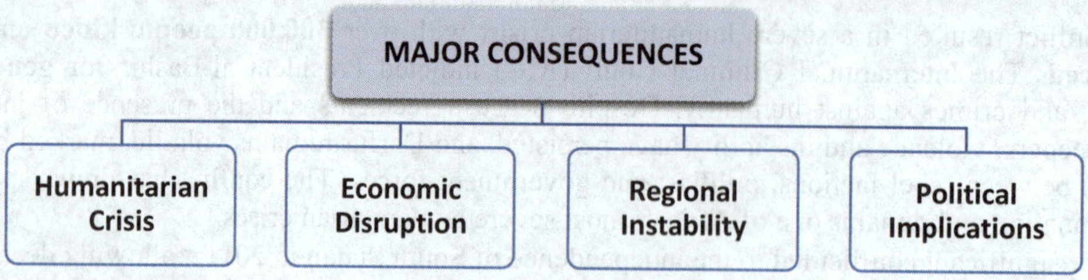

(a) **Humanitarian Crisis:**

- The conflict has led to a massive displacement of civilians, with millions forced to flee their homes.
- The humanitarian situation is dire, with many people facing food insecurity, lack of access to healthcare, and other basic necessities.
- The conflict has resulted in a significant number of civilian casualties, including deaths and injuries.

(b) **Economic Disruption:**

- The conflict has devastated Sudan's economy, leading to a sharp decline in economic activity and rising unemployment.
- The conflict has fuelled inflation, making basic goods and services more expensive for ordinary citizens.
- The destruction of infrastructure, such as roads, bridges, and factories, has further hindered economic recovery.

(c) **Regional Instability:**

- The conflict has spilled over into neighbouring countries, destabilizing the wider region.
- The conflict has created a refugee crisis, with hundreds of thousands of people fleeing to neighbouring countries.
- It has increased security challenges in the region, including the risk of terrorism and extremism.

(d) **Political Implications:**

- The conflict has weakened the central government's authority and control over the country.
- The power vacuum created by the conflict has allowed for the emergence of various armed groups and factions.
- The conflict could have long-term consequences for Sudan's political stability and development.

The international community has called for a ceasefire and a negotiated solution to the conflict. However, efforts to broker a peace deal have so far been unsuccessful. The conflict continues to have devastating consequences for the people of Sudan and the wider region.

(2) TIGRAY CONFLICT (ETHIOPIA - 2020)

The conflict began in November 2020 between the Ethiopian federal government and the Tigray People's Liberation Front (TPLF), which was the ruling party in the Tigray region. It escalated into a full-blown civil war, drawing in Eritrean forces and causing a humanitarian crisis, including widespread famine and mass displacement. A ceasefire was signed in 2022, but tensions remain high, with sporadic violence continuing.

Areas of Focus:

- The conflict has been marked by severe humanitarian issues, including famine-like conditions and mass displacement of over 2 million people.
- Allegations of war crimes and human rights abuses—such as mass killings, sexual violence, and ethnic cleansing—have drawn global attention.
- International organizations like the UN have called for investigations into these allegations. Efforts to mediate the conflict, including peace talks brokered by the African Union, garnered international attention.
- Ceasefire agreements in 2022 have somewhat eased tensions, but mistrust between parties remains a significant obstacle to lasting peace.

(3) MOZAMBIQUE INSURGENCY (CABO DELGADO - 2017)

The insurgency in Mozambique's northern Cabo Delgado province began in 2017, primarily driven by an Islamist militant group known locally as al-Shabaab (unrelated to the Somali group of the same name) that pledged allegiance to ISIS. The conflict escalated in intensity, with insurgents carrying out brutal attacks on civilians, taking control of towns, and disrupting government efforts to regain control. The discovery of large offshore natural gas reserves in the region brought significant foreign investments, but insurgent activity has threatened these projects.

Areas of Focus:

- The insurgency's impact on Mozambique's liquified natural gas (LNG) projects has been a key focus of international media, as these reserves are considered among the largest in Africa and critical to global energy markets.
- Multinational corporations, including France's TotalEnergies, were forced to suspend operations due to the insecurity.
- The humanitarian crisis has also garnered attention, with nearly 800,000 people displaced by the violence.
- International responses, including military interventions from Rwanda and regional forces from the Southern African Development Community (SADC), have been widely covered.

(4) LIBYA CIVIL WAR

Following the ousting of Muammar Gaddafi in 2011, Libya descended into chaos, with competing factions battling for control of the country. The primary conflict has been between the UN-backed Government of National Accord (GNA) based in Tripoli and forces loyal to General Khalifa Haftar's Libyan National Army (LNA), based in the east. The war peaked between 2019 and 2020, when Haftar launched a military offensive to capture Tripoli. International actors like Turkey, Russia, Egypt, and the UAE have supported different factions, leading to a proxy war scenario.

Areas of Focus:

- International involvement has kept the Libyan Civil War in the headlines. Turkey's military intervention in support of the GNA, Russia's backing of Haftar through mercenaries (notably the Wagner Group), and Egypt's strategic interests have turned Libya into a geopolitical flashpoint.
- The conflict also caused a resurgence of the migrant crisis, as Libya remains a key departure point for migrants attempting to cross the Mediterranean to Europe.
- The country's oil wealth and economic struggles have been widely reported, with various militias vying for control of oil production, further destabilizing the economy. Peace talks and the fragile ceasefire in 2020 received global coverage, but ongoing instability persists.

(5) SAHEL CONFLICT (2012)

The Sahel region, particularly in countries like Mali, Burkina Faso, and Niger, has seen escalating violence involving Islamist militant groups such as al-Qaeda and ISIS affiliates. Military coups, ethnic clashes, and insurgencies have led to widespread instability, displacement, and civilian casualties. French forces withdrew from Mali in 2022, and international peacekeeping efforts have struggled to contain the violence.

Areas of Focus:

- The rise of extremism and insurgencies in the Sahel, along with the displacement of millions, has drawn substantial global attention. Media coverage has highlighted the deteriorating security situation, with increasing attacks on civilians, soldiers, and peacekeepers.
- France's decision to withdraw its troops from Mali in 2022 was a major development, signaling shifting international strategies.
- The Sahel has also become a focal point for global counterterrorism efforts, with the U.S. and European countries involved through training programs and military assistance.
- The humanitarian consequences, including widespread food insecurity and migration crises, continue to be a pressing issue in the media.

RISING CHINESE INFLUENCE

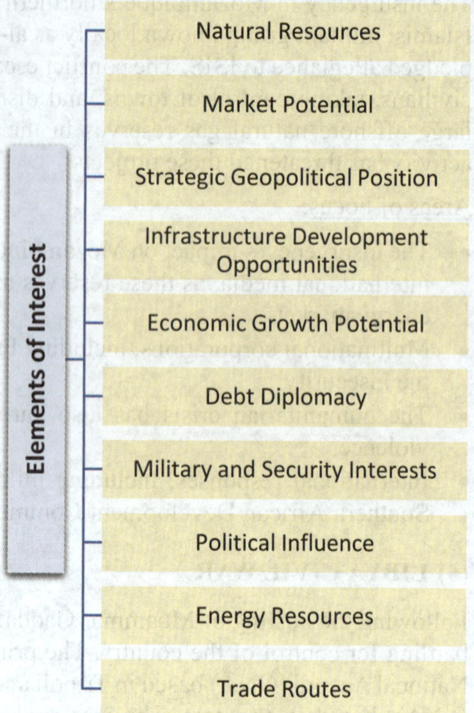

- China's relationship with Africa dates back to the **15th century** during the **Ming Dynasty**, marking the beginning of its long-standing connection with the continent. As China's **Communist leadership** consolidated power domestically, it also adopted a proactive policy toward Africa.
- Modern diplomatic ties were formally established with **South Africa in 1911**, and in **1955**, a landmark conference in **Bandung, Indonesia**, brought together African and Asian leaders to discuss shared development goals and strengthen cooperation among the "Third World," a term coined by **Mao Zedong**.
- China soon began providing development aid, exemplified by its construction of the **Tanzam railway** in the 1970s, linking **Zambia's copper belts** to **Dar es Salaam** in **Tanzania**.
- In recent decades, China has become a key political and economic force in Africa. Initially driven by ideological motivations, China's approach gradually evolved into a more consultative one, aligning its engagement with its global development objectives.
- China's trade with Africa, which was minimal in the 1990s, surged significantly by **2005**, and by **2019**, trade volumes had exceeded **$221 billion**. A report by the **Swiss-African Business Circle** revealed that, on average, **27% of China's investments** over the past decade have been directed to Africa, particularly in infrastructure, with total investments nearing **$2 trillion**.
- While China's involvement in Africa has led to major economic gains, especially in **infrastructure development**, critics argue that its focus has largely remained on **national interests**, such as **resource extraction** and **counterterrorism efforts**, rather than on Africa's long-term growth.
- This has raised concerns about **debt dependency**, as countries like **Kenya**, **Ethiopia**, and **Zambia** struggle to meet loan obligations, sparking debates around China's **"debt-trap diplomacy"**. Additionally, China's growing **military presence**, notably its base in **Djibouti**, further reflects its strategic ambitions on the continent.

INDIA AND AFRICA RELATIONS

"*For India, Africa's rise as one of the global system's poles is not just desirable, it is absolutely necessary. In fact, it is fundamental to our foreign policy thinking. Broader global rebalancing is incomplete without the genuine emergence of Africa. Only then will the world's strategic diversity come into full play*".[20]

– S Jaishankar

While India's association with Africa is of an older vintage, China which had a limited relation till the 1990s, accelerated its engagements sharply post that. In terms of money invested, volume of goods and number of projects initiated, the Chinese involvement in the continent easily overshadows the efforts of other nations over the past two decades making it the leading power in the continent.

Over the last decade and a half, India had managed to secure substantial gains in the African continent and had garnered diplomatic praise. However, the last couple of years saw the ties suffer at the hands of the pandemic and domestic troubles of India. As India enters the next phase of international relations, it must

[20] (2020, Sept 22). EAM's Remarks at the 15th CII - Exim Bank Digital Conclave on India-Africa Project Partnership, September 22, 2020. Embassy of India, Moscow, Russia. https://indianembassy-moscow.gov.in/press-releases-EAM-22-09-2020-1.php

try to recapture the momentum in the past. India's relation with Africa have to acknowledge the sharpening competition with China, not only in the African continent but also in the western Indian ocean and yet India shouldn't get bogged down in a rivalry with China in Africa. In the long run, it is therefore essential to understand Africa, what it means to India and gauge the state of India-Africa relations against the backdrop of the Great Scramble in Africa where multiple players including China, EU, UAE, Turkey along with India are vying for influence and strategic depth.

PHASES OF INDIA & AFRICA RELATIONS

1 1950s to 1970s

- India assisted the process of decolonisation in Africa.
- India's attainment of Independence through peaceful and non-violent mechanisms encouraged the Africans to look for support from India.
- Africa hadn't fallen into ideological divisions by Cold War and was a region for India to assert power politics through NAM
- Post 1962 War, India remained occupied with countering Chinese aggression, while China became more aggressive and made inroads into Africa.

2 1970s-1990s

- As African decolonisation was completed, the African nations were looking for role model for development.
- India made strategies to regain the lost path, using NAM as a tool to rework its relationship with Africa - NAM became economy oriented.
- Importance of Indian diapora increased.
- Success of India's peaceful nuclear explosion (1974) also improved India's international image.

3 Post Cold War

- India's engagement in post-cold war era owes its base to its Cold War engagement where energy concerns dominated. Economic diplomacy pushed the relationship.
- In early 2000, Africa remerged on India's strategic radar just as a first decade of reforms started to accelerate domestic economic growth, to encourage newly emerged private manufacturing, industrial and service sectors to look for foreign markets, and to force policy-makers to reduce the country's oil reliance on the Middle East.

AREAS OF COOPERATION & COLLABORATION

1. **Trade and investment**

- India is one of Africa's major trading partners, with bilateral trade between the two regions reaching around $70 billion by 2020. India exports pharmaceuticals, machinery, and manufactured goods, while Africa supplies crude oil, minerals, and agricultural products.
- Trade is set to expand with initiatives such as the **India-Africa Forum Summit** and regional trade agreements like the African Continental Free Trade Area (AfCFTA).
- Indian companies are increasingly investing in sectors such as agriculture, manufacturing, infrastructure, and energy in African nations, diversifying beyond raw materials to more value-added activities.
- India's emphasis on strengthening trade ties is complemented by its interest in digital trade and innovation, where Indian tech companies like Airtel are investing in Africa's growing telecommunications sector.

2. **Strategic and Geopolitical Partnership**

- India views Africa as a key partner in the Indo-Pacific region, sharing common interests in security, economic growth, and maritime cooperation.
- India has strengthened its presence in Africa by increasing diplomatic missions, engaging in defense cooperation through joint military exercises and training, and focusing on maritime security in the Indian Ocean.
- This partnership aligns with India's vision of a *'Free, Open, and Inclusive Indo-Pacific'*, particularly in the context of countering China's growing influence.

3. **Infrastructure and Development Assistance**

- India has been involved in building critical infrastructure across Africa, including roads, railways, ports, and government buildings.
- Indian companies have engaged in infrastructure projects like the development of **railway lines in Kenya** and the **Rufiji Dam in Tanzania**, which will improve energy and water resources. India's presence in infrastructure aligns with Africa's broader **Agenda 2063** goals, which aim for enhanced regional connectivity and sustainable infrastructure.

- India has also been providing extensive development assistance to Africa in the form of grants, concessional loans, and technical support. Indian-supported projects cover a wide array of sectors, including agriculture, health, water supply, infrastructure, and education.
- India has implemented **194 developmental projects in 37 African nations**, while over **70 additional projects in 29 countries**, with an outlay of more than **$11 billion**, are currently underway.
- These projects are geared towards sustainable development, with a focus on areas like ICT, energy, transportation infrastructure, and entrepreneurship. India's approach is aligned with South-South cooperation, emphasizing empowerment and capacity-building rather than extraction.

4. **Energy Cooperation**

- India has been collaborating with Africa in the energy sector, focusing on oil and gas exploration, as well as renewable energy projects. Indian companies are involved in building power plants, transmission lines, and solar energy projects across the continent.
- Indian involvement in African energy projects has expanded to include renewable energy, especially solar power. India has also extended its **International Solar Alliance (ISA)** to African nations, promoting solar energy development across the continent. Indian firms such as **ONGC Videsh** and **Bharat Petroleum** are exploring opportunities in oil and gas-rich regions like Mozambique, Tanzania, and Nigeria.

5. **Agriculture & Food Security**

- India has been providing technical assistance to African farmers, particularly in areas like crop improvement, soil conservation, irrigation, and food processing.
- India's contribution to Africa's agriculture has grown through capacity-building programs, including the establishment of **agricultural training centers** and the introduction of **Indian agritech solutions**.

- This collaboration supports African countries in addressing food security issues, particularly in the context of climate change.
- Indian agriculture companies are also working with African counterparts to introduce mechanization and high-yield seed varieties.

6. **Health Cooperation**

- India has been involved in the African health sector, particularly in medical infrastructure and pharmaceutical supplies. India's affordable medicines have been crucial in fighting diseases like malaria, tuberculosis, and HIV/AIDS across Africa.
- Indian companies like **Serum Institute of India** played a vital role in supplying **COVID-19 vaccines** to African nations through the **COVAX initiative**. India continues to assist African countries with healthcare training and the establishment of health facilities. Indian-supported health projects in countries like Côte d'Ivoire and Zimbabwe focus on building resilient healthcare systems and improving maternal and child health.

7. **Education, Training & ICT**

- India has been providing scholarships and training to African students and professionals, particularly in fields such as engineering, medicine, and information technology.
- India's **Indian Technical and Economic Cooperation (ITEC) program** and scholarship schemes have enabled thousands of African students to study in India. Additionally, Indian universities have partnered with African institutions for academic exchanges and joint research programs.

- The **e-VidyaBharati** and **e-ArogyaBharati (e-VBAB) Network Project** is a significant digital initiative that provides tele-education and telemedicine services across Africa.
- ICT is a growing area of cooperation between India and Africa. India has supported Africa in digital infrastructure development, including the provision of affordable mobile networks and internet connectivity.
- Indian tech firms like **Bharti Airtel** have made significant investments in expanding **telecom services** across Africa. India also supports the **Pan-African e-Network project**, which aims to bridge the digital divide by providing tele-education, telemedicine, and e-governance platforms.

8. **Climate Change & Environmental Cooperation**

- India and Africa are both vulnerable to climate change, and they have been working together on climate adaptation and mitigation efforts.
- India's push for renewable energy through initiatives like the International Solar Alliance (ISA) aligns with Africa's growing interest in green energy solutions. Joint efforts in climate resilience projects, land restoration, and the Great Green Wall initiative demonstrate the shared commitment to combating the adverse effects of climate change.

ASIA-AFRICA GROWTH CORRIDOR (AAGC)

A vision document on the AAGC was first released in Gandhinagar in 2017. It is a study jointly produced by three research institutions of India and Japan in consultation with other Asian and African think tanks. It envisages closer engagement between India and Africa for "**sustainable and innovative development**". It would be anchored on four pillars:

1. Development and cooperation projects;
2. Quality infrastructure and institutional connectivity;
3. Enhancing capacities and skills and
4. People-to-people partnership.

It will accord priority to development projects in health and pharmaceuticals, agriculture and agro-processing, disaster management, and skill enhancement. It will have ***special focus*** on **Africa, India and South Asia, Southeast Asia, East Asia and Oceania.**

8 CANADA & SOUTH AMERICA

CANADA

Canada, the world's **second-largest country by land area**, occupies a unique position on the global stage. With a population of approximately 40 million, this North American nation is not only defined by its vast and diverse landscapes but also by its significant influence in international relations. From its capital, Ottawa, to its major metropolitan centers in Toronto, Montreal, and Vancouver, Canada has emerged as a key player in global diplomacy, trade, and environmental stewardship.

IMPORTANT DETAILS	
Capital	Ottawa
Sovereign/Monarch	King Charles III
Prime Minister (September 2024)	Justin Trudeau
Population (2023)	40.09 M
Human Development Index Rank (2023)	18
GDP Growth (annual % - 2023)	1.1
Unemployment, total (% of total labour force – ILO estimate 2023)	5.4
Net Migration (2023)	249,746
*Data – World Bank & UNDP	

POLITY & GOVERNANCE

Canada is a **federal parliamentary democracy** and a **constitutional monarchy**. This means that Canada has a monarch as its head of state (*King Charles III*), but the monarch's role is mainly symbolic and ceremonial. The executive power is vested in the Crown but is exercised by the Cabinet, led by the Prime Minister (*Justin Trudeau*). Canada comprises ten provinces and three territories, each with its own government and legislative powers. The Constitution is the supreme law and includes the Constitution Act, 1867 (formerly the British North America Act, 1867) and the Constitution Act, 1982, which includes the Canadian Charter of Rights and Freedoms. Each province and territory has its own government with powers delegated by the federal constitution.

ECONOMY & TRADE

Canada has one of the largest economies in the world, known for its vast natural resources, strong financial sector, and robust trade networks. It operates under a mixed-market economy, driven by both public and private enterprises.

(a) Gross Domestic Product:

- Nominal GDP (2023): Approximately **$2.2 trillion USD**.
- Global Ranking: 9th largest economy globally by nominal GDP.
- GDP per capita (2023): Estimated to be around **$45,300 USD**, reflecting a high standard of living.

KEY ECONOMIC PILLARS

Natural Resources: Canada is rich in natural resources, including oil, gas, timber, minerals, and hydropower. These sectors form a crucial backbone of the economy.

Manufacturing: The manufacturing sector is diverse, encompassing automobiles, aerospace, and food processing.

Services: The services sector, including finance, technology, and healthcare, is a major contributor to the economy.

Agriculture: Although a smaller sector compared to the past, agriculture remains vital, with Canada being a significant exporter of grains and oilseeds.

- **Trade and Exports:**
  1) Exports (2023): Valued at approximately $750 billion USD.
  2) Major exports include crude petroleum, automobiles, aluminum, and lumber.
  3) Main trading partners: The U.S. (accounts for over 70% of exports), China, the UK, and Japan.
- Canada is a global economic player, heavily reliant on trade for its prosperity. The country is a member of various trade agreements, including –
  (a) **United States–Mexico–Canada Agreement (USMCA) (replaced NAFTA)** – As a cornerstone of Canadian trade, USMCA governs the flow of goods and services between North America's three largest economies.
  (b) **Comprehensive and Progressive Agreement for Trans-Pacific Partnership (CPTPP)** – Canada's participation in this mega-regional trade deal signifies its commitment to expanding trade in the Asia-Pacific region.
  (c) **Canada-European Union Comprehensive Economic and Trade Agreement (CETA)** – This agreement aims to deepen economic ties with the European Union, opening new markets for Canadian goods and services.
- Beyond these major agreements, Canada maintains trade relations with numerous countries, including China, India, and South Korea. While trade has been a driving force for Canada's economy, challenges such as global economic fluctuations, protectionism, and supply chain disruptions pose risks.
- In terms of foreign aid, Canada is among the top donors in the world, providing assistance to developing countries through various channels, including the Canadian International Development Agency (CIDA).
- Canada is a leader in renewable energy, with about 67% of its electricity coming from renewable sources, primarily hydroelectricity. The country has ambitious climate goals, including reaching net-zero carbon emissions by 2050. However, its reliance on oil and gas presents ongoing challenges in balancing economic growth with sustainability.

United States–Mexico–Canada Agreement (USMCA)

The USMCA is a **comprehensive trade deal** that superseded the North American Free Trade Agreement (NAFTA) in 2020. It aims to create a more balanced and reciprocal trade environment among the three North American nations.

Key features of the USMCA include:

- More stringent requirements for qualifying goods as North American, aiming to boost domestic production.
- Stronger labor standards to protect workers' rights and prevent wage suppression.
- Commitments to environmental sustainability and enforcement mechanisms.
- Provisions addressing e-commerce, data flows, and consumer protection and a modernized dispute settlement process.

DEFENCE & SECURITY

- Canada follows a policy of defence and security based on collective defence, international peacekeeping, and the protection of its sovereignty.
- The **Canadian Armed Forces (CAF)**, comprising the Army, Navy, and Air Force, focus on both national defence and international operations. The **CAF** consists of approximately 68,000 active personnel and around 27,000 reserve personnel.
- Canada's internal security is managed by the **Royal Canadian Mounted Police (RCMP)** and the **Canadian Security Intelligence Service (CSIS)**.
- Canada is a founding member of **NATO (North Atlantic Treaty Organization)** and plays a significant role in its operations. Canada supports collective defence under Article 5 of the NATO treaty, considering an attack on any NATO member an attack on all.
- Cybersecurity has become a crucial focus for Canada's national defence, with growing threats from state-sponsored actors, cyber espionage, and hacking.
- **Arctic defence** is a growing priority, as climate change opens new sea routes and resources in the Arctic region. Canada emphasizes securing its northern borders and sovereignty over the Northwest Passage, which is contested by other nations like the U.S. and Russia. Investments have been made in new Arctic patrol vessels and bases to enhance the CAF's presence in the region.

DID YOU KNOW?

As per NATO figures, in 2023, Canada spent approximately 1.38 % of its GDP on Defense. The Department of National Defence's (DND) main estimates 2023-24 are $26.5 Billion.

NORAD (North American Aerospace Defence Command)

Canada is a key partner in **NORAD**, a binational agreement with the U.S. for continental defence, focusing on aerospace warning, control, and maritime warning. This partnership ensures the protection of North America from air & missile threats, & it underscores Canada's close security ties with the U.S.

DIPLOMACY & FOREIGN RELATIONS

Canada is a prominent actor on the world stage, known for its multilateralist approach to foreign policy. As a member of the **United Nations (UN)**, the **G7**, the **G20**, the **Commonwealth of Nations**, and the **World Trade Organization (WTO)**, Canada actively participates in global governance.

The nation has a strong commitment to human rights, democracy, and multilateralism. Canada has been a leading contributor to UN peacekeeping missions worldwide, demonstrating its dedication to global peace and security. Its involvement in operations in Afghanistan, Haiti, and the Middle East underscores this commitment. Beyond peacekeeping, Canada is recognized for its role in promoting international development and humanitarian assistance. Through agencies like **Global Affairs Canada**, the country provides significant aid to developing nations, focusing on areas such as education, health, and gender equality.

RISING SIGNIFICANCE OF CANADA ON THE GLOBAL STAGE

STRATEGIC POSITION & THE ARCTIC

1. Canada shares the **longest undefended border with the United States**, making it a key partner in North American security, trade, and economic integration (including USMCA & NORAD).
2. Canada's northern territories extend into the **Arctic Circle**, giving it control over a significant portion of the Arctic region. As climate change opens up new shipping routes (like the Northwest Passage) and access to untapped natural resources (oil, gas, minerals), the Arctic has become a strategic area of global interest. Canada's claims in the Arctic, backed by its role in the Arctic Council, are crucial in shaping the future of this region.
3. With **coastlines on both the Atlantic** and **Pacific Oceans**, Canada serves as a crucial gateway for trade between Europe, Asia, and North America. Its major ports, such as Vancouver and Halifax, are key hubs for global maritime trade, enhancing Canada's strategic importance in global supply chains and international commerce.

MULTILATERAL DIPLOMACY

1. Canada's rising significance in global politics is a result of its strategic positioning, diplomatic influence, commitment to multilateralism, and leadership in key global issues.
2. Canada has been a strong advocate for **multilateralism**, frequently taking leadership roles in international organizations. For example, Canada has served multiple terms on the United Nations Security Council and has been a major contributor to UN peacekeeping missions.
3. Canada has championed **LGBTQ+ rights** on the global stage, actively promoting the inclusion of these rights in international human rights frameworks. For instance, Canada played a key role in establishing the UN's independent expert on sexual orientation and gender identity.
4. Canada has been a proactive participant in **international climate change negotiations** (including Paris Agreement). Canada has implemented a **national carbon pricing strategy**, which serves as a model for other countries.

SECURITY & DEFENCE

1. Canada's position in the **northern hemisphere**, particularly in the **Arctic**, is vital for global security. The country's military presence and surveillance capabilities in the region contribute to monitoring and defending this increasingly strategic area against potential threats, including those posed by other major powers like Russia.
2. Canada is a key member of **NATO** and plays a significant role in the **North American Aerospace Defense Command (NORAD)**. Its contributions to collective security and defense initiatives are vital to regional and global stability.
3. Canada's involvement in **global counterterrorism efforts** and its focus on **cybersecurity initiatives** is also critical.

CULTURE & SOCIETY

The Canadian population is made up of people from a wide variety of ethnic and cultural backgrounds, with the largest groups being of European, Indigenous, and Asian descent. The official languages of Canada are *English* and *French*, reflecting the country's colonial history and its close ties to both the United Kingdom and France.

Indigenous peoples, including First Nations, Inuit, and Métis, constitute a vital part of Canadian society. Their diverse cultures, languages, and spiritual beliefs have significantly shaped the nation's history and continue to influence contemporary life. Canada's multiculturalism has been enshrined in government policy, fostering a welcoming environment for immigrants and promoting intercultural understanding. This diversity is reflected in the country's vibrant arts, music, cuisine, and festivals.

Canada is renowned for its **universal healthcare system**, often referred to as **'Medicare'**. This publicly funded system ensures that all citizens and permanent residents have access to medically necessary hospital and physician services without direct out-of-pocket costs at the point of service. All residents are entitled to medically necessary services, regardless of income or health status. Each province and territory administer its own health insurance plan, leading to some variations in coverage and service delivery.

INDIA-CANADA TIES: THE EVOLVING NEXUS

Economic Cooperation

- India has emerged as a significant trading partner for Canada. In 2022, India was Canada's 10th largest merchandise trading partner globally.

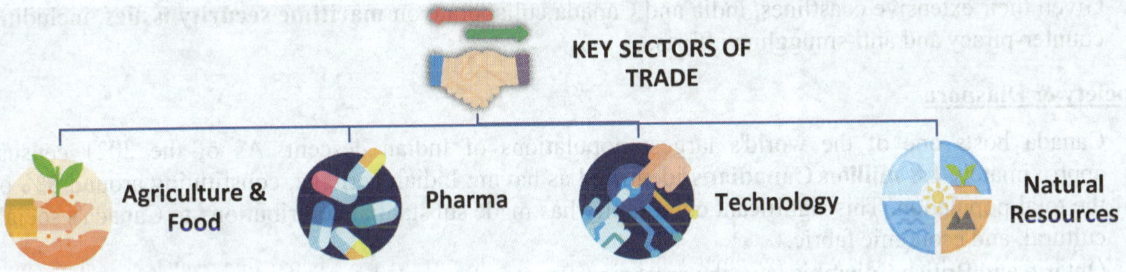

- Both nations are committed to deepening economic cooperation. India is a priority market for Canada's Indo-Pacific strategy, and the negotiation of a **Comprehensive Economic Partnership Agreement (CEPA)** is underway.
- This agreement aims to boost bilateral trade and investment substantially. Additionally, the **Foreign Investment Promotion and Protection Agreement (FIPA)** is being pursued to enhance investor confidence and facilitate business operations between the two countries. Regular **Ministerial Dialogues on Trade and Investment** further strengthen the economic relationship.

In January 2023, Canada's high commissioner to India admitted that the "bilateral trade between the two G20 economies, India and Canada, is a "seriously underperforming" economic relationship." He stated that 'the two countries are negotiating an early progress trade agreement (EPTA) as a first step towards CEPA, which will increase bilateral trade manifold.'

Education and Research

- In the field of science and technology, India and Canada have a number of joint research initiatives in areas such as clean energy, health, and advanced materials. The Canada-India Research Centre of Excellence (IC-IMPACTS) is a prime example of successful collaboration, focusing on addressing global challenges through joint research initiatives in areas such as clean energy, health, and advanced materials.
- Both countries have implemented student exchange programs to facilitate academic collaboration and cultural exchange. Numerous universities and research institutions in both countries have established partnerships for joint research, student mobility, and faculty exchange.
- Efforts are underway to foster collaboration between startups and entrepreneurs in both nations, leading to the development of innovative solutions to global challenges. Key areas of cooperation include artificial intelligence, biotechnology, agriculture, and sustainable development.
- Canada and India are increasingly collaborating on the development of emerging technologies. Areas such as hydrogen fuel cells and electric vehicles have witnessed growing cooperation. To foster innovation and address global challenges, Canada has been a significant contributor. For instance, *Grand Challenges Canada* has invested approximately $24 million between 2018 and 2019 to support over 75 projects in India, primarily focused on maternal, newborn, and child health, as well as early childhood development.

Defense and Security

- India and Canada have cultivated a robust defense and security partnership, underpinned by shared interests in regional and global stability. Both nations cooperate in areas such as counterterrorism, peacekeeping, and maritime security.
- The establishment of a **Joint Working Group on Counterterrorism** reflects the shared commitment to combating extremism and transnational threats and also helps to promote military-to-military ties.
- Canada and India are also cooperating on **defense technology** and Canada has been a supplier of military equipment to India (including aircraft and helicopters).
- Recognizing the increasing cyber threats, both countries cooperate to enhance cybersecurity capabilities and protect critical infrastructure. The establishment of the "**Joint Working Group on Cyber Security and Cybercrime**" in 2018 was a significant step in this direction.
- Given their extensive coastlines, India and Canada collaborate on **maritime security issues**, including counter-piracy and anti-smuggling efforts.

Society & Diaspora

- Canada hosts one of the world's largest populations of Indian descent. As of the 2021 census, approximately **1.8 million Canadians** identified as having Indian heritage, constituting around **5%** of the total population. This significant community has made substantial contributions to Canada's social, cultural, and economic fabric.
- Ontario and British Columbia have the most significant Indian populations, but communities are present across the country. Indian Canadians have become increasingly involved in Canadian politics, holding elected positions at various levels of government.
- Indian Canadians have made significant contributions to Canada's economy, excelling in fields like technology, medicine, and business.

RECENT ROADBLOCKS AFFECTING THE BILATERAL TIES

1. India has expressed concerns about Canadian support for *Khalistani* separatists. Furthermore, the ongoing **diplomatic standoff** between the two countries, stemming from allegations of Indian involvement in the killing of a Sikh separatist leader in Canada, has further deteriorated the bilateral relations. India views the separatist groups as a threat to its national security and accuses some Canadian politicians of being sympathetic to their cause. The ensuing diplomatic row, marked by mutual expulsions of diplomats, has further eroded trust between the two nations.
2. Trade between India and Canada is relatively modest compared to other bilateral relationships. There are ongoing discussions about how to balance **trade and investment** flows, and resolving these issues requires negotiation on trade agreements and barriers. The diplomatic issues however, have affected the ongoing trade negotiations for a Comprehensive Economic Partnership Agreement (CEPA) creating troubles for economic cooperation.
3. Indian students and professionals sometimes face challenges with **visa policies**, which can create friction. Canada's immigration policies and the processing of visas for Indian nationals can impact the relationship.
4. Differences in **human rights practices** and **domestic policies** can sometimes lead to diplomatic friction. Differing perspectives on human rights issues, particularly those related to minority groups, have created friction between the two countries.

Future and Way Ahead

The recent challenges in India-Canada relations underscore the need for a strategic reset. Both nations must prioritize diplomacy and dialogue to rebuild trust and cooperation. The key focus areas include –

(i) **De-escalation of Tensions**: Addressing the core issues, such as the Khalistan movement, through diplomatic channels and avoiding inflammatory rhetoric. Utilizing platforms like the G20, Commonwealth, and UN to build common ground and address shared challenges could prove useful for the two nations.

(ii) **Expanding Cooperation**: Revitalizing trade negotiations for the Comprehensive Economic Partnership Agreement (CEPA) and exploring new avenues for investment and collaboration. Expanding cooperation beyond trade to include areas like science, technology, defense, and climate change.

(iii) **People-to-People Ties**: Strengthening educational, cultural, and people-to-people exchanges to foster goodwill and understanding would be greatly beneficial.

India and Canada share common democratic values and can be strategic partners in a changing global order. By focusing on shared interests, addressing contentious issues through diplomacy, and building on the strong people-to-people ties, both nations can lay the foundation for a resilient and enduring partnership. It is essential to approach the relationship with a long-term perspective, recognizing that rebuilding trust takes time and consistent effort.

LATIN & SOUTH AMERICA

Source: Britannica

SOUTH AMERICA OR LATIN AMERICA?

South America is a subcontinent that is located entirely in the southern hemisphere of the Earth, while **Latin America** is a cultural and linguistic region that includes countries in both North and South America.

SOUTH AMERICA	LATIN AMERICA
It includes 12 countries: Argentina, Bolivia, Brazil, Chile, Colombia, Ecuador, Guyana, Paraguay, Peru, Suriname, Uruguay, and Venezuela.	This region is generally defined as including all of the countries in South America, as well as Mexico, Central America, and some parts of the Caribbean.
These countries are located in the southern part of the Americas, bordered by the Pacific Ocean to the	It includes countries in both North and South America that share a common language, history, and culture. In addition to Spanish and Portuguese,

west, the Atlantic Ocean to the east, and the Caribbean Sea to the north.	which are the dominant languages in the region, French, Dutch, and English are also spoken in some countries

COUNTRY	CAPITAL	GDP (CURRENT US$), 2023 (APPROX. BILLION)	HUMAN DEVELOPMENT INDEX RANK (2023)
INDIA	**NEW DELHI**	**3.5 trillion**	**134**
Argentina	Buenos Aires	640	48
Bolivia	La Paz	45.8	120
Brazil	Brasilia	2.17 trillion	89
Chile	Santiago	335	44
Colombia	Bogota	363	91
Costa Rica	San Jose	86	64
Cuba	Havana	107 (2020 fig.)	85
Dominican Republic	Santo Domingo	94.24	82
Ecuador	Quito	118.8	83
El Salvador	San Salvador	34	127
Guatemala	Guatemala City	102	136
Haiti	Port-au-Prince	19.8	158
Honduras	Tegucigalpa	34	138
Mexico	Mexico City	1.7 trillion	77
Nicaragua	Managua	17.8	130
Panama	Panama City	83	57
Paraguay	Asuncion	43	102
Peru	Lima	267	87
Uruguay	Montevideo	77	52
Venezuela	Caracas	482	119
*World Bank Data			

Historically, the Latin American and Caribbean (LAC) countries have had a very different path in comparison to India. While the LAC (Latin American and Caribbean) countries fell under the influence of US hegemony, India pursued a different path by establishing the Non-Aligned Movement and later forming a friendship treaty with the Soviet Union. In the following years, India's closed economy hindered the development of connections with the LAC region. Additionally, the LAC countries were divided and struggling with political instability, with some leaning towards capitalism and others favoring socialism. However, after the Cold War, the emergence of democracies in the region and India's economic liberalization opened up numerous opportunities for trade and commercial growth.

RISING RELEVANCE OF LATIN AMERICA

(1) **Geostrategic Location -** The strategic position of Latin America, especially with the ***Panama Canal***, is vital for global trade routes, increasing its geopolitical importance.

(2) **Rising Influence in Global Trade -** Latin America's expanding role in global trade, particularly through strategic exports like agriculture, energy, and minerals, is elevating its importance in international markets.

(3) **Growing Diplomatic Engagement -** Countries in Latin America are increasingly active in international organizations like the UN, G20, and BRICS, contributing to global discussions on issues like climate change and human rights.

(4) **Strategic Alliances and Partnerships -** Latin American nations are forming strategic alliances with global powers like the U.S., China, and the EU, strengthening their international influence and economic ties.

(5) **Regional Economic Integration -** Initiatives like ***Mercosur*** and the ***Pacific Alliance*** are boosting regional economic integration, enhancing Latin America's collective bargaining power in global negotiations.

(6) **Resource-Driven Geopolitical Importance -** The region's vast natural resources, including oil, gas, and minerals, are making it a key player in global energy and commodity markets, attracting international interest and investment.

(7) **Cultural Diplomacy and Soft Power -** Latin America's rich cultural exports, such as music, arts, film, and cuisine, are enhancing its global image and soft power, contributing to its rising relevance on the international stage.

(8) **Environmental Leadership -** Latin American countries are playing a crucial role in global environmental efforts, particularly in the preservation of the Amazon rainforest and participation in climate change negotiations.

NOTABLE TRADE BLOCS	
Pacific Alliance	The Pacific Alliance is a regional integration initiative comprised of **Chile, Colombia, Mexico,** and **Peru**. Established in 2011, it aims to create a deep integration area, fostering the free movement of goods, services, capital, and people among member states. The key objectives include: • Promoting free trade, reducing tariffs, and harmonizing regulations. • Attracting foreign investment and facilitating business operations. • Enhancing cooperation in areas such as infrastructure, energy, and education. • Strengthening the bloc's influence in the international arena.
MERCOSUR	This Southern Common Market is a South American regional trade bloc established in 1991. Its founding members include **Argentina, Brazil, Paraguay, and Uruguay**. **Bolivia** became a full member of the Mercosur in July 2024. Venezuela later joined but was suspended in 2016.

	Chile, Colombia, Ecuador, Guyana, Peru, and Suriname are associate members (They can participate in free-trade agreements, but they don't receive the benefits of the customs union).
CARICOM	The Caribbean Community (CARICOM) is a regional intergovernmental organization of 15 member states and five associate members. Its primary objectives include promoting economic integration, sustainable development, and regional cooperation. Based in Georgetown, Guyana, CARICOM has made significant strides in reducing trade barriers, harmonizing policies, and addressing regional challenges such as climate change and disaster management. The organization also plays a role in international affairs, advocating for the interests of Caribbean states.
Andean Community	Initially known as the Andean Pact, it is a regional integration bloc in South America. Its member countries are **Bolivia, Colombia, Ecuador,** and **Peru**. The bloc aims to promote free trade, economic cooperation, and social development among member nations. Despite facing challenges, the Andean Community has made progress in reducing tariffs, harmonizing regulations, and fostering regional integration.
Central American Integration System (SICA)	SICA is a regional integration organization focused on Central America. Its members include **Belize, Costa Rica, El Salvador, Guatemala, Honduras, Nicaragua,** and **Panama**. SICA aims to promote economic and social development, as well as political integration in the region. Key areas of cooperation include trade, security, and environmental protection. The organization has faced challenges due to political instability and economic disparities among member countries.

As of 2024, the Indian private sector remains actively engaged in **Latin America**, integrating the region into its global business strategies. A **Preferential Trade Agreement (PTA)** with **MERCOSUR**, established in 2004, continues to strengthen economic ties by offering mutual tariff preferences, fostering trade expansion. Several Latin American nations, including **Chile, Mexico, Guatemala, Cuba, Trinidad, and Peru**, have signed trade agreements with India, boosting bilateral trade.

Institutional mechanisms like the **India-Brazil Trade Monitoring Mechanism**, **India-Ecuador JETCO**, and **India-Argentina Joint Trade Commission** further facilitate economic collaboration. At the **2019 India-CARICOM Meet**, PM Modi announced a **$14-million grant** for community development and a **$150 million line of credit** for renewable energy projects.

Latin America accounts for **15%** of India's crude oil imports, with significant supplies from **Venezuela, Mexico, and Brazil**. Other imports include **edible oils, sugar, copper**, and **precious metals**. Latin American companies have invested **$1 billion** in India across various sectors. Additionally, India's **DRDO** continues its collaboration with **Brazil's Embraer** on airborne radar systems, with both nations cooperating in **BRICS, IBSA**, and the **International Solar Alliance**.

The Latin American region is fast becoming a beacon of hope for the global clean energy initiative. **'Decarbonization'** has been the buzz word, and while the world is skeptical of this shift, the long-term vision is clear – the future is **'renewable'**. Natural gas, in particular, plays a pivotal role in this transition.

According to Carlos Garibaldi, Executive Secretary of the Latin American and Caribbean Oil and Gas Association (Arpel), natural gas "stands at the intersection of energy security and energy transition," highlighting its dual role in providing immediate energy needs while paving the way for a cleaner future.

EMERGING CHALLENGES IN THE REGION

ECONOMIC CHALLENGES

- **Inequality**: Persistent income inequality, particularly in countries like Brazil, Colombia, and Mexico, undermines social cohesion and economic growth.
- **Middle-Income Trap**: Many countries, including Brazil, Argentina, and Chile, struggle to transition from middle-income to high-income status, facing challenges in productivity, innovation, and institutional development.
- **Debt Sustainability**: High levels of public and private debt pose risks to economic stability, as seen in Argentina and Venezuela.
- **Informal Economy**: A significant informal economy in countries like Peru and Bolivia hinders tax collection, labor regulation, and overall economic development.

SOCIAL CHALLENGES

- **Violence and Crime**: High rates of crime and violence, particularly in countries like Brazil, Mexico, and Venezuela, affect security, development, and human capital.
- **Education and Human Capital**: Inadequate education and skill development limit economic opportunities and social mobility, especially in countries like Bolivia, Ecuador, and Peru.
- **Health Disparities**: Unequal access to healthcare and persistent health issues, such as those related to malnutrition and infectious diseases, impact populations in countries like Guatemala, Honduras, and Nicaragua.
- **Migration**: Both internal and external migration, particularly from countries like El Salvador and Honduras, pose challenges and opportunities for the region.

POLITICAL CHALLENGES

- **Corruption**: Endemic corruption in countries like Venezuela, Guatemala, and Honduras erodes public trust, hinders economic development, and fuels inequality.
- **Institutional Weaknesses**: Fragile institutions and governance challenges impede effective policy implementation in countries like Bolivia, Peru, and Ecuador.
- **Populism and Polarization**: Rising political polarization and the appeal of populist leaders, as seen in Brazil, Venezuela, and other countries, can destabilize democracies.

EXTERNAL CHALLENGES

- **Global Economic Shocks**: Vulnerability to external economic downturns and commodity price fluctuations, impacting countries like Chile, Colombia, and Peru.
- **Climate Change**: The region is particularly vulnerable to the impacts of climate change, including extreme weather events and rising sea levels, affecting countries like Honduras, Nicaragua, and coastal regions of Brazil.

In the latest report presented by CAF, the Development Bank of Latin America, (released in September 2022) it was pointed out that, “Latin America's insertion at the international level is low, as is its insertion at the regional level”. It was also stated that despite efforts to implement trade opening policies by reducing tariffs, the outcomes have not been very satisfactory for the Latin American and Caribbean countries. However, the engagement of Asian economies in the region has substantially increased.

India’s engagement has been less than satisfactory due to the **lack of its uniform approach**. While India’s relations with the G20 members have been substantial, the other regions have been neglected so far. Additionally, India’s current engagement is nothing as compared to the Chinese trade with the region.

Additionally, the **intra-continent rivalry** has further deteriorated the chances of forging stable relations with the countries. Moreover, the **geographical distances** have impeded trade between India and Latin America. Some critical issues include the lack of direct shipping service from India to Latin America; difficulty in shipping heavy commodities and perishables. Whereas China has direct shipping links through the Panama Canal, giving it an upper hand.

Academic circles have hinted at a need for developing policies which could boost greater productivity and integration, including harmonisation, digitisation and standardization, apart from an urgent need to make investments in infrastructure. India and Latin America need to better understand each other’s political reality, endowments, capabilities, and priorities, beyond the experience of transitory diplomats.

INDIA AND LATIN AMERICAN NATIONS

India and Latin America have historically maintained cordial diplomatic relations, but the depth of their economic and trade ties has been limited. However, in recent years, both India and Latin American countries have shown a growing interest in strengthening their bilateral relations.

India has been making efforts to deepen its engagement with Latin America, particularly in the areas of trade, investment, and culture. The Indian government has taken steps to enhance its presence in the region by opening embassies in several Latin American countries, and Indian businesses have been investing in sectors such as IT, pharmaceuticals, and mining. On the other hand, Latin American countries have been looking to diversify their trade and investment partners beyond their traditional partners such as the US and Europe, and India has emerged as an attractive destination.

ARGENTINA BRAZIL CHILE MEXICO PERU VENEZUELA

ARGENTINA

Argentina is a key player in South America, with its rich **agricultural** resources, including soybeans, wheat, and livestock, making it a crucial part of global food supply chains. Its **industrial base**, particularly in automobiles and machinery, contributes to regional trade. As a **G20** and **UN** member, Argentina has a strategic role in international diplomacy, focusing on issues like **human rights, disarmament**, and **climate change**. However, its frequent **economic crises** and political instability have at times overshadowed its influence.

India and Argentina enjoy strong bilateral ties, particularly in areas of **trade and energy cooperation**. In 2024, trade between the two countries exceeded **$5 billion**, with India importing **soy oil** and **minerals** from Argentina, while exporting **pharmaceuticals, textiles, and chemicals**. The two nations collaborate in renewable energy, nuclear energy, and space technology. Argentina also joined the **International Solar Alliance (ISA)**, an initiative led by India. Bilateral agreements have been extended in **agriculture, defense**, and **education.**

BRAZIL

Brazil, the largest economy in **Latin America** and a **BRICS** member, is a global leader in **agriculture, mining, and energy**. Its vast natural resources, especially in **soybeans, iron ore**, and **oil**, have fueled economic growth. Brazil also plays a key role in **global diplomacy** and environmental efforts, especially in protecting the **Amazon rainforest**. Despite its economic influence, **inequality and corruption** continue to be significant challenges.

IBSA - India, Brazil and South Africa

It is an international tripartite grouping for promoting international cooperation of India, Brazil and South Africa. It was formally established by the Brasilia Declaration of **6 June 2003** by external affairs ministers of the three nations.

Objective: To focus on agriculture, education, energy, trade, culture and defence among others.

Under the IBSA Fund for 'Alleviation of Poverty and Hunger', each member country contributes $1 Million annually towards facilitation of the execution of human development projects to advance the fight against poverty and hunger in developing countries.

India and Brazil have deepened their strategic partnership, primarily through **BRICS** and the **IBSA (India-Brazil-South Africa) Dialogue Forum**. Bilateral trade crossed **$15 billion** in 2024, with Brazil exporting **crude oil, sugar, and iron ore** to India, and India exporting **pharmaceuticals, chemicals**, and **automobile**

components. The two countries also cooperate in space technology, defense, and agriculture. Both nations share common interests in **multilateral platforms**, including the **UN** and **WTO**.

CHILE

Chile is a standout in **Latin America** for its **stable democracy** and **strong economy**, largely driven by its **copper industry**, as it is the world's largest producer of copper. Chile has an extensive network of **free trade agreements (FTAs)** and is a member of the **OECD**, positioning it as a hub for international trade. Its focus on **environmental sustainability** and human rights bolsters its global image.

Chile and India maintain robust trade relations, bolstered by a **Preferential Trade Agreement (PTA)**, which has significantly increased bilateral trade, reaching **$3 billion** in 2024. India's imports from Chile mainly include **copper & lithium**, while India exports **pharmaceuticals**, **textiles**, and **IT services**. Both countries collaborate in areas such as **mining, renewable energy**, and **climate action**, with Chile being an active member of the **International Solar Alliance**.

MEXICO

Mexico is a major economic player in **North and South America** due to its strategic location and membership in trade agreements like **USMCA (formerly NAFTA)**, **OECD**, and **G20**. Mexico's economy is diverse, with significant contributions from **manufacturing, petroleum**, and **agriculture**. **Remittances** from Mexicans abroad, particularly in the U.S., are also a key component of its economy.

India and Mexico share strong economic ties, with bilateral trade reaching **$11 billion** by 2024. Mexico exports **crude oil, electronic goods**, and **silver** to India, while India exports **automobiles, pharmaceuticals**, and **IT services** to Mexico. Both countries have been enhancing cooperation in **renewable energy**, **pharmaceuticals**, and **agriculture**, and are collaborating through the **International Solar Alliance**.

PERU

Peru is known for its vast **mineral resources**, especially in **copper, gold,** and **zinc**, contributing to its economic stability. Its involvement in regional organizations like the **Pacific Alliance** and efforts in combating **climate change** have increased its influence. However, **poverty, inequality**, and **political instability** remain ongoing challenges.

India and Peru share a growing economic partnership, with trade exceeding **$4 billion** in 2024. India's imports from Peru include **copper, gold**, and **fishmeal**, while India exports **pharmaceuticals, automobiles**, and **textiles**. Cooperation extends to **mining**, **agriculture**, and **renewable energy**. Peru is an active participant in the **International Solar Alliance**.

VENEZUELA

Venezuela, once a prosperous nation due to its vast **oil reserves**, faces severe **economic and political crises**, exacerbated by government mismanagement and falling oil prices. Despite its domestic challenges, Venezuela remains important in **global energy markets** due to its vast oil reserves, though its **international standing** has diminished. The country maintains strong ties with **Russia** and **China**.

India and Venezuela maintain close energy ties, with **oil imports** from Venezuela being a significant component of the relationship. In 2024, bilateral trade stood at **$5.5 billion**, with **crude oil** being Venezuela's main export to India. India has been a key buyer of Venezuelan oil despite global sanctions. Cooperation is also seen in the areas of **education** and **healthcare**. However, political instability in Venezuela has impacted the overall bilateral relationship.

CONCLUSION

The India-Latin America relationship has grown steadily, with Brazil serving as a key anchor in India's engagement with the region. Trade between India and Brazil forms a significant portion of India's total trade with Latin America, contributing about one-fourth of the overall volume. India's investment in Brazil, valued at around **US $6 billion**, is its largest in the region, highlighting Brazil's importance in India's strategic and economic framework. Similarly, Argentina has become India's fourth-largest trading partner, following

Brazil, China, and the U.S., with trade reaching **US $7 billion** in 2022. Argentina's growing interest in BRICS and its potential purchase of India's **HAL Tejas** aircraft underscores the deepening strategic ties, particularly given Argentina's vast lithium reserves critical to renewable energy, a key area of cooperation.

Venezuela, despite its current challenges, remains another significant player, boasting the largest petroleum reserves in the world. While India halted crude oil imports from Venezuela in **October 2020** due to potential U.S. sanctions, Venezuela had been a crucial energy partner, once contributing **10% of India's oil imports**. Additionally, other Latin American countries like **Chile, Colombia**, and **Peru** play essential roles, accounting for approximately **20% of India's trade** with the region, providing key minerals and hydrocarbons. These countries, along with emerging markets such as **Ecuador, Paraguay, Panama**, and **Guatemala**, continue to grow as hubs for **Indian exports and investments**, particularly in **IT and pharmaceuticals**. Overall, India's relationship with Latin America is dynamic, driven by growing trade, strategic collaborations, and mutual interest in sectors like **renewable energy, defense**, and **technology**.

9

THE OCEANIA REGION

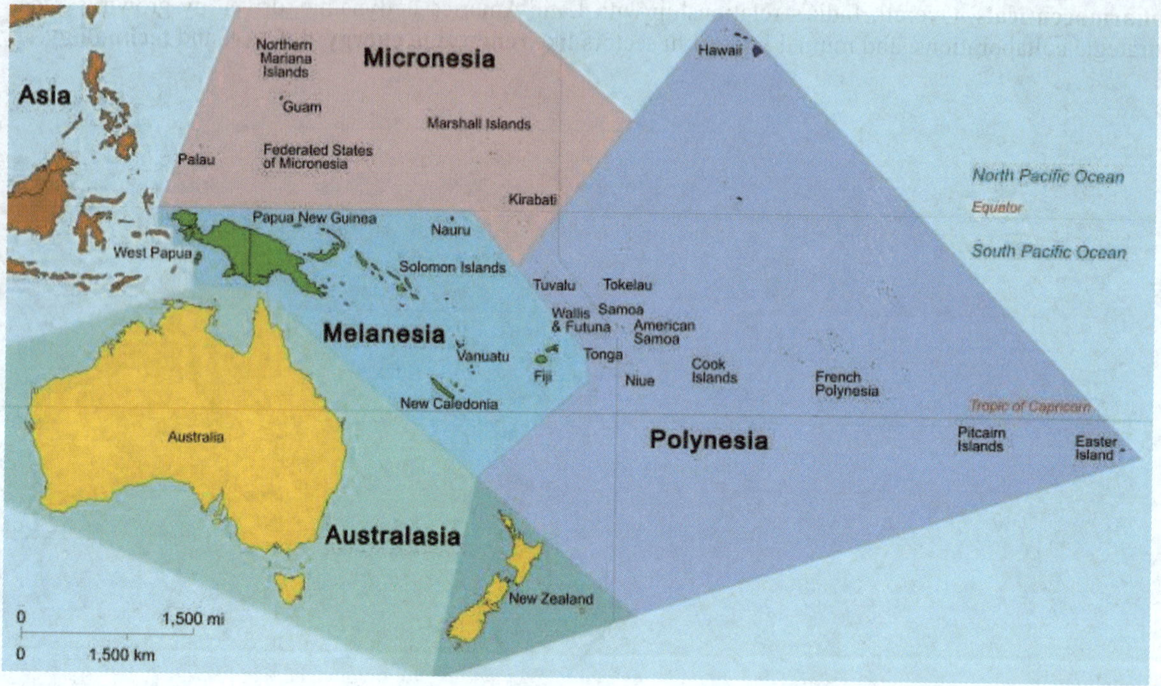

Oceania is a term that collectively refers to the islands spread across much of the Pacific Ocean. In its broadest definition, it encompasses the **entire island region between Asia and the Americas**. However, more commonly, the term excludes certain areas, such as the *Ryukyu* (also known as the *Nansei* Islands, are part of Japan), *Kuril* (ongoing territorial dispute between Russia and Japan), and *Aleutian Islands* (part of the U.S. state of Alaska), the *Japanese* archipelago, and islands with strong historical ties to mainland Asia, including Indonesia, Taiwan, and the Philippines.

'Oceania' has traditionally been divided into four parts -

- **Australasia** (Australia & New Zealand)
- **Melanesia**
- **Micronesia**
- **Polynesia**

ISLANDS OF THE PACIFIC

The regions of Melanesia, Micronesia, and Polynesia, form a vibrant tapestry of cultures, economies, and ecologies, spread across the vast Pacific Ocean. These islands, though diverse in their histories and traditions, share a deep connection to the sea, which has shaped their way of life for centuries. Economically, the region is a mix of resource-rich nations like Papua New Guinea and smaller island economies that rely heavily on tourism, fisheries, and foreign aid. Ecologically, these islands are home to some of the most unique and fragile ecosystems in the world, from coral reefs teeming with marine life to lush rainforests.

MELANESIA	MICRONESIA	POLYNESIA
Papua New Guinea, Solomon Islands, Vanuatu, Fiji, New Caledonia (French territory) & West Papua (Indonesia)	Federated States of Micronesia, Palau, Marshall Islands, Nauru, Kiribati, Guam (US territory) & Northern Mariana Islands (US territory)	Samoa, Tonga, Tuvalu, French Polynesia (French territory), Cook Islands (self-governing in free association with New Zealand), Niue (self-governing in free association with New Zealand), Easter Island (Chile), American Samoa (US territory), Tokelau (New Zealand territory) & Wallis and Futuna (French territory)

- The **Biketawa Declaration** is a set of principles and actions adopted by the Pacific Islands Forum (PIF) in 2000 (following the Fijian coup d'état) to promote regional cooperation and respond to political instability. The declaration is based on eight values, including:
  1. Commitment to Good Governance
  2. Respect for Human Rights
  3. Commitment to Democratic Processes
  4. Upkeep of the Separation of Powers
  5. Respect for the Rule of Law
  6. Peaceful Settlement of Disputes
  7. Commitment to International Norms
  8. Collaboration for Regional Stability and Security

  NOTE: The declaration also includes a commitment to respecting the principle of non-interference in the domestic affairs of other member states.
- The **2019 Boe Declaration**, adopted by Pacific Islands Forum leaders, reaffirms the region's commitment to addressing security challenges with a broadened understanding of security that includes human, environmental, and resource dimensions, alongside traditional security concerns. The Declaration underscores the significance of collective regional action in response to climate change, transnational crime, and geopolitical tensions.
- The **Teieniwa Vision** is a comprehensive anti-corruption framework adopted by Pacific Island Forum (PIF) leaders in 2020. It aims to create a corruption-free Pacific region by fostering collaboration among member states.

2050 STRATEGY FOR THE BLUE PACIFIC CONTINENT

The ***'Blue Pacific Continent'*** is a concept that envisions the Pacific Ocean and its islands as a unified entity rather than a collection of isolated nations. It emphasizes the interconnectedness of the region's people, cultures, and environments.

The **2050 Strategy** is a comprehensive blueprint developed by Pacific Island nations to secure their long-term prosperity and well-being. It aims to address the unique challenges faced by the region, including climate change, economic vulnerability, and geopolitical shifts.

Key objectives of the strategy include:

(a) **Resilience:** Building resilience to climate change, natural disasters, and economic shocks.
(b) **Sustainable development:** Promoting economic growth while preserving the environment and cultural heritage.
(c) **Regional integration:** Strengthening cooperation among Pacific Island countries to address shared challenges.
(d) **Ocean governance:** Protecting and sustainably managing marine resources.
(e) **Human development:** Investing in education, health, and social welfare.

RISING SIGNIFICANCE OF THE PACIFIC NATIONS

The Oceania region, often overlooked in global discourse, is experiencing significant geopolitical shifts. In the 21st century, Melanesia, Micronesia, and Polynesia have become increasingly significant in international relations. Several nations have garnered international attention due to various factors:

(1) **Strategic Positioning** – The Pacific nations occupy a critical location in the Indo-Pacific region, which is a focal point for global maritime trade and security. The strategic positioning of these islands influences major sea routes, making them essential for global commerce and military logistics.

> Major powers, including U.S., Russia & China aim to expand their influence in the Pacific waters, & hence the Oceanic regions are increasingly important in maintaining a balance of power in the region.

(2) **Natural resources** – The Pacific nations are endowed with valuable natural resources, including fisheries, minerals, and deep-sea mining potential. These resources are crucial for global industries and energy security, attracting significant international attention.

> For India, access to these resources, particularly in fisheries and energy, is important for its growing economy and food security.

(3) **Climate Change and Environmental concerns** – The Pacific islands are among the most vulnerable regions to the impacts of climate change, including rising sea levels and extreme weather events. Their plight has brought global attention to the urgency of addressing climate change.

> India, as a major global player and a member of the International Solar Alliance, has a vested interest in supporting climate resilience in the Pacific through renewable energy initiatives and disaster management cooperation.

(4) **Growing Political Influence** – The Pacific nations are gaining political significance in international forums, including the United Nations, where they collectively represent a substantial voting bloc. Their support can be crucial in global diplomatic efforts.

> For India, strengthening ties with Pacific nations can help in garnering support for its positions in multilateral organizations and can enhance its influence in international diplomacy, while also restoring the balance of power in the region.

(5) **Trade and Economic Opportunities** – The Pacific region offers untapped markets for trade and investment, particularly in sectors like tourism, agriculture, and infrastructure. Enhancing economic ties with these nations can diversify trade relations and open new avenues for Indian businesses.

> India's *Act East Policy & Indo-Pacific strategy* align with these goals, aiming to deepen economic engagement with the region.

(6) **Security & defense** – As maritime security becomes increasingly important, partnerships with Pacific nations are essential for maintaining peace and stability in the Indo-Pacific. Collaboration on issues such as maritime surveillance, counterterrorism, and disaster response can benefit both India and the Pacific region.

India's defense cooperation initiatives, including joint exercises and capacity-building programs, can contribute to regional security and align with India's broader strategic interests.

ISLAND GROUPINGS & FORUMS

(1) Smaller Island States (SIS)

- The SIS within the Pacific Islands Forum, comprising the **Cook Islands, Federated States of Micronesia, Kiribati, Nauru, Niue, Palau, Republic of the Marshall Islands,** and **Tuvalu**, are among the most vulnerable of the Forum Island Countries.
- These nations confront a distinct set of development challenges due to their small land size, limited natural resources, geographical remoteness and susceptibility to climate change and natural disasters, which significantly impact their resilience and capacity for sustainable development.
- The **Summit of the SIS** (discussed later) helps in addressing the issues faced by these nations by fostering regional cooperation and seeking tailored solutions.

(2) Organisation of African, Caribbean and Pacific States (OACPS)

- The OACPS is an intergovernmental organization comprising 79 countries in Africa, the Caribbean, and the Pacific.
- The Pacific members of the OACPS include **Fiji, Kiribati, Papua New Guinea, Solomon Islands, Tonga, Tuvalu, Vanuatu,** and **Samoa.**
- These nations share common interests and collaborate on a range of economic and development initiatives within the framework of the OACPS. They engage in partnerships with the *European Union*, focusing on achieving sustainable development goals, fostering economic growth, and addressing regional challenges.
- The OACPS serves as a platform for these countries to work together on issues such as trade, climate change, and development cooperation.

SAMOA AGREEMENT

The Agreement is a significant treaty within the Pacific region, particularly among **the Pacific African, Caribbean, and Pacific (PACP)** countries. The Samoa Agreement involves a total of 79 countries. Officially signed by all Pacific ACP members by July 31, 2024, the Agreement serves as the legally binding framework that guides cooperation between these countries and the European Union (EU). It aligns with the "*2050 Strategy for the Blue Pacific Continent*," which seeks to address regional challenges such as climate change and geopolitical tensions.

This Agreement is a part of the broader **EU-OACPS** (Organisation of African, Caribbean, and Pacific States) **partnership**. The Partnership Agreement is between 79 Members of the OACPS and 27 EU Member States.

REGIONAL FORUMS & SUMMITS	
EVENT or GROUPING	**DETAILS**
Pacific Islands Forum (PIF)	It is the premier political and economic policy organization in the Pacific region, comprising 18 member states, including Australia, New Zealand, and 16 independent Pacific Island countries. Established in 1971, the PIF aims to foster regional cooperation and integration, focusing on areas such as economic development, security, environmental protection, and regional stability.

	• Apart from its members, the Forum also engages in dialogue with non-member countries, including major powers like the U.S., China, and India. • The PIF addresses a range of issues critical to the region, including climate change, fisheries management, trade, and sustainable development. • The Forum has also been involved in addressing regional security issues, such as conflict resolution and maritime security, through initiatives like the **Biketawa Declaration**. • The PIF also champions the concept of the "**Blue Pacific Continent**."
Summit of the Smaller Island States (SIS)	The SIS is an important gathering within the framework of the Pacific Islands Forum (PIF), dedicated to addressing the specific needs and challenges faced by the ***Smaller Island States***. The concept of the SIS Summit emerged in 1991 when the South Pacific Forum recognized the unique development challenges faced by the smaller island nations. The inaugural SIS Summit was held in January 1992 in Rarotonga, Cook Islands. • Climate change is a central theme at the SIS Summit. Discussions often focus on securing international support for climate adaptation and mitigation efforts. • The summit explores strategies to enhance economic resilience, promote sustainable development, and diversify the economies of SIS nations. This includes discussions on fisheries, tourism, and renewable energy. • The SIS Summit provides a unified voice for the smaller island nations on the global stage, particularly in advocating for their interests in international forums, where they often seek stronger commitments to climate action and sustainable development.
Melanesian Spearhead Group (MSG)	Established in 1986, the MSG is a sub-regional organization that includes Fiji, Papua New Guinea, Solomon Islands, Vanuatu, and the Kanak Socialist National Liberation Front (FLNKS) from New Caledonia. The MSG focuses on promoting economic cooperation, trade, and cultural exchange among its members.
Polynesian Leaders Group (PLG)	The PLG was established in 2011 as a sub-regional grouping of Polynesian nations. Its members include Samoa, Tonga, Tuvalu, Cook Islands, Niue, and American Samoa, among others. It aims to strengthen cultural and historical ties among Polynesian peoples, as well as to address shared challenges, such as climate change, sustainable development, and economic cooperation.
Micronesian Presidents' Summit (MPS)	It is a forum for cooperation among Micronesian states, including the Federated States of Micronesia, Palau, Marshall Islands, Nauru, and Kiribati. The group focuses on regional issues pertinent to Micronesia, such as climate change, maritime security, and sustainable development. It provides a platform for Micronesian leaders to coordinate their positions on global and regional matters.

GLOBAL SPOTLIGHT: KEY REGIONS

(1) Papua New Guinea (PNG):

- It is the largest Melanesian country, known for its incredible biodiversity and rich cultural heritage. PNG is abundant in natural resources, including gold, copper, and timber, and has significant economic potential.
- PNG is known to have over 800 different languages spoken by its population of about 10.3 million (2023) people. This makes it the most linguistically diverse country in the world, and most of these languages are indigenous Papuan languages.

Despite its natural resources, the nation faces several challenges –

(a)Poverty, inequality, and infrastructure development are the key issues.

(b)High crime rates, particularly in urban areas, pose a significant threat to security and development.

(c)There are high rates of maternal and child mortality, infectious diseases, coupled with limited access to healthcare services.

(d)Rapid deforestation and unsustainable exploitation of natural resources is leading to biodiversity loss and climate change impacts. The rising sea levels and extreme weather events threaten coastal communities and food security.

INDIA-PNG: The nations share a growing bilateral relationship, underpinned by shared interests in economic cooperation, development, and regional stability –

- ✓ India is an increasingly important trade partner for Papua New Guinea, with significant growth in exports of commodities like palm oil and copper. India is also investing in infrastructure and development projects in the Pacific nation.
- ✓ India has been a consistent development partner, providing aid in sectors such as healthcare, education, and capacity building.
- ✓ The growing Indian diaspora in Papua New Guinea contributes to cultural exchange and economic activity.

(2) Solomon Islands:

- The Solomon Islands is a Pacific archipelago comprising over 900 islands and is home to diverse ethnic groups, each with unique customs and languages. It is widely known for its stunning beauty, including coral reefs and rainforests.
- The nation possesses abundant natural resources, including timber, gold, and fisheries, but has struggled to fully capitalize on them.
- While it is resource heavy, dependence on primary commodities, coupled with infrastructure deficits and susceptibility to natural disasters, hinders economic growth. Additionally, the country has faced political instability, ethnic tensions, and the impacts of climate change.
- The Solomon Islands' strategic location in the Pacific makes it a focal point for geopolitical competition, particularly between major powers.

Solomon island's security pact with China (2022) has raised geopolitical tensions, especially among the nations of Australia, New Zealand and the United States. It has significantly intensified strategic competition between China and Western powers for the influence in the Pacific -

- It strengthens China's strategic position in the Pacific, enabling it to expand its military (deployment of Chinese security personnel) and economic footprint (infrastructure.
- It raises concerns about the regional stability and the overall balance of power.
- The deal has sparked domestic debates in Solomon Islands about the implications for sovereignty and national security.

INDIA-SOLOMON ISLANDS: India and Solomon Islands established diplomatic relations in 1987. As part of its 'Act East' policy, India has been increasing its focus on the Pacific region, including Solomon Islands. While the relationship has traditionally been low-key, it has gained prominence in recent years due to geopolitical shifts in the Pacific.

- ✓ India has been a consistent development partner, providing aid in sectors like healthcare, education, and infrastructure. Bilateral trade has witnessed growth, with India exporting pharmaceuticals, agricultural products, and consumer goods to Solomon Islands.
- ✓ India is exploring opportunities to invest in infrastructure development in Solomon Islands, such as renewable energy and digital connectivity.
- ✓ The Island's security Pact with China has introduced new complexities into the India-Solomon Islands relationship, prompting India to reassess its engagement strategy.

(3) **Fiji:** It is an archipelago renowned for its natural beauty and diverse culture. Fiji has emerged as a **regional leader**, playing a key role in regional organizations like the Pacific Islands Forum. Fiji has experienced **political instability** in the past but has made strides in economic development and tourism. However, challenges such as climate change and natural disasters persist.

INDIA-FIJI: India and Fiji enjoy strong historical and cultural ties, with a significant Indian diaspora contributing to Fiji's economy and society. Bilateral relations have witnessed significant growth in recent years, with India emerging as a key development partner. Key areas of cooperation include infrastructure, agriculture, education, and renewable energy. The establishment of Centers of Excellence in Information Technology (CEIT) in Fiji is a testament to India's commitment to capacity building.

(4) **Marshall Islands:** The islands are a low-lying island nation in Micronesia. Known for its atoll formations, the country faces significant challenges due to climate change, including **sea-level rise** and **extreme weather events**. The Marshall Islands played a crucial role in World War II (A former US territory dealing with the legacy of nuclear testing), with the Battle of Midway being a pivotal turning point. Despite its small size, the nation has been active in international affairs, raising awareness about the impacts of climate change.

According to a **World Bank Study**, the rising sea levels in the atoll nation of Marshall Islands are projected to endanger 40 percent of existing buildings in the capital, Majuro, with 96 percent of the city at risk of frequent flooding induced by climate change.

INDIA-MARSHALL ISLANDS: The nations share cordial relations and despite geographically distant, both nations cooperate within multilateral forums like the United Nations. India has extended development assistance to the Marshall Islands, focusing on capacity building and human resource development. However, the small size of the Marshall Islands economy and its remote location pose challenges for expanding bilateral trade and investment.

(5) **Samoa**: It is located in Polynesia, and is known for its rich cultural heritage and stunning landscapes. The country has faced economic challenges and the impacts of natural disasters, but it has also made progress in areas such as education and healthcare. Samoa's strategic location in the Pacific has increased its geopolitical significance in recent years.

Samoa is at the forefront of the **global climate crisis**, with rising sea levels posing a significant threat to its existence. The country has been vocal about the need for global action to address climate change. Recovery efforts and disaster preparedness remain key issues.

INDIA-SAMOA: The nations share a growing partnership, with cooperation focused on areas such as human resource development, infrastructure, and health. India has extended Lines of Credit for various development projects in Samoa. While the relationship is developing, there is potential for further expansion in areas like trade, investment, and maritime cooperation.

(6) Tonga: Tonga, a Polynesian archipelago in the South Pacific, is renowned for its pristine natural beauty, and rich cultural heritage. Tonga is one of the world's last absolute monarchies, with the King as the head of state. Tonga's geographic isolation has contributed to the preservation of its unique culture and environment.

Despite its resources, the nation faces several challenges –

- Tonga's economy is heavily reliant on remittances from overseas workers and agriculture, making it vulnerable to external shocks.
- As a low-lying island nation, Tonga faces significant threats from sea-level rise and extreme weather events.
- Challenges in education, healthcare, and gender equality persist.

The volcanic eruption and subsequent tsunami in Tonga in early 2022 were catastrophic events that caused widespread devastation. The COVID-19 outbreak, exacerbated by the disaster, posed additional health risks to the population. Despite these setbacks, Tonga has shown resilience in its recovery efforts, with support from the international community.

INDIA-TONGA: The nations share a cordial bilateral relationship built on mutual respect and cooperation. While the relationship has traditionally been low-key, it has gained momentum in recent years.

- ✓ India has extended significant development assistance to Tonga, focusing on areas such as infrastructure, healthcare, and human resource development.
- ✓ India has been a consistent partner in supporting Tonga during times of crisis, particularly following the devastating volcanic eruption and tsunami in 2022.
- ✓ India offers scholarships and training programs to Tongan nationals, enhancing human capital development.

'HAWAII' – A PACIFIC PARADISE?

Hawaii, the **US's 50th state** comprised of a volcanic archipelago, is geographically located in ***Polynesia***, a subregion of Oceania in the Pacific Ocean. Hawaii's geographic position has made it a crucial military and transportation hub for the United States.

Hawaii has been in the global spotlight primarily due to the devastating **wildfires** that ravaged **Maui** in August 2023. The fires caused widespread destruction, loss of life, and economic hardship. The recovery process has been continuing, with challenges like rebuilding infrastructure, housing, and addressing the emotional toll on the community.

Additionally, the ongoing **volcanic activity** of **Kilauea** remains a focus of scientific and public interest.

Beyond the wildfires, Hawaii continues to grapple with issues such as tourism management, cost of living, and the preservation of native Hawaiian culture. The state is also actively involved in climate change mitigation and adaptation efforts due to its vulnerability to rising sea levels.

INDIA AND THE PACIFIC NATIONS

In the past year, India has been actively strengthening its relations with the Pacific nations in Oceania, focusing on economic, strategic, and diplomatic partnerships. This is part of a broader strategy to counterbalance China's influence in the region and enhance India's own strategic footprint.

India's outreach to smaller Pacific Island nations has also intensified, with India hosting the Forum for India-Pacific Islands Cooperation (FIPIC) and providing developmental aid and disaster relief to these nations. This is in line with India's Act East policy, which seeks to engage more deeply with Asia-Pacific nations.

There are historical and cultural ties between India and the Pacific nations, particularly through the Indian diaspora in countries like Fiji. These connections provide a strong foundation for building closer diplomatic and economic relations.

To further strengthen its relations with the Pacific nations, India should consider the following steps:

1. **Enhanced Diplomatic Engagement**: Establishing more diplomatic missions in the Pacific region and actively participating in regional forums like the **Pacific Islands Forum (PIF)** would deepen political ties.

2. **Economic Partnerships**: India should increase investments in infrastructure, renewable energy, and sustainable development projects in the Pacific. Leveraging trade agreements and economic cooperation frameworks would facilitate stronger economic linkages.
3. **Climate Change Cooperation**: Offering technological and financial assistance for climate adaptation and mitigation projects in the Pacific can position India as a leader in global environmental efforts.
4. **Defense and Security Cooperation**: Expanding defense training programs, joint exercises, and maritime security initiatives with Pacific nations can enhance regional stability and security cooperation.
5. **Cultural and Educational Exchange**: Promoting educational scholarships, cultural exchange programs, and diaspora engagement will build long-term people-to-people connections and strengthen India's soft power in the region.
6. **Multilateral Support**: Collaborating with Pacific nations in international organizations to address global challenges, such as climate change and sustainable development, will reinforce India's leadership role on the world stage.

By implementing these strategies, India can play a pivotal role in supporting the development and security of the Pacific nations, while also advancing its own strategic and economic interests in the Indo-Pacific region.

AUSTRALIA

Australia is a large country located in the southern hemisphere, bordered by the Pacific and Indian Oceans and is known globally for its diverse landscapes, including rugged outback, tropical rainforests, and stunning beaches.

IMPORTANT DETAILS	
Capital	Canberra
Monarch	King Charles III
Prime Minister	Anthony Albanese
Population (2023)	26.6 M
Human Development Index Rank (2023)	10
GDP Growth (annual % - 2023)	3.0

Polity and Governance

Australia is a **federal parliamentary democracy** and a **constitutional monarchy**. The British monarch i.e., **King Charles III** is Australia's head of state, although presently that role is largely symbolic. The Australian system of government is based on the Westminster parliamentary model, which is similar to that of the United Kingdom. The Governor-General is the representative of the Monarch of Australia and is the ceremonial head of state.

Economy & Trade

- Australia's economy is one of the most developed and diversified in the Asia-Pacific region, making it a significant player in global trade.
- The country's economic strength lies in its rich natural resources, including coal, iron ore, natural gas, and agricultural products, which are major exports. Australia is also known for its strong service sector, particularly in education, tourism, and finance.
- Australia's economy is heavily reliant on exports, particularly to Asia. China is its largest trading partner, followed by Japan, South Korea, and India. Exports of minerals and energy resources, especially iron ore and coal, are vital to Australia's economic health.

- Australia has been proactive in securing FTAs with key economies, including the Comprehensive and Progressive Agreement for Trans-Pacific Partnership (CPTPP), the Australia-United States Free Trade Agreement (AUSFTA), and the most recent Regional Comprehensive Economic Partnership (RCEP).
- Australia has demonstrated economic resilience, maintaining consistent growth over the past few decades, largely due to its robust trade policies and effective economic management. However, challenges such as reliance on commodity exports and trade tensions, particularly with China, present ongoing risks.

Australia has introduced a **"Right to Disconnect"** law, effective from August 26, 2024. This groundbreaking legislation allows workers to ignore unreasonable out-of-hours contact from their employers, promoting a healthier work-life balance.

Defense & Security

- The **Australia-United States alliance** is central to Australia's defense policy. The **ANZUS Treaty**, which includes New Zealand, solidifies this alliance, focusing on mutual defense and security cooperation. Additionally, Australia is part of the **Five Eyes intelligence-sharing alliance**.
- Australia is increasingly focused on the Indo-Pacific region, working to counterbalance China's growing influence. It has strengthened ties with regional partners through the Quadrilateral Security Dialogue (**Quad**) with the U.S., India, and Japan, and has signed the **AUKUS pact** with the U.S. and the UK to develop nuclear-powered submarines.
- Australia has been modernizing its defense capabilities, investing in advanced military technology and expanding its naval and air forces. This includes acquiring new submarines, frigates, and fighter jets to bolster its maritime and aerial defense.
- Australia is actively involved in global counterterrorism efforts and has enhanced its cybersecurity measures, recognizing the growing threat of cyberattacks to national security.

FIVE EYES INTELLIGENCE ALLIANCE

The **Five Eyes** is an intelligence-sharing alliance comprising ***the United States, the United Kingdom, Canada, Australia* and *New Zealand.*** It originated in 1946, with the US and UK forming the initial partnership. It was followed by the inclusion of Canada in 1948, and Australia and New Zealand in 1956. Rooted in the post-World War II era, this partnership facilitates the exchange of signals intelligence (SIGINT) among member nations. The alliance remains a cornerstone of Western intelligence cooperation.

Beyond SIGINT, the Five Eyes cooperation has expanded to encompass a broader range of intelligence, including counterterrorism, cyber security, and counter-proliferation. Regular summits and meetings at various levels foster close collaboration and information sharing.

Resources and S&T

- Australia is rich in natural resources, making it a global leader in mining and energy production. The country is a top producer of minerals such as **iron ore, coal, gold,** and **bauxite**, and it has vast reserves of natural gas and uranium.
- Its mining industry is highly advanced, utilizing state-of-the-art technology for extraction and processing.
- In addition to mineral wealth, Australia has significant agricultural resources, producing wheat, wool, and livestock on a large scale.
- Australia is known for its innovation in science and technology, particularly in fields such as medical research, space exploration, and environmental science.
- The country has developed world-class institutions like the **Commonwealth Scientific and Industrial Research Organisation (CSIRO)**, which has contributed groundbreaking developments in areas like Wi-Fi technology, renewable energy, and agriculture.

- Australia is also heavily invested in space research, with the Australian Space Agency aiming to become a key player in the global space industry.

WHAT SETS AUSTRALIA APART?

- **Resource Abundance**: Australia's combination of abundant mineral wealth and cutting-edge mining technology makes it a global powerhouse in natural resource production.
- **Scientific Innovation**: The country's advances in medical research, including cancer treatment and vaccine development, are globally recognized. It also leads in environmental management, tackling issues like climate change and renewable energy.
- **Strategic Location and Infrastructure**: Australia's proximity to Asia and its robust infrastructure enhance its role in global trade and technology partnerships.

Foreign Affairs & Diplomacy

- Australia's foreign policy is characterized by its commitment to multilateralism, regional engagement, and a strong alliance with the United States. The country plays an active role in international organizations and promotes global stability, free trade, and human rights (including the rights of indigenous peoples).
- Australia places significant emphasis on its relationships with Asia-Pacific nations and is considered to be a regional power in the region. It engages in regional forums such as the ASEAN Regional Forum (ARF) and the East Asia Summit (EAS), promoting economic cooperation, security, and stability in the region.
- Australia is a proactive member of international organizations, including the United Nations, the World Trade Organization (WTO), G20, and the Commonwealth of Nations.
- It is also a major contributor to global efforts to address climate change, and has implemented a range of policies aimed at reducing greenhouse gas emissions and promoting sustainability. It also advocates for global issues including disarmament and development assistance.
- Australia's foreign relations are occasionally strained by geopolitical tensions, particularly with China, its largest trading partner. Balancing economic ties with China and its strategic alliance with the U.S. presents ongoing diplomatic challenges.

Diaspora & Culture

- Australia is one of the most multicultural countries in the world, with a large portion of its population being immigrants. This diversity is reflected in Australia's cultural, culinary, and social landscapes, making it a global hub for cultural exchange.
- The Australian diaspora, particularly in countries like the UK, the U.S., and Asia, plays an essential role in its international relations, fostering cultural exchange and strengthening economic and social ties with other countries.
- Australia leverages its cultural assets, including film, music, sports, and arts, to project soft power globally.

INDIA AND AUSTRALIA ALLIANCE

India has deepened its collaboration with Australia, particularly through the Quad grouping (India, Australia, Japan, and the United States), which aims to ensure a free and open Indo-Pacific. The bilateral relations between India and Australia have grown, with increased defense cooperation, joint military exercises, and economic partnerships, especially following the Australia-India Economic Cooperation and Trade Agreement (AI-ECTA) that came into effect in December 2022.

Economy and Commerce

Australia enjoys a trade surplus of US$6.5 billion with India, indicating a trade imbalance between the two countries in 2021. The total bilateral trade in goods and services reached **US$27.5 billion** during that period, with India exporting goods and services worth US$10.5 billion and importing goods and services worth US$17 billion. **Australia ranks as India's 9th largest trading partner**, recognizing India's growing economic significance. In 2018, the Australian Government released the **India Economic Strategy to 2035**, aiming to tap into the opportunities presented by India's economic growth.

The establishment of the **India-Australia Joint Ministerial Commission (JMC)** in 1989 further facilitates interaction between the two nations at a government and business level, focusing on various trade and investment matters. The 17th India-Australia Joint Ministerial Commission meeting was held in New Delhi on 30 September 2021.

Australia and India had upgraded their bilateral relationship from 'Strategic Partnership' in 2009 to **Comprehensive Strategic Partnership** (CSP) in 2020. The Australia-India Economic Cooperation and Trade Agreement (ECTA) is a recently implemented free trade agreement that became effective on 29 December 2022. The agreement was signed in April 2022.

- Under the ECTA, more than 85 percent of Australian goods exports to India are now exempt from tariffs, with the percentage set to increase to 90 percent within six years. Additionally, significant reductions in high tariffs have been made for certain additional products.
- Furthermore, 96 percent of imports from India are currently exempt from tariffs, and this percentage will reach 100 percent within four years.

As of August 2024, India and Australia are in advanced discussions to upgrade their Economic Cooperation and Trade Agreement (ECTA) to a full **Comprehensive Economic Partnership Agreement (CEPA).**

Diaspora and Tourism

- The Indian community in Australia is one of the fastest-growing and most significant migrant groups in the country, contributing to its multicultural landscape. As of the 2021 Australian Census, over 976,000 people of Indian ancestry were living in Australia, making them the second-largest migrant group after those from England. This growth is driven by skilled migration, family reunification, and international students.
- The Indian community is predominantly urban, with the largest populations residing in Melbourne, Sydney, Brisbane, and Perth. Melbourne has the highest concentration of Indian-born residents.
- Indians in Australia are among the most highly educated and skilled migrant groups. A large proportion of the Indian population is employed in professional fields such as IT, engineering, healthcare, and finance.
- In 2018, both nations entered into a Memorandum of Understanding (MOU) to enhance cooperation in the field of tourism.
- India is the **second-largest source of international students** in Australia. In 2022, over 120,000 Indian students were enrolled in Australian educational institutions, contributing significantly to the education sector.
- Indian tourists spent around AUD 1.6 billion in Australia in 2019, making India one of the top ten markets for tourism expenditure in Australia.
- People of India and Australia also have a long-standing sporting relationship, with cricket being a particularly significant sport in both countries. A Letter of Intent dealing with **Migration and Mobility Partnership Agreement** (MMPA) was signed during Leaders' Summit in March 2022.

> Despite their professional and personal success, members of the Indian community have occasionally faced incidents of racism and discrimination. These issues have been acknowledged and addressed through government and community initiatives aimed at promoting multiculturalism and social cohesion

Education and Science & Technology

India and Australia signed an **Educational Exchange Programme (EEP)** in 2003. Indian students are the second-largest group of international students in Australia, and several Australian universities have set up campuses in India.

India and Australia have established formal scientific and technological cooperation through an Inter-Governmental Agreement signed in October 1986. The Australia-India Strategic Research Fund (AISRF), established in 2006, facilitates advanced research collaboration between experts from both countries.

- The fund comprises various components such as the India Australia Biotechnology Fund, India-Australia Science & Technology Fund, Grand Challenge Fund, and Fellowship Schemes.
- To administer the fund, Joint Committees on S&T and Biotechnology have been established.

In August 2022, the 6th meeting of the **Australia-India Education Council (AIEC)** was co-chaired by the Ministers for Education of both nations. Furthermore, a Letter of Intent was signed between the **University of Wollongong** and **Gujarat International Finance Tec-City (GIFT City)** in July 2022, marking the University of Wollongong as the first Australian university to establish a campus in India.

Energy and Resources

Australia is a significant producer and exporter of **coal**. India imports a substantial amount of coal from Australia, with the two countries collaborating to develop cleaner coal technologies. India's growing demand for **natural gas** has also received backing from Australia that has vast natural gas reserves. The two countries have signed several agreements for the supply of liquefied natural gas (LNG) from Australia to India.

Indian companies have invested in Australian **mining projects**, and the two countries have signed agreements for collaboration in the mining sector. The important minerals include copper, gold and iron ore. Australia's known **uranium resources (reserves)** are the world's largest – almost **one-third of the world total** and is the world's third largest producer. The **2014 Civil Nuclear deal** allows the export of Australian import to India for peaceful purposes. The **Fourth India-Australia Energy Dialogue** took place in a virtual format on 15 February **2022**.

During the 2nd **Virtual Leaders' Summit** on 21 March 2022, a Memorandum of Understanding (MoU) was signed between Khanij Bidesh India Ltd. (KABIL) from India and the Critical Minerals Facilitation Office (CMFO) from Australia. This MoU focused on co-investment in Australian critical minerals projects. On 1 November 2022, the **3rd Joint Working Group (JWG)** on cooperation in the mining and processing of critical and strategic minerals was held in Sydney, alongside the International Mining and Resources Conference & Expo (IMARC).

A **Civil Nuclear Cooperation Agreement** between India and Australia was signed in September 2014 and the agreement came into force in November 2015. The Australian Parliament passed the "Civil Nuclear Transfer to India Bill 2016" on 01 December, 2016 which enables Australian uranium mining companies to fulfil contracts to supply Australian uranium to India for civil use with certainty that exports will not be hampered by domestic legal action challenging the consistency of the IAEA's safeguards in India and Australia's international non-proliferation obligations.

Diplomatic interactions

The **First India-Australia 2+2 Ministerial Dialogue** that was held in **September 2021** in New Delhi saw in attendance the respective ministers of both nations. **Foreign Ministers' Framework Dialogue (FMFD)** is the central mechanism for advancing the bilateral agenda and is held annually, alternatively in India and Australia. The **12th FMFD** and **1st Foreign Ministers' Cyber Framework Dialogue** was conducted in Melbourne on 12 February 2022. The **13th FMFD** was held in Canberra on 10 October 2022

The Prime Minister of both nations held the **2nd India-Australia Virtual Summit** on 21 March 2022, which was followed up with certain crucial announcements, which included[21] –

(1) **Return of 29 artefacts** by Government of Australia
(2) Establishment of **General Rawat India-Australia Young Defence Officers' Exchange Programme**
(3) Letter of Arrangement between India and Australia for **Educational Qualifications Recognition**
(4) **MoU for cooperation and collaboration on broadcasting** between Prasar Bharati, India and Special Broadcasting Service (SBS), Australia
(5) Matching funds as Australia of the amount of AUD 10 million for Pacific Island Countries under **Infrastructure for Resilient Island States** (IRIS) and;
(6) Matching funds as Australia of the amount of AUD 10 million for Pacific Island Countries under **International Solar Alliance** (ISA).

Australia supports India's candidature in an expanded UN Security Council. Both India and Australia are members of the Commonwealth, IORA, ASEAN Regional Forum, Asia Pacific Partnership on Climate and Clean Development, International Solar Alliance, Coalition for Disaster Resilient Infrastructure, Indo-Pacific Economic Framework and have participated in the East Asia Summits.

Defence and Strategic Relations

India and Australia have a flourishing defence relationship underpinned by the **2006 Memorandum on Defence Cooperation** and the **2009 Joint Declaration on Security Cooperation.** India and Australia share concerns about regional security, particularly in the Indo-Pacific region. The two countries participate in joint military exercises, such as the bilateral naval exercise **AUSINDEX**, and have signed a range of defense agreements, including the Mutual Logistics Support Agreement (MLSA).

Important Military exercises –

- In 2018, the Indian Air Force took part in **Exercise Pitch Black** in Australia for the first time, which occurred from 27 July to 17 August.
- During March 2018, the Australian Naval ship HMAS Larrakia participated in the **'MILAN'** Naval exercise in the Andaman & Nicobar Islands.
- In April 2021, India joined the French-led naval exercises called La Perouse in the Bay of Bengal, along with Australia, the USA, and Japan.
- The navies of India, Australia, Japan, and the USA participated in Phase I of **Exercise Malabar** 2021, hold from 26-29 August 2021 off Guam, and in Phase II in the Bay of Bengal from 12-15 October 2021.
- The India-Australia Joint Military Exercise **AUSTRAHIND** 2022 took place in Rajasthan from 28 November to 11 December 2022. This exercise marked the first time that all arms and services contingents from both armies participated in the series.

Bilateral mechanisms between the nations include Joint Trade & Commerce Ministerial Commission, Defence Policy Talks, Defence Services Staff Talks, Energy Dialogue, etc. Australia's Quad partnership with India, Japan and the United States is a key pillar in Australia's foreign policy.

Foreign Minister Wong attended a **Quad Foreign Ministers' meeting** in New Delhi on 3 March 2023, which took place after the G20 Foreign Ministers' Meeting. India and Australia share the view that the Indian Ocean region holds great strategic importance, and they are actively working together to enhance regional stability. Their collaborative efforts involve fostering deeper regional cooperation, establishing norms, and strengthening regional capabilities to peacefully address various challenges.

NEW ZEALAND

New Zealand is a small island country located in the southwestern Pacific Ocean and is known for its stunning natural landscapes, diverse wildlife, and vibrant culture. New Zealand is often seen as a leader in many areas, including environmental sustainability, human rights, and social justice. The country has a long

[21] Prime Minister's Office – Government of India. (2022, Mar 21). Joint Statement: India-Australia Virtual Summit. https://pib.gov.in/Pressreleaseshare.aspx?PRID=1808418

history of promoting peace and disarmament, and has been an active participant in various international organizations and initiatives.

It also has a strong and positive reputation around the world, and is often viewed as a progressive and inclusive society. The country has a highly developed economy, with a focus on industries such as agriculture, tourism, and technology. It is also known for its high quality of life, excellent healthcare system, and strong social safety net.

IMPORTANT DETAILS	
Capital	Wellington
Monarch	King Charles III
Prime Minister	Christopher Luxon
Population (2023)	5.2 M
Human Development Index Rank (2023)	16
GDP Growth (annual % - 2023)	0.6

Polity and Governance

- New Zealand is a **parliamentary democracy** and a **constitutional monarchy**, with the monarch of the United Kingdom as its head of state, i.e., **King Charles III**. However, the real political power in New Zealand is held by elected officials who operate within a framework of constitutional rules and procedures.
- The Governor-General is the representative of the Monarch of New Zealand and is the ceremonial head of state. The Prime Minister is the head of government and leads the Cabinet.
- The unicameral Parliament, known as the House of Representatives, is the legislative body.
- New Zealand continues to maintain a robust democratic governance system with a strong emphasis on transparency, rule of law, and civil liberties.
- The country is known for its effective management of public resources and ranks highly on global governance indices.
- Additionally, there have been ongoing efforts to improve the rights and representation of the ***Māori***, the indigenous people of New Zealand.

Economy & Trade

- New Zealand is a developed economy, known for its high standard of living. Key sectors include agriculture, tourism, and manufacturing. New Zealand's economy has been resilient post-pandemic, with a focus on recovery and sustainable growth.
- The government has invested in infrastructure, technology, and the green economy to stimulate development.
- New Zealand continues to strengthen its trade relationships, particularly with China, Australia, and ASEAN countries.
- The country is a member of the Comprehensive and Progressive Agreement for Trans-Pacific Partnership (CPTPP) and has signed free trade agreements with various countries.
- The country faces economic challenges such as housing affordability, inflation, and labor shortages.
- The agricultural sector, a significant contributor to the economy, is under pressure to adopt sustainable practices due to climate change concerns.

Defense & Security

New Zealand maintains a defense policy focused on regional stability, disaster response and international peacekeeping. The country's defense strategy emphasizes cooperation with allies such as Australia, the United States, and regional partners in the Pacific. The New Zealand Defence Force (NZDF) is undergoing modernization, with investments in upgrading its naval and air capabilities. The country has also been participating in joint military exercises with allies to enhance its defense readiness.

New Zealand has been strengthening its cybersecurity infrastructure to protect against emerging threats.

Foreign Affairs & Diplomacy

New Zealand's foreign policy is characterized by its commitment to multilateralism, international law, and human rights. The country plays an active role in international organizations such as the United Nations, World Trade Organization, the Asia-Pacific Economic Cooperation (APEC) forum and the Pacific Islands Forum. New Zealand continues to engage with Pacific Island nations, focusing on development aid, climate change mitigation, and regional security. The country has also been working to deepen its ties with Southeast Asia and maintain a balanced approach in its relations with major powers like China and the United States.

The country is also a founding member of the **Five Eyes intelligence alliance**, along with the United States, Canada, the United Kingdom, and Australia. As a vocal advocate for climate action, New Zealand has been pushing for more ambitious global climate goals. The government has set a target for net-zero carbon emissions by 2050.

Diaspora & Culture

New Zealand has a diverse population, with a significant ***Maori*** population and immigrants from various countries. ***Maori*** culture plays a central role in New Zealand's identity, with traditional arts, language, and customs being preserved and celebrated. The country's multiculturalism and geographic location have fostered strong connections with other nations.

The ***Māori*** are the indigenous people of New Zealand, descended from Polynesian migrants who arrived in canoes between the 13th and 14th centuries. The arrival of European settlers in the 18th century led to significant changes in Māori society, including land loss, cultural suppression, and conflict.

Māori culture is deeply rooted in traditions like carving, weaving, tattooing, and performing arts. Māori have been actively involved in advocating for their rights and self-determination, leading to significant progress in recent decades.

INDIA AND NEW ZEALAND RELATIONS

India and New Zealand have a long-standing relationship, based on shared values of democracy, rule of law, and multiculturalism. Bilateral relations between the two countries have strengthened in recent years, driven by growing economic, political, and cultural ties.

Trade and Commerce

The bilateral trade relationship between India and New Zealand has grown significantly in recent years. In terms of exports, India's main exports to New Zealand include textiles, clothing, and footwear, followed by machinery, chemicals, and pharmaceuticals. New Zealand's main exports to India include dairy products, wood, and meat, followed by edible fruits and nuts.

India is also a significant supplier of information technology services to New Zealand, with Indian IT companies playing a key role in the country's digital economy. **The India-New Zealand Joint Trade Committee meeting** took place on 24 June 2022, aiming to review and enhance bilateral trade partnership and cooperation in various sectors such as agriculture, pharmaceuticals, textiles, renewable energy, and services. **The India-New Zealand 2025: Investing in the Relationship** is a strategic document launched in 2020, outlining a future-oriented approach for New Zealand government agencies and partners to strengthen the relationship with India in the coming years. The **India NZ Business Council (INZBC)** and **India NZ Trade Alliance (INZTA)** are two prominent organizations dedicated to promoting trade and investment relations between India and New Zealand.

Areas of disconnect –

- Despite the ongoing maintenance of bilateral relations, the economic data reflects a concerning trend. In 2017, New Zealand's exports to India were reaching nearly 2 billion New Zealand dollars per year, but they have since experienced a significant decline, now standing at less than NZ$800 million.
- The deterioration could also be seen from the fact that India, which was the 10th biggest of the island nation in 2016, now holds a meagre 15th spot.

Politics and Diplomacy

India and New Zealand share a warm and amicable relationship based on their commonalities as Commonwealth nations, their adherence to parliamentary democracy, and the use of the English language. Both countries gained independence in the same year, and India established diplomatic representation with the opening of a **Trade Commission** in 1950, which was later upgraded to a **High Commission**.

The **4th Foreign Ministry Consultations** between India and New Zealand took place in New Delhi on 23 June 2022. While New Zealand recognizes the significant market potential and services sector of India, India also acknowledges New Zealand's strategic position in the Asia-Pacific region and its growing influence in various global and regional forums. New Zealand is a respected and influential player on the global stage, and is committed to working with other nations to address common challenges and promote greater prosperity and stability around the world. Over the past five years, the once-ambitious plans of both the nations regarding bilateral cooperation have gradually stagnated if not declined outrightly.

Education and Research

Indian students are the third-largest group of international students in New Zealand, and several New Zealand universities have set up campuses in India. Indian students numbering approximately 15000 (before the pandemic) are the 2nd largest source of international students for NZ. Many Indian students come to New Zealand to pursue degrees in fields such as information technology, engineering, and business.

Another area of cooperation is in the field of **agricultural research**. India and New Zealand have a joint research program focused on improving the productivity and sustainability of agriculture in both countries. The program includes research into areas such as dairy farming, crop management, and food processing.

India and New Zealand have signed a Memorandum of Understanding (MoU) to establish a joint research program focused on **developing new technologies for renewable energy generation and storage**. The program includes research into areas such as solar energy, wind energy, and hydrogen fuel cells. Additionally, New Zealand government has established a fund to support international research collaborations, which includes opportunities for Indian researchers to participate.

Population and Culture

India and New Zealand have a strong and growing people-to-people relationship, with significant ties in areas such as education, tourism, and culture. India is a growing market for New Zealand tourism, with more than 70,000 Indian tourists visiting the country each year. New Zealand is a popular destination for Indian tourists due to its natural beauty, adventure sports, and friendly people. Cultural ties between India and New Zealand are also strong, with a growing interest in Indian culture and arts in New Zealand. There are several Indian cultural associations and organizations in the country, which promote Indian dance, music, and cuisine.

Thus, India's relations with New Zealand have been marked by efforts to boost trade, investment, and people-to-people ties, though this relationship is less strategically driven compared to India's ties with Australia. These moves are seen as part of India's broader Indo-Pacific strategy, which seeks to build alliances and partnerships that can contribute to regional stability and counter the growing influence of China in Oceania

10 GLOBAL WATERS & MARITIME OUTLOOK

MARITIME REGION – POWER AND PRESTIGE

'Whoever rules the waves rules the world'

\- Alfred T. Mahan

The notion of 'sea power' has its roots in the 19th century, but in essence the phrase mirrors the scenarios of this decade. While the context then was mainly maritime commerce, naval power today has become the cornerstone of all foreign policies. Alfred Thayer Mahan's *The Influence of Sea Power upon History* was published in the 1800s but continues to drive national policies today. It had argued in favour of military buildup as a means to secure national prosperity.

> The world's oceans are regulated mainly under the **United Nations Convention on the Law of the Sea (UNCLOS), 1982** (came into force in November 1994) apart from other treaties. The UNCLOS ensures freedom of shipping navigation at the sea and provides the right to access the open seas.

The oceans, covering over 70 percent of the surface of Earth, provides a big portion of resources and livelihood. The maritime domain is becoming prominent due to an enhanced focus on security, economic and environmental reasons surrounding it. '**Blue Economy**' is an important feature of the economic development for the coming years. It has been estimated that the Blue Economy could contribute to around thirteen billion UD dollars to South Africa's GDP and create a million jobs by 2033. The Indian Ocean has specifically been hailed as a treasure of untapped opportunities, mainly surrounding maritime connectivity and renewable energy

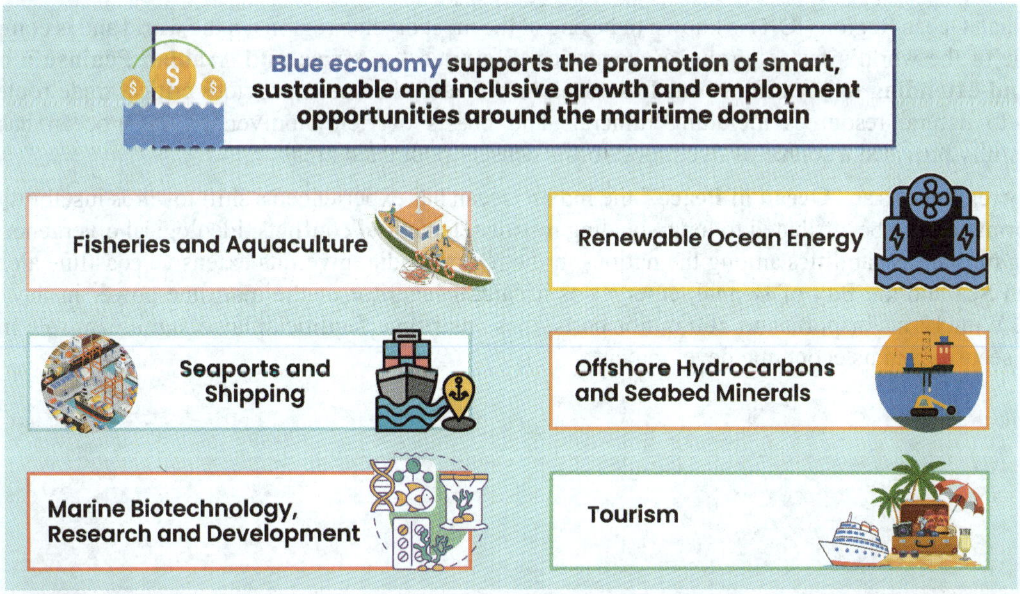

It includes, among other facets - Fisheries and aquaculture, renewable ocean energy, seaports and shipping, offshore hydrocarbons and seabed minerals, marine biotechnology, research and development and tourism.

In June 2022, UN Secretary-General Antonio Guterres referred to an **'ocean emergency'**, highlighting the lack of a dedicated treaty to protect marine and ocean health. The **UN High Seas Treaty,** also known as the Paris Agreement for the Ocean, was proposed to address biodiversity beyond national jurisdiction and ocean protection. However, negotiations with 168 countries failed to yield satisfactory results. In June 2023, 193 UN members ratified the treaty, which aims to preserve marine biodiversity, clean waters, sustainable fish stock management, temperature reduction, and global warming mitigation. The treaty is crucial for tackling ocean threats and achieving the 2030 Agenda for Sustainable Development.

While maritime diplomacy includes a wide range of operations, from cooperative measures like port visits, drills, and humanitarian aid to persuasive deployment and coercion, it is however, no longer restricted exclusively to warships.Today, it is also undertaken by coast guards, private vessels, and non-state organisations. On one hand, the use of such diplomacy can reflect changes in the international order, and on the other hand, it acts as an excellent gauge for the existence and severity of international tension. Thus, as the nations walk further into the 21st century, maritime diplomacy could become an integral tool in their diplomatic relations which could ensure stability and security without rushing headfirst into an outright conflict with each other.

INDIAN OCEAN REGION

"*Whoever controls the Indian Ocean will dominate Asia, the destiny of the world will be decided on its waters*"

\- Alfred T. Mahan

The Indian Ocean, ranking as the third largest ocean globally, holds a significant population, approximately **one-third of the world's total, despite covering only about 25% of the Earth's land mass**. This region boasts abundant human resources. Notably, the Indian Ocean serves as a crucial pathway for global activities, including **70% of the world's oil transportation**, **33% of global trade**, and **50% of container traffic through its Sea Lines of Communication (SLOCs)**. Beyond its geographical significance, the Indian Ocean acts as a connecting link between the emerging economies of Southeast Asia, South Asia, the Middle East, and North Africa (MENA). Its presence directly influences international trade and connectivity between Asia and Africa, as well as Asia and Europe.

The Indian Ocean Region (IOR) is known to be one of the most diverse regions in the world and is comprised of some of the world's fastest growing economies. **Bounded by Africa and Arabian Peninsula on the west and extending to Myanmar and Indonesia in the east**, the ocean provides critical trade routes and access to natural resources including minerals and boasts of rich biodiversity. This ocean has thus successfully provided a source of livelihood for its densely populated areas.

Initially regarded as an "**Ocean of Peace**," the Indian Ocean has experienced a shift towards instability. This transformation can be attributed to long-standing mistrust, territorial conflicts, ideological divergences, and varying military capabilities among the nations in the region. India, given its extensive coastline along the Arabian Sea and the Bay of Bengal, emerges as a natural inheritor of the maritime power in the Indian Ocean. With 12 major ports and 200 minor ports, these maritime facilities play a significant role in both India's security and its economic development.

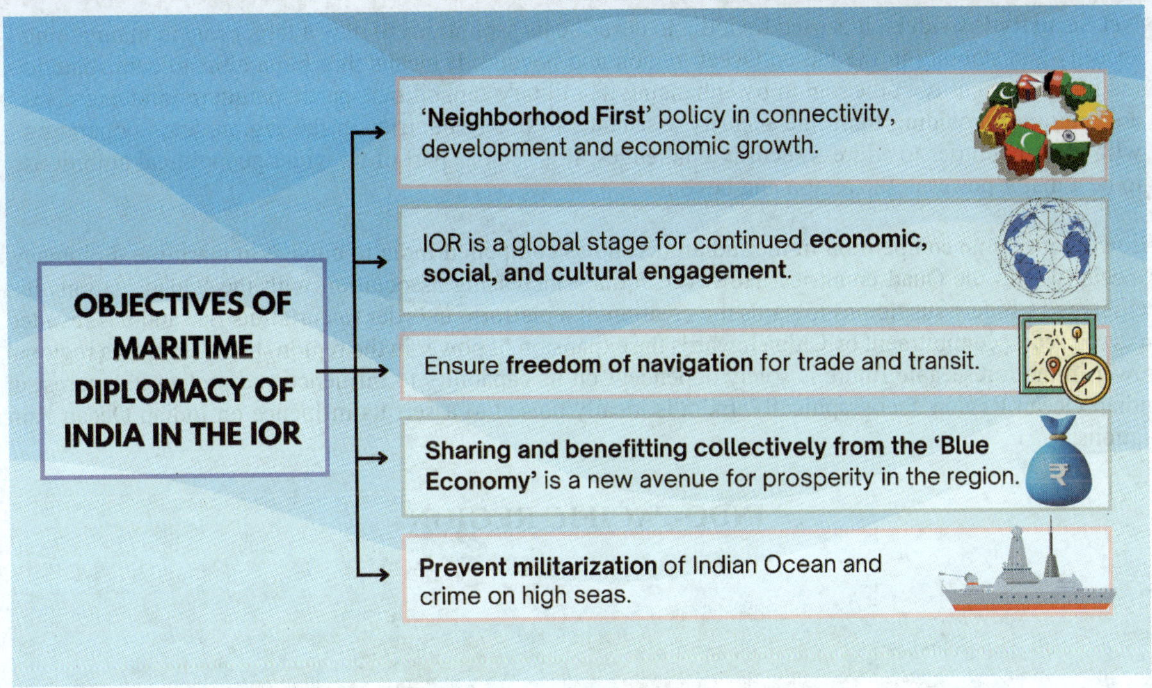

SIGNIFICANCE OF THE IOR

The Indian Ocean Region (IOR) continues to hold great significance for India -

- Economic Significance - The IOR is critical **economically** since it is an important trade route and hosts the world's most important strategic chokepoints, including the **Straits of Hormuz** and **Malacca**. Approximately **95 per cent of India's trade by volume** and **68 per cent of trade by value come via the Indian Ocean**. This includes trade with countries in the Middle East, Africa, and Southeast Asia. The Indian Ocean is also rich in natural resources, including oil and gas, and India has been actively pursuing exploration and extraction of these resources.
- Geostrategic and Geopolitical factors - India derives its **geo-strategic importance** principally from its geographic location in the Northern Indian Ocean. The Indian Ocean is strategically significant in terms of global geopolitics, as it **connects the major centers of power in the world**, including the **Middle East, Africa,** and **Asia**. The growing competition for influence in the region, particularly between China and India, has important implications for the global balance of power, and India's presence and influence in the Indian Ocean region will play a critical role in shaping the future of this competition.
- Security interests - The IOR faces its own diverse set **of traditional** and **non-traditional security challenges**, whether by non-state actors like smugglers, terrorists and pirates or by competitive naval states. The third-largest body of water in the world is currently facing turbulence over issues of contestation, mainly around power and influence over the region. From a military standpoint, India is a significant regional force in maintaining stability along critical Maritime or **Sea Lines of Communication (SLOC)**. As a result, India is developing as a key regional maritime force capable of affecting the future trajectory of the Indian Ocean Region's security environment.

  The two major regional powers, India and China, have been engaging with each other and the nations in the region in order to exert their share of influence over the ocean. While the engagement has not necessarily been overt, with the possibility of a military conflict being almost inconsequential, the rising infrastructure development including port development and military engagement including exercises and patrols, threatens to destabilize the region.
- International standing - India's influence and engagement in the region is seen as an important factor in **shaping the regional security order and promoting economic growth and development**. India has also been actively building partnerships and alliances in the region, including with countries such as the United States, Japan, and Australia, which has helped to enhance its influence and standing in the international community.

Net Security Provider– It is used by India to describe its aspirations to play a larger role in maintaining security and stability in the Indian Ocean region and beyond. It means that India aims to contribute to maintaining security in the region by enhancing its military capabilities, participating in joint exercises and training, providing maritime security assistance to other countries in the region, and cooperating with other countries to address security challenges. It is seen as part of its wider geopolitical ambitions to be a major power in the region and beyond.

Growing maritime competition in the Indian ocean has compelled India to engage in maritime diplomacy, especially with the Quad countries. However, India's increasing association with the 'Quad' nations has heightened Chinese suspicions towards the creation of a platform in order to curtail its rise and has resulted in even greater commitment by China towards the expansion of power in the region. India's rise as a regional power in the foreseeable future is solely dependent on its capability to influence and protect its interest in Indian Ocean Region. Geographically, India is ideally poised to assert its influence on Indian Ocean Rim Nations.

INDO-PACIFIC REGION

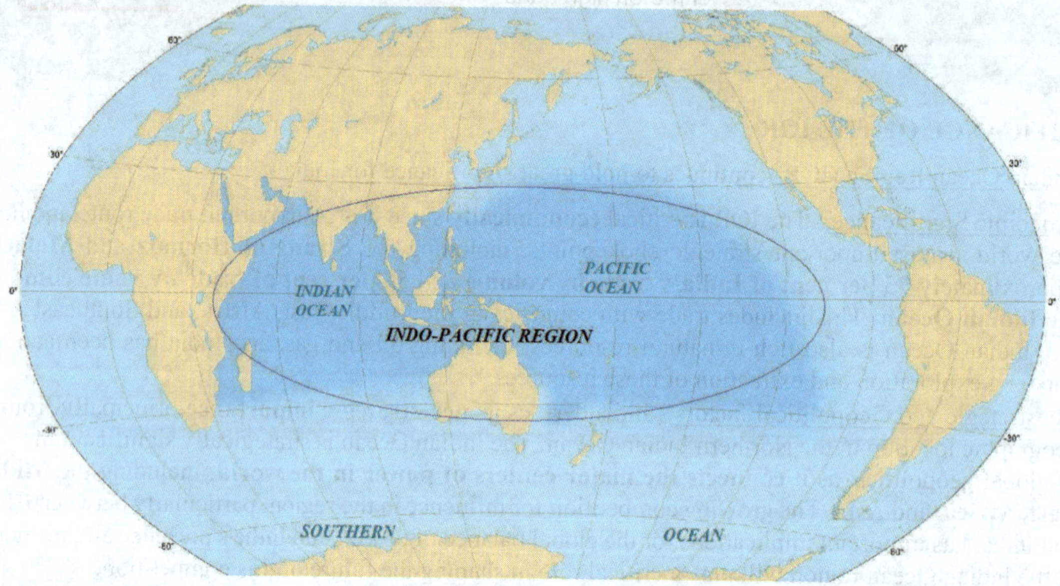

'The future of each of our nations, and indeed the world, depends on a free and open Indo-Pacific enduring and flourishing in the decades ahead.'

– President Joe Biden, Quad Leaders' Summit, September 2021

The 'Indo-Pacific' was previously used as a spatial concept to reference the bio-geographical region for the purposes of studies. The geopolitical gravity is shifting from the old 'Asia-Pacific' and giving way to 'Indo-Pacific' as the new framework for regional order. The term has widened to cover the geographical area between the western shores of the United States and the eastern coast of Africa. This simple change in nomenclature carries substantial conceptual significance. The scale of the Indo-Pacific presently, dilutes the ability of any one country unilaterally to shape the regional order. This confluence of the seas has resulted in economic and strategic interconnectedness of the interested parties and translates into mutual benefit and mutual vulnerability.

Asia Pacific	Indo-Pacific
It relates to the part of Asia that lies in the Pacific Ocean.	An integrated theatre that combines the Pacific Ocean and the Indian Ocean along with the landmasses surrounding them.
Coverage - North-East Asia, South-East Asia and Oceania (South-Western Pacific)	Coverage- Ranges from the coast of East Africa, across the Indian Ocean, to the Western Pacific, including countries like Japan, Australia and New Zealand.
Domain - Economic conception rather than a security related grouping	Domain – It has strategic and economic dimensions. It also includes maritime security and cooperation.
India is not considered a part of this region	India is an integral part of this region

Indo-Pacific Region

- **Population**: Over 70% of the world's population, including 58% of the youth
- **Economy**: 60% of the global GDP
- **Growth**: 2/3rd of global economic growth
- **Geography**: 65% of the world's oceans and 25% of its land

Over time the nations have come up with different perspectives on the Indo-Pacific construct and molded ways to better understand the changes to effectively balance their regional matters. Japanese Prime Minister Shinzo Abe's visionary speech in the Indian Parliament in 2007 on the ***'confluence of the two seas'*** became the guiding light for the concept of a **'Free and Open Indo-Pacific'**. Overtime, nations including India and the United States reiterated their 'commitment towards a free and open, connected, prosperous, secure and resilient Indo-Pacific'. The region has transformed into a geo-economic and geopolitical arena in this age of globalization where security and development form the backbone, with most nations contesting to gain an upper hand while remaining mutually dependent.

GLOBAL SHIFT TOWARDS THE INDO-PACIFIC REGION

Indo-Pacific Order

'Rules' are a primary constituent of all the major international orders and the Indo-Pacific has also followed suit. However, the regional actors are increasingly becoming disenchanted with such structures and are in serious disagreement over the kind of rules to be applied, the implementing authority and the resultant decisions surrounding default. The official details of the incipient Indo-Pacific rulebook give prominence to the principles of state sovereignty, non-interference and territorial integrity, which has been collectively termed as the **'Eastphalia'** by scholars. However, the rules-based order is becoming a contested framework mainly due to the hijacking of power by a select few and the consequential asymmetrical representation of interested parties.

Over the last decade itself, the Indo-Pacific region has seen strong and sustained economic growth spreading across the Pacific rim, South Asia, Southeast Asia, the Gulf region and coasts of Africa. The Indo-Pacific as a concept has been effectively modified by the nations to suit their diverse ambitions. For India, it is the next logical step beyond 'Act East', while for the US, it is viewed as a 'unified theatre' which provides a platform for global convergences against future threats. For Russia and Japan, it is a part of their strategic evolution towards the East, while for China, a strong influence in the region is critical in its rise as a global power. In general, the region plays an important role in trade and global economy for all major players. According to S. Jaishankar, "**Indo-Pacific is now a 'fact of life', and the question of convergence is therefore, more of a perception than of reality**". More importantly, the Indo-Pacific Region has been referred to as 'the theatre of World War III".

Main points of significance of the region –

(1) Strategic Hub for Economic Growth:

In 2023-2024, the Indo-Pacific continued to be a driving force in global economic growth. The region hosts some of the world's most dynamic economies, including China, India, Japan, and Australia. ASEAN countries also contribute to the momentum with their collective GDP growing steadily, driven by trade, manufacturing, and digital economies. The Indo-Pacific accounts for over **60% of the world's GDP and 46% of global merchandise trade**, making it an economic powerhouse. For instance, India and Australia's push to upgrade their **Economic Cooperation and Trade Agreement (ECTA)** highlights the growing economic interconnectivity across the region.

(2) Critical for Global Supply Chains:

The Indo-Pacific is a key player in global supply chains, especially in technology, manufacturing, and raw materials. Countries such as Japan and South Korea are expanding partnerships with Southeast Asian nations to diversify supply chains and reduce over-reliance on China. The region's importance is underscored by its **Sea Lines of Communication (SLOC),** which include crucial maritime routes like the **Mozambique Channel, Bab-el-Mandeb,** and **the Lombok Strait.** These chokepoints are vital for global trade, ensuring the smooth flow of goods and energy. India's "**Production Linked Incentive (PLI)**" scheme for electronics manufacturing aims to leverage its strategic position in these supply chains.

(3) Geopolitical Rivalry and Power Balancing:

The Indo-Pacific has become a battleground for geopolitical influence, particularly between the U.S. and China. The **U.S. Indo-Pacific Strategy of 2022-2023** aims to strengthen alliances with regional powers like Japan, India, and Australia (under the Quad framework) to counterbalance China's growing assertiveness. Despite the Permanent Court of Arbitration's 2016 ruling that invalidated China's claim in the South China Sea, China has continued militarizing the region, conducting aggressive patrols, and expanding island features. Its development of ports in ***Gwadar*** (Pakistan), ***Hambantota*** (Sri Lanka), and a naval base in ***Djibouti*** raises concerns about potential military use, increasing tensions and prompting countermeasures from regional powers.

(4) Military and Security Focus:

Security concerns have heightened in the Indo-Pacific due to rising tensions in the **South China Sea** and **the Taiwan Strait**. The U.S. has increased its military presence in the region, conducting **joint naval exercises** with Japan and Australia in 2023 to ensure freedom of navigation. India, recognizing the strategic importance of the region's maritime routes and SLOCs, has enhanced its naval capabilities, focusing on the Indian Ocean to counter China's increasing presence. The strategic positioning of ports and naval bases in the region, such as China's base in ***Djibouti***, has added to the escalating militarization, emphasizing the need for collaborative efforts from all nations involved.

(5) Energy and Maritime Security:

The Indo-Pacific is vital for global energy flows, with crucial maritime routes such as the **Strait of Malacca** facilitating a significant portion of the world's oil and gas transport. The region's expansive marine resources, including **hydrocarbons, methane hydrates, and rare earth metals**, have made it a focal point for energy security. In 2023-2024, energy security has become even more critical as the global push for decarbonization intensifies. Nations in the region, such as Australia, are investing heavily in renewable energy infrastructure and green hydrogen. India, along with ASEAN countries, is working on establishing a green energy corridor, while the extensive **Exclusive Economic Zones (EEZs)** are fostering a competitive environment for resource exploration.

(6) Environmental and Climate Challenges:

The Indo-Pacific is particularly vulnerable to climate change, with rising sea levels and extreme weather events threatening island nations like the **Maldives** and **Pacific Islands**. Regional cooperation on climate resilience has intensified. The **2023 Indo-Pacific Islands Forum** brought together countries to address shared environmental challenges, while nations like Japan and Australia have pledged financial and technological assistance to build resilience. Additionally, the region faces threats such as piracy, trafficking, and illicit fishing, which require coordinated efforts from governments to tackle these multidimensional challenges.

(7) Expanding Multilateralism:

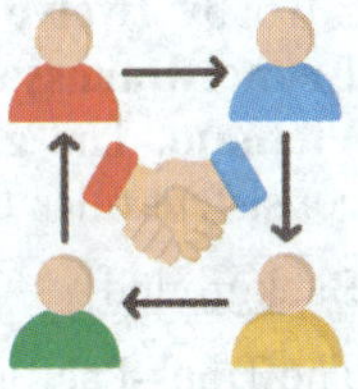

Multilateral engagement in the Indo-Pacific has grown in significance through platforms like the **Quadrilateral Security Dialogue (Quad)** and the **Association of Southeast Asian Nations (ASEAN)**. In 2024, the Quad—comprising India, Australia, Japan, and the U.S.—continued to focus on defense cooperation, vaccine diplomacy, and infrastructure development, reflecting its increasing role in regional security. The coordinated efforts to ensure freedom of navigation and a rules-based order in the region are partly a response to China's growing military assertiveness and disregard for international rulings in the South China Sea. These multilateral initiatives are pivotal for maintaining peace and stability.

(8) Digital Economy and Technological Innovation:

With rapid digital transformation in Indo-Pacific economies, the region has become a focal point for technological innovation. India's digital economy, projected to reach **$1 trillion by 2025**, is leading this shift alongside ASEAN countries, which are embracing e-commerce and digital trade. Investments in 5G infrastructure, AI, and cybersecurity in countries like South Korea and Singapore are creating new trade opportunities. The region's technological advancements are shaping global supply chains and governance structures, with new digital partnerships becoming critical for economic growth.

(9) China's Expanding Influence and Counterstrategies:

China's growing dominance in the Indo-Pacific, particularly through its aggressive stance in the **South China Sea**, continues to be a significant concern for regional powers. China's refusal to accept the **Permanent Court of Arbitration's** ruling and its militarization of disputed territories have provoked stronger opposition from countries like the **Philippines** and **Vietnam**. China's establishment of ports with dual-use potential in *Gwadar* and *Hambantota* underscores the strategic importance of the Indo-Pacific, prompting counterstrategies from India, the U.S., and Japan to ensure a free and inclusive region.

(10) Emerging Role of Smaller Nations:

Smaller Indo-Pacific nations are increasingly asserting their relevance in the region's geopolitical landscape. The security agreement between **Solomon Islands** and **China** in 2023 raised alarms about China's military ambitions in the Pacific, while Sri Lanka's economic crisis and debt dependence on China have highlighted vulnerabilities in the region. These smaller nations are critical as larger powers vie for influence, and their strategic positioning around key maritime routes makes them essential players in Indo-Pacific diplomacy.

In conclusion, the Indo-Pacific's rising significance in 2023-2024 is shaped by a combination of economic growth, geopolitical competition, technological innovation, and environmental challenges. Major powers, including the U.S., China, India, Japan, and Australia, continue to vie for influence in this critical region, recognizing its pivotal role in global trade, security, and governance.

Following China's push in the region, the **Pacific Island Forum (PIF)** was reborn. The problems which had previously created hurdles in functioning were resolved after a quorum of leaders met in June. The result of the meeting, the "Suva Agreement", enshrines a power-sharing agreement where the three subregions – Polynesia, Melanesia, and Micronesia – rotate the PIF secretary general role, supported by two newly created deputy secretary general positions.

TRANS-PACIFIC PARTNERSHIP (TPP)

The Trans-Pacific Partnership was a trade agreement which was concluded in 2015 and was signed in early 2016 by **twelve participating members**, which included **The United States of America, Australia, Brunei Darussalam, Canada, Chile, Japan, Malaysia, Mexico, Peru, New Zealand, Singapore and Vietnam**. The goal of this ambitious deal was to create a fully integrated economic area and establish consistent rules for global investment.

Background

The Trans-Pacific Partnership (TPP) was a trade agreement in 2005 between a group of Pacific Rim nations, including Brunei, Chile, New Zealand, and Singapore. Under President Bush's administration, the TPP expanded to twelve countries, including Canada, Japan, Malaysia, and Mexico. Under the Obama administration, the TPP was framed as the centerpiece of the USA's strategic pivot to the Asia-Pacific region. After negotiations, the participating members reached an agreement in 2015 and signed the pact in 2016. The TPP's size was seen as a game-changer, accounting for approximately 40% of global trade.

The agreement consisted of thirty chapters, covering tariffs on goods and services, intellectual property rights, e-commerce rules, labor and environmental standards, dispute resolution mechanisms, and other aspects of global trade. However, the deal faced opposition from the US Congress, including a loss of employment at home and an increase in trade deficit. **In 2017, the US withdrew from the TPP under President Trump. The remaining eleven signatories (TPP-11)** continued discussions to salvage the trade deal, leading to the signing of the Comprehensive and Progressive Agreement for Trans-Pacific Partnership (CPTPP) in 2018.

Despite the US withdrawal, the CPTPP has continued to attract interest from other countries. In February 2021, the UK applied for membership, followed by China in September 2021. Japan, the 2021 chair of the CPTPP, indicated that it would consult with member countries to respond to China's request. In July 2023, the CPTPP members formally accepted the United Kingdom as the 12th member. India, which had initially kept a safe distance from the grouping, is now eyeing the platform due to its increasing economic and geostrategic relevance. With its 12 members accounting for **approximately 40% of global trade,** the CPTPP remains a significant force in global trade, shaping the economic landscape of the Asia-Pacific region and beyond.

FORUM FOR INDIA-PACIFIC ISLANDS COOPERATION (FIPIC)

In Suva, Fiji, the Forum for India-Pacific Islands Cooperation (FIPIC) was founded in 2014 with the goal of advancing strategic collaboration, sustainable development, and reciprocal prosperity between India and the Pacific Islands. It gives governments a forum to have fruitful conversations, exchange best practices, and look into joint ventures that fit with their development goals. On May 22, 2023, in Papua New Guinea, the third FIPIC summit highlighted the importance of Pacific Island countries as "large ocean states" and India's backing for them. By supporting India's Act East Policy and its application, backed by Pacific Island nations, for a permanent seat at the UN Security Council, the FIPIC has the ability to impact international relations. Additionally, the forum acts as a check on China's expanding sway over the area.

SOUTH CHINA SEA

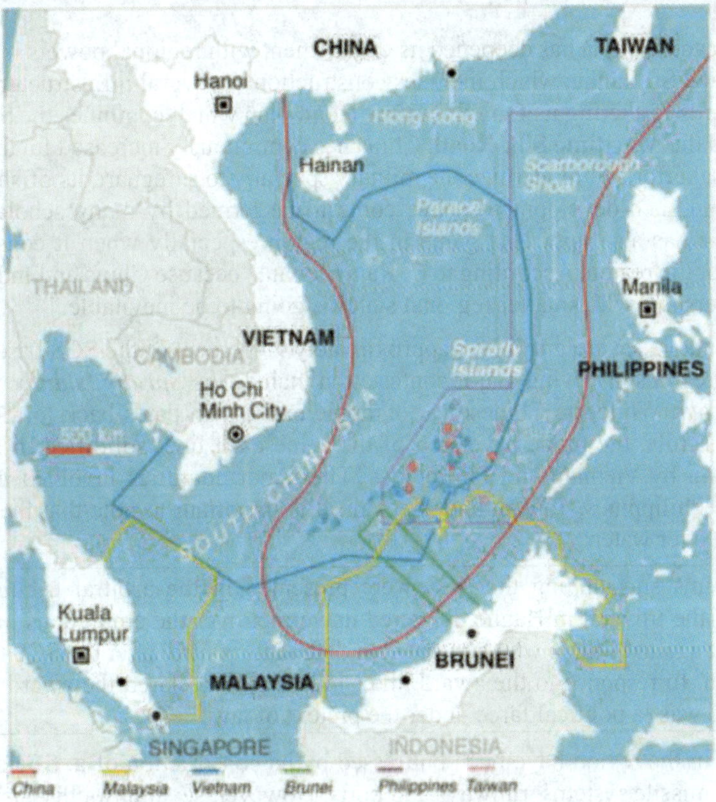

Source http://blogs.voanews.com/state-department-news/2012/07/31/challenging-beijing-in-the-south-china-sea/)

The **South China Sea (SCS)** is a marginal sea in the Pacific Ocean, littoral to the South-East Asian Nations. The SCS is a strategically important body of water and borders several nations including China, Vietnam, the Philippines, and Malaysia, among others.The SCS has over two hundred land features over varying proportions, many of which are presently contested by the bordering nations including China due to the overlapping claims over the territorial waters.

Relevance of South China Sea

- Commercial gateway for merchant shipping
- Rich source of hydrocarbons & natural resources
- Military presence
- Territorial Disputes

- The SCS is one of the **busiest shipping routes** in the world, with an estimated one-third of global shipping passing through its waters. The SCSis a crucial waterway with over US$ 5 trillion trade passing through the sea lanes in the region.
- The SCS is also **rich in natural resources** such as oil and natural gas, making it an important economic zone for countries in the region.
- Several countries, including China and the United States, have a military presence in the region, with naval vessels conducting regular patrols in the area. This has led to concerns about potential military conflict and escalation in the region.
- The SCS is the subject of several **territorial disputes**, particularly between China and neighboring countries such as Vietnam and the Philippines. China has claimed most of the South China Sea as its own, and has built several artificial islands in the region, leading to tensions and conflict with other countries in the area.

Over the past two decades, China has deepened its engagement with regional powers including Bangladesh, Myanmar, Pakistan and Sri Lanka, which includes construction of several infrastructure projects and ports. They are aimed towards furthering its **One Belt, One Road** plan which combines the **Silk Road Economic Belt** (land based) and the **Maritime Silk Road**. China has continuously increased funding in the region and has undertaken several efforts to modernize the military specially to safeguard its offshore investments and overseas interests, and such developments have come to be termed by many scholars as the '***string of pearls***'. In turn, India has also upped its game in the region especially when it considers itself the '**net security provider**' for the region. According to C. Raja Mohan, "because China and India are rising powers, their pursuit of partnerships with smaller regional states is going to be inevitable."

China claims 'indisputable sovereignty' over approximately 90 percent of the SCS based on its '**Nine Dash Line**' principle. The regions involving major contestation include the ***Spratly Islands***, ***Paracel Islands*** and the ***Scarborough Shoal***. While the Chinese cartographic expression dates back to a 1947 map produced during the Nationalist rule, the modern version of the 'nine dash line' solidified in 2009 in response to continental shelf claim by Vietnam and Philippines. The major countries involved in disputes include - China, Malaysia, the Philippines, Taiwan and Vietnam. It is important to note that the UNCLOS does not recognize such a line over water.

The most recent claims surrounding the SCS were presented in the arbitral tribunal of UNCLOS by Philippines. In 2016, the tribunal in Hague delivered its verdict over the ambiguous line over water in the SCS. The award went against China, who continued to defend its control over the SCS through its historical linkages to the region. In response to the award, the Chinese side declared the award null and void while adding that the award was 'a political farce under the pretext of law'.

The claims of China in the region have been buttressed by its construction of **artificial islands** which are being enhanced with missile systems, runways and ports. However, several South Asian nations have been discussing their grievances surrounding the unilateral changes undertaken by China on ground in the SCS. It is widely acknowledged in academic circles that 'while the world was busy tackling a global pandemic, China was working on enhancing its presence in this region'.

In the 55th ASEAN Foreign Ministers' Meeting (AMM) held in August 2022, the representatives 'reaffirmed the need to enhance mutual trust and exercise constraint in the conduct of activities that could escalate disputes or affect stability'.

India's approach

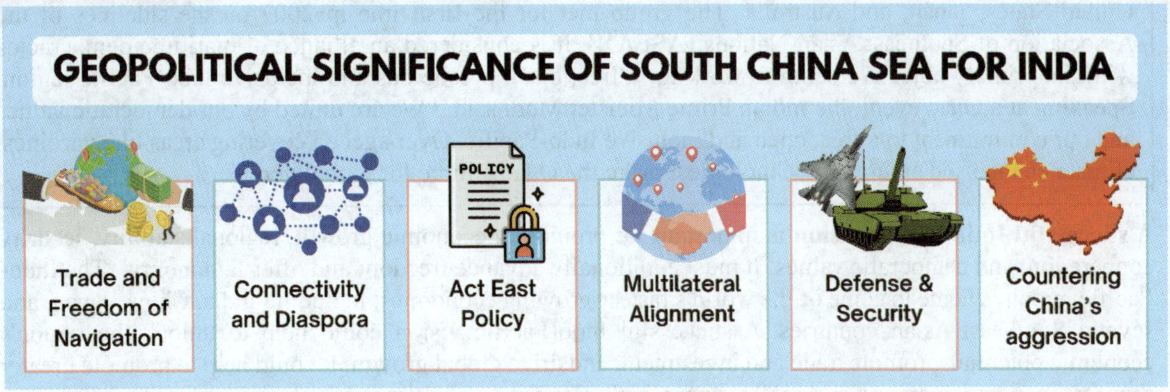

In a reply to a question in the Lok Sabha, Dr. Rajkumar Ranjan Singh, the Minister of State in the Ministry of External Affairs reiterated India's commitment towards international obligations and stated that, "**India supports freedom of navigation and overflight, and unimpeded commerce, based on the principles of international law, as reflected notably in the UNCLOS**. As a State Party to the UNCLOS, India urged all parties to show utmost respect for the UNCLOS, which establishes the international legal order of the seas and oceans."

India is heavily dependent on oil and gas imports, and the South China Sea is a major source of oil and natural gas. Any disruption in the region could have a significant impact on India's energy security.According to reports, **over 55 percent of India's trade with the Indo-Pacific region passes through the Malacca Straits and South China Sea.** Due to such wide stakes, New Delhi has reiterated its objective of keeping the sea lanes safe while pushing for a **rules-based order towards freedom of navigation.**

For the **Act East Policy** to be successful, India must ensure that the SCS region is stable and secure. In order to counter China's assertive stance and maintain its status as the 'Net Security Provider', India has been solidifying partnerships with countries in the region, including Vietnam and Philippines. Any conflict in the region, particularly involving China and the United States, could have a significant impact on **India's security environment**, given India's growing strategic partnership with the United States and its own territorial disputes with China.

The bigger goal of creating the **Indo-Pacific as a single maritime zone** would remain incomplete without securing stability in the South China Sea, which includes observing the Chinese manoeuvres in the region. Chinese aggression has prompted the other nations to project greater levels of activism in the region, both diplomatic and military. India is now seen partnering with the nations like the US to keep the Chinese aggression at bay.

Thus, the South China Sea remains a critical geopolitical flashpoint in the contemporary era, with ongoing disputes and competing claims to territory, natural resources, and strategic influence. The rise of Chinese presence in the critical waters has been at the cost of the neighboring states and the nations with interests in the region. The coercive attitude of China is bound to rattle diplomatic relations with other nations and may hamper its plan for supremacy. India is also waking up to the challenge and securing its interests while curtailing the rising dragon. The ASEAN group had also reaffirmed the need to pursue peaceful resolution of disputes in accordance with the universally recognized principles of international law, including the UNCLOS.

China's assertive and expansive foreign policy, backed by its massive economic and military prowess is being widely perceived as a potential threat to the rules-based multilateral order in the Indo-Pacific region. The idea of a **Quadrilateral Security Dialogue (or Quad)** comprising of the US, Japan, India and Australia, was resuscitated around 2017 with the objective of ensuring a free and open Indo-Pacific region based on the rule of law. While for India the Quad has been a prominent plurilateral platform to address contemporary challenges and opportunities in the Indo-Pacific, China has always viewed this grouping with suspicion and sees it as a strategy aimed at 'containing China'.

Quadrilateral Security Dialogue (QUAD) is the strategic dialogue between the four countries viz. India, United States, Japan, and Australia. The group met for the first time in 2007 on the sidelines of the Association of Southeast Asian Nations (ASEAN). It is considered an alliance of maritime democracies with the primary objective being to work for a free, open, prosperous and inclusive Indo-Pacific region. Speaking at a Quad event, the Indian Prime Minister Modi said, "We are united by our democratic values and our commitment to a free, open and inclusive Indo-Pacific. Over agenda covering areas like vaccines, climate change and emerging technologies, make the Quad a force for global good".

A **successful Indo-Pacific vision** is important for promoting economic growth, regional stability, security cooperation, and democratic values. It must additionally advance freedom and offer 'autonomy'. The Indo-Pacific region is home to some of the world's fastest-growing economies, including India, China, Japan, and several Southeast Asian countries. A successful Indo-Pacific vision could help to unlock the region's economic potential, promote trade and investment, and drive global growth. It could help to promote greater security cooperation among regional partners, including through initiatives such as joint military exercises and intelligence-sharing arrangements.

The Indo-Pacific region includes a number of democracies, such as India, Japan, and Australia. A successful Indo-Pacific vision could help to promote democratic values, such as the rule of law, freedom of speech, and human rights, in a region where these values are not universally respected. The region would thus continue to be an area of focus for many countries in the region, as well as for the broader global community.

INDIAN APPROACH – HYDRO DIPLOMACY

In 2003, PM Atal Vihari Vajpayee while laying down the contours of India's strategic area of interest and extended neighbourhood, had stated,

"As we grow in international stature, our defence strategies should naturally reflect our political, economic and security concerns, extending well beyond the geographical confines of South Asia. Our security environment ranges from the Persian Gulf to the Straits of Malacca across the Indian Ocean, includes Central Asia and Afghanistan in the North West, China in the North East and South East Asia. Our strategic thinking has also to extend to these horizons."

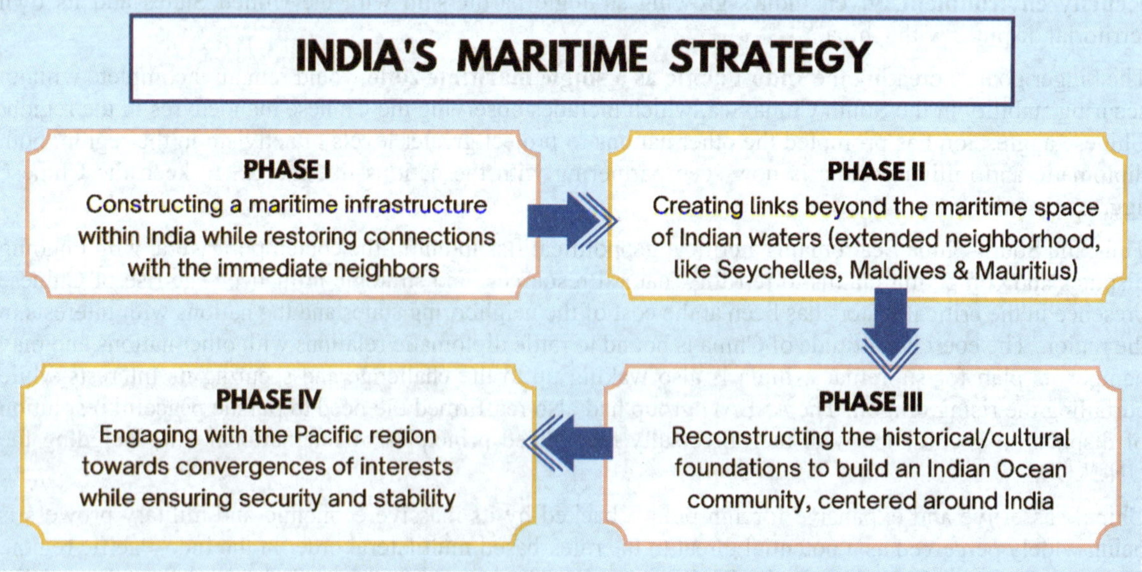

India calls for a free, open and inclusive order in the Indo-Pacific, based upon respect for sovereignty and territorial integrity of all nations, peaceful resolution of disputes through dialogue and adherence to

international rules and laws. India's concept of the Indo-Pacific is inclusive in nature and supports an approach that respects the right to freedom of navigation and overflight for all in the international seas.

The theme for the **12th Delhi Dialogue** (June 2022) – **"Building Bridges in Indo-Pacific"**, reinforced India's commitment to the region. It was held against the backdrop of several other nations converging their interests to build a rules-based global order. In order to get its India-Pacific strategy correct, India would have to secure its credibility in the Indian Ocean region, which not only is a natural arena for influence but also holds substantial security repercussions.

Given the increasing prominence of the Indio-Pacific issue in global discourse, the Ministry of External Affairs (India) established a new **'Indo-Pacific Division'** in 2019. This helps to demonstrate the nation's priority to the region and would assist in building coherence around this region.

Indo-Pacific Division deals with matters relating to the Indo-Pacific, India-ASEAN relations, East Asia Summit, Indian Ocean Rim Association (IORA), Asia-Europe Meeting (ASEM), Mekong-Ganga Cooperation (MGC) and Ayeyawady-Chao Phraya-Mekong Economic Cooperation Strategy (ACMECS).

SAGAR (SECURITY AND GROWTH FOR ALL IN THE REGION) INITIATIVE

"You cannot cross the sea merely by standing and staring at the water"

- Rabindranath Tagore

The Indian External Affairs Minister repeated these words in his speech at the fourth Indian Ocean Conference in 2019 to elaborate on the relevance of maritime geography, its changing facets and India's role in the ever-evolving Indian Ocean Region. India's policy on maritime cooperation in the Indian Ocean Region (IOR) has come to be based on the approach of **SAGAR - Security and Growth for All in the Region**, which was unveiled by Prime Minister Modi in 2015 during his tour of the Indian Ocean island states. While there hasn't been a single officially released document that lays down this approach, it has been reiterated through numerous maritime events and initiatives. S. Jaishankar has previously highlighted that India's SAGAR vision -was to be 'consultative, democratic and equitable'.

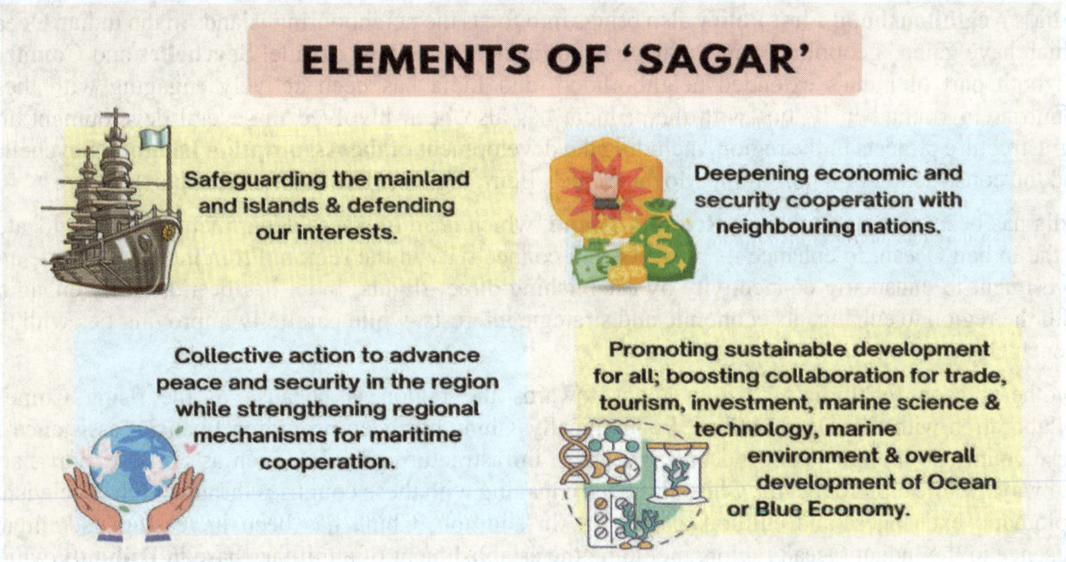

Indian Ocean Rim Association (IORA) is an inter-governmental organization which was formed with an aim of strengthening regional cooperation and sustainable development within the Indian Ocean region through its **23 Member States** and **10 Dialogue Partners**. India is a founding member of IORA that was established in 1997. The Secretariat is in Port Louis, Mauritius. The priority areas include – (1) Disaster Risk Management, Maritime Safety and Security (2) Science and Technology (3) Fisheries Management (4) Tourism and Cultural Exchanges (5) Academic (6) Trade and Investment Facilitation; with two cross-cutting issues – (i) Blue Economy and (ii) Women's Economic Empowerment. India has been an active participant of the IORA events, while occasionally playing host to conferences and capacity building workshops under the IORA umbrella.

Another significant development in the direction of maritime cooperation was the admission of India to the **Indian Ocean Commission (IOC)** as the fifth 'observer', with the others being China, Malta, European Union and International Organisation of La Francophonie (OIF). This step holds strategic significance and would allow collective engagement with the island nations of Western Indian Ocean (WIO) and help to sustain ties with another ally, France.

> The IOC was set up in 1982 and comprises Seychelles, Madagascar, Comoros, Mauritius, and Reunion Island, France's overseas territory in the region.

The year 2012 witnessed the launch of the **MASE Programme** by IOC and three other regional organizations. It is a European Union-funded programme to promote Maritime Security in Eastern and Southern Africa and Indian Ocean. The IOC has provided mechanism for the surveillance and control of the Western Indian Ocean, with two regional centres-

1) Regional Maritime Information Fusion Center (RMIFC), based in Madagascar: To deepen maritime domain awareness and promote information sharing.
2) Regional Coordination Operations Centre (RCOC), based in Seychelles: To facilitate jointly coordinated interventions at sea using information provided by the RMIFC.

The IOC has thus provided a deterrent against unabated maritime crime which wasn't being effectively handled by independent or national forces alone. As an 'observer' to the IOC, India can benefit from the resources provided by the IOC, while it also has much to contribute in terms of extending the expertise regarding the region. The sub-regional efforts including those of the IOC can greatly benefit India in developing its maritime domain awareness and capacity building to safeguard its people and assets in the region.

Rising significance of the neighbouring islands

India's **Neighbourhood First Policy** also brings into focus the neighbouring islands in the Indian Ocean which have gained geopolitical and strategic significance in the past decade. **Seychelles** and **Comoros** are both part of India's extended neighborhood, and India has been actively engaging with these countries to strengthen its ties with them. India has also been involved in several development and infrastructure projects in the region, including the development of the **Assumption Island** in Seychelles and the construction of a port in the Mozambique's Beira region (mainly for coal export).

India has been engaging with the **Reunion Island**, which is an overseas department of France located in the Indian Ocean, to enhance its presence and connectivity in the region. From increasing trade and investment to enhancing connectivity by establishing direct flights, India has been actively engaging with the region to enhance its economic and strategic interests, while parallelly improving ties with the French Government.

Another reason for India's shift in focus towards the region is because of the rising Chinese collaboration with the island nations. Economically, China has been providing financial assistance to these countries through loans and investments in infrastructure projects, such as ports, airports, and highways; while diplomatically, China has been engaging with these countries through high-level visits, diplomatic exchanges, and cultural exchanges. In addition, China has been increasing its military presence in the Indian Ocean region, including the establishment of a military base in **Djibouti**, which is located near the entrance to the Red Sea.

OPPORTUNITIES IN FUTURE

Whether it is security perspective, economic interests, geopolitical scenarios or other influential factors, the maritime region would play a critical role in molding the international and bilateral relations in future. Addressing the challenges and opportunities presented by the maritime region requires effective international cooperation and coordination, and the region will continue to be a critical area of focus for the international community. Therefore, the global community should ensure cooperation in the region for greater stability that could enhance prosperity for all.

The Indian Ocean is increasingly becoming a focal point in the 21st century, serving as a significant arena for global strategic pursuits and regional military interests of various world and regional powers. The extent to which India evolves as a comprehensive national power relies heavily on its ability to develop and showcase its maritime capabilities.

India with a coastline of over 7,500 kilometers, cannot understate the significance of maritime diplomacy in pursuing national interests. The maritime diplomacy will be critical for India's security, economic interests, regional influence, and environmental sustainability. However, diplomacy will only work if India is able to keep pace with development of maritime capabilities. Effective maritime diplomacy would help India build partnerships and alliances with other countries in the region, promote greater regional stability and security, and enhance India's strategic importance on the global stage.

11

MULTI-ALIGNMENT & REGIONAL GROUPINGS

FROM BILATERALISM TO MULTI-ALIGNMENT

When contrasted with unilateralism, which relates to the actions of a single party, **bilateralism** concerns relations or policies of joint action between two parties or nations. This form of diplomacy has been in place for centuries and continues to form a key building block of the international relations in the present day and age. Bilateralism works by recognizing differences and taking prompt action to minimize issues between the two nations. Post-World War II (WWII), the **multilateral system** was designed and put in place to foster cooperation among states. The basis of the approach was, 'principles of conduct', 'indivisibility' and expectations of 'diffused reciprocity'. The multilateral architecture which began as a set of frameworks for effective functioning, gradually grew to encompass issues of economic development, international security, human rights, global health and environmental issues. Several formal and informal forums cropped up over the next decades, which included the UN, World Bank, WTO, OECD etc. The multilateral system gained a new momentum around the end of the Cold War due to the acceleration of global exchanges and the enhanced multistakeholder approaches allowed for further participation of new actors, which included the civil society organisations and the private enterprises.

'Minilaterals' are partnerships between like-minded nations, which are currently proving to be more effective in international diplomacy than much larger multilateral arrangements. For example, the I2U2 grouping (India, Israel, the UAE, and the United States).

Bilateralism	Multilateralism	Multi-Alignment
It consists of the political, economic, or cultural relations between two sovereign or independent states.	Collaboration between several countries (at least three), in formal or informal institutional settings, to discuss issues of mutual interest and coordinate their policies.	The policy of creating parallel alliances, encompassing not only military aspects but also addressing a range of national interests, including tangible security and development concerns as well as intangible ideological factors.
Bilateral diplomacy works with individual foreign states on a variety of topics to further one's own domestic and international goals. It helps to reduce conflict and secure mutual trust.	Focus is on generalized principles of conduct which ensure that decision-making in international governance institutions is not based on the particularistic interests of a few or powerful players.	This philosophy is meant to strengthen multilateral partnerships and seeks to align with multiple blocs (rivals) in order to gain influence or secure interests.

Examples: Free Trade Agreements (FTA) or Foreign Direct Investment (FDI) agreements between two nations or cultural ties between India and Bhutan etc.	Examples: United Nations, South Asian Association for Regional Cooperation (SAARC), Gulf Cooperation Council (GCC) etc.	Examples: India's involvement in Shanghai Cooperation Organisation (SCO) and BRICS and parallel engagement with Quadrilateral Security Dialogue (Quad).

Recent geopolitical changes have led to a shift toward multi-alignment. Unlike **non-alignment**, which focused on not taking sides in conflicts and promoting peace, **multi-alignment involves engaging with multiple, sometimes opposing, parties or blocs in global rivalries**. This approach has gained importance, particularly after the COVID-19 pandemic, which saw nations closing borders and focusing inward. While some experts argue that bilateralism better serves national interests, others advocate for mutually beneficial multilateral frameworks.

However, recent decades have seen declining trust in multilateralism and growing dissatisfaction with the liberal international order. The post-World War II vision of a universal multilateral system that would address global issues equitably has not materialized, with divisions between the Global North and South still persisting.

Despite these challenges, multi-alignment and multilateralism are not mutually exclusive; they should operate together as key geopolitical strategies. For example, India's involvement in both the Quad and BRICS, despite their differing agendas, demonstrates how multilateralism and multi-alignment can overlap. While Quad focuses on countering Chinese aggression in the Indo-Pacific, BRICS represents the developing world's perspective, including China and Russia. India's participation in these opposing groups highlights its strategic approach to global engagement.

INDIAN CONTEXT

1. **Non-Alignment in the Cold War Era** - During the Cold War, India adopted a policy of "non-alignment," which meant not joining either of the two superpower camps (the US or the Soviet Union). This was intended to maintain India's strategic autonomy and avoid being drawn into global conflicts. However, this strict policy saw a shift in 1971 when India signed the Indo-Soviet Treaty of Peace, Friendship, and Cooperation. The treaty marked a partial alignment with the Soviet Union, as India realized that the US would not support it or deter China in the event of a conflict.
2. **Criticism and Adaptation** - India's closer ties with the Soviet Union were criticized as being contrary to the principles of non-alignment, of which India was a founding member. Despite this, India maintained its relationships with the US and China, ensuring that it continued to be seen as a non-aligned nation overall. This approach marked the beginning of India's gradual shift towards "multi-alignment.".

> ***Multi-alignment*** involves engaging with multiple global powers, even those with conflicting interests. It's important to note that multi-alignment is distinct from multilateralism. ***Multilateralism*** refers to India's engagement with international institutions and forums, and for India, it is an extension of its multi-alignment strategy. Both serve to protect and advance Indian interests on the global stage.

3. **Shift Towards Multi-Alignment** - In the last decade, under Prime Minister Modi, India has reoriented its foreign policy from strict non-alignment to a more flexible and proactive approach known as "multi-alignment." This strategy has been praised by experts as it allows India to navigate the complex geopolitical landscape effectively. India's multilateral engagements, such as participation in the United Nations, the World Trade Organization, and regional groups like the Shanghai Cooperation Organization (SCO), complement its multi-alignment policy by projecting soft power and addressing global challenges.
4. **Reformed Multilateralism** - Prime Minister Modi, during the 20th Summit of the SCO in 2020, emphasized the need for "reformed multilateralism." This concept focuses on ensuring that multilateral institutions, like the United Nations, reflect current global realities and give India a more significant role

in decision-making processes. Reformed multilateralism aligns with India's multi-alignment strategy, ensuring that India can continue to balance its relationships with major powers like China, Russia, and the USA, while advocating for reforms in global governance structures.

MAJOR GLOBAL GROUPINGS

NORTH ATLANTIC TREATY ORGANISATION (NATO)

Military and security alliances have historically been a tool to counterbalance a dominant power or a perceived threat surrounding it. With such an aim in mind, the North Atlantic Treaty Organization (NATO) was established in 1949 to balance the rising Soviet power and aggression post World War II. NATO is a transatlantic security alliance composed of thirty member nations, including the United States of America. While it was originally created to deter Russian aggression, it gradually became a pillar of US-Europe military cooperation. Since the close of the Cold War, NATO along with its allies have taken on a wide range of missions and have conducted several security operations in countries like Afghanistan, Iraq and Libya.

Usually, security alliances tend to collapse once the threat perceptions change, however, even after the demise of the Union of Soviet Socialist Republics (USSR), NATO continued to thrive after members debated on the future direction of the alliance and made appropriate changes. U.S. Senator Richard Lugar had stated in a 1993 speech that "the common denominator of all the new security problems in Europe is that they all lie beyond NATO's current borders". Hence, with the changing geopolitical scenario, the idea of 'collective defence' seemed too restrictive. The idea to restructure NATO to hedge against an uncertain future was effectively summarized by Margaret Thatcher when she had remarked that, "You don't cancel your home insurance policy just because there have been fewer burglaries on your street in the last 12 months".

COLLECTIVE DEFENCE

Article V of the North Atlantic Treaty - An armed attack against one or more [member states] in Europe or North America shall be considered an attack against them all.

NATO is a **consensus-based alliance** in which decisions taken are unanimous. The individual states or subgroups of allies can initiate action outside the ambit of the alliance. Additionally, the member states are not coerced into participating in every NATO operation.

Over the years the Russian leaders have observed with mounting resentment as the NATO has nearly doubled its membership since the close of the Cold War. According to the pledges made in the early 1990s, the alliance was not to expand into the former Soviet bloc. Initially, the NATO members were split on the issue of expansion of the alliance eastwards. The dispute between Russia and NATO began escalating when the alliance opened its doors to ex-Soviet Republics and former **Warsaw Pact** states starting late 1990s including Hungary, Poland, Latvia, Romania and Slovenia among others. While the two continued to exist parallelly, more nations were being brought under the NATO's umbrella, including Albania and Croatia (2009), Montenegro (2017) and North Macedonia (2020). However, fears of a conflict grew stronger when the alliance stated its intent to admit Georgia and Ukraine sometime in future. The Russian officials however have warned that such a development would "be an act of hostility against Russia". Eventually, a more direct confrontation was witnessed when NATO got involved in the Russia-Ukraine war.

Developments in 2024

Sweden became the most recent member of NATO on **March 7, 2024**, making it the **32nd member** of the alliance. In **April 2023**, the **Republic of Finland** had become the **31st member** of the NATO.

The major repercussions of the expansion of NATO include the following –

(1) Increased Security for Member States

- Sweden's entry into NATO bolsters the alliance's presence in Northern Europe and the Baltic region, which has become an area of heightened strategic importance due to tensions with Russia. Sweden's geography, with its proximity to Russia and control over key areas such as the Baltic Sea, enhances NATO's ability to defend its northern flank and safeguard Baltic countries.
- As a NATO member, Sweden benefits from Article 5 of the NATO treaty, which ensures collective defense, meaning an attack on one member is considered an attack on all. This security guarantee provides a strong deterrence against potential aggressors, particularly Russia, whose actions in Ukraine have raised concerns throughout Europe.

(2) Worsening Relations with Russia

- Russia has consistently opposed NATO's eastward expansion, viewing it as a threat to its security. The inclusion of Sweden, along with earlier expansions to the Baltic States and Eastern Europe, has been a major source of friction. Moscow may perceive NATO's enlargement as encirclement, leading to heightened military posturing, aggressive rhetoric, and retaliatory actions.

- Russia could increase its military presence in regions bordering NATO countries, such as Kaliningrad or the Arctic, and strengthen its alliances with countries outside NATO, like Belarus. This could result in a further militarization of Europe, increasing the risk of direct confrontation or miscalculation.

(3) Strengthening of NATO's Capabilities

- Sweden's military, though traditionally neutral, is highly developed and adds significant capacity to NATO. Sweden has modern air and naval forces, with expertise in submarine warfare and Arctic defense, which strengthens NATO's collective military capabilities in the North Atlantic and the Arctic.
- Sweden is also a major defense technology exporter and has significant expertise in areas such as aerospace, surveillance, and cybersecurity, which could benefit NATO's overall defense infrastructure and future military developments.

(4) Enhanced Security Cooperation in the Nordic Region

- Sweden's accession to NATO, following Finland's recent membership, leads to a more unified defense posture in the Nordic region. Norway, Denmark, Iceland, Sweden, and Finland, all now part of NATO, can work more cohesively on regional security matters, including joint military exercises, intelligence sharing, and Arctic security.
- With both Sweden and Finland in NATO, the Baltic Sea effectively becomes a "NATO lake." This strategic advantage allows for greater control over this critical maritime region and facilitates the movement of NATO forces and resources in the event of a crisis.

(5) Shift in European Security Architecture

- Sweden's decision to join NATO marks a significant shift from its long-standing policy of military non-alignment, which dates back to the Napoleonic Wars. This shift signals a broader transformation in European security architecture, where formerly neutral or non-aligned states are re-evaluating their positions in response to growing external threats, particularly from Russia.
- As a member of both the European Union and NATO, Sweden's inclusion may also lead to greater integration between the two organizations in areas like defense coordination and countering hybrid threats. This could accelerate discussions on a more unified European defense identity, with closer cooperation between NATO and EU security mechanisms.

(6) Implications for Global Security

- NATO's expansion, particularly in the context of growing US-China competition and Russia's opposition, contributes to a more polarized global security environment. Countries outside NATO, particularly in Asia and Africa, may feel compelled to align more clearly with one side, leading to greater geopolitical divisions and the potential for new alliances to emerge as counterbalances to NATO.
- Countries like Ukraine and Georgia, which have expressed interest in joining NATO but face strong opposition from Russia, may see Sweden's accession as a positive sign but also as a potential source of increased tensions. Russia has already made it clear that it will not tolerate further NATO expansion into what it considers its sphere of influence, potentially exacerbating conflicts in regions such as the Black Sea.

(7) Economic and Defence Industry Effects

- NATO's expansion will likely lead to further increases in defense spending, particularly from new members like Sweden, which will need to meet NATO's defense expenditure requirements. This could stimulate the defense industries of NATO countries, particularly in sectors like aerospace, cybersecurity, and military technology.
- Russia's response to NATO's expansion, including potential economic sanctions or trade disruptions, could have broader economic repercussions. Countries closely tied to both Russia and NATO members may face difficult economic choices as they navigate the fallout from increased tensions.

(8) Impact on Arctic Geopolitics

Sweden's NATO membership may also influence Arctic geopolitics. The Arctic is increasingly becoming a contested region, with Russia, NATO countries, and other global powers vying for influence. Sweden's accession strengthens NATO's presence in the Arctic, a region rich in resources and strategic shipping routes, potentially leading to more military deployments and competition in the far north.

India's engagement with the North Atlantic Treaty Organization (NATO) has been limited, as **India is NOT a member of NATO** and is not located in the North Atlantic region. India's non-alignment policy has been a constraint on its engagement with NATO, as it seeks to maintain neutrality in conflicts between major powers.

ASSOCIATION OF SOUTHEAST ASIAN NATIONS (ASEAN)

The Association of South-East Asian Nations (ASEAN) was formed on 8 August 1967 in Bangkok, Thailand, through the signing of the ASEAN declaration, also known as the Bangkok declaration. It serves as a regional organization for promoting economic and social development in Southeast Asia. The founding members of ASEAN were Indonesia, Malaysia, Philippines, Singapore, and Thailand. Subsequently, Brunei, Vietnam, Laos, Myanmar, and Cambodia joined the group.

In 2003, ASEAN moved along the path of the EU by agreeing to establish an ASEAN Community comprising three pillars, namely –

(i) ASEAN Political-Security Community (APSC)
(ii) ASEAN Economic Community (AEC)
(iii)ASEAN Socio-Cultural Community (ASCC)

The **objectives** of ASEAN were primarily focused on **enhancing economic growth to achieve social progress and cultural development**. Additionally, the organization aimed to **foster regional peace and stability by upholding the rule of law and the principles outlined in the United Nations Charter**.

ASEAN countries have celebrated what has become known as the 'ASEAN Way', a form of interaction that is informal, non-confrontationist and cooperative. The respect for national sovereignty is critical to the functioning of ASEAN.

India's Association

ASEAN forms an integral part of India's 'Act East Policy'. India's engagement with ASEAN is aimed at enhancing its presence and connectivity in the region and promoting economic cooperation, strategic partnerships, and cultural exchanges.

India is NOT a member of ASEAN

India is part of the **ASEAN Plus Six** grouping, which includes China, Japan, South Korea, New Zealand and Australia

India joined ASEAN as a **sectoral dialogue partner** in 1992, and due to shared interests, ASEAN extended an invitation to India to become a **full dialogue partner** at the fifth ASEAN Summit in Bangkok in 1995. **India also became a member of the ASEAN Regional Forum (ARF) in 1996.** Furthermore, in 2010, India and ASEAN signed a Free Trade Agreement that came into effect. Although India participated in negotiations to join the Regional Comprehensive Economic Partnership (RCEP) in 2020, it ultimately chose not to be a part of it.

GROUP OF SEVEN (G-7)

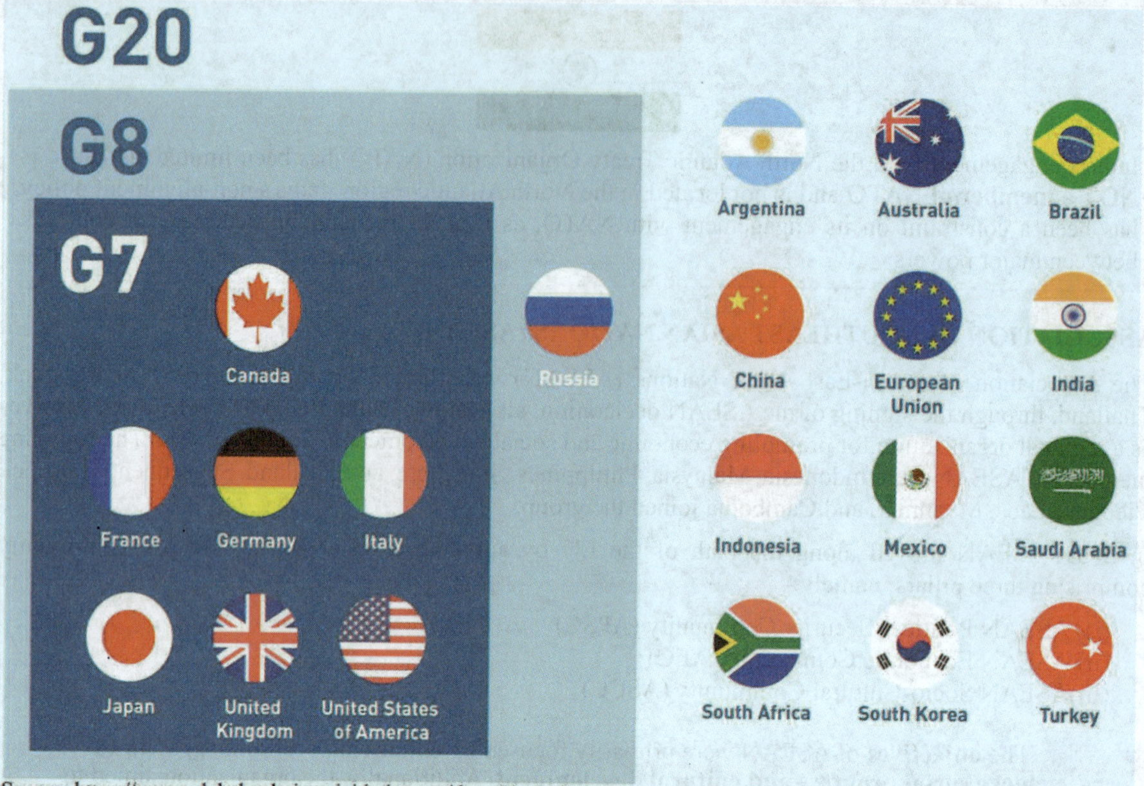

Source: https://www.global-solutions-initiative.org/the-g20-t20/

The **G7** is an **informal grouping** of seven of the **world's advanced economies**- Canada, France, Germany, Italy, Japan, the United Kingdom, the United States. The European Union (EU) is not a member of the G7 but has attended the summits since 1977.

Founded	G7 was originally known as the "**World Economic Summit**," was established in **1975** by former French President Valéry Giscard d'Estaing and then Federal Chancellor Helmut Schmidt.
Secretariat/HQ	G7 is not based on a treaty and has **no permanent secretariat**. The group's presidency rotates annually among the seven member countries.
Members	Canada, France, Germany, Italy, Japan, the United Kingdom, the United States
Summits	• The 1st Summit was held in 1976 in Puerto Rico • The **49th Summit was held in 2023 in Hiroshima, Japan**; the focus issues included - global security, the war in Ukraine, nuclear disarmament, climate change, economic resilience, and promoting a free and open Indo-Pacific. • **The 50th Summit was held in June 2024, in Borgo Egnazia, Italy**; the focus areas included – support to Ukraine, climate change, economic security, artificial intelligence, health & food security and building partnerships to promote resilient supply chains and reduce critical dependencies.

The G7 initially consisted of the heads of state and government from Germany, France, the UK, Italy, Japan, and the USA, collectively known as the '***Group of Six***'. The purpose of the summit was to **address global**

economic challenges, specifically the issues of the 1970s such as the first oil crisis and the breakdown of the fixed exchange rate system known as **Bretton Woods.**

The **Group of Five (G5)** consisting of the **major industrial nations** was established in mid 1970s to coordinate the economic policies of **France, Germany, Japan, the United Kingdom, and the United States**. The nations coordinated through the Plaza Agreement of September 1985. However, G5 was subsequently superseded by the G7.

Canada was invited to join in 1976 and the Group of Seven met for the first time for the 1976 Summit in Puerto Rico. The **European Community** (now European Union) conducted its first talks with the G7 in London in 1977. The European Community (now European Union) has regularly participated in all working sessions since the Ottawa Summit in 1981. As of 2022, the G7 continues to function as a forum for discussion of economic and financial issues among the major industrial countries.

IMPORTANT FACTS:

- Association bound by shared values whose members are committed to freedom and human rights, democracy and the rule of law, prosperity and sustainable development.
- Decisions made by the group are **not legally binding** but have tangible political impact.
- Focus Areas -
  (a) Monetary Policy issues
  (b) Foreign Policy
  (c) Security Policy
- Consists of **40% of the Global GDP** and accounts for **1/10th of the world's population.**

CASE OF RUSSIA

In 1991, Soviet General Secretary Gorbachev was invited to talks on the fringes of the London Summit. The **Group of Eight** was constituted after Russia became a member after the Birmingham Summit in 1998. The group **reverted to G7** in 2014 after Russia violated Ukraine's sovereignty and territorial integrity (Annexation of Crimea).

RELEVANCE OF G7

Economic Leadership: The G7 countries collectively represent a significant portion of the global economy. Their actions and policies can have a profound impact on global economic stability and growth. It provides a platform to coordinate their economic policies, address global economic challenges, promote international trade and prevent economic crisis.

Global Governance: The G7 addresses a wide range of global challenges, including climate change, poverty, and inequality. The G7 supports multilateralism and the role of international organizations in addressing global challenges.

Shaping the Global Agenda: It helps to set the global agenda, identifying key issues that require international attention and cooperation. The G7's collective voice can significantly influence international debates on various topics, from trade to climate change. They also wield significant soft power which could eb used to promote their values and interests on a global scale.

The **50th Summit (2024)** that was held in Borgo Egnazia (Italy), focused on several key issues –

1. **Ukraine:** G7 leaders reaffirmed their support for Ukraine in its fight against Russia's invasion, imposing further sanctions and providing military aid.
2. **Economic Challenges:** The G7 addressed issues such as inflation, supply chain disruptions, and the global debt crisis, seeking to promote economic stability and growth.
3. **Climate Change:** G7 members committed to ambitious climate goals, including phasing out unabated coal power and increasing renewable energy capacity.
4. **Global Health:** The G7 focused on strengthening global health systems and addressing health security challenges, particularly in the context of pandemics.
5. **Food and Health Security:** G7 leaders discussed strategies to address food insecurity and malnutrition, particularly in developing countries.
6. **Supporting Developing Countries:** The G7 pledged to scale up support for developing countries, including through debt relief and infrastructure investment.

India & the 'Group of Seven'

Although **India is NOT a formal member of the G7 grouping**, India's increasing presence in the global conversations has been acknowledged by the G7 grouping which has been inviting the country to attend its Summits as a guest regularly, with the **2024 G7 Summit** being no exception. This reflects India's growing economic and diplomatic influence on the global stage –

India is NOT a member of G7

(a) **Shared Interests**: India shares many of the G7 countries' interests, including economic growth, climate change, and global governance.

(b) **Cooperation on Global Issues**: India collaborates with the G7 on various global challenges, such as counterterrorism, humanitarian aid, and sustainable development.

The possibility of India joining the G7 in the future is a subject of ongoing debate. While some argue that India's economic size and global influence warrant its inclusion, others contend that the group's membership should remain exclusive to developed economies. As India's economy continues to grow and its global role expands, its relationship with the G7 is likely to evolve. While the world is getting increasingly polarized, India's engagement with the G7 is a step towards its vision of a truly multipolar world including the achievement of other vital self-interests

SOUTH ASIAN ASSOCIATION FOR REGIONAL COOPERATION (SAARC)

Founded	1985 with the signing of the SAARC Charter in Dhaka on 8th December 1985
Secretariat/HQ	Kathmandu, Nepal
Members	Afghanistan, Bangladesh, Bhutan, **India**, the Maldives, Nepal, Pakistan and Sri Lanka
Observers	Australia, China, European Union, Japan, Iran, Mauritius, Myanmar, South Korea and USA
Summits	• The 1st Summit was held in1985 in Dhaka, Bangladesh • The 18th Summit was held in 2014 in Nepal • The 19th Summit was to be held in 2016 in Pakistan but was cancelled.

For long, South Asia had been a region which boasted of rich resources, both human and natural, but remained neglected in terms of unity and security which made it increasingly volatile and unstable. The lack of collaboration between the nations has been used to their advantage by many, including terrorist groups, drug cartels, human trafficking agencies among others.

Eventually, it was in **November 1980 that the idea of regional cooperation for the region was first raised**. After consultations between the representatives of the South Asian nations, the foreign secretaries of the seven founding countries, Bangladesh, Bhutan, India, Maldives, Nepal, Pakistan, and Sri Lanka met for the first time in Colombo in April 1981. Soon, five broad areas for regional cooperation were identified.

In **August 1983**, a significant meeting took place in New Delhi for two main reasons. Firstly, the **adoption of the Declaration on South Asian Association Regional Cooperation (SAARC)** occurred during the meeting. Secondly, the **formal launch of the Integrated Program of Action (IPA)** took place, focusing on five areas of cooperation: agriculture, rural development, telecommunications, meteorology, and health and population activities.

OBJECTIVES

- Promoting the welfare of the people of South Asia
- Strengthening collective self-reliance
- Promoting active collaboration and mutual assistance in various fields
- Cooperating with international and regional organizations

India is a member of SAARC

Areas of Cooperation

The IPA launched in 1983 had initially referred to five areas of cooperation, but eventually, more areas was amalgamated within the ambit. Presently, **eleven areas of cooperation** have been agreed on between the member nations.

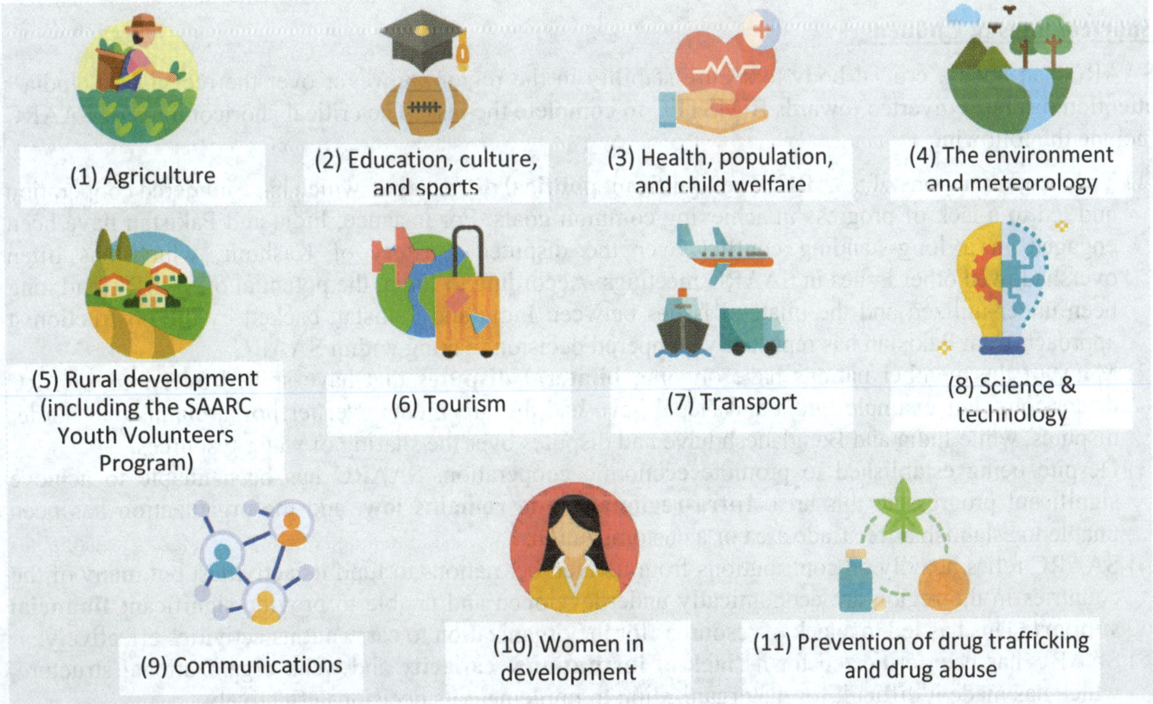

Principal Organs

- The meetings of the grouping are held at the **Summit** level, usually on an annual basis. The first Summit was held in1985 in Dhaka, Bangladesh and the last, 18th Summit was held in 2014 in Nepal.
- The Foreign Ministers of Member States together comprise **the Council**, which generally meets twice a year.
- There also exists a **Standing Committee of Foreign Secretaries** to provide overall monitoring and coordination and mobilize resources and approve financing.
- The SAARC Secretariat was set up in Kathmandu in 1987 to fulfill the purpose of coordinating and overseeing the implementation of SAARC initiatives and acting as a communication bridge between SAARC and other international organizations. The secretary-general is chosen by the Council of Ministers based on a rotational system and serves a non-renewable term of three years.

Significance

- As of 2024, SAARC approximately represents **3% of the total land area** worldwide, approximately **21% of the global population**, and contributes around **5.21% (US$ 4.47 trillion)** to the global economy.
- The member countries are often referred to as "natural allies" due to their shared geographical features, including the Himalayas and the Indian Ocean, which serve as natural boundaries. The group is working to enhance peace, prosperity and stability within the region.
- While India had been initially apprehensive in joining the regional association, when western powers began eyeing the region to enhance their influence, India eventually had to put its foot down.
- Before becoming a member, India had proposed two principles – (1) that the organization **would not discuss bilateral issues** and (2) that all the decisions would be taken based on **unanimity**. Such a stance allowed the organisation to work independently of the bilateral relations between the member nations.

The 19th Summit, which was to be held in Pakistan in 2016 had to be cancelled when 6 countries (all except Nepal and Pakistan) pulled out of the summit in the aftermath of the Uri attack in India. The regional grouping has not been very effective since 2016 and all efforts to resuscitate it have been futile. India continues to maintain that unless Pakistan stops terrorist activities in India, there will be no dialogue and it will not participate in SAARC Summits.

Shortcomings & Challenges

SAARC had been a crucial body to secure stability in the region, however over the recent past, India's attention has been diverted towards BIMSTEC to complete the task. The critical shortcomings of SAARC include the following -

(1) The member nations of SAARC have significant **political differences**, which have hindered cooperation and led to a lack of progress in achieving common goals. For instance, India and Pakistan have been engaged in a long-standing conflict over the disputed territory of Kashmir, which has often overshadowed other issues in SAARC meetings. According to India, the potential of SAARC had long been under-utilized and the bilateral issues between India and Pakistan backed by the obstructionist approach from Pakistan has repeatedly hampered decision making within SAARC.

(2) Many of the member nations have ongoing **bilateral disputes** that have spilled over into SAARC discussions. For example, India and Nepal have had disagreements over territorial claims and border disputes, while India and Bangladesh have had disputes over the sharing of water resources.

(3) Despite being established to promote economic cooperation, SAARC has been unable to achieve significant progress in this area. **Intra-regional trade remains low**, and the organization has been unable to establish a free trade area or a customs union.

(4) SAARC relies heavily on contributions from its member nations to fund its activities, but many of the countries in the region are economically underdeveloped and unable to provide significant **financial support**. This has led to a lack of resources for the organization to carry out its activities effectively.

(5) SAARC has been criticized for its **lack of institutional capacity** and weak organizational structure, which has made it difficult for the organization to implement its decisions effectively.

SHANGHAI COOPERATION ORGANISATION (SCO)

The SCO was established in 2001 by China & Russia as a **regional strategy grouping** which was aimed at combating separatist unrest. Since then, the SCO has evolved into a forum for discussion on regional security and economic issues. More importantly, the organisation has been playing a critical role in reimagining Central Asia's role going ahead in the 21st century.

As of 2024, the SCO is a political, economic, and defense organization. It's the world's largest regional organization by population and geographic scope, covering around 40% of the world's population and 80% of Eurasia.

Founded	June 2001
Secretariat/HQ	Beijing, China
Members	China, Kazakhstan, Kyrgyzstan, Russia, Tajikistan, Uzbekistan (2001), India and Pakistan (2017), Iran (2023, officially joined as the 9th member)
Observers	Belarus and Mongolia [Afghanistan is an observer state that has been inactive since September 2021]
Summits	• The 1st meeting of SCO was held in **Beijing (China)** in **September 2003.** • The **23rd Meeting** of the SCO Council of Heads of State was hosted by India, (under its first-ever presidency of SCO) in **July 2023** in a virtual format. • The **24th Summit** of the Council of Heads of State of SCO was held in **Astana, Kazakhstan in July 2024**. It focused on the major theme of 'Strengthening Multilateral Dialogue-Striving Towards a Sustainable Peace and Prosperity'.

Major goals and objectives

(1) Strengthening friendly relations and mutual trust among member states
(2) Protecting regional peace, security, and stability
(3) Fighting against terrorism, radicalism, and organized crime
(4) Strengthening cooperation in political, economic, scientific, and environmental issues.

Regional Anti-Terrorism Structure (RATS)

RATS is a **counterterrorism body** established by the Shanghai Cooperation Organization (SCO) in 2004. RATS is headquartered in Tashkent, Uzbekistan (2022) however there are discussion of moving its headquarters to Moscow, Russia. RATS was created to enhance cooperation among member countries in the areas of counterterrorism, intelligence sharing, and law enforcement. The main objective of RATS is to strengthen the capacity of member countries to combat the "three evils" of **terrorism, separatism, and extremism**. In addition, RATS provides technical assistance and support to member countries to enhance their border security and prevent the illegal trafficking of weapons, drugs, and other illicit goods.

Rising significance of the SCO

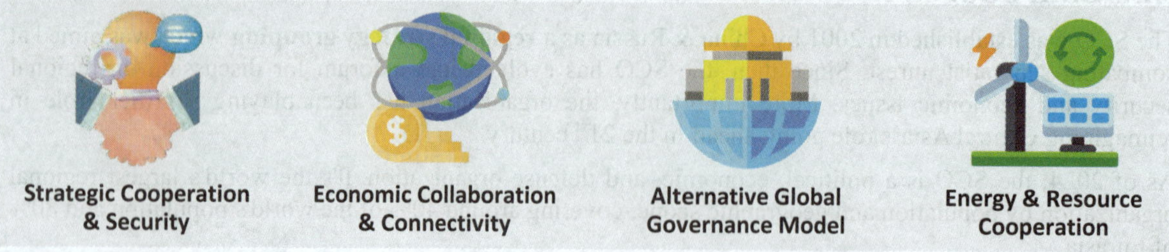

(i) The SCO, initially founded in 2001, has evolved from a regional security pact into a **comprehensive organization** that focuses on counterterrorism, combating extremism, and drug trafficking. This has led to the establishment of joint military exercises and intelligence-sharing mechanisms, enhancing its role as a security-oriented body in Asia.

(ii) The inclusion of countries like India and Pakistan in 2017 expanded the SCO's **economic footprint**, with these nations representing a significant portion of the world's population and economic output. The SCO promotes initiatives like the Belt and Road Initiative (BRI), which aims to enhance connectivity and trade across Asia, Europe, and Africa. This also helps to reduce dependence on western-dominated trade networks.

(iii) The SCO offers an **alternative model of global governance** and provides a platform for member states to advocate for a multipolar world order, challenging the dominance of Western institutions like NATO and the G7.

(iv) The SCO's member states are rich in **natural resources**, particularly in Central Asia. The organization has facilitated energy cooperation, with members collaborating on pipelines, energy markets, and joint ventures. This further reduces their dependence on western energy markets.

THE WEST IS CONCERNED !

1) The growing influence of the SCO in regions like Central Asia, South Asia, and the Middle East threatens to **diminish Western strategic interests and alliances.**

2) The SCO is seen as a **counterbalance to Western alliances like NATO and the European Union**. With China and Russia as leading members, the SCO represents a challenge to Western influence in Eurasia.

3) The SCO's advocacy for a multipolar world directly **challenges the unipolar world order led by the United States and its allies** since the end of the Cold War.

4) The SCO's support for initiatives like the BRI poses **economic competition to Western-led economic projects**. The development of alternative financial systems and trade routes could weaken the influence of institutions like the IMF and World Bank.

5) The increasing military cooperation within the SCO, including joint exercises and arms development, is viewed as a **potential threat to Western military interests**. It may lead to the formation of a military bloc that could rival NATO in certain regions.

India and the SCO

India became a full member of SCO in 2017

1) China's Ambivalence: While China publicly expressed support for India's full membership in the SCO, its underlying concerns about India's growing influence and regional ambitions were evident.

2) Russia's Crucial Role: Russia's consistent support for India's SCO membership was instrumental in overcoming Chinese objections and securing India's full membership in 2017.

3) Bilateral Issues Set Aside: SCO membership provides a platform for member states to address regional challenges and foster cooperation, setting aside bilateral disputes.

4) Counterterrorism and Regional Stability: The SCO has been instrumental in addressing issues such as terrorism, drug trafficking, and regional instability.

5) Afghanistan: India's SCO membership has provided a platform for shaping the post-US withdrawal landscape in Afghanistan, promoting regional stability and countering extremist threats.
6) Central Asia: The SCO offers India an opportunity to enhance its engagement with Central Asian countries, fostering economic and cultural ties.

India's membership in the SCO has significantly enhanced its regional standing and provided a platform for addressing shared challenges. While the relationship with China remains complex, India's participation in the SCO offers opportunities for cooperation and mutual benefit.

THE BAY OF BENGAL INITIATIVE FOR MULTI-SECTORAL TECHNICAL AND ECONOMIC COOPERATION (BIMSTEC)

The Bay of Bengal Initiative for Multi-Sectoral Technical and Economic Cooperation (BIMSTEC) is a regional organization that includes seven member states located in the coastal and neighboring areas of the Bay of Bengal, creating a connected regional unity. **Initially established as BIST-EC** (Bangladesh, India, Sri Lanka, and Thailand Economic Cooperation) in 1997, it later became **BIMST-EC** with the addition of Myanmar, and eventually transformed into **BIMSTEC** in 2004 with the inclusion of Nepal and Bhutan.

Founded	1997 through the Bangkok Declaration
Secretariat/HQ	Dhaka, Bangladesh
Members	People's Republic of Bangladesh, the Kingdom of Bhutan, the Republic of India, the Republic of the Union of Myanmar, Nepal, the Democratic Socialist Republic of Sri Lanka, and the Kingdom of Thailand
Summits	• 1st Summit was held in 2004 in Bangkok, Thailand • 2nd Summit was held in 2008 in New Delhi, India • The most recent (last) summit was the **5th Summit** which was hosted virtually by Sri Lanka in March **2022**. [The **19th BIMSTEC Ministerial Meeting**, was convened virtually from Bangkok, Thailand, in March 2023].

Until the early 20th century, the Bay of Bengal region was highly interconnected and integrated. However, with the independence of its member countries and their pursuit of individual goals and alliances starting from the 1940s, the sense of community in the region significantly diminished. Therefore, the establishment of the regional grouping, BIMSTEC, aimed **to revive the connectivity and shared interests among the countries in the Bay of Bengal region.** The first Secretary General of BIMSTEC, ***Sumith Nakandala***, emphasized that the goal was not to create something entirely new but rather to rediscover and strengthen the common heritage of the Bay of Bengal.

As stated on the official BIMSTEC website, the group serves as a **bridge between South and Southeast Asia, fostering stronger relations among its member countries.** The **BIMSTEC Charter** was signed and adopted during the 5th BIMSTEC Summit held in virtual format in Colombo, Sri Lanka, in March 2022. According to the Charter, it is an **inter-governmental organization consisting of seven members.** The nations together account for 22 percent of the world's population with a combined GDP of approximately $2.7 trillion.

Initially, when formed in 1997, the main areas of focus for the group were trade, technology, energy, transport, tourism, and fisheries. However, in 2008, these focus areas were expanded to include agriculture, public health, poverty alleviation, counterterrorism, environment, culture, people-to-people contact, and climate change.

The sectors were last reorganized in 2021, led by member states as follows –

- **Bangladesh**: Trade, Investment and Development
- **Bhutan**: Environment and Climate Change
- **India**: Security; Sub-sectors: Counterterrorism and Transnational Crime, Disaster Management, Energy
- **Myanmar**: Agriculture and Food Security; Sub-sectors: Agriculture, Fisheries and Livestock
- **Nepal**: People-to-People Contact; Sub-sectors: Culture, Tourism, People-to-People Contact (forums of think tanks, media etc.)
- **Sri Lanka**: Science, Technology & Innovation ; Sub-sectors: Technology, Health, Human Resource Development
- **Thailand**: Connectivity

Principles and Objectives

According to the BIMSTEC Charter, cooperation within the BIMSTEC is to be based on respect for the principle of sovereign equality, territorial integrity, political independence, non-interference in internal affairs, non-aggression, peaceful co-existence, mutual respect and mutual benefit. **Article 1 of the Charter lists out certain 'Purposes' of the grouping.** Some of these include[22]-

1) To create an enabling environment for rapid economic development through identification and implementation of specific cooperation projects in the already agreed areas of cooperation and such other areas that may be agreed upon by the Member States.
2) To maintain peace and stability in the Bay of Bengal region through close collaboration in combating international terrorism, transnational organized crimes as well as natural disasters, climate change and communicable diseases.
3) To accelerate the economic growth and social progress in the Bay of Bengal region through joint endeavours in a spirit of equality and partnership.
4) To promote active collaboration and mutual assistance on matters of common interest in the economic, social, technical and scientific fields.
5) To endeavor to eradicate poverty from the Bay of Bengal region.
6) To establish multidimensional connectivity, promote synergy among connectivity frameworks in the region, as a key enabler to economic integration for shared prosperity.

BIMSTEC Summit

- The highest governing body of BIMSTEC is composed of the **Heads of State or Government of the Member States.** It serves as both a deliberative and decision-making body, providing policy guidance and making important decisions related to the objectives of BIMSTEC, member interests, and other relevant issues.
- The **Summit meetings take place every two years** and are **preceded by the Ministerial Meeting**. The hosting Member State holding the Chairmanship is responsible for organizing the Summit.
- **Consensus** is the basis for all decisions made during the Summit Meetings.

The Ministerial Meeting comprise the Ministers dealing with foreign relations of the Member states. During the **19th BIMSTEC Ministerial Meeting** held virtually in **March 2023**, several decisions were made regarding the inclusion of new sub-sectors within different sectors of the organization. The meeting approved the **addition of the Blue Economy as a sub-sector under the Trade, Investment, and Development Sector.**

[22] BIMSTEC Charter, https://mea.gov.in/Portal/LegalTreatiesDoc/022M3847.pdf

Significance of BIMSTEC

(1) BIMSTEC **connects South Asia with Southeast Asia**, making it a crucial bridge between two of the world's most dynamic regions. This strategic position enhances its role in fostering regional integration and cooperation. The **Bay of Bengal**, which lies at the heart of BIMSTEC, is a critical maritime space for global trade, with significant sea lanes that are vital for international shipping, energy supplies, and regional security.

(2) It emphasizes **multi-sectoral cooperation**, including trade, investment, technology, energy, and infrastructure development. This focus is crucial for the **economic development** of its member states, many of which are developing economies. Projects like the BIMSTEC Transport Connectivity Master Plan, which are aimed at enhancing connectivity, help to facilitate trade and people-to-people exchanges.

(3) It plays a pivotal role in **addressing non-traditional security challenges** in the region, such as terrorism, drug trafficking, human trafficking, and natural disasters. By fostering collaboration among member states, BIMSTEC contributes to regional stability. The organization also serves as a platform for **dialogue and cooperation on security matters**.

(4) BIMSTEC **complements other regional groupings like the SAARC and ASEAN**. It provides an alternative platform for regional cooperation, especially when other organizations face political or operational challenges. For ex: it was seen as a way to bypass the deadlock often encountered in SAARC due to political tensions, particularly between India and Pakistan.

Thus, the grouping has been assisting its members in several ways. It allows Bangladesh to project itself more than a small extension of the Indian subcontinent; it provides an opportunity for Sri Lanka to connect with the landmass; for Bhutan and Nepal it provides them a window to the Bay of Bengal and the connected regions, away from their landlocked positions; for Myanmar and Thailand it provides them an access to a rising consumer market while balancing China's aggression in South Asia.

India and BIMSTEC

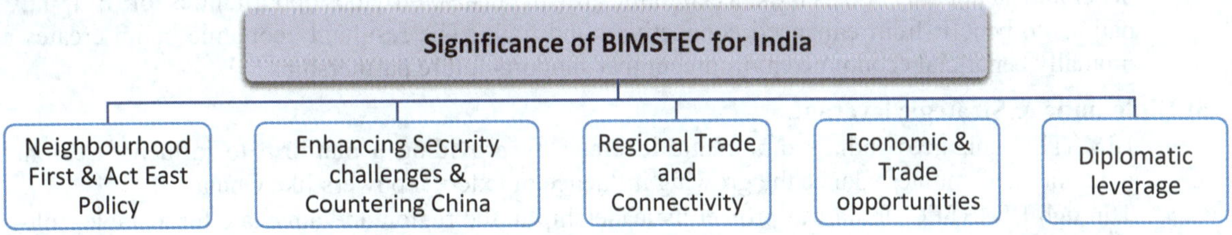

(1) Neighbourhood First and Act East Policy

Founding Member

- BIMSTEC plays a pivotal role in advancing India's "*Neighbourhood First*" and "*Act East*" policies, which are central to its foreign policy objectives. The organization provides an ideal platform for India to strengthen ties with its immediate neighbors in South Asia while simultaneously enhancing engagement with Southeast Asian countries.
- Prime Minister Modi emphasized the importance of regional security during the last BIMSTEC summit, asserting that "**regional security is of top priority**" amidst changing geopolitics in Europe. He proposed transforming the Bay of Bengal into a "**bridge of connectivity, prosperity, and security**," which aligns with India's strategic vision of fostering closer relationships with neighboring countries and deepening its influence in the East.

(2) Enhancing Security challenges & Countering China

- India's strategic concerns in the Bay of Bengal region are closely linked to the growing influence of China, particularly through initiatives like the Belt and Road Initiative (BRI). China's "debt trap diplomacy" has been a significant issue. BIMSTEC offers India a platform to counter China's assertiveness by promoting a rules-based order in the region, rooted in recognized international norms.
- Prime Minister Modi's vision of the Bay of Bengal as a zone of peace and security contrasts sharply with the militarized and contested waters of the South China Sea. Through BIMSTEC, India can advocate for a code of conduct that ensures freedom of navigation and minimizes military disturbances, thereby preserving regional stability.
- Through BIMSTEC, India can address common regional challenges, promote development, and build trust with its neighbors. The organization's focus on non-traditional security issues, such as terrorism, climate change, and natural disasters, also supports India's goal of creating a stable and secure regional environment.

(3) Regional Trade and Connectivity

- The organization supports various infrastructure projects that facilitate seamless connectivity across the region, including the **India-Myanmar-Thailand Trilateral Highway** and the **Kaladan Multi-Modal Transit Transport Project**. These initiatives align with India's broader goals of improving regional integration and reducing logistical bottlenecks.
- India's proximity to the **Malacca Strait**, one of the world's busiest trade routes, positions it strategically within BIMSTEC. The Bay of Bengal's connection to the Strait of Malacca directly impacts the security and economic interests of BIMSTEC members.
- Moreover, India's ***Sagarmala* Project**, which aims to develop ports and improve inland connectivity, can significantly boost trade with BIMSTEC countries, further integrating regional economies and enhancing India's trade footprint.

(4) Economic & Trade opportunities

- BIMSTEC helps India by facilitating greater market access and fostering economic cooperation with its member states. The organization represents a combined market of over 1.5 billion people, offering significant potential for expanding trade and investment. BIMSTEC's focus on multi-sectoral cooperation, including energy, technology, and infrastructure development, aligns with India's economic goals.
- The **Sagarmala Project** exemplifies India's efforts to utilize its extensive 7,500 km coastline by developing ports and connecting them with inland highways and railways. This infrastructure development not only boosts India's economic growth but also provides opportunities for BIMSTEC nations to benefit from enhanced connectivity and trade. The resultant economic boom creates a mutually beneficial economic environment that supports future partnerships.

(5) Diplomatic & Strategic leverage

- BIMSTEC enhances India's diplomatic leverage by providing a platform to influence regional dynamics and counterbalance the growing influence of external powers like China.
- Through BIMSTEC, India can project its leadership in the region and advocate for a stable, rules-based order that aligns with its strategic interests.
- Such a leverage is crucial amidst the rising tensions and geopolitical shifts in the broader Indo-Pacific region.

GROUP OF 20 (G-20)

The G-20 is an international forum that serves as a **platform for major developed and emerging economies to collaborate.**

Founded	1999
Secretariat/HQ	The G20 does not have a permanent secretariat or headquarters. Instead, the presidency of the G20 rotates annually among its member countries, which are responsible for organizing the annual summit and setting the agenda for that year.
Members	As of August 2024, the G20 consists of **19 nations and 2 Regional Unions.** • **Nations**: Argentina, Australia, Brazil, Canada, China, France, Germany, **India**, Indonesia, Italy, Japan, Republic of Korea, Mexico, Russia, Saudi Arabia, South Africa, Turkey, the United Kingdom, the United States. • **Regional Unions**: The European Union and the African Union (2023). Additionally, Spain has been invited as a permanent guest.
Summits	• The 1st **G20 summit** was held in **Washington, D.C.**, in November 2008 (in the wake of the subprime mortgage crisis). • The 17th **Summit** was held in Nov 2022 in Bali, Indonesia. The **Bali Declaration** was adopted. • The 18th **Summit was held in Sept 2023 in New Delhi, India**. The theme for the summit was "*One Earth, One Family, One Future*," reflecting India's emphasis on inclusivity and global cooperation. • The 19th Heads of State and Government Summit of the Group of 20 (G20) will take place in **November 2024 in Rio de Janeiro, Brazil.**

Origin Story

In 1997-99, the world witnessed a global financial crisis which rattled the entire economic framework. The G-20 was **established in 1999** to **facilitate discussions and formulate policies aimed at ensuring global financial stability**. Initially, the G20 Finance Ministers and Central Bank Governors held meetings on the advice of the G7 Finance Ministers to address the financial crisis. However, it was not until 2008 that the leaders of the G-20 nations convened for the inaugural G-20 Summit. During this summit, the leaders collaborated to address the repercussions of the financial crisis that originated in the United States. The leaders designated the G-20 as "the premier forum for our international economic cooperation" during their **Pittsburgh Summit** in 2009. The grouping is considered a broader international platform due to the inclusion of both the developed and developing nations.

Initially, the G20 primarily concentrated on macroeconomic policies but gradually broadened its scope to address a wide range of global economic growth-related issues. These include finance, trade, infrastructure, investment, energy, employment, combating corruption, development, agriculture, as well as technology, innovation, and the digital economy. The G20 consists of 80% of the Global GDP and accounts for 60% of the world's population and supports 75% of global exports.

NOTE

To ensure the continuity of the agendas, every year the **'Troika'** which consists of the previous presidency, the current year presidency, and the upcoming presidency, conduct intensive communication.

The G20 Troika during the **Brazilian G20 Presidency in 2024** will comprise India, Brazil, and South Africa.

The G20 meetings regularly invite international organizations to participate. These organizations include the International Labour Organization (ILO), the International Monetary Fund (IMF), the Financial Stability Board (FSB), the World Bank (WB), the World Trade Organization (WTO), the Organisation for Economic Cooperation and Development (OECD), and the United Nations (UN). Additionally, the World Health Organization (WHO) was invited by the German G20 Presidency in 2017.

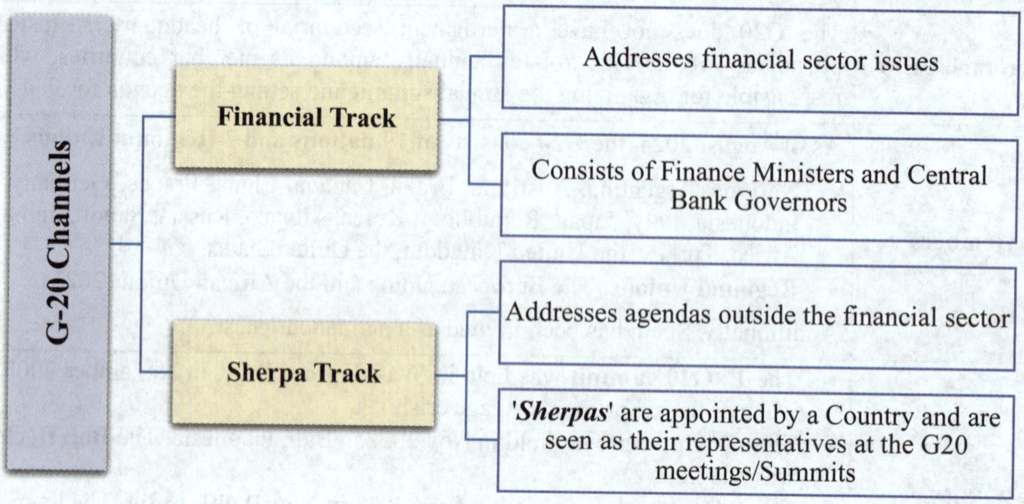

Think 20 (T20)

The T20 was initiated in 2012 as an engagement group independent of the national governments. In simpler terms, it is the "ideas bank" for the G20. It is a key mechanism through which G20 policymakers engage the pooled resources of the global academic, research and think tank community to solve global problems. The T20 Summit took place in Bali on September 4-6, 2022, under the Presidency of Indonesia.

*Each year, under a new G20 Presidency, the T20 creates **Task Forces** to structure their proposals around the most critical issues, driving policy innovation.

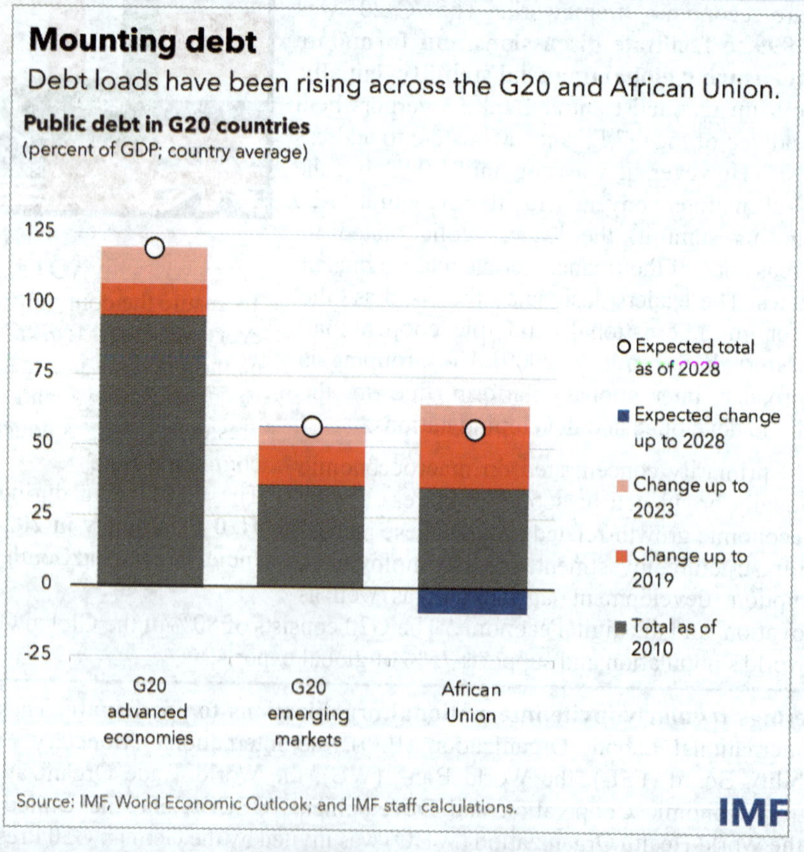

India and G-20

Member of G20 since 1999

India has been a member of the G20 since its inception in 1999 and has constantly contributed towards its discussions on issues of global importance. G20 plays a critical role in shaping the global governance on all major issues and hence India's engagement with the grouping is crucial due to the interlinking of economic opportunities and challenges.

In a major boost to the ties, India had assumed the **Presidency** of the G20 for one year from **01 December 2022** to **30 November 2023** and also hosted the **G-20 Leaders' Summit** in New Delhi in **September 2023**. India's G20 presidency was also special, because for the first time the 'Troika' comprised only developing countries that had set the agenda for two-thirds of the world population, representing around 85 per cent of the global GDP and over 75 per cent of the global trade.

The theme of India's Presidency (2023) - "*Vasudhaiva Kutumbakam*" or "One Earth · One Family · One Future". The theme affirmed the value of all life on the planet Earth and spotlights **LiFE (Lifestyle for Environment)**, both at the level of individual lifestyles as well as national development.

During a statement in the Rajya Sabha, Dr. Rajkumar Ranjan Singh, Minister of State in the Ministry of External Affairs (2023), expressed that **as the G20 Presidency, India will have the opportunity to identify, emphasize, enhance, and garner international support for crucial priorities of developing countries across various social and economic sectors**. These sectors encompass energy, agriculture, trade, digital economy, health, environment, employment, tourism, anti-corruption, and women empowerment. The focus will particularly be on areas that affect the most vulnerable and disadvantaged populations.

INDIA, BRAZIL, SOUTH AFRICA DIALOGUE FORUM (IBSA)

The IBSA Dialogue forum is an international tripartite grouping that was established in 2003 as a platform for the three large, multicultural, and developing democracies, India, Brazil and South Africa to engage in dialogue and cooperation on global issues. The grouping was formed based on shared values of democracy, human rights, and the rule of law, as well as a commitment to promoting *South-South cooperation*.

Establishment	IBSA was established in 2003 through the adoption of the "***Brasilia Declaration***" by the foreign ministers of the three countries.
Secretariat/HQ	IBSA does not have a headquarters or a permanent executive secretariat.
Institutional Mechanism	• **IBSA Summit**: At the highest level, the heads of state and government of the three countries meet regularly to set the agenda and provide political guidance for the group. • **Ministerial Meetings**: Ministers from various sectors, including foreign affairs, defense, trade, and health, meet to discuss specific areas of cooperation. • **Working Groups**: There are 14 sectoral working groups that focus on specific areas of cooperation, such as agriculture, environment, education, energy, and information technology. • **IBSA Fund**: This fund finances South-South cooperation projects in other developing countries, particularly in areas related to poverty alleviation and capacity building. The IBSA Fund has been recognized for its work in contributing to development goals.

Main Objectives & Areas of Cooperation

Political coordination: The three countries work together to promote their interests on the international stage, particularly in forums like the United Nations, where they advocate for the reform of the Security Council to include more representation from developing countries.

Economic cooperation: IBSA seeks to enhance trade and investment among the member countries, which are all significant players in their respective regions.

Social development: The forum promotes the sharing of best practices in areas like health, education, and social welfare, addressing issues such as poverty alleviation, gender equality, and sustainable development.

Knowledge Exchange: The grouping focuses on facilitating the exchange of information, technology, & expertise. IBSA encourages collaboration in research and development, with a focus on innovation and technology transfer.

Rising Significance

(a) **Geopolitical Shifts:** The evolving geopolitical landscape, including the rise of China and shifts in U.S. foreign policy, has given renewed relevance to IBSA as a platform for like-minded democracies in the Global South to collaborate.

(b) **Global Governance and Multilateralism**: As emerging powers, India, Brazil, and South Africa have used IBSA to advocate for a more equitable global governance structure. The group has consistently called for the reform of international institutions, such as the United Nations Security Council, to better reflect the current global order.

(c) **IBSA and BRICS:** While IBSA and BRICS (Brazil, Russia, India, China, and South Africa) share overlapping memberships, IBSA's significance lies in its focus on democratic governance and development cooperation. The grouping offers an alternative space for India, Brazil, and South Africa to address issues without the influence of China and Russia, allowing them to maintain their strategic autonomy.

(d) **Pandemic Response:** In the wake of the COVID-19 pandemic, IBSA countries have coordinated efforts to manage the health crisis, share knowledge on pandemic management, and advocate for equitable access to vaccines and treatments. The pandemic has highlighted the importance of South-South cooperation in addressing global challenges.

Main Challenges

(i) Despite the potential for increased trade and investment, economic ties between the IBSA countries have not grown as significantly as expected. There is still a **lack of deep economic integration**, with trade flows remaining below their potential.

(ii) IBSA's **institutional mechanisms**, such as working groups and ministerial meetings, have sometimes been criticized for their **lack of efficiency** and follow-through on initiatives. The grouping's activities have occasionally been perceived as slow-moving, limiting its impact on the global stage.

(iii)The **rise of BRICS** has somewhat overshadowed IBSA, given the former's larger economic and geopolitical weight due to the inclusion of China and Russia. This has led to questions about the continued relevance of IBSA, even though it remains a distinct forum for promoting democratic values and South-South cooperation.

India & IBSA

IBSA is a critical platform for India to promote its strategic, economic, and geopolitical interests on the global stage. As the world faces shifting power dynamics, India's role in IBSA becomes even more significant in advocating for democratic values, enhancing South-South cooperation, and countering the influence of emerging powers like China.

1) **Strategic Autonomy in Global Governance**
   - India's active participation in IBSA allows it to assert leadership in promoting democratic values and reforming global governance institutions. It provides a platform to advocate its agenda for UNSC reform and an inclusive global order.
   - As a member of both IBSA and BRICS, India can use IBSA to maintain strategic autonomy, balancing the influence of China and Russia within BRICS. IBSA's focus on democratic governance and South-South cooperation offers India an alternative forum to pursue its interests without compromising its democratic values.
2) **Economic and Development Cooperation**
   - IBSA is crucial for India's efforts to enhance South-South cooperation, particularly in areas such as poverty alleviation, healthcare, education, and sustainable development. The IBSA Fund, which finances development projects in other developing countries, showcases India's commitment to sharing its development experience and fostering global solidarity.
   - While there is much to be achieved, the grouping provides opportunities for India to strengthen trade and investment with Brazil and South Africa.
3) **Geopolitical Significance**
   - In the evolving geopolitical landscape (influenced by initiatives like China's BRI), IBSA allows India to collaborate with like-minded democracies to promote a rules-based international order. This collaboration is crucial for India's strategy to counterbalance China's growing influence, particularly in the Global South.
   - India's leadership in IBSA enhances its diplomatic leverage and helps it build alliances with other developing nations on key global issues, such as climate change, trade, and development.
4) **People-to-People Ties**
   - IBSA provides a framework for India to enhance cultural and people-to-people exchanges with Brazil and South Africa. This is important for promoting Indian culture, education, and technology in these regions, thereby strengthening India's soft power and global influence.
   - India can collaborate and share expertise in areas like information technology, space research, and pharmaceuticals. This collaboration can lead to mutual benefits, including capacity building and innovation.

QUADRILATERAL SECURITY DIALOGUE (QUAD)

About	The Quadrilateral Security Dialogue, commonly referred to as the Quad, is an **informal strategic alliance** between four major democratic nations: **India, the United States, Japan, and Australia.**
Aims & Objectives	The Quad seeks to promote a free, open, inclusive, and prosperous Indo-Pacific, grounded in a rules-based international order. Its key objectives include upholding freedom of navigation, advocating for peaceful dispute resolution, and ensuring adherence to international law. Member nations are committed to strengthening regional cooperation to foster stability and prosperity in the Indo-Pacific.
Areas of focus	Maritime security, counterterrorism, humanitarian assistance and disaster relief, cybersecurity, and economic development. The Quad has conducted joint military exercises, held high-level diplomatic talks, and engaged in economic cooperation to achieve its goals.
Secretariat/HQ	The Quad does not have a permanent headquarters. Instead, the Quad is a strategic forum that holds diplomatic and strategic discussions in various locations.
Institutional Mechanism	• The first ever QUAD Summit was held *virtually* in **March 2021.** • The first ever **in-person Quad Summit** was held on **24th September 2021** in Washington D.C., USA. • The **third in-person Quad Leaders' Summit** was conducted in Hiroshima, Japan in May 2023.

	• **2024 Quad Summit** – The United States will be hosting the fourth (4th) in-person Leaders' meeting on 21st September 2024 in Wilmington, Delaware.

- The idea for the alliance was first introduced by then-Japanese **Prime Minister Shinzo Abe** in 2007, but its roots trace back to the aftermath of the 2004 Indian Ocean tsunami. Following the disaster, the four nations collaborated to provide humanitarian aid and relief, laying the foundation for future cooperation.
- Though initially informal, the Quad faded from focus due to objections from China, which viewed the group as a countermeasure to its growing influence. However, in 2017, the alliance was revived in response to China's increasingly assertive actions in the Indo-Pacific, signaling a shift in regional dynamics.
- For the United States, the Quad represents a strategic pivot toward the Indo-Pacific, reinforcing its efforts to counterbalance China's influence. By fostering economic, military, and diplomatic collaboration, the Quad aims to create a regional environment that supports peace, security, and sustainable development.

In recent years, the Quad has gained renewed significance due to increasing geopolitical tensions in the region, particularly with China's growing military and economic influence. The Quad has been described as a "mini NATO" in the Indo-Pacific, and its members share a common vision of a free, open, and prosperous Indo-Pacific.

The **Quad Vaccine Partnership and Global Health Security** was launched in 2021. As of mid-2022, the Quad partners had collectively pledged approximately USD 5.2 billion to the COVAX AMC, approximately 40 per cent of the total contributions from government donors

In **May 2022**, the Indian PM participated in the **second in-person Quad Leaders' Summit** in Tokyo, Japan. The highlights include[23] –

- The Leaders reiterated their desire to **combat terrorism**, denounced the use of terrorist proxies and emphasized the importance of denying any logistical, financial, or military support to terrorist groups which could be used to launch or plan terror attacks, including cross-border attacks.
- A **Quad Climate Change Action and Mitigation Package (Q-CHAMP)** was announced to enhance efforts in promoting environmentally friendly shipping, clean energy, including green hydrogen, and the development of climate-resilient infrastructure.
- In the field of critical and emerging technologies, the Quad launched the Common Statement of Principles on Critical Technology Supply Chains, as part of their ongoing collaborative work.
- The Quad Leaders announced the establishment of the **Quad Partnership on Humanitarian Assistance and Disaster Relief (HADR)** for the Indo-Pacific, aiming to facilitate more efficient and timely responses to disasters in the region.
- The Quad Leaders expressed their support for **the Indo-Pacific Maritime Domain Awareness Initiative (IPMDA)**, which aims to strengthen countries' capabilities in responding to humanitarian and disaster relief incidents and combating illegal fishing. The IPMDA will provide a comprehensive and cost-effective maritime domain awareness system in near-real-time.

While China has communicated its displeasure that the group represents an attempt at forming an "Asian NATO," though unlike the European alliance there is no mutual-defence pact in effect, the Quad members have officially reiterated that the group is meant to deepen economic, diplomatic and military ties among the four countries.

[23] Prime Minister's Office. (2022, May 24). Prime Minister's participation in the Quad Leaders' Summit. PIB Delhi. https://pib.gov.in/PressReleaseIframePage.aspx?PRID=1827884

Significance of QUAD for India

(1) **Counterbalancing China's Influence**: One of the primary reasons for India's active involvement in the Quad is to counter China's assertive behavior in the Indo-Pacific region, particularly in the Indian Ocean. As India faces territorial challenges along its northern borders and increasing Chinese influence in neighboring countries, the Quad offers a platform for India to align with like-minded democracies to ensure a free and open Indo-Pacific. This enhances India's strategic position in balancing China's expansionism, especially through initiatives like the Belt and Road.

(2) **Maritime Security**: With India's strategic interests in the Indian Ocean and broader Indo-Pacific region, the Quad helps boost maritime security. India, along with the U.S., Japan, and Australia, has increased maritime cooperation, naval exercises (like the Malabar Exercise), and intelligence-sharing to ensure freedom of navigation, counter piracy, and tackle illegal fishing. These efforts reinforce India's role as a net security provider in the Indian Ocean.

(3) **Technological and Economic Collaboration**: The Quad provides India with an avenue to collaborate on emerging technologies like 5G, artificial intelligence, and cybersecurity, offering alternatives to Chinese technology. The group also facilitates economic cooperation, investment in infrastructure, and resilient supply chains, helping India to diversify trade and reduce its dependence on China. Moreover, the Quad's focus on vaccine diplomacy, particularly during the COVID-19 pandemic, has strengthened India's pharmaceutical industry and regional influence.

(4) **Geopolitical Leverage**: The Quad enhances India's geopolitical standing by positioning it as a critical player in global power dynamics. By aligning with the U.S., Japan, and Australia, India strengthens its diplomatic clout and influence in multilateral forums such as the UN, G20, and BRICS. It also provides India with strategic partnerships that bolster its foreign policy objectives, especially in regional stability and counterterrorism efforts.

(5) **Energy and Infrastructure Cooperation**: With India's growing energy needs, the Quad facilitates cooperation on energy security, renewable energy, and infrastructure development. Through joint initiatives, the Quad can support sustainable development projects in South and Southeast Asia, aligning with India's interests in regional connectivity and infrastructure growth.

Furthermore, India's SAGAR initiative aims to establish itself as a net security provider in the Indian Ocean region. Through cooperation within the Quad framework, India can gain access to strategic locations for establishing naval bases. Additionally, India advocates for a multipolar world governed by rules, and the Quad partnership can contribute to India's aspirations of becoming a regional superpower.

Thus, the Quad enhances India's security, economic interests, and geopolitical influence, offering a crucial platform to address its regional challenges and global aspirations.

BRAZIL, RUSSIA, INDIA, CHINA AND SOUTH AFRICA (BRICS)

BRICS is an intergovernmental organisation working in the field of international politics. The concept of BRICS emerged from the idea of grouping the world's leading emerging economies that were seen as the main drivers of global economic growth. Each of the five members of BRICS is a prominent developing or newly industrialized country, characterized by their substantial economic growth and influential role in regional affairs. The five nations collectively represent approximately **2% of the world's population, 23% of global GDP, 30% of the land area,** and **18% of global trade**.

Establishment	The discussion around BRICS started in 2001 as BRIC, an acronym coined by Goldman Sachs for Brazil, Russia, India, and China. BRICS was formally established in 2009 and South Africa was added in 2010.

Members	As of August 2024, there are a total of **9 members** ▪ **Original members**: Brazil, Russia, India, China, South Africa ▪ **Latest Additions**: Iran, Egypt, Ethiopia and the United Arab Emirates.
Interested Nations	Argentina, Bangladesh, Indonesia, Mexico, and Turkey have conveyed keen interest in becoming full members of BRICS, while Egypt, Iran, Nigeria, Sudan, Syria, Pakistan, and Greece have also expressed their desire to join the group.
Critical Summits	• 1st Summit: Russia, 2009 • 4th Summit: India, 2012 (New Delhi Summit: Proposal to create a joint BRICS Development Bank was introduced) • 6th Summit: Brazil, 2014 (Fortaleza Summit: This summit led to creation of the New Development Bank or BRICS Bank) • 12th Summit (Virtual): Hosted by Russia, 2020 (Theme: "Global Stability, Shared Security, and Innovative Growth") • 14th Summit (2022): Convened under the Chairmanship of China, in virtual format. • **15th Summit (2023): Held in South Africa** → The South African President announced that 6 emerging market group nations (Argentina, Egypt, Ethiopia, Iran, Saudi Arabia, and the UAE) had been invited to join BRICS. (Argentina declined & Saudi Arabia hasn't confirmed acceptance) • **16th Summit (Oct 2024): To be held in Russia**
BRICS Economy	**New Development Bank** – Based in Shanghai (China): The bank was established in 2014 and finances infrastructure and sustainable development projects in BRICS and other emerging economies. **BRICS Contingent Reserve Arrangement** – It is a framework for the provision of support through liquidity and precautionary instruments in response to actual or potential short-term balance of payments pressures

Principles And Objectives

- The core principles of the BRICS platform include respecting the sovereignty of member states, upholding international law, and recognizing the United Nations as the central body for peace, security, and development. The platform promotes openness, information sharing, and consensus-based decision-making, while acknowledging the multipolar nature of the global economic and financial system.
- The BRICS mechanism is designed to advance peace, security, development, and cooperation. While initially centered on economic interests, the grouping has since broadened its agenda to address a range of global issues.
- The group aims to enhance its influence in global governance by aligning positions on key international matters, advocating for reforms in global financial institutions such as the International Monetary Fund (IMF) and the World Bank, and supporting a multipolar world order.
- A key objective is to increase market access opportunities and strengthen the interconnections among member states' markets. The focus is on boosting mutual trade, investment, and creating a favorable business environment for entrepreneurs and investors across all BRICS nations.
- Members are dedicated to achieving inclusive economic growth that addresses poverty, reduces unemployment, and promotes social inclusion.
- The platform aspires to foster peace, prosperity, security, and development in a world characterized by interconnectedness, globalization, and multiple centers of power.
- BRICS also emphasizes the importance of cultural exchange and building people-to-people ties among its members, encouraging collaboration in education, healthcare, and science and technology.

Significance

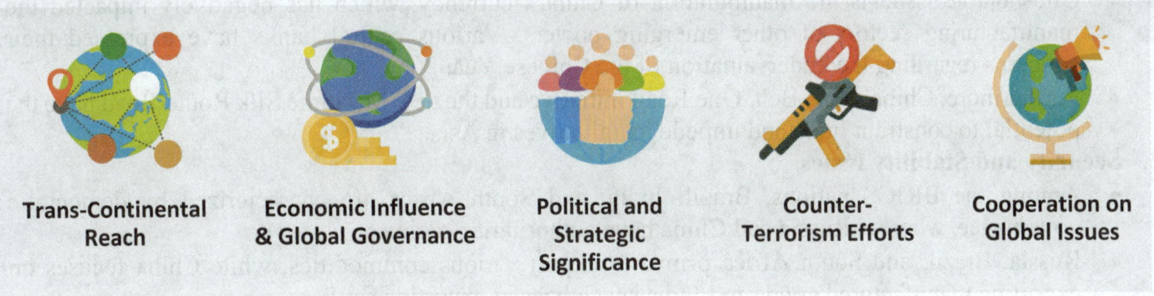

(1) **Trans-Continental Reach**: The BRICS grouping spans across multiple continents, including Asia, Europe, Africa, and Latin America, giving it a unique and valuable trans-continental dimension. This broad geographical representation allows BRICS to address a wide range of global issues and perspectives, making it a significant force in international relations.

(2) **Economic Influence**: In the wake of the recent financial crisis, BRICS countries played a pivotal role in shaping macroeconomic policies during G-20 meetings. Their collective influence in global economic governance is growing, particularly as BRICS has now surpassed the G7 in terms of its share of global GDP.

(3) **Global Governance:** As global negotiations on critical issues like the World Trade Organization (WTO) reforms and climate change intensify, the unity of the BRICS group becomes increasingly significant. BRICS members work together to advocate for the interests of developing nations and ensure that global policies are more inclusive and representative.

(4) **Rising Political and Strategic Significance**: The grouping's pursuit of multipolarity and a redefined global order challenges the dominance of Western-led institutions and promotes a more balanced distribution of power. By advocating for reforms in global financial and political institutions, BRICS aims to create a more equitable and just international system.

(5) **Support for India's Counter-Terrorism Efforts**: BRICS has consistently supported India's stance on countering terrorism, emphasizing a collective commitment to rejecting terrorism in all its forms and manifestations. The group has specifically identified and condemned terrorist organizations such as Lashkar-e-Taiba (LeT), Jaish-e-Mohammed (JeM), and Tehrik-i-Taliban Pakistan (TTP) as perpetrators of violence. This support enhances India's efforts to combat terrorism and strengthens its diplomatic position on the global stage.

(6) **Enhanced Cooperation on Global Issues:** BRICS serves as a crucial platform for member countries to collaborate on a wide range of global issues, including sustainable development, health, education, and technology. The group's collective efforts in these areas contribute to addressing some of the most pressing challenges facing the world today. The bloc's emphasis on cultural exchange and people-to-people ties further strengthens the bonds among member countries

BRICS Plus

BRICS Plus is a concept that expands the BRICS grouping to include other emerging economies from different regions of the world. The idea was first proposed by China, the host of the 2017 BRICS summit, as a way to broaden the group's influence and strengthen ties with other developing countries. Under the BRICS Plus concept, other emerging economies are invited to participate in the BRICS summit as guests.

The first BRICS Plus meeting was held in 2017, where leaders from Egypt, Guinea, Mexico, Tajikistan, and Thailand were invited to attend as guests. The main objective of BRICS Plus is to promote greater cooperation between the BRICS countries and other emerging economies, particularly those from Africa, Asia, and Latin America. Iran has recently applied to join BRICS Plus.

Areas of Concern

1. **Dominance of China**: Currently, the Chinese economy not only holds the position of the second-largest globally but also surpasses the combined economies of all other BRICS nations. However, China's political ambitions have presented challenges, making it difficult to reach consensus within the group.

- One notable issue is the manipulation of China's currency, which has negatively impacted the manufacturing sectors of other emerging powers. Various central banks have expressed their concerns regarding the undervaluation of the Chinese Yuan.
- Furthermore, China's One Belt, One Road initiative and the new Maritime Silk Route/Road have the potential to constrain India and impede its initiatives in Asia.

2. **Security and Stability issues**:
   - Among the BRICS nations, Brazil, India, and South Africa are characterized by democratic governance, whereas Russia and China have authoritarian regimes.
   - Russia, Brazil, and South Africa primarily export various commodities, while China focuses on exporting manufactured goods and India specializes in exporting services.
   - The diminishing strength of the strategic triangle involving Russia, China, and India has an impact on the perception of the group.
   - The Chinese economy is significantly larger than South Africa's, with a size that is 28 times greater. Additionally, the income per capita in India is one-tenth of that in Russia.

I2U2

I2U2 is a strategic grouping involving **India, Israel, the United Arab Emirates (UAE), and the United States**. It was originally conceptualized as the "*West Asian Quad*" in 2021 and later officially named I2U2 during the group's first summit in July 2022.

- **Focus**: This grouping aims to address economic cooperation, food security, energy, and other critical areas of shared interest among the member states.
- **Goals**:
  (a) To leverage the strengths of the four nations in areas like innovation, technology, and infrastructure development.
  (b) Foster collaboration in sustainable projects, food security, and renewable energy, especially by combining Israeli technological prowess, UAE capital, U.S. expertise, and India's large-scale developmental needs.
- **Key Projects:**
  1) One of the first initiatives is a food corridor in India, involving investments from the UAE, technological inputs from Israel, and U.S. expertise.
  2) Renewable energy projects in India, aiming to enhance sustainable infrastructure.

I2U2 serves as a platform for the integration of economic, technological, and diplomatic resources of these four nations, promoting regional stability and addressing shared concerns related to sustainable development, trade, and energy security.

AUKUS

AUKUS is a trilateral security pact announced in September 2021 between **Australia, the United Kingdom, and the United States.**

- **Focus**: Its primary aim is to enhance security cooperation in the Indo-Pacific, with a particular focus on military and technological advancements, including the sharing of defense capabilities and nuclear-powered submarine technology.
- **Goals**:
  (i) Strengthen the Indo-Pacific region's defense against growing threats, particularly China's assertiveness.
  (ii) Facilitate the transfer of U.S. and UK expertise to enable Australia to acquire nuclear-powered submarines.
  (iii) Boost cooperation in advanced technologies like cyber capabilities, artificial intelligence (AI), quantum technologies, and undersea warfare.
- **Key Features:**
  1. **Nuclear-Powered Submarines**: One of the hallmark agreements under AUKUS is the U.S. and UK helping Australia acquire nuclear-powered submarines, which will enhance Australia's maritime capabilities in the Indo-Pacific.

2. **Technological Collaboration**: AUKUS focuses on collaboration in areas such as cyber capabilities, undersea technologies, and advanced missile systems.

AUKUS is seen as a significant shift in global defense alliances, strengthening the security architecture in the Indo-Pacific region and signalling the U.S.'s long-term commitment to countering China's influence. It also represents an unprecedented level of military collaboration among these three countries.

OTHER IMPORTANT GROUPINGS & CONNECTIVITY PROJECTS

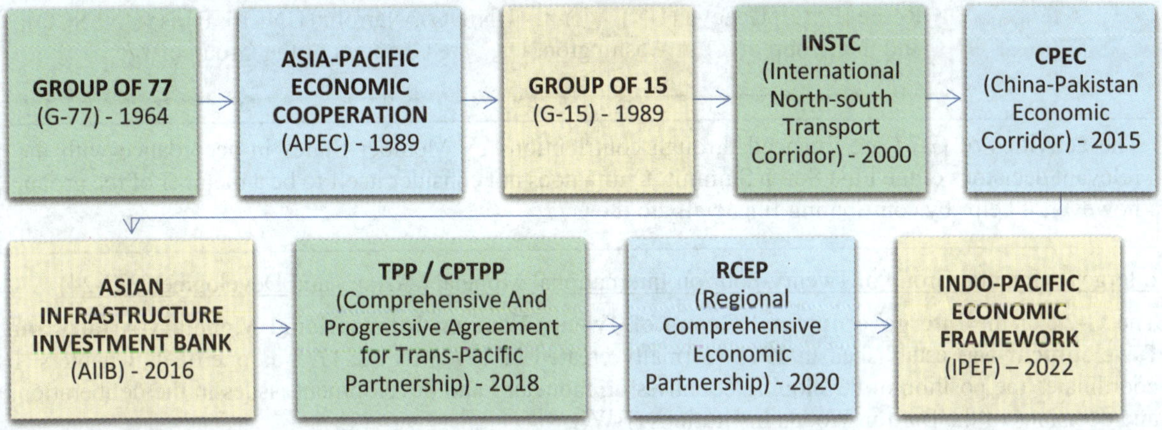

GROUP OF 77 (G-77)

It is the largest **intergovernmental organization of developing countries** aimed at the promotion of the collective interests of the countries of the 'South'. The primary purpose of its formation was to represent and advance the shared economic interests of its member nations and to enhance their collective ability to negotiate on major global economic matters within the United Nations framework.

The Group of 77 (G-77) came into existence on **15 June 1964**, consisting of seventy-seven developing countries that had endorsed the "Joint Declaration of the Seventy-Seven Developing Countries." This declaration was issued at the conclusion of the inaugural session of the United Nations Conference on Trade and Development (UNCTAD) in Geneva.

While the membership has expanded to include **134 member nations**, the original name was retained due to its historical significance. While China continues to provide political and financial support to the G77, it doesn't consider itself a member as a result of which, the official statements are delivered in the name of The **Group of 77 and China** or **G77+China**.

The **inaugural meeting** of the G-77 took place in **Algiers** in 1967, during which the significant **Charter of Algiers** was formally adopted. This event marked a milestone in the group's development, leading to the establishment of a more structured institutional framework. Through collective action, the G-77 enables member countries to enhance their negotiating power on global economic issues. Additionally, the group strives to foster South-South cooperation to expedite economic growth. The **Chairmanship**, serving as the highest political authority within the organization, rotates among regional representatives from Africa, Asia-Pacific, and Latin America and the Caribbean. Each Chairmanship tenure lasts for one year across all G-77 Chapters.

Points to remember

- The **Republic of Uganda** holds the chairmanship of the G77 (in New York) for 2024, succeeding Cuba.
- The South Summit is the supreme decision-making body and the first and the second south summits were held in Havana, Cuba, in April 2000 and in Doha, Qatar, in June 2005, respectively. The Third Summit is scheduled to be held in December 2023 in Kampala (Uganda).
- The 46th Annual Meeting of Ministers for Foreign Affairs of the G-77 was held in September 2022 in New York.
- Rome (FAO), Geneva (UN), Vienna (UNIDO), Nairobi (UNEP), Paris (UNESCO), and the Group of 24 in Washington, D.C. are Chapters of the Group of 77.

The activities of G-77 are financed through contributions by Member States in accordance with the relevant decisions of the First South Summit. **China** does not consider itself to be a member of the group, however, it helps by contributing financially to the G77.

Intergovernmental Group of Twenty-Four on International Monetary Affairs and Development (G-24)

The **G-24** or the **Intergovernmental Group of Twenty-Four on International Monetary Affairs and Development** was established in **1971** (formally created in 1972) by the G77 as one of its Chapters. It coordinates the position of developing countries on monetary and development issues in the deliberations and decisions of the Bretton Woods Institutions (BWI).

The **members** include Algeria, Argentina, Brazil, China, Colombia, Congo, Cote D'ivoire, Ecuador, Egypt, Ethiopia, Gabon, Ghana, Guatemala, Haiti, India, Iran, Kenya, Lebanon, Mexico, Morocco, Nigeria, Pakistan, Peru, Philippines, South Africa, Sri Lanka, Syria, Trinidad & Tobago and Venezuela. Every member of the G-24, except for Mexico, is also a member of the G77.

The **Caracas Programme of Action (CPA)** in 1981 brought the concept of collective self-reliance to the operational stage. The CPA identifies a set of priority actions in the fields of trade, technology, food and agriculture, energy, raw materials, finance, industrialization and technical cooperation. The **Perez-Guerrero Trust Fund on Economic and Technical Cooperation among Developing Countries (PGTF)** was established in 1986 with an initial core capital of US$ 5 million with the condition that only interest accrued on PGTF could be used to support projects so as to preserve intact the core capital. The PFTG has been very successful in providing an independent funding source for the grouping.

India and G77

The G77 nations have successfully demanded greater participation of developing nations in international politics while arguing that the negotiations should lead to international agreements which enhance their growth. While the G77 continued to work towards its agendas, some nations grew more than the others over time and wished to take up larger roles. The consequence of such a demand was the creation of the **BASIC** coalition.

The BASIC nations which included Brazil, China, India and South Africa formed a grouping in **2009** to team up and address the climate change negotiations together. Together with the G77, they've worked to achieve certain central goals in the negotiations, which includes mainly – (1) a greater participation in the global governance structure and (2) an equitable access to resources which could support their sustainable development aspirations. India has been supporting the efforts and participating in the activities of both G77 and the BASIC grouping. The relationship between the members of G77 and BASIC has been one of mutual benefit or even mutual dependency.

ASIA-PACIFIC ECONOMIC COOPERATION (APEC)

- APEC is a **regional economic forum** that was established in **1989**.

- Members: It consists of **21 member economies**, including Australia, Brunei Darussalam, Canada, Chile, China, Hong Kong (China), Indonesia, Japan, Korea, Malaysia, Mexico, New Zealand, Papua New Guinea, Peru, the Philippines, Russia, Singapore, Chinese Taipei, Thailand, the United States, and Vietnam.
  - The term 'economies' is used for the members since the forum has a cooperative process which is mainly concerned with economic issues. Hence, the members engage with each other as economic entities.

- Aims and Objectives: To promote and enhance the interdependence of the Asia-Pacific region and facilitate the development of a prosperous regional economy. APEC aims to achieve balanced, inclusive, sustainable, innovative, and secure growth within the region.
- The **APEC Secretariat, headquartered in Singapore**, serves as the central support mechanism for the APEC process. It plays a crucial role in coordinating, providing technical assistance, and offering advisory services to promote sustainable economic growth and prosperity in the Asia-Pacific region.
- It is **not a donor organisation** and the activities are centrally funded – by **annual contributions** from member economies. The decisions of the forum are reached by **consensus** and are **not binding in nature**; additionally, the **commitments** are made on a **voluntary** basis.
- Decision-Making Body: Operates on a consensus-based approach, with decisions made by member economies at the APEC Economic Leaders' Meeting and Ministerial Meetings.

NOTE - The last APEC Economic Leaders' Meeting took place in **San Francisco, USA**, in November 2023. The upcoming APEC host include Peru (2024), the Republic of Korea (2025), and Viet Nam (2027).

- Major Hurdles: Divergent economic policies among members, geopolitical tensions (especially U.S.-China relations), and varying levels of commitment to APEC's non-binding goals.
- Future Prospects: APEC continues to play a critical role in fostering economic cooperation, with an increased focus on digital economy, green growth, and inclusive development.

The APEC region generated a nominal GDP of USD 52 trillion in 2020, accounting for 62% of the global nominal GDP. APEC's work is guided by the **Putrajaya Vision 2040** which aims at creating an open, resilient, dynamic and peaceful Asia-Pacific community by 2040. Three economic drivers are to be targeted – (1) Trade and investment (2) Innovation and digitalization (3) Strong, balanced, secure, sustainable and inclusive growth.

India and APEC

India is presently not a full member of the APEC and holds an 'observer status' (as of April 2023). While India has been keen on joining the economic grouping as a member, it has failed to garner substantial support so far. A reason which is usually presented for India's non-inclusion in the grouping is **APEC's extra-regional status**. In contrast to the term 'Indo-Pacific' which is much wider, the term 'Asia Pacific' relates only to that part of Asia which lies in the Pacific Ocean and India doesn't effectively fall under the ambit of APEC and hence, cannot be a full member.

Benfits of joining APEC

- Natural extension of India's **Act East Policy** and could help in the growth of our North-Eastern region.
- Provides a pathway for **greater integration into the regions's economy**, while additionally **attracting investments**.
- Makes **'trade' a unifying force** in the region, in the face of competing trade regimes straining the ties.
- Helps to boost **strategic and geopolitical interests** surrounding the Pacific region.
- Helps to **tap the potential of the demographic dividend** through a wider market.
- Potential to **reform our trade structure** and incorporate global best practices and benchmarks.
- It acts as a step towards gaining access to the **Trans-Pacific Partnership (TPP)**

Certain challenges which have been cited in India's journey to becoming a member of APEC

The standards of India's goods and services being exported, which include the recent issues of **Sanitary and Phytosanitary (SPS) measures** and **Technical Barriers to Trade (TBT).**

India's **inability to align with the global standards** in terms of its intellectual property regime.

India's **management of the policies** relating to land acquisition, labour reforms and other ease of doing business targets.

After the APEC leaders' decision in 2012 to not extend the moratorium on new membership, there has been a **renewed effort to include India as a member of APEC**. The present decade has again seen a revival of discussions on the issue of India's membership to the APEC, however, the country continues to face impediments in the form of opposition from members who do not consider India's record on economic reform satisfactory or worthy of meriting inclusion.

GROUP OF 15 (G-15)

G15 is an **informal forum** which was established at the Ninth Non-Aligned Summit Meeting in Belgrade, then Yugoslavia, in **September 1989** as an 'Action Group' to support the Third World. The first Summit was held in Malaysia in 1990. It is composed of countries from Latin America, Africa, and Asia with a common agenda of enhanced growth and prosperity. The summit-level Group encourages **South-South cooperation** and **North-South dialogue**.

- <u>Membership</u>: It has expanded and includes Algeria, Argentina, Brazil, Chile, Egypt, India, Indonesia, Iran, Jamaica, Kenya, Malaysia, Mexico, Nigeria, Senegal, Sri Lanka, Venezuela, Zimbabwe.
- <u>Focus Areas</u>: The Group focuses on **cooperation** among developing countries in the areas of investment, trade, and technology. It aims to serve as a **forum for regular consultations** among developing countries with a view to coordinate policies and actions.
- <u>Decision Making</u>: The highest decision-making body of the G-15 is the **annual Summit Meeting** of its **Head of State and Government (HOS/G)** which is chaired by the country hosting the summit.
  - The G-15 Summit takes place every two years and is hosted in rotation among the three developing regions represented in the G-15 membership.
  - The summit is overseen and coordinated by a steering committee, known as the ***Troika***, consisting of the foreign ministers of the preceding host country, the current host country, and the anticipated future host country.

- Last Summit: The **15th G-15 Summit** was held in Colombo, Sri Lanka in 2012.

Although the G-15 does not have an established administrative structure, it benefits from the Technical Support Facility (TSF) located in Geneva. Furthermore, the Federation of Chambers of Commerce, Industry, and Services (FCCIS) serves as a private sector forum for G-15 member countries. The FCCIS aims to facilitate coordination and collaboration in promoting business, economic development, and joint investments among G-15 nations.

India and G-15

India was a founder member of the G-15 grouping and along with other members, it had conceived the grouping as an economic forum designed to foster South-South cooperation. G-15 has taken up cooperative projects in diverse sectoral areas such as food production, population, energy, geological research, family planning, telecom, gene banks, medicinal and aromatic plants, solar energy, Information Technology etc. India continues to support the endeavours of the group, and although the grouping hasn't been very active over the last decade and there have been differences of opinions in relation to trade and financial issues, the members continue to engage in discussions to support the greater cause of South-South cooperation and growth of the Third World.

CPEC (CHINA-PAKISTAN ECONOMIC CORRIDOR)

- Members: China and Pakistan.
- Aims & Objectives: Enhance infrastructure, boost economic development, and strengthen bilateral ties through a series of infrastructure and energy projects.
- Focus Areas: Infrastructure development, energy projects, Gwadar port development, and economic zones.
- Decision-Making Body: Joint Cooperation Committee (JCC) between China and Pakistan oversees the implementation and progress of CPEC projects.

NOTE

The 11th Joint Cooperation Committee meeting was held in Islamabad in October 2023, focusing on expanding the scope of CPEC to include more sectors.

MAJOR TROUBLES & HURDLES - CPEC	
Security Concerns	▪ The CPEC passes through regions like Balochistan and Khyber Pakhtunkhwa, which are prone to insurgencies and terrorist activities. Several attacks on Chinese workers and infrastructure projects have raised concerns about the safety of investments and personnel. ▪ There is resistance from local communities in Balochistan who feel marginalized and fear that the benefits of CPEC projects will not trickle down to them. These communities have occasionally targeted CPEC projects to express their grievances.
Political and Economic Instability in Pakistan	▪ Political instability and frequent changes in government in Pakistan affect the continuity and smooth implementation of CPEC projects. ▪ Pakistan's economic instability, including a high debt burden, has raised concerns about the country's ability to sustain the financial commitments required by CPEC. The possibility of a debt trap similar to what some other countries have experienced with Chinese loans is a significant worry. ▪ Some projects within CPEC, particularly in energy and infrastructure, have faced criticism for their economic viability. There are concerns that these projects may not generate the expected returns, leading to financial strain on Pakistan.
Environmental & Social Impact	▪ Large-scale infrastructure projects under CPEC, such as road construction and port development, have raised concerns about environmental degradation, particularly in ecologically sensitive areas. ▪ The construction of CPEC projects has led to the displacement of local populations, particularly in Balochistan. This has exacerbated social tensions and fueled opposition to the projects.

International Criticism and Geopolitical Tensions	▪ The U.S. and other Western nations have criticized CPEC as part of China's broader Belt and Road Initiative (BRI), viewing it as a tool for expanding Chinese influence in the region. ▪ CPEC is a significant element in the broader geopolitical rivalry between China and other major powers, particularly the United States and India. This rivalry could complicate the progress of CPEC projects.

Implications of CPEC on India

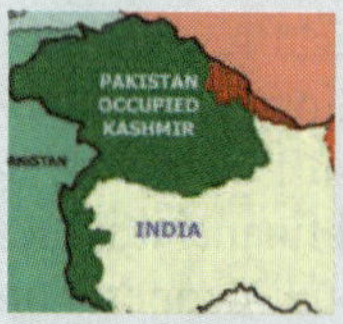

PoK & Sovereignty Concerns

Chinese Strategic presence

Economic & Diplomatic Response

India and BRI

1) **CPEC's Passage Through Pakistan-Occupied Kashmir (PoK)**
   - **India strongly opposes CPEC** because it passes through Pakistan-Occupied Kashmir (PoK), a region India claims as its own. India views CPEC as a **violation of its sovereignty and territorial integrity**. The construction of infrastructure in PoK, such as roads and power plants, is seen as an endorsement of Pakistan's control over the region.
   - India has lodged **formal diplomatic protests** with both Pakistan and China regarding CPEC, particularly the projects in PoK. India has consistently maintained that the region is an integral part of its territory and that any projects undertaken there without its consent are illegal.

2) **Strategic Implications**
   - CPEC is a key component of China's **Belt and Road Initiative (BRI)**, which India views as a strategic encirclement. The development of ***Gwadar*** port and other infrastructure projects in Pakistan gives China a strategic foothold in South Asia, which could be used for military purposes in the future.
   - CPEC has **deepened economic and military ties between China and Pakistan**, two countries that already have a close strategic partnership. This increased cooperation poses a **challenge to India's security**, particularly in the context of the long-standing rivalry with Pakistan.

3) **Economic and Diplomatic Responses**
   - In response to CPEC, India has pursued **alternative connectivity projects** in the region. For instance, India is developing the ***Chabahar*** port in Iran, which provides a route to Afghanistan and Central Asia, bypassing Pakistan. This project is seen as a counterbalance to ***Gwadar*** port under CPEC.
   - India has **strengthened its diplomatic and economic ties** with countries in the Indo-Pacific region, including through initiatives like the Quad (India, the United States, Japan, and Australia). This is part of a broader strategy to counterbalance China's influence in the region.

4) **India's Position on the Belt and Road Initiative (BRI)**
   - India is one of the few major countries that have outrightly rejected China's Belt and Road Initiative, primarily because of CPEC. India has **refused to participate in BRI summits** and has criticized the initiative for lacking transparency, sustainability, and respect for sovereignty.
   - India has advocated for a **rule-based international order** and emphasized the importance of respecting sovereignty and territorial integrity in global projects. India's stance on CPEC is aligned with its broader position on the BRI.

INSTC (INTERNATIONAL NORTH-SOUTH TRANSPORT CORRIDOR)

- Members: India, Iran, Russia, Turkey, Azerbaijan, Kazakhstan, Armenia, Belarus, Tajikistan, Kyrgyzstan, Oman, Ukraine, and Syria. [One Observer State: Bulgaria].
- Aims & Objectives: Develop a multimodal transportation network to enhance trade connectivity between India, Russia, Europe, and Central Asia.
- Focus areas: Infrastructure development, reducing transport costs and time, facilitating trade between member states.
- Decision Making body: Governed by intergovernmental agreements and regular meetings of member state representatives.
- Major Hurdles: Political instability in member regions, logistical challenges, and competition with other trade corridors (e.g., China's Belt and Road Initiative).
- Future Prospects: Potential for increased trade between Europe and Asia, particularly in light of geopolitical shifts and supply chain diversification.

> **NOTE**
> The most recent discussions on INSTC took place in 2023, with a focus on expanding the corridor and integrating it with other regional initiatives.

ASIAN INFRASTRUCTURE INVESTMENT BANK (AIIB)

The **Asian Infrastructure Investment Bank (AIIB)**, founded in 2016, is a multilateral development bank based in Beijing. Its mission is to improve social and economic outcomes in Asia by financing infrastructure projects that promote sustainable development.

- **Members**: As of May 2024, the total number of countries approved for membership of AIIB is 109 (Regional Members: 48, Non-Regional Members: 48, Prospective Members: 13), with participation from regions beyond Asia, including Europe and Africa.
- **Objectives**:
  (a) To promote sustainable infrastructure and facilitate economic development in Asia and other regions.
  (b) Finance projects related to energy, transport, urban development, water supply, and environmental sustainability.
- **Key Projects**:
  (i) AIIB has funded projects in sectors like transportation, renewable energy, water, and urban infrastructure across Asia and parts of Africa.
  (ii) Major investments in green infrastructure projects like solar and wind energy in countries such as India, Pakistan, and Turkey.

AIIB represents China's vision of a multilateral financial institution capable of addressing the infrastructure gaps in developing countries, rivaling Western-dominated institutions like the World Bank and Asian Development Bank. It has become a key player in financing sustainable development in Asia and beyond.

> **NINTH ANNUAL MEETING (2024)**
> The 2024 AIIB Annual Meeting of the Board of Governors of AIIB (9th Annual meeting) will take place in the historic city of Samarkand, Uzbekistan, on Sep. 25-26, 2024. The theme for this year's meeting is, "*Building Resilient Infrastructure for All*".

COMPREHENSIVE AND PROGRESSIVE AGREEMENT FOR TRANS-PACIFIC PARTNERSHIP (CPTPP)

The CPTPP is a major free trade agreement (FTA) among 11 Pacific Rim countries aimed at promoting economic integration, trade liberalization, and investment across the Asia-Pacific region.

- **Members**: 11 Pacific Rim countries (excluding the United States)
- **Focus**: A trade agreement that evolved from the original Trans-Pacific Partnership, focusing on trade liberalization and economic integration across the Pacific region.

- Origins and Evolution –
  - In 2016, twelve nations—including the **United States**—signed the **Trans-Pacific Partnership (TPP)**, a comprehensive trade agreement that aimed to enhance trade and economic cooperation by addressing investment, intellectual property rights, labor standards, and environmental concerns.
  - The original signatories included **Australia, Brunei, Canada, Chile, Japan, Malaysia, Mexico, Peru, New Zealand, Singapore, Vietnam**, and the **United States**.
  - However, after the U.S. withdrew from the TPP in 2017, the remaining 11 countries moved forward with a revised version of the agreement, renaming it the **Comprehensive and Progressive Agreement for Trans-Pacific Partnership (CPTPP)**.
  - The CPTPP was officially signed in **March 2018** in **Santiago, Chile**, as a continuation of the TPP, but with key provisions suspended to accommodate the absence of the U.S. This agreement preserves the core objectives of the original TPP, while offering flexibility for other nations to join in the future.
- **Nations involved** - Australia, Brunei Darussalam, Canada, Chile, Japan, Malaysia, Mexico, Peru, New Zealand, Singapore and Vietnam. More recently, China, Taiwan and the United Kingdom have shown interest in joining the partnership.
- **Objective** - The CPTPP seeks to:

1) **Promote Regional Economic Integration**: The agreement aims to foster deeper economic cooperation among member nations by reducing or eliminating tariffs and non-tariff barriers on goods and services. This trade liberalization enhances market access and economic growth across the Asia-Pacific region.
2) **Enhance Investment Opportunities**: By creating transparent and predictable rules for investment, the CPTPP encourages foreign direct investment (FDI) between member countries, promoting long-term economic development.
3) **Address Broader Economic Cooperation**: Beyond trade, the CPTPP sets standards on intellectual property rights, labor practices, environmental protection, and dispute resolution mechanisms, providing a modern, comprehensive framework for economic governance.

The CPTPP is a landmark in trade diplomacy, serving as a model for future trade agreements. Its comprehensive nature addresses not only tariffs but also modern challenges like intellectual property, labor rights, and environmental sustainability. The inclusion of major economies in the Asia-Pacific region gives it significant economic and geopolitical weight, positioning it as a counterbalance to other regional agreements, such as the Regional Comprehensive Economic Partnership (RCEP) and China's Belt and Road Initiative.

By encouraging an open and inclusive trading environment, the CPTPP provides an opportunity for countries to benefit from the rapidly growing economies of the Asia-Pacific while adhering to high standards in trade and economic cooperation.

RCEP (REGIONAL COMPREHENSIVE ECONOMIC PARTNERSHIP)

- The RCEP is a **Free Trade Agreement (FTA)** which was signed by **15 nations – 10 ASEAN members** and five key partners including **China, South Korea, Japan, Australia and New Zealand**, at the **4th RCEP leaders' summit** in **November 2020**.
- **Focus**: A free trade agreement that creates the world's largest trading bloc by GDP, aiming to reduce tariffs and facilitate trade among member countries.

It has been hailed as the world's largest FTA and has the potential to increase the global national income by USD 186 billion annually by 2030 and add 0.2% to the economy of its participating members.

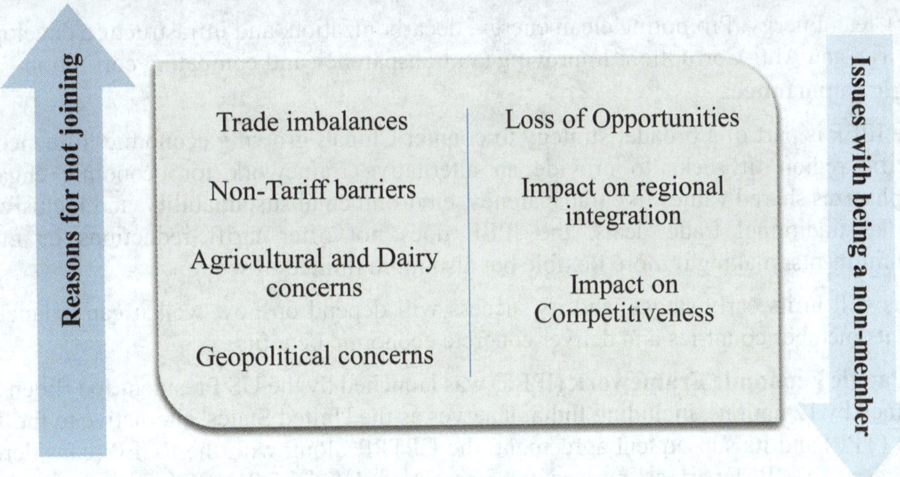

India was originally part of the RCEP negotiations but decided not to join the agreement.
Additionally, the US has also not joined the grouping.

India was concerned about the potential **trade imbalances** that could arise from the RCEP agreement. India's trade deficit with many of the RCEP member countries, particularly China, has been a long-standing issue. India was concerned that the RCEP agreement would lead to further imbalances and harm its domestic industries. The **non-tariff barriers** were another point of conflict that was a potential threat. India was worried that the RCEP could lead to an influx of cheaper imports from other countries that could harm its domestic industries, particularly its small and medium-sized enterprises (SMEs). Additionally, the influx of cheaper **agricultural and dairy imports** from other countries was another cause of concern for India's domestic farmers. Lastly, India was worried about the **growing influence of China** in the Asia-Pacific region and did not want to be seen as aligning itself too closely with China.

While the decision to stay out could seem rational for now, however, India's absence from the RCEP could have some negative repercussions in the long run. This decision could lead to a **loss of trade opportunities** with the member countries since the RCEP is expected to create the world's largest trading bloc, with a combined GDP of around $26 trillion. Staying out of the FTA could mean that Indian businesses may find it harder to access markets in the RCEP countries, putting them at a disadvantage compared to competitors in other countries that are part of the agreement. An absence could also impact India's **regional integration** in the Asia-Pacific region. It could also limit India's ability to shape the direction of economic integration in the region. The RCEP is expected to reduce trade barriers among the member countries, making it easier for businesses to trade and invest across borders. India's absence from the agreement could make it harder for Indian businesses to **compete** with those in the RCEP countries, particularly in sectors such as manufacturing and services.

INDO-PACIFIC ECONOMIC FRAMEWORK (IPEF)

The **Indo-Pacific Economic Framework (IPEF)** was launched in May 2022 by U.S. President Joe Biden as part of Washington's efforts to re-engage economically with the Indo-Pacific region, which is increasingly seen as the geopolitical center of gravity.

- **Members**: 14 countries, including the United States, India, Japan, Australia, South Korea, and several ASEAN members.
- **Focus**:
  - **Economic Cooperation**: The IPEF aims to deepen economic engagement and cooperation among its members in the Indo-Pacific region. It is not a traditional free trade agreement but a strategic framework focusing on broader economic issues.
  - **Key Pillars**: The framework is organized around four key pillars:
    1) Trade: Enhancing digital trade, labor standards, and environmental sustainability.
    2) Supply Chains: Improving supply chain resilience and reducing vulnerabilities.

3) Clean Energy: Promoting clean energy, decarbonization, and infrastructure development.
4) Tax and Anti-Corruption: Improving tax transparency and combating corruption.

- **Strategic Importance**:
  (a) The IPEF is part of a broader strategy to counter China's growing economic influence in the Indo-Pacific region. It seeks to provide an alternative framework for economic engagement that emphasizes shared values like transparency, environmental sustainability, and inclusivity.
  (b) Unlike traditional trade deals, the IPEF does not offer tariff reductions or market access commitments, making it more flexible but also more limited in scope.

The IPEF is still in its early stages, and its success will depend on how well it can balance the diverse interests of its member countries and deliver concrete economic benefits.

The **Indo-Pacific Economic Framework** (IPEF) was launched by the US President Joe Biden in **May 2023** and was joined by 12 nations, including India. It serves as the United States' alternative to the Trans-Pacific Partnership (TPP) and its subsequent agreement, the CPTPP, along with the RCEP (considered as China-led). The (present) 14 IPEF partners represent 40 percent of global GDP and 28 percent of global goods and services trade.

- Nations involved (as of 30th May 2023)- Australia, Brunei, Fiji, India, Indonesia, Japan, Republic of Korea, Malaysia, New Zealand, Philippines, Singapore, Thailand, Vietnam & USA.
- Objective - IPEF seeks to strengthen economic engagement among partner countries with the goal of advancing growth, peace and prosperity in the region.

INDIAN PERSPECTIVE

- India has been engaged in a dispute with the United States for the past couple of years regarding the matter of **data localisation**, which is a major concern for the country. In 2019, the Indian government presented a Bill in the Lok Sabha that outlines a structure for keeping Indian data within the country and the creation of a Data Protection Authority.
- However, as per the statement made by the Ministry of External Affairs, "**India is committed to a free, open, and inclusive Indo-Pacific region** and believes that deepening economic engagement among partners is crucial for continued growth, peace, and prosperity. India is keen to collaborate with partner countries under the IPEF and work towards advancing regional economic connectivity, integration and boosting trade and investment within the region".
- **India has joined Pillars II to IV of IPEF while it has an observer status in Pillar-I.**

12 GLOBAL GOVERNANCE INSTITUTIONS

GLOBAL GOVERNANCE

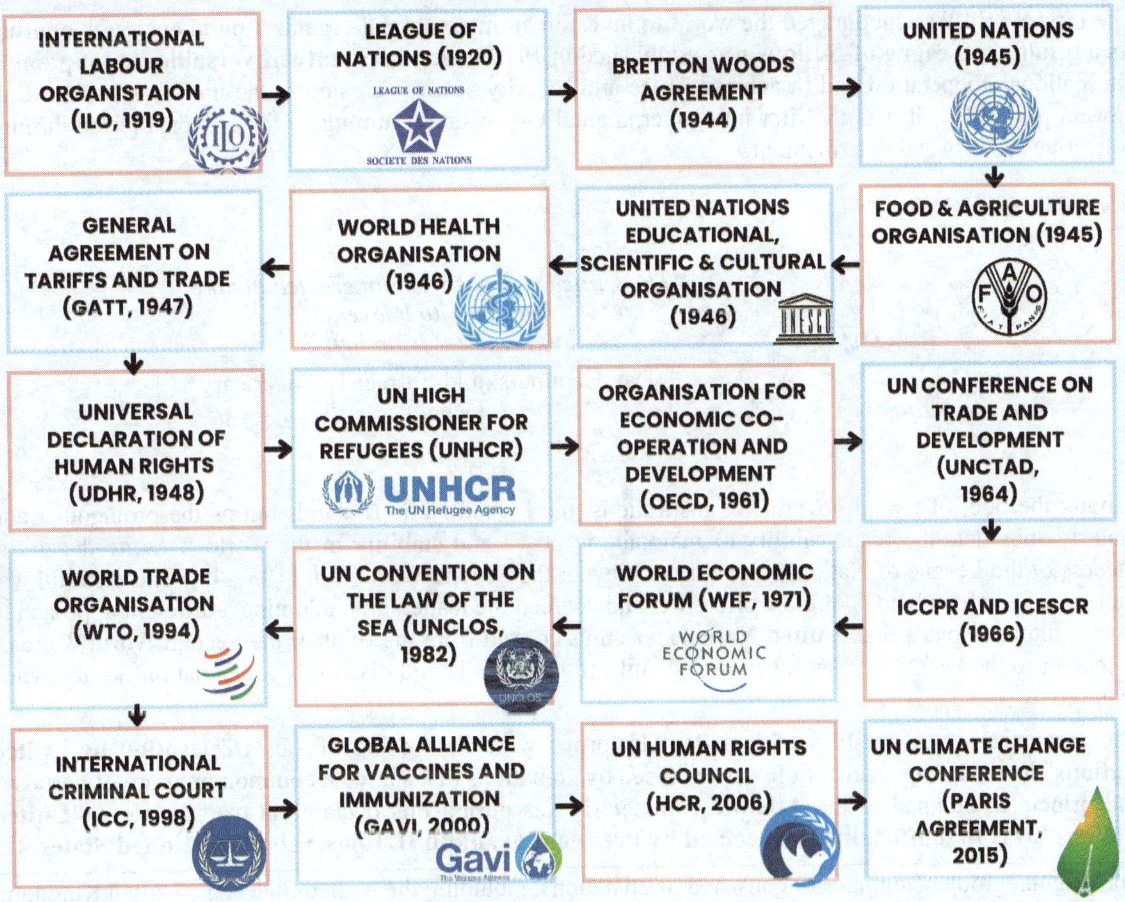

The international institutions for global governance are in no way a silver bullet for all the discrepancies and hindrances obstructing the smooth course of events on the globe, however their existence is indispensable. Only after gruesome wars were fought for power and dominance did the world leaders realise that '**shared progress**' was the only way forward. While national governments were well equipped to tackle domestic complications, resolving issues on a global level required convergence of ideas on a larger scale. States therefore agreed to discuss contentious issues and find peaceful solutions under the umbrella of an international organization instead of going headfirst into war. Such organizations, contrary to popular belief, are not 'Super States' which hold complete authority over its members, but in fact owe their creation to the states and respond to their grievances while remaining neutral in the process of offering their services.

Some issues in the recent decades have had **transboundary effects** which require the commitment of several nations to effectively counter them. The matters which require a multilateral approach include epidemics and pandemics, climate change and global warming, piracy and free passage of the seas, space and use of global commons among others. The international organizations thus provide a durable **platform to brainstorm ideas** and helps to produce information for effective coordination. Such organizations enable the creation of mechanisms, rules and bureaucracy to handle international affairs and helps in confidence-building about cost-sharing, division of benefits and commitment to honor the terms and conditions of the award or decision, as it relates. They therefore assist to coordinate the actions of transnational actors and alleviate collective action problems, provide global public goods especially peace and security, establish mediation systems for conflict and provide unified standards for trade and industry.

LEAGUE OF NATIONS AND THE UNITED NATIONS

Origin Story

The First World War encouraged the world to invest in an international organization to deal with conflict. As a result, the **League of Nations** was established in 1919 under the **Treaty of Versailles** to 'to promote international cooperation and to achieve peace and security'. It was created at the initiative of the Allied powers post WWI. It was the first intergovernmental Organisation aiming to foster world peace through collective security and disarmament.

UNITED NATIONS

UNITED NATIONS

"The United Nations was not created to take humanity to heaven, but to save it from hell."

— Dag Hammarskjold, former UN Secretary-General

Among the pool of global governance institutions, the United Nations stands out as the protagonist and majorly shoulders the responsibility of maintaining peace and stability in the world. Despite the initial success of the League of Nations, it could not prevent the Second World War (1939-45). The dreadful war shook the very foundations of the world order and coerced the leaders into adopting a different approach to handle future disputes. The **United Nations** was thus created from the ruins of the Second World War as a successor to the League of Nations to remedy bilateral or multilateral discord between nations as and when required.

The organization was established in a flexible format with the signing of the **"Declaration by United Nations"** in **1942**. This declaration was endorsed by 26 nations that shared a common program of purposes and principles outlined in the **Atlantic Charter**. It was during this declaration that **the term "United Nations" was first officially used, coined by President Franklin D. Roosevelt of the United States**.

The original group of signatories consisted of 26 nations, including the United States, the United Kingdom, the Soviet Union, China, Australia, Belgium, Canada, Costa Rica, Cuba, Czechoslovakia, the Dominican Republic, El Salvador, Greece, Guatemala, Haiti, Honduras, India, Luxembourg, the Netherlands, New Zealand, Nicaragua, Norway, Panama, Poland, South Africa, and Yugoslavia.

San Francisco Conference

Representatives from fifty nations convened in San Francisco, USA, from 25 April to 26 June 1945 for the United Nations Conference on International Organization. During the conference, the objective was to conclude the drafting of the Charter of the United Nations and establish the Statute of the newly-formed International Court of Justice. It is worth noting that at the time of the conference, there was no universally recognized Polish Government. However, on 28 June, such a government was announced, bringing the total number of nations represented to fifty-one. There were over 850 delegates apart from the advisers and staff which brought the count to approximately 3500. While being an important Conference in the pages of history, it was also the largest international gathering of the time. The voting procedure was critical, and every section of the Charter had to be passed by a two-thirds majority.

While the Charter was signed at the San Francisco Conference on 26 June 1945, the UN didn't immediately come into existence, since in many countries it had to be approved by their parliaments. On **24 October**

1945 (observed as the United Nations Day), when the five permanent members and a majority of other signatory states had ratified the Charter and notified the State Department of the United States, the United Nations came into existence.

The current membership of the UN is of **193 members** and two 'non-member observer states' namely Palestine and Vatican City.

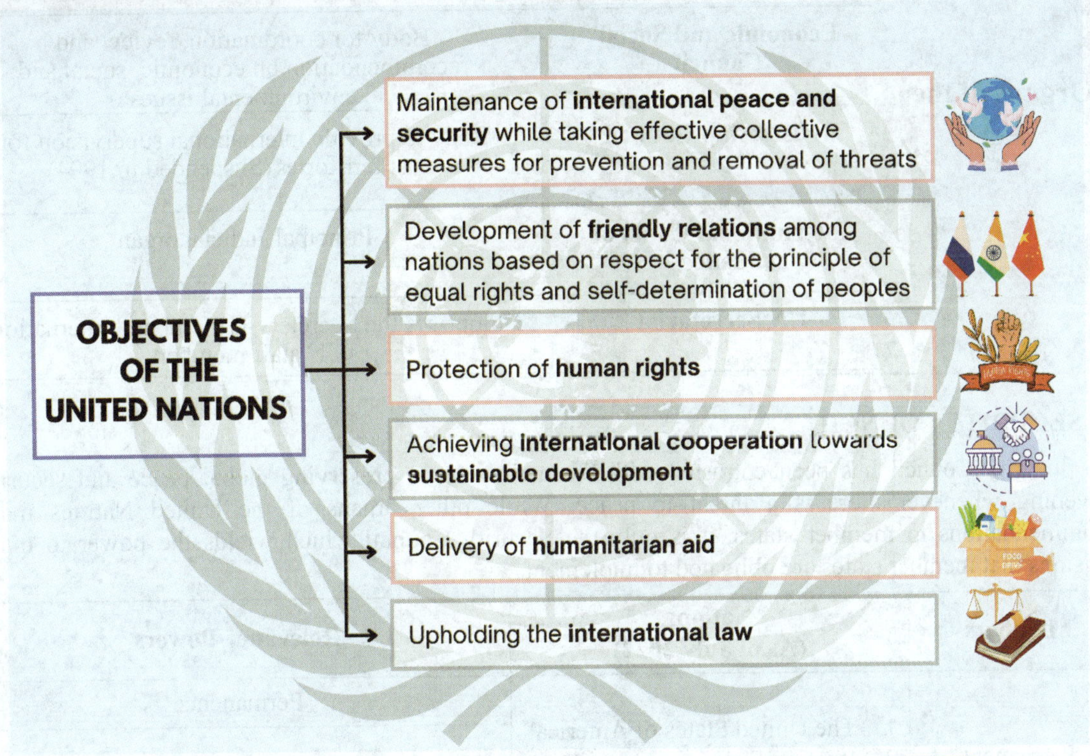

- Negotiation
- Investigation commissions
- Mediation
- Judicial settlements
- Resorting to regional institutions or treaties
- Other peaceful means of their own choice

Mechanisms for peaceful settlement of conflicts

Organs of the UN	General Assembly	Deliberative and representative organ
	Security Council	Body primarily responsible for maintaining peace and security
	Economic and Social Council	Body for coordination, review and recommendation on economic, social and environmental issues
	Trusteeship Council	Body to provide international supervision for 'trust territories'(Suspended in 1994)
	International Court of Justice	Principal Judicial organ
	UN Secretariat	Comprises the Secretary-General and international UN staff members

UN SECURITY COUNCIL

The Security Council has been entrusted with the main role of preserving global peace and security, convening whenever there is a threat to peace. While other organs of the United Nations make recommendations to member states, it is only the Security Council which wields the power to make decisions that member states are obligated to implement.

Members	Nations (As of July 2022)	Relevance/Powers
Permanent Members (5)	1. The United States of America 2. Russian Federation 3. China 4. The United Kingdom 5. France	Permanence 'Veto' Power: If any of the five permanent members of the 15-member Security Council casts a dissenting vote, the resolution or decision would not be authorized.
Non-Permanent Members (10)	1) Algeria (end of the term: 2025) 2) Ecuador (2024) 3) Guyana (2025) 4) Japan (2024) 5) Malta (2024) 6) Mozambique (2024) 7) Republic of Korea (2025) 8) Sierra Leone (2025) 9) Slovenia (2025) 10) Switzerland (2024)	Each year the General Assembly elects five non-permanent members (out of 10 in total) for a **two-year term.** In accordance with the General Assembly resolution of 1963, the 10 non-permanent seats are **distributed on a regional basis-** • Five for African and Asian States • One for Eastern European States • Two for the Latin American and Caribbean States • Two for Western European and other States.

Voting System

- As per Article 27 of the UN Charter:
- Each member of the Security Council is entitled to one vote.
- Procedural matters are decided by an affirmative vote of nine members.
- For all other matters, an affirmative vote of nine members is required, including the concurring votes of the permanent members. However, in decisions related to Chapter VI and paragraph 3 of Article 52, a party involved in a dispute must abstain from voting.

NOTE

The five permanent states were selected on the pretext of being the **most powerful nations immediately after the Second World War** and also because they constituted the victors in the War. The UN Charter gave the permanent members a privileged position to bring about stability in the world after the Second World War.

The **International Telecommunication Union was founded in 1865**. The **International Telegraph Union, and the Universal Postal Union were established in 1874** and both are presently United Nations specialized agencies.

The reality of the 21st century is in stark contrast to the time when the UN was born. The Soviet Union has disintegrated, paving the way for the Russian Federation, the status of the United States as the sole superpower is fast diluting, China is emerging as a great power, while locking horns with the US, the withdrawal of US forces and a regime change in Afghanistan has raised humanitarian issues, the pandemic has significantly altered the way people lead their lives and the unabated use of fossil fuels has exacerbated the climate change with the repercussions being truly felt by all. Meanwhile other issues continue to destabilize the world order including the Russia-Ukraine War, Syria-Palestine conflict, terrorism, nuclear proliferation, refugee and migrant related issues, food insecurity, wildfires, coral bleaching and economic depressions among other things.

Therefore, the UN has its work cut out for itself.

INDIA AND THE UNITED NATIONS

India, a founding member of the UN and signatory to the 1942 Declaration by United Nations, has played a proactive role in the organization since its inception. This active involvement reflected Jawaharlal Nehru's internationalist vision at independence. India's foreign policy goals, aligned with UN principles, facilitated a harmonious relationship between the two. During the Cold War, India viewed the UN as crucial for maintaining peace and took a leading stance on issues such as anti-colonialism and global economic fairness. The Kashmir issue was also brought before the UN in 1948. In the 1970s and 80s, India advocated for a more equitable, multilateral world order, proposing concepts like the Indian Ocean as a peace zone and a new International Economic Order. Rajiv Gandhi's 1988 proposal for a "Nuclear-Weapon Free and Non-violent World Order" was a landmark initiative.

India has significantly contributed to the UNDP and peacekeeping forces and has served as a non-permanent Security Council member eight times, including the 2021-22 term. It continues to push for UN reforms to enhance its representativeness and relevance.

Arguments for India's permanent membership include –

Global Leadership & Influence

Economic Prowess & Global Trade

Contributions to the UN

Global Issues

I. Global Leadership and Influence

- **Rising Power:** India's emergence as the world's largest democracy and its growing economic and political influence makes it a natural candidate for permanent membership.
- **Regional Leadership:** India's strategic location and its role as a regional power necessitate its inclusion in the UN Security Council to address challenges and promote cooperation in the region.

II. Economic Prowess and Global Trade

- **Economic Influence:** India's growing economy and its increasing role in global trade make it a vital player in international affairs.
- **Trade Negotiations:** India's participation in the UN Security Council would enhance its ability to influence global trade negotiations and address trade-related disputes.

III. Contributions to the UN

- **Financial Contributions:** India is a significant contributor to the UN's budget and peacekeeping missions.
- **Human Resources:** India provides a large number of troops and police officers to UN peacekeeping operations.

IV. Global Issues

- **Climate Change:** India has been a vocal advocate for addressing climate change and has taken steps to promote renewable energy.
- **Nuclear Disarmament:** India has championed nuclear disarmament and non-proliferation efforts.
- **Regional Representation:** India's diversity and its connections to neighboring countries make it well-suited to represent the interests of the South Asian region.

India has been advocating for "**constructive reforms**" in the United Nations and various international organizations like the IMF, WHO, and WTO. The objective is to adapt these institutions to the present realities and ensure that India and other developing nations have a fair voice. Harsh V Pant highlights that India's push for restructuring global multilateral institutions includes the need for institutional accountability and broader representation of developing countries.

Peacekeeping Missions

Since 1948, over one million women and men from 125 countries have served in 71 Peacekeeping Missions. The peacekeepers have proven to be the saviors for some of the world's most vulnerable people. Their efforts and sacrifices on the field has made the '**Blue Helmet**' or '**Blue Beret**' an epitome of hope and justice for millions. The United Nations Missions and Peacekeeping forces have been deployed in several nations over the years including Lebanon (1958), Congo (1960), Yemen (1963), Cyprus (1964), Iran-Iraq (1988), Central America (1989), El Salvador (1991), Somalia (1992), Haiti (1993), Bosnia and Herzegovina (1995), Angola (1997), Sierra Leone (1999), Tajikistan (2000), Sudan (2005), etc. Presently, more than 100,000 military, police and civilian personnel from 125 nations are serving in 14 peacekeeping operations. The following table presents the timeline of some important developments of the UN Peacekeeping Forces.

Year	Particulars
May 29, 1948	The **UN Truce Supervision Organisation (UNTSO)** was established to call for cessation of hostilities in Palestine. It was decided that the truce should be supervised by the UN Mediator, with the assistance of a group of military observers.
Jan 24, 1949	The first team of unarmed military observers, who later formed the nucleus of the **UN Military Observer Group in India and Pakistan (UNMOGIP)** arrived to assist the Military adviser of the UN Commission for India and Pakistan.

Nov 5, 1956	The **United Nations Emergency Force (UNEFI)** was established to secure an end to the Suez Crisis and supervise the withdrawal of armed forces of France, Israel and UK from Egypt and later act as a buffer between Egyptian forces and provide impartial supervision of the ceasefire.
Sept 20, 1965	The **UN India-Pakistan Observation Mission (UNIPOM)** was established to supervise the ceasefire along the India-Pakistan border except in J&K (UNMOGIP operated here). The UNIPOM was closed in March 1966.
Oct 25, 1973	The **Second UN Emergency Force (UNEFII)** was established to supervise an immediate and complete ceasefire between Egyptian and Israeli forces. It was assisted by the military observers of the UNTSO
Sept 29, 1988	UN Peacekeeping Forces won the **Nobel Peace Prize**
Nov 8, 1994	The **International Criminal Tribunal for Rwanda (ICTR)** was established to prosecute persons responsible for genocide and other violations of humanitarian law. The ICTR was closed in 2015.
Aug 21, 2000	The **Brahimi Report** was submitted by the high-level Panel on UN peace and security activities, chaired by Lakhdar Brahimi. The report noted that the peacekeeping operations must be equipped fully and should operate under credible mandates.
Mar 28, 2018	Secretary-General Antonio Guterres launched the **Action for Peacekeeping (A4P)** initiative at a Security Council High-Level Debate.
Apr 2022	UN Secretary-General António Guterres traveled to Kyiv (Ukraine) and visited sites of suspected war crimes in the region.

India's Contribution

India has had a long association with the UN Peacekeeping forces and has provided more than 2,00,000 military and police officers to UN peacekeeping missions. They have altogether served in 49 of the 71 missions established since 1948. India has also contributed eminent Force Commanders for the missions and is presently (as of August 2022) the fifth largest troop contributor (TCC) with 5,323 personnel deployed in 8 out of 13 active missions. The other important services provided by the Indian side include medical care, veterinary support and engineering services. Additionally, India garnered accolades when it became the first country in 2007 to deploy an all-women contingent to a UN Peacekeeping Mission (Liberia). On the flip side, India has lost more peacekeepers than any other UN member state, a staggering 175 in number.

> In July 2022, two BSF personnel who were part of a Mission in the Democratic Republic of Congo (DRC) were among the five who lost their lives during a protest near the border with Uganda.

The Secretary Generals of the UN have been known to work towards continuously adapting to new challenges in peace, security and development areas. Continuing the momentum, in January 2019 António Guterres with the support of Member States launched an unprecedented reform to the UN system. A new 'Department of Peace Operations' (DPO) was created to act as the centre of excellence for the UN peace operations. The main goals of the reforms related to –

- Prioritizing prevention and peace
- Strengthening the effectiveness and coherence of peacekeeping operations and special political missions
- Aligning more closely with the development and human rights pillars.

India has been discussing the need to create linkages between the nature of contemporary peacekeeping operations and the ground realities. The Indian representatives have highlighted the need to co-relate the resources provided with the rapid changes on the surface.

Reformation of the United Nations

While the UN has assisted in tackling the issues plaguing the world, the situation on ground has been drastically altered and the reformation of the body has thus long been overdue. Previously in 1992, on a debate surrounding the reformation of UN Security Council, the UN General Assembly adopted a resolution. The resolution reflected three main complaints:

(i) The Security Council **does not accurately represent the current political landscape**.
(ii) Its **decisions primarily align with Western values** and interests and are heavily influenced by a small group of powerful countries.
(iii) It **lacks fair and balanced representation.**

The nations have also been pressing to give effect to the reforms in question. The major discussions in the international circles revolve around the following key issues -

United Nations Reform Agendas	Question of the veto held by the permanent members
	Regional representation
	Categories of Membership
	The working methods of an enlarged Council
	The Security Council and General Assembly relationship

NOTE

In **September 2024**, the United States announced its support for **adding two permanent seats for African nations** on the U.N. Security Council, along with the introduction of a **non-permanent seat for a small island developing state** for the first time. The U.S. Ambassador to the U.N. highlighted that, "*While Africa has three non-permanent seats on the Security Council, that doesn't allow African countries "to deliver the full benefit of their knowledge and voices*."

UNITED NATIONS EDUCATIONAL, SCIENTIFIC AND CULTURAL ORGANIZATION (UNESCO)

UNESCO, established in **November 1945** (with its constitution taking effect in 1946), is a specialized agency of the United Nations. Its primary objective is to foster global cooperation in the fields of education, science, culture, and communication in order to promote peace and security. **India has been a member of UNESCO since 1946.**

The Organization has 193 Members and 12 Associate Members [The US and Israel officially withdrew from the UNESCO in December 2018] and is governed by the General Conference and the Executive Board (58 Members). The Secretariat, led by the **Director-General**, is responsible for executing the decisions made by these two entities. With over 50 field offices worldwide, the organization's headquarters are situated in Paris.

UNESCO is also responsible for designating and protecting **World Heritage Sites, Biosphere Reserves**, and **Intangible Cultural Heritage**, and it plays a critical role in advancing the UN's global agenda for sustainable development.

UNIVERSAL DECLARATION OF HUMAN RIGHTS (UDHR)

The UDHR is a historic document adopted by the **United Nations General Assembly** on **December 10, 1948**. It was drafted by representatives from different legal and cultural backgrounds from all regions of the world. The UDHR is considered a milestone in the history of human rights as it recognizes the inherent dignity and worth of all human beings, and sets out fundamental human rights to be universally protected.

These rights include civil and political rights, such as the right to life, liberty, and equality before the law, as well as economic, social, and cultural rights, such as the right to education, work, and social security.

The **UDHR is not binding on the governments**. However, it led to the drafting of **two legally binding covenants – ICCPR and ICESCR.**

ICCPR & ICESCR

International Covenant for Civil and Political Rights (ICCPR) and International Covenant for Economic, Social and Cultural Rights (ICESCR) are multilateral treaties adopted by the United Nations General Assembly in **1966**. Together, they form the **International Bill of Human Rights.**

The **ICCPR** recognizes civil and political rights, such as the right to life, freedom of speech, and freedom of religion. It also includes protections against torture, slavery, and arbitrary detention. The **ICESCR** recognizes economic, social, and cultural rights, such as the right to education, work, and healthcare. It also recognizes the right to an adequate standard of living, including food, clothing, and housing. The ICESCR obliges states parties to promote and protect these rights without discrimination and provides for a treaty body, the Committee on Economic, Social and Cultural Rights, to monitor its implementation.

> The **United Nations Development Programme (UNDP)** is a United Nations agency that focuses on promoting sustainable development and reducing poverty worldwide. The UNDP operates in more than 170 countries and territories, working with national governments, civil society organizations, and the private sector to address development challenges and promote human development. The UNDP's work is guided by the **Sustainable Development Goals (SDGs)**, which are a universal call to action to end poverty, protect the planet, and ensure that all people enjoy peace and prosperity. The SDGs are **17 goals** with 169 targets that all 193 UN Member States have agreed to try to achieve by the year **2030**.

UN HIGH COMMISSIONER FOR REFUGEES (UNHCR)

It is a specialized agency of the UN that is responsible for protecting and assisting refugees, asylum seekers, stateless persons, and other forcibly displaced people around the world. The UNHCR was established in 1950 and is headquartered in Geneva, Switzerland. The UNHCR also works to promote durable solutions for refugees, including voluntary repatriation to their home countries, resettlement in third countries, and local integration in countries of asylum. The UNHCR works closely with national governments, civil society organizations, and other partners to find lasting solutions for refugees and other forcibly displaced people.

Even though **India is not officially a signatory to the Refugee Convention and the Protocol**, and also does not have a national refugee protection framework, it has been hosting varied refugee groups for decades and has found solutions for many forcibly displaced persons.

INTERNATIONAL CRIMINAL COURT (ICC)

The International Criminal Court (ICC) operates as an **autonomous global organization** and **operates separately from the United Nations**. Its primary function is to **investigate** and, if necessary, **prosecute individuals accused of the most serious international crimes**.

The ICC is governed by the **Rome Statute**, its founding treaty. While the Court's funding primarily comes from States Parties to the Rome Statute, it also receives voluntary contributions from various sources such as governments, international organizations, individuals, corporations, and other entities. **The Court is headquartered in The Hague, Netherlands**, which is also known as the host State.

Rome Statute (1998)

It was adopted at a diplomatic conference in Rome, Italy on 17 July 1998 and it **entered into force on 1 July 2002**. There are presently **123 states** that are party to the statute. Out of them, 33 are African States, 19 are Asia-Pacific States, 18 are from Eastern Europe, 28 are from Latin American and Caribbean States, and 25 are from Western European and other States.

India has neither signed nor ratified the Rome Statute and is thus, not a member of the ICC.

The Court has jurisdiction in accordance with this Statute with respect to the following crimes[24]:

(1) **Crime of Genocide** - the specific intent to destroy in whole or in part a national, ethnic, racial or religious group by killing its members or by other means: causing serious bodily or mental harm to members of the group etc.
(2) **War crimes** - grave breaches of the Geneva conventions in the context of armed conflict and include, for instance, the use of child soldiers; the killing or torture of persons such as civilians or prisoners of war etc.
(3) **Crimes against humanity** - serious violations committed as part of a large-scale attack against any civilian population and includes offences like murder, rape, imprisonment, enforced disappearances, torture, apartheid etc.
(4) **Crime of aggression** - use of armed force by a State against the sovereignty, integrity or independence of another State.

Being a judicial organization, the **ICC does not possess its own police force or enforcement mechanism**. Consequently, it depends on cooperation from countries worldwide to assist with various tasks, including–

- making arrests,
- transferring arrested persons to the ICC detention centre in The Hague
- freezing suspects' assets, and
- enforcing sentences.

Principle of 'NO IMMUNITY'

According to the principle, 'Persons acting in an official capacity as a head of state, member of government or parliament or as an elected representative or public official are in no manner exempted from prosecution or criminal responsibility'. Additionally, superiors or military commanders may be held responsible for criminal offences committed by persons under their effective command and control or effective authority and control.

By virtue of this principle, on 17 March 2023, Pre-Trial Chamber II of the International Criminal Court (ICC) issued a warrant of arrest for **Mr. Vladimir Vladimirovich Putin** in the context of the **situation in Ukraine**. The charges read – "the President of the Russian Federation, is allegedly responsible for the **war crime of unlawful deportation of population (children)** and that of **unlawful transfer of population (children) from occupied areas of Ukraine to the Russian Federation**".

WORLD HEALTH ORGANISATION (WHO)

WHO is a specialized agency of the United Nations that is responsible for promoting and protecting public health worldwide. The WHO was established in **1948** and is headquartered in **Geneva, Switzerland**. The WHO works with governments, civil society organizations, and other partners to promote and support global health initiatives, and to provide leadership on key public health issues. The WHO also works to promote **universal health coverage**, which means ensuring that all people have access to the health services they need without facing financial hardship. The organization is committed to promoting equity in health, and to addressing the social, economic, and environmental factors that can impact health outcomes.

NOTE

The **Food and Agriculture Organisation (FAO)** is a specialised agency of the UN, based in **Rome** (Italy), which works for alleviation of poverty and hunger by promoting agriculture development, improved nutrition and easy access of food.

The WHO played a key role in the global response to the **COVID-19 pandemic**. It provided technical guidance and support to countries on a range of issues related to COVID-19, including testing, contact tracing, treatment, and public health measures. The WHO also worked to ensure that countries had access to the necessary medical supplies

[24] Rome Statute of the International Criminal Court. https://www.icc-cpi.int/sites/default/files/RS-Eng.pdf

and equipment, including personal protective equipment (PPE) for healthcare workers. It also established the COVID-19 **Solidarity Response Fund** to support the global response to the pandemic.

OTHER IMPORTANT TREATIES AND ORGANISATIONS

WORLD TRADE ORGANISATION (WTO)

General Agreement on Tariffs and Trade or GATT was a multilateral treaty that was signed in 1947 with the goal of promoting international trade by reducing trade barriers such as tariffs and quotas. The GATT was the first agreement of its kind, and it played a key role in shaping the global trading system. It was originally a legal agreement designed to accelerate economic recovery after WWII. **The GATT served as a basis for the creation of the World Trade Organization (WTO) in 1995.**

The World Trade Organisation (WTO) is an international organization which sets the rules for global trade. This organization was set up in 1995 as the successor to the General Agreement on Trade and Tariffs (GATT). The WTO's **164 members** represent 98 per cent of world trade.

India has been a member of the WTO since its establishment in 1995. India has been a strong advocate for developing countries, and has worked to ensure that the WTO's rules and policies take into account the specific needs and challenges of developing countries. India has also been involved in a number of disputes at the WTO, both as a complainant and as a respondent. The major areas of discord include issues of agricultural subsidies, export restrictions, Information Technology etc.

ORGANISATION FOR ECONOMIC CO-OPERATION AND DEVELOPMENT (OECD, 1961)

The Organisation for Economic Co-operation and Development (OECD) is an **intergovernmental economic organization** founded in 1961 to promote economic growth, prosperity, and sustainable development. It is headquartered in Paris, France, and has 38 member countries, mainly developed countries from Europe, North America, and the Asia-Pacific region.

The OECD works to promote policies that will improve the economic and social well-being of people around the world. It conducts research, provides economic data, and makes policy recommendations on a wide range of issues, including trade, investment, innovation, tax, education, environment, and social issues. The OECD's work is based on the principles of democracy, market economy, and human rights.

India is one of the many **non-member economies** with which the OECD has working relationships in addition to its member countries. The OECD has been co-operating with India since 1995.

UN CONFERENCE ON TRADE AND DEVELOPMENT (UNCTAD, 1964)

A **permanent intergovernmental body established by the UN** in 1946 with an aim to formulate policies relating to all aspects of development including trade, aid, transport, finance and technology. Its permanent secretariat is in Geneva, Switzerland. The UNCTAD reports to the UN General Assembly and United Nations Economic and Social Council.

One of the principal achievements of UNCTAD (1964) has been to conceive and implement the **Generalised System of Preferences** (It is a preferential tariff system which provides tariff reduction in developed countries to promote exports of manufactured goods from developing countries) UNCTAD has also been financing research and development activities; It has provided development assistance for low-income countries and debt relief.

WORLD INTELLECTUAL PROPERTY ORGANISATION (WIPO, 1970)

The World Intellectual Property Organization (WIPO) is a **specialized agency of the United Nations** that promotes the protection of intellectual property (IP) throughout the world. WIPO was established in 1967 and is headquartered in Geneva, Switzerland. Its main goal is to encourage innovation and creativity by providing a balanced and effective international IP system.

WIPO administers several treaties that establish international standards for IP protection and enforcement, including the Patent Cooperation Treaty (PCT), the Madrid System for the International Registration of

Marks, and the Hague System for the International Registration of Industrial Designs. It also provides a range of services to help individuals and organizations protect their IP, including registration services, legal advice, and capacity-building programs.

WIPO also plays a significant role in promoting IP protection and enforcement in developing countries. It provides technical assistance, training, and capacity-building programs to help these countries develop and implement effective IP policies and systems. In addition, WIPO works to raise awareness of the importance of IP protection and the value of innovation and creativity in promoting economic growth and development.

WORLD ECONOMIC FORUM (WEF, 1971)

The World Economic Forum (WEF) is a **non-profit international organization** that is committed to improving the state of the world by engaging business, political, academic, and other leaders of society to shape global, regional, and industry agendas. It was founded in 1971 and is headquartered in Geneva, Switzerland.

The WEF organizes an annual meeting in Davos, Switzerland, which brings together global leaders from various sectors to discuss the most pressing issues facing the world today. The meeting has become a high-profile event, attracting government officials, business leaders, and other influential individuals from around the world.

UN CONVENTION ON THE LAW OF THE SEA (UNCLOS, 1982)

The United Nations Convention on the Law of the Sea (UNCLOS) is an international treaty that was adopted in 1982 and entered into force in 1994. It is widely regarded as the cornerstone of modern international maritime law, providing a comprehensive framework for the management and conservation of the world's oceans and their resources.

UNCLOS establishes the legal rights and responsibilities of nations in their use of the world's oceans, establishing guidelines for businesses, the environment, and the management of marine natural resources. It sets out the maritime zones that coastal states can claim, including the territorial sea, contiguous zone, exclusive economic zone (EEZ), and continental shelf. The treaty also provides for the protection and conservation of the marine environment and the management of marine living resources, including fish stocks.

UNCLOS has been signed by over 160 countries, including most major maritime powers. **India and China are state parties to the UNCLOS** – India ratified the treaty in 1995. The United States has not ratified the treaty.

OTHER NON-STATE ACTORS

Non-state actors include those organisations and individual(s) that aren't affiliated with or directly funded through the government. They, however, have powerful political, economic or social power and are able to influence at national and where possible, international level but don't align themselves to any particular country and its government.

According to Pearlman and Cunningham, **non-state actors** are defined as **"an organized political actor not directly connected to the state but pursing aims that affect vital state interests"** (Pearlman & Cunningham, 2011)

Such non-state actors are increasingly playing a critical role in international relations and wielding substantial influence over international relations, however, unlike the state – a well organised and internationally recognized sovereign body, the non-state bodies lack formal government support.

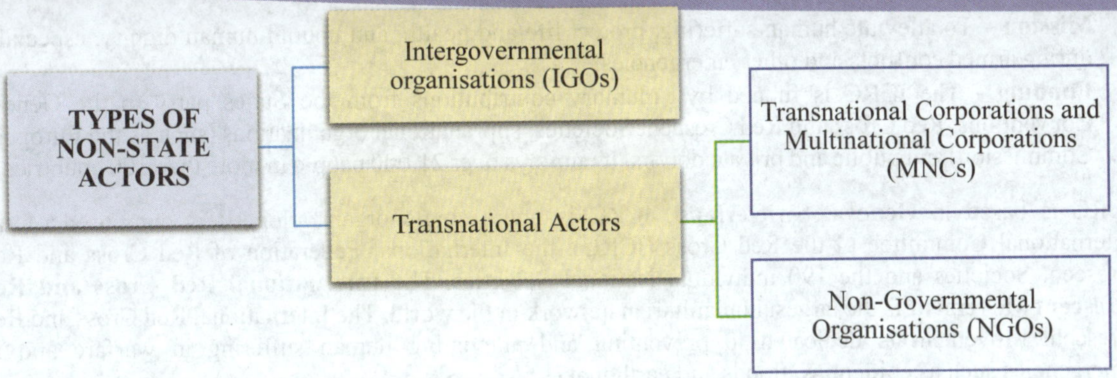

Intergovernmental organisations (IGOs)

These are organisations whose members consist of three or more nations/states. They are created to resolve shared problems and give the IGOs authority to make collective decisions while managing issues on the global agenda. Global IGOs include UN, WTO, IMF etc. Regional IGOs include ASEAN, EU etc.

Transnational Actors

These bodies/individuals work below the state level but function beyond the state borders as well. They are of two types –

(1) Transnational Corporations (TNCs) / Multinational Corporations (MNCs)

These are companies/corporations that have headquarters in one state but invest and operate extensively in other states. They operate globally with several branches and subsidiaries. Numerous multinational corporations (MNCs) generate annual sales in the tens of billions of dollars, with some top corporations like Wal-Mart reaching hundreds of billions of dollars. These MNCs establish and maintain a global business infrastructure that connects a transnational network of business professionals. Moreover, MNCs play a role in supporting the development of the countries in which they operate. By operating in foreign states, MNCs create employment opportunities for local residents, thereby contributing to economic stability in those areas.

(2) Non-governmental Organizations (NGOs)

They are private international actors that are composed of volunteers from the population of two or more states. The members of the NGOs establish such organisations to promote common interests and ideals that influence the policies of state governments and intergovernmental organizations (IGOs) rather than the state. The major issues that the NGOS deal with include - disarmament, environmental protection, human rights, women and children rights and LGBTQ rights etc. NGOs are increasingly being recognized in the UN and other forums, as legitimate actors along with states but is not equal to them. Many people discovered that they could take part in the global system and lobby to influence international organisations after joining NGOs.

INTERNATIONAL COMMITTEE OF THE RED CROSS (ICRC)

The ICRC is an independent and neutral organization ensuring humanitarian protection and assistance for victims of war and armed violence. It was established in **1863** and operates worldwide, helping people affected by conflict and armed violence and promoting the laws that protect victims of war. ICRC's mandate stems essentially from the **Geneva Conventions of 1949.** It takes action in response to emergencies and promotes respect for international humanitarian law and its implementation in national law.[25]

INTERNATIONAL MOVEMENT

[25] International Committee of the Red Cross, https://www.icrc.org/en/who-we-are

- **Mission** – To alleviate human suffering, protect life and health, and uphold human dignity, especially during armed conflicts and other emergencies.
- **Funding** - The ICRC is funded by voluntary contributions from the States party to the Geneva Conventions, Red Cross and Red Crescent Societies, supranational organizations (such as the European Commission) and public and private donors. It employs over 21,000 people in more than 100 countries.[26]

ICRC is based in **Geneva, Switzerland**. ICRC is not a single organization. It is composed of the International Committee of the Red Cross (ICRC), the International Federation of Red Cross and Red Crescent Societies and the 190 individual National Societies. The **International Red Cross and Red Crescent Movement** is the largest humanitarian network in the world. The International Red Cross and Red Crescent Movement is dedicated to preventing and alleviating human suffering in warfare and in emergencies such as epidemics, floods and earthquakes.[27]

AMNESTY INTERNATIONAL

Amnesty International is an **NGO** (Non-Government Organisation) that campaigns for the **protection of human rights** all over the world. It was formed in London in **1961** by its founder **Peter Benson**. It promotes respect for all the human rights in the Universal Declaration of Human Rights. Additionally, the organization produces and releases human rights reports that hold significant value in the field of human rights research and advocacy. With a presence in 150 countries worldwide, it boasts a membership, signatory, and supporter base exceeding 2.2 million individuals.

Major objectives –

- Protection of women, Children & refugees
- Ending illegal torture and execution
- Abolishing the death penalty, torture and other cruel treatment has held prisoners. Fair (fair and fast) trials for political prisoners
- Protection of prisoners of conscience.
- Protection of human rights violations related to his physical and psychological integrity
- Regulation of the global arms trade.
- Overcoming discrimination on grounds of caste, religion, race etc.

Amnesty International was awarded the **Nobel Peace Prize** (1977) for its **campaign against torture**.

OXFAM

Oxfam International emerged in **1995** when several independent non-governmental organizations decided to collaborate as a confederation. Their purpose was to enhance efficiency and make a more significant impact in their efforts to **alleviate worldwide poverty and address issues of injustice**. The official website describes Oxfam as a global movement of individuals dedicated to combating inequality, with the ultimate goal of eradicating poverty and injustice.

- **Oxfam International Secretariate** – Nairobi, Kenya.
- **Offices** - The Secretariat runs offices in Addis Ababa, Oxford, Brussels, Geneva, New York, Moscow and Washington DC.

The name **'Oxfam'** comes from the **Oxford Committee for Famine Relief**, founded in Britain in **1942**. The group campaigned for food supplies to be sent through an allied naval blockade to starving women and children in enemy-occupied Greece during the **Second World War**. While the organisation was established to cater to war ravaged areas, post war, it continued its work, sending materials and financial aid to groups

[26] International Committee of the Red Cross, https://www.icrc.org/en/who-we-are
[27] International Committee of the Red Cross, https://www.icrc.org/en/who-we-are

aiding poor people throughout Europe. As the situation in Europe improved, Oxfam's attention shifted to the needs of people in developing countries.[28]

The Oxfam International confederation comprises 21 member organizations, situated in various countries such as **Australia, Belgium, Brazil, Canada, Colombia, Denmark, France, Germany, Great Britain, Hong Kong, Ireland, India, Italy, Mexico, The Netherlands, New Zealand, Quebec, South Africa, Spain, Turkey, and the United States**. Currently, Oxfam operates in approximately 70 nations, collaborating with numerous partners, allies, and communities. Their focus is on saving and safeguarding lives during emergencies, assisting in the restoration of livelihoods, and advocating for enduring and meaningful change. Central to their endeavors is a commitment to upholding women's rights in all aspects of their work.

Oxfam India in its report, **'India: Extreme inequality in numbers'**[29] laid down some critical statistics –

1 % increase in wealth	The top 10% of the Indian population holds 77% of the total national wealth. 73% of the wealth generated in 2017 went to the richest 1%, while **670 million Indians (approx.) who comprise the poorest half of the population saw only a 1% increase in their wealth**.
70 millionaires/day	There are 119 billionaires in India. Their number has increased from only 9 in 2000 to 101 in 2017. Between 2018 and 2022, **India is estimated to produce 70 new millionaires every day.**
Fortune increased by 10 times	**Billionaires' fortunes increased by almost 10 times over a decade** and their total wealth is higher than the entire Union budget of India for the fiscal year 2018-19, which was at INR 24422 billion.
63 Million pushed into poverty	Many ordinary Indians are not able to access the health care they need. **63 million of them are pushed into poverty because of healthcare costs** every year - almost two people every second.
941 years gap	It would take **941 years for a minimum wage worker in rural India to earn what the top paid executive** at a leading Indian garment company earns in a year.
Source: Oxfam.org	

In January 2023, Oxfam India released its report, **Survival of the Richest: The India story.** The important observations include –

- A mere **5 percent of individuals in India possess over 60 percent of the nation's wealth**, while the bottom 50 percent of the population holds a mere 3 percent of the wealth.
- Between 2012 and 2021, **40 percent of the wealth generated in India was acquired by just 1 percent of the population**, whereas only 3 percent of the wealth reached the bottom 50 percent.
- India holds the unfortunate distinction of having the **highest number of poor individuals** in the world, **totaling 228.9 million**. Conversely, the number of billionaires in India increased from 102 in 2020 to 166 in 2022.
- The **combined wealth of India's top 100 wealthiest individuals** has reached a staggering **$660 billion (Rs 54.12 lakh crore).**

GREENPEACE

GREENPEACE

It is a **non-governmental environmental Organisation** with offices in over 39 countries and an international coordinating body in **Amsterdam**, the Netherlands. This independent global campaigning network was founded in Canada in **1971** by **Irving Stowe** and **Dorothy Stowe**.

---

[28] Oxfam – Our History. https://www.oxfam.org/ar/node/7405

[29] India: extreme inequality in numbers. Oxfam International. https://www.oxfam.org/en/india-extreme-inequality-numbers

Objective – Greenpeace directs its advocacy efforts towards global concerns that impact the Earth's capacity to sustain diverse forms of life. These encompass a range of issues including climate change, deforestation, overfishing, commercial whaling, genetic engineering, and opposition to nuclear activities.

Methods used – It uses s direct action, lobbying, research, and ecotage to achieve its goals.

The global Organisation **does not accept funding from governments, corporations, or political parties** and relies on its three million individual supporters and foundation grants.

HUMAN RIGHTS WATCH

HUMAN RIGHTS WATCH

Human Rights Watch (HRW) is a prominent international non-governmental organization dedicated to the **investigation, research, and advocacy of human rights.** Its inception dates back to **1978** when the Europe and Central Asia Division, originally known as the **Helsinki Watch**, was established. HRW has grown to become the largest US-based international human rights organization. It has played a pivotal role in the formation of global coalitions such as campaigns against landmines, the use of child soldiers, and the establishment of the International Criminal Court.

HRW publishes over 100 reports annually, covering human rights practices in approximately 90 countries worldwide. The organization currently operates through thematic divisions or programs that address various aspects of human rights, including arms, business and human rights, children's rights, disability rights, environmental issues in relation to human rights, health and human rights, international justice, LGBTQ+ rights, refugees, terrorism and counterterrorism, women's rights, and emergency situations.

> Human Rights Watch has won the **2008 United Nations Prize for Human Rights**, in recognition of the vital role played by the Human Rights movement in trying to end abuses over the past 60 years. The award given every five years, was bestowed in New York on December 10, 2008, the 60th anniversary of the Universal Declaration of Human Rights.

13

NUCLEAR POWER & INTERNATIONAL PERSPECTIVE

UNITED NATIONS AND NUCLEAR DISARMAMENT

"Disarmament is at the heart of the system of collective security set out in the UN Charter. The purpose of this system was nothing less than the elimination of war as an instrument of foreign policy 'to save succeeding generations from the scourge of war'."

- **Securing Our Common Future: An Agenda for Disarmament(2018)**

The United Nations has consistently advocated for the elimination of weapons of mass destruction, particularly nuclear weapons, since its inception. The UN General Assembly's first resolution in 1946 created a Commission to address atomic energy issues, focusing on controlling its use for peaceful purposes and proposing measures to eliminate atomic and other mass destruction weapons from national arsenals.

In response to the nuclear arms race and the Cuban Missile Crisis, Latin American governments led negotiations that resulted in the Treaty of Tlatelolco, establishing the first nuclear weapons-free zone in Latin America and the Caribbean. This initiative inspired the creation of additional Regional Nuclear-Weapon-Free Zones (NWFZ) in regions like the South Pacific, Southeast Asia, Africa, and Central Asia. These zones aimed to reinforce global norms against nuclear proliferation and disarmament, promoting peace and security.

The United Nations Office for Disarmament Affairs plays a crucial role in supporting the disarmament of weapons of mass destruction, including nuclear, chemical, and biological weapons. It collaborates with intergovernmental organizations and specialized UN agencies to strengthen non-proliferation efforts. Various multilateral treaties have been established to prevent nuclear proliferation and testing while advancing nuclear disarmament, as discussed further.[30]

- On **December 2, 2009**, during the **64th session of the United Nations General Assembly**, August 29 was designated as the International Day against Nuclear Tests. This declaration aimed to raise awareness and promote actions against nuclear testing.
- In **2013**, the General Assembly organized its inaugural **high-level meeting on nuclear disarmament.** By adopting resolution 68/32, September 26 was designated as the **International Day for the Total Elimination of Nuclear Weapons**. This day serves as an opportunity for the international community to reassert its dedication to prioritizing global nuclear disarmament.

NOTABLE DEVELOPMENTS SURROUNDING NUCLEAR POWER	
1945	The two atomic bombs destroyed the cities of **Hiroshima** and **Nagasaki** and are estimated to have killed a total of 213,000 people immediately.
1946	First resolution of UN, the General Assembly (GA) identified nuclear disarmament as a leading goal of the UN.

[30] United Nations Office for Disarmament Affairs Programmes Financed From Voluntary Contributions 2021-2022, https://reliefweb.int/report/world/united-nations-office-disarmament-affairs-programmes-financed-voluntary-contributions-2021-2022

1959	The GA included nuclear disarmament as part of the more comprehensive goal of general and complete disarmament under effective international control (resolution 1378(XIV)) – it was the first GA resolution ever to be sponsored by the entire membership of the UN.
1962	**Cuban Missile Crisis,** bringing the world to the brink of nuclear war.
1963	The Treaty Banning Nuclear Weapon Tests in the Atmosphere, in Outer Space and Under Water, or the **Partial Test Ban Treaty**, was opened for signature.
1967	**First nuclear weapons-free zone (NWFZ) established – Treaty of Tlatelolco**
1968	The **Treaty on the Non-Proliferation of Nuclear Weapons (NPT)** was opened for signature.
1970	The **NPT entered into force,** [The Treaty was extended indefinitely in May 1995].
1978	A GA Special session dedicated to disarmament was held. The member states noted that 'effective measures of nuclear disarmament and the prevention of nuclear war would have the highest priority'.
1991	**South Africa** voluntarily **renounced** its nuclear weapons programme.
1992	By the **Lisbon Protocol** to the **Strategic Arms Reduction Treaty (START I), Belarus, Kazakhstan and Ukraine voluntarily renounced nuclear weapons in their possession following** the dissolution of the Soviet Union.
1996	The **Comprehensive Nuclear-Test-Ban Treaty (CTBT)** opened for signature.
2010	During the **2010 NPT Review Conference,** States parties established a 64-point action plan encompassing nuclear disarmament, nuclear non-proliferation, and the peaceful utilization of nuclear energy.
2017	On July 7, the **Treaty on the Prohibition of Nuclear Weapons** was adopted, marking the first legally binding multilateral instrument for nuclear disarmament in two decades.
2018	The Secretary-General launched "**Securing Our Common Future: An Agenda for Disarmament**," which focuses on nuclear weapons elimination within the framework of "disarmament to save humanity."
2020	The **fiftieth anniversary of the Treaty on the Non-Proliferation of Nuclear Weapons** (NPT) entering into force was commemorated.
2021	On January 22, the **Treaty on the Prohibition of Nuclear Weapons** came into effect. On February 3, the **Parties agreed to extend the Treaty between the United States of America and the Russian Federation** on Measures for the Further Reduction and Limitation of Strategic Offensive Arms, known as "**new START**," until February 4, 2026.
2022	▪ During the First Meeting of the States parties to the Treaty on the Prohibition of Nuclear Weapons (TPNW), the adoption of the "**Vienna Declaration**" reaffirmed their commitment to achieving the total elimination of nuclear weapons. ▪ The Vienna Action Plan was also adopted to **support the efficient and timely implementation of the Treaty and its objectives**. ▪ The **Tenth Review Conference of the Treaty on the Non-Proliferation of Nuclear Weapons (NPT)** occurred from August 1st to 26th at the United Nations Headquarters.

2023	▪ **AUKUS Agreement and Nuclear Submarine Deal:** The trilateral security pact between Australia, the United Kingdom, and the United States, known as AUKUS, moved forward with a deal to supply Australia with nuclear-powered submarines. ▪ **China's Expansion of Nuclear Arsenal:** Reports indicated that China significantly expanded its nuclear arsenal in 2023, leading to heightened global security concerns and impacting arms control discussions.
2024	Global tensions around nuclear weapons remain high, with countries like North Korea continuing to develop their nuclear capabilities. Meanwhile, diplomatic efforts to strengthen treaties like the NPT and the CTBT are ongoing, though challenges persist in achieving universal compliance and disarmament.

Source: Al-Baidar Centre for Studies & Planning; Federation of American Scientists

NUCLEAR SUPPLIERS GROUP (NSG)

The Nuclear Suppliers Group (NSG) is an association of countries that supply nuclear materials and technology. Its main objective is to prevent the proliferation of nuclear weapons by enforcing guidelines for nuclear exports and related activities.

GUIDELINES

The first set of NSG Guidelines governs the export of **items that are especially designed or prepared for nuclear use.** These include- Nuclear material; Nuclear reactors and equipment therefore; Non-nuclear material for reactors; Plant and equipment for the reprocessing, enrichment, and conversion of nuclear material and for fuel fabrication and heavy water production; and Technology associated with each of the above items.

The second set of NSG Guidelines governs the export of **nuclear-related dual-use items and technologies** (items that have both nuclear and non-nuclear applications), which could make a significant contribution to an unsafeguarded nuclear fuel cycle or nuclear explosive activity.

The NSG was established in response to the **detonation of a nuclear device by a non-nuclear-weapon State (India's Pokhran-I) in 1974**, which highlighted the potential misuse of peaceful nuclear technology. It is a **voluntary and non-legally binding association of major supplier governments**, **not formed through a treaty**. Each participating government implements the NSG Guidelines according to its own national laws and practices. States have the option to voluntarily adhere to the guidelines without officially becoming a participating government of the NSG.

- 2023-2024 NSG Chair Country: **BRAZIL**
- 48 Participating Governments (Members)- Argentina, Australia, Austria, Belarus, Belgium, Brazil, Bulgaria, Canada, China, Croatia, Cyprus, Czech Republic, Denmark, Estonia, Finland, France, Germany, Greece, Hungary, Iceland, Ireland, Italy, Japan, Kazakhstan, Republic of Korea, Latvia, Lithuania, Luxembourg, Malta, Mexico, Netherlands, New Zealand, Norway, Poland, Portugal, Romania, Russian federation, Serbia, Slovakia, Slovenia, South Africa, Spain, Sweden, Switzerland, Turkey, Ukraine, United kingdom and United states.
- Observers - The **European Commission** and the **Chair of the Zangger Committee** (also known as Nuclear Exporters Committee) participate as observers.

India is NOT a participating member of the NSG

- Decisions, including on membership, are made by consensus. Decisions on export applications are taken at the national level in accordance with national export licensing requirements.
- The NSG Guidelines contain the so-called "**Non-Proliferation Principle**," adopted in 1994, whereby a supplier, notwithstanding other provisions in the NSG Guidelines, authorises a transfer only when satisfied that the transfer would not contribute to the proliferation of nuclear weapons.
- The NSG Guidelines align with and supplement several internationally recognized and legally binding agreements concerning nuclear non-proliferation. These include the following -

NUCLEAR WEAPONS-FREE ZONES		
Zone	**Treaty**	**Geographical area covered**
First	Treaty of Tlatelolco	Latin America and the Caribbean
Second	Treaty of Rarotonga	South Pacific

Third	Bangkok Treaty	Southeast Asia
Fourth	Pelindaba Treaty	Africa
Fifth	Treaty of Semipalatinsk	Central Asia

DUAL USE CONTROLS

[Dual-use items include nuclear fuel cycle activities and weaponization]

At the beginning of the 1990's, it became apparent that export control provisions then in force had not prevented Iraq, a party to the NPT, from pursuing a clandestine nuclear weapons program, which later prompted UN Security Council action. A large part of Iraq's effort had been to acquire dual-use items not covered by the Guidelines and then to build materials within Iraq needed for a nuclear weapons program. Iraq's program gave substantial impetus to the NSG's development of its dual-use Guidelines. It ensured that these items would remain available for peaceful nuclear activities subject to IAEA safeguards, as well as for other industrial activities that would not contribute to nuclear proliferation.

The NSG decided in 1992 to establish Guidelines for transfers of nuclear-related dual-use equipment, material, and technology (items that have both nuclear and non-nuclear applications), which could make a significant contribution to an unsafeguarded nuclear fuel cycle or nuclear explosive activity.

NUCLEAR NON-PROLIFERATION TREATY (NPT)

NPT is an international treaty, which came into force in 1970. The main objective was to prevent the spread of nuclear weapons and weapons technology.

Three pillars

Non-proliferation: The NPT prohibits the spread of nuclear weapons to states that do not already possess them. States that do possess nuclear weapons (China, France, Russia, the United Kingdom, and the United States) commit to not transferring these weapons to other states and to working towards disarmament.

Disarmament: States that possess nuclear weapons commit to working towards disarmament and eventual elimination of their nuclear arsenals.

Peaceful uses of nuclear energy: The NPT recognizes the right of states to develop nuclear energy for peaceful purposes, subject to international safeguards to ensure that these activities are not used for military purposes.

An international conference to review the **Nuclear Non-proliferation Trea**ty was concluded at the UN (New York) in August 2022. It however ended without a consensus document, highlighting the growing power conflict in the current decade.

India is NOT a signatory to the NPT

Note: The topic of Indian Nuclear Power has been discussed later in detail.

PARTIAL TEST BAN TREATY (PTBT)

The Partial Test Ban Treaty (PTBT) is an international treaty that **prohibits all nuclear weapon tests in the atmosphere, in outer space, and underwater**. The treaty was signed on August 5, 1963, by the United States, the United Kingdom, and the Soviet Union, and entered into force on October 10, 1963.

The PTBT has three main provisions:

- Prohibition on nuclear weapons tests in the atmosphere, in outer space, and underwater.
- Obligation to prevent the dumping of nuclear waste in the ocean or other bodies of water.
- Promotion of the peaceful use of nuclear energy.

The PTBT was a significant achievement in the effort to limit nuclear weapons testing and the spread of nuclear weapons. Prior to the treaty's adoption, nuclear weapons tests were conducted openly and extensively in the atmosphere, causing widespread concern about the health and environmental impacts of radioactive fallout.

Signature – 8 August 1963
Deposit of instruments of ratification – October 1963

COMPREHENSIVE NUCLEAR-TEST-BAN TREATY (CTBT)

The Comprehensive Nuclear-Test-Ban Treaty (CTBT) is an international treaty that prohibits all nuclear weapons test explosions and any other nuclear explosions, whether for military or civilian purposes. The treaty was opened for signature on September 24, 1996, and has been signed by 185 countries, including all five of the recognized nuclear-weapon states.

The CTBT aims to prevent the spread of nuclear weapons and to promote disarmament by prohibiting the testing of nuclear weapons. The treaty provides for the establishment of a comprehensive international monitoring system (IMS) to detect and verify any nuclear explosions, using a network of monitoring stations located around the world.

Despite the widespread support for the CTBT, it has not yet entered into force, as it has not been ratified by all of the necessary countries, including some of the nuclear-armed countries. However, the treaty's monitoring system is operational, and its data is used for a range of purposes, including disaster warning and scientific research.

India is NOT a signatory to the CTBT

TREATY ON THE PROHIBITION OF NUCLEAR WEAPONS (TPNW)

The Treaty on the Prohibition of Nuclear Weapons (TPNW) is an international treaty that bans the development, testing, production, stockpiling, transfer, use, and threat of use of nuclear weapons. The treaty was adopted by the United Nations General Assembly on July 7, 2017, and opened for signature on September 20, 2017. It **entered into force on January 22, 2021**, after it was ratified by 50 countries.

The TPNW is the first treaty to comprehensively prohibit nuclear weapons, and it was adopted in response to the growing concerns about the risks posed by nuclear weapons and the slow pace of disarmament by the nuclear-armed countries.

THREE PILLARS

- **Prohibition**: The treaty prohibits the development, testing, production, stockpiling, transfer, use, and threat of use of nuclear weapons.
- **Disarmament**: The treaty calls for the complete elimination of nuclear weapons and requires states that possess nuclear weapons to take steps towards disarmament.
- **Victim assistance and environmental remediation**: The treaty recognizes the harm caused by the use and testing of nuclear weapons and requires states to provide assistance to victims and to take measures to remediate contaminated environments.

India did not participate in these negotiations for the TPNW. India also clarified that it would not become a party to the treaty.

India is not a member

INTERNATIONAL CONVENTION FOR THE SUPPRESSION OF ACTS OF NUCLEAR TERRORISM (ICSANT)

- The multilateral Convention covers a broad range of acts and possible targets, including nuclear power plants and nuclear reactors. It criminalizes the planning, threatening, or carrying out acts of nuclear terrorism.
  - Adopted - 13 April 2005
  - Opened for Signature - 14 September 2005
  - Entered into Force - 7 July 2007

Signature (UN) – 24 July 2006
Deposit of instruments of ratification – 01 December 2006

The convention defines the **act of nuclear terrorism** as the '**use or threat to use nuclear material, nuclear fuel, radioactive products or waste, or any other radioactive substances with toxic, explosive, or other dangerous properties**.' The definition includes the use or threat to use any nuclear installations, nuclear explosive, or radiation devices in order to kill or injure persons, damage property, or the environment, or to compel persons, States, or international organizations to do or to refrain from doing any act.[31]

[31] First Session Of Ad Hoc Committee On Terrorist Bombings And Nuclear Terrorism To Be Held At Headquarters, 24 February - 7 March, https://press.un.org/en/1997/19970221.l2823.html

INTERNATIONAL ATOMIC ENERGY AGENCY (IAEA)

- The International Atomic Energy Agency is an **intergovernmental organization that seeks to promote the peaceful use of nuclear energy and to inhibit its use for any military purpose, including nuclear weapons.**
- It was established as an autonomous organization through its own international treaty, the **IAEA Statute on 29 July 1957.**
- **Headquarter**: Vienna, Austria
- **Objectives**:
    - o The IAEA came into being to implement **US President Dwight Eisenhower's "Atoms for Peace" proposal.**
- The primary objective of the NSG is to **encourage the peaceful utilization of nuclear energy** and prevent its military applications, specifically in relation to nuclear weapons.
- The NSG also functions as an intergovernmental platform for **promoting scientific and technical collaboration in the peaceful application of nuclear technology and nuclear power**.
- IAEA teams regularly inspect nuclear facilities all over the world to **ensure that civilian reactors are not being used for military purposes.**
- Though established independently of the UN through its own international treaty - the **IAEA Statute,** the IAEA reports to both the UNGA & UNSC.

India is a member

In **2009**, an Agreement between the Government of India and the IAEA for the **Application of Safeguards to Civilian Nuclear Facilities** was signed.

In **2014**, India ratified an Additional Protocol (as part of its commitments under US-India Nuclear Deal) to its safeguards agreements with the IAEA.

- The IAEA has two "**Regional Safeguards Offices**": in Toronto, Canada & in Tokyo, Japan.
- The IAEA and its former Director General, **Mohamed ElBaradei**, were jointly awarded the **Nobel Peace Prize in 2005**.

MULTILATERAL EXPORT CONTROL REGIME

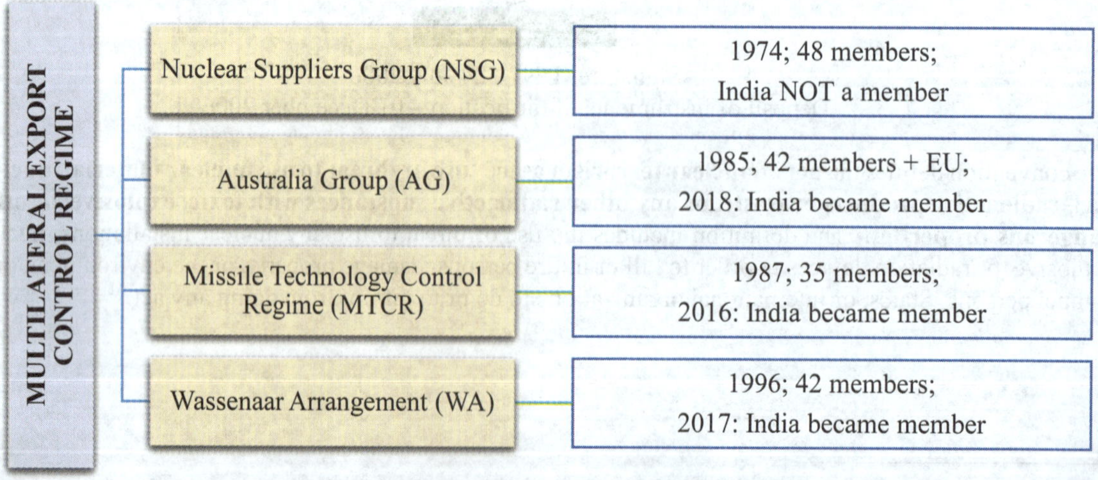

AUSTRALIA GROUP (AG)

It is an informal forum of countries which seeks to ensure that **exports do not contribute to the development of chemical and biological weapons (CBW)** through the **harmonisation of export controls.**

> **NOTE**
> The 37th **Australia Group Plenary** was held in Paris, France, from June 3-7, 2024. Participants expressed concerns about past uses of chemical weapons in Syria.

- Backdrop - The formation of the AG in **1985** was prompted by Iraq's use of chemical weapons during the **Iran-Iraq War (1980-1988).**Australia became alarmed by Iraq's efforts in developing chemical weapons and advocated for the alignment of global export controls on precursor chemicals used in chemical weapons. With the expansion of its membership, the Australia Group (AG) broadened its scope to encompass chemical production equipment and technologies, as well as measures to prevent the proliferation of biological weapons.
- Aim&Objective - The Australia Group **employs licensing measures to prevent the proliferation of chemical and biological weapons (CBW)** by ensuring that the export of specific chemicals, biological agents, and dual-use manufacturing facilities and equipment does not contribute to their spread. This is accomplished through the harmonization of export licensing measures among participating countries.
- 42Members + EU- Argentina, Australia, Austria, Belgium, Bulgaria, Canada, Croatia, Republic of Cyprus, Czech Republic, Denmark, Estonia, **European Union**, Finland, France, Germany, Greece, Hungary, Iceland, India, Ireland, Italy, Japan, Republic of Korea, Latvia, Lithuania, Luxembourg, Malta, Mexico, Netherlands, New Zealand, Norway, Poland, Portugal, Romania, Slovak Republic, Slovenia, Spain, Sweden, Switzerland, Republic of Turkey, Ukraine, United Kingdom and United States.

All participants have licensing measures over 89 chemical weapons precursors.
Participants also require licences for the export of specific:

- Dual-use chemical manufacturing facilities, equipment and related technology;
- Plant pathogens;
- Animal pathogens;
- Biological agents; and
- Dual-use biological equipment and related technology.

- Participants have recognised from the outset that export licensing measures are not a substitute for the strict and universal observance of the **1925 Geneva Protocol**, the **1972 Biological and Toxin Weapons Convention (BWC)** and the **Chemical Weapons Convention (CWC).**

India and Australia Group

On **19 January 2018** India formally became the **43rd member** of the Australia Group (AG). According to the Government of India, the entry into the Group would be mutually beneficial and would contribute further to international security and non-proliferation objectives. With its admission into the AG, India has demonstrated the will to implement rigorous controls of high standards in international trade, and its capacity to adapt its national regulatory system to meet the necessities of its expanding economy.

MISSILE TECHNOLOGY CONTROL REGIME (MTCR)

- Established in **1987**, by **G-7 countries** – USA, UK, France, Germany, Canada, Italy, and Japan
- The MTCR is an **informal** and **voluntary alliance** where all decisions, including membership, require a consensus among current members. The Regime does not have an official secretariat, with **France serving as the designated Point of Contact (POC)** for the MTCR.
- Chairmanship – In 2022, **Switzerland took the MTCR chair for a one-year term,** replacing Russia.
- Objective —In 1992, the MTCR expanded its original scope from missiles designed for nuclear weapons delivery to include missiles intended for the delivery of all types of weapons of mass destruction (WMD), including nuclear, chemical, and biological weapons. The proliferation of such missiles has been recognized as a threat to global peace and security.

> **NOTE**
>
> The 36th **Plenary Meeting** of the Missile Technology Control Regime (MTCR) took place in Rio de Janeiro, Brazil from October 30 to November 3, 2023. During the meeting, Japan raised regional concerns such as North Korea's missile activities, Russia's invasion of Ukraine, and Iran's missile proliferation.

- Legal Status-The MTCR is **not a legally binding treaty** and does not impose obligatory commitments on its partner countries. The Guidelines, to which all 35 partner countries voluntarily adhere, only explicitly prohibit the export of production facilities for Category I MTCR Annex items.
- Focus – The MTCR pays special attention to rockets and unmanned aerial vehicles that have the capability to carry a payload of 500 kg or more and travel a distance of at least 300 km. It also focuses on the equipment, software, and technology associated with such systems.
- **35 Members (Partners)**: Argentina (1993); Australia (1990); Austria (1991); Belgium (1990); Brazil (1995); Bulgaria (2004); Canada (1987); Czech Republic (1998); Denmark (1990); Finland (1991); France (1987); Germany (1987); Greece 1992); Hungary (1993); Iceland (1993); India (2016); Ireland (1992); Italy (1987); Japan (1987); Luxemburg (1990); Netherlands (1990); New Zealand (1991); Norway (1990); Poland (1998); Portugal (1992); Republic of Korea (2001); Russian Federation (1995); South Africa (1995); Spain (1990); Sweden (1991); Switzerland (1992); Turkey (1997); Ukraine (1998); United Kingdom (1987); United States of America (1987).
- Chairmanship — Rotates on an ad hoc basis. Normally the country that hosts the Plenary serves as Chair for the ensuing year.
- Decision Making –The WA's Plenary is the decision-making body of the Arrangement, which operates based on consensus. All MTCR decisions including decisions on membership require a consensus decision by all current Regime members.
- The MTCR led to the formation of the **International Code of Conduct against Ballistic Missile Proliferation (the Hague Code of Conduct).**

> **India and MTCR**
>
> India had formally applied for membership in 2015 and got **admitted in 2016**. India got access to the latest state of the art technologies.
>
> India can now build missile systems capable of carrying a 500-kilogram payload at least 300 kilometers and even take assistance from other MTCR members like India did in increasing the range of **Brahmos** (supersonic missile) with the help of Russia. Additionally, ISRO can now access the forbidden cryogenic technology from Russia which is required for the space exploration operations. India can also transfer technology and missiles to non-MTCR members.
>
> In 2022, **India** and **Philippines** inked a US$ 375 million deal for the procurement of BrahMos shore-based anti-ship missile system. Potential export customers for the missile system include Vietnam and Indonesia where advanced discussions are going on.

WASSENAAR ARRANGEMENT (WA)

The Wassenaar Arrangement (WA) was established in 1996 as the world's first multilateral arrangement to address the regulation of both conventional weapons and sensitive dual-use goods and technologies. It operates as a **voluntary international export control regime**.

> **NOTE**
>
> The 27th Wassenaar Arrangement (WA) Plenary meeting was held in Vienna on November 30, 2023, and was chaired by **Ambassador Jaideep Mazumdar of India**.

- Objective - To contribute to regional and international security and stability, by promoting transparency and greater responsibility in transfers of conventional arms and dual-use goods and technologies, thus preventing destabilizing accumulations.
- Chairmanship – **India**assumed the chairmanship of the plenary of the Wassenaar Arrangement on 1st January 2023 for one year.

The Arrangement is considered a replacement for the **Coordinating Committee for Multilateral Export Controls (COCOM)**, which was disbanded in 1994. COCOM was discontinued by its member countries due to limitations in its export control methods.

- 42 Members – Argentina, Australia, Austria, Belgium, Bulgaria, Canada, Croatia, the Czech Republic, Denmark, Estonia, Finland, France, Germany, Greece, Hungary, India, Ireland, Italy, Japan, Latvia, Lithuania, Luxembourg, Malta, Mexico, Netherlands, New Zealand, Norway, Poland, Portugal, Romania, Russia, Slovakia, Slovenia, South Africa, South Korea, Spain, Sweden, Switzerland, Turkey, Ukraine, the United Kingdom, and the United States.

With the exception of **China**, all the other permanent members of the U.N. Security Council are signatories of the WA.
Other notable absentees from the Wassenaar Arrangement include –Israel, Belarus, North Korea and Iran.

In order to enhance openness, the Wassenaar Arrangement encourages states to engage in voluntary exchanges of information and notifications regarding their export activities involving weapons and items listed under the arrangement's control lists-

(1) **For the Munitions List (Conventional Weapons)**[32]: Every six months, members exchange information on deliveries of conventional arms to non-Wassenaar members that fall under eight broad weapon categories: battle tanks, armored combat vehicles (ACVs), large-caliber artillery, military aircraft/unmanned aerial vehicles, military and attack helicopters, warships, missiles or missile systems, and small arms and light weapons. The ACV, aircraft, and helicopter categories include models designed to perform reconnaissance or conduct command of troops missions.

(2) For the Dual-Use Goods and Technologies List[33]:

- **Tier 1: Basic Items** - Twice per year, members exchange information on all export licenses denied on proposed transfers to non-Wassenaar members.
- **Tier 2: Sensitive items and subsets of Very Sensitive items**
  - (i) For the subset of Very Sensitive items, such as stealth technology materials and advanced radar, members are called on to "exert extreme vigilance" in exports.
  - (ii) Twice per year, members exchange information on all export licenses issued or transfers made to non-Wassenaar members.

- Members of the Wassenaar Arrangement have established non-binding criteria to provide guidance for the export of man-portable air defense systems (MANPADS), commonly known as shoulder-fired, surface-to-air missiles. They have also endorsed voluntary "best practices" concerning the disposal of surplus military equipment, the enforcement of national export controls, and the regulation of highly sensitive dual-use exports.

---

[32] The Wassenaar Arrangement, Arms Control Association, https://www.armscontrol.org/factsheets/wassenaar

[33] The Wassenaar Arrangement, Arms Control Association, https://www.armscontrol.org/factsheets/wassenaar

OTHER WEAPONS OF MASS DESTRUCTION

BIOLOGICAL WEAPONS

Main elements

- These weapons disperse disease-causing organisms or toxins to harm or kill humans, animals or plants.
- They can be fatal and are highly contagious.
- The diseases caused by such weapons are transboundary and wouldn't confine themselves to national borders and can spread rapidly around the globe.
- The deliberate release of such biological toxins by state or non-state actors would result in catastrophic consequences. Apart from the loss of lives, such toxins could result in food shortages, environmental catastrophes, devastating economic loss, and widespread illness.
- The terrorist and other illegal organisations could even misuse the same to induce fear and mistrust among the general public.

Biological Weapons Convention (BWC)

The BWC, also known as the **Convention on the Prohibition of the Development, Production and Stockpiling of Bacteriological (Biological) and Toxin Weapons and on their Destruction**, was negotiated in Geneva, Switzerland by the Conference of the Committee on Disarmament. It was opened for signature on April 10, 1972, and came into effect on March 26, 1975. Currently, the BWC has 183 state-parties. The BWC **complements the 1925 Geneva Protocol**, which only prohibited the use of biological weapons and did not address the development, production, or possession of chemical weapons.

The **1925 Protocol for the Prohibition of the Use of Asphyxiating, Poisonous or Other Gases, and of Bacteriological Methods of Warfare**, commonly known as the **1925 Geneva Protocol**, bans the use of chemical and bacteriological (biological) weapons in war. The Protocol (1925) was drawn up and signed at a conference under the auspices of the League of Nations from 4 May to 17 June 1925.

Signature – 17 June 1925
Deposit of instruments if ratification – 09 April 1930

- States Parties to the Biological Weapons Convention undertook never in any circumstances to develop, produce, stockpile or otherwise acquire or retain:
  1. microbial or other biological agents, or toxins whatever their origin or method of production, of types and in quantities that have no justification for prophylactic, protective or other peaceful purposes;
  2. weapons, equipment or means of delivery designed to use such agents or toxins for hostile purposes or in armed conflict.[34]

(BWC)
Signature – 15 January 1973
Deposit of instruments of ratification – 15 July 1974

[34] Biological Weapons Convention, United Nations, https://disarmament.unoda.org/biological-weapons

CHEMICAL WEAPONS

Main elements

- The modern use of such weapons began with the World War I, when both sides began using poisonous gas to cause significant battlefield casualties.
- Such weapons consist of commercial chemicals that are put into standard munitions such as grenades and artillery shells.
- The major chemicals used historically, include chlorine, phosgene (a choking agent) and mustard gas (which inflicts painful burns on the skin).
- The use of such toxins resulted in over 1,00,000 deaths during World War I. According to UN estimates, since World War I, chemical weapons have caused more than one million casualties globally.

Chemical Weapons Convention (CWC), 1992

While the Geneva Protocol had been enacted in 1925 to prohibit the use of chemicals, it had a several drawbacks especially the fact that it didn't prohibit the development, production or stockpiling of chemical weapons. As a result, the Cold War era saw a significant rise in the manufacture and stockpiling of such chemical weapons. To redress the vacuum in legislation, the CWC was adopted after 12 years.

After negotiations that lasted over a decade, the **Convention on the Prohibition of the Development, Production, Stockpiling and Use of Chemical Weapons and on Their Destruction** or the **Chemical Weapons Convention (CWC)** was adopted by the Conference on Disarmament in Geneva on **3 September 1992**. The CWC opened for signature in Paris on 13 January 1993 and entered into force on 29 April 1997.

The CWC, or Chemical Weapons Convention, is a landmark disarmament agreement that was negotiated through a multilateral process. It is the first agreement of its kind to address the complete elimination of a specific category of weapons of mass destruction under global oversight and control.

(CWC)
Signature (UN) – 14 January 1993
Deposit of instruments of ratification – 03 September 1996

Organisation for the Prohibition of Chemical Weapons (OPCW)

With the entry-into-force of the Chemical Weapons Convention (CWC) on 29 April 1997, the Organisation for the Prohibition of Chemical Weapons (OPCW) was formally established.

- **Technical Secretariat** - The Hague, the Netherlands.
- **Membership** –
  - States Parties to the Convention: 193
  - Signatory States: 1
  - Non-signatory States: 3
- **Population covered** - 98% of the global population.
- **Objectives -**
  - to ensure a credible, transparent regime to verify the destruction of chemical weapons;
  - to prevent their re-emergence in any member State;
  - to provide protection and assistance against chemical weapons;
  - to encourage international cooperation in the peaceful uses of chemistry; and
  - to achieve universal membership of the OPCW.
- **Destruction Progress** (As of Dec 2022)
  - World's declared chemical weapons stockpiles destroyed: 99%
  - Total declared stockpiles of chemical agents: 72,304 metric tonnes

- Total destroyed stockpiles of chemical agents: 71,946 metric tonnes

(OPCW)
Signature – 14 January 1993
Deposit – 03 September 1996
Entry into force – 29 April 1997

- In recognition of its extensive efforts to eliminate chemical weapons, **the OPCW was awarded the Nobel Peace Prize in 2013**.

INDIA – A NUCLEAR STATE

One significant aspect of India's industrialization plans was the establishment of a **nuclear program in the late 1940s**, led by **Homi J. Bhabha**. The aim was to utilize atomic energy for peaceful purposes. Jawaharlal Nehru, the Prime Minister of India at the time, opposed the development of nuclear weapons and advocated for comprehensive nuclear disarmament. However, his pleas for disarmament were unsuccessful. In October 1964, when Communist China conducted nuclear tests, the five nuclear-armed countries (the US, USSR, UK, France, and China) attempted to impose the Nuclear Non-Proliferation Treaty (NPT) of 1968 on the international community. **India viewed the NPT as discriminatory and chose not to sign it.**

MAJOR EVENTS OF NUCLEAR PROGRAMME – INDIA SPECIFIC	
1947	Post-independence, PM Nehru entrusted the development of the nuclear programme to **Homi Bhabha.**
1948	The Energy Act, 1948 stressed on peaceful development of nuclear energy.
1970	**Non-Proliferation Treaty (NPT) comes into force.**
May 18, 1974	**Pokhran-I (Rajasthan)**
1974	**Nuclear Suppliers Group (NSG) created.**
1978	The International Atomic Energy Agency (IAEA) released the **NSG Guidelines** to regulate the transfer of nuclear materials for peaceful purposes, with the aim of preventing their diversion towards unsafeguarded nuclear activities or the development of nuclear weapons.
1992	The NSG expanded the Guidelines to include transfers of dual-use equipment, materials, and technology that could potentially support unsafeguarded nuclear fuel cycles or activities related to nuclear explosives.
May 1998	**Pokhran-II**
2005	The framework for a US-India nuclear deal forms part of the 2005 statement between former PM Manmohan Singh and former President George Bush.
Aug 2008	Board of Governors of IAEA adopts India specific safeguards agreement.
Sept 6, 2008	**India gets waiver from guidelines of NSG (Nuclear Suppliers Group).**
Oct 8, 2008	President Bush signs legislation to enact the landmark **US-India Civilian nuclear agreement.**

Oct 10, 2008	The deal is signed between external affairs minister Pranab Mukherjee and Secretary of State C. Rice, in Washington DC.

Important Nuclear-related events

Pokhran I	Smiling Buddha	1974	• **India's first successful nuclear bomb test** • **Peaceful Nuclear Explosion** conducted in Rajasthan
Pokhran II	Operation Shakti	1998	• A series of **five nuclear bomb test explosions** conducted by India (Rajasthan) • The tests achieved their main objective of giving India the **capability to build fission and thermonuclear weapons** with yields up to 200 Kilotons. • PM AB Vajpayee declared a voluntary moratorium on tests.
Indo-US Nuclear Deal		2006-07	India consented to the **segregation of its civilian and military nuclear installations**, and committed to subject all its civilian nuclear facilities to the oversight of the International Atomic Energy Agency (IAEA).
Nuclear Suppliers Group (NSG) Waiver		2008	• The **civil nuclear agreement acknowledges India's "de facto" status**, despite its non-membership in the NPT. • It was an exceptional measure to grant an **exemption to a country that has not ratified the NPT and the CTBT.**

- In 1974, India carried out its inaugural nuclear test, known as Pokhran I or 'Smiling Buddha,' which was described as a peaceful detonation. India maintained its stance of utilizing nuclear energy solely for peaceful objectives. However, the tests were not taken in a good spirit by all nations and **new sanctions were imposed on India** by Western nations including the USA.
- **India didn't take part in the Comprehensive Nuclear Test Ban Treaty** (CTBT) that was adopted in 1996. The multilateral treaty that aims to ban all nuclear explosions (civilian or military purpose) has been regarded by India as discriminatory in nature. India refused to support the CTBT because it **does not address complete disarmament** and is discriminatory in nature with permanent UNSC members. Another major concern was the Entry- Into Force (EIF) clause, which India considered a violation of its right to voluntarily withhold participation in an international treaty.
    - o India has also maintained that it will not be bound by the CTBT until the major nuclear powers, including the United States, Russia, China, France, and the United Kingdom, have ratified the treaty and demonstrated their commitment to nuclear disarmament.
- The leading brain behind **Pokhran II** (1998) explosions as the chief of the Defence Research and Development Organisation, was Dr. APJ Abdul Kalam. With this India successfully ushered in the nuclear era. The 'Missile Man of India' had proclaimed in 2009 that, "India needs to be a nuclear-weapon state, as other nations are well-equipped and only strength respects strength". After successfully demonstrating the capability to build fission and thermonuclear weapons, PM AB Vajpayee declared a **voluntary moratorium** on tests. India pledged to continue to work for inaugural and non-discriminably nuclear disarmament.
- **Indo-US Nuclear Deal (2006-2008)** – This deal helped to undo the sanctions imposed on India by the global community and ushered a new nuclear image. Under this, India signed a civil-military separation plan and India-IAEA safeguard agreement. In return, US diplomacy helped us to get **NSG waiver**.

July 18, 2005	The U.S. and India announced the launch of the Civil Nuclear Cooperation Initiative.
August 1, 2008	The IAEA Board of Governors approved India's safeguards agreement, paving the way for India's consideration at the Nuclear Suppliers Group (NSG).
September 2008	After much lobbying by President Bush's administration, the Nuclear Suppliers Group (NSG) approved the India-specific exemption.
October 1, 2008	The U.S. Congress gave the final approval to an agreement facilitating nuclear cooperation between the United States and India.

Key features of the Indo-US Nuclear Deal were as follows:

1. India undertook the **separation of its civil and military nuclear facilities** and subjected all its civil nuclear facilities to **oversight by the International Atomic Energy Agency (IAEA).**
2. India committed to signing an **Additional Protocol**, enabling more extensive inspections of its civilian nuclear facilities by the IAEA.
3. India pledged to maintain its **voluntary moratorium on nuclear weapons testing**.
4. India agreed to **enhance the security of its nuclear arsenals**.
5. India aimed to engage in discussions with the United States towards the negotiation of a **Fissile Material Cutoff Treaty (FMCT)**, which aims to prohibit the production of fissile material for weapons purposes.
6. India agreed to prevent the proliferation of enrichment and reprocessing technologies to countries that do not possess them and to **support global non-proliferation efforts**.
7. **US companies were granted permission to construct nuclear reactors in India** and supply nuclear fuel for its civilian energy program.
8. **India became eligible to procure dual-use nuclear technology from the United States**, including materials and equipment that could be utilized for uranium enrichment or plutonium reprocessing, potentially contributing to the production of nuclear weapons material.

Importance of Nuclear Suppliers Group Membership

- It would give India **access to nuclear technology**, which would help the country to develop its nuclear energy sector. This would enable India to meet its growing energy demands and reduce its dependence on fossil fuels.
- It would **strengthen the global non-proliferation regime** by bringing India into the fold of responsible nuclear suppliers.
- It would **enhance India's diplomatic influence**, as it would give India a platform to engage with other nuclear suppliers and shape global nuclear policy.
- It would also have **economic benefits** for India, as it would open up new markets for Indian nuclear technology and expertise.

In 2008, the participating governments of the **Nuclear Suppliers Group (NSG)** reached a consensus to grant India a "clean waiver" from the group's regulations, which generally prohibit nuclear trade with countries that are not parties to the **Nuclear Non-Proliferation Treaty (NPT).** This waiver enabled India to engage in nuclear trade and access advanced nuclear technologies, including those used for uranium enrichment and plutonium reprocessing.

In 2016, India formally applied for membership in the NSG. This move was soon followed by similar applications from Pakistan and Namibia. India's application has sparked significant debate, primarily because India is not a signatory to the NPT. Instead, India maintains a unilateral moratorium on nuclear testing. Despite strong support from several NSG members, such as the United States, France, and Russia, opposition from countries like China, which advocates for a criteria-based approach to NSG membership, has stalled India's accession.

As of August 2024, India's membership in the NSG remains a contentious issue, with ongoing negotiations and no final resolution yet in sight. Additionally, recent developments have seen renewed diplomatic efforts by India to gain broader international support for its NSG bid, emphasizing its strong non-proliferation record and the strategic benefits of including India in the group. However, the geopolitical dynamics, particularly the strategic competition between India and China, continue to complicate India's path to full NSG membership.

India refused to sign NPT because –

(1) The NPT defines "nuclear weapons states" as those that tested devices before 1967, which means India would not be included.

(2) No fixed timelines have been mentioned for disarmament.

(3) NPT is an unfair treaty as nuclear weapon states have no obligation to give up the weapons while non-nuclear states are not allowed to have them.

Challenges and Strategic Implications

(1) **India's Quest for NSG Membership** - While a majority of nations support India's bid for membership in the Nuclear Suppliers Group (NSG), a coalition of countries, led by China and including New Zealand, Ireland, Turkey, South Africa, and Austria, has consistently opposed India's admission. China argues that India must first sign the Nuclear Non-Proliferation Treaty (NPT) to be eligible for NSG membership and advocates for a non-discriminatory criterion for the admission of countries that are not party to the NPT.

(2) **India's Position as a Responsible Nuclear Power** - India's standing as a 'responsible nuclear power' among the small group of nuclear-armed states is significantly influenced by the civil relationships it fosters with other nuclear powers. India's unique position on the global stage is marked by its status as a non-signatory to the NPT, the Comprehensive Nuclear-Test-Ban Treaty (CTBT), and its current exclusion from the NSG. While some nations, particularly the five recognized nuclear-weapon states under the NPT, have expressed disappointment with India's decision to remain outside these frameworks, other allies and partners have shown understanding, criticizing the discriminatory nature of these treaties. These countries acknowledge India's status as a nuclear-armed state and recognize its contributions to global non-proliferation efforts.

(3) **Evolving International Reception** - In recent years, there has been a gradual shift in the international community's reception of India's position. However, as India navigates these complex dynamics, it must pay close attention to the evolving global nuclear debate and reassess its domestic civilian and military nuclear programs. The current geopolitical landscape has underscored the continuing relevance of nuclear weapons as instruments of power and military strategy. The unfolding nuclear discourse, with

its unpredictable and paradoxical undertones, echoes the Cold War era, where nations pledge cooperation towards nuclear disarmament but their actions suggest otherwise.

(4) **India's Strategic Path Forward -** Under the stated circumstances, India must carve out its own strategic path, balancing its international commitments with domestic needs. As the global nuclear debate intensifies, India's ability to navigate these challenges will be crucial in maintaining its status as a responsible nuclear power while advancing its national interests in a complex and often contradictory international environment.

IS THE FUTURE NUCLEAR?

"As a global family, we can no longer allow the cloud of nuclear conflict to shadow our work to spur development, achieve the Sustainable Development Goals and end the COVID-19 pandemic. Now is the time to lift this cloud for good, eliminate nuclear weapons from our world, and usher in a new era of dialogue, trust and peace for all people."

\- António Guterres, Secretary-General of the United Nations

Energy security has emerged as one of the most critical issues confronting the international community in the 21st century. Amid this backdrop, nuclear energy has experienced resurgence, often referred to as a "nuclear renaissance" by experts. Touted as a low-carbon energy source, nuclear energy presents a viable option for mitigating climate change. Countries investing in nuclear energy are often perceived as taking proactive steps toward addressing environmental concerns, which, in turn, influences their diplomatic relations with other nations.

(a) **A Source of Cooperation and Conflict:** Nuclear energy serves as both a catalyst for cooperation and a potential source of conflict. On one hand, nations may collaborate on developing and sharing nuclear energy technologies, fostering closer ties and enhancing mutual trust. On the other hand, competition over access to nuclear resources or technological advancements can lead to geopolitical tensions and conflicts. It is important to remember that nuclear technology was originally developed for military purposes, and nations with access to such technology possess a strategic advantage in terms of energy security, which inevitably impacts their international relations.

(b) **The Dual-Use Dilemma:** The dual-use nature of nuclear technology—capable of being harnessed for both civilian energy production and military applications—raises significant concerns about non-proliferation and the potential for nuclear weapons development. Countries with nuclear energy capabilities may also possess the latent ability to develop nuclear weapons, prompting fears among other nations regarding their intentions and military capabilities.

(c) **Prestige and Power:** Nuclear energy is often seen as a symbol of prestige and power, leading to the emergence of the term "nuclear power." Despite the existence of numerous treaties and agreements aimed at promoting non-proliferation, the divide between "nuclear" and "non-nuclear" states persists, contributing to an imbalanced global order marked by insecurity and fuelling the ongoing race for nuclear dominance.

(d) **The Dark Side of nuclear weapons:** The catastrophic consequences of nuclear weapons, from the immediate devastation to long-term health effects like cancer and chronic illnesses, as well as widespread environmental destruction, cannot be overlooked. The paradoxical debate surrounding the concept of "war for peace" continues, as the international community remains unable to reach a consensus on the complete elimination of all Weapons of Mass Destruction (WMD).

Thus, the future of nuclear energy in international relations will hinge on a complex interplay of factors, including access to nuclear technology and resources, non-proliferation concerns, the potential for either cooperation or conflict, and the role of nuclear energy in combating climate change. As nations navigate these challenges, the trajectory of nuclear energy will significantly shape the contours of global diplomacy and security.

14

INDIA'S GLOBAL FOOTPRINT - THE DIASPORA

THE DIASPORA: A GLOBAL PHENOMENON

ETYMOLOGY

The term "diaspora" originates from the Greek word ***diaspeirein***, which means "**to scatter**." Historically, it was used to describe the dispersion of people from their original homeland, especially the Jewish diaspora after the Babylonian exile.

In the modern context, diaspora refers to a population that has migrated from its homeland to other parts of the world, either voluntarily (for work, education, or other opportunities) or involuntarily (due to conflict, persecution, or natural disasters). This term encompasses not only the original migrants but also their descendants who may maintain a connection, whether emotional, cultural, or economic, to their ancestral homeland.

Major characteristics of a diaspora include the following –

Dispersed Population: Diasporas are typically characterized by a population that is dispersed across multiple geographic regions but maintains a shared identity.

Sense of Community: Despite being geographically dispersed, members often maintain a strong sense of community and shared identity, often revolving around common cultural, religious, linguistic, or national ties.

Connection to Homeland: Diasporas often maintain a connection to their homeland, which may manifest in various forms - remittances, cultural exchanges, advocacy, & political lobbying.

Transnationalism: Diasporas embody the concept of transnationalism, as they live across borders but maintain multiple identities and connections to more than one nation.

THE INDIAN DIASPORA

The Indian diaspora represents a vast and dynamic network of individuals of Indian origin residing outside India. Spanning across continents, this global community is characterized by its diverse socio-economic backgrounds, cultures, and experiences. With roots tracing back to historical migrations and colonial labor practices, the Indian diaspora has evolved into one of the largest and most influential diaspora groups worldwide.

Comprising over 30 million people, the Indian diaspora is spread across countries in North America, Europe, the Middle East, Africa, Southeast Asia, and beyond. This global dispersion has led to a rich tapestry of cultural exchanges and economic contributions. Indian expatriates have established vibrant communities in their host countries, significantly influencing local economies, politics, and cultural landscapes.

PRAVASI BHARATIYA DIVAS

It is a national event celebrated by India on **January 9th** each year to honour the contributions of the Indian diaspora to the nation's development.The day commemorates the return of Mahatma Gandhi from South Africa to India on this date in 1915.

The key objectives of Pravasi Bharatiya Divas include:

1. **Recognizing the diaspora's contributions**: Appreciating the efforts of Overseas Indians in various fields, including business, technology, and culture.
2. **Strengthening ties**: Fostering stronger connections between India and the Indian diaspora worldwide.
3. **Facilitating knowledge exchange**: Providing a platform for dialogue and collaboration between the diaspora and the Indian government.
4. **Encouraging investment**: Attracting investment from the diaspora to support India's economic growth.

CLASSIFICATION OF INDIAN DIASPORA

NRI (NON-RESIDENT OF INDIA)

NRIs are Indian citizens who live & work outside of India for 182 days in a fiscal year while maintaining strong ties to their home country.

OCI (OVERSEAS CITIZEN OF INDIA)

OCI is a permanent residency form that allows Indians and their spouses to live and work in India for an indefinite period of time.

PIO (PEOPLE OF INDIA)

PIOs, or non-Indian citizens of other countries, were combined under OCI in 2015.

LEADING DESTINATIONS

The Indian diaspora is one of the largest and most influential in the world, with millions of people of Indian origin living in various countries. Major countries with significant Indian diaspora populations include:

	**THE UNITED STATES OF AMERICA**	The Indian diaspora in the US is one of the largest and most successful, with over 4.5 million people of Indian origin contributing to various sectors, including technology, healthcare, academia, and entrepreneurship.
	**UNITED ARAB EMIRATES**	The UAE is home to a significant Indian population, with approximately 3.5 million Indians, making up nearly 30% of the country's population. Indians are crucial to the UAE's economy, particularly in construction, healthcare, retail, and technology sectors.

	**SAUDI ARABIA**	Saudi Arabia has a large Indian diaspora, estimated at around 2.6 million people. Indians are primarily employed in construction, healthcare, and the service industry, playing a vital role in the country's development.
	**MALAYSIA**	Malaysia has a longstanding Indian community, with over 2.1 million people of Indian origin, primarily descendants of laborers brought during the British colonial period. The Indian diaspora has significantly influenced the country's culture, politics, and economy.
	**THE UNITED KINGDOM**	The UK has a large and influential Indian diaspora, with over 1.9 million people of Indian descent. This community has made substantial contributions to British society, particularly in business, politics, healthcare, and education.
	**CANADA**	Canada is home to a growing Indian diaspora, with around 1.8 million people of Indian origin. The Indian community is active in various sectors, including technology, healthcare, and education, and has a significant political presence.
	**SOUTH AFRICA**	South Africa has an Indian diaspora population of approximately 1.5 million, primarily descendants of indentured labourers brought during the 19th century. The community has had a profound impact on the country's culture, politics, and economy.
	**AUSTRALIA**	Australia has seen a rapid increase in its Indian diaspora, with around 1.1 million people of Indian origin. Indians in Australia are well-represented in sectors like education, healthcare, and IT, and have a growing influence in Australian society.
	**SINGAPORE**	Singapore is home to around 600,000 people of Indian origin. The Indian diaspora is well-integrated into society and plays a vital role in Singapore's economic development, particularly in finance, technology, and trade.
	**QATAR**	Qatar hosts a sizable Indian diaspora, with around 700,000 Indians working in various sectors, including construction, healthcare, and services, contributing significantly to the country's economy.

THE SIGNIFICANCE OF DIASPORAS

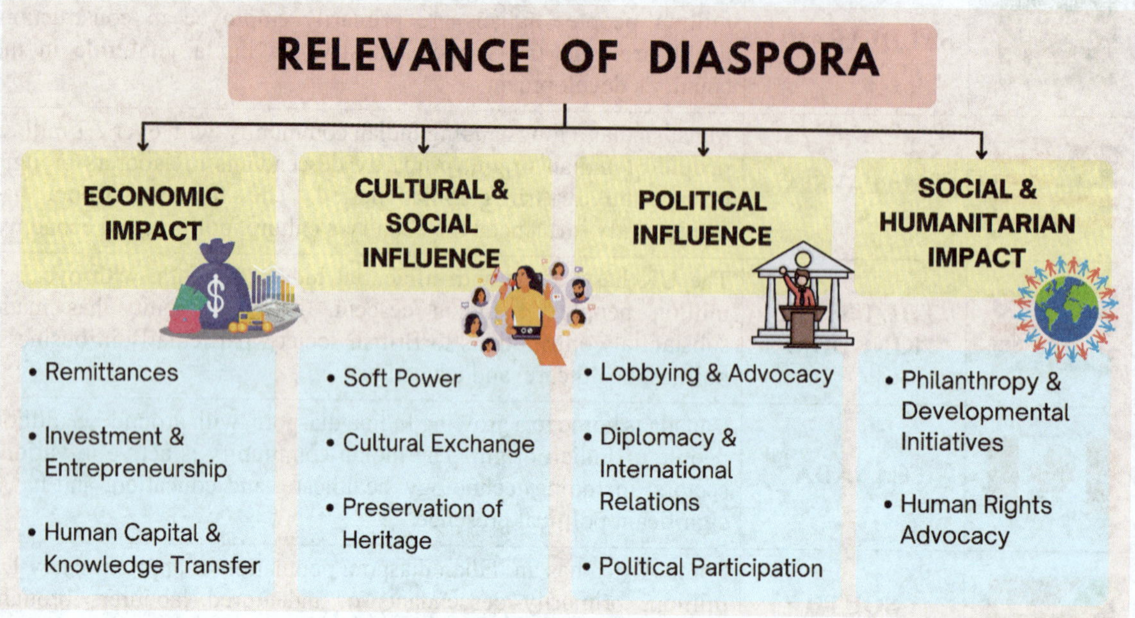

(1) Economic Impact

- One of the most tangible impacts of diasporas is the **remittances** they send back to their home countries. According to the World Bank, global remittances are a significant source of income for many developing countries, often surpassing foreign direct investment (FDI) and official development assistance (ODA).

REMITTANCES

As of 2023, **India remains the world's largest recipient of remittances**. The Indian diaspora, numbering over 35 million people, sent an unprecedented **$107 billion** back to their families in India during the financial year 2023-24 (World Bank).

The **United States** remains the primary source of remittances to India, followed by the United Arab Emirates, the United Kingdom, Singapore, and Malaysia.

- Diasporas often serve as **investors and entrepreneurs**, channeling funds into business ventures in their countries of origin. They play a crucial role in fostering economic ties between their host and home countries. Ex: The Indian diaspora has been instrumental in the growth of the IT sector in India through investments, business collaborations, and knowledge transfer.
- Diaspora communities contribute to the development of their homelands by **transferring skills, knowledge, and technology**. Many highly skilled professionals in the diaspora, such as doctors, engineers, and academics, participate in initiatives to improve education, healthcare, and infrastructure in their countries of origin.

(2) Cultural and Social Influence

- Diasporas can enhance the **soft power** of their home countries by acting as **cultural ambassadors**. Through their professional achievements, artistic contributions, and social engagement, members of the diaspora can shape positive perceptions of their homeland and influence global public opinion.
- Diasporas are key agents of **cultural exchange**, introducing elements of their native cultures into host societies while simultaneously adopting aspects of the host culture. This cultural blending enriches the social fabric of both the homeland and the host country. For example, the global

popularity of Indian cuisine, music, and films can be partly attributed to the influence of the Indian diaspora.

- Diasporas play a crucial role in **preserving and promoting their cultural heritage**. Through festivals, language schools, religious institutions, and community organizations, diaspora communities ensure that future generations remain connected to their cultural roots.

(3) Political Influence

- Diaspora communities often engage in **lobbying** and **advocacy** efforts to influence the policies of both their host and home countries. They can mobilize resources, organize campaigns, and exert pressure on governments to address issues of concern, such as immigration policies, human rights, and international trade. Ex: The Indian American community has been actively involved in lobbying for immigration reform in the United States, particularly concerning the H-1B visa program and green card backlog issues.
- They can serve as bridges between their host and home countries, facilitating **diplomacy and fostering bilateral relations.** They often act as informal diplomats, promoting dialogue, cooperation, and understanding between nations. Ex: Prime Minister Narendra Modi has actively engaged with the Indian diaspora as part of his diplomatic strategy to strengthen India's global ties.
- Many countries allow their diaspora to participate in **national elections**, either by voting from abroad or through special representation. This inclusion of the diaspora in the political process ensures that their voices are heard and that they remain connected to the governance of their homeland. Ex: The Indian government has recognized the importance of the diaspora in the political process and has taken steps to allow Non-Resident Indians (NRIs) to participate in national elections.

(4) Social and Humanitarian Impact

- Diaspora communities are often involved in **philanthropic activities**, supporting charitable organizations, disaster relief efforts, and development projects in their home countries. This philanthropic engagement contributes to social welfare and development, particularly in areas such as education, healthcare, and poverty alleviation. Ex: **Pratham USA**, supported by Indian-Americans, focuses on improving literacy and education outcomes for children in India.
- Diasporas can play a crucial role in advocating for **human rights and social justice** in their home countries. By raising awareness, organizing campaigns, and leveraging international networks, they can draw attention to human rights abuses and support movements for social and political change. Ex: During the **2012 Delhi gang rape case**, the Indian diaspora globally organized protests, candlelight vigils, and online campaigns to demand justice and reforms in India's legal and social systems regarding women's safety.

MAKING HEADLINES - PERSONS OF INDIAN ORIGIN

In recent years, individuals of Indian origin have increasingly made headlines across the globe, distinguishing themselves in various fields such as politics, business, science, arts, and technology. From leading multinational corporations to holding high-ranking political offices in foreign governments, these trailblazers have not only broken glass ceilings but have also significantly contributed to shaping global narratives. Their achievements reflect the immense potential and influence of the Indian diaspora, underscoring the far-reaching impact of India's global presence. As they continue to rise to prominence, these individuals embody the spirit of resilience, innovation, and leadership, bringing pride to their heritage while influencing the world at large.

<u>Some important individuals making headlines over the years include the following –</u>

1. **Rishi Sunak**, of Indian descent, became the first person of Indian origin to serve as the Prime Minister of the United Kingdom. His rise to power was celebrated by the Indian diaspora worldwide as a significant milestone in global politics and representation.

2. **Kamala Harris**, the first woman of Indian and African-American descent to become the Vice President of the United States, has continued to be a prominent figure in global politics. Her position has empowered the Indian diaspora and brought attention to the contributions of Indian-Americans in U.S. governance. Kamala Harris officially announced her 2024 presidential candidacy (Democratic presidential)in August 2024.

3. Indian-American astronaut **Sunita Williams**, known for her record-setting spaceflights, remains a key figure in NASA's missions. Her legacy and involvement in training future astronauts, including missions to the ISS, continue to inspire both the Indian diaspora and aspiring scientists worldwide. In August 2024, NASA formally broke the news that astronauts Butch Wilmore and Sunita Williams were stranded on the ISS (till early 2025) due to technical issues with the Boeing Starliner spacecraft, delaying their return to Earth.
4. **Indra Nooyi**, former CEO of PepsiCo, remains a significant figure in global business. Her memoir, "*My Life in Full: Work, Family, and Our Future*," published in 2022, became a bestseller and was widely discussed for its insights into leadership, work-life balance, and the challenges faced by women in corporate America. Her story continues to inspire the Indian diaspora, particularly women aspiring to leadership roles.
5. Ajay Banga is a prominent Indian-American business executive who currently serves as the **President of the World Bank Group**. As World Bank President, Banga is focused on driving sustainable development, addressing global challenges, and leveraging technology to improve the lives of people around the world.He was previously the executive chairman of *Mastercard*.
6. **Gitanjali Rao**, a young Indian-American scientist and inventor, continued to gain global recognition in 2023 for her work in science and innovation. She has been featured on various global platforms for her inventions aimed at solving pressing social issues, such as water contamination and cyberbullying.
7. Leaders of Indian descent, such as **Sundar Pichai** (Google), **Satya Nadella** (Microsoft), and **Arvind Krishna** (IBM), continued to dominate headlines in 2023. Their leadership in navigating challenges like AI development, cybersecurity, and global digital inclusion highlights the significant influence of the Indian diaspora in shaping the tech industry's future.
8. Throughout 2023, Indian-American scientists played crucial roles in advancing COVID-19 research and vaccine development. Figures like **Dr. Vivek Murthy**, the U.S. Surgeon General, and **Dr. Kizzmekia Corbett**, who contributed to the development of the Moderna vaccine, were central in the global fight against the pandemic, showcasing the diaspora's impact on public health.

CHALLENGES FOR DIASPORAS

1) **Identity and Integration**: Diasporas often face challenges related to identity and integration, particularly in balancing their connection to their homeland with their assimilation into the host country. Issues of dual identity, cultural assimilation, and discrimination can affect the well-being and social cohesion of diaspora communities.
2) **Political and Social Tensions**: Diasporas may find themselves caught in political or social tensions between their home and host countries. For instance, geopolitical conflicts, trade disputes, or diplomatic

tensions can create challenges for diaspora communities, who may face divided loyalties or discrimination based on their national origin.

3) **Economic Vulnerabilities**: While diasporas contribute significantly to the economies of their home and host countries, they may also face economic vulnerabilities, such as precarious employment, lack of access to social services, and economic exploitation in the host country.

RECENT ISSUES FACED BYTHE INDIAN DIASPORA

The Indian diaspora has faced various challenges in recent times, including:

1) **Economic Hardships:** The COVID-19 pandemic and the subsequent global economic downturn have had a profound impact on the Indian diaspora, particularly those in sectors like hospitality, retail, and healthcare.
   - For instance, in the Gulf countries, where a significant portion of the Indian diaspora is employed in construction and service industries, thousands faced job losses and had to return to India. The situation was further exacerbated by the lack of social security nets in these host countries, leaving many without financial support during the crisis.

XENOPHOBIA

It is a form of prejudice & discrimination that often manifests in negative attitudes, behaviors, or policies towards people from other cultures, countries, or ethnicities. Xenophobia can lead to social exclusion, discrimination, & violence.

2) **Racial Discrimination:** Racial discrimination and ***xenophobia*** have emerged as significant issues for the Indian diaspora, particularly in Western countries.
   - For example, in the United States, there have been numerous reports of hate crimes against people of Indian origin. The tragic shooting of *Srinivas Kuchibhotla*, an Indian engineer in Kansas in 2017, highlighted the dangers of rising xenophobia.
3) **Political Issues:** Political affiliations and citizenship status have also become areas of concern for the Indian diaspora.
   - For instance, the changes in immigration policies in the United States under the Trump administration created uncertainty for many Indian professionals working on H-1B visas. The sudden imposition of travel bans and visa restrictions left many in limbo, unable to return to their jobs or join their families.
4) **Cultural Integration:** Balancing cultural identity with integration into host societies remains a persistent challenge for the Indian diaspora. In countries like the United Kingdom and Canada, where multiculturalism is celebrated, the diaspora has managed to maintain its cultural practices while integrating into the broader society. However, in other regions, especially where assimilation is expected, the pressure to conform can lead to identity conflicts.
   - For example, younger generations of the Indian diaspora in the United States often grapple with maintaining their cultural heritage while navigating the expectations of an American lifestyle. This struggle is evident in areas like marriage, where traditional practices may clash with modern values, or in education, where the emphasis on certain career paths may differ from those valued in Indian culture.
5) **Health and Well-being:** Mental health has become an increasingly pressing issue within the Indian diaspora, particularly among the youth. The pressure to succeed, combined with the challenges of cultural dislocation and discrimination, has led to rising cases of anxiety, depression, and other mental health issues.
   - For example, in the United States, studies have shown that Indian-American teens and young adults experience higher levels of stress and mental health challenges compared to their peers from other backgrounds.
6) **Diaspora Engagement with India:** The relationship between the Indian government and its diaspora has also faced strains. While the Indian government has made efforts to engage the diaspora through initiatives like ***Pravasi Bharatiya Divas***, there have been instances where the diaspora's concerns have not been adequately addressed.

- For example, during the COVID-19 pandemic, there were criticisms of the Indian government's repatriation efforts, with many stranded abroad feeling abandoned. Additionally, the introduction of new taxation policies on Non-Resident Indians (NRIs) has sparked debates within the diaspora about their rights and obligations to their homeland.

REPATRIATION OF INDIANS DURING CONFLICTS

India has a robust mechanism for the repatriation of its citizens during conflicts, war-like situations, or other emergencies abroad. This process involves coordinated efforts by various government agencies, particularly the Ministry of External Affairs (MEA), Indian embassies and consulates, the Indian Armed Forces, and other stakeholders. The Indian government has historically undertaken several large-scale operations to bring its citizens back safely from conflict zones or areas experiencing political instability.

The **Indian Embassies and Consulates** play a crucial role in organizing and facilitating the repatriation process. They provide shelter, food, and necessary documentation to stranded citizens and coordinate with local authorities for their safe departure. The MEA sets up 24/7 helplines and establishes control rooms to assist citizens in distress, providing them with the latest updates and guidance.

Key Features of India's Evacuation Efforts -

- **Swift Response:** The Indian government has demonstrated a swift and efficient response to crises, mobilizing resources and coordinating with local authorities to ensure the safety of its citizens.
- **Comprehensive Planning:** Evacuation operations involve meticulous planning, including coordination with foreign governments, airlines, and ground transportation.
- **Robust Support Systems:** The Indian government provides essential services, such as accommodation, food, and medical assistance, to evacuated citizens.
- **Collaboration with International Partners:** India often collaborates with other countries and international organizations to facilitate evacuations and provide humanitarian aid.

NOTABLE EVACUATION OPERATIONS

OPERATION	DETAILS
Operation SAFE HOMECOMING (Libya, 2011)	It was a large-scale evacuation mission conducted by the Indian government in 2011 to rescue Indian nationals stranded in Libya during the Libyan Civil War. The operation was launched in response to the violent unrest and civil conflict that erupted in Libya following anti-government protests against the regime of Muammar Gaddafi. Over 15,000 Indian nationals were successfully evacuated from Libya during the Operation. The operation was one of the largest and most complex evacuation missions undertaken by India in recent history.
Operation RAAHAT (Yemen, 2015)	Amidst the Yemeni Civil War, India successfully evacuated thousands of Indian citizens from the conflict-ridden country. The operation showcased India's ability to mount large-scale rescue missions in complex and volatile environments. Over 4,600 Indian citizens were evacuated along with over 900 foreign nationals from 41 countries.
Operation MAITRI (Nepal, 2015)	Following the devastating earthquake in Nepal, India launched Operation Maitri to provide humanitarian aid and support to the affected population.Although primarily a humanitarian mission, it also involved evacuating Indian citizens from Nepal.
VANDE BHARAT MISSION (COVID-19, 2020)	It was a repatriation operation launched by the Indian government to bring back Indian citizens stranded abroad during the COVID-19 pandemic. The mission was launched in May 2020, and was a success, helping to repatriate over 1.83 million Indian nationals from more than 100 countries. The mission is considered one of the largest civilian repatriation exercises in recent history.

Operation DEVI SHAKTI (Afghanistan, 2021)	As the Taliban regained control of Afghanistan, India conducted a complex evacuation operation to rescue Indian citizens and Afghan collaborators. The operation involved coordination with multiple governments and international organizations.Under the operation, a total of 669 people were evacuated from Afghanistan. This comprises of 448 Indians and 206 Afghans.
Operation GANGA (Neighbouring nations of Ukraine, 2022)	It was a large-scale evacuation mission undertaken by the Indian government in February and March 2022 to rescue Indian nationals stranded in Ukraine during the Russian invasion. The operation was launched in response to the sudden and escalating conflict, which left thousands of Indians, particularly students, in precarious situations across Ukraine.Due to the closure of Ukrainian airspace, Indian nationals were evacuated by land to neighboring countries like Romania, Hungary, Poland, Moldova, and Slovakia.Over 22,500 Indian nationals were safely evacuated from Ukraine and neighboring countries.
Operation KAVERI (Sudan, April 2023)	Amidst the ongoing conflict in Sudan, India successfully evacuated its citizens, demonstrating its ability to respond to rapidly evolving crises. The operation successfully brought back over 4,090 people, including 136 foreign nations, from Sudan.
Operation AJAY (Israel, Oct 2023)	The operation was launched by the Indian government to evacuate Indian citizens from conflict-hit Israel. The operation was initiated in response to the outbreak of severe conflict between Israel and militant groups, which led to a dangerous and unstable environment for foreign nationals, including Indians. Special evacuation flights were arranged to bring back Indian citizens from Israel.

RETURN MIGRATION &'BRAIN GAIN'

Return migration refers to the phenomenon where individuals who had previously migrated to another country choose to return to their home country, often bringing back valuable skills, experiences, and networks. In the context of the Indian diaspora, return migration has the potential to contribute significantly to India's economic and social development, a concept often termed as "*brain gain.*"

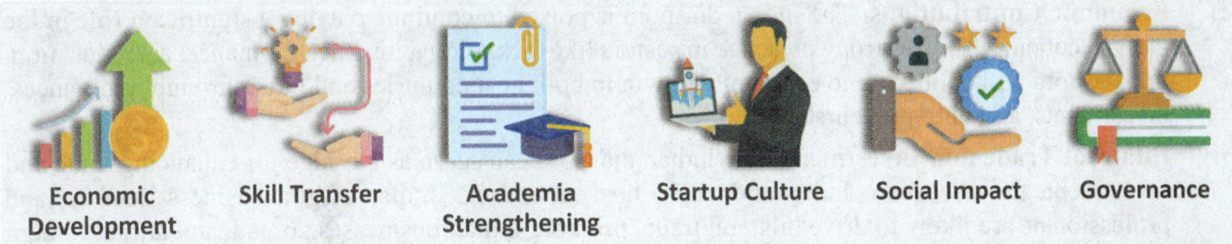

(a) **Economic Development**: Returnees bring advanced skills and global exposure, driving innovation and economic growth. Examples include tech entrepreneurs from Silicon Valley who have launched successful startups in India (Companies like **Flipkart**, founded by ex-Amazon employees Sachin and Binny Bansal), contributing to the country's growing tech ecosystem.

(b) **Skill Transfer and Innovation**: Returning professionals introduce global best practices and technologies, enhancing sectors like healthcare, technology, and research. Their contributions help bridge skill gaps and foster innovation in India's key industries.

(c) **Strengthening Institutions and Academia**: Returnees bolster academic and research institutions by raising standards, mentoring talent, and fostering international collaborations. Their involvement can enhance the global reputation of Indian universities and research centers.

(d) **Entrepreneurship and Startups**: Many returnees launch startups, bringing capital, global market insights, and innovative ideas. Their ventures drive employment and economic growth, particularly in

India's thriving startup ecosystem. The rise of India's startup ecosystem, particularly in cities like Bangalore, Hyderabad, and Pune, is partly driven by returnees who have played a key role in shaping this dynamic environment.

(e) **Cultural and Social Impact**: Returnees introduce diverse perspectives, promoting modern values like gender equality, corporate social responsibility and environmental sustainability. Their influence can lead to progressive social changes within their communities in India.

(f) **Policy and Governance**: Returnees can shape policies and governance by applying their international experience. Their involvement in public service and advisory roles can drive economic growth and strengthen India's global relations. Additionally, returnees can play a role in strengthening India's relations with other countries, leveraging their international networks to facilitate trade, investment, and diplomatic ties.

While return migration offers many benefits, it also presents challenges. Returnees may face difficulties in re-integrating into the local culture and professional environment, which can differ significantly from what they experienced abroad. However, with the right support systems, including government policies that facilitate reintegration, professional networks, and mentorship programs, these challenges can be mitigated. The Indian government has recognized the potential of return migration and has implemented initiatives to attract diaspora members back to India, such as the ***Vibrant Gujarat Global Summit*** and the ***Pravasi Bharatiya Divas***.

Return migration and brain gain represent a significant opportunity for India to harness the skills, knowledge, and global networks of its diaspora. By encouraging and supporting the return of talented professionals, entrepreneurs, and academics, India can accelerate its development, enhance its global competitiveness, and address critical challenges in various sectors.

WORD MIGRATION REPORT 2024

According to **World Migration Report 2024**, India is the country of origin for **the greatest number of foreign migrants globally (almost 18 million),** with sizable diasporas spread across the US, Saudi Arabia, UAE, and other nations.

The research states that there are somewhat more female immigrants from India than male immigrants. In India, Bangladesh, and Pakistan, the percentage of male emigrants is notably high.

FUTURE PROSPECTS AND OPPORTUNITIES

(i) **Economic Contributions**: The Indian diaspora is poised to continue playing a significant role in the global economy. With a strong presence in sectors like technology, healthcare, finance, and education, the diaspora will contribute to economic growth in both host countries and India through remittances, investments, and entrepreneurship.

(ii) **Bilateral Trade and Investment**: The Indian diaspora can serve as a bridge for enhancing trade and investment ties between India and their host countries. Indian-origin business leaders and professionals are likely to drive bilateral trade, promote Indian businesses abroad, and attract foreign direct investment (FDI) into India.

(iii) **Technological Innovation**: With a large number of Indian professionals working in the global tech industry, the diaspora will continue to be at the forefront of technological innovation. This will create opportunities for collaboration in areas such as artificial intelligence, fintech, biotech, and renewable energy between India and other nations.

(iv) **Educational Collaboration**: The Indian diaspora can play a crucial role in strengthening educational ties between India and other countries. Opportunities include establishing academic partnerships, facilitating student exchanges, and creating scholarships that enable greater access to global education for Indian students.

(v) **Diaspora Engagement Policies**: Recognizing the importance of their diaspora, many countries are developing policies and initiatives to engage and support their diaspora communities. These may include programs for investment facilitation, cultural exchange, and political participation. Such policies can help harness the potential of the diaspora for national development.

(vi) **Digital Connectivity and Global Networks**: Advances in technology and communication have enhanced the ability of diaspora communities to stay connected with their homeland and with each other. Social media, digital platforms, and global networks have made it easier for diasporas to mobilize resources, share knowledge, and engage in transnational activities.

(vii) **Diaspora Networks and Professional Associations**: Strengthening and expanding diaspora networks and professional associations can create new opportunities for collaboration and knowledge-sharing. These networks can facilitate mentorship, business development, and innovation across borders.

(viii) **Sustainable Development Goals (SDGs)**: Diasporas can play a significant role in achieving the United Nations' Sustainable Development Goals (SDGs) by contributing to economic growth, social inclusion, and environmental sustainability. Their involvement in development initiatives, knowledge transfer, and advocacy can support efforts to build a more equitable and sustainable world.

In today's globalized world, diasporas are more relevant and significant than ever before. They serve as vital connectors between nations, contributing to economic growth, cultural exchange, and political diplomacy. Their role in shaping global dynamics, fostering development, and preserving cultural heritage makes them indispensable players in the international arena. As the world becomes increasingly interconnected, the influence and importance of diaspora communities are likely to continue growing, offering new opportunities for collaboration, innovation, and global progress.

15 CHANGING PERCEPTIONS OF THREAT & NEW WORLD ORDER

THREATS AND SECURITY

Threat is an indication of potential or imminent danger. It is a situation or activity that could cause harm or has the potential to cause harm. While **security** means **freedom from threats**. In the context of the issues at hand, discussions around security wouldn't include any threats, but only those acts that threaten or have the potential to threaten the 'core values'. Security can be categorized into two groups - traditional and non-traditional conceptions.

1. TRADITIONAL NOTIONS

Traditional conceptions of security are principally concerned with the use, or threat of use, of military force. Here, force is both the principal threat to security and the principal means of achieving security. Here, the referent is the state with its territory and governing institutions.

(a) Internal: The concept of state sovereignty according to which no one is above the state implies political authority which is based on territory and autonomy. Territoriality is the right of exclusive political authority over a particular geographic area (internal sovereignty) and autonomy means that no external factor – such as another state – has authority within the borders of a defined state (external sovereignty).

The concept of national security has been developed over the years. The following table enumerates some highlights surrounding the growth of concepts.

Particulars	Pre-Westphalian concept	Westphalian concept	Post-Cold War concept
Main values and interests	Territory, agriculture and food, property of community members	Sovereignty, territorial integrity, economy, peace, freedoms, diplomatic affairs	The separation of power, rule of law, national identity and honour, human rights and freedoms, quality of life, information resources, environment and biodiversity, international order etc.
Major threats	Conflicts among groups, diseases, natural disasters	Military related threats (war etc.), political threats/crimes, uprisings against regimes, intelligence subversion, interference in foreign affairs	Non-military threats (terrorism and organized crime), epidemics, climate change and natural hazards, environmental degradation, decline in human development, poverty, hunger, economic instability, technology related threats, nuclear weapons etc.

Regulations for protection	Common Law	National and Domestic legislations; International Law (under development)	National and International Laws; International Judicial pronouncements; decisions of International Bodies, commissions and Arbitral authorities

Presently, national security includes security of the society (heterogenous group) and security of the state, but also their participation in international and global security. It implies the unhindered development, enjoyment and protection of sovereign values which is improved through the function of security of citizens supranational security mechanisms, the absence of (individual, group, and collective) fear of being endangered, as well as collective sense of serenity, certainty and control over the future events and developments of importance for the life of society and the state.

(b) External:

EXTERNAL			
Deterrence: Preventing war	**Defence**: Limiting or ending war	**Balance of Power**: Countries with bigger and stronger neighbouring countries must be wary of a potential future aggression. A good part of maintaining a balance of power is to build up one's military power, although economic and technological power are also important.	**Alliance Building**: It is a coalition of states that coordinate their actions to deter or defend against military attack. Countries form alliances to increase their effective power relative to another country or alliance.

WAR INDUCED THREATS AND THEIR RESPECTIVE LINKAGES

Type of Threat	Affected parties	Outcomes and pressures
High and volatile International Food Prices	Heavily import-dependent states with urbanized societies, like Mexico, Pakistan, Azerbaijan, Syria, Philippines, Egypt etc. Producer states which could impose export restrictions due to soaring prices, like Argentina, Russia, China, Brazil, Thailand, Indonesia etc.	• Excessive burden on the exchequer • High inflation • Economic collapse • Riots coupled with political instability • Panic buying by consumers which could further push up prices
High and volatile International Energy Prices	High import-dependent developing nations, like India, Eastern European nations, Chile, Turkey etc.	• Deteriorating public finances leading to economic crisis • Spiraling inflation • Possible regime collapse • Conflicts and social disruptions • Disincentive to invest

Disruption of access to resources and minerals	High-tech manufacturing sectors in import-dependent countries, like Germany and other European manufacturers, Japan, South Korea, Taiwan etc.	• Disruption of supply chains and resultant fall in income/profits • Panic buying and creation of stockpiles which could further exacerbate tensions

2. NON-TRADITIONAL NOTIONS

Non-traditional concepts of security extend beyond conventional military risks and encompass a broad spectrum of threats and hazards that impact the overall well-being of individuals. These alternative perspectives on security are often described as "human security" or "global security."

- **Human security** pertains to **safeguarding individuals rather than solely prioritizing the security of states.** While a "narrow" understanding of human security concentrates on violent perils faced by individuals or communities, advocates of a "broader" perspective contend that the scope of threats should encompass issues such as hunger, disease, and natural disasters. This broader view is justified by the fact that these factors collectively claim more lives than warfare, genocide, and terrorism combined.
- The concept of **global security** emerged in the 1990s in response to the global nature of threats such as global warming, international terrorism, and health epidemics like AIDS and bird flu. It suggests that no individual nation can resolve these threats alone due to their transboundary nature. The biggest example in the present decade is the COVID-19 which shook the well-established medical fraternity, both in developed and developing nations. Since the new-age problems are global in nature, international cooperation is vital, even though it is difficult to achieve.

Some of the issues which are hampering security efforts in the present decade are as follows-

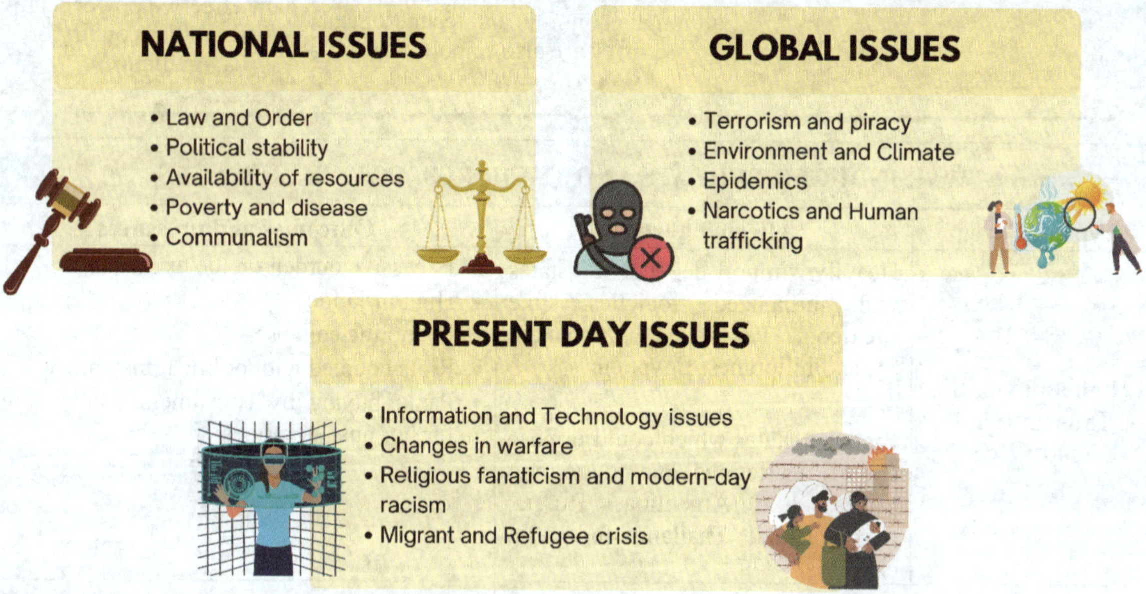

NEW SOURCES OF THREATS – CONTEMPORARY WORLD

(a) Terrorism

Terrorism refers to **political violence that targets civilians deliberately and indiscriminately**. The terrorist groups work with an objective of instilling fear in the minds of the people in order to bring about changes in their favour whether by force or threat of force. Terrorism poses a direct threat to the security of citizens globally and to international stability and prosperity. Terrorist organizations motivate individuals, particularly young people, to abandon their communities worldwide and journey to regions of conflict, predominantly in Iraq and Syria, and increasingly in Libya. The utilization of **CBRNE materials (chemical, biological, radiological, nuclear, and explosive)** in terrorist attacks has the potential for devastating repercussions on communities and critical infrastructure.

(b) **Global Poverty**

World population has reached **8 billion** on November 15, 2022 according to the United Nations, with India overtaking China to become the world's most populous country (estimated population – 1,425,771,530 people). According to the World Bank, about 9.2% of the world, **or 719 million people, live in extreme poverty**, on less than $2.15 a day. In the coming 50 years, the population of the world's poorest nations is projected to triple, while several wealthy countries will experience a decline in population. This disparity in population growth is accompanied by a situation where affluent states or privileged social groups with high per capita income tend to become even wealthier. In contrast, low incomes combined with high population growth create a reinforcing cycle that contributes to the impoverishment of poorer nations and marginalized groups.

According to World Bank's report, **'Poverty and Shared Prosperity 2022', by 2030 nearly 7 percent of the world's population—nearly 600 million people—will still struggle in extreme poverty.** 2020 saw the biggest setback to global poverty in decades which was exacerbated by the pandemic.

(c) **Migration**

The prevalence of extreme poverty has led to significant migration, as individuals seek improved living conditions and greater economic prospects. This phenomenon has resulted in political tensions on an international scale. International legal frameworks and norms draw a distinction between migrants, who choose to leave their home countries, and refugees, who flee due to factors such as war, natural disasters, or political persecution. While nations generally accept and provide assistance to refugees, they are not obligated to accept migrants. Furthermore, individuals who have been displaced from their homes but remain within national borders, referred to as "**internally displaced people**," lack internationally recognized rights to address their grievances.

(d) Zoonotic diseases

Zoonoses are diseases and infections that naturally pass between humans and vertebrate animals. They can be categorized into three classes:

1. Endemic zoonoses: These are prevalent in multiple locations and affect a significant number of people and animals.
2. Epidemic zoonoses: These occur sporadically in terms of their timing and geographical distribution.
3. Emerging and re-emerging zoonoses: These are either newly identified in a population or have previously existed but are rapidly increasing in their incidence or expanding their geographical range. Some examples of such zoonoses reported in recent times include Rift Valley fever, SARS, pandemic influenza H1N1 2009, Yellow fever, Avian Influenza (H5N1) and (H7N9), West Nile virus, and the Middle East respiratory syndrome coronavirus (MERS-CoV).

Evidence suggests that novel pathogens, especially viruses, originating from animals display unpredictable behavior and continue to emerge and spread globally. In our increasingly interconnected world, the occurrence of emerging zoonoses in one country poses a potential threat to global health security. These diseases are concerning due to their capacity for rapid epidemic spread, high fatality rates, and the lack of specific treatments and vaccines available to effectively control their transmission.

- It is estimated that, globally, about **one billion cases of illness and millions of deaths occur every year from zoonoses.**
- Some **60% of emerging infectious diseases that are reported globally are zoonoses.**
- Over **30 new human pathogens have been detected in the last three decades**, 75% of which have originated in animals.

ENVIRONMENT AND RESOURCE GEOPOLITICS

Thomas Malthus discouraged the idea of 'endless progress' and considered it a threat because of the inexorable pressures of population growth and Earth's limited capacity to support it. In his ***Essay on the Principle of Population***, he argued that the impact of growing population on a fixed supply of land and other resources would result in starvation. **David Ricardo** shared his belief that diminishing natural resources because of expanding economic activity would eventually halt both population and economic growth.

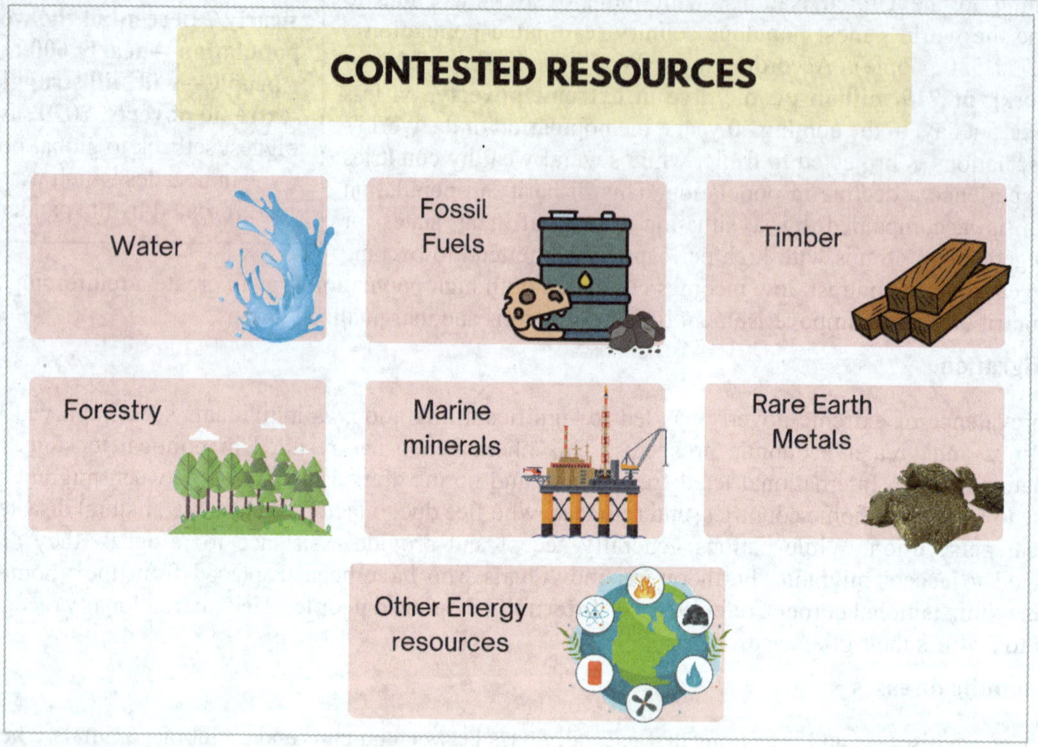

Natural resources may be defined as "stocks of materials that exist in the natural environment that are both scarce and economically useful in production or consumption, either in their raw state or after a minimal amount of processing".

The significance of resources in shaping the rise and fall of dynasties and regimes is deeply rooted in history. Discussions surrounding "*Resource Geopolitics*" date back to ancient times, reflecting the enduring importance of access to and control over resources. During the era of Mercantilism, the reliance on sea power highlighted the critical need for timber, a resource that became a strategic priority for European powers starting in the 17th century. The First and Second World Wars further underscored the necessity of maintaining a steady supply of strategic commodities, particularly oil, which played a pivotal role in military operations and national security.

(a) **Modern Geopolitical Thinking on Resources**

- Contemporary Western geopolitical thought continues to emphasize the interconnectedness of trade, war, and power, with a focus on maritime navigation and the control of overseas resources. This approach remains central to understanding the dynamics of resource geopolitics in the modern era.
- The past two centuries, particularly the recent decades, have seen a significant expansion in the range and volume of natural resources traded internationally, reflecting the growing demand and advancements in transportation technologies.

(b) **Transition to Renewable Energy and Its Challenges**

- While the global energy landscape is gradually shifting from fossil fuels to renewable energy, this transition is still in its early stages. Technological advancements in renewable energy generation and storage are crucial to making this shift sustainable and affordable for all.
- Until these technological leaps are achieved, gas and fossil fuels will continue to meet the increasing energy demands, highlighting the ongoing reliance on traditional energy sources.

(c) **Globalization of Natural Resource Trade**

- The globalization of natural resource trade continues unabated, raising concerns about the impact of economic growth on the Earth's finite resources. This has led to intensified debates on the sustainability of current practices and the need for more responsible resource management.

(d) **Environmental Concerns in International Affairs**

- Natural disasters and environmental changes are increasingly influencing international relations, as their effects are not confined by national borders. This has made environmental issues a critical component of world politics.
- Since the 1960s, the environmental consequences of economic growth have gained political prominence, leading to a growing recognition of the need for collective action to address these challenges.

(e) **Urgency of Addressing Climate Change**

- According to the IPCC Report, to limit global warming to around 1.5°C (2.7°F), global greenhouse gas emissions must peak before 2025 and be reduced by 43% by 2030. This underscores the urgent need for coordinated global efforts to mitigate the impacts of climate change and protect the planet's resources for future generations.

As per the latest findings of **IPCC** (Working Group III Sixth Assessment Report – April 2022), "the harmful carbon emissions from 2010-2019 have never been higher in human history, is proof that the world is on a 'fast track' to disaster".

Major environmental issues

- Agricultural land losing fertility
- Overgrazed grasslands
- Extensive pollution and depletion of water bodies
- Poor water leading to restricted food production
- Less or no access to safe water in developing nations
- Heavy deforestation
- Coastal Pollution and coral bleaching
- Global warming and decline in amount of ozone in stratosphere
- Extreme weather events due to climate change

Relevant developments around environment protection

- **Club of Rome:** This global think-tank gained recognition for its publication of the book "Limits to Growth" in 1972, which highlighted the potential depletion risks associated with the rapidly increasing world population. In response, international organizations like the United Nations Environment Programme (UNEP) initiated international conferences and promoted in-depth studies to foster a more coordinated and impactful approach to addressing environmental challenges. Subsequently, the environment has gained prominence as a significant and pressing issue.

- **Brundtland Report, 1987 – '*Our Common Future*':** The report issued a cautionary message that traditional models of economic growth were not viable in the long run, particularly considering the aspirations of developing countries in the South for additional industrial progress.

- **Earth Summit, 1992:** The **United Nations Conference on Environment and Development**, known as the Earth Summit, held in Rio de Janeiro, Brazil, in **June 1992**, marked a significant consolidation of attention towards environmental issues. The summit witnessed the participation of 170 countries, numerous non-governmental organizations (NGOs), and multinational corporations. A notable observation made during the Rio Summit was the divergence in environmental agendas between the affluent and developed nations of the **global North** and the impoverished and developing nations of the **global South**. The Northern states primarily focused on concerns related to ozone depletion and global warming, while the Southern states were primarily interested in addressing the interplay between economic development and environmental management.

- **Agenda 21:** The Rio Summit resulted in the establishment of conventions addressing climate change, biodiversity, forestry, and a set of recommended development practices known as 'Agenda 21'. One of the key outcomes of the summit was a consensus on the integration of economic growth with ecological responsibility. This approach to development, widely known as 'sustainable development', emphasizes the importance of balancing economic progress with environmental stewardship.'
- **1992 United Nations Framework Convention on Climate Change (UNFCCC):** According to the agreement, parties involved should take actions to safeguard the climate system based on fairness and in line with their **common but differentiated responsibilities and respective capabilities (CBDR-RC)**. The parties recognized that developed countries have been primarily responsible for the majority of historical and current global greenhouse gas emissions. Additionally, it was acknowledged that per capita emissions in developing countries remain comparatively low. As a result, certain developing countries such as China and India were exempted from the obligations outlined in the **Kyoto Protocol**.
- **The Paris Agreement**: It was adopted in December 2015 at the UN Climate Change Conference (COP21), is a landmark international accord aimed at combating climate change. It seeks to limit global temperature rise to well below 2°C above pre-industrial levels, while pursuing efforts to keep it to **1.5°C.** The agreement emphasizes reducing greenhouse gas emissions, enhancing climate resilience, and providing financial support to developing nations. Countries set their own climate action plans, known as **Nationally Determined Contributions (NDCs),** and are expected to review and strengthen them every five years. The Paris Agreement represents a unified global effort to mitigate climate impacts.

THE GLOBAL COMMONS

'Commons' refers to resources that are **not privately owned but instead shared by a community.** Likewise, certain regions or areas in the world are not under the jurisdiction of any particular state and necessitate shared governance by the international community. These areas are referred to as ***res communis humanitatis*** or **global commons.**

Earth's Atmosphere

Antarctica

Ocean Floor

Outer Space

The Global Commons are areas that transcend national borders, making their governance and protection crucial to global stability and sustainability. The significance of the global commons lies in their role in supporting life on Earth, promoting economic growth, and providing opportunities for scientific exploration.

Effective management of these commons is essential for addressing issues like climate change, resource scarcity, and equitable access to benefits from global resources.

(a) Challenges in Managing the Global Commons

Despite various international agreements aimed at safeguarding the global commons, challenges remain in reaching consensus on environmental goals due to differing priorities, timelines, and interpretations of scientific data. For instance, the discovery of the Antarctic ozone hole in the 1980s marked a pivotal moment in global environmental governance, demonstrating both the risks of inaction and the potential for international cooperation to address ecological threats. This issue exemplified the complexities of balancing economic growth with environmental protection on a global scale.

(b) Inequalities in Outer Space

The management of outer space reflects disparities between developed and developing nations, with the Global North benefiting more from space exploration and technological advancements. These inequities extend to future generations, raising concerns about the long-term sustainability of space activities. The recent "race to space" has intensified debates around the equitable use of outer space resources, prompting discussions among academics and diplomats about ensuring fair access and benefit-sharing.

(c) Strain on the Earth's Atmosphere and Oceans

The atmosphere and ocean floors, both essential components of the global commons, are under immense pressure from industrial activities and technological developments. Rapid industrialization and unsustainable practices have led to pollution, overfishing, and climate change, threatening the balance of these ecosystems. The impact of human activities on these commons underscores the need for global cooperation in managing and protecting shared resources for current and future generations.

In conclusion, the global commons are vital to the planet's well-being, and their protection requires collaborative international efforts. The issues around environment degradation, climate change and resource depletion can no longer be brushed under the carpet and the direct and indirect ramifications, including the externalities must be considered going ahead. The issues require a head-on approach consisting of a collaboration between nations in order to safeguard the future of the upcoming generations. Going ahead, the nations must join forces to effectively manage their domestic progress while catering to the needs of the larger globe.

INDIA'S STAND

The **India Energy Outlook 2021** (World Energy Outlook Special Report, IEA) had shed light on the opportunities and challenges for India in its path to ensuring reliable, affordable and sustainable energy to growing population. The rise in incomes and improvement in standards of living have resulted in India becoming the world's third-largest energy consuming country. Certain highlights have been listed below-

- India's **energy demand** is projected to increase by almost 35% between 2019 and 2030.
- India is witnessing a loosening of the hold of **coal in the energy mix**. The share of coal as it stood in 2019 was 44% and is projected to fall to 34% by 2040.
- The **Solar power** will witness an explosive growth in the next two decades driven by policy ambitions, innovative regulatory approaches, and the cost-competitiveness of solar. It may soon match coal's share in the power generation mix.
- India is expected to experience a **rapid increase in electricity demand** compared to overall energy demand. However, there is a projected significant increase in variability in both electricity output from solar PV and wind, as well as daily consumption. Some Indian states are anticipated to witness a regular surplus in renewable energy output, particularly around midday, before the year 2030.
- As per the Stated Policies Scenario (STEPS), **India is poised to surpass the targets outlined in its Nationally Determined Contribution (NDC) under the Paris Agreement**. The emissions intensity of India's economy is projected to improve by 40% from 2005 to 2030, exceeding the 33-35% target set in its existing NDC. Furthermore, the share of non-fossil fuels in electricity generation capacity could potentially reach nearly 60%, surpassing the 40% commitment made by India.

INTERNATIONAL SOLAR ALLIANCE (ISI)

The **ISA** is a global initiative launched in 2015 during the Paris Climate Conference (COP21) by India and France to promote solar energy adoption and combat climate change. The alliance aims to bring together countries with high solar potential to foster cooperation in harnessing solar energy, making it affordable, reliable, and sustainable for all. The ISA is a significant element of global climate diplomacy, as it seeks to address energy needs, reduce greenhouse gas emissions, and advance the United Nations' Sustainable Development Goals (SDGs).

As per reports, in 2023 approximately $300 billion was invested in the solar sector.

The important elements of ISA include the following –

1) Formation: It was launched by Indian Prime Minister Narendra Modi and then-French President François Hollande on November 30, 2015. Initially aimed at 121 solar-rich countries located between the Tropic of Cancer and Tropic of Capricorn, the membership criteria were later expanded to include any United Nations member country. By 2024, the alliance has grown to 123 member countries, with a focus on countries with high solar energy potential.
2) Global Energy Transition: The ISA facilitates the global shift toward renewable energy, aiming to mobilize $1 trillion in investments by 2030 for solar energy promotion. It supports financial mechanisms and provides technical assistance, particularly for developing nations like those in Africa. India's solar investments in Africa have improved energy access in areas facing energy poverty.
3) One Sun, One World, One Grid (OSOWOG): India's OSOWOG initiative seeks to establish a globally interconnected solar grid to transfer solar energy across regions. It aims to enhance cross-border energy distribution between Asia, Africa, and Europe. Backed by the World Bank and other nations, this initiative is pivotal in addressing global energy needs through solar power.
4) Blended Financial Mechanisms: ISA's Solar Risk Mitigation Initiative (SRMI) collaborates with institutions like the World Bank to de-risk solar investments in developing regions. Affordable Finance at Scale aggregates smaller solar projects into larger ones, making them more appealing to investors and promoting solar deployment in low-income countries.
5) Increased participation from the private sector: ISA partners with private enterprises to advance solar deployment. Collaborations with corporations and solar companies have boosted funding and scaling of projects like India's **Rewa** and **Bhadla** Solar Parks.
6) Major solar projects in developing nations: ISA has led numerous solar initiatives in Africa and the Pacific Islands. The Solar Grandmothers Initiative empowers rural African women with solar engineering skills. India's collaboration with Pacific Island nations supports cleaner energy transitions through solar plants, reducing reliance on fossil fuels in Small Island Developing States (SIDS).
7) COP26 And COP28 Momentum: At COP26, ISA launched the Green Grids Initiative under OSOWOG, gaining global support. With continued momentum through COP27 and COP28, ISA has reinforced its role in the renewable energy landscape. These summits have mobilized international support, furthering the role of solar energy in achieving global climate objectives.

MAJOR HIGHLIGHTS OF 2024

In September, 2024 **Nepal** became the **101st country** to join the ISA as a full member.

Paraguay had become the 100th full member in June 2024.

In September, ***Ajay Mathur***, Director General of the ISA, announced a partnership with **Africa50** to launch the first regional fund in Africa as part of ISA's flagship private sector initiative, the **Global Solar Facility**.

TECHNOLOGY, SPACE AND WARFARE

"...if we are to play a meaningful role nationally and in the comity of nations, we must be second to none in the application of advanced technologies."

\- *Vikram Sarabhai* (02 Feb 1968)

Wars are as old as civilization itself, however the methods have constantly evolved to keep pace with changing times. It has been rightly stated that 'necessity is the mother of invention' and there is nobody who better understood this dictum than the 21st century nation-states. Scarcity of resources and technological advancements provided impetus to evolve the methods of warfare. The race to 'innovate' has in turn provided an upper hand to countries and even proved decisive during conflicts.

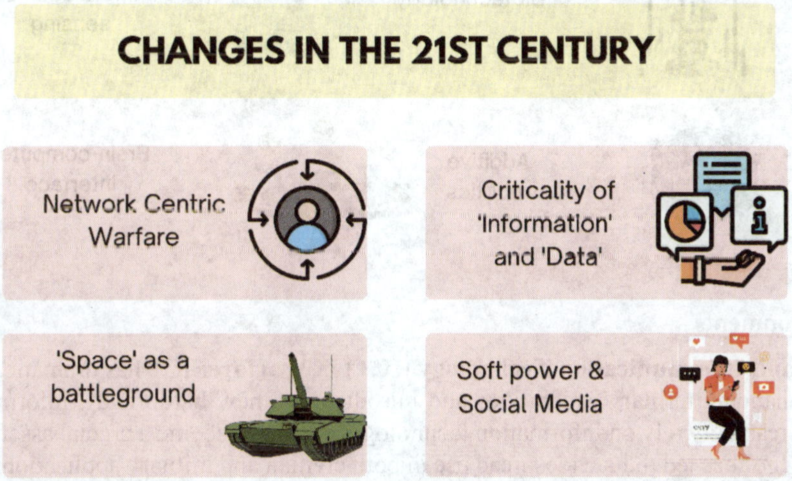

Over the past decades, technology has witnessed growth in quick succession. Such transformational equipment designs complemented the already existing materials to carefully adapt to the new paradigm. **Information and Communication Technology (ICT)** drastically changed the methods of connectivity and warfare. The information technology has become an indispensable part of military establishments today enabling the creation of a platform that effectively integrates, generates and assimilates information and allows application of combat power beyond visual range. Such a doctrine is being commonly termed **'Network Centric Warfare' (NCW)**. The NCW allows the synchronization of combat power of geographically dispersed forces through shared situational awareness and better control. A famous example includes the doctrine of **'*Blitzkrieg*'**, whereby German tanks were fitted with a wireless set to improve command.

Blitzkrieg is defined as a war conducted with great speed and force; a violent surprise offensive by massed air forces and mechanized ground forces in close coordination. Blitzkrieg (In German: "lightning war") is most commonly associated with Nazi Germany during the Second World War as a method of offensive warfare responsible for Nazi Germany's military successes in the early years of World War II.

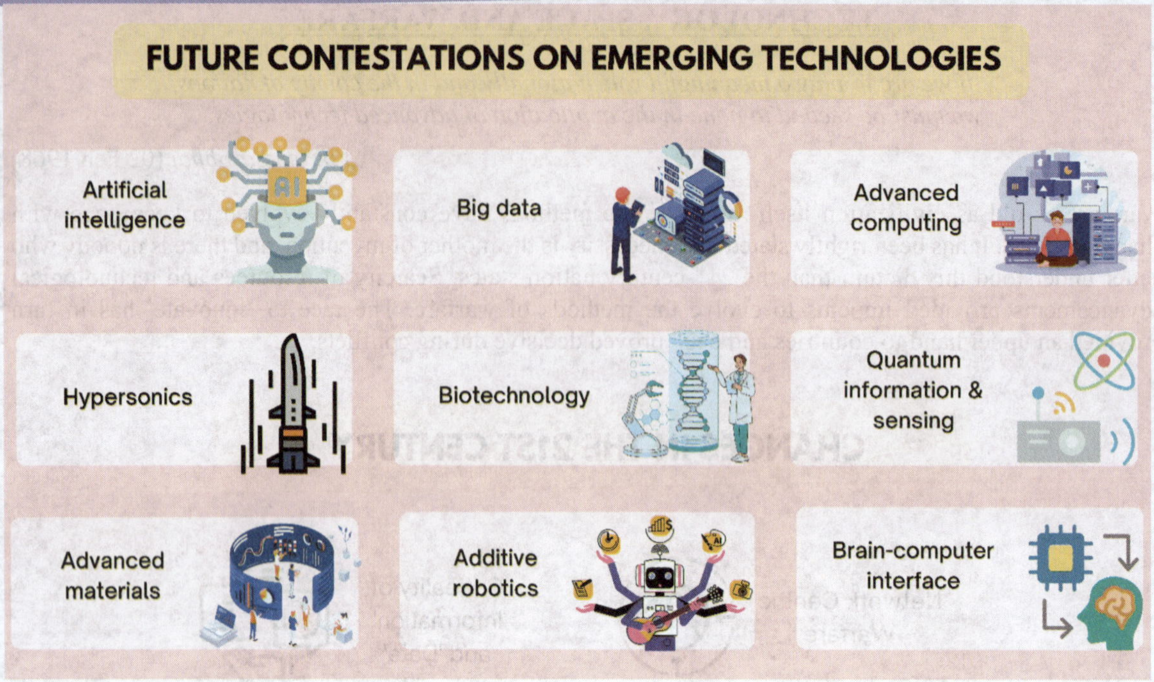

<u>**Significant developments**</u> -

1. **Information and Communication Technology (ICT) in Warfare:** ICT has dramatically transformed warfare by enhancing military capabilities and introducing a new battlefield—information space. As economies increasingly rely on information technology, data has become a crucial asset. The shift to the "*Information Age*" has led to its widespread use in both civilian and military applications. Countries that leverage ICT advancements can gain a significant edge in trade and defense, shaping the future global economic order.
2. **Impact on Social Media and Diplomacy:** Social media has reshaped the interaction between governments and citizens, offering both a platform for public voice and a tool for governance. Social media allows citizens to organize politically and question leaders' decisions. It also enables "***digital diplomacy***," where global summits and diplomatic interactions have shifted online, especially during the COVID-19 pandemic. Platforms like Twitter allow real-time diplomatic dialogues, challenging traditional diplomacy by providing a global stage for state communication and public scrutiny. We're in a world today where '***Data is the new Oil***' and the uniqueness of 'information' as a battlespace lies in the all-pervasive and ubiquitous nature. According to Beth Simmons, "the possibilities for mobilizing social forces and affecting governance within and across nations have never before seemed as significant as they do in the modern Global Information Age."
3. **Challenges of Information Warfare:** Information warfare has emerged as a modern-day threat, involving large-scale attacks on technological systems supporting critical infrastructure, such as power grids and communications networks. Unlike conventional warfare, these attacks often have no specific platform, making them hard to defend against. Examples include Russia's alleged interference in the 2016 U.S. elections, ISIS's online recruitment, and Edward Snowden's NSA revelations. Such instances highlight the vulnerabilities of nations in the Information Age.
4. **The Threat of Cyber Warfare:** Cyber warfare has become a growing concern as defenders work tirelessly to safeguard crucial systems from attackers. The ***Pegasus*** spyware case, where governments allegedly used spyware against their own citizens, has raised ethical concerns worldwide. Misuse of technology, including instances in India, like insurgency promotion in Kashmir and unauthorized hacking, demonstrates the dangers of unchecked cyber capabilities.
5. **Space as a New Frontier for Warfare:** The 21st century has seen space emerge as a potential battleground. Nations are developing capabilities to safeguard commercial satellites and prepare for future space warfare. Although space is heavily militarized, overt weaponization is limited due to the

1967 Outer Space Treaty. The race to militarize space is a response to the growing importance of satellite communication, navigation, and surveillance systems in modern warfare. Nations like the U.S., Russia, and China are competing to dominate this new battlefield, investing in space-based defense technologies.

Owing to the swift shift in favour of the ICT domain, the World Bank has stressed on the need for 'open data' and 'data sharing initiatives' for a positive developmental impact in future. It even dealt with the need for a 'new social contract for data' in its publications to enable the low-income nations to voice their opinions equally in the global debate of data governance.

The ***Outer Space Treaty*** was largely based on the Declaration of Legal Principles Governing the Activities of States in the Exploration and Use of Outer Space (1963). The Treaty was opened for signature by the three depository Governments (the Russian Federation, the UK and the USA) in January 1967, and it entered into force in October 1967. The crucial principles include –

- the exploration and use of outer space shall be carried out for the benefit and in the interests of all countries and shall be the province of all mankind
- outer space shall be free for exploration and use by all States
- States shall not place nuclear weapons or other weapons of mass destruction in orbit or on celestial bodies or station them in outer space in any other manner
- States shall avoid harmful contamination of space and celestial bodies

Signature – 3 March 1967
Deposit of instruments of ratification – January 1982

While nations have been covertly working on developing extensive space related machinery since the launch of '***Sputnik***' (USSR) in 1957, it was in 2019 when the **US Space Force** was established which took the 'race to space' to a whole different level. The US created a new branch of the armed services which was the result of the recognition that 'Space' was now a national security imperative. Since 1957, Russia, US, China, India, Germany and Japan among others have made extensive research into developing space exploration capabilities. Several smaller nations including South Korea, Libya, South Africa, Iran etc. are believed to be developing indigenous satellites and space launch capabilities. Global superiority is fast fading away, giving way to pursuing superiority in the space domain.

Among India's neighbours, China has been actively pursuing the space race. In 2007, China conducted the ASAT test and successfully launched a land-based interceptor in 2013. The country has a robust civil space program and is closing in on the two powers, Russia and US, in space capabilities. India also has a growing space program, rooted in ISRO (1969), which has tested an ASAT missile (anti-satellite weapon) under the '***Mission Shakti***' and has high-power lasers known as the **KALI** to tackle incoming space threats.

While the economic dependence on space technology could prove to be disastrous if techniques aren't evolved to defend the resources, however there are **several arguments against space weaponization-**

1. It could undermine the international and national sovereignty and security.
2. The treaties protecting the global commons and prescribing their peaceful use would be undermined and would result in
3. It could potentially disrupt the active arms control instruments especially the ones relating to nuclear arsenal.
4. The pollution via the space debris is both hazardous for space and the satellites orbiting the Earth.

5. The arms race could prove counter-productive and would lead to placement of even more satellites to keep track of new developments on the military front.

Thus, presently cyberspace is the new frontier of warfare and 'digital diplomacy' the new public diplomacy with ICT being the indispensable weapon for every nation in its international relation arsenal. While technology is fast unfolding in every arena, efforts must be made to balance the digital diplomacy with the traditional face-to-face diplomacy to create effective linkages with the world leaders.

Mission DefSpace was launched at the annual Defense Expo held in Gandhinagar, Gujarat in October 2022. It aims to **develop innovative solutions for the Armed Forces in the space domain** through industry and start-ups at DefExpo 2022. The goal of Mission DefSpace is to make India Atmanirbhar in defence technologies in the space domain. It will encourage technology development in space for defence applications by startups and young entrepreneurs through 75 Defence Space Challenges launched across various Department for Defence Production (DDP) initiatives viz iDEX, 'Make 1', and 'Make 2'. These technologies, with dual-use applications, will accelerate the all-round development of India while safeguarding our national interests.

COLLABORATIVE SECURITY

While 'force' played a critical role in structuring the international order in the past, the strategic landscape now demands an approach that looks at collaborative security. Cooperation may be bilateral (i.e., between any two countries), regional, continental, or global and may involve a variety of other players, both international and national. International organisations like the UN, the World Health Organisation, the World Bank, the IMF etc. and non-governmental organisations like Amnesty International, the Red Cross, private foundations and charities, churches and religious organisations, trade unions, associations, etc. can play a significant role in securing global peace. **While force is frowned upon in the current scenario, it hasn't been completely taken off from the discussion table, as an act of last resort**. Non-traditional security i.e., the use of dialogue, discussions and consensus is regarded better than the use of traditional security methods, including an outright war. Similarly, force which is sanctioned and applied collectively by the international community rather than by an individual country would most probably be considered ethical.

In the current situation, it is crucial to prioritize multilateral cooperation and engagement. However, it is important to be cautious to prevent the formation of military alliances resembling the NATO and Warsaw Pact. Establishing supportive connections with ASEAN countries, particularly Indonesia, which holds potential as a maritime anchor in the region due to its geographical location, is necessary. Engaging positively with Vietnam is also a proactive and strategic step for the future.

SECURITY BODIES AND ORGANISATIONS

(1) INTERPOL

INTERPOL is the **International Criminal Police Organization**, an intergovernmental organization that facilitates cooperation among law enforcement agencies across the world. It was established in **1923** and is headquartered in Lyon, France. The organization's mission is to promote cross-border police cooperation and coordination in preventing and combating international crime, including terrorism, organized crime, cybercrime, and other serious offenses. It presently has 195 member countries.

> The 90th Interpol General Assembly meeting was held in New Delhi in October 2022.

INTERPOL Notices are international requests for cooperation or alerts allowing police in member countries to share critical crime-related information. Notices are issued by the General Secretariat at the request of a member country's INTERPOL National Central Bureau and are made available for all the member countries to consult in the Notices database. Notices can also be issued at the request of International Criminal Tribunals and the International Criminal Court to seek persons wanted for committing crimes within their jurisdiction, notably genocide, war crimes, and crimes against humanity.[35]

(a) **Red Notice**: To seek the location and arrest of persons wanted for prosecution or to serve a sentence.
(b) **Yellow Notice**: To help locate missing persons, often minors, or to help identify persons who are unable to identify themselves.
(c) **Blue Notice**: To collect additional information about a person's identity, location or activities in relation to a criminal investigation.
(d) **Black Notice**: To seek information on unidentified bodies.
(e) **Green Notice**: To provide warning about a person's criminal activities, where the person is considered to be a possible threat to public safety.
(f) **Orange Notice**: To warn of an event, a person, an object or a process representing a serious and imminent threat to public safety.
(g) **Purple Notice**: To seek or provide information on modus operandi, objects, devices and concealment methods used by criminals.[36]

(2) Financial Action Task Force

The Financial Action Task Force (FATF) is an intergovernmental organization established in 1989 to combat money laundering, terrorist financing, and other threats to the integrity of the international financial system. The FATF comprises 39 member countries and two regional organizations, and it **operates under the guidance of the G7**. Its recommendations and guidelines are widely recognized as the global standard for anti-money laundering and counter-terrorism financing measures.

The FATF is responsible for developing and promoting international standards and best practices to prevent and combat money laundering and terrorist financing. It also conducts evaluations of countries' compliance with these standards and provides technical assistance to countries that need help in implementing them.

DID YOU KNOW?

Pakistan was removed from the FATF 'grey list' on terror funding in October 2022. The removal was announced after a consensus decision of all 39-members, including India to accept the review of Pakistan's efforts on strengthening its anti-money laundering and combating terror financing (AML/CFT) mechanisms.
As of August 2024, Pakistan remains out of the FATF Grey List.

The FATF maintains two lists to identify countries that are not implementing its recommendations effectively:

GREY LIST

The FATF Grey List, also known as the "list of jurisdictions under increased monitoring," identifies countries that have deficiencies in their **anti-money laundering and counter-terrorism financing (AML/CFT)** regimes but have committed to addressing those deficiencies. Countries on the Grey List are subject to increased monitoring and scrutiny by the FATF, and they must report on their progress in addressing the identified deficiencies.

BLACK LIST

The FATF Black List, also known as the "list of high-risk and non-cooperative jurisdictions," identifies countries that have significant deficiencies in their AML/CFT regimes and have not made sufficient efforts to address them. Countries on the Black List are subject to various sanctions and restrictions, such as restrictions on financial transactions, increased duc diligence requirements, and potential expulsion from the international financial system.

Being on the Grey or Black List can have significant consequences for a country's economy and international reputation, as it can deter foreign investment, harm trade relationships, and lead to increased scrutiny and regulatory requirements.

---

[35] INTERPOL. About Notices. https://www.interpol.int/How-we-work/Notices/About-Notices
[36] INTERPOL. About Notices. https://www.interpol.int/How-we-work/Notices/About-Notices

(3) Global Partnership on Artificial Intelligence (GPAI)

GPAI is a multilateral initiative launched in 2020 that aims to promote the responsible development and use of artificial intelligence (AI) in ways that are consistent with human rights, democratic values, and ethical principles. GPAI was founded by a group of countries, including Canada, France, Germany, Japan, the United Kingdom, the United States, and the European Union. Its members represent more than half of the world's economy and population, and they work together to support the development and deployment of AI technologies that are safe, trustworthy, and inclusive. GPAI focuses on several key areas, including responsible AI governance, data governance, AI and innovation, and the future of work. Its activities include research, policy development, capacity building, and cooperation among its members and with other stakeholders, such as industry, civil society, and academia.

INDIA AND ITS SECURITY STRATEGY

Strengthening the military capabilities

- India has been involved in conflicts with its neighbours — Pakistan in 1947–48, 1965, 1971 and 1999; and China in 1962.
- Since it is surrounded by nuclear- armed countries in the South Asian region, India's decision to conduct nuclear tests in 1998 was justified by the Indian government in terms of safeguarding national security.

Strengthening international norms and international institutions

- J. L. Nehru supported the cause of Asian solidarity, decolonisation, disarmament, and the UN as a forum in which international conflicts could be settled.
- India also took initiatives to bring about a universal and non-discriminatory non-proliferation regime with respect to nuclear weapons. It argued for an equitable New International Economic Order (NIEO).
- India joined 160 countries that have signed and ratified the 1997 Kyoto Protocol, which provides a roadmap for reducing the emissions of greenhouse gases to check global warming.

Meeting security challenges within the country

- Several militant groups from areas such as the Nagaland, Mizoram, the Punjab, and Kashmir among others have, from time to time, sought to break away from India. India has tried to preserve national unity by adopting a democratic political system.

Adopting Democratic Politics

- There has been an attempt in India to develop its economy in a way that the vast mass of citizens are lifted out of poverty and misery and huge economic inequalities are not allowed to exist. Democratic politics allows spaces for articulating the voice of the poor and the deprived citizens. Democracy is not just a political ideal; a democratic government is also a way to provide greater security.

CERT-IN

CERT-In (Computer Emergency Response Team-India) is the national agency responsible for cybersecurity in India. It is a government agency established in 2004 under the Ministry of Electronics and Information Technology (MeitY), and it serves as the national nodal agency for responding to cybersecurity incidents and for mitigating their impact.

CERT-In is responsible for:

- Collecting, analyzing, and disseminating information on cybersecurity incidents, threats, and vulnerabilities.
- Responding to and mitigating cybersecurity incidents and providing technical assistance to organizations and individuals affected by them.
- Developing and promoting best practices for information security and cybersecurity.
- Conducting research and development activities in the field of cybersecurity.

CERT-In works closely with other government agencies, law enforcement agencies, and international organizations to promote a safe and secure cyberspace in India. It also provides training and capacity-building programs for government agencies, critical infrastructure operators, and other stakeholders to enhance their cybersecurity capabilities.

NATIONAL INTELLIGENCE GRID (NATGRID)

The National Intelligence Grid (NATGRID) is a networked system that connects various databases of multiple intelligence agencies of India to collect and analyze intelligence data to counter terrorism and other threats to national security. It is an ambitious project of the Indian government that aims to enhance India's national security and counter-terrorism capabilities by providing a framework for data sharing among various intelligence agencies.

NATGRID was proposed after the 2008 Mumbai attacks, as a response to the need for better intelligence sharing and coordination among different security agencies in India. The project aims to link 21 different databases, including airline and railway passenger information, bank account details, and mobile phone records, to provide a comprehensive picture of any individual or organization's activities.

The NATGRID project is supervised by the Ministry of Home Affairs (MHA) and is expected to be implemented in a phased manner. The project is expected to play a crucial role in countering terrorism, tracking money laundering, and preventing other threats to national security.

NATIONAL CRITICAL INFORMATION INFRASTRUCTURE PROTECTION CENTRE (NCIIPC)

The National Critical Information Infrastructure Protection Centre (NCIIPC) is a specialized organization in India that is responsible for protecting critical information infrastructure (CII) from cyber threats. It is an agency of the Indian government's Ministry of Electronics and Information Technology (MeitY).

NCIIPC's primary role is to identify, assess, and mitigate cybersecurity risks to critical information infrastructure in India. The agency works in close collaboration with various stakeholders, including government departments, public and private sector organizations, and international agencies, to develop policies, standards, and guidelines for protecting critical information infrastructure. NCIIPC focuses on various critical sectors, such as energy, banking and finance, telecommunications, transportation, and government services. It provides cybersecurity-related advisory services to organizations in these sectors and conducts regular risk assessments to identify potential vulnerabilities and threats.

NCIIPC is also responsible for facilitating incident response and recovery in case of cybersecurity incidents affecting critical information infrastructure. The agency collaborates with other agencies such as the Indian Computer Emergency Response Team (CERT-In) and law enforcement agencies to investigate and mitigate cyber threats and attacks.

NEW WORLD ORDER

The developments since the second World war, including the disintegration of the Soviet empire, the emergence of 'tiger' economies in East Asia and ASEAN and the rise of China as a global power, among other things, have left the west and the Eurasian powers playing catch-up. Apart from this, India is the only one to have undertaken the journey more arduously on a democratic vehicle.

The manner of dealing with nations has drastically been altered. While previously wars and muscle power were the determining factors for asserting influence, in the new world order, financial instruments, displays of strength and connectivity projects have provided opportunities to assert power without the need for physical clashes with competitors.

An important domain which experienced negative ramifications due to the ongoing changes, is the provisioning of 'global goods'. The rise of China and the parsimony projected by the United States over the past few years, has severely affected the availability of global resources towards a larger global cause. For instance, the hesitance in continuing troop commitments in the Middle East and Afghanistan or more recently the apathetic response by the developed nations during the corona pandemic and their lukewarm approach to tackle the actions of the terrorists globally, have together resulted in a narrower approach to international relations. This further threatens to destabilize the status quo of the international systems along with the creation of a disconnected world order that lacks trust in global institutions to effectively create order from chaos.

The world stands disenchanted with globalization and holds a major grudge towards mercantilism. The key principles which formed the backbone but were taken for granted - access to global markets, reliance on global talent mobility and value of global supply chains, are all under stress.

CONTEMPORARY CHANGES AND CHALLENGES

"Loose and practical arrangements of cooperation will proliferate across geographies. Some would be like-minded, other could be opportunistic and many more, a mix of the two."

- S. Jaishankar, 'The India Way' (2020)

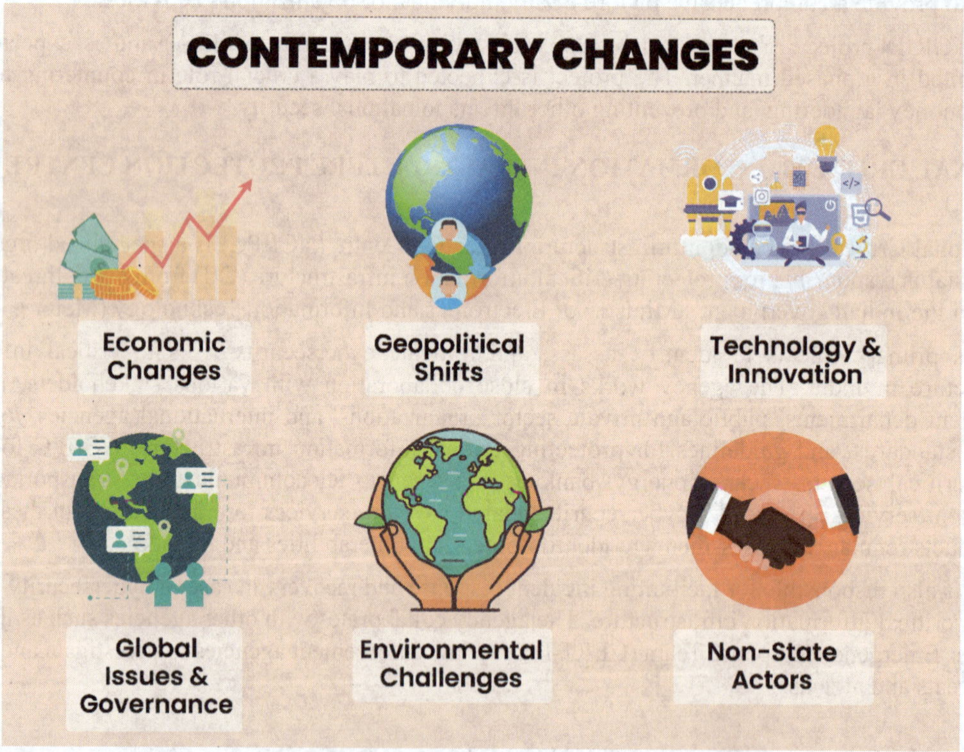

1. **Globalization and Interdependence:** The deepening interconnectedness of economies, cultures, and political systems worldwide has created unprecedented opportunities for trade, innovation, and cultural exchange. However, it also presents challenges, such as economic vulnerabilities, supply chain disruptions, and the rapid spread of crises, such as pandemics or financial collapses, across borders.
2. **Technological Advancements:** The rapid pace of technological innovation, particularly in areas like artificial intelligence, automation, and biotechnology, is fundamentally transforming industries, labor

markets, and societal norms. These advancements bring efficiency and growth but also raise concerns about job displacement, ethical dilemmas, and the digital divide between and within nations.

3. **Economic Inequality:** The growing disparity in wealth and income both within countries and between developed and developing nations is becoming a central issue. Economic inequality exacerbates social tensions, fuels political instability, and undermines efforts towards inclusive and sustainable development.
4. **Multipolarity:** The rise of emerging powers, especially China and India, is reshaping the global power structure. This shift towards a more multipolar world order challenges the dominance of traditional Western powers and introduces new dynamics in international diplomacy, economic competition, and security alliances.
5. **Emerging Markets:** The increasing economic and political influence of emerging markets, such as Brazil, Russia, India, China, and South Africa (BRICS), is altering the balance of power in international relations. These nations are asserting themselves in global governance, trade negotiations, and regional security matters, challenging the established order.
6. **Regionalism:** The formation and strengthening of regional blocs and alliances, such as the European Union, ASEAN, and the African Union, reflect a growing trend towards regional cooperation. While these blocs aim to enhance economic integration and collective security, they also raise questions about the potential fragmentation of global governance.
7. **Cybersecurity Threats:** As nations become more reliant on digital technologies, the risk of cyberattacks, cyber warfare, and data breaches has escalated. These threats undermine national security, disrupt economies, and erode public trust in digital systems, making cybersecurity a critical aspect of national and international security strategies.
8. **Artificial Intelligence and Automation:** The integration of AI and automation into various sectors is not only transforming the global economy but also driving geopolitical shifts and creating social challenges. These technologies have the potential to increase productivity and innovation, but they also pose risks related to job displacement, privacy concerns, and the ethical use of AI.
9. **Multilateralism vs. Unilateralism:** The rise of unilateral actions by powerful states and the weakening of multilateral institutions, such as the United Nations and World Trade Organization, have strained the traditional framework of international cooperation. This shift challenges global governance, undermines collective problem-solving efforts, and increases the potential for conflicts.
10. **Global Health Governance:** The COVID-19 pandemic exposed the weaknesses in global health governance and highlighted the need for stronger international cooperation to address health crises. Effective global health governance is crucial for coordinating responses to pandemics, improving health systems, and ensuring equitable access to vaccines and treatments
11. **Climate Change:** Climate change is one of the most pressing global challenges, with far-reaching economic, social, and political consequences. The impacts of climate change, including extreme weather events, rising sea levels, and resource scarcity, are reshaping international relations, prompting calls for urgent collective action.
12. **Resource Scarcity:** The increasing competition for essential resources, such as water, energy, and arable land, is intensifying tensions between nations and regions. Resource scarcity can lead to conflicts, exacerbate existing geopolitical disputes, and drive migration, creating complex challenges for global stability.
13. **Rise of Non-State Actors:** The growing influence of non-state actors, including transnational corporations, international organizations, NGOs, and terrorist groups, is altering the dynamics of international relations. These entities can wield significant power, often operating across borders and challenging traditional state-centric governance structures.
14. **Global Governance Challenges:** The rise of non-state actors and the increasing complexity of global issues have made it more difficult for governments to maintain stability and address challenges effectively. Traditional governance structures are being tested, requiring new approaches to international cooperation and policy-making to manage global risks and opportunities.

THE TENSIONS BETWEEN NATIONALISM AND MULTILATERALISM

International politics in 2023 and 2024 is increasingly defined by the **complexities of a decentralized and fragmented global landscape.** The absence of a unifying global authority has left nation-states to contend with an enduring sense of anarchy, deepened by mutual distrust. These challenges are magnified by the rise of nationalism and populism, trends that continue to erode the foundations of liberal democracy while empowering autocratic regimes.

Recent global crises have only intensified this instability. The **war in Ukraine** has reignited Cold War-era tensions, with Russia's assertive actions not only threatening European security but also testing the resilience and unity of Western alliances. In the Middle East, the unresolved conflict in **Palestine** remains a flashpoint, as escalating violence and political paralysis destabilize the region and complicate international peace efforts. Meanwhile, the **UK's immigration crisis**—exacerbated by **Brexit**, economic strains, and a lack of cohesive policy—underscores a growing global tension between the desire for national sovereignty and the responsibilities tied to humanitarian obligations. These issues point to a broader crisis in global migration, where the balance between security and compassion is increasingly fraught.

Together, these crises reflect a retreat from the principles of "**liberal internationalism**," as faith in multilateral approaches to global challenges continues to diminish. Once the primary architects of the post-World War II order, the United States and the United Kingdom have seen their global leadership roles diminish, particularly as nationalism and internal challenges—like economic stagnation and the aftershocks of the COVID-19 pandemic—have taken hold. The European Union, grappling with its own internal divisions, has also been caught in the crosswinds of these shifts.

During Donald Trump's presidency, the U.S. openly challenged **liberal internationalism**, further eroding trust in global institutions and traditional alliances. While President Biden has made efforts to restore international cooperation, the damage to the liberal world order appears extensive and difficult to repair. Meanwhile, emerging powers like China and Russia are increasingly assertive on the global stage, pushing **sovereignty** and **nationalism** as guiding principles, often in opposition to established international norms and governance structures. This rebalancing of power complicates efforts to address pressing global challenges, from security threats to climate change, as the traditional role of **hegemonic powers** is increasingly diluted by the influence of new state and non-state actors.

The **global power dynamics** of today reflect a significant shift from the past. Where nations once climbed the ranks of international influence through a blend of national strength, strategic alliances, and global leadership, the present era is marked by increasing multipolarity. **Power is more diffused, alliances are more fluid, and national interests increasingly drive foreign policy decisions**. This evolving world order is inherently unstable, with countries pursuing more inward-looking, nationalist strategies that prioritize domestic needs over international collaboration. Such approaches, often at odds with multilateral governance, risk further fragmenting global institutions and weakening collective efforts to tackle shared challenges.

Looking ahead, **the concept of collective action and long-standing alliances is likely to become more flexible and transactional**. This shift is particularly evident in security and defense, where changes in nuclear policy, military exercises like the ***Malabar***, and evolving partnerships in regions like Afghanistan illustrate a more pragmatic approach. Rising nationalism and geopolitical competition mean that allies may diverge on key issues, while traditional adversaries may find themselves cooperating in response to shared global threats. The future of international politics will be shaped by a pragmatic realignment of interests, where cooperation and competition are increasingly fluid, and the pursuit of sovereignty and national interest drives much of the global agenda.

COVID AFTERSHOCKS AND DIPLOMACY

The COVID-19 pandemic has had a profound impact on the way the world functions, affecting nearly every aspect of human life and changing the very paradigm of international relations. It continues to bring about sweeping changes in the world order and the interactions among the nations in general. The political boundaries that were once considered the blueprint for discrimination, steadily became more porous due to the transboundary effect of the pandemic, that left every nation on the planet helpless, without exception.

As per reports, the fallout from the COVID-19 pandemic threatens to push over **70 million people into extreme poverty**. As per a statement by Guy Ryder, the Director of ILO, 23 percent of young people currently are not in employment, education or training. The number of young people globally who can't find a job in 2022 could reach a staggering 73 million.

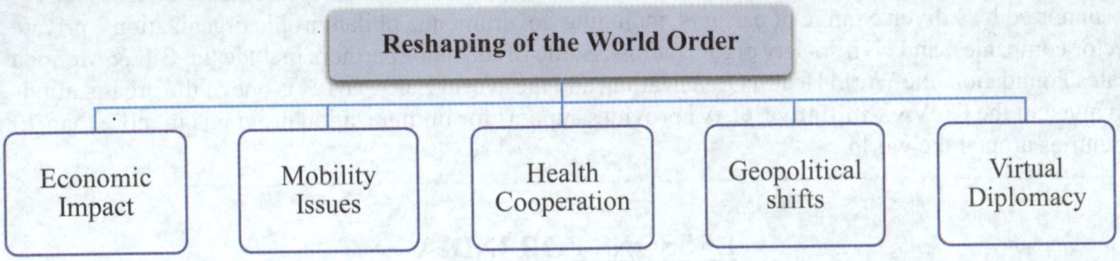

- COVID-19 has led to a global economic downturn, with many countries experiencing recessions and rising unemployment rates. This has led to a significant shift in the global economic balance, with some countries experiencing more severe economic impacts than others.
- The pandemic has severely impacted global travel and mobility, with many countries closing their borders and imposing strict travel restrictions. This has disrupted international trade, supply chains, and tourism, and has significantly reduced the movement of people across borders.
- The pandemic has highlighted the need for greater international cooperation in the field of health, with countries working together to share information and resources to combat the spread of the virus. The World Health Organization (WHO) has played a key role in coordinating international efforts to combat the pandemic.
- COVID-19 led to geopolitical shifts, with some countries using the crisis to expand their influence and pursue their strategic interests. For example, China has sought to increase its influence in the global arena by providing aid to countries struggling with the pandemic.
- The COVID phase saw a sudden shift towards virtual diplomacy, with many high-level meetings and conferences being held online. This has reduced the need for travel and has made it easier for countries to engage with one another from a distance. The pandemic accelerated the trend towards remote work and increased reliance on technology for communication and collaboration.

The COVID-19 led to economic, social, and geopolitical shifts that are likely to shape the global landscape for years to come. It coerced the nations to work together to combat the spread of the virus while also pursuing their own interests. While it has had a negative effect on all areas of life in general, it has also highlighted the need for greater international cooperation and the importance of global health as a shared priority. It has provided the much needed precent for tackling future pandemics and epidemics.

COVAX INITIATIVE

The COVAX initiative was launched in **2020** and is a global effort aimed at ensuring equitable access to COVID-19 vaccines around the world. The initiative is led by **GAVI, the Vaccine Alliance, the World Health Organization (WHO),** and the **Coalition for Epidemic Preparedness Innovations (CEPI).** It was launched in response to concerns about the unequal distribution of COVID-19 vaccines. The initiative aims to accelerate the development and manufacture of COVID-19 vaccines and to ensure that they are distributed fairly to people in all countries, regardless of their income level. As of April 2023, more than 200 countries have joined the COVAX initiative, which has helped to distribute millions of vaccine doses around the world.

Global Alliance for Vaccines and Immunization (GAVI, 2000)

It is **public-private partnership** that was established in **2000** with the goal of improving access to vaccines in the world's poorest countries. Since its establishment, GAVI has helped to immunize over 760 million children and prevent more than 13 million deaths from vaccine-preventable diseases. GAVI is supported by a diverse range of partners, including governments, philanthropic organizations, private sector companies, and civil society organizations. Some of its major partners include the Bill & Melinda Gates Foundation, the World Health Organization, and the World Bank. GAVI is one of the organizations involved in the **COVAX initiative**. GAVI provides support for immunization programs in more than 70 countries around the world.

LESSONS FOR INDIA

In the journey which began in 1947, India as a nation has overcome the Cold war era, got embroiled in several wars and conflicts, an economic overhaul, the development of a unique nuclear policy and a progressive space exploration strategy, among other critical changes within the country. Through the experiences over these past decades, the leaders have acquired critical insight into the functioning of the global order and world politics. More importantly, the events have helped us to learn from past mistakes in order to chart a pathway for success in the future. The following points summarize India's viewpoint of the world and itself as it enters the next phase of development –

> The term ***Realpolitik*** was coined in the 19th century to elaborate on the system of diplomacy or politics which is based on practical considerations of the current situation rather than ideological considerations, to meet the needs of the country.

1. **Significant stress on realism in policy making** – Realism is a modified form of ***realpolitik*** which focuses on the idea of pursuit, possession and application of power to secure the interests of a nation. It has been observed that Indian policies were previously shrouded in skepticism regarding the global turbulence and its possible ramifications on our development. The implicit belief regarding India's high standing in world affairs because it pursued policies backed by principles of morality and sovereignty often led India to undermine the influence of **competitive politics** on the country. India's policy of strict non-alignment, the poor understanding of the strategic discourse and the discomfort regarding the use of hard power resulted in creating an image of a 'reluctant power'. For instance, India's blind optimism regarding its relations with Pakistan backfired in 1965, while recurring terrorist activities continue to dislodge the confidence we reposed in the nation time and again. The need of the hour is to formalize our diplomatic stance based on realistic principles while focusing on presenting a strong global image backed by a robust security and military force which help to prioritize national goals. Moreover, given the many shocks of the last few years, India has proven resilient, managing the pandemic, internal protests, climate-induced disasters and economic shocks. As India is raising its international profile, it must do so while being certain of its principles and priorities in order to successfully manage the country's rise to global prominence.
2. **Nurturing Multi-alignment** – India has been actively nurturing diplomatic ties with multiple players in recent years. India's foreign policy under the current government has focused on building stronger ties with both traditional allies and emerging powers, as well as deepening economic and strategic partnerships. India engagement with several regions is a reflection of its growing strategic and economic interests. The recent areas of focus include the Indo-Pacific, West Asia, Central Asia and Africa. Apart from bilateral relations, India has also been deepening cooperation through 'minilaterals' like Quad, I2U2, SCO, BIMSTEC etc.

India's future steps were summarized well by Dr. S. Jaishankar in his book, *'The India Way'*-

"This is the best time for us to engage America, manage China, cultivate Europe, reassure Russia, bring Japan into play, draw neighbours in, extend the neighbourhood and expand traditional constituencies of support."

3. **Ensuring sovereign autonomy in its engagements**– India has been blamed for its cognitive dissonance. For examples, India appears to hold mutually contradictory beliefs about its ties with both Moscow and Beijing, leaving others, including U.S. policymakers and sometimes even the Indian public, unclear about where India really stands. However, it has been repeatedly said that India is a sovereign nation that cannot be dictated as per the whims of a third nation. According to India, it has been interacting with the international community with the prime objective of pursuing national interest. Going forward, India must ensure that it maintains its autonomy in the face of global conflicts and disturbances.
4. **Leveraging the global environment to pursue leadership goals** – Since India aims to become a stronger and more influential power in future, it must ensure that it can work alongside the global institutions to address global challenges and emerge as a leader in the process. By playing an active role in these institutions (UN, WTO etc.), India can help to shape the global perspective and promote its own interests. India can leverage the global environment by addressing global challenges such as climate change and terrorism. By working with other countries to address these challenges, India can help to build a safer, more stable, and more prosperous world.
5. **Greater risk-taking in diplomacy** – Undertaking risks and their management are inherent aspects of diplomacy. While being risk averse is usually preferred, it doesn't always reap positive results on a global platform. Risk-taking offers a greater pool of rewards, whilst a low-risk foreign policy could lead to stagnation or even debasement. The understanding of the risks involved while engaging with the global players and the subsequent decision making has the potential to alter the growth trajectory of a nation. A flexible posture to the changing global dimensions, would help to leverage the changing ideologies in our favour. While India must introduce new systems to adopt the dynamic approaches of the 21st century, it is not necessary to abandon the existing set of principles that govern the country. The climb to the top would, however, require calling the shots on riskier strategies and policies, whether economic, political or diplomatic. While being profitable, the moves must be well-calculated in order to avert any obvious misfortune for the country.

Given the velocity of change underway, India has work cut out for itself – it must shape an inclusive and equitable international order. This can only be achieved if India builds up on its state capacity, industrial and economic heft and strategic culture that would befit its status as a leading power. While doing so, India must forge alliances based on consensus that could do both – guide its own trajectory for future and also appeal to the communities, especially the developing nations, around the world. India could by the end, prepare a successful model for the developing world to emulate that has its roots in internationalism and liberalism.

Thus, to summarize, the present decade is witnessing a '**crisis of transition**' in which leadership and institutions including coalitions are being renegotiated towards a 'less western' order, while remaining relatively open and rules-based. The rise of new leaders and regions is symptomatic of the redistribution of authority and roles across the globe owing to the faltering of American hegemony and the unwillingness of old leaders to lead a global order based on rules of international propriety.

Although several nations have garnered substantial influence and power in certain aspects of foreign policy and economy, the global challenges that were presented in the last decade have made one thing clear – one nation or a small group of nations cannot emerge as great power(s) because it excels in one or another kind of capability. It is now widely accepted that the nations will have to rely on the combined capabilities of a larger community in order to serve their domestic and international interests and which is why the military, territorial, economic and political capabilities of a sovereign country cannot be weighed in isolation of each other going forward.

"International relation is something not to be taken for granted, but something to be understood and to be changed and, more particularly, to be changed beyond the present limits of its political structure and organization. Here lies indeed the ultimate theoretical and practical justification for our interest in a theory of international relations."

- Hans Morgenthau

16 APPENDIX

PRELIMS PREVIOUS YEAR QUESTIONS

YEAR - 2024

1. **Consider the following countries:**
   1. Italy
   2. Japan
   3. Nigeria
   4. South Korea
   5. South Africa

   Which of the above countries are frequently mentioned in the media for their low birth rates, or ageing population, or declining population?
   (a) **1, 2 and 4**
   (b) 1, 3 and 5
   (c) 2 and 4 only
   (d) 3 and 5 only

2. **Consider the following pairs:**

Country	Reason for being in the news
Argentina	Worst economic crisis
Sudan	War between the country's regular army and paramilitary forces
Turkey	Rescinded its membership of NATO

   How many of the pairs given above are correctly matched?
   a. Only one pair
   b. **Only two pairs**
   c. All three pairs
   d. None of the pairs

3. **Statement-I:** Sumed pipeline is a strategic route for Persian Gulf oil and natural gas shipments to Europe.
   Statement-II: Sumed pipeline connects the Red Sea with the Mediterranean Sea.
   Which one of the following is correct in respect of the above statements?
   (a) **Both Statement-I and Statement-II are and Statement-II explains correct Statement-I.**
   (b) Both Statement-I and Statement-II are, correct, but Statement-II does not explain Statement-I.
   (c) Statement I is correct, but Statement I is incorrect.
   (d) Statement I is incorrect, but Statement II is correct.

4. **Consider the following statements:**
   1. India is a member of the International Grains Council.
   2. A country needs to be a member of the International Grains Council for exporting or importing rice and wheat.

   Which of the statements given above is/are correct?
   (a) **1 only**
   (b) 2 only
   (c) Both 1 and 2

(d) Neither 1 nor 2

5. **Consider the following statements:**
Statement-I: The European Parliament approved The Net-Zero Industry Act recently.
Statement-II: The European Union intends to achieve carbon neutrality by 2040 and therefore aims to develop all of its own clean technology by that time.
Which one of the following is correct in respect of the above statements?
(a) Both Statement-I and Statement-II are correct and Statement-II explains Statement-I.
(b) Both Statement-I and Statement-II are correct, but Statement-II does *not* explain Statement-I
(c) **Statement I is correct, but Statement II is incorrect**
(d) Statement I is incorrect, but Statement II is correct

6. **Consider the following statements:**
Statement-1: Recently, Venezuela has achieved a rapid recovery from its economic crisis and succeeded in preventing its people from fleeing/emigrating to other countries.
Statement II: Venezuela has the world's largest oil reserves
Which one of the following is correct in respect of the above statements?
(a) Both Statement-I and Statement-II are correct and Statement-II explains Statement-I
(b) Both Statement-I and Statement-II are correct, but Statement-II does not explain Statement-I
(c) Statement I is correct, but Statement II is incorrect
(d) **Statement I is incorrect, but Statement II is correct**

7. **Consider the following statements regarding World Toilet Organization:**
1. It is one of the agencies of the United Nations.
2. World Toilet Summit, World Toilet Day and World Toilet College are the initiatives of this organization, to inspire action to tackle the global sanitation crisis.
3. The main focus of its function is to grant funds to the least developed countries and developing countries to achieve the end of open defecation.

Which of the statements given above is/are correct?
(a) 2 only
(b) 3 only
(c) 1 and 2
(d) 2 and 3

<u>YEAR - 2023</u>

1. **About three-fourths of world's cobalt, a metal required for the manufacture of batteries for electric motor vehicles, is produced by**
(a) Argentina
(b) Botswana
(c) the Democratic Republic of the Congo
(d) Kazakhstan

2. **Which one of the following is a part of the Congo Basin?**
(a) Cameroon
(b) Nigeria
(c) South Sudan
(d) Uganda

3. **With reference to India's projects on connectivity, consider the following statements :**
1. East-West Corridor under Golden Quadrilateral Project connects Dibrugarh and Surat.
2. The Trilateral Highway connects Moreh in Manipur and Chiang Mai in Thailand via Myanmar.
3. Bangladesh-China-India-Myanmar Economic Corridor connects Varanasi in Uttar Pradesh with Kunming in China.

How many of the above statements are correct?
(a) Only one

(b) Only two
(c) All three
(d) None

4. Consider the following pairs:

	Region often mentioned in news	Reason for being in news
1.	North Kivu and Ituri	War between Armenia and Azerbaijan
2.	Nagorno-Karabakh	Insurgency in Mozambique
3.	Kherson and Zaporizhzhia	Dispute between Israel and Lebanon

How many of the above pairs are correctly matched?
(a) Only one
(b) Only two
(c) All three
(d) None

5. Consider the following statements:
Statement-I: Israel has established diplomatic relations with some Arab States.
Statement-II: The 'Arab Peace Initiative' mediated by Saudi Arabia was signed by Israel and Arab League.
Which one of the following is correct in respect of the above statements?
(a) Both Statement-I and Statement-II are correct and Statement-II is the correct explanation for Statement-I
(b) Both Statement-I & Statement-II are correct & Statement II is not the correct explanation for Statement-I
(c) **Statement-I is correct but Statement-II is incorrect**
(d) Statement-I is incorrect but Statement-II is correct

6. Consider the following pairs with regard to sports awards:

1.	Major Dhyan Chand Khel Ratna Award	For the most spectacular and outstanding performance by a sportsperson over period of last four years
2.	Arjuna Award	For the lifetime achievement by sportsperson
3.	Dronacharya Award	To honour eminent coaches who have successfully trained sportspersons or teams
4.	Rashtriya Khel Protsahan Puraskar	To recognize the contribution made by sportspersons even after their retirement

How many of the above pairs are correctly matched?
(a) Only one
(b) Only two
(c) Only three
(d) All four

7. Consider the following statements in respect of the 44th Chess Olympiad, 2022:

1. It was the first time that the Chess Olympiad was held in India.
2. The official mascot was named 'Thambi'.
3. The trophy for the winning team in the open section is the Vera Menchik Cup.
4. The trophy for the winning team in the women's section is the Hamilton-Russell Cup.

How many of the statements given above are correct?

(a) Only one
(b) Only two
(c) Only three
(d) All four

8. Consider the following pairs:

	Area of conflict mentioned in news	**Country where it is located**
1.	Donbas	Syria
2.	Kachin	Ethiopia
3.	Tigray	North Yemen

How many of the above pairs are correctly matched?

(a) Only one
(b) Only two
(c) All three
(d) None

9. In recent years Chad, Guinea, Mali and Sudan caught international attention for which one of the following reasons common to all of them?

(a) Discovery of rich deposits of rare earth elements
(b) Establishment of Chinese military bases
(c) Southward expansion of Sahara Desert
(d) Successful coups

10. Consider the following statements about G-20:

1. The G-20 group was originally established as a platform for the Finance Ministers and Central Bank Governors to discuss international economic and financial issues.
2. Digital public infrastructure is one of India's G-20 priorities.

Which of the statements given above is/are correct?

(a) 1 only
(b) 2 only
(c) Both 1 and 2
(d) Neither 1 nor 2

11. Consider the following statements:

Statement-I: Switzerland is one of the leading exporters of gold in terms of value.

Statement-II: Switzerland has the second largest gold reserves in the world.

Which one of the following is correct in respect of the above statements?

(a) Both Statement-I and Statement-II are correct and Statement-II is the correct explanation for Statement-I
(b) Both Statement-I & Statement-II are correct & Statement-II is not the correct explanation for Statement-I
(c) **Statement-I is correct but Statement-II is incorrect**
(d) Statement-I is incorrect but Statement-II is correct

12. Consider the following statements:

Statements-I: Recently, the United States of America (USA) and the European Union (EU) have launched the 'Trade and Technology Council'.

Statement-II: The USA and the EU claim that through this they are trying to bring technological progress and physical productivity under their control.

Which one of the following is correct in respect of the above statements?

(a) Both Statement-I and Statement-II are correct and Statement-II is the correct explanation for Statement-I

(b) Both Statement-I & Statement-II are correct & Statement-II is not the correct explanation for Statement-I

(c) **Statement-I is correct but Statement-II is incorrect**

(d) Statement-I is incorrect but Statement-II is correct

13. Consider the following statements:

The 'Stability and Growth Pact' of the European Union is a treaty that

1. limits the levels of the budgetary deficit of the countries of the European Union
2. makes the countries of the European Union to share their infrastructure facilities
3. enables the countries of the European Union to share their technologies

How many of the above statements are correct?

(a) Only one

(b) Only two

(c) All three

(d) None

14. Consider the following statements:

1. Recently, all the countries of the United Nations have adopted the first-ever compact for international migration, the 'Global Compact for Safe, Orderly and Regular Migration (GCM)'.
2. The objectives and commitments stated in the GCM are binding on the UN member countries.
3. The GCM addresses internal migration or internally displaced people also in its objectives and commitments.

How many of the above statements are

(a) Only one

(b) Only two

(c) All three

(d) None

15. Consider the following countries:

1. Bulgaria
2. Czech Republic
3. Hungary
4. Latvia
5. Lithuania
6. Romania

How many of the above-mentioned countries share a land border with Ukraine?

(a) Only two

(b) Only three

(c) Only four

(d) Only five

16. Which one of the following countries has its own Satellite Navigation System?

(a) Australia

(b) Canada

(c) Israel

(d) Japan

17. Consider the following statements:

Statement-I: According to the United Nations 'World Water Development Report, 2022'. India extracts more than a quarter of the world's groundwater withdrawal each year.

Statement-II: India needs to extract more than a quarter of the world's groundwater each year to satisfy the drinking water and sanitation needs of almost 18% of world's population living in its territory.

Which one of the following is correct in respect of the above statements?

(a) Both Statement-I and Statement-II are correct and Statement-II is the correct explanation for Statement-I

(b) Both Statement-I and Statement-II are correct and Statement-II is not the correct explanation for Statement-I

(c) **Statement-I is correct but Statement-II is incorrect**

(d) Statement-I is incorrect but Statement-II is correct

18. Which one of the following countries has been suffering from decades of civil strife and food shortages and was in news in the recent past for its very severe famine?

(a) Angola

(b) Costa Rica

(c) Ecuador

(d) Somalia

YEAR - 2022

1. Consider the following statements:

1. Bidibidi is a large refugee settlement in north-western Kenya.
2. Some people who fled from South Sudan civil war live in Bidibidi.
3. Some people who fled from civil war in Somalia live in Dadaab refugee complex in Kenya.

Which of the statements given above is/are correct?

(a) 1 and 2

(b) 2 only

(c) 2 and 3

(d) 3 only

2. Consider the following countries:

1. Armenia
2. Azerbaijan
3. Croatia
4. Romania
5. Uzbekistan

Which of the above are members of the Organization of Turkic States?

(a) 1, 2 and 4

(b) 1 and 3

(c) 2 and 5

(d) 3, 4 and 5

3.

With reference to the United Nations Convention on the Law of Sea, consider the following statements:

1. A coastal state has the right to establish the breadth of its territorial sea up to a limit not exceeding 12 nautical miles, measured from baseline determined in accordance with the convention.
2. Ships of all states, whether coastal or land-locked, enjoy the right of innocent passage through the territorial sea.
3. The Exclusive Economic Zone shall not extend beyond 200 nautical miles from the baseline from which the breadth of the territorial sea is measured.

Which of the statements given above are correct?

(a) 1 and 2 only

(b) 2 and 3 only

(c) 1 and 3 only
(d) 1, 2 and 3

4.
Which one of the following statements best reflects the issue with Senkaku Islands, sometimes mentioned in the news?
(a) It is generally believed that they are artificial islands made by a country around South China Sea.
(b) **China and Japan engage in maritime disputes over these islands in East China Sea.**
(c) A permanent American military base has been set up there to help Taiwan to increase its defence capabilities.
(d) Though International Court of Justice declared them as no man's land, some South-East Asian countries claim them.

5. Consider the following pairs:

	Country		Important reason for being in the news recently
1.	Chad	—	Setting up of permanent military base by China
2.	Guinea	—	Suspension of Constitution and Government by military
3.	Lebanon	—	Severe and prolonged economic depression
4.	Tunisia	—	Suspension of Parliament by President

How many pairs given above are correctly, matched?
(a) Only one pair
(b) Only two pairs
(c) Only three pairs
(d) All four pairs

6. Consider the following pairs:

	Country		Region often mentioned in the news
1.	Anatolia	—	Turkey
2.	Amhara	—	Ethiopia
3.	Cabo Delgado	—	Spain
4.	Catalonia	—	Italy

How many pairs given above are correctly matched?
(a) Only one pair
(b) Only two pairs
(c) Only three pairs
(d) All four pairs

7. With reference to the "United Nations Credentials Committee", consider the following statements:
1. It is a committee set up by the UN Security Council and works under its supervision.
2. It traditionally meets in March, June and September every year.
3. It assesses the credentials of all UN members before submitting a report to the General Assembly for approval.
Which of the statements given above is/are correct?

(a) 3 only
(b) 1 and 3
(c) 2 and 3
(d) 1 and 2

8. Which one of the following statements best describes the 'Polar Code'?
(a) **It is the international code of safety for ships operating in polar waters.**
(b) It is the agreement of the countries around the North Pole regarding the demarcation of their territories in the polar region.
(c) It is a set of norms to be followed by the countries whose scientists undertake research studies in the North Pole and South Pole.
(d) It is a trade and security agreement of the member countries of the Arctic Council.

9. With reference to the United Nations General Assembly, consider the following statements:
1. The UN General Assembly can grant observer status to the non-member States.
2. Inter-governmental organisations can seek observer status in the UN General Assembly.
3. Permanent Observers in the UN General Assembly can maintain missions at the UN headquarters.
Which of the statements given above are correct?
(a) 1 and 2 only
(b) 2 and 3 only
(c) 1 and 3 only
(d) 1, 2 and 3

10. Consider the following:
1. Asian Infrastructure Investment Bank
2. Missile Technology Control Regime
3. Shanghai Cooperation Organisation
India is a member of which of the above?
(a) 1 and 2 only
(b) 3 only
(c) 2 and 3 only
(d) 1, 2 and 3

11. Consider the following statements:
1. Vietnam has been one of the fastest growing economies in the world in the recent years.
2. Vietnam is led by a multi-party political system.
3. Vietnam's economic growth is linked to its integration with global supply chains and focus on exports.
4. For a long time Vietnam's low labour costs and stable exchange rates have attracted global manufacturers.
5. Vietnam has the most productive e-service sector in the Indo-Pacific region.
Which of the statements given above are correct?
(a) 2 and 4
(b) 3 and 5
(c) 1, 3 and 4
(d) 1 and 2

12. Consider the following statements:
1. "The Climate Group" is an international non-profit organization that drives climate action by building large networks and runs them.
2. The International Energy Agency in partnership with the Climate Group launched a global initiative "EP100".
3. EP100 brings together leading companies committed to driving innovation in energy efficiency and increasing competitiveness while delivering on emission reduction goals.

4. Some Indian companies are members of EP100.
5. The International Energy Agency is the Secretariat to the 'Under2 Coalition'.

Which of the statements given above are correct?

(a) 1, 2, 4 and 5
(b) 1, 3 and 4 only
(c) 2, 3 and 5 only
(d) 1, 2, 3, 4 and 5

13. "Rapid Financing Instrument" and "Rapid Credit Facility" are related to the provisions of lending by which one of the following?

(a) Asian Development Bank
(b) International Monetary Fund
(c) United Nations Environment Programme Finance Initiative
(d) World Bank

14. With reference to the "G20 Common Framework", consider the following statements:

1. It is an initiative endorsed by the G20 together with the Paris Club.
2. It is an initiavtive to support Low Income Countries with unsustainable debt.

Which of the statements given above is/are correct?

(a) 1 only
(b) 2 only
(c) Both 1 and 2
(d) Neither 1 nor 2

YEAR - 2021

1. Consider the following statements:

1. 'Right to the City' is an agreed human right and the UN-Habitat monitors the commitments made by each country in this regard.
2. 'Right to the City' gives every occupant of the city the right to reclaim public spaces and public participation in the city.
3. 'Right to the City' means that the State cannot deny any public service or facility to the unauthorized colonies in the city.

Which of the statements given above is/are correct?

(a) 1 only
(b) 3 only
(c) 1 and 2
(d) 2 and 3

2. Consider the following statements:

1. The Global Ocean Commission grants licences for seabed exploration and mining in international waters.
2. India has received licences for seabed mineral exploration in international waters.
3. 'Rare earth minerals' are present on seafloor in international waters.

Which of the statements given above are correct?

(a) 1 and 2 only
(b) 2 and 3 only
(c) 1 and 3 only
(d) 1, 2 and 3

3. Consider the following statements:

1. 21st February is declared to be the International Mother Language Day by UNICEF.
2. The demand that Bangla has to be one of the national languages was raised in the Constituent Assembly of Pakistan.

Which of the above statements is/are correct?
(a) 1 only
(b) 2 only
(c) Both 1 and 2
(d) Neither 1 nor 2

4. With reference to 'Water Credit', consider the following statements:
1. It puts microfinance tools to work in the water and sanitation sector.
2. It is a global initiative launched under the aegis of the World Health Organization and the World Bank
3. It aims to enable the poor people to meet their water needs without depending on subsidies.

Which of the statements given above are correct?
(a) 1 and 2 only
(b) 2 and 3 only
(c) 1 and 3 only
(d) 1, 2 and 3

5. Consider the following statements in respect of the Laureus World Sports Award which was instituted in the year 2000:
1. American golfer Tiger Woods was the first winner of this award.
2. The award was received mostly by 'Formula One' players so far.
3. Roger Federer received this award maximum number of times compared to others.

Which of the above statements are correct?
(a) 1 and 2 only
(b) 2 and 3 only
(c) 1 and 3 only
(d) 1, 2 and 3

6. Consider the following statements in respect of the 32nd Summer Olympics:
1. The official motto for this Olympics is 'A New World'.
2. Sport Climbing, Surfing, Skateboarding, Karate and Baseball are included in this

Which of the above statements is/are correct?
(a) 1 only
(b) 2 only
(c) Both 1 and 2
(d) Neither 1 nor 2

7. Consider the following statements in respect of the ICC World Test Championship:
1. The finalists were decided by the number of matches they won.
2. New Zealand was ranked ahead of England because it won more matches than England.

Which of the above statements is/are correct?
(a) 1 only
(b) 2 only
(c) Both 1 and 2
(d) Neither 1 nor 2

YEAR - 2020

1. Consider the following pairs:

	International Agreement/set-up	Subject
1.	Alma-Ata Declaration	Healthcare of the people
2.	Hague Convention	Biological and chemical weapons
3.	Talanoa Dialogue	Global climate change
4.	Under2 Coalition	Child rights

Which of the pairs above is/are correctly matched?

(a) 1 and 2 only
(b) 4 only
(c) 1 and 3 only
(d) 2, 3 and 4 only

2. In which one of the following groups are all the four countries members of G20?

(a) Argentina, Mexico, South Africa and Turkey
(b) Australia, Canada, Malaysia and New Zealand
(c) Brazil, Iran, Saudi Arabia and Vietnam
(d) Indonesia, Japan, Singapore and South Korea

YEAR - 2019

1. The Global Competitiveness Report is published by the

(a) International Monetary Fund
(b) United Nations Conference on Trade and Development
(c) World Economic Forum
(d) World Bank

2. With reference to Asian Infrastructure Investment Bank (AIIB), consider the following statements:

1. AIIB has more than 80-member nations.
2. India is the largest shareholder in AIIB.
3. AIIB does not have any members from outside Asia.

Which of the statements given above is/are correct?

(a) 1 only
(b) 2 and 3 only
(c) 1 and 3 only
(d) 1, 2 and 3

3. Which of the following adopted a law on data protection and privacy for its citizens known as General Data Protection Regulation' in April 2016 and started implementation of it from 25th May, 2018?

(a) Australia
(b) Canada
(c) The European Union
(d) The United States of America

4. Recently, India signed a deal known as 'Action Plan for Prioritization and Implementation of Cooperation Areas in the Nuclear Field' with which of the following countries?

(a) Japan
(b) Russia
(c) The United Kingdom
(d) The United States of America

YEAR - 2018

1. What is/are the consequence /consequences of a country becoming the member of the 'Nuclear Suppliers Group'?

1. It will have access to the latest and most efficient nuclear technologies.
2. It automatically becomes a member of "The Treaty on the Non-Proliferation of Nuclear Weapons (NPT)".

Which of the statements given above is/are correct?

(a) **1 only**
(b) 2 only
(c) Both 1 and 2
(d) Neither 1 nor 2

2. The term "two-state solution" is sometimes mentioned in the news in the context of the affairs of

(a) China
(b) Israel
(c) Iraq
(d) Yemen

3. International Labour Organization's Conventions 138 and 182 are related to

(a) Child labour
(b) Adaptation of agriculture practices to global climate change
(c) Regulation of food prices and food security
(d) Gender parity at the workplace

4. In the Indian context, what is the implication of ratifying the 'Additional Protocol' with the 'International Atomic Energy Agency (IAEA)'?

(a) The civilian nuclear reactors come under IAEA safeguards.
(b) The military nuclear installations come under the inspection of IAEA
(c) The country will have the privilege to buy uranium from the Nuclear Suppliers Group (NSG).
(d) The country automatically becomes a member of the NSG.

5. Consider the following countries:

1. Australia
2. Canada
3. China
4. India
5. Japan
6. USA

Which of the above are among the 'free-trade partners' of ASEAN ?

(a) 1, 2, 4 and 5
(b) 3, 4, 5 and 6
(c) **1, 3, 4 and 5**
(d) 2, 3, 4 and 6

6. "Rule of Law Index" is released by which of the following ?

(a) Amnesty International
(b) International Court of Justice
(c) The Office of UN Commissioner for Human Rights
(d) World Justice Project

YEAR - 2017

1. Consider the following in respect of Indian Ocean Naval Symposium (IONS):
1. Inaugural IONS was held in India in 2015 under the chairmanship of the Indian Navy.
2. IONS are a voluntary initiative that seeks to increase maritime co-operation among navies of the littoral states of the Indian Ocean Region.

Which of the above statements is/are correct?
(a) 1 only
(b) **2 only**
(c) both 1 and 2
(d) neither 1 nor 2

2. 'Broad-based Trade and Investment Agreement (BTIA)' is sometimes seen in the news in the context of negotiations held between India and
(a) European Union
(b) Gulf Cooperation Council
(c) Organization for Economic Cooperation and Development
(d) Shanghai Cooperation Organization

3. What is the importance of developing Chabahar Port by India?
(a) India's trade with African countries will enormously increase.
(b) India's relations with oil producing Arab countries will be strengthened.
(c) India will not depend on Pakistan for access to Afghanistan and Central Asia.
(d) Pakistan will facilitate and protect the installation of a gas pipeline between Iraq and India

4. Consider the following statements:
1. The Nuclear Security Summits are periodically held under the aegis of the United Nations.
2. The International Panel on Fissile Materials is an organ of International Atomic Energy Agency.

Which of the statements given above is/are correct?
(a) 1 only
(b) 2 only
(c) Both 1 and 2
(d) Neither 1 nor 2

5. The term 'Digital Single Market Strategy' seen in the news refers to
(a) ASEAN
(b) BRICS
(c) EU
(d) G20

YEAR - 2016

1. 'Belt and road Initiative' is sometimes mentioned in the news in the context of the affairs of
(a) African Union
(b) Brazil
(c) European union
(d) China

2. Which of the following is not a member of 'Gulf Cooperation Council'?
(a) **Iran**
(b) Saudi Arabia
(c) Oman
(d) Kuwait

3. 'European Stability Mechanism', sometimes seen in the news, is an
(a) agency created by EU to deal with the impact of millions of refugees arriving from Middle East
(b) agency of EU that provides financial assistance to eurozone countries

(c) agency of EU to deal with all the bilateral and multilateral agreements on trade
(d) agency of EU to deal with the conflict arising among the member countries

4. 'Doctors Without Borders (Medecins Sans Frontiercs)', often in the news, is
(a) A division of World Health Organization
(b) A non-governmental international organization
(c) And inter-government agency sponsored by European Union
(d) A specialized agency of the United Nations

5. Consider the following statements:
The India-Africa Summit -
1. Held in 2015 was the third such Summit
2. Was actually initiated by Jawaharlal Nehru in 1951
Which of the statements given above is/are correct?
(a) 1 only
(b) 2 only
(c) Both 1 and 2
(d) Neither 1 nor 2

6. With reference to 'Organization for the prohibition of Chemical Weapons (OPCW)' consider the following statements:
1. It is an organization of European Union in working relation with NATO and WHO
2. It monitors chemical industry to prevent new weapons free emerging
3. It provides assistance and protection to Stated Parties against chemical weapons threats.
Which of the statements given above is/are correct?
(a) 1 only
(b) 2 and 3 only
(c) 1 and 3 only
(d) 1,2 and 3

7. Community sometimes mentioned in the news In the affairs of
1. Kurd : Bangladesh
2. Madhesi : Nepal
3. Robingya : Myanmar
Which of the pairs given above is/are correctly matched?
(a) 1 and 2
(b) 2 only
(c) 2 and 3
(d) 3 only

INTERNATIONAL RELATIONS MAINS PYQ

YEAR - 2023

1. 'Virus of Conflict is affecting the functioning of the SCO'. In the light of the above statement point out the role of India in mitigating the problems.
2. Indian diaspora has scaled new heights in the West. Describe its economic and political benefits for India.
3. 'The expansion and strengthening of NATO and a stronger US-Europe strategic partnership works well for India'. What is your opinion about this statement? Give reasons and examples to support your answer.
4. Q.4) Sea is an important Component of the Cosmos". Discuss in the light of the above statement the role of the IMO (International Maritime Organization) in protecting environment and enhancing maritime safety and security.

YEAR - 2022

1. 'India is an age-old friend of Sri Lanka.' Discuss India's role in the recent crisis in Sri Lanka in the light of the preceding statement.
2. Do you think that BIMSTEC is a parallel organisation like the SAARC? What are the similarities and dissimilarities between the two? How are Indian foreign policy objectives realized by forming this new organisation?
3. How will I2U2 (India, Israel, UAE and USA) grouping transform India's position in global politics?
4. 'Clean energy is the order of the day.' Describe briefly India's changing policy towards climate change in various international fora in the context of geopolitics.

YEAR - 2021

1. "If the last few decades were of Asia's growth story, the next few are expected to be of Africa's." In the light of this statement, examine India's influence in Africa in recent years.
2. "The USA is facing an existential threat in the form of a China, that is much more challenging than the erstwhile Soviet Union." Explain.
3. Critically examine the aims and objectives of SCO. What importance does it hold for India?
4. The newly tri-nation partnership AUKUS is aimed at countering China's ambitions in the Indo-Pacific region. Is it going to supersede the existing partnerships in the region? Discuss the strength and impact of AUKUS in the present scenario.

YEAR - 2020

1. Critically examine the role of WHO in providing global health security during the COVID-19 pandemic.
2. 'Indian diaspora has a decisive role to play in the politics and economy of America and European Countries'. Comment with examples.
3. 'Quadrilateral Security Dialogue (QUAD)' is the transforming itself into a trade bloc from a military alliance, in present times – Discuss.
4. What is the significance of Indo-US defence deals over Indo-Russian defence deals? Discuss with reference to stability in the Indo-Pacific region.

YEAR - 2019

1. 'The time has come for India and Japan to build a strong contemporary relationship, one involving global and strategic partnership that will have a great significance for Asia and the world as a whole.' Comment.
2. 'Too little cash, too much politics, leaves UNESCO fighting for life.' Discuss the statement in the light of US' withdrawal and its accusation of the cultural body as being 'anti-Israel bias'.
3. "What introduces friction into the ties between India and the United States is that Washington is still unable to find for India a position in its global strategy, which would satisfy India's National self- esteem and ambitions" Explain with suitable examples.

YEAR - 2018

1. "India's relations with Israel have, of late, acquired a depth and diversity, which cannot be roiled back." Discuss.
2. A number of outside powers have entrenched themselves in Central Asia, which is a zone of interest to India. Discuss the implications, in this context, of India's joining the Ashgabat Agreement, 2018.
3. What are the key areas of reform if the WTO has to survive in the present context of Trade War', especially keeping in mind the interest of India?
4. In what ways would the ongoing US-Iran Nuclear Pact Controversy affect the national interest of India? How should India respond to this situation?

YEAR - 2017

1. 'China is using its economic relations and positive trade surplus as tools to develop potential military power status in Asia', In the light of this statement, discuss its impact on India as her neighbor. (150 words)
2. What are the main functions of the United Nations Economic and Social Council (ECOSOC)? Explain different functional commissions attached to it. (150 words)
3. The question of India's Energy Security constitutes the most important part of India's economic progress. Analyze India's energy policy cooperation with West Asian Countries. (250 words)
4. Indian Diaspora has an important role to play in South-East Asian countries' economy and society. Appraise the role of Indian Diaspora in South- East Asia in this context (250 words)

YEAR - 2016

1. "The broader aims and objectives of WTO are to manage and promote international trade in the era of globalization. But the Doha round of negotiations seem doomed due to differences between the developed and the developing countries." Discuss in the Indian perspective.
2. Evaluate the economic and strategic dimensions of India's Look East Policy in the context of the post-Cold War international scenario.
3. "Increasing cross-border terrorist attacks in India and growing interference in the internal affairs of several member-states by Pakistan are not conducive for the future of SAARC (South Asian Association for Regional Cooperation)." Explain with suitable.
4. What are the aims and objectives of the McBride Commission of the UNESCO? What is India's position on these?

MAJOR MILITARY EXERCISES OF INDIA 2023-2024

IMPORTANT MILITARY EXERCISE OF INDIA: BILATERAL EXERCISE

Participating Countries	Army/Navy/ Air force	Bilateral Exercise Name
India and Australia	Army	AUSTRA HIND
	Navy	AUSINDEX-23
India and Bangladesh	Army	SAMPRITI
	Navy	BONGOSAGAR-23
	Air force	TABLE TOP EX
India and China	Army	HAND IN HAND
India and France	Army	SHAKTI
	Navy	VARUNA
	Air force	GARUDA
India and Indonesia	Army	GARUDA SHAKTI
	Navy	SAMUDRA SHAKTI-23
India and Japan	Army	DHARMA GAURDIAN
	Navy	JIMEX
	Air force	VEER GAURDIAN
India and Kazakhstan	Army	KAZIND
India and Kyrgyzstan	Army	KHANJAR
India and Maldives	Army	EKUVERIN
	Navy	EKATHA
India and Mongolia	Army	NOMADIC ELEPHANT
India and Myanmar	Army	IMBEX
	Navy	IMCOR
India and Nepal	Army	SURYA KIRAN

India and Oman	Army	AL NAGAH
	Navy	NASEEM-AL-BAHR
	Air force	EASTERN BRIDGE- IV
India and Russia	Army	INDRA
	Navy	INDRA NAVY
	Air force	INDRA
India and Seychelles	Army	LAMITIYE
India and Sri Lanka	Army	MITRA SHAKTI
	Navy	SLINEX
India and Thailand	Army	MAITRI
		INDO-THAI CORPAT
	Air force	SIAM BHARAT
India and The United Kingdom	Army	AJEYA WARRIOR
	Navy	KONKAN
	Air force	INDRADHANUSH-IV
India and the USA	Army	YUDHABHAYAS AND VAJRA PRAHAR
	Navy	SALVEX
	Air force	RED FLAG 16-1
India and Vietnam	Army	VINBAX
India and UAE	Navy	ZAYED TALWAR
India and Saudi Arabia	Navy	AL MOHED AL HIND
India and Egypt	Army	CYCLONE-I

MILITARY EXERCISE OF INDIA 2024: MULTILATERAL EXERCISE

S. No.	Multilateral Exercise	Participating Countries
1.	RIMPAC	Australia, Brunei, Canada, Chile, China, Colombia, Denmark, France, Germany, India, Indonesia, Italy, Japan, Malaysia, Mexico, Netherlands, New Zealand, Norway, Peru, Philippines, South Korea Singapore, Thailand, Tonga, the United Kingdom, and the United States
2.	MALABAR	India, the United States, and Japan
3.	COBRA - GOLD	Asia-Pacific countries
4.	Samvedna	South Asian Region Nations

IMPORTANT BILATERAL AND TRILATERAL SUMMIT

Summit Name	Year	Participating Countries	Key Outcomes
G-24	2024	28 members (including India) plus China (special invitee).	The proposals of an independent expert panel on the reform of multilateral development banks have been adopted by the G24, a group of developing countries. In the Bretton Woods Institutions, G24 coordinates developing nations' stances on monetary and development-related issues.
G-77	2024	Members: 134 members (including India)	India stressed its support for the Global South during the G77 + China Summit held in Cuba. The G77 is the largest intergovernmental organization of developing nations, with 134 members, including India, and was founded in 1964 with the goal of advancing collective economic interests and combined negotiation power.
GCC	2023	The Kingdom of Bahrain, the State of Kuwait, the Sultanate of Oman, the State of Qatar, the Kingdom of Saudi Arabia and the United Arab Emirates	India's bilateral trade with the Gulf Cooperation Council (GCC) is growing rapidly, with GCC accounting for over USD 154 billion in FY 2021-22. India-GCC relations are significant for trade, energy security, remittance, and attracting expatriates, with Saudi Arabia, UAE, and Kuwait being key sources of crude oil imports.
GSP	2024	Denmark and India	The Green Strategic Partnership (GSP) between Denmark and India is to advance global cooperation, job creation, economic growth, green growth, and political cooperation with a particular emphasis on the Paris Agreement and UN Sustainable Development Goals.
I2U2	2024	India, Israel, USA and UAE.	Under the I2U2 group, India, Israel, and the United Arab Emirates have established a

			collaborative space venture with the goal of developing a special space-based tool for decision-makers, organizations, and businesspeople, with an emphasis on infrastructure, transport, and maritime security.
India-Australia Leaders' Virtual Summit	2022	India, Australia	Defense cooperation, trade relations, and regional security.
India-France joint statement	2023	India and France	In order to strengthen collaboration in the areas of defense, security, space exploration, civil nuclear energy, and maritime security in the Indian Ocean region, France and India have inked a strategic partnership statement. The statement is important for India because it shows off the country's expanding role in regional security, fortifies relations with a crucial European ally, and advances India's defense capabilities in addition to supporting its goals in space exploration and civil nuclear energy. Future initiatives include having strategic conversations and strengthening cooperation in international organizations.
India-France Strategic Dialogue	2022	India, France	Defense and security cooperation, counter-terrorism, and climate change.
India-France-UAE trilateral	2024	India, France and UAE	In February 2024, India, France, and the United Arab Emirates established a trilateral cooperation project centered on energy, defense, health, and technology. The gathering promotes collaboration, fortifies relationships with key allies like France and the United Arab Emirates, and demonstrates India's dedication to addressing global issues. Future plans call for arranging trilateral meetings on topics like food security, desertification, and single-use plastic pollution in 2023, when the UAE is hosting the COP28 and India is hosting the G20.
India-Germany Inter-Governmental Consultations	2022	India, Germany	Trade, climate change, and sustainable development.
India-Gulf Cooperation Council (GCC) Summit	2023	India, GCC member states	Trade relations, energy security, and strategic cooperation.
India-Indonesia-	2024	India, Indonesia and Australia	In order to improve collaboration in the Indo-Pacific area, Australia, Indonesia, and India convened a trilateral meeting in May 2024.

Australia trilateral			Important results included agreements on disinformation, cyber security, maritime cooperation, and counterterrorism, as well as cooperative initiatives to support regional economic growth and connectivity. The summit highlights India's commitment to regional cooperation and stability, enhances its relationship with important allies, and supports its "Act East" policy.
India-Japan Annual Summit	2022	India, Japan	Economic cooperation, infrastructure development, and regional security.
India-Nordic Summit	2022	India, Nordic countries	Climate change, renewable energy, and digital transformation.
India-South Korea-US	2024	India, South Korea and US	In March 2024, the US, South Korea, and India convened a trilateral technology dialogue with an emphasis on developing tech areas like semiconductors, 5G, and artificial intelligence. The establishment of a trilateral innovation hub, cooperative efforts to address global supply chain concerns, and fortifying relationships with important Indo-Pacific partners were among the main results. In 2025, there are plans to hold regular trilateral meetings.
India-UAE joint statement	2023	India and UAE	A comprehensive strategic agreement has been linked by India and the UAE, with an emphasis on commerce, investment, energy, defense, nuclear energy, space exploration, and climate change. The declaration is important for India since it highlights India's expanding position in regional security and defense cooperation, improves energy security, promotes space exploration and nuclear energy goals, and fortifies ties with the Gulf area.
India-US Leaders' Summit	2022	India, United States	Trade relations, defense cooperation, and Indo-Pacific strategy.
INSTC	2023	India, Iran, Russia, Turkey, Azerbaijan, Kazakhstan, Armenia, Belarus, Tajikistan, Kyrgyzstan, Oman, Ukraine, Syria.	Iran has started transferring Russian goods to India through the International North-South Transit Corridor (INSTC), a 7200 km multi-modal transportation network. INSTC connects the Indian Ocean, Persian Gulf, Caspian Sea, Saint Petersburg, and North Europe. It aims to reduce transportation costs and transit time between India and Russia by 30% and half compared to the Suez Canal. It also aims to reduce dependence on current trading partners and serve as India's response to China's Belt and Road Initiative.
SWP	2024	India and Netherlands	In 2022, the Ministry of Jal Shakti, India, and the Ministry of Infrastructure and Water

				Management, Netherlands, signed the Strategic Water Partnership (SWP). SWP seeks to promote cooperative research of creative and sustainable technology solutions/nature based solutions, knowledge exchange, and the utilization of Dutch experience in sustainable water initiatives in India.

REGIONS WITH INTERNAL DISPUTES

Region or Country	Conflict	Involved Countries/Parties	Year	Conclusion/Current Status
		AFRICA		
Ethiopia	Tigray War	Ethiopia, Tigray People's Liberation Front (TPLF)	2020-2022	An ethnic rebel group called the TPLF fought the Ethiopian government. The humanitarian crisis was caused by the fighting. Though tensions still exist, a ceasefire was proclaimed in November 2022.
Sudan	Darfur Conflict	Sudan, Various Rebel Groups	2020-2024	Political unrest and economic instability have made the confrontation between the Sudanese government and several rebel groups worse.
Burkina Faso	Coup D'état	Burkina Faso, Military Junta	2022	President Roch Marc Christian Kaboré was overthrown by a military coup. The Patriotic Movement for Safeguard and Restoration (MPSR), which is the junta in charge, has had difficulty dealing with the insurgency and continuous security threats.
Mozambique	Insurgency in Cabo Delgado	Mozambique, Islamic State-linked Militants	2020-2024	The Cabo Delgado region has been under attack by insurgents associated with ISIS. Although insecurity endures, the government keeps up its efforts to quell the insurgency with help from abroad.
Central African Republic	(CAR) Ongoing Conflict	CAR Government, Rebel Groups, Various Militant Groups	2020-2024	Many armed groups and rebel factions continue to inflict bloodshed on the Central African Republic. Despite continuous efforts at peace, there are still occasional conflicts and an unstable situation.
South Sudan	Ongoing civil war, humanitarian crisis, and political tensions	South Sudanese government, opposition groups (e.g., SPLM-IO), UN peacekeepers	2024	Rival factions and ethnic groups' power struggles are the main cause of the conflict. Vice President Machar's dismissal by President Kiir set off a civil war that has resulted in massive violence, mass displacement, and humanitarian disasters. This has been one of the

				deadliest wars in Africa due to resource competition, ethnic tensions, and outside interference.
Uganda	Political instability, opposition protests, and security crackdown	Ugandan government, opposition groups (e.g., NUP), security forces	2024	Security crackdowns, opposition protests, and political repression are the main causes of the conflict. Dissent has been exacerbated by President Museveni's protracted rule and limitations on political freedoms. Following the arrest of opposition leader Bobi Wine, demonstrations against electoral fraud turned violent, with security forces being accused of violating human rights.
Somalia	Ongoing Islamist insurgency and terrorist attacks	Al-Shabaab, Somali government, African Union forces	2023	The Islamist insurgency led by Al-Shabaab persists in terrorizing the nation, specifically focusing on civilians and government personnel. The conflict, which has resulted in extensive destruction and displacement, is fueled by the group's extreme ideology and desire for control.
Mali	Mali Insurgency	Mali, Various Rebel Groups, Jihadist Militants	2020-2024	Jihadist organizations such as Al-Qaeda and ISIS affiliates are engaged in combat against the government of Mali. There are still continuous insurgencies, and the situation is unstable despite foreign assistance. .
Nigeria	Insurgency in the Northeast	Nigeria, Boko Haram, ISWAP	2020-2024	The Islamic State West Africa Province (ISWAP), a branch of Boko Haram, and its affiliate organization still carry out insurgent operations. Stabilizing the area and tackling humanitarian issues are persistent challenges for the Nigerian government.
Libya	Libyan Civil War	Libya, Various Militias, GNA, LNA	2020-2024	Libya is still split, with competing groups fighting for dominance, such as the Libyan National Army (LNA) and the Government of National Unity (GNA). Although there is a tenuous ceasefire in place, the political landscape is still complicated and unstable.

SOUTH ASIA				
Afghanistan	Taliban insurgency, political instability, and humanitarian crisis	Taliban, Afghan government, US, NATO	2023	The Taliban's takeover of Afghanistan in 2021 was facilitated by the withdrawal of US and NATO forces, creating a power vacuum. A weak and corrupt Afghan government, unable to counter the Taliban, and Pakistan's support for the group, further contributed to their success. The international community's lack of engagement and the Doha Agreement, which excluded the Afghan government, also emboldened the Taliban. The Afghan military's sudden collapse allowed the Taliban to swiftly seize control, regaining power after two decades.
Myanmar	Coup d'état and Civil Unrest	Myanmar, Military Junta (Tatmadaw), Pro-Democracy Groups	2021	The democratically elected government was overthrown by a military takeover. After the military launched harsh crackdowns, there were protests and civil unrest. The situation is still tense since there is still resistance and criticism from around the world.
CENTRAL ASIA				
Kazakhstan	Protests and Unrest	Kazakhstan, Government, Various Protest Groups	2022	Violent altercations resulted from protests against increases in petrol prices and general unrest. The CSTO forces, commanded by Russia, helped the government regain control, but the underlying problems have not been addressed.
Democratic of Congo	Ongoing rebel fighting, humanitarian crisis, and political instability	DRC government, rebel groups (e.g., M23), UN peackeepers	2023	Rivalries for resources, political unrest, and ethnic tensions are the main causes of the conflict. Rebel groups, militias, and supporters of former President Kabila pose threats to President Tshisekedi's precarious administration. Amid competing interests for influence between foreign powers and neighboring countries, the eastern regions are beset by violence, displacement, and humanitarian crises. It is one of the longest-running conflicts in Africa as a result of decades of corruption, poor leadership, and outside intervention.

MIDDLE EAST				
Syria	Syrian Civil War	Syria, Assad Regime, Various Rebel Groups, ISIS	2020-2024	The conflict, which involves a number of parties including ISIS, the Kurdish forces, and the Assad administration, has lessened in severity but is still ongoing. There is still a need for political solutions.
Iran	Protests and Repression	Iran, Various Protest Groups	2020-2024	Serious crackdowns have been implemented in response to protests against the Iranian regime, which are motivated by political and economic grievances. There is still a great deal of instability in the situation.
Lebanon	Political instability, economic crisis, and sectarian tensions	Lebanese government, opposition groups (e.g., Hezbollah), international community	2024	Political corruption, economic hardship, and sectarian divisions are the main causes of the conflict. The government's economic policies and corruption has been the target of violent protests, which have been made worse by Hezbollah's influence and Iran's support. Lebanon's instability has also been exacerbated by the spillover from the Syrian civil war.
Turkey- Syria Border	Ongoing conflict, refugee crisis, and cross-border tensions	Turkish government, Syrian government, Kurdish groups (e.g., YPG)	2024	The civil war in Syria and Turkey's worries about Kurdish separatism are the main causes of the conflict. Turkey has militarily intervened in Syria in an effort to thwart the establishment of a Kurdish state along its border. Clashes, displaced people, and humanitarian crises have resulted from tensions between Syrian government forces and the US-backed Kurdish YPG.
Yemen	Civil war, humanitarian crisis, and Saudi-led intervention	Yemeni government, Houthi rebels, Saudi Arabia, UAE	2023	The humanitarian crisis resulting from the Houthi rebels' and the government's civil war has been made worse by Saudi Arabia's intervention. Widespread displacement and destruction have resulted from the fighting.
Israel-Palestine	Ongoing war	Israel, Palestine, Hamas, Fatah	2024	A long-standing disagreement over political rights, territory, and identity is the root of the conflict. Israelis claim their right to a safe homeland, while Palestinians demand statehood and self-determination. Tensions have been exacerbated by decades of occupation, settlement growth, and violence; unresolved issues

				include Jerusalem's status and refugee rights.
SOUTH CHINA SEA				
South China Sea	Territorial Disputes	China, Vietnam, Philippines, Malaysia, Brunei	2020-2024	Several nations are involved in disputes over marine area in the South China Sea. Periodic military and diplomatic conflicts reflect the ongoing tensions.